C000020791

British Crime Writing

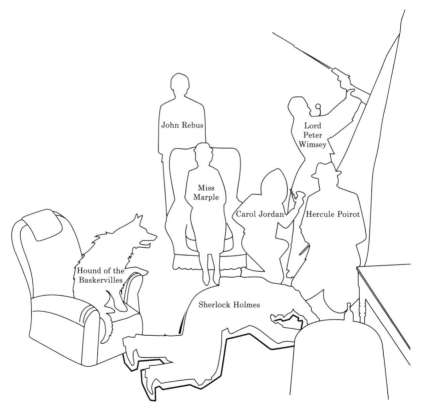

John Rebus

Lord
Peter
Wimsey

Miss
Marple

Carol Jordan

Hercule Poirot

Hound of the
Baskervilles

Sherlock Holmes

Key to cover illustration.

British Crime Writing

An Encyclopedia

Volume II: I–Z

Edited by Barry Forshaw

Greenwood World Publishing
Oxford / Westport Connecticut
2009

First published by Greenwood World Publishing 2009

1 2 3 4 5 6 7 8 9 10

Greenwood World Publishing
Prama House
267 Banbury Road
Oxford OX2 7HT
An imprint of Greenwood Publishing Group, Inc
www.greenwood.com

British Library Cataloguing-in-Publication Data: a catalogue record for this book is available from the British Library

Library of Congress Cataloging-in-Publication Data

British crime writing : an encyclopedia / [edited by] Barry Forshaw.
    p. cm.
  Includes bibliographical references and index.
  ISBN 978-1-84645-022-8 (set: alk. paper); ISBN 978-1-84645-030-3 (vol. 1: alk. paper); ISBN 978-1-84645-031-0 (vol. 2: alk. paper)
  1. Detective and mystery stories, English – Encyclopedias.   2. Crime writing – Great Britain – Encyclopedias.   3. Authors, English – Biography – Encyclopedias.   I. Forshaw, Barry.

  PR19B67   2009
  823'.087209003 – dc22   2008030713

ISBN 978-1-84645-022-8 (set)
ISBN 978-1-84645-030-3 (vol. 1)
ISBN 978-1-84645-031-0 (vol. 2)

Designed by Fraser Muggeridge studio
Pictures researched by Zooid Pictures
Typeset by TexTech International
Printed and bound by South China Printing Company

Contents

Acknowledgements

In addition to my appreciation of the inestimable industry and scholarship of the contributors (notably Mark Campbell, Russell James and Geoff Bradley, who provided much added value), I owe a special debt of gratitude to two Mikes, Ashley and Ripley, whose knowledge of the crime genre is prodigious. In fact, Mike Ashley's contribution to the encyclopedia has – in many ways – been nonpareil. Simon Mason at Greenwood has been a constant source of inspiration and literary erudition, while Liane Escorza has provided invaluable liaison expertise. Finally, my thanks to Judith Forshaw for her invaluable administrative help.

Alphabetical List of Entries

Guide to Related Topics

Golden Age Crime Fiction

Allingham, Margery (1904–1966)
Bentley, E[dmund] C[lerihew] (1875–1956)
Blake, Nicholas (1904–1972)
Charteris, Leslie (1907–1993)
Cheyney, Peter (1896–1951)
Creasey, John (1908–1973)
Crispin, Edmund (1921–1978)
Crofts, Freeman Wills (1879–1957)
Dickinson, Peter (b.1927)
Dudley, Ernest (1908–2006)
Freeman, R. Austin (1862–1943)
Golden Age Crime Fiction
Goodchild, George (1888–1969)
Graeme, Bruce (1900–1982)
Heyer, Georgette (1902–1974)
Hornung, E.W. (1866–1921)
Household, Geoffrey (1900–1988)
Iles, Francis (1893–1971)
Knox, Ronald (1888–1957)
Marsh, Ngaio (1895–1982)
Mason, A[lfred] E[dward] W[oodley] (1865–1948)
Mitchell, Gladys (1901–1983)
Morland, Nigel (1905–1986)
Rohmer, Sax (1883–1959)
Tey, Josephine (1896–1952)
Vickers, Roy (1889–1965)
Wallace, Edgar (1875–1932)
Wentworth, Patricia (1878–1961)
Wheatley, Dennis (1897–1977)
Whitechurch, V[ictor] L[orenzo] (1868–1933)

Thrillers

Archer, Geoffrey (b.1944)
Bagley, Desmond (1923–1983)
Child, Lee (b.1954)
Creed, John (b.1961)
Davidson, Lionel (b.1922)
Egleton, Clive (1927–2006)
Follett, Ken (b.1949)
Forsyth, Frederick (b.1938)
Fullerton, John (b.1949)
Gadney, Reg (b.1941)
Harris, Robert (b.1957)
Higgins, Jack (b.1929)
Innes, Hammond (1913–1998)
Leather, Stephen (b.1956)
Lyall, Gavin (1932–2003)
McLaren, John (b.1951)

McNab, Andy (b.1959)
Ryan, Chris (b.1961)
Seymour, Gerald (b.1941)
Thrillers: Novels of Action
Williams, Alan (b.1935)

Academic Crime

Academe, Death in
Blake, Victoria (b.1963)
Dexter, Colin (b.1930)
Innes, Michael (1906–1994)
Stallwood, Veronica

Espionage

Allbeury, Ted (1917–2005)
Ambler, Eric (1909-1998)
Canning, Victor (1911–1986)
Childers, Erskine (1870–1922)
Clifford, Francis (1917–1975)
Cumming, Charles (b.1971)
Deighton, Len (b.1929)
Espionage Fiction
Fleming, Ian (1908–1964)
Freemantle, Brian (b.1936)
Gardner, John Edmund (1926–2007)
Haggard, William (1907–1993)
Leasor, James (1923–2008)
le Carré, John (b.1931)
Le Queux, William (1864–1927)
MacLean, Alistair (1922–1987)
Markstein, George (1929–1987)
Mitchell, James (1926–2002)
O'Donnell, Peter (b.1920)
Oppenheim, Edward Phillips (1866–1946)
Porter, Henry (b.1953)
Price, Anthony (b.1928)
Rimington, Stella (b.1935)
Trevor, Elleston (1920–1995)

Comic Crime

Brahms, Caryl (1901–1982)
Brookmyre, Christopher (b.1968)
Caudwell, Sarah (1939–2000)
Edwards, Ruth Dudley (b.1944)
Fforde, Jasper (b.1961)
Guttridge, Peter (b.1951)
Humour and Crime Fiction
Lindsay, Douglas (b.1964)
Porter, Joyce (1924–1990)
Pryce, Malcolm (b.1960)
Ripley, Mike (b.1952)

Trow, M.J. (b.1949)
Watson, Colin (1920–1982)

Detectives

Blake, Sexton
Campion, Albert
Dalgliesh, Adam
Frost, Inspector
The Great Detectives: The Mass Appeal
    of Holmes, Poirot and Wimsey
Holmes, Sherlock
Holmes, The Rivals of
Marple, Jane
Poirot, Hercule
Psychic Detectives
Rebus, Inspector
TV Detectives: Small-Screen Adaptations
Wexford, Inspector
Wimsey, Lord Peter

Foreign Settings

Binyon, T[imothy] J[ohn] (1936–2004)
Dibdin, Michael (1947–2007)
Freeling, Nicolas (1927–2003)
Hewson, David (b.1953)
Keating, H.R.F. (b.1926)
Nabb, Magdalen (1947–2007)
Nadel, Barbara
Pearce, Michael (b.1933)
Rathbone, Julian (1935–2008)
Smith, Alexander McCall (b.1948)
Wilson, Robert (b.1957)

Historical Crime

Bell, Josephine (1897–1987)
Cleverly, Barbara
Davis, Lindsey (b.1949)
Doherty, Paul (b.1946)
Gregory, Susanna (b.1958)
Historical Crime
Jackson, Lee (b.1971)
Jecks, Michael (b.1960)
Knight, Bernard (b.1931)
Lake, Deryn
Levack, Simon (b.1965)
Marston, Edward (b.1940)
Morson, Ian (b.1947)
Peters, Ellis (1913–1995)
Pirie, David (b.1953)
Rowe, Rosemary (b.1942)
Sansom, C.J. (b.1952)
Tallis, Frank (b.1958)
Taylor, Andrew (b.1951)
Tremayne, Peter (b.1943)
Wishart, David (b.1952)

Literary Crime

Ackroyd, Peter (b.1949)
Amis, Martin (b.1949)
Atkinson, Kate (b.1951)
Banville, John (b.1945)
Barnes, Julian (b.1946)
Chesterton, G[ilbert] K[eith] (1874–1936)
Greene, Graham (1904–1991)
Hamilton, Patrick (1904–1962)
Ishiguro, Kazuo (b.1954)
Literature and Crime Fiction
Maugham, W. Somerset (1874–1965)
Sinclair, Iain (b.1943)
Waters, Sarah (b.1966)

True Crime

Burn, Gordon (b.1948)
Davis, Carol Anne (b.1961)
Innes, Brian (b.1928)
Kennedy, Sir Ludovic (b.1919)
Masters, Brian (b.1939)
Pearson, John (b.1930)
True Crime
Wilson, Colin (b.1931)

Anthologists

Adrian, Jack (b.1945)
Anthologies
Ashley, Mike (b.1948)
Edwards, Martin (b.1955)
Haining, Peter (1940–2007)
Hale, Hilary (b.1949)
Hardinge, George (1921–1997)
Harris, Herbert (1911–1995)
Jakubowski, Maxim (b.1944)

Magazines

CADS
Creasey Mystery Magazine
Crime Time
Crimewave
Detective Magazine
Edgar Wallace Mystery Magazine
Hutchinson's Mystery Story Magazine
London Mystery Magazine, The
MacKill's Mystery Magazine
Magazines
Saint Mystery Magazine
Scorpion Magazine
Sherlock Magazine
Shots Magazine
The Strand Magazine
Suspense
Union Jack (and *Detective Weekly*)

Film

Beat Girl (film, 1960)
Brighton Rock (film, 1947)
Bulldog Jack (film, 1935)
Criminal, The (film, 1960)
Dead Man's Shoes (film, 2004)
Film and Crime: Page to Screen
Frenzy (film, 1972)
Frightened City, The (film, 1961)
Gangster No. 1 (film, 2000)
Get Carter (film, 1971)
Gumshoe (film, 1971)
Hell Drivers (film, 1957)
Hell Is a City (film, 1960)
It Always Rains on Sunday (film, 1947)
League of Gentlemen, The (film, 1960)
Lock, Stock and Two Smoking Barrels
    (film, 1998)
Long Good Friday, The (film, 1980)
Mona Lisa (film, 1986)
Murder on the Orient Express (film, 1974)
Night and the City (film, 1950)
No Orchids for Miss Blandish (film, 1948)
Performance (film, 1970)
Sexy Beast (film, 2000)
Tiger in the Smoke (film, 1956)
Villain (film, 1971)

Television

The Bill (television series, 1984–)
Brother Cadfael (television series, 1994–1998)
Cracker (television series, 1993–2006)
Cribb (television series, 1980–1981)
Dalgliesh, Adam
Dalziel & Pascoe (television series, 1996–)
Frost, Inspector
Hazell (television series, 1978–1980)
Holmes on TV
Inspector Morse (television series, 1987–2000)
Marple, Jane
Police Procedurals
Prime Suspect (television series, 1991–2006)
Rebus, Inspector
The Saint on Television
Sharman (television series, 1995–1996)
TV Detectives: Small-Screen Adaptations
Wexford, Inspector
Wimsey, Lord Peter
Wire in the Blood (television series, 2002–)

Introduction

There are few genres in popular fiction that have such a hold on readers' affections as has crime fiction, and however accomplished the American titans of the genre (past and present), the amazing flowering of talent in Great Britain (since the genesis of the genre in the nineteenth century) has no equal. Hardly surprising, given that Charles **Dickens** and Wilkie **Collins** were the progenitors of the genre, producing (*inter alia*) its key elements: dogged detective, complex plotting and surprising revelations. Although it has to be said that Arthur Conan **Doyle** modelled Sherlock **Holmes** on the American Edgar Allan Poe's super-intelligent detective Auguste Dupin, he added in the process rich layers of the eccentric characterisation and accoutrements that have made Holmes one of the best-loved figures in fiction.

Coordinating an encyclopedia such as this is a daunting task, given the range of British crime fiction across the centuries. Remarkably, this range is broad, despite the apparent geographical limitations of the British Isles compared to the vast canvas of the United States. But perhaps the very parochialism of much British crime fiction is precisely what imbues it with its customary sharpness, particularly when murderous secrets confined in British suburban spaces are set free. And then, there is the received perception of the British love of order (although such stereotypes are in flux at present); crime novels are particularly satisfying in that we are invited to relish the chaos unleashed by the crime and criminals before the status quo is re-established – a process that has a particular resonance for the British character (more so than for, say, Americans – the barely contained pandemonium of the large American city is never really tamed). Of course, when (as mentioned earlier) Charles Dickens and Wilkie Collins introduced several of the key tropes of crime fiction (in such classics as *Bleak House* (1853) and *The Moonstone* (1868)), neither author had any thoughts of creating a genre (although it is instructive to remember that their books, while massively popular, lacked the literary gravitas in their day that later scholarship dressed them with; this was the popular fare of the day, dealing in the suspense and delayed revelation that was later to become the *sine qua non* of the genre). In generic fiction, the violin-playing denizen of 221b Baker Street and his celebrated creator are, of course, the single most important factors in terms of generating an army of imitators – notably Agatha **Christie**'s Hercule **Poirot** (although Holmes clones continue to surface to this day, dressed in contemporary garb rather than deerstalker and Inverness cape but still demonstrating impressive ratiocination skills).

Apart from the sheer pleasure of reading a good crime novel, the 'added value' in many of the best examples has long been the implicit (or sometimes explicit) element of social criticism freighted in by the more challenging writers. Among popular literary genres, only science fiction has rivalled the crime novel in 'holding the mirror up to nature' (or society). Best-selling modern writers such as Ruth **Rendell**, Minette **Walters** and Ian **Rankin** have kept alive (and developed) the tradition of social commentary, which was always a key element in the genre, although rarely at the expense of sheer storytelling skill, the area in which the crime field virtually demolishes all its rivals. When (in the early twenty-first century) crime fiction became quantifiably the most popular of popular genres (comprehensively seeing off such rivals as romance fiction), it was only the inevitable coda to a process that had been long underway, all the more to be celebrated for this added value of social responsibility.

The crime novels that appeared in Britain between the First World War and the Second World War enjoyed immense success, but the fact that these books constituted a **Golden Age** in British crime fiction was not immediately apparent – something that may seem surprising today, given the iconic status of Ngaio **Marsh**, Dorothy L. **Sayers** and the doyenne of the field, Agatha Christie. Interestingly, all of these writers are still consumed avidly, but their male counterparts (including Freeman Wills **Crofts**, Francis **Iles** (*aka* Anthony Berkeley), Edgar Wallace and honorary Brit John Dickson **Carr**), while still read, have not maintained a grip on the public imagination to the same degree.

But was it a Golden Age? Unquestionably, yes. While the innovations of the day ultimately became clichés (an inevitable process in any field in which subtly varied repetition is a key strategy), the most striking fact about British crime writing in the 1920s and 1930s is the sheer craftsmanship and invention that inform the work of all the best writers. If today the tropes of these writers appear calcified with overuse, such devices as the cloistered setting (for example, the isolated island in Agatha Christie's *And Then There Were None* (1940), also published and filmed as *Ten Little Indians*) were new to readers of the day. Not only do the Golden Age novels afford massive pleasure when read (in the right spirit) even now, their themes and strategies have been highly durable – a fact highlighted by their continuing use by modern writers such as P.D. **James** (although it is debatable whether such riffs on familiar themes will continue in the hands of a generation of writers not brought up on Christie, Sayers and co.).

Interestingly, one of the principal appeals of Golden Age British crime writing – the opportunities afforded to the reader to enjoy the blandishments of sybaritic country-house living – has been hijacked by adaptations in visual media. Audiences perhaps prefer to see big-budget location shooting in a lovingly preserved country pile than rely on the written word. But despite the appeal of adaptations in other media, there is no denying the continuing interest in this remarkable period of British crime writing. Similarly, the fog-shrouded Victorian **London** of Sherlock Holmes may be more familiar to audiences these days from the legion of television and film adaptations (ranging from the out-of-period but exuberant Basil Rathbone Universal series to the exemplary and faithful adaptations featuring the late Jeremy Brett). Sherlock Holmes was the principal *locus classicus* for the Golden Age writers, and the intuitive sleuth became a key figure (notably, of course, in the hands of Agatha Christie). Elements of social criticism were to be found, but these were less important than the construction of a narrative with the precision of the Swiss watch – although writers such as Josephine **Tey**, in *The Franchise Affair* (1948), incorporated more sophisticated material addressing contemporary mores (with their often crippling moral strictures). And while true evil remained almost a metaphysical concept, often divorced from reality (Holmes's arch nemesis, the 'Napoleon of Crime' Professor Moriarty, is undoubtedly one of the great creations of crime literature and possessed no real-life counterpart), writers such as Margery **Allingham** (in *The Tiger in the Smoke* (1952), with its psychopathic protagonist) introduced dark psychopathology into the genteel world of the British crime thriller and transformed it into something far more disturbing (giving the lie, in fact, to Dulwich-educated Raymond **Chandler**'s dismissal of the classic British mystery in *The Simple Art of Murder* as always etiolated and divorced from reality).

The dividing line between crime and **espionage** fiction is often hard to detect, and more strict delineations between genres are a relatively recent phenomenon. Raymond Chandler and Ian **Fleming** maintained a lively correspondence, comparing notes on both their working methods and the careers of their respective protagonists (the fact that one wrote about a private detective and the other about a counter-espionage agent worried neither man). In the Golden Age, there were few worries about whether the exploits of John **Buchan**'s Richard Hannay, in such books as *The Thirty-Nine Steps* (1915), should be classified as espionage or crime; such divisions did not exist, and (in any case) the attentions of the moral guardians of the day were concentrated on the corrupting effects of these 'shockers' (the fact that Buchan and his civilised adventurer-hero now seem the most traditional and comforting of fictions would no doubt inspire bemusement in the author).

Espionage fiction, with its potentially wider canvas than crime novels, has been able to make more pertinent points about the society that produced it than most crime fiction – inevitable, of course, given that the fate of nations is at stake rather than that of individuals caught up in more parochial criminal activities. Similarly, the political stance of the authors has often been far more germane to the fiction they produced than that of crime writers – and the leftwards, anti-establishment drift from the conservative tradition of John Buchan is notable. At the beginning of the twentieth century, novels such as Erskine **Childers**'s classic *The Riddle of the Sands* (1903) located the source of the threat in Germany, and (inevitably) Germany provided British writers with a useful resource to draw upon for many years. However, it was not long before the growling of the Soviet bear became the soundtrack to espionage fiction, and there is an argument for stating that the dispiriting years of the Cold War produced a fine flourishing of the genre, notably in the magnificent early novels of John le Carré and Len **Deighton** (the case for Ian Fleming's durable spy James Bond is a more controversial one these days, but Fleming remains an exceptional writer, his energetic narratives and evocations of luxurious living still holding a great appeal, whatever else has dated in the novels).

There is an argument for suggesting that the first great British spy novel is Joseph **Conrad**'s *The Secret Agent* (1907), although his *Under Western Eyes* (1911) bids a fair claim to the title, and this phantasmagorical picture of a nest of anarchists has moved through a variety of perceptions, from shopworn and overfamiliar to all-too-terrifyingly relevant in the twenty-first century (notably the figure of The Professor, who is a walking bomb – the modern terrorist parallels are not difficult to discern). But while early espionage heroes such as Buchan's Hannay defended the Empire (without too much introspection) against sinister foreign threats, it was to be a later generation of writers that infused equivocation and ambiguity into the narratives, shaking forever the certainties of an earlier generation (it should be noted, however, that Buchan was one of the earliest writers to see how thin the veneer of civilisation was, even in the West – a fact not lost on Buchan admirers of a later generation such as Graham **Greene**).

The Ashenden stories of W. Somerset **Maugham** introduced a whole new level of sophistication into the spy story and removed at a stroke the simple antithesis between good and evil that had powered so much of the genre. And apart from the sense of realpolitik that Maugham inaugurated, he also placed far greater stress on multifaceted characterisation – after him, it was nigh on impossible for writers (even those of a populist stamp) to return to the two-dimensional stereotypes of earlier books. Such writers as William **le Queux** and Sapper (creator of the proto-Bond

Bulldog Drummond) lost their lustre – they are read these days mostly as historical curiosities, and this is leaving aside the anti-Semitism to be found in even the best writing from that era.

The next significant development in espionage fiction came in the work of Eric **Ambler** in the 1930s. Building on the innovations of his great predecessor, Ambler destabilised forever comfortable notions of 'us' and 'them', dispensing with the former certainties. But Ambler's most significant innovation was a radical move across the political spectrum from the right-wing ethos of his predecessors towards a more left-leaning orientation in his heroes. Certainly, the antagonists whom the central characters in Ambler's novels came up against could be pretty nasty specimens, but there were several to be found on 'our' side. And the brave causes of earlier generations were now much more murky affairs, with the moral line to be taken by the protagonists far less easy to discern. Ambler (who enjoyed a second career as a highly successful screenwriter) also introduced a new sense of genuine danger into his narratives that made many of his predecessors' narratives look contrived and thin. His most celebrated successors are, of course, Graham Greene and John le Carré, who adapted and developed the tropes found in Ambler's work and produced a stronger case for the espionage thriller to be taken seriously as literature. But the unglamorous approach that had now become the norm did not preclude black and sardonic humour – a key element in such critically acclaimed novels as those of Len **Deighton** – coming to the fore, with a wisecracking protagonist pointing out the absurdity of the espionage game. The end of the Cold War created problems for writers such as le Carré, but by their moving into new areas (such as the untrammelled influence of big business in the Third World), new avenues were forged for the spy novel. And even as the le Carré generation grew older, fresh talents began to appear, such as the highly skilled Charles **Cumming**, whose assiduously detailed novels of espionage – while indebted to his great predecessors – continue to demonstrate that there is much life in the genre.

British crime fiction can (and often does) divide into two distinct (although not mutually exclusive) genres. The first is the undemanding divertissement, wherein the puzzle (and its ingenious solving) is central: in this area, British writers have few equals, notably Christie and the like. But the other stream, that of the dark investigation of psychological states, is quite as strong in the United Kingdom and has been as far back as Conan Doyle. Since the 1940s, this examination of the nether regions of the human psyche (and its inevitable derogation of our behaviour) has been a British speciality, made all the more acute by the carefully preserved decorum of appearance (however turbulent the mental states beneath), which, until recently, was the *sine qua non* of middle-class British society. Such writers as Patrick **Hamilton** have stripped bare this national consciousness with quite as much unsparing rigour as novelists working in more overtly 'literary' fields. And while the sexual arena was *hors de combat* for an earlier generation of writers, modern crime specialists such as Laura **Wilson** have dragged sexual mores into the daylight. If most crime novels hardly suggest sexuality as an ameliorative, life-affirming force, this has more to do with the demand of drama than healing psychoanalytical imperatives.

Addressing the mainstream of crime fiction today (and leaving aside the legacy of the past), it is clear that the field is in ruder health than it has ever been – such is the range of trenchant and galvanic work now that an argument could be made that we are living in a second Golden Age. Take, for instance, the formidable duo of P.D. James and Ruth Rendell. James took the mechanics of the genre as forged by her great predecessors and enriched all the key elements: plotting, setting and (most of all) characterisation – her tenacious protagonist, Commander Adam **Dalgliesh**, is one of the most rounded and plausible series characters in crime fiction, even persuading the reader of the unlikely premise that a copper could also be a respected poet. Ruth Rendell ploughed similar territory in her reliable Inspector **Wexford** novels, but mined a far more disturbing psychological vein in her non-series, standalone crime novels, set in a world of dark criminality and betrayal – quite the equal of the American Patricia Highsmith. Rendell's novels under the pseudonym Barbara Vine have the same queasy concerns, with an even more cold-eyed take on human foibles. The hitherto unquestioned supremacy of the James–Rendell duo is being challenged by such remarkable novelists as Minette Walters and Frances **Fyfield**, who have folded a new social incisiveness into the contemporary British crime novel.

And there are the male writers: the older generation, such as Frederick **Forsyth** and Dick **Francis**, whose productivity has barely faltered over the years; and the younger writers, who have reinvigorated the genre with resolutely non-parochial crime epics as full of exuberance and invention as they are of violence, such as Mark **Billingham**, Michael **Marshall** and Christopher **Brookmyre**. And, of course, there is the male writer who comfortably outsells all his rivals, the formidable Ian Rankin, whose Edinburgh-set novels featuring his doughty copper Jack **Rebus** have propelled him to the upper echelons both in reader numbers and in critical acclaim (the Rebus series has also been distinguished by Rankin's refusal to simply repeat well-loved ideas, as his ex-alcoholic copper takes on new and cogent problems in society).

The remit of this encyclopedia has been as wide as possible: every possible genre that is subsumed under the heading of crime fiction is here, from the novel of detection to the blockbuster thriller to the novel of espionage. The dark worlds of **Noir** and **True Crime** treated, but the more ingratiating fields of Romance and **Humour** are also referenced. And while criminals are central to the text, the police are given their appropriate due. The reader will discover many familiar names, but hopefully the encyclopedia will act as a guide to much unfamiliar terrain.

The experts who wrote this book were chosen on the basis of their boundless enthusiasm for the genre, and (largely speaking) the authors they cover (all entries have individual credits) have their virtues rather than their demerits maximised in the essays. But while there are no hatchet jobs here, many a dispassionate view is given. Generally speaking, though, contributors have been requested to extol the virtues of writers they admire. Working with the brief that the readers will be seeking to extend their knowledge and pleasure in the genre, the assumption was made that positive recommendations would be preferred to adverse criticism – however, anodyne praise has been discouraged, and those elements that have dated badly in certain writers' works are duly noted. And as the contributors include such top British crime writers as Andrew **Taylor**, Natasha **Cooper**, Russell **James**, Carol Anne **Davis**, Philip **Gooden**, Mark **Timlin**, Lauren **Milne-Henderson**, Martin **Edwards**, Carla **Banks**, Nicholas **Royle**, Laura **Wilson** and Michael **Jecks** (along with a variety of key crime reviewers and editors), nonpareil critical writing is the order of the day. The experts here know virtually everything there is to know about the genre – from writers who produced a single long-out-of-print novel in the 1920s to what trends are likely to develop in a healthy, organically expanding genre.

About this Book

Entries are laid out alphabetically. Biographical entries appear under the subjects' surnames (the surname by which they are best-known), and other sorts of entries (on themes, periods, genres, associations, magazines, films, television adaptations and characters) are listed by key word – e.g. **Literature and Crime Fiction** under 'L', **TV Detectives** under 'T', Espionage Fiction under 'E', etc.

When a subject is known by more than one name, dummy entries cover the alternatives (e.g. 'Vine, Barbara see Rendell, Ruth'). When a book is known by different titles in the UK and US, the British title is used in the entry, and the American title given as a variant in the Selected Works section at the entry's end. Dates of publication are usually the dates of first book publication, though the dates of serialisation or magazine publication are given instead when the context demands it. Acronyms (e.g. CWA, MWA, etc.) are spelled out in entries.

One of the pleasures of a good encyclopedia is following lines of enquiry across entries. Here, cross-references to other entries are given in **bold**; in addition, many entries contain, at the end, '*see also*' suggestions. There are also recommendations for further reading after the Selected Works sections at the ends of entries, and, at the end of the encyclopedia, a Select Bibliography which lists key sources of information about British crime fiction in general. Finally, for readers who want to explore a topic in all its aspects, the index provides a detailed listing.

Whether they are seeking general or specific information, a guide to the best (or even the enjoyably meretricious) in crime fiction to add to their shopping list, or looking for a debriefing after enjoying a particular book, I hope they will be comfortably accommodated here.

I

Iles, Francis (1893–1971)

Francis Iles is the best-known pseudonym of Anthony Berkeley Cox. Under this pseudonym, he wrote *Malice Aforethought* (1931), one of the key crime novels of the twentieth century. And he is now best remembered by the Iles pseudonym, even though he used the name for only three of his twenty-six novels. As Anthony Berkeley, he wrote ten novels about his amateur detective, Roger Sheringham. He also wrote eleven non-series novels under either that name, or as A.B. Cox or under the curious pseudonym A. Monmouth Platts. He was educated at Sherbourne School, passed through London's University College and became a journalist and book reviewer (he reviewed crime as Francis Iles).

The importance of *Malice Aforethought* is revealed in its first sentence: 'It was not until several weeks after he had decided to murder his wife that Dr Bickleigh took any active steps in the matter.' Here is a crime novel in which we know immediately 'whodunit'. We know who the victim is, who the murderer is, and all that remains is to learn how he kills her and whether he will get away with it. We also quickly find that we are on the side of the murderer. His wife is a termagant with no redeeming qualities, and although Doctor Bickleigh is no saint, we are happy to sit in our armchairs and wish him well.

At the time of the book's publication, by which time mystery stories were long established and hugely popular, this was an unexpected and unusual way to tell a story (though not original; there had been 'inverted' plots before from writers such as R. Austin **Freeman**). If we do not find Iles's approach a shock today, it is only because the idea has had many imitators; however, in 1931, it stood apart and revealed a potentially more effective way of writing about crime, one in which the reader lived with the perpetrator and watched with him while the detectives tried to unravel his perfect plan. It was a masterly book, taking us through the crime, the investigation and a splendid trial scene, right up to a clever last-minute twist and wry epilogue. It showed the way for a new kind of book, the psychological crime story, in which the author explored the criminal mind. Many subsequent crime writers owe him a debt. And the change of direction was no accident, for in his preface to *The Second Shot*, published the year before, Anthony Berkeley had predicted the movement towards the psychological crime novel: 'I personally am convinced that the days of the old crime-puzzle pure and simple, relying entirely upon plot and without any added attractions of character, style or even humour, are, if not numbered, at any rate in the hands of the auditors.' He, however, did not mean to sweep *everything* away: 'The puzzle element will no doubt remain, but it will become a puzzle of character rather than a puzzle of time, place, motive and opportunity.' Berkeley astutely saw where the crime novel had to go. And before his experimental book's success was clear, he had begun work on a second, overtly psychological crime novel, *Before the Fact*. (The Hitchcock film *Suspicion* (1941) was based on this book.) In the first paragraph of this novel comes the line: 'Lina Aysgarth had lived with her husband for nearly eight years before she realised that she was married to a murderer.' Inverted crime again. And if *Malice Aforethought* borrowed from a real-life murder case

(Armstrong, in 1921), another Iles book, *As for the Woman* (1939), can equally be said to have been inspired by the Bywaters and Thompson case in 1922, a case (like the book) in which intimate details of a sexual nature were laid before the court. That the details seem less shocking today is no reflection on the original book.

By 1931, Anthony Berkeley was already an established crime writer. He had published six Roger Sheringham novels, five others and several short stories. The following year, he would be one of the founding members of the by-invitation-only Detection Club. Yet in a few years time, at the outbreak of the Second World War, he would, as a novelist, lay down his pen.

Roger Sheringham was devised as a journo-novelist-turned amateur detective. (The diffident Ambrose Chitterwick replaces Sheringham for two later books and a short story.) The Sheringham mysteries began in 1925 with *The Layton Court Mystery*, and from Berkeley's second Sheringham novel, *The Wychford Poisoning Case* (1926), there were clear signs that the author was not content to write routine whodunits. Puzzles they were certainly, and ingenious, but the second Sheringham novel revisited the real-life Victorian cause célèbre of Florence Maybrick. In the fifth one, *The Poisoned Chocolates Case* (1929), Berkeley gently lampooned his own Detection Club, and rather than have a case solved by a master detective, he served a collation of six separate cases swarmed over by six investigators, one of whom was Berkeley's Roger Sheringham (who, to add to the confusion, came up with the wrong answer).

One mystery concerning Iles himself is why he gave up writing fiction so soon, at the age of only forty-eight. Peter **Lovesey**, in a preface to a reprint of *Malice Aforethought* (1996), unearthed two conflicting explanations: that Iles lost what he called the *gusto* ('Believe me, it goes,' he confessed to fellow writer George Bellairs) or that he inherited a private fortune. Berkeley himself gave no explanation. But he did continue to write for radio and work as a journalist, reviewing crime fiction till shortly before his death in 1971. *See also* The Detective in British Fiction.

Selected Works by the Author

As Francis Iles
Malice Aforethought (1931)
Before the Fact (1932)
As for the Woman (1939)

As Anthony Berkeley – Roger Sheringham Novels
The Wychford Poisoning Case (1926)
The Poisoned Chocolates Case (1929)
Top Storey Murder (1931)
The Silk Stocking Murders (1941)

As Anthony Berkeley – Ambrose Chitterwick Novels
The Piccadilly Murder (1928)
Trial and Error (1937)

Further Reading
Johns, Ayresome. 1993. *The Anthony Berkeley Cox Files*. Ferret Fantasy.

Russell James

Innes, Brian (b.1928)

Dr Brian Innes is an award-winning author who specialises in true crime and forensics. Born in London and educated at King's College, Innes holds a BSc (Special) and MRSC and spent some years conducting laboratory research before turning to writing as a career.

One of his most popular titles, *Fakes and Forgeries* (2005), covers (amongst other curiosities) some fascinating hoaxes and forgeries, including (1) the 1991 discovery of a diary purportedly written by Jack the Ripper, which appeared to offer a final solution to the mystery of the Whitechapel Murders of 1888 when James Maybrick claimed to be the serial killer; (2) the publication of the Hitler diaries in 1981 by *Stern* magazine, which made no notable attempt to authenticate them (in 1983, it was proved that the diaries were fakes produced by Konrad Kujau, a petty thief and smuggler); (3) the discovery of the Vinland Map in 1957, which is thought to have been produced in the fifteenth century and copied from the original thirteenth-century map but remains unauthenticated. The book also discusses techniques for creating forgeries: artists' strokes, how to age paper and how modern desktop publishing has made fake currency so much easier to make.

The Body in Question (2005) deals with forensics and related areas of criminal justice. Case studies from around the world are used to demonstrate the ways in which forensic science has been used to solve many a perplexing crime. Biographical essays highlight important people in the history and development of forensics. In fact, it could be read alongside the earlier *Bodies of Evidence* (2001). Innes discusses the first time an expert (Oliver Wendell Holmes) proved in court that a specific gun used for a murder was in America in 1902. The book also charts the progress of forensic science from the first ballistics efforts in 1835 to modern DNA testing. Innes cites the O.J. Simpson case when important evidence may have been mishandled and the chain-of-custody requirements ignored. *Serial Killer* (2006) addresses the public's insatiable appetite for stories of human predators; it is a study of fifty killers and their victims. The book goes hand-in-hand with his 2003 publication *Profile of a Criminal Mind*, which explores the areas of criminal profiling used to detect offenders.

Innes's credentials for compiling works dealing with, amongst other subjects, unidentified flying objects, the occult, secret societies and the supernatural, came from his rigorous journalistic background. After seven years on Fleet Street, Innes became the art director for the Hamlyn Group. Next, he became the art director for part works at BPC Publishing, and then joined Orbis Publishing as creative director and deputy chairman. After this, he was a director of Mirror Publishing, before becoming an independent consultant to the Brown Reference Group. *See also* True Crime.

Selected Works by the Author
Bodies of Evidence (2001)
Fakes and Forgeries (2005)
The Body in Question (2005)
Serial Killer (2006)

Mike Stotter

Innes, Hammond (1913–1998)

Although now considered unfashionable, Hammond Innes was one of the most adroit purveyors of the action adventure yarn during the 1940s and 1950s.

Ralph Hammond Innes was born on 15 July 1913 in Horsham, Sussex, and was educated at Cranbrook School in Kent. After graduating in 1931, he worked as a journalist for *The Financial News* (which later merged with *The Financial Times*), during which time he married Dorothy Mary Lange.

He began by writing in his spare time, and his first book, *The Doppelganger*, appeared in 1937. Later that year, he followed it with *Air Disaster*, a thrilling tale involving narrow escapes, rooftop chases and sinister dope smugglers.

During the Second World War, he served in the Royal Artillery, witnessing at first hand the Battle of Britain, an event that inspired his 1941 war novel *Attack Alarm*. His other wartime novels were *Wreckers Must Breathe* (1940; also known as *Trapped*) and *The Trojan Horse* (1940). After spending three years overseas, he returned to England in 1945 and began writing full-time.

Many of Innes's novels are characterised by atmospheric, first-person accounts of the sea, reflecting his love of this elemental force. *Maddon's Rock* (1948) concerned the strange return of the ship *Trikkala*, missing for over a year, while *The Wreck of the Mary Deare* (1956) told a similar story about the sudden appearance of a 6,000-ton freighter in the English channel. (It was turned into a 1959 film starring Charlton Heston, after a mooted Hitchcock adaptation fell through.) In *Atlantic Fury* (1961), Innes tells a more human story of a man discovering his long-lost brother, although the windswept backdrop of a Hebridean island is still lovingly described.

A repeated theme in Innes's work is his pitting of Man against Nature. His heroes often have to fend for themselves in dangerous and isolated locations, fighting the malevolent forces of nature, as well as human enemies, to discover a secret buried in the past. Innes always meticulously researched the places he wrote about, travelling the world in his quest for authenticity. These included Antarctica (*The White South*, 1949), the Indian Ocean (*The Strode Adventurer*, 1965) and the Australian outback (*Golden Soak*, 1973).

Innes is most famous for *Campbell's Kingdom* (1952), a rugged tale of oil prospecting in the Canadian Rockies; its success is due in no small part to the well-made big-screen adaptation that followed five years later, starring Dirk Bogarde and Stanley Baker.

Innes also penned historical fiction, travel articles and children's books (under the pseudonym Ralph Hammond). He was also an experienced yachtsman, and along his wife, he took part in many ocean races in their boat *Mary Deare*, named after his 1956 novel. He was awarded a CBE in 1978. He died on 10 June 1998, leaving the bulk of his estate to the Association of Sea Training Organisations.

Selected Works by the Author
Attack Alarm (1941)
The Blue Ice (1948)
The Angry Mountain (1950)
Campbell's Kingdom (1952)
The Mary Deare (1956; also published in the United States as *The Wreck of the Mary Deare*)
The Strode Venturer (1965)
Solomon's Seal (1980)

Mark Campbell

Innes, Michael (1906–1994)

Michael Innes is the pseudonym of J.I.M. Stewart (John Innes Mackintosh Stewart), under which name he wrote novels, biographies and several important books of criticism and essays. As Michael Innes, he is best known for his long-running series built around Inspector Appleby; one of his early books, paradoxically, was *Appleby's End* (1945), although the series was to continue sporadically until the 1980s.

Innes (or Stewart) was educated at Edinburgh Academy and Oriel College, Oxford, and after graduation in 1929, he went to Vienna, where he studied Freudian psychoanalysis. From 1930 to 1935, he lectured in English at the University of Leeds where he became a Jury Professor of English. He moved to Australia to work at the University of Adelaide from 1935 to 1945, and returned in 1946 to lecture at Queens University Belfast until 1948. He then became Reader in English Literature at Christ Church, Oxford, in 1949 and remained there until his retirement in 1973. He had five children, one of whom, Angus Stewart, also became a novelist.

The year 1949 saw the publication of Stewart's *Character and Motive in Shakespeare*. His 'serious' novels began with *Mark Lambert's Supper* (1954) and included a fine series of five linked novels about Oxford life, published from 1974 to 1978 as a quintet: *A Staircase in Surrey*. Stewart contributed to the twelfth volume of the *Oxford History of English Literature* (subtitled *Eight Modern Writers*) in 1963 and wrote biographies of Rudyard Kipling (1966), Joseph **Conrad** (1968) and Thomas Hardy (1971).

The Appleby series featured the impeccably educated Inspector John Appleby (later to become commissioner and finally to be retired as Sir John Appleby). The first book in the series, *Death in the President's Lodging*, appeared before the war (1936), in which the young Inspector Appleby investigates an ancient university where the president of a group of devious dons had been found dead, his body surrounded by small piles of human bones. Any idea that detective stories were beneath the intellectual Stewart were dispelled the following year when, as Innes again, he produced one of his finest Appleby books, *Hamlet, Revenge!* (1937), set, as the title suggests, within the confines of a theatrical company – thereby closing down the list of suspects. (Both of these early titles were included in Penguin's first *Michael Innes Omnibus* (1983), along with *The Daffodil Affair* (1942), a somewhat manic tale involving a missing girl, a lost horse and a haunted house, and in which the Innes humour was overstretched.) From distant South Australia, Innes despatched his third Appleby novel, *Lament for a Maker* (1938), in which he paid obvious homage to one of the fathers of the detective story, Wilkie **Collins**, who in *The Woman in White* (1860) had made effective use of multiple narrators to show a crime from different points of view. Opinions vary on whether this experiment paid off. Either way, Innes was now clearly established as one of the leading **Golden Age** detective writers. He was back the following year, 1939, with *Stop Press*.

Not only was Innes a Golden Age writer but he was also one of the small but successful band of Oxford authors, setting their novels in a setting many of their readers knew well – the university town of Oxford itself. But, perhaps as part of the post-war democratic shift, Innes was brave enough to shift his focus from Oxford and to set some later Appleby novels around more mundane provincial universities. Oxford, though, remained superior, in his view.

Appleby appeared in over thirty novels, holding various ranks – indeed the sequence in which he gained them amused some critics – and his final appearance (retired and knighted) came as late as 1986, in *Appleby and the Ospreys*. Perhaps his oddest appearance came in Marion Mainwaring's *Murder in Pastiche* (1954; also known as *Nine Detectives all at Sea*). In the suitably closed environment of a transatlantic liner, nine famous detectives compete to solve the murder of a gossip columnist. Each detective was given a play upon their name; Appleby's being Sir Jon Nappleby.

Innes produced a few non-Appleby novels, the best of which revolve around the comic art dealer Hildebert Braunkopf, spawned out of the Appleby story *A Private View* (1952), and later, the artist Charles Honeybath, who first appeared in *The Mysterious Commission* (1974). In these, as in the main series, Michael Innes showed his quirky humour and inventiveness. He delighted in oddly named characters, eccentric and at times malevolent dons, ancient aristocrats and quintessentially English locations. (*Appleby's End* revolved around the villages of Sleeps Hill, Linger, Boxer's Bottom and Snarl. *The Journeying Boy*, 1949, introduced Inspector Cadover.) If Innes included too many literary jokes, the sheer exuberance of his comic invention was memorable.

It is to the credit of Innes that, unlike some from the Golden Age period, his John Appleby grew and developed with the books. One might say that Appleby lasted so long – fifty years, from 1936 to 1986 – that he *had* to develop. He changed as the world about him changed. War perhaps was the biggest change of all; and in *The Secret Vanguard* (1940), Innes moved from the mere solving of puzzles to adventure. This was a 'chase' novel, the first of several such. *The Journeying Boy* – not an Appleby story – and *Appleby Plays Chicken* (1957) are two that notably continue the chase theme, although none of Innes's books should be approached with the hope of finding all-out action and adventure. His metier is entertainment of a more lasting and refined nature, and he remains rooted in the best traditions of the classic police detective story. *See also* Golden Age Crime Fiction.

Selected Works by the Author

As J.I.M. Stewart
A Staircase in Surrey (1974 to 1978) comprising: *The Gaudy, Young Pattullo, A Memorial Service, The Madonna of the Astrolabe, Full Term*
Myself and Michael Innes (autobiography, 1987)

As Michael Innes
Death at the President's Lodging (1936; also published in the United States as *Seven Suspects*)
Hamlet, Revenge! (1937)
There Came Both Mist and Snow (1940; also published in the United States as *A Comedy of Terrors*)
The Journeying Boy (1949; also published in the United States as *The Case of the Journeying Boy*)
Operation Pax (1951; also published in the United States as *The Paper Thunderbolt*)
The Man from the Sea (1955; also published in the United States as *Death by Moonlight*)
The Mysterious Commission (1974)

Russell James

Inspector Morse (television series, 1987–2000)

Inspector Morse is widely regarded as the most successful British television detective series. It was based on the ingenious novels of Colin **Dexter**, but it owed much to a felicitous combination of first-rate screenplays, the photogenic Oxford backdrop and outstanding performances by John Thaw and Kevin Whately as Morse and the long-suffering Sergeant Lewis.

Ted Childs of Central Television had noted the success of BBC TV's *Miss Marple* series starring Joan Hickson, which benefited from high-calibre writers translating cleverly constructed stories for the screen – boldly and yet with respect for the source material. Dexter's books are strong in setting, plot and *mise-en-scène*; he has little interest in police procedure, but that mattered little when it came to adapting his stories for the small screen. Producer Kenny McBain persuaded Childs that each episode should last for two hours rather than the conventional one hour; the series was conceived of as a collection of films, rather than a routine cop drama. This increased the cost, but it also resulted in high production values and afforded room for the leisurely exploration of character and locale.

John Thaw was best known for his highly successful role as the tough cop Jack Regan in 'The Sweeney', although he had appeared in a variety of dramas, including 'Redcap', as a military policeman, and the excellent, although now almost forgotten, Francis Durbridge serial *Bat out of Hell* (1966). It was a risky casting decision, given that Thaw was so closely associated with Regan, but Childs, who had worked on 'The Sweeney', recognised the actor's subtlety and range. Whately was far from an obvious choice for the role of Lewis, not least because he was so much younger than Dexter's sergeant and was a Geordie, rather than a Welshman. At the time, his main claim to fame was playing the bricklayer Neville Hope in the popular series *Auf Wiedersehen Pet*. But the decision to reinvent Morse's sidekick proved masterly, as the interplay between the gruff, cerebral chief inspector and his amiable sergeant became one of the joys of each programme.

At the outset, McBain secured the services of two writers of distinction, Anthony Minghella and Julian Mitchell. Minghella wrote the first screenplay, 'The Dead of Jericho', based on Dexter's third Morse novel, which he chose because 'it had a very real sense of place'. Shown on 6 January 1987, it established Morse's prime characteristics: not only his love of cars, crosswords, women, alcohol and classical music, but also his doggedness as a detective. The relationship with Lewis is firmly grounded: Morse is rude and patronising, but there is an undercurrent of affection. The stunning camera work, directed by Alastair Reed, set a new standard for television detective drama, while Barrington Pheloung's distinctive original music made an immediate impact (the theme spells out Morse's name in Morse code, and in some shows, the music provides a similar clue to the culprit's identity.) Colin Dexter made a fleeting cameo appearance, walking past Thaw in a college. These disparate elements became integral to the series as a whole.

The first series was completed by two screenplays from Mitchell: 'The Silent World of Nicholas Quinn' and 'Service of All the Dead'. Mitchell regards the latter as Dexter's finest novel; like *The Dead of Jericho*, it earned a **Crime Writers' Association** Silver Dagger. Excellent audience ratings and critical acclaim – not an invariable combination where television cop shows are concerned – guaranteed that Morse would investigate again. The second series ran to four films and by the time it came to an end, the reputation of Inspector Morse for accessible yet sophisticated entertainment was firmly established.

Dexter had never been a prolific writer, and it was soon clear that original storylines would be required. In a couple of episodes, a touch improbably, Morse ventured abroad, to Italy and Australia, but like most detectives who venture far from home, he seemed like a fish out of water. Intriguingly, 'The Wolvercote Tongue' – based on an idea by Dexter, written by Mitchell and first shown on Christmas Day 1987 – provided the basis for the later novel *The Jewel That Was Ours* (1991). Other writers were recruited, including Alma Cullen and Daniel Boyle; and although McBain left after the second series, his replacement, Chris Burt, ensured that the quality of the programmes never slipped. As the years passed, the relationship between Morse and Lewis developed until it resembled that between father and son. Morse was unorthodox and indifferent to authority, but his longing for romance was portrayed by Thaw with great sensitivity, above all in 'Dead on Time', scripted by Boyle, in which the detective encounters Susan Fallon (Joanna David gave a compelling performance in the part) to whom he was once engaged to be married.

For the thirty-third and final episode, 'The Remorseful Day', in which Morse dies, the award-winning director Jack Gold was brought in; the result, screened on 15 November 2000, was a poignant programme of a quality to match the best in the series. Thirteen million viewers tuned in, and overall, the series is said to have attracted over a billion viewers worldwide. When Thaw himself died in 2002, a nation mourned; he had become one of Britain's best-loved actors.

The Morse phenomenon was such that it spawned countless spin-offs, including record albums, documentaries, a concert of the music performed at the Royal Albert Hall, toy-replica Jaguars, jig-saw puzzles and a board game. Ultimately, Sergeant Lewis took centre stage in a television programme of his own, first aired on 26 January 2006; its popularity was such that further episodes followed. The lasting legacy of *Inspector Morse*, however, was the proof that, in skilful hands, a detective series could entertain a global audience whilst at the same time satisfying viewers who wanted something a little more than just a well-contrived whodunit mystery. *See also* TV Detectives: Small-Screen Adaptations.

Further Reading
Bird, Christopher. 1998. *The World of Inspector Morse: A Complete A–Z Reference for the Morse Enthusiast*. Boxtree.
Bishop, David. 2006. *The Complete Inspector Morse*, rev. ed. Reynolds & Hearn.
Sanderson, Mark. 1995. *The Making of Inspector Morse*, 2nd ed. Macmillan.

Martin Edwards

Ishiguro, Kazuo (b.1954)

Kazuo Ishiguro is an outstanding literary novelist. He is perhaps best known for his third novel, *The Remains of the Day* (1989), which won the Booker Prize, became a bestseller and was made into a highly successful film. With his fifth novel, *When We Were Orphans* (2000, nominated for the Booker Prize), he played in fascinating ways with the conventions of classic detective fiction.

Ishiguro was born in 1954, in Nagasaki, Japan, and came to England with his parents when he was five. His writing explores cultural identity – especially, of course, with reference to Japan, where his first two novels are set, and England. His typically unreliable narrators introspectively worry at the reliability of their memories, at whether they are fitting in to whatever society they find themselves and at making sense of their childhood experiences. The narrator of *When We Were Orphans* matches this profile perfectly: Christopher Banks, the child of English parents, grows up in the International Settlement, Shanghai, at the very beginning of the twentieth century.

His best friend is Japanese; both live in fear of going 'back home'. After the mysterious disappearance of his parents, Banks does indeed return to England, an orphan. The story opens as he thinks back to his schooldays in England; he believes himself to have been a well-adjusted boy and is puzzled by his friends' memories of him as odd. And one of his schoolboy eccentricities was his ambition to become a private detective; his classmates buy him a magnifying glass for his birthday.

Now an adult, Banks has fulfilled his ambition, and as a hugely successful and renowned investigator, he is welcomed into and feted by high society. His profile is distinctly Holmesian: he lives, alone, in rooms, at 14b Bedford Gardens, and has a string of celebrated cases to his name. When recalling his childhood, his patterns of speech continually echo the jargon of detective fiction: he interrogates, he makes enquiries, he believes he has witnessed significant incidents. But his greatest case lies ahead of him: to 'solve' the disappearance of his parents in Shanghai.

To some extent, Ishiguro pokes fun at the figure of the great detective. As a boy, Banks seems to have cut a comical figure: he overhears another boy mock him as 'too short to be a Sherlock'. A beautiful woman comes across the adult Banks clownishly lying flat on the floor peering at the ground with his magnifying glass. And Banks's investigative abilities are called into question by his hopelessly wrong readings of what was going on in his childhood, as we learn in a classic denouement scene which almost parodies its counterpart in the traditional whodunit. Somewhat grandiosely, Banks believes that the role of the detective is a profoundly significant one: to 'root out single-handedly all the evil in the world'. Ishiguro has himself said that classic detective fiction, so popular after the First World War, provided an escapist alternative to the unpleasant realisation that 'evil and suffering in the modern world wasn't about a master criminal or a clever vicar who was poisoning people for someone's inheritance'. Banks finds himself faced with the horrors of actual war – the early stages of the Japanese invasion of China – and turning his magnifying glass on to one of its bloody victims is a shocking irrelevance in the context of the carnage. Banks's most damaging delusion is that solving his personal mystery will somehow avert the war itself.

However, Ishiguro does not merely deride the figure and mission of the traditional detective. The investigative process in *When We Were Orphans* functions as an allegory for the process at work in all his novels: the minute analysis of society; the mysteries of childhood under a magnifying glass; and perhaps most strikingly, what Frank Kermode has called 'the occult narrative' – the story based on a secret which the writer gradually uncovers – which is fundamental to both crime fiction and to Ishiguro's other novels. *See also* The Detective in British Fiction.

Selected Works by the Author
A Pale View of Hills (1982)
An Artist of the Floating World (1986)
The Remains of the Day (1989)
The Unconsoled (1995)
When We Were Orphans (2001)
Never Let Me Go (2005)

Further Reading
Lewis, Barry. 2000. *Kazuo Ishiguro*. Manchester University Press.
Wong, Cynthia F. 2005. *Kazuo Ishiguro*, rev. ed. Northcote House.

Heather O'Donoghue

It Always Rains on Sunday (film, 1947)

Robert Hamer, director

This uncharacteristically gloomy Ealing film – somewhere between film noir and neo-realism – was based on a novel by Arthur La Bern, who also wrote *Goodbye Piccadilly, Farewell Leicester Square* (source for Alfred Hitchcock's **Frenzy**) and *Night Darkens the Streets* (filmed as *Good Time Girl*).

Tommy Swann (John McCallum), a smash-and-grab man, breaks out of Dartmoor and returns to his old manor, Bethnal Green, hoping to be sheltered by his ex-girlfriend Rose (Googie Withers) until he can hop on a ship for Cape Town. Rose, a former barmaid who remembers Tommy as a sharp-suited, pre-war, flash character, is shocked to find an unshaven, worn-out escapee lurking in the disused Anderson shelter in her tiny back garden but does her best to take him in – though his presence only serves to remind her how drab and petty her current life is. Rose has married older, bluff widower George Sandigate (Edward Chapman) and has trouble with Vi (Susan Shaw) and Doris (Patricia Plunkett) – Sandigate's daughters from a previous marriage – and her own tearaway son Alfie (David Lines), who blackmails Vi and her would-be lover, bandleader Morry Hyams (Sydney Tafler), for a mouth organ. Morry's brother (John Slater), the local big spiv, fixes a fight and kicks back cash to a youth club gymnasium, though he is still despised by his father (Meier Tzelniker) and sister (Jane Hylton) while three petty crooks (Alfie Bass, Jimmy Hanley and John Carol) scurry around trying to offload a haul of roller skates. Sergeant Fothergill (inevitably played by Jack Warner) cruises blandly around his patch, missing nothing and knowing everyone, keeping a lid on minor criminal activities while tracking down the jail-hardened Tommy, who is finally apprehended in a night-time pursuit through the railway shunting yards.

Directed and co-written by Robert Hamer, the most pessimistic director of Ealing stable, the movie evokes the kind of busy, fussy community values found in the studio's 'little England' films (*Passport to Pimlico*, *The Lavender Hill Mob*), but also homes in mercilessly on everyday desperation. This is a world of cheese rationing, darts down the pub before an overcooked lunch, dance-hall Lotharios (Morry is billed as 'The Man with Sax Appeal'), puritanical fences who gouge their customers, busy markets which leave the streets choked with rubbish when they move on, rip-off slot-machine arcades, smoky boozers and – as the title suggests – the miseries of the British weather. There is a working-class vibrancy to much of the activity – the film is full of picturesque criminal slang and Yiddish expressions – but Hamer, who chronicled a suffocating Victorian family crime in the underrated *Pink String and Sealing Wax* (1945) and dealt with a social-climbing serial killer in the justly classic *Kind Hearts and Coronets* (1949), is most concerned with trapped, doomed souls like Rose and Tommy, who misremember a pre-war idyll and now have to cope with the sordid practicalities of life on the run. Although much of the film is stage bound, several on-location sequences provide a valuable panorama of post-blitzed **London**. *See also* Film and Crime: Page to Screen *and* Realism and Crime Fiction.

Kim Newman

J

Jackson, Lee (b.1971)

Lee Jackson is a Victorian **London** obsessive. He is the author of a series
of historical thrillers as well as two non-fiction studies of London in the Victorian
period and also maintains a comprehensive historical website.

While living and working as a librarian in London, Jackson became fascinated by
the city's Victorian past. This soon became his passion, and his research led to him pen
the period thriller *London Dust* (2003). This well-received novel, full of vivid descriptions of the dark side of Victorian society, was shortlisted for the Ellis Peters Historical
Dagger Award. The Victorian milieu remains the basis of his literary career with
further novels, two non-fiction books and an impressive website, which is as much a
resource for anyone interested in social history as it is for information about the author.

Jackson's Victorian-set mysteries take the reader through the metropolis,
exploring the oddities of Victorian life and aspects of the period that the reader
may know little about, such as mourning department stores (in *The Welfare of the
Dead*, 2005) or Victorian pleasure gardens (in *The Last Pleasure Garden*, 2006). His
narratives are full of wry commentary on the absurdities of the class system, and
he is not frightened to explore the darker side of society (pornography, prostitution
or unwanted children). His novels are detailed and evocative, with eccentric and
well-drawn characters, many of them strong-willed women like the heroine of his
first novel, *London Dust*.

London Dust (2003) follows Natalie Meadows in her attempts to uncover the
murderer of her best friend and music-hall star, Nellie Warwick. Natalie's journey
brings her into contact with the seedier parts of the city and with religious
Salvationists, who may be less righteous than the people they are trying to save.

Jackson's next three novels centre on the eccentric Inspector Decimus Webb and
his assistant, Sergeant Bartley. The first, *A Metropolitan Murder* (2004), sees them
investigating the brutal murder on the London Underground. How Victorians deal
with death is explored in *The Welfare of the Dead* (2005), in which the detectives are
called in to investigate the murder of two prostitutes while also investigating a case
of grave robbing. The third novel in the series, *The Last Pleasure Garden* (2006),
revolves around the Cremorne Pleasure Gardens, which is being terrorised by 'The
Cutter' (who attacks young women by removing a lock of their hair). After two
murders, Webb's investigations lead him to a crusading vicar and to the secrets
of the wife and daughter of a respectable stockbroker.

Jackson introduced a new heroine in *A Most Dangerous Woman* (2007), in the
shape of coffee-shop proprietor Sarah Tanner, drawn back into the dark underworld
of the metropolis after witnessing the murder of an old friend. She returned in *The
Mesmerist's Apprentice* (2008), foiling the schemes of a conniving physician while
dodging a gang of Lambeth 'roughs' bent on vengeance.

Selected Works by the Author
London Dust (2003)
A Metropolitan Murder (2004)
The Welfare of the Dead (2005)
The Last Pleasure Garden (2006)

Jackson, Lee

A Most Dangerous Woman (2007)
The Mesmerist's Apprentice (2008)

Website
www.victorianlondon.org

Terry Fountain

Jakeman, Jane (b.1941)

Not so well known as many of her contemporaries in the field, Jane Jakeman is the highly regarded author of meticulously researched historical mystery stories, in particular her 1990s trilogy featuring the Byronic nineteenth-century sleuth Lord Ambrose Malfine.

Born in Wales, Jakeman studied in Oxford and received a PhD in Islamic Art from Oxford University. She is married to eminent Egyptologist Jaromir Malek. She is the author of numerous articles in academic journals and has contributed to *The New Statesman*, *The Sunday Times* and *The Independent*, for which she has reviewed crime fiction.

Her first novel, *Let There Be Blood* (1997), is a highly impressive piece, beginning with the once-dashing figure of Lord Ambrose Malfine returning to his West Country ancestral home in 1830 to recover from the privations of war in Greece, aided by his faithful Greek manservant, Belos. However, his much-needed solitude is spoilt by the murder of a nearby farmer and his son, and Malfine reluctantly leaves his comfortable estate to investigate the case. Having turned amateur sleuth, he soon finds that the job of unmasking the murderer is not as easy as it might at first seem.

With an elegant prose style echoing that of the Brontës and with a protagonist not a million miles away from *Pride and Prejudice*'s Mr Rochester, the book was an instant hit with those seeking a literary edge to their crime fiction, and a follow-up appeared later that year. *The Egyptian Coffin* had Malfine decamp from the bleak Dartmoor tors to the dusty alleyways of Cairo in a sinister tale of an Egyptian curse that threatens the life of a young heiress in thrall to her wicked uncle. Written in the form of letters and bearing several plot elements akin to *The Woman in White*, Jakeman's literary inspirations this time appeared to be such **Gothic** mystery writers as Wilkie **Collins** and Sheridan Le Fanu.

The final novel in the sequence, *Fool's Gold* (1998), centres on Ambrose's seemingly unrequited love for Elisabeth Anstruther, governess of a recently orphaned young boy. Although Elisabeth refuses Ambrose's gentlemanly advances, he is soon at her side investigating a series of suspicious deaths, and it is not long before he has to protect her against some very dangerous opponents.

Enormously popular in the United States, the trilogy was followed by a contemporary European series featuring French magistrate Cecile Galant, opening with a murder at the Cannes Film Festival in *Death in the South of France* (2001). Artist Claude Monet features heavily in the atmospheric Victorian mystery *In the Kingdom of Mists* (2002). Jakeman has also written ghost stories set in Oxford and edited a sumptuous book of English recipes dating from the 1770s. *See also* Historical Crime.

Selected Works by the Author
Let There Be Blood (1997)
The Egyptian Coffin (1997)

Mark Campbell

Jakubowski, Maxim (b.1944)

In the world of contemporary British crime writing, few figures are so influential as this author, editor and book dealer.

Born in Britain of Polish and Russo-British parents, Maxim Jakubowski was raised and educated in France. Jakubowski's earliest published works were primarily in the field of science fiction – his first book being an anthology of French science fiction, *Travelling towards Epsilon* (1976). He subsequently produced other anthologies of science fiction and fantasy plus a couple of reference books, but by the early 1980s, his emphasis had shifted to crime fiction. His interests lie primarily in the cause and effect of crime rather than in the detection, although he does profess a fascination for locked-room puzzles. Among his few crime novels, only one, *On Tenderness Express* (2000), actually involves a detective, in this case a private detective looking for a lost girl, and even here, his interest is more in what causes people to do what they do. His other crime novels show the shiftless nature of individuals who can become sucked into criminal activity, such as in *It's You That I Want to Kiss* (1996), where a psychopath pursues a couple across America seeking to retrieve his stolen property, and in *Because She Thought She Loved Me* (1997), which, although dealing with Internet pornography, involves a chase across Europe. These three books have been included in the omnibus *Skin in Darkness* (2006). Jakubowksi's interest in this transitory life leading to either self-discovery or self-destruction is reflected in the anthology *The Mammoth Book of On the Road* (2002; also published in the United States as *The Mammoth Book of Tales of the Road*).

His anthologies, like his novels, show Jakubowski's interest in noir fiction, the darkness of the soul and the psychology of crime. In the early 1980s, as editor (and managing director) of Zomba Books, he initiated the Black Box line of thrillers, publishing a series of omnibus volumes of collected novels by David Goodis, Cornell Woolrich, W.R. Burnett, Jim Thompson and others. In the late 1980s, he produced a similar series, Blue Murder, for Simon & Schuster, this time reprinting classic novels by Davis Grubb, Newton Thornburg, Cornell Woolrich and others. These volumes brought American noir of the 1940s and 1950s to a new British generation and were influential in opening a new source for British writers to mine. Such work was reflected in his anthologies *London Noir* (1994), *No Alibi* (1995) and the *Fresh Blood* trilogy (1996–1999), compiled with Mike **Ripley**. He also presented selections of representative crime fiction from the American **pulp** magazines in *The Mammoth Book of Pulp Fiction* (1996) and *The Mammoth Book of Pulp Action* (2001).

Jakubowski left the publishing world in 1988 and established Murder One, Britain's first and biggest specialist crime fiction bookshop. The shop helped Jakubowski remain on top of developments in crime fiction and also became a focal point for writers as well as book collectors. When markets for new short fiction dwindled in Britain, especially with the passing of the annual *Winter's Crimes* in 1992, Jakubowski tried to encourage new markets. He compiled a selection of the best fiction from that series as *Murders for the Fireside* (1992). A second selection, *More Murders for the Fireside* (1994), reprinted other recent fiction that had been nominated for or had won awards. He initiated his own series for new fiction with *New Crimes* (1990), which ran for three volumes with Constable; there was a further volume, *Crime Yellow* (1994), with Gollancz. Several stories from these series were nominated for or won awards. However, difficulties in sustaining a regular new market led Jakubowski to switch to selecting the best British crime fiction published each year, with *Best British Mysteries*, which began in 2003.

Jakubowksi's interest in modern crime, plus his many excursions into erotic fiction, has not lessened his interest in more traditional fiction, especially historical crime. In addition to *Royal Crimes* (1994), Jakubowski compiled three bumper anthologies of historical crime fiction: *Past Poisons* (1998), *Chronicles of Crime* (1999) and *Murder through the Ages* (2001). He also assembled the best of classic crime in *The Mammoth Book of Vintage Whodunnits* (2006) and *Great TV and Film Detectives* (2006). In a more light-hearted vein, he compiled *The Mammoth Book of Comic Crime* (2002), while *The Mammoth Book of Future Cops* (2003) combined his interest in crime and science fiction.

Amongst his non-fiction books, the Anthony Award-winning *100 Great Detectives* (1991) is a useful summary whilst *The Mammoth Book of Jack the Ripper* (1999), with Nathan Braund, brought together all the current thinking on the notorious murderer.

Jakubowski's anthologies continue to be amongst the best markets in Britain for state-of-the-art crime fiction, with the editor encouraging authors to continue to push the barriers. *See also* Anthologies *and* Science Fiction and Crime Fiction.

Selected Works by the Author

Novels
It's You That I Want to Kiss (1996)
Because She Thought She loved Me (1997)
On Tenderness Express (2000)
Confessions of a Romantic Pornographer (2006)

Edited
100 Great Detectives (1990)
Murders for the Fireside (1992)
More Murders for the Fireside (1994)
Fresh Blood (1996–1999; three volumes), with Mike Ripley
Mammoth Book of Pulp Fiction (1999)
Best British Mysteries series (2003–)

Mike Ashley

James, Bill (b.1929)

Bill James is one of the pseudonyms of James Tucker (he also writes as David Craig and Judith Jones). As Bill James, he has written a long series of crime novels set in an unnamed dockland town featuring police detectives Colin Harpur and Desmond Iles. The fourth novel in the series was turned into a television drama, but was only modestly successful, perhaps because the distinctive qualities of James's work are not readily translatable to drama or indeed palatable to a television audience: a brilliant but idiosyncratic prose style, oblique, loaded dialogue, blackly comic and sometimes surreal characters, and extraordinarily subtle and complex plots, in which the tightly knit criminal fraternity watch the local police watching them.

Assistant Chief Constable Desmond Iles is a natty dresser, a bigoted Orangeman, paranoid – especially with regard to his wife's fidelity (or lack of it) – and ambitious to the point of insanity. He also has an unhealthy and predatory interest in the precocious teenage daughters of his subordinate Colin Harpur. At the beginning of the series, Harpur is only fairly happily married to an idealistic English teacher, who hosts a book club from their house; Harpur feels very acutely his cultural inferiority. But his key strength is his relationship with a weirdly eccentric police informer, Jack Lamb, who attends fine-art auctions, both buying and, more worryingly, selling, and is the chief conduit for information passing in both directions between the police and the criminals.

49. Bill James.

The criminal community is depicted with humour, insight and complete contempt. But the structures and concerns of their alternative society are disturbingly analogous to those of the police force, with their outward respectability, cut-throat jockeying for position behind the scenes and cynical sexual liaisons. For instance, we see Panicking Ralph, a prosperous and skilful getaway car driver, whose daughters (unlike Harpur's) are at an expensive private school. The comedy lies not in a demonstration of this weakness in action, but in the way shifts of power amongst his colleagues are registered by who dares to use his nickname to his face.

James is also the author of two **espionage** novels, featuring black Welsh Oxford graduate Simon Abelard (*Split*, 2002 and *A Man's Enemies*, 2004) and a number of other crime novels, such as *Middleman* (2003) or *Letters from Carthage* (2006), a typically off-beat take on the epistolary novel, which are not in the Harpur and Iles series, but demonstrate James's unique and wholly unmistakeable literary features. Some characters move between the David Craig and Bill James books (such as police psychiatrist Andrew Rockmain). *See also* Humour and Crime Fiction *and* Police Procedurals.

Selected Works by the Author
You'd Better Believe It (1985)
The Lolita Man (1986)
Halo Parade (1987)
Protection (1988)
Come Clean (1989)
Take (1990)
The Detective Is Dead (1995)
Panicking Ralph (1997)
Eton Crop (1999)
Easy Streets (2004)
Wolves of Memory (2005)
In the Absence of Iles (2008)

Heather O'Donoghue

James, P.D. (b.1920)

Phyllis Dorothy James is considered by many to be the leading writer of British detective fiction of the post–Agatha **Christie** generation. Although her output is smaller than most other practitioners – minuscule compared with Dame Agatha herself – her superb characterisations, solidly constructed mysteries and expert knowledge of the British criminal system more than make up for any brevity of material.

P.D. James was born on 3 August 1920 in Oxford. Her father, Sidney Victor, was a tax officer, and she was the eldest of three. From an early age, family holidays at the seaside resort of Lowestoft instilled in her a love of the East Anglian countryside. She was educated at the prestigious Cambridge High School for Girls, but the academic life was not for her, and she left at sixteen, foregoing the prospect of further education to work instead in her father's tax office.

Shortly after the outbreak of the Second World War, she met and married Dr Ernest Connor Bantry White, just before his departure for the Royal Army Medical Corps. They had two daughters, Claire and Jane, born during the war, and Phyllis stayed at home and looked after them herself – coping as best she could on a frugal army stipend. But when her husband returned from the front, it became apparent that he had been deeply affected by his combat experiences. Tragically, he had developed schizophrenia and spent his remaining years being admitted to various mental hospitals until his death in 1964.

Apart from the difficulty in looking after her husband, she also suffered terrible financial pressures. White received no war pension, and so Phyllis had to rely on her in-laws to help them scrape by. She enrolled as a hospital clerk to bring in enough money and took evening classes to fill in educational gaps that were caused by her early departure from school. And alongside these classes, she began to write fiction.

She decided to write a crime story, as she felt this would have a good chance of being accepted by a publisher. She based the location of *Cover Her Face* (1962) on the Essex country house in which she was living at the time. 'It was a country house murder story rather like Agatha Christie – perhaps more Agatha Christie than any of my subsequent books,' she recalled in a 2005 interview (*Crime Time*). Naming her protagonist after her old English teacher, Miss Dalgliesh, she gave Scotland Yard detective Adam **Dalgliesh** many of the artistic qualities she herself admired, including the ability to write poetry. 'I was very much aware of the problem that Dorothy L. **Sayers** and

Agatha Christie had in making their detectives too eccentric and getting rather tired of them,' she said in the same interview. 'So I decided to have a character who could develop; from the beginning I had in mind that he might be a serial character.'

At a weekend house party in Kent, actor and writer Miles Malleson suggested she send her manuscript – written as 'P D James' – to his agent, Elaine Greene. Elaine immediately accepted it. Later, while she and her husband, Hugh Carlton Greene, then director general of the BBC, were dining at All Souls College, they found themselves sitting next to one of the directors of Faber and Faber, Charles Montieth. Montieth mentioned that their detective writer Cyril **Hare** (whose best-known novels include *Tragedy at Law*, 1942, and *An English Murder*, 1951) had died recently, and they were looking for a replacement. Elaine suggested P.D. James, and the rest is history.

James's original intention was that *Cover Her Face* would act as a practice run for what she intended to be a 'serious' novel the following year. However, by the time she finished it, she already had had an idea for a second, and the plaudits from critics and readers alike strengthened her desire to continue writing in the same genre. Indeed, she considered the format's conventions to be an aid to imagination, rather than a straightjacket. 'As I continued, I came to believe that I could stay within the conventions and the structure of the classical detective story whilst also stretching it,' she recalled. 'I could use it to say something psychologically true about men and women and also about the society in which they live' (***Crime Time***, 2005).

Two years later, James had worked her way up the British Civil Service to become a principal in the Criminal Department of the Home Office. She was responsible for the appointment of scientists to Britain's forensics laboratories and advised ministers on juvenile crime issues. These experiences she used to great effect in *Death of an Expert Witness* (1977), a book that saw her popularity as a crime writer increase dramatically in the United Kingdom. Her next book, the stand-alone *Innocent Blood* (1980), became a number one bestseller in the United States, with 20th Century Fox buying the film rights for a large (undisclosed) sum.

The financial rewards of such popularity allowed her to take early retirement from the Home Office in 1979 and move to a cottage in Southwold in Essex. However, the quantity of her output remained much as before, with only three books produced during the 1980s. This concern for quality over quantity marks her out as a distinctive writer in the field – her books seem to improve with every passing year. Recent offerings, such as the darkly atmospheric *Devices and Desires* (1989) and the ecclesiastical skulduggery of *Death in Holy Orders* (2001), show that she is every bit as powerful a writer as she was when she first started out, and certainly unafraid to explore in ever more vivid detail the flawed psychological make-up of her characters.

Her sole contribution to the science fiction genre was *The Children of Men* (1992), which postulated an infertile future world and the activities of a rebel group who oppose the dictator of 2021 England, one Xan Lyppiatt. Seen by many as a Christian allegory (the world saved by a seemingly miraculous birth), the novel was adapted into a visually stunning 2006 film, starring Clive Owen and directed by Alfonso Cuarón. But although the film succeeded magnificently in portraying a grim and violent future Britain, it omitted the (admittedly complex) political background of the book, with James's main storyline pared down so much that it was almost unrecognisable.

James's other series detective, young, amateur sleuth Cordelia Gray, has appeared in two novels: *An Unsuitable Job for a Woman* (1972) and *The Skull Beneath the Skin* (1982). While both are eminently readable, neither shares the psychological insight of her Dalgliesh titles, and they must be considered lesser works. Gray was played by Pippa Guard in a 1982 film version of *An Unsuitable Job for a Woman*, while a short-lived television series (1997–2001) featured Helen Baxendale as the feisty investigator.

Roy Marsden has become synonymous with the character of Adam Dalgliesh on television, playing the part in a series of solidly presented adaptations from 1983 to 1998 for Anglia TV. Since then, Martin Shaw has appeared as the laconic detective in BBC adaptations of two more recent works, *Death in Holy Orders* (2001) and *The Murder Room* (2003).

James's non-writing activities have included chairing the British Society of Authors and the 1987 Booker Prize panel, serving as a local magistrate and sitting on the BBC Board of Governors from 1988 to 1993. She was awarded an OBE in 1983 and a life peerage in 1991; her official title is thus Baroness James of Holland Park. She currently holds seven honorary doctorates from various British universities and has won numerous awards for her books, including CWA Silver Daggers for *Shroud for a Nightingale* (1971), *The Black Tower* (1975) and *A Taste for Death* (1986). A revealing volume of memoirs, *Time to Be in Earnest*, appeared in 2001. *See also* Crime Writers' Association *and* Women Crime Writers.

Selected Works by the Author
Cover Her Face (1962)
Shroud for a Nightingale (1971)
The Black Tower (1975)
Death of an Expert Witness (1977)
Devices and Desires (1989)
The Murder Room (2003)

Mark Campbell

James, Peter (b.1948)

James's early writing spans the spy-fiction, supernatural and science fiction genres. For many years, he was also a film and television writer and producer. Eventually, however, he decided to focus all his creative energies on writing crime fiction, spurred by the instant global success of his Detective Superintendent Roy Grace series.

James nurtured a desire to be a crime writer after a youthful reading of Graham **Greene**'s ***Brighton Rock***, which was set in his home town (now city) of Brighton. But success in fiction did not come quickly or easily to him. His first attempt at a novel, written at the age of nineteen, *Ride Down a Roller Coaster*, although never published, did secure him an agent in 1969 (Kurt Hellmer in New York). After a film-school education (against Hellmer's advice for a would-be novelist, believing that he would be too distracted and that his creative energies would be dissipated), James went first into the television then subsequently into the film business. Among his first film productions as a producer was the highly acclaimed *Death Dream* (1973) directed by Bob Clark. But the first film James created as a writer, *Spanish Fly* (1976), was savaged by the Britain's most powerful critic, Barry Norman, as being 'the least funny British funny film ever made' and 'probably the worst British film since the Second World War'.

At the age of twenty-nine (in 1979), James read an article in *The Times*, noting a shortage of spy thrillers. Although hankering to write a detective novel, he was concerned that the world of crime fiction was overcrowded and decided to write a piece of spy fiction and came out with *Dead Letter Drop* (1981). To his delight, the manuscript secured him a new agent (Kurt Hellmer having died in the meantime), and the book was accepted for publication by W.H. Allen. But disappointment and disenchantment were soon to set in.

This novel and his next, *Atom Bomb Angel* (1982), sold only a few thousand copies. Both were spy thrillers featuring MI6 agent Max Flynn. *Dead Letter Drop* dealt with the discovery of a mole at the very top of the British Security Services, and *Atom Bomb Angel* dealt with the horrors of a terrorist attack on a nuclear power station on the UK mainland. While lacking the characterisation, which is one of the major strengths of James's latter novels, the books reveal his early narrative and plotting skills and, perhaps even more significantly, his prodigious and rigorously accurate research, which contribute greatly to the authenticity of his later writing, particularly in the crime genre.

His third novel, *Billionaire* (1983), a financial thriller set in the murky international world of metal broking, revolved around a plot to mine the Persian Gulf and force up the price of gold. The same uneven characterisation as with the first two applies to this book, but the plotting and research were masterly. But like the first two and despite some decent reviews, this novel failed to get attraction.

When James poured his heart out to a friend, Elizabeth Buchan, then a jacket blurb writer at Penguin (and now a successful novelist), she chided him for writing spy thrillers just because they were the kind of books that would sell. 'Write what you are passionate about,' she told him. It was a piece of advice that was to change his life.

In 1983, the tragic death of the son of close friends, who subsequently began consulting mediums, inspired *Possession* (1988). The elegant urban ghost story instantly became James's first real breakthrough book and was subsequently translated into twenty-three languages. A series of well-researched and chilling novels, exploring different areas of the paranormal, followed: *Dreamer* (1989), *Sweet Heart* (1990), *Twilight* (1991) and *Prophecy* (1992).

Denial (1999), a psychological thriller in which a psychiatrist is stalked by a patient's son after his mother commits suicide following a session with him, is notable for the first appearance of Glenn Branson, who would reappear as Detective Superintendent Roy Grace's sidekick and foil – in many ways Watson to Grace's Holmes in the Roy Grace novels.

Following a lengthy gap, James finally produced his first crime fiction novel, *Dead Simple* (2005) and, in doing so, discovered his true métier. *Dead Simple*, in which Roy Grace makes his first appearance, is considered by some people to be James's finest novel to date. It works both as a highly charged thriller and as an impeccably researched **police procedural**. And in the novel, James finally claims his native Brighton as his landscape and backdrop. *Dead Simple* is masterfully plotted and filled with sharp, shocking twists, but it is the rounded character of Detective Superintendent Roy Grace that captivated James's readers even more than the story itself.

Dead Simple, translated into twenty-eight languages, achieved James's largest sales to that time, both in the United Kingdom and internationally, and won him three awards – the Germany Krimi Blitz Crimewriter of the Year (2005), the French Prix Polar International (2007) and the French Prix Coeur Noir (2007).

Looking Good Dead (2006), the second Grace novel, continued with James's format of mixing a fast-moving thriller plot with police procedural – Tom Bryce, a decent man, commuting daily from Brighton to London discovers a CD left behind on the train. When he inserts it into his computer in an attempt to trace its owner, he finds himself driven to a website in which he witnesses a savage murder.

James's third Grace novel, *Not Dead Enough* (2007), centres around the theme of identity theft. Through the introduction of a deprived, young drug addict, James shows a sharp insight into the underbelly of Grace – and of James – Brighton and Hove, creating through the novel a chiaroscuro contrast between the gilded life of Brian Bishop and the no-hoper world of Brighton street life. *See also* Espionage Fiction *and* Thrillers: Novels of Action.

Selected Works by the Author
The Truth (1997)
Denial (1998)
Faith (2000)
Dead Simple (2005)
Looking Good Dead (2006)
Not Dead Enough (2007)

Barry Forshaw

James, Russell (b.1942)

When everyone else on the British crime-writing scene seemed to be writing **police procedurals**, Russell James wrote about victims and low-life criminals. In his novels, the police barely appeared. In a short time, James had established himself as one of Britain's leading hard-boiled writers.

Russell James had seven years of military education before drifting into various jobs, including working on a Mediterranean radio station and being a stagehand at the Old Vic. His debut novel, *Underground* (1989), was told in the first person by a villain lying low, biding his time for the propitious moment – but as (inevitably) his enemies trace him, he finds himself on the run. The book's pungently realised setting was South **London**, an area James would return to in other novels. *Daylight* (1990) explored the world of debt-collectors and Russian gangs, while in *Payback* (1991), Floyd Carter returns home to avenge his murdered brother but is pulled back into a world of drug dealing, loan sharks and murder. James continued to impress with hard-boiled writing in *Slaughter Music* (1995), in which jealousy and revenge suck the young hit-man protagonist into an emotional quagmire. Although the plotline sounds well trodden, the result was violent and kinetic.

Count Me Out (1996) is a novel of honour and conflict, set in the fairgrounds of Devon, although the story begins in South East London. The chance to abscond with half-a-million pounds is too much for Scott, even if it means abandoning his family. But it proves problematic for his brother, who tries not to be drawn into a world of criminality. This is a dark and powerful novel with a strong storytelling ethos. But it is surpassed by *Painting in the Dark* (2000), a study of evil and deceit, considered by many to be James's landmark novel. The book spans seventy years and is linked by two connected strands. One explores the Nazis and fascist Britain in the 1930s; the second is structured as a more conventional crime novel set against the background of the 1997 general election with an enigmatic Tony Blair sweeping into power. For large sections of the novel, Naomi, the female protagonist, appears to argue the case for fascism, and she gives sympathetic portraits of Mosley, Goering and Adolf Hitler. This is counterbalanced with the modern-day art fence Gottfleisch (a recurring James character and a likeable rogue), who wants to get his hands on sought-after paintings of Hitler owned by Naomi.

50. Russell James.

James's novels force the readers to confront their own reaction to the text. Although he offers humanised villains, he tempers his books with cold-eyed black humour and tight prose. Another of his trademarks is to examine the dark underbelly of the criminal life and anatomise it, with all sentimentality brushed aside. He favours the loner who is strong, sometimes emotionally damaged, who must fight on all fronts to stay alive. His novels include some of the best crime fiction written in the United Kingdom.

Selected Works by the Author
Underground (1989)
Payback (1991)
Slaughter Music (1995)
Count Me Out (1996)
Painting in the Dark (2000)
Pick Any Title (2002)
No One Gets Hurt (2003)
Sleuth – Britain's Greatest Fictional Detectives (non-fiction, 2008)

Mike Stotter

Janson, Hank (1917–1989)

In his day, Hank Janson (pseudonym of Stephen Frances) was a publishing phenomenon. Between 1946 and 1971, his hard-boiled tales of glamorous America sold over twenty million copies. Not only was he the master of seamy pulps, but his Spanish Civil War saga – *La Guerra*, written over two years in the mid-1960s – was praised by one reviewer as the best historical novel since *Gone with the Wind*, and comparable with *For Whom the Bell Tolls* and *Dr Zhivago*. Yet when Frances died in 1989 of emphysema at his home in Spain, few people knew about it, apart from some close friends. His name had not appeared on a book for over ten years, and during the last years of his life, it was his wife, Theresa, who supported the family.

Stephen Daniel Frances was born in Lambeth, South London, in 1917. His father, also called Stephen, was a shop assistant who had married May Isabel Abbott in 1916, but was soon to be conscripted into the army. On the day his son reached one year of age, he was killed while serving in France, and Steve was raised by his mother on the pittance of an army pension.

51. Cover of *When Dames Get Tough* (originally published in 1946).

'Hank Janson' first appeared in the days of Pendulum Publications in the 1940s. A printer had phoned up with the news that he had enough paper for a 25,000 print run on a twenty-four-page book. This was manna to any publisher, but the manuscript had to be in on Monday. It was Friday. 'I rang around,' Frances recalled. 'No writer I contacted had any manuscript available of the length required.' Unable to find a suitable manuscript, Frances turned to a friend, Muriel. 'I asked her if she was willing to work over the weekend. She was. "It's going to be hard work," I warned. "I'll dictate and you'll type." We worked all Saturday and until after midnight on Sunday. But by then we had the exact number of typed pages the printer needed. I was hoarse from walking up and down while dictating and Muriel's shoulders ached from hunching over the typewriter.'

The book was delivered, titled *When Dames Get Tough* (1946), the author given as Hank Janson, and was quickly followed by *Scarred Faces* (1946), a sixty-four pager containing two short novels ('Scarred Faces' and 'Kitty Takes the Rap'). The three stories were relatively well written, with each story continuing from where the last left off. However, it was not until the next series of books was launched that Janson became the bestseller of his time.

With the lukewarm reception of a western novel, Frances quickly turned back to the gangster novel, and over the next few weeks, wrote *This Woman Is Death* (1948). While waiting for the printers, he wrote another, *Lady Mind That Corpse* (1948), and even as the first title was being delivered, he was already into a third. He delivered the second novel to Reiter and offered him *Gun Moll for Hire*, and was given the news that sales were good. Reiter wanted 15,000 of the third book, and another 5,000 each of the first two. However good this news was, it was tempered by the knowledge that Frances had the finance to print only 10,000. Reiter immediately offered to finance the additional printing, and a bond of friendship was formed between the two. 'I couldn't believe it,' Frances later said. 'In almost all my dealings in business everybody was obsessed with getting their hands on money and then never letting go of it. I never forgot this, and later on, when powerful book distributors made extremely tempting offers I never for a moment considered taking the distribution of Hank Janson away from him.'

Janson's success was phenomenal. At the time, the books of James Hadley **Chase** and other hard-hitting crime novelists were bestsellers (*No Orchids for Miss Blandish*, 1939, sold a million copies in five years and has continued to sell ever since), and the popularity of 'Yank' magazines and **pulps** had been known since the 1930s. War-time import restrictions meant that the genuine article was not available, and a massive market for British editions of magazines was created. The glamour of Hollywood had taken Britain by storm as well, with film magazines and glossy photo magazines selling in their many thousands. The war had seen a massive influx of American influence, whether from films, magazines or the thousands of American servicemen drafted into the country. The Janson novels were a series, which made them stand out from the one-off novels of Ben Sarto (another best-seller of the late 1940s, the pen-name of Frank Dubrez Fawcett) or Darcy Glinto (Harold Kelly). Concentrating on his one creation, Steve was able to build up Janson's character from one book to the next, and readership loyalty proved his ability to tell a good yarn. The fourth novel, *No Regrets for Clara* (1949), had a first printing of 20,000.

Janson was another reflection of a fictionalised Steve Frances. The stories were violent, fast-paced and written in a style that was easily read. Janson was a traveller who roamed America finding women and adventure in equal quantities. The fictional America he travelled was culled from travel brochures, but its glamour was a stark contrast to an England still in the grip of rationing. Frances tried to think himself into Janson's shoes:

> I aimed at making Hank Janson seem a real living person. I invented a biography for him which was widely accepted as true. So many readers believed Hank Janson was flesh and blood that Hank Janson fan clubs were formed around Britain that appealed for Hank to pay them a visit. When writing, I completely identified myself with Hank Janson. If a girl slapped his face my cheek stung. If he smelled rotting fish I felt nauseated and if he exhausted himself I had to gulp whiskey to revive myself. Because I could identify myself so thoroughly with Hank Janson, my readers were probably also helped to identify with the book's hero, which is what many readers like to do.

The books were becoming a runaway success, the print run soon went up to 30,000 and Reiter was asking for a more regular supply. 'I am a very slow and very bad typist,'

Frances admitted. 'But I was being urged to provide more Hank Janson books, more quickly.' The answer was a second-hand Dictaphone, which recorded on a wax cylinder.

> When I completed a stack of cylinders I carried them around the corner to a typing agency. I developed my own writing method. I dictate the book hot and fast. I put in everything that bubbles into my mind. Often the sentences don't make sense but the words conjure up an emotion. I can dictate so very much more quickly than I can type that I can quickly record a first 'rough' novel. Then, when I get back the mass of typed material from the typist I cut drastically, edit ruthlessly, change, adapt, correct and edit until I feel I can send the amended copy for its final typing.

Hank Janson had risen to the leagues of the multi-million sellers when the climate in British publishing was showing a downswing. Paper rationing was deregulated in 1951, and more and more books jostled in the bookstands. Publishers were collapsing regularly as competition became fiercer, yet Janson's sales were increasing. The success story of Hank Janson was summed up by Frances: 'Writing is hard work and very demanding, but I enjoy it. And those who are lucky and can enjoy their work are lucky indeed. I was content to work hard and have the advantages of a simple, natural life, far away from the hustle, bustle and greyness of city life.' It was as perfect an existence for him as he had ever hoped for. 'I had no dreams of attaining wealth and fame.' To which statement he added the fateful words, 'Which was just as well!' *See also* Historical Crime *and* Pulp.

Selected Works by the Author
When Dames Get Tough (1946)
Scarred Faces (1946)
Lady, Mind That Corpse (1948)
This Woman Is Death (1948)
No Regrets for Clara (1949)
Sweetie, Hold Me Tight (1952)
Downtown Doll (1961)

Steve Holland

Jardine, Quintin (b.1947)

At the time of writing, the leading lights of Scottish noir are undoubtedly Ian **Rankin** and Quentin Jardine. The latter, who is unafraid to touch on real-life events such as the 9/11 bombings, may have entered the fray late, but his two series detectives, Bob Skinner and Oz Blackstone, have been delighting readers since the early 1990s.

Jardine was born in Motherwell, once the steel-making capital of Scotland, and studied law at the University of Glasgow. He worked as a journalist in Lanarkshire for seven years and then joined the Scottish Office's government information service in 1971, where he spent nine years as an information officer, advising ministers and senior civil servants. He also worked briefly as a public relations officer for the Conservative Party in Scotland (or, more colourfully, a spin doctor) during the tenure of Margaret Thatcher.

In the late 1980s, he found himself on holiday in Spain with 'a particularly execrable book', and deciding that he could do better himself, he began writing the first case for Bob Skinner, head of Edinburgh Criminal Investigation Department.

Skinner's Rules was published in 1993, the first of seventeen novels featuring the acerbic Scotsman. A serial killer is at loose in the winding alleyways of Edinburgh, but as Skinner delves into the background of his victims, he finds a conspiracy of silence sheltering the 'real' criminal. Unsurprisingly, Edinburgh's topography is described in loving detail, and the book garnered praise from locals as well as from wider afield. As the series swiftly progressed, sometimes at more than one book a year, Skinner rose through the ranks, becoming, by the time of the twelfth book, *Head Shot* (2002), deputy chief constable. His tangled domestic life is also well documented, although it rarely takes centre stage.

52. Quintin Jardine.

Jardine's other series character, Oz Blackstone, is a wealthy 'private enquiry agent' happily living in Glasgow with his childhood sweetheart Primavera Philips. Sharing traits in common with the author, he has a fondness for his Spanish holiday home in L'Escala and a love of golf. His first two appearances – *Blackstone's Pursuits* (1996) and *A Coffin for Two* (1997) – were written under the name Matthew Reid. Series featuring Blackstone are more playful than the grittier Skinner series and are all written in the first person. Blackstone's other career as Hollywood movie actor allowed him, in a surreal authorial conceit, to star in a filmed adaptation of a Bob Skinner novel in *Poisoned Cherries* (2002).

Sadly, televised versions of Jardine's works have never materialised (to date), although the author's preferred choice of Christopher Eccleston or Liam Neeson as Skinner would surely guarantee high viewing figures. A lifelong supporter of Motherwell Football Club, Jardine currently shares his time between homes in East Lothian and the Costa Brava.

Selected Works by the Author
Skinner's Rules (1993)
A Coffin for Two (1996)
Murmuring the Judges (1998)

Jardine, Quintin

Head Shot (2002)
Poisoned Cherries (2002)
For the Death of Me (2005)
Dead and Buried (2006)

Website
www.quintinjardine.com

Mark Campbell

Jecks, Michael (b.1960)

Michael Jecks is the author of a best-selling series of historical mysteries that began with *The Last Templar* (1995).

There is something deliciously paradoxical about Jecks, for thirteen years earning a living in the ultramodern information-technology industry while plunging himself into the distant past. It was in 1993 when the creative juices began to flow. While on honeymoon in Devon, he conceived the idea for a medieval murder story. Finding himself unemployed and with the support of his wife and parents, he decided to write the novel, which became *The Last Templar*. It was finished in March 1994, and Headline bought it, commissioning two more in the series, which has grown to twenty-four novels and counting.

The series is set in Devon (where Jecks now lives) of the early fourteenth century, during the reign of Edward II. The novels feature his sleuthing heroes, Simon Puttock, bailiff of Lydford Castle, who is responsible for law and order across the Stannaries (the tin mines) of Dartmoor, and Sir Baldwin Furnshill, a disposed and a somewhat grumpy and irascible former Templar Knight and now Keeper of the King's Peace in Crediton. The characters have grown in strength and personality through the series and attract a large following.

The novels are a very clever amalgam of the whodunit format with clues and suspects and a rich, vibrant presentation of the turbulent period in which they are set. The books are meticulously researched – Jecks is forever adding to his growing library of books on the period – but he uses the information he gleans to aid and enrich the characters and the story, rather than hold up the plot for a brief history lesson as some historical novelists do. His cleverness lies in his ability to take aspects of contemporary life and create a mystery out of them. For example, country fairs (*The Abbott's Gibbet*, 1998), leper hospitals (*The Leper's Return*, 1998), Christmas celebrations (*The Boy-Bishop's Glove Maker*, 2000) and piracy (*The Death Ship of Dartmouth*, 2006) all feature as a backdrop to mystery and murder.

Jecks has also taken his heroes away from Devon in a sequential group of novels. After the unpleasant repercussions experienced in *The Mad Monk of Gidleigh* (2002), Baldwin and Simon decide to make a pilgrimage to Santiago de Compostela in Galicia, but even here they find that murder is not far away. A group of pilgrims is attacked by outlaws, then a young girl is found murdered near Santiago and the local pesquisidore asks Simon and Baldwin to find the killer. In the next novel, *The Outlaws of Ennor* (2004), Simon and Baldwin are returning from their pilgrimage when they are thrown from their course by pirates and foul weather and end up stranded on the strange island of Ennor, where Simon is asked to help seek the murderer of the hated local tax collector. In *The Tolls of Death* (2004), Simon and

Baldwin are once more on the mainland, but while journeying home, they become involved in savage murders in a Cornish village.

With great aplomb, Jecks keeps his series fresh and entertaining. It will, without any doubt, have a long and healthy existence. *See also* Historical Crime.

Selected Works by the Author
The Last Templar (1995)
The Leper's Return (1998)
Squire Throwleigh's Heir (1998)
The Boy-Bishop's Glovemaker (2000)
The Devil's Acolyte (2002)
The Mad Monk of Gidleigh (2002)
The Outlaws of Ennor (2004)
The Death Ship of Dartmouth (2006)
Dispensation of Death (2007)

David Stuart Davies

Johnston, Paul (b.1957)

Paul Johnston became a full-time writer after the critical and commercial success of *Body Politic* (1997), a book set in Edinburgh some twenty-five years into an imaginary future. It won the **Crime Writers' Association** John Creasey Award for best first novel for 1997. Four subsequent novels, *The Bone Yard* (1998), *Water of Death* (1999), *The Blood Tree* (2000) and *The House of Dust* (2001), continued the futuristic crime theme. Each featured maverick investigator Quintilian Dalrymple. Interestingly, who Dalrymple was investigating on behalf of whom was as much a mystery to the detective as to the reader. To create a straightforward mystery had never been Johnston's aim.

53. Paul Johnston.

Born in Edinburgh, educated at Fettes, he attended Oxford University. After a spell as a tourist guide in Greece and working for shipping companies in London, Belgium and Greece, he moved to a newspaper in Athens, thence to the small Aegean island of Antiparos in 1989, teaching English to pay the bills. He returned to Edinburgh in 1995 to take a master's degree. Throughout, he sought to fulfil a long-held ambition to write fiction. (The fact that his father Ronald Johnston was a successful thriller writer may have encouraged him.) Johnston used his time abroad to inform his work – increasingly so beyond the first novels, when he moved back from the future, as it were, to set tales in Greece. He has claimed that living away from Scotland helped him to cut through the myths about his homeland, and certainly his first books mocked the nationalistic myths of Scotland and the greater British Isles through his fictional device of a newly independent Edinburgh ruled by a supposedly benevolent dictatorship. Most readers will have recognised the allusions to our present state.

The Dalrymple novels were followed by a set of three entirely different and more conventional crime novels set in Greece and based around the detective Alex Mavros: *A Deeper Shade of Blue* (2002), *The Last Red Death* (2003) and *The Golden Silence* (2005). In *A Deeper Shade of Blue*, Mavros set out to trace a missing tourist, only to find that she was not the only one who had disappeared. *The Last Red Death* won the prestigious **Sherlock** Award for Best Detective Novel in 2004 and told of modern-day and Second World War terrorism, the memories and effects of which lie semi-dormant beneath hot Greek soil. Shortly after it was published, a real-life terrorist arrest occurred in Greece, apparently straight out of the book. Johnston followed the three novels with a stand-alone, *The Death List* (2007), a revenge thriller set in contemporary **London**, in which a crime novelist unwittingly let a fan into his life, with devastating consequences. It was another change of direction from an author who is never content to settle for what worked last time. *See also* Thrillers: Novels of Action.

Selected Works by the Author
Body Politic (1997)
The Bone Yard (1998)
The House of Dust (2001)
The Last Red Death (2003)
The Death List (2007)

Russell James

Jones, Russell Celyn (b.1955)

Although he has avoided being pigeonholed as a crime writer, Celyn Jones has flitted in and out of criminal activity, in a fictional sense. In his first novel, *Soldiers and Innocents* (1990), Captain Evan Price snatches his young son from his estranged wife and goes on the run from military police. The protagonist of *Small Times* (1992) is a pickpocket called Harry Langland, and the novel opens with a pickpocket gang at work in a major shopping street, a scene expertly choreographed and authenticated by close description of technique and shrewd use of insider's vocabulary, such as 'joey' and 'dip squad'. *The Eros Hunter* (1998), which begins with the discovery of a mutilated corpse hoisted high in the rigging of a yacht in **London**'s upscale

St Katharine's Dock, is a **police procedural** with a seductive casual style ('Clyne, Ridley and Stokes are all police and ride around in unmarked cars'), although, as in Celyn Jones's other novels, what really interests him are the relationships under scrutiny, between parent and child, between man and woman, between investigating officers. Between good and bad, right and wrong, truth and lies. In each of his novels, he asks searching moral questions, and the answers usually have something to do with responsibility and redemption.

In *Ten Seconds from the Sun* (2005), Thames river pilot Ray Greenland is a man forced to kiss his wife with his eyes wide open and sit in front of the mirror trying on new faces ('I practised a look that wasn't my own'). No one is actively pursuing him, but if they knew who he was, they would be. Harmless comments from strangers ('You look like someone I know') threaten to destroy the haven of family life he has built with his wife Lily and two much-cherished children. It is Ray's probation officer, Tom, who offers a survival strategy ('He told me how to tell stories') once Ray emerges after almost ten years in prison for an unspeakable crime he committed as a child with a different name. Protected by his new identity and alternative biography, Ray meets Lily, and they embark on a relationship that, according to the law, should be disclosed to the probation service, just as Ray's past is required to be disclosed to Lily. Neither disclosure is made, for fear of break-up of the relationship, and Ray is caught in a rip tide of potentially tragic consequences.

Watermen do not drive and Ray holds no licence of that sort, so he is only a passenger in Lily's car when it shunts into another vehicle as they return from their children's school fête, the accident presaging a deadlier collision between past and present, one which Ray is powerless to prevent. However, Tom assures Ray, 'If you can tell stories well, people tend to believe you.'

Selected Works by the Author
Soldiers and Innocents (1990)
Small Times (1992)
An Interference of Light (1995)
The Eros Hunter (1998)
Surface Tension (2001)
Ten Seconds from the Sun (2005)

Nicholas Royle

Joseph, Alison (b.1958)

Alison Joseph is the author of the intriguing clerical detective series featuring Sister Agnes Bourdillon, an independently minded nun living in present-day **London**.

Joseph was born in North London and graduated in French and Philosophy at Leeds University before becoming a producer and presenter in a local radio station. She then returned to London to make short documentaries for the fledging television station Channel 4 and, in 1985, founded her own production company, Works on Screen, alongside producer Sue Conte. One of the series the company produced, *Through the Devil's Gateway* (1990), documented the history of women in organised religion, leading to a book of essays on the subject edited by Joseph.

Her fascination with the role of women in the church underpins her first novel, *Sacred Hearts* (1994). The novel introduced Sister Agnes Bourdillon, a far-from-temperate Benedictine nun brought up in France, now living in a bedsit in London, working on a project for runaway teenagers. When she reads in a newspaper that her aggressive former husband Hugh Bourdillon is accused of murdering his new wife Philippa, she heads off to his tiny Gloucestershire village to investigate personally.

Sister Agnes is no Miss Marple-style spinster in a flowery cotton dress. She may have taken holy orders, but that does not curtail her love of cars, clothes and sex. However, despite confessing to her old friend Father Julius that she is beyond saving, she still exhibits a strong religious faith that forms the backbone of her character. In this aspect, she shares traits similar to those of G.K. **Chesterton**'s detective priest Father Brown. It is the tension between (religious) faith and (practical, sometimes immoral) actions that makes Agnes such an interesting, if at times slightly far-fetched, figure.

Her second outing, *The Hour of Our Death* (1995), sees Agnes working as a hospital visitor in the London teaching hospital of St Hugh's, where the death of an administrative assistant, followed by an irregular post-mortem, convinces her that her detective skills are once more required. Falling in love with a suspect adds piquancy to her solitary lifestyle, but her religious calling wins out – just.

Other books have taken her to a girls' boarding school (*A Dark and Sinful Death*, 1997), a women's prison (*The Dying Light*, 1999) and a drug-rehabilitation clinic (*The Darkening Sky*, 2004). *Shadow of Death* (2007) brings a supernatural tinge to the proceedings as Agnes stumbles on a tranche of seventeenth-century occultist texts; Agnes has recently made the transition to television.

Joseph also writes short stories and plays for radio and has penned abridged versions of best-selling novels – such as Louis de Bernières's *Captain Corelli's Mandolin* and Phillipa Gregory's *Earthly Joys* – for BBC Radio 4. She lives in London with her husband and three children. *See also* London in Crime Fiction *and* Women Crime Writers.

Selected Works by the Author
Sacred Hearts (1994)
A Dark and Sinful Death (1997)
The Night Watch (2000)
The Darkening Sky (2005)
Shadow of Death (2007)
A Violent Act (2008)

Website
www.alisonjoseph.com

Mark Campbell

Joss, Morag

Morag Joss has described her first three novels – which feature Sarah Selkirk, a professional cellist and amateur sleuth living in Bath – as 'fairly light-hearted', and her later novels have moved increasingly towards literary fiction. Nevertheless, even in the second Selkirk novel, *Fearful Symmetry* (1999), the use of multiple viewpoints and a sensitive handling of autism indicated that Joss was writing something more than traditional cosies.

Joss grew up on the west coast of Scotland, graduated in English from St Andrew's University and then studied singing at the Guildhall School of Music and Drama. She has worked in museums, galleries and higher education and has been an adviser to the National Trust in arts education.

The plot of her first novel, *Funeral Music* (1998), was prompted by a conversation with P.D. **James** at the Roman Baths in Bath. When Joss joked that the baths would be a good place to find a body, P.D. James agreed and said that Joss must go and write the story – which she did, gaining a Dilys Award nomination from the Independent Mystery Booksellers Association.

Before completing the Selkirk series, Joss realised that she wanted to write something deeper and darker. The result was *Half Broken Things* (2003), which won the **Crime Writers' Association** Silver Dagger. Three damaged and lonely misfits – Jean (a house-sitter nearing retirement), Michael (loner and thief) and Steph (pregnant and on the run from an abusive boyfriend) – form a surrogate family based on self-deceptions and gradually appropriate the house that Jean is house-sitting. The arrival of someone from Michael's past and the rightful owners of the house tip an uneasy equilibrium towards a devastating climax. Joss has commented in an interview that she likes the part often played by 'the house' in English novels, as opposed to 'the road' in American fiction.

Joss's literary explorations of psychological suspense have prompted comparisons with Ruth **Rendell** and Minette **Walters**, but she confesses to being only 'a very patchy reader of crime'. She has also said that she is 'very, very interested in people who live lives of quiet desperation'. This interest, already apparent in *Half Broken Things*, also revealed itself in *Puccini's Ghosts* (2005), in which the theme of music reoccurs. The heroine is Lila, a fifteen-year-old who has a singing talent but who is trapped in a dreary seaside town with a mother who is hysterical and a father who is a failed lawyer. Returning as a woman in her 1950s to bury her father, Lila's grip on her sanity loosens as she recalls the summer of 1960 and the ill-fated amateur production of Puccini's *Turandot* that blighted her family's lives.

In *The Night Following* (2008), Joss further examines the repercussions of loss and deception, and the relationship between accidental wrongdoing, conscience and responsibility. On a blustery April day, a doctor's wife driving along a quiet country road hits a cyclist, killing her instantly. She drives away. The story, a study of a killer's journey into the shadows of guilt and isolation, follows her bizarre and sinister attempts to atone for what she did. *See also* Crime Writers' Association.

Selected Works by the Author
Funeral Music (1998)
Fearful Symmetry (1999)
Fruitful Bodies (2001)
Half Broken Things (2003)
Puccini's Ghosts (2005)
The Night Following (2008)

Julian Maynard-Smith

K

Kavanagh, Dan

See Barnes, Julian

Keating, H.R.F. (b.1926)

H.R.F. Keating is one of Britain's most highly acclaimed crime novelists. Not only is he creator of Inspector Ghote of the Bombay (now Mumbai) Criminal Investigation Department, the hero of twenty-one crime novels, but he is also the author of eleven other crime novels, four mainstream novels and several non-fiction works. Two of his Ghote books – the first, *The Perfect Murder* (1964), made into a film by Merchant Ivory, and a later book, *The Murder of the Maharajah* (1980) – were awarded the **Crime Writers' Association** (CWA) Gold Dagger, and in 1996, he received Cartier Diamond Dagger for a lifetime's achievement. He was the chairman of the CWA from 1970 to 1971 and, in 1985, was elected President of (by invitation only) the Detection Club, a position he held until 2001. For work beyond his fiction writing, he won the George N. Dove award for 'Outstanding Contribution to the Serious Study of Mystery and Crime Fiction' in 1995. He is a Fellow of the Royal Society of Literature and served on its council.

Keating was born in St Leonards-on-Sea, son of a headmaster, and when he attended his father's school, his one privilege was that he could bathe in the family bathroom rather than in the communal school baths. He took a degree at Trinity College, Dublin, won the vice chancellor's prose prize and embarked on a career in journalism. After three years as a regional subeditor, he moved to *The Daily Telegraph* in 1956, then to *The Times* in 1958. His first novel, *Death and the Visiting Firemen*, was published in 1959. He met his wife-to-be (actress Sheila Mitchell) that year. From 1959, he published a book practically every year until the 1980s when after his only two-year gap, he went back to writing a book a year into the new millennium.

His first book displayed a fondness for unusual settings, a fondness which endeared him to readers throughout his career. *Death and the Visiting Firemen* brought a visiting team of American fire-prevention officers to a conference in modern-day Britain, where on arrival at Southampton they were met by a team of coach and horses. (Such a journey might seem more bizarre to an Englishman than to an American.) It was Keating's search for different settings that led him to set his fifth book – a one-off, he had intended – in exotic India. This was *The Perfect Murder*, featuring a Bombay policeman Ganesh Ghote, and won the Gold Dagger. People told him, 'You should go on with Inspector Ghote.' At the time, Keating had famously never been to India. He researched through films, books and newspaper articles and created an India so lifelike and lovable that much of his fan base was in that subcontinent. But his famous lack of first-hand knowledge could not continue.

In 1975, Air India offered him a free return flight, and having seen his adopted country, Keating returned to it six months later with a television crew.

His Inspector Ghote (pronounced 'hoe-tay', although practically no one outside India pronounces it correctly) is polite and diffident, if persistent, and survived through some two dozen delightful books (with a new book appearing, after an interval, in 2008). Ghote has been helped on his cases by several assistants, including Axel Svennson, a Swede, and Gregory Strongbow, an American. The film version of *The Perfect Murder* was less than perfect, but Ghote's various television incarnations have been more successful.

Although Ghote dominates Keating's reputation, Keating has created other memorable characters, including the charlady Mrs Craggs in *Death of a Fat God* (1963) and star of many short stories (collected in 1985 as, perhaps inevitably, *Mrs Craggs: Crimes Cleaned Up*). She featured also in stories for BBC's *Woman's Hour*. Keating's *The Rich Detective* (1993) had a detective inspector winning a million pounds, and the idea of a *rich* detective inspired a loose series to follow it, comprising *The Good Detective* (1995), *The Bad Detective* (1996), *The Soft Detective* (1997), then more successfully *The Hard Detective* (2000), which debuted the more hard-bitten Harriet Martens, who warranted a return in *A Detective in Love* (2001). Even with Ms Martens in his repertoire, Keating is a writer who eschews violence – in so far as a crime writer can. He prefers dilemmas and mysteries to guns and punch-ups. Nevertheless, the more recent Keatings contain unexpected grit and swearing. A sign of the times perhaps, or a sign that a professional writer moves with the times.

Keating began as a journalist and while writing fiction continued as a crime fiction reviewer for *The Times* from 1967 to 1983. He admitted once that the real challenge, as any writer would guess, was to bring his mini-reviews down to the prescribed thirty words. His main tip for achieving it was that 'words you can reasonably put a hyphen between count as one'. As his George N. Dove award attests, he has written numerous articles and several respected books *about* crime fiction, from anthologies (he edited several) to the eminently practical *Writing Crime Fiction* (1994). He wrote a comprehensive *Sherlock Holmes, the Man and His World* in 1979. Other reference works include *Murder Must Appetize* (1975), *Crime and Mystery: The 100 Best Books* (1987) and *The Bedside Companion to Crime* (1989), whilst he edited the anthology *The Man Who...* (1992) for the Detection Club in honour of Julian Symons's 80th birthday. *See also* Conventions *and* TV Detectives: Small-Screen Adaptations.

Selected Works by the Author
Death and the Visiting Firemen (1959)
The Dog It Was That Died (1962)
The Perfect Murder (1964)
Inspector Ghote Breaks an Egg (1970)
Sherlock Holmes, the Man and His World (non-fiction, 1979)
The Murder of the Maharajah (1980)
Mrs Craggs: Crimes Cleaned Up (stories, 1985)
Writing Crime Fiction (non-fiction, 1994)
The Hard Detective (2000)

Russell James

Kelly, Jim (b.1957)

Jim Kelly is one of the most provocative and ambitious of contemporary crime novelists, author of the Philip Dryden series, atmospherically set in Ely, Cambridgeshire. His chosen career was journalism, but he turned to full-time crime writing in 2003, leaving the *Financial Times* where he was education correspondent.

Like his subsequent novels, his first book, *The Water Clock* (2002), nominated for the **Crime Writers' Association** [CWA] John Creasey Memorial Award for first crime novel by an author, is set in 'The Black Fen' – that area of misty marsh and isolated communities first used as a crime landscape by Dorothy L. **Sayers** in her classic *The Nine Tailors* (1930). *The Water Clock* introduced a trio of characters who have appeared throughout the series so far. Philip Dryden is an amateur sleuth who is reluctantly drawn into a series of mysteries as he goes about his chosen trade as a journalist on *The Crow*, a mythical newspaper created by Kelly for the tiny cathedral city of Ely. The author spent ten years in provincial journalism in Bedford and York before moving to Fleet Street and draws heavily on his experiences, to produce a flavour of the inherently bizarre, lonely and quirky life of the local newspaper hack. Dryden's sidekick is Humphrey H. Holt, an overweight cab driver who fills an empty life by trundling around the Fens in a two-door Ford Capri looking for business. Humph, divorced, morose and taciturn, combats loneliness with incessant motion and finds in Dryden someone equally happy to avoid personal tragedy by immersing himself in the lives of others. Dryden's promising career as a national journalist has been interrupted by a horrific car accident which has left his wife – Laura – in a coma.

Laura is the silent partner in the trio. She is a prisoner of locked-in syndrome, a form of coma induced by trauma, which involves the victim having no outward signs of life while having to endure an unknown level of consciousness. She is a patient at The Tower, a private hospital in Ely, and Dryden's wanderings always end with a visit to her bedside, where he tells her of his day in the hope that somewhere, on some level, she is listening.

The books in the series each have a distinct character, often determined by elemental forces. *The Water Clock*, in which a series of crimes is set in motion by the discovery of a rotting corpse on the roof of Ely cathedral, is told against the backdrop of Fen floods. *The Fire Baby* (2004), the second in the series, takes place during a sweltering summer heatwave. All the books deal to some extent with crimes past, as well as present, and in *The Fire Baby*, Dryden has to go back to the infamous drought of 1976 to find the clues he needs to unravel a modern mystery.

As the books progress, Laura emerges painfully from coma and is able to contribute to Dryden's fascination with uncovering the truth about the past. In *The Moon Tunnel* (2005), she plays a key role by researching – from her bedside computer – the story behind a 1940s prisoner-of-war (PoW) camp set up in Ely to take Italian and German PoWs. Archaeological work on the site has uncovered an escape tunnel and the skeleton of a man trapped within. Dryden traces the story forward into the heart of the local Italian community and finds a family still prepared to kill to protect the secrets of the past.

In *The Coldest Blood* (2006), Dryden finds himself involved in a mystery which stretches back into his childhood. An icy winter cold snap claims the life of a recluse, frozen to death on his own doorstep. As Dryden delves into his past, a trail begins to lead back to a forgotten summer murder at a seaside holiday camp. Dryden, Humph and Laura set out for the scene of the crime as a lethal ice storm grips the coast. *The Skeleton Man* (2007), the fifth in the series, shifts the scene to the once thriving village of Jude's Ferry – empty and deserted for years since the army requisitioned the area for a firing range. Dryden is among a group of soldiers which uncovers a grisly secret hanging beneath the village's old pub – the eponymous skeleton man.

In 2006, Kelly was awarded the CWA's Dagger in the Library for his body of work.

Selected Works by the Author
The Water Clock (2002)
The Fire Baby (2004)
The Moon Tunnel (2005)
The Coldest Blood (2006)
The Skeleton Man (2007)

Barry Forshaw

Kelly, Mary (b.1927)

Mary Kelly is the author of a number of sensitively drawn and emotionally involving crime novels, in particular the quartet of novels beginning with *The Spoilt Kill* (1961), for which she won the **Crime Writers' Association** (CWA) Gold Dagger.

Kelly was born in London, studied English at Edinburgh University, married a fellow student in 1950 and graduated in 1951. She taught English in the south of England for a few years, before writing her first book one summer between jobs. *A Cold Coming* (1956), the first of three conventional detective stories featuring Detective Chief Inspector Brett Nightingale, was, she said quoting A.S. Byatt, an attempt to re-create a remembered literary pleasure – adding, however, how far short it fell.

It is on the quartet of books that the crime reader should first focus. Nicholson, the narrator of the first book, is a detective working undercover in the closed community of a Midlands pottery, to pinpoint the employee that is passing new designs to competitors. The chief suspect is Corinna, the most talented of the designers with whom, it is clear from the start, Nicholson has fallen in love. During the period of his undercover, a body is found within the pottery precincts.

The Spoilt Kill is a beautifully constructed detective story, given weight and substance by Kelly's superb writing. The pottery is brought to miraculous life (place and time is always key to Kelly); her prose is full of detail and insight; and her dialogue scenes smartly reveal the shifting tensions within the community, culminating in the heartbreaking final episodes.

Due to a Death (1962) is even more deeply tragic. Here the locale shifts to a run-down Thames estuary town, where the protagonists, narrator Agnes and the mysterious Hedley finally stumble over the truth behind the female body found on the nearby marshes. A **London** suburb, rife with class (and racial) tensions, is the backdrop for *March to the Gallows* (1964). Nicholson here is a spectral presence, his memory influencing the narrator as she sets out to recover some stolen property and finds herself. *Dead Corse* (1966), initially an investigation of a suicide in a Northern steel-making community, is perhaps her most accomplished book.

Write on Both Sides of the Paper (1969) is the book of which Kelly is proudest. It is also the one which most divides her supporters. But cast aside genre conventions, this atmospheric, unclassifiable story of the years-old conflict between its two key characters, set against the background of a theft at a Scottish paper mill, shows many of the characteristic strengths of Kelly at her best. *The Twenty-Fifth Hour* (1971), although well worth reading, is perhaps the weakest of the latter novels. Finally in her last book, the 1930s-set *The Girl in the Alley* (1974), she succeeded in breaking every rule of the Detection Club of which she is a member.

In *The Girl in the Alley*, the narrator remarks, 'People's houses and people's lives…they're the chief thing worth learning about anywhere. What else is there?' Against a backdrop of the fevered imaginings of today's crime fiction that is surely a notion worth revisiting. *See also* Conventions *and* Women Crime Writers.

Selected Works by the Author
The Spoilt Kill (1961)
Due to a Death (1962)
March to the Gallows (1964)
Dead Corse (1966)
Write on Both Sides of the Paper (1969)
The Twenty-Fifth Hour (1971)
The Girl in the Alley (1974)

Further Reading
Kelly, Mary. 1996. 'The CADS Questionnaire'. *CADS* 27 January.

Bob Cornwell

Kennedy, Sir Ludovic (b.1919)

Although Ludovic Kennedy is best known as a broadcaster and as one of ITN's first presenters, his trenchant and strongly researched books have exposed some of the twentieth century's worst miscarriages of justice.

He was born in Edinburgh and educated at Eton College and Christ Church, Oxford, an experience he enjoyed as it gave him respite from his hypercritical mother. He joined the navy during the Second World War, later writing about his experiences in four naval books, *Sub-Lieutenant* (1942), *Nelson's Band of Brothers* (1975), *Pursuit* (1974) and *Menace* (1979). He also remained fascinated by **true crime**, a genre he discovered as a teenager when he found the *Notable British Trials* series in his grandfather's library.

Decades later, Kennedy found the transcript of Timothy Evans trial and became convinced of his innocence. Evans, who was illiterate and had an IQ of 68, had been hanged in 1950 for the alleged murder of his baby daughter. The culprit was his necrophiliac landlord, John Reginald Christie, who also killed Evan's pregnant wife and six other women for sexual gratification. While studying the evidence, Kennedy discovered various anomalies. The resultant book, *10 Rillington Place* (1961; the title taken from the address of the murder house), created a public outcry, although it was thirteen years before Evans was granted a posthumous pardon.

His subsequent book, *The Trial of Stephen Ward* (1965), explored the Profumo scandal, finding that Stephen Ward, a masseur who committed suicide when accused of living off immoral earnings, had been made a scapegoat by his employer. It was followed by *A Presumption of Innocence* (1976), questioning the evidence in the Patrick Meehan case. Meehan was in jail for supposedly murdering a bingo hall owner called Rachel Ross, attacked with her husband during a botched burglary.

But numerous pieces of evidence suggested that Meehan was not at the scene. After seven years, he was given a free pardon, another man having admitted to the homicide. Kennedy's pursuit of justice upset many lawyers and solicitors, and he was barred from several golf and social clubs run by members of the legal profession.

He resolved not to get involved in any more exhausting miscarriages of justice but was persuaded otherwise when he received heartfelt missives from two men serving life for the Luton Post Office murder. His expose, *Wicked Beyond Belief* (1980), showed that the police had fabricated evidence. The men were freed, having spent ten years in jail.

His research then took him overseas to meet Anna Hauptmann, the widow of Richard Hauptmann, who had been executed fifty years before for the kidnap and murder of the Lindbergh baby. Although numerous people were convinced of Hauptmann's innocence after reading Kennedy's exhaustive study, *The Airman and the Carpenter* (1985), the State of New Jersey continued to assert that Hauptmann was the murderer.

Kennedy's other specialist subjects include atheism (he spent decades studying religious tracts before concluding that there is not a deity) and euthanasia. He was knighted in 1994.

Selected Non-fiction Works by the Author
10 Rillington Place (1961)
The Trial of Stephen Ward (1965)
A Presumption of Innocence (1976)
Wicked beyond Belief (1980)
The Airman and the Carpenter (1985)
On My Way to the Club (1989)
Euthanasia: The Good Death (1990)
All in the Mind: Farewell to God (1999)

Carol Ann Davis

Kernick, Simon (b.1966)

Simon Kernick belongs to the recent crop of self-made crime writers of the hard-knocks school – a writer with little formal education who has turned his real-life experience of the grittier aspects of suburbia into a fertile breeding ground for violent suspense novels.

Born in Slough, a suburb of London so dreary that poet John Betjeman called on the Luftwaffe to bomb it, Kernick has made his origins work for him. After spells as a manual labourer and computer-software salesman, he turned to crime writing as a means to escape from the suburban rut he seemed destined for. He produced *The Business of Dying* (2001), which catapulted him into a new life. A clever tale written in the first person, narrated by Dennis Milne, a police detective sergeant who moonlights as a hit man, it draws the reader into an accidental complicity with a tortuous plot line in which the distinction between the right and wrong become increasingly blurred.

The Murder Exchange (2003) and *The Crime Trade* (2004) continued a loosely linked series set in and around north London's gangland, featuring Kernick's rising star detective John Gallan and feisty partner Tina Boyd. It is a world of contract killings, protection rackets, endemic corruption and drug stings that go disastrously wrong.

A Good Day to Die (2005), shortlisted for the **Crime Writers' Association** Steel Dagger, starts out exotically in the Philippines but only because that is where his ex-hit man/ex-copper has been hiding out. He is, thankfully, rapidly brought back to Kernick's **London** suburban stomping ground in an attempt to solve the murder of an old friend, now a vigilante rather than a policeman.

Relentless (2006) marked a departure from his established characters in a taut, stand-alone suspense thriller in which Kernick's lead character is on the run from the moment he hears a friend on the phone reveal his address to the men torturing him to death. What Kernick utilises may be something of a formula, but it does what it says on the jacket: makes for a relentless read, notably true of *Severed* (2007), which works in similar vein when an ex-soldier wakes up to see a girl's corpse next to him and a DVD that appears to show him killing her.

Kernick is a talented master of the set-piece, who knows how to press the action buttons while keeping a tight rein on the suspense factor. He has been compared to American crime writer Dennis Lehane, but his feel for his milieu – the seedy side of affluent southern England – is, if anything, more acute. He will keep pulling in fans of hard-bitten crime fiction for decades. *See also* Crime Writers' Association *and* London in Crime Fiction.

Selected Works by the Author
The Business of Dying (2001)
The Murder Exchange (2003)
The Crime Trade (2004)
Relentless (2006)
Severed (2007)

Peter Millar

Kerr, Philip (b.1956)

A wide-ranging author who has conquered a variety of genres, Philip Kerr has written novels as diverse as the Berlin Noir series set in Nazi Germany; the highly acclaimed and thought-provoking near-future thriller *A Philosophical Investigation* (1992); a John F. Kennedy assassination thriller, *The Shot* (1999); and a mystery novel set in the seventeenth century, *Dark Matter: The Private Life of Sir Isaac Newton* (2002). Born in Edinburgh, he trained as a lawyer and did a postgraduate degree in German law. He spent most of the 1980s working as a copywriter for a number of advertising agencies, including Saatchi & Saatchi, before becoming a full-time novelist.

His first novel, *March Violets* (1989), relocated the 1930s hard-boiled tradition to the Berlin of the same decade and led to the Berlin Noir series featuring private eye Bernie Gunther. The series has drawn comparisons to Raymond **Chandler**, an influence (along with Dashiell Hammett) that Kerr himself acknowledges. Bernie, despite his past as a Schutzstaffel officer, is basically decent but pragmatic enough to work the system to his advantage. *March Violets* (a term of derision used by original Nazis for late converts) starts just before the Berlin Olympics, and Bernie is on a murder investigation that takes him to the highest echelons of the Nazi party and lands him in Dachau. In *The Pale Criminal* (1990), it is 1938, little girls are being murdered and Gunther is blackmailed into rejoining the police. *A German Requiem* (1991) explores the hardships in post-war Germany, and the corruption, duplicity and violence that occur on both sides when a nation is vanquished – a theme continued in *The One from the Other* (2006), when even in 1949, friend and foe can be as immoral as each other and where it is impossible to tell 'the one from the other'.

Social hardships, but in modern-day St Petersburg, underpinned *Dead Meat* (1995). The book, praised for its realistic portrayal of the daily struggles of Russians, won Kerr a CWA Gold Dagger nomination. The investigation of the murder of an anti-Mafia journalist leads to the uncovering of a Mafia plot that could harm the entire Russian populace.

Kerr is also well known for thrillers exploring dystopian futures. These include *Gridiron* (1995), in which a computer sets out to destroy its human creators, and *The Second Angel* (1998), in which a virus makes blood more valuable than gold.

Under the name P.B. Kerr, he has written the 'Children of the Lamp' series of children's novels. He has three children of his own and is married to the novelist Jane Thynne. *See also* Thrillers: Novels of Action *and* Science Fiction and Crime Fiction.

Selected Works by the Author
March Violets (1989)
The Pale Criminal (1990)
A German Requiem (1991)
A Philosophical Investigation (1992)
A Five Year Plan (1997)
The Second Angel (1998)
The One from the Other (2006)
A Quiet Flame (2008)
One Small Step (2008)

Julian Maynard Smith

Kersh, Gerald (1911–1968)

One of the founding fathers of British noir, Gerald Kersh has been sadly neglected since his death (despite a cult following), and his crime novels and short stories are hard to find. Born in Teddington-on-Thames to a large, immigrant Jewish family packed with larger-than-life characters – some of whom he would immortalise in print – Kersh endured a morose and tearful childhood, nearly dying of lung congestion when he was still an infant. This brush with death seems to give him the strength of character to combat the vicissitudes of fate that dogged his later life. Right from childhood, Kersh had a compulsion to write – producing his first story 'Tommy and Tilly Tadpole' at the age of eight – and later claimed that hardly a day passed when he was not scribbling a story or article. Educated at the Regent Street Polytechnic, he took a variety of jobs while struggling to fulfil his literary ambition, including as cook, salesman, cinema manager, night-club bouncer, debt collector and even, briefly, wrestler. Cheekily, Kersh approached Edgar **Wallace** for advice, but claiming to be a better writer can hardly have been surprised at the great man's lack of encouragement. Nevertheless, his love of the bizarre and his fascination with the Soho of petty crooks and streetwalkers – not to mention his propensity for getting into fights – provided him with the raw materials for his first success.

Night and the City (1938) is the story of Harry Fabian, would-be gangster and part-time pimp, whose life in Soho is one long round of self-deception and schemes that come to nothing. In particular, a plan to promote wrestling by bringing a retired veteran back to the ring which backfires when the fighter dies, and Harry, out of cash, plans to sell his girlfriend to a white slave-trafficker. The novel, with its vivid picture of **London** low-life, was a bestseller and earned its struggling young author $40,000 for the film rights. The subsequent movie with Richard Widmark did not impress the critics – or Kersh, who hated the script – but still stands as a key entry among the small group of British noir pictures. In 1992, the film was re-made starring Robert de Niro with the setting transposed from London to New York – which would probably have annoyed Kersh even more. The author released some of his spleen in *The Song of the Flea* (1948), also set in seamy London and recounting the degradation a writer is forced to endure to write with integrity.

During the Second World War, Kersh served in the Coldstream Guards, had what can only be described as a 'colourful war' that included desertion and a part in the liberation of Paris, and turned his experiences into a classic tale of Army life, *They Die with Their Boots Clean* (1941). In 1947, Kersh, who was once again a familiar sight around Soho in his colourful suits and bow-ties, wrote another outstanding crime novel, *Prelude to a Certain Midnight* (1947), the story of a hunt for a child-murderer which has a terrible sense of inevitability darkening every page. Despite these early successes, Kersh was forever hard up and constantly searching for new markets or keeping ahead of the taxman. In the 1950s, he became an American citizen and settled in a remote home in the Shawangunk Mountains in New York State. Although his health was declining, he continued to write prolifically for a number of the most numerous prestigious US magazines including *The Saturday Evening Post,* which published 'The Secret of the Bottle' about the disappearance of Ambrose Bierce in the issue of 7 December 1957, winning Kersh an Edgar Award from the Mystery Writers of America the following year. His output of crime stories included the comical novel, *A Long Cool Day in Hell* (1965); and a series featuring crime reporter, 'Swindle Sheet' Morris, and seventeen tales of the Falstaffian villain, Karmesin, an unregenerate rogue who relates stories of his outlandish exploits to the author. Ellery Queen, who published many of these short stories, referred to the fat, deceitful and nimble-fingered Karmesin as 'either the greatest criminal or the greatest liar of all time'. *See also* Humour and Crime Fiction; Tart Noir *and* Pulp.

Selected Works by the Author
Night and the City (1938; also published in the United States as *Dishonor*)
The Song of the Flea (1948)
Prelude to a Certain Midnight (1953)
A Long Cool Day in Hell (1966)
Karmesin: The World's Greatest Criminal – Or Most Outrageous Liar (2003)

Website
The Nights and Cities of Gerald Kersh by Paul Duncan at http://harlanellison.com/kersh/

Peter Haining

Knight, Bernard (b.1931)

One of Britain's leading forensic pathologists (he was at the forefront of the Fred and Rosemary West case) and a barrister, Bernard Knight has since become an established crime writer. His first detective novel, *The Lately Deceased* (1961), led to a string of others, including some in Welsh, but his more recent **historical** strand is the Crowner John series of medieval mysteries.

Knight was born in Cardiff and spent much of his life around there. He began as a farmer, became a medical student and, after qualifying in 1954, served in Malaya for three years during the terrorist Emergency. He entered forensic pathology in 1959 and became a Home Office pathologist in 1965. After being called to the Bar at Gray's Inn in 1966, he retired in 1996 as professor of Forensic Pathology. He has been a consultant to Amnesty, for which he went on missions to Uganda to examine torture victims and to Kuwait at the end of the Gulf War to investigate atrocities. He received Commander of the British Empire in 1993.

The favourable response to his first crime novel led him to produce a string of others, including *Thread of Evidence* (1965), *Mistress Murder* (1966), *Russian Roulette* (1968), *Policeman's Progress* (1969) and *Tiger at Bay* (1970). All these early novels appeared under the alias Bernard Picton. He first turned to historical novels in the 1970s, with *Lion Rampant* and then *Madoc, Prince of America*, both about twelfth-century Wales. In 1977, he wrote the biography of Milton Helpern, the famous chief medical examiner of New York City. He has written radio plays and television scripts. He contributed storylines and a linked novel for *The Expert* on BBC TV and wrote for *District Nurse*, *Bergerac*, and so on. Between 1971 and 2002, Knight also wrote or edited twelve reference books (some in collaboration) on forensic medicine and pathology, including *Murder, Suicide or Accident* (1971; as Picton) and *Lawyers Guide to Forensic Medicine* (1982).

Knight's unique blend of experience as Home Office pathologist and time at the bar has ensured great veracity in his novels. His Crowner John series, set in 1194, is based around the first coroner for Devon, Sir John de Wolfe (the eponymous Crowner John, *Crowner* meaning coroner), and begins with *The Sanctuary Seeker* (1998), immediately followed by *The Poisoned Chalice* (1998), *Crowner's Quest* (1999) and *The Awful Secret* (2000). In *The Sanctuary Seeker*, Sir John, fresh back from the crusades, has to deal with the more mundane business of holding an inquest on an unidentified body. The dead man turns out to be a fellow crusader, from one of Devon's most honourable families – and Sir John's brother-in-law Sheriff Richard de Revelle is a deliberate obstacle to the investigation. In *The Poisoned Chalice*, Christina, the daughter of an Exeter businessman, is raped, and Crowner John must bring the unknown assailant to justice. As becomes clear throughout the series, the tales are, in effect, timeless crime stories, suffused with the events and colour of the twelfth century. *Figure of Hate* (2005), his ninth book, begins with a jousting day in which an altercation breaks out between Hugh Peverel, Lord of Sampford Peverel, and Reginald de Charterai, a stranger. Two days later, Hugh's body is found in a barn, stabbed in the back. Is de Charterai to blame? Again, the setting is medieval but the mystery is not. By the time of *The Elixir of Death* (2006), medieval politics have forced their way through: a Norman knight named Peter le Calve is murdered, and his severed head is discovered stuck on the rood screen of Exeter cathedral. Crowner John investigates, and his unscrupulous brother-in-law, Richard de Revelle, is once again involved.

Although Knight uses his extensive experience and knowledge of pathology to inform his books, they are far more than casebooks dramatised; they are vigorous, stirring tales enlivened and liberated by their medieval setting. Two have been BBC radio plays (*The Sanctuary Seeker* and *The Tinner's Corpse*, 2001). For some years, Knight appeared in Medieval Murderers (a group consisting of Michael **Jecks**, Susanna **Gregory**, Philip **Gooden** and Ian **Morson**), giving readings in libraries and bookshops. The group collaborated in *The Tainted Relic* (2005), *The Sword of Shame* (2006) and *The House of Shadows* (2007). As a break from his medieval series, but again using his real-life experience, Knight has also written *Dead in the Dog* (2009), a 1950s whodunit based in a military hospital during the Malayan terrorist emergency. *See also* Conventions *and* Historical Crime.

Selected Works by the Author
The Sanctuary Seeker (1998)
The Poisoned Chalice (1998)
The Tinner's Corpse (2001)
The Elixir of Death (2006)

Russell James

Knox, Ronald (1888–1957)

Ronald Knox's writings in crime fiction were relatively few: six detective novels, one short story, three contributions to Detection Club co-operatives, essays in the 'higher criticism', particularly relating to Sherlock **Holmes** – a field in which he was a pioneer – even an apocryphal Holmes story of his own, 'The Adventure of the First Class Carriage', published in *The Strand* 1947 (February), and the celebrated Decalogue of 'dos and don'ts' for crime writers, which had considerable influence in the **Golden Age** era, was published in 1929. He said that detective fiction was 'a highly specialist art form which deserves its own literature'; he would be pleased with the appearance of this encyclopedia.

54. Portrait of Ronald Knox by caricaturist Powys Evans ('Quiz'), 1922.

He was (like Sayers's Lord Peter **Wimsey**) educated at Eton and Balliol, later becoming an honorary fellow in the latter. Initially, he was an Anglican priest, who converted to Roman Catholicism in 1917 – a large proportion of his writings comprise apologia for the Catholic church. He served in Military Intelligence in the Great War. His Decalogue (1927) forbade, in detective stories, supernatural agencies, poisons unknown to science, fortuitous accidents, unaccountable intuitions, clues not identified to the reader, identical twins, detective themselves committing the crime and, curiously, Chinamen, and insisted on a strict rationing of secret rooms and passages and that the culprit must be mentioned in the early part of the story. By and large, although one can identify exceptions, these taboos were observed, consciously or not, by authors. He was a keen Detection Club member.

Arguably, Decalogue and his Sherlockian 'scholarship' were of greater significance than the detective novels, which appeared between 1925 and 1937. His first, *The Viaduct Murder* (1925), is something of a romp, a skit on detective fiction – much more so than E.C. **Bentley**'s *Trent's Last Case* (1913, which was intended as such) and even more than A.A. Milne's once-popular *The Red House Mystery* (1922). The remaining five novels feature Miles Bredon, an investigator for the Indescribable Insurance Co. Bredon is a big man, good humoured, absent-minded and slightly lethargic. His mind works in a desultory way, rendering his service for his employers uncertain. Playing patience, which he does regularly, apparently helps his intuition, and his charming wife Angela supplied the common sense, which is largely lacking in her husband. His recorded cases mostly do not turn out well for the insurance company.

The Three Taps (1927) is better for its atmosphere – a rural inn, engagingly named The Load of Mischief – and characterisation than its mystery, which is confusingly presented (the 'taps' control the gas supply in the victim's bedroom). *The Footsteps at the Lock* (1928), whose setting is the upper reaches of the Thames, features a canoeing expedition by two brothers who dislike each other. One is found dead, but can it be murder? And, if so, can it be brought home to the other brother, who has an alibi? *The Body in the Silo* (1934), set in the Wye Valley, is better as a mystery than any other Knoxes, even the last two, *Still Dead* (1934) and *Double Cross Purposes* (1937), both set in Scotland. Generally, Knox seemed to like rural settings.

Knox's work is little read nowadays, but he had a key influence on the detective story's development and for this reason should not be forgotten.

Selected Works by the Author
The Viaduct Murder (1925)
The Three Taps (1927)
The Footsteps at the Lock (1928)
The Body in the Silo (1934)
Still Dead (1934)
The Fallen Idol (1936)
Double Cross Purposes (1937)

Philip Scowcroft

L

Lacey, Tony (b.1948)

Tony Lacey is senior editor at Penguin and the man behind some of the most successful books of the last three decades, with some prestigious credits in crime fiction. He joined Penguin straight from university and has been with the publisher for over thirty years. Initially, he worked in the children's division and was publishing director of Puffin from 1980 to 1983, taking the list in a more male direction, subsequently achieving success with several international bestsellers. He moved over to adult books, becoming the first publishing director of Penguin's new UK adult imprint, Viking (the company had earlier bought the US publishing house Viking, so this was a move to inaugurate a worldwide hardcover imprint). Lacey held this job for ten years, then became publishing director of paperbacks, in 1990s. He is now a floating publishing director, whose authors include Nick Hornby, Will Self, Jonathan Coe and William Trevor.

Lacey is not a specific crime publisher, but he published all of Ruth **Rendell**'s novels written as Barbara Vine, generally considered to be among her best works (*The Birthday Present*, the thirteenth novel as Barbara Vine, was published in 2008). He has been John Mortimer's editor since 2000, overseeing the delightful Rumpole books, and published the early novels of John **Harvey** and Philip **Kerr** in the new Viking list (both authors are now firmly among the most acclaimed writers in the crime/thriller field). Lacey was behind Philip Kerr's remarkable trilogy Berlin Noir. As Harvey's editor, he published his first four novels – *Lonely Hearts* (1989), *Rough Treatment* (1990), *Cutting Edge* (1991) and *Off Minor* (1992). These novels, featuring Harvey's signature character Charlie Resnick, were filmed by the BBC, starring Tom Wilkinson before the actor became famous (*Off Minor* is a book that Lacey feels did not quite work – perhaps erring on the side of being too moody).

Regarding his work on the Barbara Vine books, Lacey notes that Ruth Rendell wanted to write a more complex crime-based novel and felt it ought to be a different publisher from her customary Random House, to separate out the books – and the Barbara Vine books started with *A Dark-Adapted Eye* (1986). He remembers lightly questioning Rendell's nom de plume at their first meeting – a colleague half-jokingly said that 'Vine' would be stacked on the less-seen bottom shelves of bookshops! However, it is a name with family connections for the author. The Vine novels have sold 1.6 million altogether in Penguin. Lacey has noted that Paul **Sidey** (Rendell's Random House editor for the novels written under her own name) and he are unusual in the competitive world of publishing in being friends, despite sharing an author, and that they sometimes have dinner together with Ruth Rendell. *See also* Thrillers: Novels in Action.

Barry Forshaw

Lake, Deryn

Deryn Lake, the pseudonym of the romantic and historical novelist Dinah Lampitt, is the author of the John Rawlings historical mysteries. She has also worked as a director of plays and musicals for local theatrical groups in the south of England, where she lives.

Lampitt's early career was as a journalist, working on various magazines and newspapers, including *The Evening News* and *The Times*, but she gave up that career when she married and raised a family. However, after her husband's death in 1982, she turned again to writing and produced her first historical novel, *Sutton Place* (1983). This book and its two sequels, *The Silver Swan* (1984) and *Fortune's Soldier* (1985), trace the accursed history of the Weston family through the generations. Two other historical novels are of interest to the mystery devotee. *To Sleep No More* (1987) is a tale of witchcraft and disturbed souls, again down through the generations, while *The King's Women* (1991) explores the life of Joan of Arc and her connection to the mysterious Priory of Sion.

With a downturn in the historical-fiction market, Lampitt turned to **historical** crime, writing under the pseudonym Deryn Lake. In 1983, Lampitt undertook some research to establish the precedence of the company H.D. Rawlings in the manufacture of carbonated water, and her work identified the originator of the company, John Rawlings, an apothecary, living in the 1760s. Further investigation revealed that this was the same period in which John Fielding was developing London's first police force out of the Bow Street Runners, founded by his brother, the novelist Henry Fielding. John Fielding was the chief magistrate and was known as the 'Blind Beak of Bow'. In the first of the series, *Death in the Dark Walk* (1994), Rawlings stumbled across a body and is under suspicion as the murderer, and needs to prove his innocence. Fielding is impressed by Rawlings's knowledge and profound memory, and a formidable team is formed. Thereafter, Rawlings becomes Fielding's investigator.

The series has reached twelve books as of 2007. All are faithful re-creations of the late eighteenth century and all are well-crafted mysteries, some with the atmosphere of historical romances or the gothic novels of the period. Lake has been dubbed the 'Queen of the Georgian Mystery' by *The Times*. *See also* Historical Crime *and* London in Crime Writing.

Selected Works by the Author
The King's Women (1992)
Death in the Dark Walk (1994)
Death on the Romney Marsh (1997)
Death at St James's Palace (2002)
Death in Hellfire (2007)

Websites
www.derynlake.com/index.php
'Tangled Web' entry at www.twbooks.co.uk/authors/derynlake.html

Mike Ashley

La Plante, Lynda (b.1946)

The most prolific female crime fiction scriptwriter on British television, Lynda La Plante is the creator of the hugely successful and award-winning series *Prime Suspect* and *Trial and Retribution*.

Born Lynda Titchmarsh on 15 March 1946 in Formby, near Liverpool, the author trained first as an actress at Royal Academy of Dramatic Art and worked for the National Theatre and the Royal Shakespeare Company. Under the stage name of Lynda Marchal, she appeared in various television series, including *Z Cars* (1963), *Out of the Unknown* (1969), *The Sweeney* (1978) and *The Professionals* (1980), and as hay fever–suffering ghost Tamara Novak in *Rentaghost* (1980).

As Lynda Marchal, she wrote three episodes of a 1973 children's series, *The Kids from 4A*, but it was not until 1980, just after she married musician Richard La Plante, that she submitted plotlines for the adult crime series *The Gentle Touch*. Although ultimately rejected, the plotlines led to the commissioning of her first television series as writer, *Widows* (1983), which was nominated for two British Academy Awards (BAFTAs). A sequel followed, but it was not until *Prime Suspect* (1991) that her fame really took off. Starring Helen Mirren as the iconic Detective Chief Inspector Jane Tennison, the hard-hitting drama won a slew of awards, including four BAFTAs and an Edgar Award.

Conceived initially for the one-off story, Tennison returned by popular demand in a further six instalments over the next decade and a half, concluding with an explosive two-part finale in 2006. During this period, La Plante authored many stand-alone dramas, including *Comics* (1993) and *Killer Net* (1998), but it was to be a 1997 teleplay, *Trial and Retribution*, that proves to be her most long-lasting creation. Featuring Detective Sergeant Michael Walker, as played by David Hayman, the self-contained plots are characterised by their psychologically dark and violent subject matter, usually involving sexual crimes, alongside a unique three- or four-image narrative style that allows the viewer to see the unfolding police investigation from a variety of viewpoints.

Besides adapting several of her television stories, La Plante has also written a number of original novels. Her first two, *The Legacy* (1987) and *The Talisman* (1989), formed a rollicking family saga about a Welsh miner's daughter who inherits a fortune. With *Cold Shoulder* (1994), she moved into straightforward thriller territory with an edgy novel about an embittered ex-Pasadena cop, Lorraine Page, hunting down a serial killer. *Cold Blood* (1996) and *Cold Heart* (1998) completed the trilogy.

Other noteworthy novels include *Bella Mafia* (1991), a *Godfather*-style gangster story from a female perspective; *Royal Flush* (2002), in which a daring diamond theft is attempted; and the two Detective Inspector Anna Travis novels, *Above Suspicion* (2004) and *The Red Dahlia* (2006), both clearly inspired by her television counterpart, Jane Tennison.

In 1994, she created her own company, La Plante Productions, to oversee all future television productions of her works. *See also* TV Detectives: Small-Screen Adaptations.

Selected Works by the Author
Widows (1983)
Prime Suspect (1991)
Prime Suspect 2 (1992)
Cold Shoulder (1994)
Trial and Retribution (1997)
Royal Flush (2002; also published in the United States as *Royal Heist*)
The Red Dahlia (2006)

Website
www.laplanteproductions.com

Mark Campbell

Laurence, Janet (b.1937)

Known principally for her Darina Lisle series, which is enriched by gourmet recipes and juicy titbits from the world of high gastronomy, Janet Laurence later went on to add a second, historical, series based around the Venetian artist Canaletto.

She began as a cookery writer, producing a weekly column for *The Daily Telegraph* from 1984 to 1986. Among a considerable journalistic output, she wrote six cookery books and a series on historical cooking for *Country Life,* and outside of crime writing, she continues to write contemporary women's fiction under the pseudonym Julia Lisle. In 2007, Laurence published a writer's guide: *Writing Crime Fiction.* She was chairman of the **Crime Writers' Association** during 1998–1999.

55. Janet Laurence.

The Darina Lisle series began in 1989 with *A Deepe Coffyn* (immediately showing Laurence's twin interests in history and cuisine). Darina, an apprentice chef, is hired by the Society of Historical Gastronomes to prepare authentic feasts for the society's annual weekend. Two people die mysteriously – although neither is poisoned – and suspicion falls on the young chef Darina. The novel is as much a satire on the higher echelons of catering as it is a satisfying whodunit. Seven more Darina Lisle titles followed at the rate of one a year, with a further two titles being served in 1998 and 2000. By the time of the tenth book (*The Mermaid's Feast*, 2002), Darina was, conveniently for the series, comfortably married to the Detective William Pigram. For this adventure, Davina drags him away with her for two weeks on a luxury liner, where her only light duty will be to advise the owners on the most suitable menus. Or so she thinks. A lovelorn purser disappears – and it does not look like suicide. Once again Darina and her husband have a succulent mystery on their hands.

In 1997, Laurence overlapped her Lisle series with a new one featuring the real-life artist Canaletto – the mysteries of whose life have engaged art historians for centuries. In the first book, *Canaletto and the Case of Westminster Bridge* (1997), set in 1746, the flamboyant artist visits Georgian **London** peopled, he hopes, with his enthusiastic would-be collectors. Unfortunately, the city is also home to those who wish him dead. Two years later, Laurence brought Canaletto back to London, and two years later again she brought him back a third time to become embroiled in an expected visit to the capital by Bonnie Prince Charlie.

In each of her series, Laurence aims at an educated readership who will appreciate seeing their tastes reflected in what they read. The books are deft and humorous and remain sharp in observation. Not for nothing did Ian **Rankin** call her the 'Silver Fox' of crime writing. *See also* Historical Crime Writing.

Selected Works by the Author
A Deepe Coffyn (1989)
Hotel Morgue (1992)
Death à la Provencale (1994)
Canaletto and the Case of Westminster Bridge (1997)
Canaletto and the Case of Bonnie Prince Charlie (2002)
The Mermaid's Feast (2002)

Russell James

Lawrence, David (b.1942)

David Lawrence is the pseudonym of the poet David Harsent. He is also a television scriptwriter and was at one time editorial director of Arrow Books. Harsent also uses two other pseudonyms: as David Pascoe he wrote the stand-alone *Fox on the Run* (1999), before which, as Jack Curtis, he wrote half a dozen dark and intense thrillers beginning with *Crow's Parliament* (1988) and continuing to *The Confessor* (1997). As a crime writer, he then softened the tone a little and was warmly praised for the resultant Stella Mooney series.

The son of a bricklayer, Lawrence was born in Devon, grew up in Buckinghamshire, left school at sixteen and worked for ten years in a bookshop. After working in publishing while writing as a poet, he embarked on a parallel life as a crime and thriller writer under the names Jack Curtis and David Lawrence. His poetry collections include *A Violent Country* (1969), *Mister Punch* (1984), *Selected Poems* (1989), *News from the Front* (1993), *A Bird's Idea of Flight* (1998) and *Marriage* (2002). *Legion* (2005) was shortlisted for the Whitbread poetry award, won the Forward Prize and was shortlisted for the T.S. Eliot Prize. As David Harsent, he has collaborated on operas and song cycles with Sir Harrison Birtwhistle and has written for stage and television. He lives in Barnes with his wife, the actor Julia Watson, and their daughter Hannah.

His debut novel as David Lawrence, *The Dead Sit Round in a Ring* (2002), opens with four dead bodies sitting in a ring in a room in Notting Hill Gate. Three of the four appear to have committed suicide, but the fourth has been professionally despatched. Investigator Detective Sergeant Stella Mooney appears as a splendidly credible heroine, whose private life is crumbling in non-cliché ways, but like a dog with a succulent bone she will not let go. The case, she finds, involves a turf war between London and Bosnian gangs fighting to control a lucrative trade in imported prostitutes, and the stakes are high enough for both sides to have summoned top-level help. The book was well written, violent and surprisingly well informed, and Stella at the end of the book clung to the only security in her life – the man she lived with: older, undemanding and supportive. Next in the series, *Nothing Like the Night* (2003), saw this romantic interest threatened by her attraction towards another man, but it was a mere backdrop to the challenge in her professional life, where she and her colleagues struggled to find and stop a pair of vicious serial killers. Again the tale was superbly told, with the poet's taut prose propelling a strong story. *Cold Kill* (2005) saw Stella out on her own: a young man had confessed to the slaying of a young woman. Case closed? Not for Stella. As ever, honing of the narrative is razor-sharp. *See also* Literature and Crime Writing.

Selected Works by the Author
The Dead Sit Round in a Ring (2002)
Nothing Like the Night (2003)
Cold Kill (2005)
Down into Darkness (2007)

Russell James

League of Gentlemen, The (film, 1960)

Basil Dearden, director

The League of Gentlemen – not to be confused with the grotesquely comic television series or the comic/film *The League of Extraordinary Gentlemen* – is an adaptation of an interesting, if sketchy, novel (1958) by John Boland (1913–1976). The title is an ironic reference to the associates of the novel *The Scarlet Pimpernel* (1905) by Baroness Orczy (1865–1947), and the storyline is almost a realistic version of *The Lavender Hill Mob* (1951). The film, wittily scripted by Bryan Forbes (b.1926), is less interesting for its efficient but standardised they-don't-quite-get-away-with-it bank heist than as a cynical and darkly satirical re-reading of the stiff-upper-lip war films it borrows its stars from. Hyde (Jack Hawkins), booted out of the army after twenty-five years, assembles a squad of cashiered ex-officers unable to fit into civilian society and trains them to commit a robbery with the exact military efficiency British viewers would have expected if they were, as in earlier films, planning the retaking of Malta or the destruction of the bridge on the river Kwai. Interestingly, he first approaches his recruits by sending them a crime novel about a perfect heist – which Boland identifies as *Clean Break* (1955) by Lionel White (1905–1985?), source for Kubrick's *The Killing*. A succession of familiar officer material types are introduced in acid vignettes which undermine their images: Nigel Patrick (very free with the 'old love') worries about the overdraft and flits from one gaff (and mistress, Melissa Stribling) in search of the next easy score; Terence Alexander ('I had a bloody good war, *actually!*') exchanges innuendo with sex-kitten Nanette Newman; Richard Attenborough fixes one-armed bandits; Roger Livesey, a padre cashiered for 'gross indecency', slobbers over a collection of 'health' magazines (many Harrison Marks titles are visible); Keiron Moore, a 'Mosleyite backroom boy' exposed as gay by the newspapers, runs a gym, which enables him to massage Dinsdale Landen; and Norman Bird, a henpecked nobody who wants to ditch his cramping wife and her senile father, tinkers with explosives in a shed. This deliberate corruption of cherished national myth is a curious mirror image of *The Dirty Dozen* (1967), in which crooks become soldiers, which suggests just how skewed the peacetime dreams of Britain's filmland heroes had become by 1960, recovering their pride and a sense of camaraderie through dirty tricks and criminal enterprises – not a suspense-filled but comic raid on the slack, peacetime army undertaken to rustle up an arsenal. Director Basil Dearden – who often used the plodding policier as a way into social issues (race in *Sapphire*, homosexuality in *Victim*) – stages the robbery with flair, but this film belongs to its cast: note the interplay between a gruff Hawkins and the criminally undervalued Patrick as they rustle up a meal in the grubby kitchen of Hawkins's huge but dilapidated mansion. A favourite moment: Patrick noticing an idealised portrait of Hawkins's wife and asking if the woman is dead only to be told off-handedly and with disappointment, 'No, the bitch is still going strong.' In the end, all these self-pitying stiff-upper-lippies are undone by a little boy who collects number plates. *See also* Film and Crime: Page to Screen.

Kim Newman

Leasor, James (1923–2008)

There were various attempts to shoehorn James Leasor's resourceful hero Dr Jason Love into the James Bond category – the most forceful progenitor of this endeavour being, of course, Leasor's publisher. And it is clear that Leasor had the Fleming ethos clearly in mind when chronicling the adventures of his globetrotting hero. But Love was cut from a rather different cloth, and the author's love of vintage cars transmuted the sequence of **espionage** adventures featuring the character into something quite individual, even though the inevitable cinema adaptation stressed the Bond connection.

After studying in London and Oxford, Leasor served in Army in Malaya and India during the Second World War as a captain in the Royal Berkshire Regiment. His early literary endeavours included the editorship of the *Isis* before the obligatory stint (for so many aspiring thriller writers) as a journalist; Leasor wrote for the *The Daily Express*. After well-received early books such as *Not Such a Bad Day* (1946) and a penetrating study of Rudolph Hess (*Rudolph Hess: The Uninvited Envoy*, 1961), Leasor set about to create a series that would both make his name and finesse his bank balance. Dr Jason Love, who debuted in *Passport to Oblivion* (1964), was different in many ways from his obvious prototype, Fleming's James Bond. Love was a country doctor with a successful practice (and sometime judo expert), inveigled into espionage by an ex-colleague from the Burmese campaign (inveigled under duress, of course, a sine qua non for recruitments in the espionage genre). And while Fleming cannily associated Bond with expensive, high-end cars, Leasor made a love of vintage automobiles central to his conception (this, however, hardly represented a stretch for the author, given that it was his own passionate interest). Those who enjoyed the Jason Love adventures will be familiar with the splendid Cord roadster, Love's vehicle of choice, treated with the care and attention reserved for a lover.

In fact, Leasor's picaresque globetrotting narratives suggest Richard Hannay adventures as much as any of the latter's descendants – due, no doubt, to Leasor's admiration of this godfather of the genre. *Passport to Oblivion* also betrays a nod to John **Buchan** with the death of a mysterious figure that sets the narrative in train. In an office above a wholesale fruiterer in Covent Garden, a red-haired Scot is searching through a filing cabinet for the name of a man he knew in Burma some twenty years earlier. The latter is, of course, Jason Love. After being dragooned into dangerous clandestine activities, Love finds that his comfortable bucolic existence is gone, perhaps forever. The novel was indifferently filmed with David Niven as *Where the Spies Are* (1965), but Leasor admirers did not hold this against him, and the second outing for Jason Love, *Passport to Peril* (1966), developed the exuberant storytelling of its predecessor, with Love finding himself in Pakistan, where a Nawab's son is being blinded by long-distance laser at the behest of the Chinese intelligence services. By now, critics were routinely comparing the effortless speed of Leasor's narratives with the fabulous Cord car driven by Love – in fact, the car became almost as important a protagonist as the hero. After several more titles beginning with the buzzword 'Passport' (*Passport in Suspense*, 1967, and *Passport for a Pilgrim*, 1968), Leasor, now comfortable with his character, expanded the length of the books and felt able to slow down the hectic pace in such novels as *Love Down Under* (1992) – and the publication date of the latter (along with *Frozen Assets*, 1989) demonstrated that Jason Love had considerably more longevity than most Bond imitators (most of whom have fallen by the wayside). But Leasor's books, although seeming dated today, are still highly coloured, skilfully crafted entertainments.

Selected Works by the Author

Passport to Oblivion (1964)
Passport to Peril (1966)
Passport in Suspense (1967)
Passport for a Pilgrim (1968)
Frozen Assets (1989)
Love Down Under (1992)

Barry Forshaw

Leather, Stephen (b.1956)

Stephen Leather is a journalist-turned crime writer, who began writing fiction full-time in 1992, on publication of his fourth book. His books are tough-minded, all-action stories, guaranteed of healthy sales, and have been translated into more than ten languages. Leather also writes for television, contributing to such series as *London's Burning*, *The Knock* and the BBC's *Murder in Mind*. For ten years, he worked as a journalist on newspapers such as *The Times*, the *Daily Mail* and the *South China Morning Post* in Hong Kong. In a mixed career, he was earlier a biochemist, a quarry worker, a baker, a petrol-pump attendant, a barman and a clerk for the Inland Revenue.

Most Leather books stand alone, although in 2004 he began a series based around Dan Shepherd. In none of his books does Leather leave much room for poetic policemen or wisecracking villains. The books are usually set in a dangerous world of vicious criminals and their uncompromising pursuers, where death seldom comes prettily. One unfortunate, for example, is thrown into a swimming pool alive with a concrete block tied to his leg. His killers stand beside the pool to watch him drown.

Although Leather often engages with modern-day issues, he uses them more as a background – even a killing ground – than as an opportunity to preach. In *The Eyewitness* (2003), set in war-wrecked Yugoslavia, a charity worker tries to trace the girl who escaped when two dozen people were murdered in a bout of ethnic cleansing. But rather than interest the reader in the good work of this charity, Leather has his hero go off to a bar on his own, where the first girl he meets leads him to his quarry. Diversions en route include hard sex and violence, and the search ends with predictable 'betrayal from within'. Leather's hard-bitten approach works far better

56. Stephen Leather.

in *Tango One* (2002). 'Tango One' means Police Target Number One, who in this case is Den Donovan, a tough and Teflon-skinned drugs czar. In an elaborate scheme to ensnare him, the police and MI6 put three rookie cops into deep, deep cover. It takes three years for the agents to get close to Donovan, by which time he has massive problems of his own: his wife and his accountant have run off together, taking all of his money (some £60 million) at the very time that his Columbian debtors are after him for the £10 million he owes them. Donovan is a vicious villain, and villains have to take their punishment, but the real surprise comes as Leather's morally ambiguous thriller turns the fundamental tenets of story-telling upside down. Here we see Leather at his best: the writing is efficient, credible and endlessly informative and, more importantly, remains full of twists and excitement.

Selected Works by the Author
Pay Off (1987)
The Long Shot (1994)
The Birthday Girl (1995)
Tango One (2002)
Soft Target (2005)
Cold Kill (2006)
Hot Blood (2006)
Dead Men (2008)

Russell James

le Carré, John (b.1931)

John le Carré is the defining figure in the evolution of the literary thriller at the end of the twentieth century and the beginning of the twenty-first century. More than any writer, he took the relatively recent niche genre of the espionage thriller, developed it, reinvented it and made it, in a highly individual manner, into a mainstream form of literature which dealt with themes that were political, historical, psychological and autobiographical.

His large – and still growing – oeuvre will unavoidably and correctly be seen to centre on the 'Karla trilogy', which encapsulated the justifiable paranoia of the Cold War; the central novel, *Tinker, Tailor, Soldier, Spy* (1974), stands on a par with any work of fiction of the late twentieth century. If his early and middle years were marked primarily by autobiographical influences, from his years in British intelligence to the bohemian lifestyle of his errant father (most blatantly exorcised in his 1986 novel *A Perfect Spy*), his later years have taken on a more deliberately political, almost didactic tone. The later books, in particular, have verged on the polemical in places, proselytising the author's left-liberal political stance and growing anger at the Western world's brutal globalisation. But even here, a vibrant sense of outrage has been massaged into masterful prose and meshed with vividly drawn characters who channel the politics into their own experience.

John le Carré was born David John Moore Cornwell in Poole, Dorset, on 19 October 1931 to Ronald Cornwell (known as Ronnie), a character of dubious reputation, and Olive (Gussy) Cornwell whom le Carré was hardly to see until he reached adulthood. He went to school first at St Andrew's prep school near Pangbourne and then for a while at Sherborne School. His mother abandoned her errant husband when young David was six years old, and he was brought up mainly by his father, who was a semi-successful confidence trickster, would-be politician and full-time rogue, who attracted an entourage of exotic and eccentric characters. Unsurprisingly, the teenage David was unsettled at Sherborne; he disliked his strict housemaster, which gave him a lasting distrust of hidebound British institutions. At the age of sixteen, he persuaded his father – then going through a relatively wealthy phase – to send him to school in Switzerland, where he studied German at Berne University from 1948 to 1949. Having come across an English diplomat almost certainly involved in intelligence, when he was called up to do military service he elected to serve with the Intelligence Corps in Austria. In 1952, he returned to England to resume his education, reading Modern Languages at Lincoln College, Oxford, where he met the college rector Vivian H.H. Greene, whom he would later claim to have been one of the models for fictional spymaster George Smiley.

Le Carré's studies had to be interrupted in 1954 when his father went bankrupt; forced to find a job, he started teaching at Milford Junior School. When family circumstances improved, he returned to Oxford and graduated with a first-class degree in 1956. After an unsatisfying two years' teaching at Eton (building up the knowledge of English public-school life, which would form the basis of the seminal first chapter of *Tinker, Tailor*), he left and tried out a variety of jobs, including, according to his own account, selling bath towels and washing elephants. In 1959, he joined the British Foreign Office and was sent to West Germany, where he became second secretary in the British Embassy in Bonn, the immediate background for *A Small Town in Germany* (1968). It was in this role that he became intimately familiar with the front line of the Cold War, getting to know West German politicians and visiting Berlin. His experiences here would form the backdrop to *The Spy Who Came in from the Cold* (1963) and *The Looking-Glass War* (1965).

It is accepted that his real employer at this time was Britain's Secret Intelligence Service (SIS) or MI6 and that one of the reasons he was unable to further a career with the service was that his was one of the names betrayed to the Soviet Union by the notorious double agent Kim Philby. He met Philby, and there are traces of the spy in the double agent unearthed in *Tinker, Tailor*. Le Carré himself refutes the idea that he remains a spy-turned writer: 'I am a writer who when I was very young spent a few ineffectual but extremely formative years in British intelligence.' While he was still in Bonn, he wrote and published his first two novels *Call for the Dead* (1961) and *A Murder of Quality* (1962). It was because members of the Foreign Office were not supposed to publish under their own names that he first took the pseudonym John le Carré.

Obviously a first novel and bearing little signs as yet of the mastery of later years, *Call for the Dead* is still a striking and enjoyable murder mystery set in the world le Carré knew so well: where the secret world of espionage blends into ordinary life. It is of particular significance, however, that this very first effort already introduces the character who would emerge as the central pillar of the mature le Carré opus: George Smiley. It also features other characters that would appear again: bit parts for Peter Guillam, who would become a major aide to Smiley in the Karla books, as well as police inspector Albert Mendel and East German spy Hans-Dieter Mundt. In this book, although he does kill the spy at the end, emphasising his ruthlessness when necessary, Smiley is already the antithesis of the action hero: self-effacing and quiet-spoken. He has already fallen from grace – which was to become a habit – and at the end of the book retires altogether from the service. In *A Murder of Quality*, Smiley is semi-retired and involved in scholastic research (his speciality, which recurs repeatedly, is baroque German literature) when he is called in to investigate a murder at a minor public school (based in Sherborne). This is essentially a detective story – possibly an experiment with a new genre – and merits attention only to those who wish to reconstruct George Smiley's biography.

It was le Carré's third novel that changed everything, and it also featured Smiley, although only in a minor role, now back in harness in a senior position at what we will come to know as The Circus. *The Spy Who Came in from the Cold* was a breakthrough book not just for its author but for the genre. At the time, Ian **Fleming**'s books and the early James Bond movies were the height of fashion. There was a counterweight to be found in Len **Deighton**'s hard-bitten working-class spook in *The Ipcress File* (1962), but le Carré's Alec Leamas inhabited a more sombre, bleaker world determined by realpolitik and betrayal. Graham **Greene**, to whom le Carré would come to be compared, called it 'the best spy novel I have ever read'.

Leamas's mission is to fake disgrace and alcoholic collapse and let himself be turned by the East German secret service in order to get close enough to kill Mundt, now their spymaster, but it ends in a grim web of double-cross. Its 1965 film adaptation starred Richard Burton in a gritty, harsh, appropriately black-and-white antidote to Sean Connery's Technicolor exploits in *Thunderball*, released months earlier. Where Bond bedded exotic beauties, Leamas's love is a shy ex-communist librarian. The book won the Somerset Maugham Award and changed le Carré's life, propelling him into the big time and allowing him to give up his 'day job' with the Foreign Office, return to England and devote himself full-time to writing.

His recent career was, however, much in evidence in the next two books, *The Looking-Glass War*, an equally bleak, grim story of a doomed British espionage plot in East Germany, and *A Small Town in Germany*, set in the contemporary Bonn he had just left, involving a neo-Nazi threat.

By now established in his genre, le Carré was to take the biggest gamble of his career – to leap into mainstream literature with a book wholly unrelated to anything he had done before that will deal with human relationships, life, death and philosophy. The result was *The Naïve and Sentimental Lover* (1971), and it was a bold disaster. His laudable determination 'not to plod around the same track like an old athlete just because it makes money' came unstuck in a novel that critics called 'maudlin and overwritten'. It actually deserves more attention, if only for its relevance to the author's subsequent trajectory. His hero, Aldo Cassidy, is a pram manufacturer, a romantic with a childhood overshadowed by his untrustworthy father, a married man insecure about his responsibilities to wife and family, all characteristics that could loosely be ascribed to the author (he divorced from his first wife in the year of the book's publication). Cassidy falls in with would-be bohemian artist and author Shamus and his adoring, abused woman Helen, to become involved in a ménage à trois that he hopes will change his life and give meaning to the title, a realisation of the German philosopher Schiller's concept of the artist. The plan ends sordidly in betrayal and recrimination. The book confronts head-on – and clumsily – many of the themes the author considered most important in literature. Its critical failure, happily, sent him back to the genre he knew, where he was to succeed in dealing with all those themes – and more – bruised but honed by his well-meaning but ill-fated excursion.

It was another three years before his masterpiece saw the light of day. *Tinker, Tailor* begins with one of the finest first chapters in English literature, a masterpiece of oblique introduction that, if read carefully, encapsulates the whole novel and provides the vital clue as to the means and reason for the death of the traitor. Jim Prideaux, when we first meet him, is a bruised veteran of we-know-not-what come to take over as stand-in master in a minor public school, befriends a fat boy, gives his pupils lessons in life and deals brusquely with an owl fallen down a chimney. An unlikely beginning for one of the greatest espionage novels of all time. Gradually, we enter the world of The Circus – named for Shaftesbury Circus, where le Carré situates MI6's fictional headquarters – and witness the return of George Smiley. Once again in retirement after the death of his mentor, 'Control', following a failed secret operation by Prideaux in Czechoslovakia to find a mole in the heart of the Circus, Smiley is recalled when an AWOL agent turns up new information proving that the mole exists. Smiley is tasked to interview, sift and sort information, to uncover which of his former high-ranking colleagues is the traitor. A dumpy, owlish man, plagued by the infidelities of his high-born wife (she is having an affair with one of the suspects), he cuts a sad, lonely role as a hero whose success will only unearth lies and treason. A huge critical success, the book tapped into the psychology of post-imperial Britain, of a generation stripped of its old values and searching in vain for new ones, of moral vacuity, hollow friendships and cynicism in the place of sincerity. *Tinker, Tailor* subsequently became not just a literary icon but a broadcast masterpiece when it was turned into a television series featuring Alec Guinness as Smiley. Having originally pictured the actor Arthur Lowe (better known for his comedy roles), le Carré would later admit that Guinness's masterly depiction coloured his image of the character.

He followed the novel up with *The Honourable Schoolboy* (1977), which shifted the focus from the Soviet Union to China and questions Britain's slavish relationship towards the United States. The story ends in tragedy and treachery with Smiley and co. dismissed from the service once again in favour of American puppets. *Smiley's People* (1980) saw the apotheosis of his plump hero as Smiley is once again brought back into the loop to investigate the death of a retired Russian general in London and ends up discovering a secret that could entrap his nemesis, the Soviet spymaster Karla. Smiley's victory is attained by means that call into question his morality that leaves a bitter rather than sweet taste in his mouth and proves a fitting finale to a series of books that have unofficially become known as the 'Karla trilogy'.

In *The Little Drummer Girl* (1983), le Carré ventured into bold, new territory of the Middle East with the story of a left-wing actress enlisted by her lover as an Israeli plant in a Palestinian terror group with which she comes to sympathise. Her resultant breakdown is itself an allegory of the intractable schizophrenia of the conflict.

A Perfect Spy (1986) is, by le Carré's own admission, his autobiographical novel – in theory a memoir by a long-time British spy Rick Pym, but in fact largely a portrait of his father. Pym's multiple manifestations of himself, as he himself and others recount them, reveal a man with many exteriors but in the end lacking an essential core. A fine, complex book, in which the espionage element is incidental and the world we are immersed in is unrelated to the universe of Smiley and the Circus.

In *The Russia House* (1989), we are back more distinctively in the espionage field, with publisher Barley Blair drawn into a game of intrigue set in the dying days of the Soviet Union, which the book all but anticipates. *The Secret Pilgrim* (1991) is le Carré's epitaph for the Cold War, in which a first-person narrator Ned invites the retired Smiley to speak to new recruits. But the book serves to illustrate the developing persona of Ned as he recounts his mentor's exploits and examines the amoral world in which they occurred.

The Night Manager (1993) had a hint of le Carré's exotic childhood as well as his adult success in its cosmopolitanism. His first post–Cold War novel, it involves international racketeering and a turf war by intelligence agencies at a loose end. In *Our Game* (1995), he returns to an ostensibly domestic British scene with the disappearance of a lecturer from Bath University, except that he was a former SIS man and his handler must track him down. The trail leads to the wilds of the disintegrating Soviet Union and the autonomous republics of Ossetia and Ingushetia, an astute comment on the post-Soviet anarchy.

The Tailor of Panama (1996) is perhaps le Carré's most light-hearted book and centres on the wonderfully well-rounded character of Harry Pendel, a tailor with pretensions, money problems and social aspirations. His nemesis is Andy Osnard, an amoral British spy who bribes Pendel to use his connections to spy on the status of the canal – soon to be handed over by the Americans – but believes the cash-strapped tailor's spiralling exaggerations. It was made into a film in 2001, directed by John Boorman, with Pierce Brosnan (then fresh from his 007 role) playing Osnard as an almost anti-Bond with a cameo role by Harold Pinter, and le Carré writing the script. By the time of shooting the film, some of the politics required alteration because the canal handover had taken place. Nonetheless, there were critics who felt that the film's overly upbeat ending had been arranged to pander to Hollywood and dilute the novel's harsh condemnation of US expansionism.

Single and Single (1999) is ostensibly – and intelligently – a tale set in the unsavoury new world of the financially unscrupulous, post-Soviet mafia in Georgia and Turkey and their immoral Western partners, reaping millions from marketing 'clean' blood from the Caucasus. It is also a return to the complex family relationships between father and son pitting the unscrupulous elder Tiger Single against his son Oliver, who discovers himself to be a surprisingly honest lawyer. In not-dissimilar vein, *The Constant Gardener* (2001) was an unabashed attack on Western drugs companies profiteering in Africa, woven into a plot about the wife of a British diplomat in Kenya who is found raped and murdered in the bush. In what has by now become typical of the late le Carré, this is a gripping novel with a complex plot based on corruption and highly critical of money-grabbing under the guise of globalisation.

Absolute Friends (2003) revisits the Cold War in retrospective and is one of the less successful later books. Its hero, Ted Mundy, renews his acquaintance with Sasha, a former East German spy, whom he has known since student days in 1960s West Berlin, who worked together across the ideological divide to contribute towards the Cold War's end. But in the harsh new world, they become pawns and then victims in the US 'war on terror'. An overambitious book, it suggested le Carré had lost some of his grip on the realities of modern Europe.

The Mission Song (2006) returns, in its heart if not in its actual setting, to Africa. Narrated with convincing fluency by a multilingual African interpreter drawn into a corrupt coup attempt, it describes a conspiracy to defraud the Congo of mineral resources, disguised as benign redistribution of wealth. Most remarkable is le Carré's research and the strength of characterisation needed to get so successfully inside the head of his protagonist.

For all his convincing sense of time and place, le Carré – or perhaps, one should say, David Cornwell – has never quite acclimatised to the modern world with which his novels have by and large so distinctively kept pace. By his own admission, he hates the telephone and has never learned to type, preferring to write his manuscripts by hand. He dislikes city life and much prefers the relative seclusion of Cornwall, where he has lived for more than forty years. He has been married twice, from 1954 to 1971 to Alison Sharp, with whom he has three sons, and since 1972 to Valerie Eustace with whom he has one son. In recent years, he has been politically more active in the views reflected both in his novels and in articles for newspapers where he has vociferously attacked the United States–led invasion of Iraq and condemned the evils of profiteering globalisation.

His work has come to be the benchmark by which all other espionage fiction aspires to be judged. 'As good as le Carré' or occasionally 'better than...' is the reviewer's quote most longed-for by publishers. 'The new le Carré' is a title doled out on rare occasions to the most aspirational new prophets of the genre, but to date none have proved more than mere disciples. He has been compared to Graham Greene, although he is said to dislike the comparison. It is imprecise because the two writers have vastly differing literary styles, yet it is true that both have bridged the gap between 'serious' and 'popular' fiction, proving that a supremely skilful author can combine both. *See also* Espionage Fiction *and* Thrillers: Novels of Action.

Selected Works by the Author
The Spy Who Came in from the Cold (1963)
Tinker, Tailor, Soldier, Spy (1974)
The Honourable Schoolboy (1977)
Smiley's People (1980)
A Perfect Spy (1986)
The Tailor of Panama (1996)
The Constant Gardener (2001)
The Mission Song (2006)

Website
www.randomhouse.com/features/lecarre/author.html

Peter Millar

Lemarchand, Elizabeth (1906–2000)

Elizabeth Lemarchand described her books as classical detective stories: 'old hat, but there are still a surprising number of old hatters around'. For example, all feature a map or plan, and most of them contain a list of characters; several of them take place in her native Devon, although not in real places; and many show an interest in history, education or other 'cultural' matters.

Born in Barnstaple, Lemarchand was a schoolteacher in Bristol and elsewhere before becoming deputy headmistress at Godolphin School, Salisbury (1940–1960), then was briefly a head teacher in North Wales, and retired early because of serious illness and took up writing – short stories initially, five being published – as a convalescence hobby. They were followed by sixteen novels, all featuring the Scotland Yard Detective Superintendent Tom Pollard and Detective Sergeant Gregory Toye (who later becomes inspector), both decent police officers (Toye is rather sentimental) and family men.

Unsurprisingly, the first (and arguably the best) of them, *Death of an Old Girl* (1967), is set in a school, its art department turning out to be connected, unwittingly, with international art smuggling – Pollard's wife is artistic and (unofficially) helps him in this case. *Let or Hindrance* (1973; published in the United States as *No Vacation for Murder*) is also set in school, but the school is being used for a cultural activity holiday. The setting of *Death on Doomsday* (1971) is a stately home; that of *Step in the Dark* (1976), a library-cum-museum of a local learned society. *Buried in the Past* (1974) and *Suddenly while Gardening* (1978) have archaeological backgrounds – in the latter, a modern skeleton is found in an ancient tomb. Local history comes into *The Affacombe Affair* (1968) and ancient superstition into *Troubled Waters* (1982). For part of the action of *Cyanide with Compliments* (1972), which shares some characters with *Affacombe*, we visit a Mediterranean cruise ship.

Lemarchand's books make enjoyable reading (and re-reading), exploring a warm, cosy world with pleasant, if two-dimensional, characterisation and, most importantly, solid detection. *See also* Conventions *and* True Crime.

Selected Works by the Author
Alibi for a Corpse (1969)
Unhappy Returns (1978)
Change for the Worse (1980)
Nothing to Do with the Case (1981)
The Wheel Turns (1984)
Who Goes Home? (1986)

Philip Scowcroft

Le Queux, William (1864–1927)

William Le Queux was a British journalist and author who was a pioneer creator of influential spy novels, warning of the likelihood of the First World War. Le Queux also served as an intelligence agent for the government both before and during the First World War, although he was apparently self-funded and responsible for recruiting others – all amateurs – to assist him.

Although of French descent, Le Queux (pronounced 'kew') was an ardent anglophile and a powerful advocate of the need for greater awareness in Britain of the vulnerability in its military defences. In his youth, he had travelled extensively with his parents, gaining a cosmopolitan education and fluency in several European languages. Although he studied art, he continued to travel and became a journalist, establishing his reputation for a series of articles in *The Times* on the Russian revolutionary movement and also gaining the support of Emile Zola for further reportage in the French press. His first book, *Guilty Bonds* (1890), drew upon Russian political intrigue, as did the stories in *Strange Tales of a Nihilist* (1892). Le Queux's interest in Russian espionage led him to deduce that Jack the Ripper was Dr Alexander Pedachenko, who he believed had been sent to Britain by Russia's secret police to identify weaknesses in Britain's police force. He did not reveal this until his book of reminiscences, *Things I Know about Kings, Celebrities and Crooks* (1923).

Le Queux's fame, or (to some) notoriety, began with *The Great War in England in 1897* (1894), which tells of the invasion of Britain by a combined Franco-Russian force. France is again the enemy in *England's Peril* (1899), but after the *entente cordiale*, Germany became the enemy in *The Invasion of 1910* (1906). This was written with the help of Britain's national hero Lord Roberts. Its serialisation in Lord Northcliffe's *Daily Mail* led to such an outcry that the government felt compelled to review Britain's security. Le Queux repeated the idea again in the thinly disguised novel, *Spies of the Kaiser* (1909).

Although these were Le Queux's best-known books, they are but 4 out of almost 200. A quarter of them deal with international espionage, and many more contain some criminal element or accounts of real criminal activities.

Le Queux was also a dedicated criminologist, who spent time with various law enforcement or surveillance agencies to understand their methods and learn their stories. Books inspired by such activities include *Secrets of Monte Carlo* (1899) and *Mysteries of a Great City* (1919) – set in Paris and featuring the detective Monsieur Becq – and *The Crimes Club* (1927), stories based on an actual organisation that included Le Queux and Arthur Conan **Doyle** among its members. Other books of interest include *The Three Knots* (1922), which features a female detective, and *The Bronze Face* (1923), which explores the mystery behind an epidemic of suicides. The protagonist in *The Secrets of the Foreign Office* (1903) is Duckworth Drew, a detective involved in espionage on behalf of his chief, the Marquis of Macclesfield. The character is generally regarded to have sewn the seeds for Ian **Fleming**'s James Bond, although Fleming had plenty of other sources of inspiration. Le Queux also wrote books about both Rasputin and the French master criminal Landru.

Le Queux was an early pioneer of radio, even setting up his own broadcasting unit after the war. He saw its potential in espionage and incorporated the wireless into several of his books, notably *Tracked by Wireless* (1922), *The Voice from the Void* (1922), subtitled 'The Great Wireless Mystery' and *The Broadcast Mystery* (1924). Le Queux wrote right up to his death at the age of sixty-three, always active and interested in new developments and fighting one crusade or another. There were those who believed that he had lost touch with reality, and it is generally accepted that his autobiography, *Things I Know*, does not let facts get in the way of a good story.

Few of Le Queux's books have passed the test of time and are marred by over-exuberance and his desire to lecture, but at their best they are memorable period pieces of a time when the Intelligence Services were in their infancy. *See also* Espionage Fiction.

Selected Works by the Author
Strange Tales of a Nihilist (1892)
England's Peril (1899)
Secrets of Monte Carlo (1899)
Mysteries of a Great City (1919)
The Voice from the Void (1922)
The Marked Man (1925)
The Crimes Club (1927)

Further Reading
Patrick, Chris, and Stephen Baister. 2007. *William Le Queux: Master of Mystery*.
Woods, Brett F. 'War, Propaganda and the Fiction of William Le Queux', www.critiquemagazine.com/article/lequeux.html.

Mike Ashley

Levack, Simon (b.1965)

Simon Levack writes quirky and colourful historical crime fiction set in a vividly realised Aztec Mexico, on the eve of the Spanish conquest in the early sixteenth century. His first novel, *Demon of the Air* (2004), won the **Crime Writers' Association** Debut Dagger in 2000 and established Levack in an increasingly overcrowded field.

Levack was brought up in Kent. He trained as a lawyer and worked in and around the legal profession before taking up writing full-time in 2003. He still lives in Kent and is married with one son.

To date, Levack has published four books – *Shadow of the Lords* (2005), *City of Spies* (2006) and *Tribute of Death* (2007), being the other three. All feature the same hero – Cemiquiztli Yaotl – a fictitious slave to Aztec Emperor Montezuma's chief minister. The character is allowed to subtly develop throughout the series, although the forward trajectory of the narrative remains paramount.

Levack has also published a number of short stories, featuring the same character and setting in *Ellery Queen's Mystery Magazine*.

Selected Works by the Author
Demon of the Air (2004)
Shadow of the Lords (2005)
City of Spies (2006)
Tribute of Death (2007)

Barry Forshaw

Lewin, Michael Z. (b.1942)

The first great wave of neo-Chandlerian novels came in the early 1970s, as writers such as Jonathan Valin, Loren Estleman, Roger Simon and Michael Lewin divvied up America's major cities and populated them with hard-boiled private eyes. But by the time *Ask the Right Question* (1971), which introduced Indianapolis-based Albert Samson, was nominated for Edgar, Lewin was already living in England, where he has remained ever since.

Michael Zinn Lewin was born in Springfield, Massachusetts, and raised in Indianapolis; Zinn was his mother's family name – one of his ancestors named the plant genus Zinnia. Lewin was educated at Harvard, then at Cambridge, where the Footlights revue consumed most of his energy. He returned to America and taught, until E.L. Doctorow, an editor at Dial Press, bought his first book, *How to Ace College Exams* (1971). Its success freed him to become a full-time writer.

Albert Samson was a brilliant creation, influenced as much by Ross Macdonald as Chandler. A shrewd observer, Samson never carried a gun; his cases reflected the boring reality of everyday private-eye work, at least at first. He is a dedicated wisecracker, and his chaotic relationships, particularly with his mother, provided a strain of humour, which increased as the series moved on, foreshadowing his later Lunghi series. The tone of easy humour comes closest to Stuart Kaminsky's Toby Peters series, but initially with a sharper edge, which grew softer until Samson was reduced to putting on 'mystery' events for wealthy dinner-party guests and lost his private investigator ticket. Lewin spun off characters for other novels set in Indianapolis, three featuring the cynical cop Leroy Powder, another starring Samson's social-worker girlfriend Adele Buffington and one with the homeless dwarf Jan Moro, which co-stars Powder.

Lewin's other fiction includes the novelisation of the Sean Connery movie *The Next Man* (1976) and a young-adult historical mystery, *Cutting Loose* (1999), in which a girl disguises herself as a boy to play baseball and travels to London to investigate her father's death.

Long resident in the West Country, Lewin, in the 1990s, began writing about the Bath-based Lunghi family detective agency, where three generations of Anglo-Italians mix family relations with crime solving. He has appeared, performed and written with the West Country–based writers Peter **Lovesey** and Liza **Cody** and, at one point, coached a local women's basketball team.

Lewin's humour helps make him an effective short-story writer, and he has been a frequent contributor to anthologies and the *Ellery Queen* and *Alfred Hitchcock* magazines. His collection *The Reluctant Detective* (2001) includes the title story (a 1984 Edgar nominee), and *If the Glove Fits* (2002) was nominated after it appeared. He has also written two collections of off-beat short stories written as a dog's narration. Lewin has scripted many radio plays, based on his novels and stories as well as adapting Lovesey's, and written the screenplays for two Japanese television movie adaptations of the novels, *Missing Woman* (1981) and *And Baby Will Fall* (1988). His novel *Hard Line* (1982) won a Japanese Maltese Falcon award as best foreign novel, and *Called By a Panther* (1991) received a similar Marlowe award in Germany. His website is informative and entertaining. *See also* Film and Crime: Page to Screen *and* Humour and Crime Fiction.

Selected Works by the Author
Ask the Right Question (1971)
The Next Man (1976)
Hard Line (1982)
Out of Time (1984; also published in the United States as *Out of Season*)
Telling Tales (stories, 1994)
Family Business (1995)
Rover's Tales (stories, 1998)

Lewin, Michael Z.

The Reluctant Detective (stories, 2001)
Eye Opener (2004)

Website
http://michaelzlewin.com

Michael Carlson

Lewis, Ted (1940–1982)

Ted Lewis's legacy as a cult crime writer is arguably a result of Mike Hodges's iconic 1971 gangster movie ***Get Carter***. His *Jack's Return Home* (1970) formed the basis for the film, but in his short lifetime he also produced several other equally readable books, as well as writing for the BBC cop series *Z Cars* (1962–1978).

Lewis was born in Manchester on 15 January 1940 and moved to Barton-upon-Humber as a child when his father became manager of the Quarry and Lime Works at the nearby village of Melton Ross. Educated at Barton Grammar School under the aegis of historical novelist Henry Treece, Lewis began writing as soon as he left school. He was also an accomplished artist, attending Hull Art School (against the wishes of his parents) and working for a short time as a film and television animator, most notably on the Beatles's 1968 film *Yellow Submarine*.

His first novel was an autobiographical romance with the somewhat clumsy title *All the Way Home and All the Night Through* (1965), but it was his 1970 follow-up, *Jack's Return Home*, that proved a turning point in his career. The latter narrates the story of London gangster Jack Carter's return to his Northern hometown (Doncaster in all but name) to arrange his brother's funeral. The book's evocation of a grim industrial milieu peopled with corrupt politicians and avaricious businessman garnered quietly impressive reviews. The ultimate seal of approval came from the *Doncaster Evening Post*, which described the novel as 'completely believable'.

Fledgling British film-maker Mike Hodges seized on the story for his movie debut, writing the screenplay and changing the title to *Get Carter*; it was released the following year with Michael Caine giving a career-defining performance in the title role. Relocating to Newcastle, the documentary-style direction, naturalistic performances and raw depictions of sex and violence, coupled with a distinctive jazz score by Roy Budd, helped the film overcome a hostile critical backlash (mirroring that which greeted *A Clockwork Orange* the same year) to become what is now regarded as the best British gangster movie of the twentieth century.

Despite writing two further books about Carter, and several other novels, of which the best is *Billy Rags* (1973), about an escaped bank robber, Lewis never achieved the same level of success. He died at the young age of forty-two, in relative obscurity. *See also* TV Detectives: Small-Screen Adaptations.

Selected Works by the Author
Jack's Return Home (1970; later reissued as *Get Carter*)
Plender (1971)
Billy Rags (1973)
Jack Carter's Law (1974; also published in the United States as *Jack Carter and the Law*)
G.B.H. (1980; also published in the United States as *Grievous Bodily Harm*)

Mark Campbell

Lindsay, Douglas (b.1964)

Scottish-born Douglas Lindsay is the writer of a series of absurd but affectionate satires of the serial killer genre, all featuring the hapless barber Barney Thomson.

Lindsay had always had a 'vague inkling to write books, but could never really be bothered' and landed a job with the Ministry of Defence after leaving university. He only found the time to attempt a novel when he took unpaid leave to join his wife who was working at Senegal, West Africa. After a false start, Lindsay wrote *The Long Midnight of Barney Thomson* (1999) and 'sent it out to every publisher on the planet; and every publisher on the planet raced back to tell me to clear off'. Lindsay continued to write, and finally Piatkus Books published the novel. Lindsay, then, started Long Midnight Publishing to chronicle Barney's misadventures and acquired a German publisher who is translating the series to great success.

Lindsay's serial killer satires are comedy thrillers of the darkest order. The eponymous hero – who accidentally kills his employer and ends up on the run as a suspected serial killer – is always up to his neck in murder. The unfortunate barber never seems to find a respite from the mayhem, which is hardly surprising, as the Scotland he inhabits is rife with mass murders! Barney even finds a monastery full of them in the second novel, *The Cutting Edge of Barney Thomson* (2000). His death at the end of *A Prayer for Barney Thomson* (2001) does not seem to bring him peace as he is brought back to life in *The King Was in His Counting House* (2004) to deal with a killer stalking the Scottish Cabinet. Settling on the Isle of Cumbrae, Barney finally thinks that he has found the quiet life. However, death is not far behind in *The Da Vinci Code*–inspired *The Last Fish Supper* (2006) and the ghostly *The Haunting of Barney Thomson* (2007).

Throughout the series you can see the influence of the author's love of film, television (from Tarantino to surrealistic US television serials such as *Northern Exposure*) and popular culture in general. The novels are full of absurdly witty dialogue – although you may need help to decipher the Glaswegian accent – with characters expounding aimlessly on irrelevant subjects, while others quote lines of classical literature and philosophy to great comic effect. Lindsay also uses the Barney Thomson novels as a platform to deride his current pet hates and is not above making fun of Scottish politics (*The King Was in His Counting House*), support groups (Murders Anonymous from *A Prayer for Barney Thomson*), murder mysteries (*Barney Thomson and the Face of Death*, 2002) or the publishing phenomenon *The Da Vinci Code* (*The Last Fish Supper*).

The Barney Thomson novels are blackly entertaining and a nicely twisted absurd satire on the serial killer genre.

Selected Works by the Author
The Long Midnight of Barney Thomson (1999)
The Cutting Edge of Barney Thomson (2000)
A Prayer for Barney Thomson (2001)
Barney Thomson and the Face of Death (2002)
The King Was in His Counting House (2004)
The Last Fish Supper (2006)
The Haunting of Barney Thomson (2007)

Website
www.barney-thomson.com

Terry Fountain

Linscott, Gillian (b.1944)

Though known mainly for her historical crime series featuring the suffragette Nell Bray, Gillian Linscott has written several other crime books, including a separate series about ex-cop Birdie Linnet. She won the **Crime Writers' Association** Ellis Peters Historical Dagger for *Absent Friends* in 2000. The following year's *The Perfect Daughter* was shortlisted for the same prize.

A graduate of Somerville College, Oxford, Linscott began her career as a reporter for *The Guardian*, working for seven years. She also worked for the *Liverpool Post* and the *Birmingham Post* and was a BBC parliamentary reporter for local radio stations. In the 1980s, she began writing crime fiction part-time, and her first published book was *A Healthy Body* (1984), launching the four-book Birdie Linnet series. Linnet was an ex-cop who in this book nipped across to France to track his wife and her lover. The lover, inevitably, was soon found murdered, with Birdie being the prime suspect. The series remained firmly rooted in the 1980s. However, for her next series, by which time she was writing full-time, Linscott used her knowledge of history and politics to help create the feisty Edwardian suffragette Nell Bray. In *Sister Beneath the Sheet* (1991), Bray was encountered fresh from Holloway prison, where she had been held for throwing a half brick through the window of Number 10 Downing Street. Despite her imprisonment, Nell, like many suffragettes, was passionately concerned with what was right, rather than in simply doing wrong. Her suffragist politics were central to the plots, in the first of which Bray is engaged by Mrs Pankhurst, no less, to collect a large sum of money from a prostitute in Biarritz who was later murdered. Equally juicy plots followed at the rate of one a year culminating in 2003 with the last of the series, *Blood on the Wood* (2003). During the series, Nell moved through suffragette history – the demonstrations, the First World War – although the books were written and published in a non-chronological sequence. For example, the second last published, *Dead Man Riding* (2002), was set earliest, in 1900. In Linscott's award-winning *Absent Friends*, women had finally won the right to vote, and Nell stood as a candidate at the 1919 General Election. But it was still a crime book: the previous candidate had been murdered.

Lively, well informed, intelligent and barbed, the Nell Bray series never broke through to achieve the popular success it deserved. Perhaps it needed a television series. One exception to the Bray series should also be mentioned: *The Garden* (2003) traces the fortunes of a Rhondda mining family and the mine owners from the Edwardian period into the 1920s. It is Linscott's rarest title.

Selected Works by the Author
A Healthy Body (1984)
Murder Makes Tracks (1985)
Knightfall (1986)
A Whiff of Sulphur (1987)
Sister Beneath the Sheet (1991)
Hanging on the Wire (1992)
Widow's Peak (1994)
Absent Friends (1999)
The Perfect Daughter (2000)
Dead Man Riding (2002)
Blood on the Wood (2003)

Russell James

Literature and Crime Fiction

'You can go back to every classic that's ever been written, and it's about good and evil. The crime novel is just the simple form of that. What's better as a moral and dramatic question than somebody who decides to murder someone' (Gerald Petievich).

There are literary crime writers, and there are literary novelists whose books contain crimes of one sort or another. While judging the former is necessarily subjective – on what criteria does one call it a crime novel, or any other type of novel, literary? – the latter is easier to identify if only because the criteria seem more straightforward: not so much the nature or extent of the crimes contained in a particular novel, but whether the investigation of such crimes constitutes the subject of the novel. However, separating crime and literary novels is more often than not the province of publishers and booksellers, who seek such categories to assist them in marketing their books or placing them in shops to ensure that maximum copies are sold. Consequently, any discussion of literature as, or separate from, crime fiction is irrevocably linked to the economics of publishing and, in Britain, subsumed in assumptions relating to class, aesthetics and questions regarding popular, as opposed to literary, culture.

Boldly stated, anyone investigating crimes, be they personal or public, is a crime writer. However, the more literal minded would insist on a murder, as well as the obligatory investigation no matter where it might lead. But what, in fact, constitutes a crime, much less an investigation? Are we talking about state crimes as much as crimes against individuals, a war as much as a personal slight, a cold-blooded murder as much as an act of petty revenge? And does an investigation simply entail pursuing a culprit, or is it the examination of the culture that has produced the culprit? Could it be that doing either accomplishes both? One might even go so far as to say that if one is not investigating the culture, the end result could, in itself, be criminal, or at least barely worth the effort put into writing a novel, whether crime, literary or something in-between.

At the same time, anyone writing coherently can be said to be literary, even if the term *literary* is difficult to define. Yesterday's literary style can easily become tomorrow's cliché, while today's literariness might only be a passing phase proclaimed by those responsible for selling the novel or a critic's infatuation with a pretty face or a half-decent turn of phrase. What was written 50–100 years ago might today seem stilted to some, but stylish to others. At the same time, modern writings, from Derek **Raymond**'s *Factory* novels to Irish writer Ken Bruen's (b.1951) high-energy prose, might appear highly literary to those impressed by their verisimilitude and honesty, which to others might come across as overblown, if not ridiculous. In such matters, even time tends to be an uncertain arbiter, as illustrated by Gerald **Kersh**'s vernacular novels, such as his 1957 *Fowler's End* or his 1938 ***Night and the City***. While the latter is termed a classic and as fresh as it was the day it was written, some critics have called the former overly vernacular and dated. All one can say, finally, is that literary style is subjective, residing, like tarnished beauty, in the private eye of the beholder.

Although crime fiction tends to function best outside the parameters of mainstream literary fiction, it has long been co-opted by middlebrow literary types. That past crime writers have been not only leaned on, but accepted into the literary canon only means that their writing has been acknowledged as yet a standard literary format, at least to the extent that it can be identified, copied and parodied. This has been the case in the United States regarding the works of Raymond **Chandler** and Dashiell Hammett, while in Britain, such writers as Arthur **Conan Doyle**, Wilkie **Collins** and Graham **Greene** (although the latter is too mutable to be linked to any one particular style or genre) have passed the test of time and become stylists, or, if you will, objects of literary discernment, appreciated by critics as well as the general reading public.

In fact, there has always been a literary element to British crime fiction, as well as a criminal element to a great deal of literary fiction. There have long been literary writers who dabble in crime, particularly if one includes in this category anyone who puts their writing at the service of self-styled investigations and muckraking instincts. No matter how you look at it, the origins of British crime fiction are found as much in the work of those who might be called literary, as in the annals of *Newgate*, penny bloods or the pages of pulp magazines that would later appear.

It was social reformer William Godwin (1756–1836), for his *The Adventure of Caleb Williams* (1794), who is credited with writing the first novel to use murder as the central incident. In 1824, James Hogg's (1770–1835) Scottish masterpiece, *The Private Memoirs and Confessions of a Justified Sinner*, appeared, as grisly and terrifying a novel as anything that would later be written by the likes of James Ellroy. Determined to investigate the culture, Charles **Dickens** was among the first to write about the dark and criminal side of Victorian London in such narratives as *Oliver Twist* (1838), *Bleak House* (1853), *Barnaby Rudge* (1841) and *The Mystery of Edwin Drood* (1870). When it comes to the first literary crime novelist, Dickens's friend, Wilkie **Collins**, is often singled out, having written (among others) *The Woman in White* (1859) – 'The first, the longest, and the best of modern English detective novels,' according to T.S. Eliot – and *The Moonstone* (1868), both containing convoluted plots and determined investigatory work. Around the same time, Robert Louis Stevenson (1850–1894) was writing 'The Suicide Club' (1878), *The Strange Case of Dr Jekyll and Mr Hyde* (1886) and the unfinished 'Weir of Hermiston' (1896), which would influence a number of future crime and suspense writers, including Ian **Rankin**. George Gissing (1857–1903), in such books as *New Grub Street* (1891) and *The Odd Women* (1893), detailed pest-stricken London and those living on the margins (whether reviewers scrambling for money to pay for their next meal or women attempting to pursue independent lives); Gissing was not so much a crime writer as a chronicler of Edwardian noir. Equally important was Joseph **Conrad** (1857–1924) – *Secret Agent* (1907) and *Under Western Skies* (1911) – who would also hold sway among crime and spy-fiction writers, from Eric **Ambler** to Raymond Chandler.

In the early years of the twentieth century, various writers composed impeccable, if middle-class, crime fiction cloaked (to varying degrees) in literary clothing. One such writer was G.K. **Chesterton**, who wrote the essay 'In Defence of Detective Stories' (1901) followed by Father Brown narratives, the first of which appeared in 1910. These books were read by aficionados, including those later attracted to Agatha **Christie**, Dorothy L. **Sayers**, Georgette **Heyer** and purveyors of what would be known as the British cosy crime novel that would prove popular from the 1920s onwards. Another literary writer interested in crime fiction was Somerset **Maugham**. Known for his spy stories (*Ashenden*, 1928), Maugham worked as a secret agent during the First World War and wrote crime narratives such as *Up at the Villa* (1941), about a woman who has a one-night stand with a total stranger who ends up killing himself, leaving the woman to dispose of the body, and *Christmas Holiday* (1944), in which a young woman discovers that her husband is an assassin.

While most crime writers, whether literary or hard-boiled, come from middle-class backgrounds, they do not necessarily share the perspectives one might associate with their class. One of the first to offer a more substantial representation of the whole spectrum of society was Graham Greene. Without sacrificing his more salient stylistic qualities, Greene wrote a number of what he described as entertainments, including a number of taut thrillers. Another literary genre writer was Eric Ambler, who was five years younger than Greene. He virtually invented the modern spy novel. Greene and Ambler, respectively, in such novels as ***Brighton Rock*** (1938) and *The Mask of Dimitrios* (1939), fashioned a pathway that future writers as diverse as John le Carré, Philip **Kerr** and Chris **Petit** would follow. Political yet never dogmatic, literary but unpretentious, political yet never doctrinaire, stylish yet gritty, they would take British crime and spy fiction outside its claustrophobic, middle-class boundaries, to investigate the seedier side of British and European life and, in doing so, articulate the prevailing cynicism of the pre- and post-war era.

Various critics acknowledged Greene's pre-eminence, notably short-story writer Julian Maclaren-Ross (1912–1964). In an essay published in the *Times Literary Supplement*, in February 1955, entitled 'Out of the Ordinary: The Novel of Pursuit and Suspense', Maclaren-Ross discusses the merits of everyone from Sexton **Blake** to Ivy Compton-Burnett (1884–1969). But it is Greene who merits pride of place. According to Maclaren-Ross, it was Greene's personal contribution that appealed to the interwar generation: '[The] ruthless violence and suspense that seemed to symbolise the impending calamity of which all were conscious; the seediness and squalor, the cinematic narrative technique and swift-moving impressionistic prose; the varied settings and minor characters so brilliantly sketched in; and the sense of love and pity, despairing but still alive in a world well lost for hate.'

Demonstrating his eclectic tastes, Maclaren-Ross spends much of the essay discussing not only the importance of Greene, but the influence of Buchan, Stevenson and Maugham, before moving on to other stylish suspense writers of the era, including former left-wingers Nicholas **Blake** (*The Whisper in the Gloom*, 1954), Julian **Symons** (*The Broken Penny*, 1953) and Roy Fuller (1912–1991) (*The Second Curtain*, 1953). He also attempts to update the genre, citing Geoffrey **Household**, Richard Collier (b.1924) (*Pay Off in Calcutta*, 1948), Michael **Innes** (*The Secret Vanguard*, 1940), **Allingham** (***Tiger in the Smoke***, 1952 and *Traitor's Purse*, 1941), Edmund **Crispin** (*The Moving Toyshop*, 1946 and *Holy Disorders*, 1945), Kevin Fitzgerald (1902–1993) (*Quiet Under the Sun*, 1953), Richard Parker (1915–1990) (*Gingerbread Man*, 1953), Margot Bennett (1912–1980) (*Farewell Crown and Goodbye King*, 1952) and Bernard Glemser (1908–1990) (*The Dove on His Shoulder*, 1953), all of them, given the era, literary in their approach, at a time when the '"straight" or "serious" novel has become a vehicle for ponderous philosophical or sociological theory and seems in danger of forfeiting its claim to be considered as literature'.

Maclaren-Ross implies that no matter how literary, the writers who have had the greatest influence are those who have been able to look beyond their class. Thus the latter group differs considerably from literary toffs such as Michael Innes, Julian Symons and Edmund Crispin – or British judge Arthur Alexander Gordon Clark, who, in the 1930s and 1940s, published Cyril **Hare** books such as *Tragedy at Law* (1942) that showed off his knowledge of the legal system, but from the perspective of the suites rather than the streets. Not to mention those who, after the First World War, wrote about a way of life featuring village greens and dreaming spires (along with locked rooms and convoluted plots) that was foreign to most inhabitants of the British Isles.

Literature and Crime Fiction

There was yet another type of literary novel, one that is often unacknowledged, written around that time, influenced not only by Greene but by various Americans, including that era's proletariat writers. Vernacular and part of a nascent noir tradition, it sought to address the relationship between crime and class, but written from the point of view of those scrambling to survive. Examples include the likes of *Low Company* (1936) and *What Rough Beast* (1939) by Mark Benney (b.1910), *They Drive by Night* (1938) and *There Ain't No Justice* (1939) by James **Curtis** or *Wide Boys Never Work* (1937) by Robert Westerby (1909–1968).

It was a type of novel invigorated by the war and subsequent egalitarian ideas that followed from it, which resulted in noir thrillers by Patrick **Hamilton** and Gerald **Kersh**. Although Hamilton and Kersh had published before the war – *Twenty Thousand Streets under the Sky* and *Night and the City*, respectively – Hamilton's *Slaves of Solitude* and Kersh's *Prelude to an Uncertain Midnight* depicted a down-at-the-heels picture of post-war Britain. Thus Greene, Ambler, Hamilton, Kersh and lesser writers such as Gerald Butler (1907–1988) (*Kiss the Blood Off My Hands*, 1940; *Mad with Much Heart*, 1949), would turn crime fiction – in fact, closer to noir than crime fiction – into something interesting regarding style, content, politics, mores and manners. In turn, these writers would go on to facilitate 1950s kitchen-sink narratives by John Braine (1922–1986), Allan Sillitoe (b.1928) and David Storey (b.1933), which helped bridge the gap between working-class literary fiction and crime fiction. One could even draw a line from Kersh to a bohemian outsider Alexander Trocchi (1925–1984) – the latter's *Young Adam* (1954) and *Cain's Book* (1961) may be classified as crime novels – and a subsequent wave of working-class writers, such as Alexander Baron (1917–1999) (*Low Life*, 1963) and Emanuel Litvinoff (b.1915) (*Journey through a Small Planet*, 1972), who, like Benney, were intent on exploring the relationship between crime and working-class life.

Not that one can be completely accurate when differentiating crime fiction along class lines, although it remains a predominantly middle-class pursuit. At least this is true so far as writers are concerned. Readers are another matter. According to Ken Worpole, 'working class reading tastes have often been more adventurist and internationalist than patterns of middle-class reading' (1983, 21). It is certainly not hard to imagine working-class readers looking forward to the latest novel by that fierce upholder of the class system, John **Buchan**, as well as the more egalitarian Eric Ambler, while middle-class readers might go so far as to seek out such youthful literary indiscretions as Sexton Blake, Sapper, Bulldog Drummond, Zenith the Albino or Sherlock **Holmes**. At the same time, these days class plays a notably smaller role in both the writing and the reading of a crime novel. Which is not to say that writers or, for that matter, readers are not the products of their class. Working-class readers might devour the latest Martina **Cole**, but they, like their middle-class counterparts, might equally opt for Val **McDermid**, John le Carré, Philip Kerr or Sarah Waters (b.1966). Or vice versa. Although one appreciates how contemporary crime fiction has crossed class lines, one cannot help but notice that it has accomplished this at the expense of a certain voyeurism, particularly when it comes to crime fiction which seeks verisimilitude, a quality largely absent from past crime fiction, literary or otherwise, or literary fiction in which crimes occur.

Any discussion surrounding literature and crime fiction must also address the subject of highbrow versus middlebrow culture. While, in another context, this would amount to nothing more than matters of taste, or what differentiates the high-minded from the pedestrian, in Britain it is a topic that invariably leads to a discussion about the politics of class. Although, for better or worse, the latter is a subject that, in recent decades, has been sideswiped by the expansion of the British middle class, making any reference to middlebrow versus highbrow culture a lesser concern, ameliorated by such negatives as economic necessity and the search for new markets. Publishers, whether or not they pass into the hands of multinationals, have had to adopt strategies that ensure profitability. This has meant even literary fiction must now demonstrate a degree of mass appeal if only so it can be placed in a recognisable category and retail context. This often results in a hit-and-run collision with crime fiction. No wonder there are some who see the plethora of literary prizes, three-for-two offers, overabundance of bookstore chains and decline of independent sellers, supermarket markdowns, and so on as adversely affecting the quality of that which is published. As both saviour and curse of publishing, crime fiction stands in the thick of this new economics. In *The Guardian*'s bestsellers for 2006, out of the 100 books listed, less than 10 might be called literary novels, half of which co-opt elements of crime fiction; at the same time, at least 20 books could be categorised as crime fiction. Moreover, among *The Guardian*'s '100 Most Borrowed Books 2005–2006' from libraries, some two-fifths are crime novels. Is it surprising, then, that literary fiction is being sold as intelligent crime fiction or that crime fiction is touted as the new literature?

Even so, few crime aficionados would consider literary dabblers such as Martin **Amis** or Peter **Ackroyd** true crime writers, if only because their style belies their background and perspective. Conversely, a crime writer, no matter how critics might rave about their style, ear for dialogue, or ingenious plots, has little chance of becoming a literary writer. Literary writer Iain **Sinclair** might celebrate the novels of Derek Raymond, but that does not mean Raymond, despite his public-school education, dark humour and mock-poetic style, will ever be considered a literary writer. Likewise, Sinclair, although he writes about Jack the Ripper (*Down River*) and others inhabiting London's *demimonde*, will never be categorised as a crime writer. Sinclair's judgement simply makes Raymond acceptable to those who consider crime fiction to be lowbrow lit, a genre read by those who are too lazy or ill-educated to read real fiction. Likewise, Martin Amis's endorsement of American crime writer Elmore Leonard, or *Granta's* publishing James Ellroy's account of his mother's death, simply gives these writers a particular currency, making them, to their publishers delight, palatable to a wider readership, while certifying their democratic tastes. Meanwhile, literary novelists writing about crime can gloss over what is often a severe lack of immediacy or inability to confront the culture head-on. Crime, after all, is pandemic, both as a genre and as an unfortunate, if often understandable, cultural phenomenon, its politics open to all concerned parties, residing in its investigatory process rather than in its voyeurism or literary flourishes. On the other hand, the likes of Sinclair or Ackroyd are able to attract the interest of those crime readers with an appetite for the dark side of London's history, or who have approached the genre through avant-garde literature, which has made them receptive to prose styles that bear little resemblance to the terse, hard-boiled style normally found on the pages of most crime novels.

Along with the 1919 Public Libraries Act, the popularity of the paperback allowed the general public access to a cross-section of crime and literary fiction. Despite considerable resistance from mainstream publishers, Penguin paperbacks were introduced in 1935 and gained mass appeal during the 1940s, at a time when more crime novels than ever were being published. Yet, from the outset, Penguin sought to separate crime and literary fiction, deploying their green covers and spines for the former and orange covers and spines for the latter. Consequently, even though it allowed the public greater access to literature, Penguin wound up perpetuating the divide between crime, no matter how stuffy or middle-class, and literary fiction. This divide did not begin to change until the economic upswing of the 1960s when young people began to emerge as influential consumers, if not arbiters of taste, causing distinctions between highbrow and middlebrow culture to blur. Not surprisingly, this came at a time when critical opinion regarding the legitimacy of such hard-boilers as Chandler and Hammett were in the process of being revised. However, even though hardcore practitioners such as Ted **Lewis** (***Get Carter***), John le Carré and Robin Cook (also known as Derek Raymond) were publishing novels in the United Kingdom, none, with the possible exception of le Carré, were to gain the same recognition as their American counterparts.

Consequently, the demands of the market, tweaked by the politics of the subsequent years, were factors in the resurgence, however muted, of British crime fiction. But although more British authors than ever were investigating an assortment of criminal activities, few, whether literary writers or crime novelists, would adopt the language of hard-boiled fiction. This particular format was too stylised, too confining and too American to flow comfortably from the pens and typewriters of British writers. With rare exceptions – including James Hadley **Chase**, Peter **Cheyney** and James Curtis – this was to persist until British crime writers emerged in the mid-1990s influenced by contemporary American stylists such as Crumley, Ellroy, Higgins and Leonard.

Related to any discussion about crime and literature, or popular culture and the politics of social class, is the time-honoured tradition of literary writers publishing crime novels under pseudonyms. For example, C. Day Lewis wrote crime puzzle novels as Nicholas Blake, Agatha Christie as Mary Westmacott and John Dickson **Carr** as Carter Dickson. More recently, Julian **Barnes** has written crime fiction as Dan Kavanagh, Tim Parks as John MacDowell and John **Banville**, whose literary work often contains a criminal element anyway, as Benjamin Black. Then there is Ruth **Rendell**, who, when distinguishing between page-turners and more psychological, if not literary, efforts, writes as Barbara Vine. Clearly, adopting a pseudonym, like differentiating between crime and literary fiction, might have more to do with marketing than with the improper use of literature, or an author's desire to keep secret the fact that they writing crime fiction. With the added implication that a given author might be down-swinging for financial, rather than artistic, reasons, the cynicism of which could easily result in an author losing some of their readership.

British crime writers will no doubt continue to wrestle with the history and stylisation of the genre as well as the legacy of their culture. That is what keeps British crime fiction interesting. The fact is, British crime fiction has always had a literary dimension and – as illustrated by the work of such writers as Nicolas **Freeling**, Michael **Dibdin**, Ruth Rendell, John **Harvey**, Philip Kerr and John le Carré – continues to do so. This is not to say that their hard-boiled counterparts such as Ted Lewis, Derek Raymond, David **Peace**, Lee **Child**, John **Connolly** or Mark **Timlin** are any less literary. It is just that they derive from a different tradition, one that has come to us not so much from Sexton Blake, Anthony Skene (1886–1972) or even Hank **Janson**, as Graham Greene and American noirists such as Goodis, Thompson, Ellroy and Leonard. Meanwhile, mainstream literary writers, such as Martin Amis, Sarah Waters, John Banville, Iain Pears, Pete Ackroyd, Iain Sinclair, Ian McEwan (b.1948), whose novels contain an assortment of crimes, past and present, retain their class credentials by borrowing more from literary crime fiction rather than from hard-boiled novels. One might even conclude that, with its disasters, corruption, death, wars and pestilence, the world has hopefully turned every novelist, literary or otherwise, who writes honestly about contemporary life, into a crime writer of one sort or another. *See also* Golden Age Crime Fiction *and* Origins of British Crime Fiction.

Further Reading

Haining, Peter. 1977. *Mystery! An Illustrated History of Crime and Detective Fiction.* Souvenir Press.
Haut, Woody. 2002. *Heartbreak and Vine: The Fate of Hardboiled Writers in Hollywood.* Serpent's Tail.
Maclaren-Ross, Julian. 2005. *Bitten by the Tarantula and Other Writing.* Black Spring Press.
Mesplede, Claude. 2003. *Dictionaire des literatures policieres.* Joseph K. Press.
Worpole, Ken. 1983. *Dockers and Detectives.* Verso.
Worpole, Ken. 1984. *Reading by Numbers.* Verso.

Woody Haut

Lock, Stock and Two Smoking Barrels (film, 1998)

Guy Ritchie, director

In the 1990s, thanks to the success of Guy Ritchie's debut feature (and as British hard-boiled crime fiction enjoyed a renaissance), many British writer-directors tried to put a Tarantinoid spin on the British gangster movie. The sub-genre mushroomed so quickly, tossing off the likes of Circus (2000), *Essex Boys* (2000), *Going Off Big Time* (2000), *Quality Indigo* (2005), etc., etc., that it became instantly tiresome, allowing a few more unusual efforts (***Sexy Beast***, 2000, ***Gangster No. 1***, 2000) to rise like cream. In his subsequent career, Ritchie has been unable to recapture the *Lock, Stock* buzz – see-sawing from inflated gangland follow-ups (*Snatch, Revolver*) to a famously disastrous vehicle for his wife, Madonna (*Swept Away*) – but the fact that the style was soon run into the ground should not detract from the modest, refreshing achievement of his first film. It is at heart an extended shaggy dog story, as is revealed by snippets of cockney narration that introduce minor characters or prod the plot along, but the writer-director and his cast show enough freestyle energy and bizarre confidence to get away with it.

Set entirely in a fantasy East End where women almost do not exist and shot through with a drunken all-night haze, the movie creates a world related to reality and to old crime movies and fiction but also self-contained and original. The plot is a complex collision of several sets of crooked characters. Eddy (Nick Moran), Tom (Jason Flemyng), Soap (Dexter Fletcher) and Bacon (Jason Statham) are harmless wide boys who find themselves in a pickle when demon card-player Eddy loses a rigged three-card brag game with local mob boss, porn baron Hatchet Harry (P.H. Moriarty). The men are required to hand over half a million quid by the end of the week or suffer from the attentions of Harry's debt-collectors, a bald head-dunker called Barry the Baptist (bare-knucks champ Lenny McClean) and the fearsome but paternal Big Chris (football hard man Vinnie Jones). The quartet overhear their nastier neighbours planning on robbing a group of public-school dope cultivators (led by former Young Sherlock **Holmes** Nicholas Rowe) and decide to rip off the rip-off artists.

In the mean time, Barry has hired a pair of Mancunian thickos to steal some antique shotguns which they stupidly sell to the good-guy gang. Also mixed up in the escalating mess are an Afro-haired drugs czar, Eddy's bar-owning Dad (Sting), middle-man Nick the Greek (Stephen Marcus) and an extremely unlucky traffic warden. *Lock, Stock and Two Smoking Barrels* is too mixed-up to synopsise easily and too rickety to think about closely but gets plenty of laughs as it rushes from scene to scene. Ritchie's colour-desaturated style, use of unusual background music, scattershot slang (some subtitled) and mostly tasteful black comedy give the whole film the feel of an altered state of perception, whether it be Eddy's shaky devastation at running up the debt or various spells of drunkenness, trancing, drugginess or adrenalin rush which smite all the characters. It ends in homage to *The Italian Job* (1969) with the cast dangling. Besides the many big-screen imitations, the film spun off a seven-episode television series, *Lock, Stock. See also* London in Crime Fiction *and* TV Detectives: Small-Screen Adaptations.

Kim Newman

London in Crime Fiction

Twenty thousand streets under the sky. This was how Patrick **Hamilton** described London in the title of his mordant 1935 trilogy about the capital's deluded and downwardly mobile. The implication is that London's many streets can divide as well as unite, while on each street it is likely that a crime has been, or will be, committed, each interesting enough to constitute a novel on its own.

So many streets. So many crimes.

But London has long been associated with crime, at least since the *Newgate Calendar*, the production of which began in the latter part of the eighteenth century.

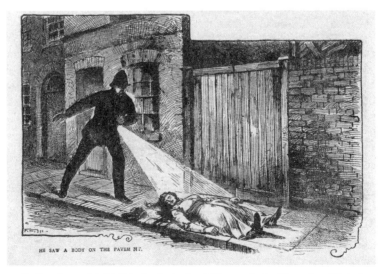

HE SAW A BODY ON THE PAVEMENT.

57. Police Constable Neil finds the body of Ripper victim Mary Ann Nicholas in Bucks Row, Whitechapel, in the East End of London.

Particularly murder, the fascination of which might have been first articulated by Thomas De Quincey (1785–1859) in his 1827 essay 'On Murder, Considered as One of the Fine Arts', in which he relates the story of the Radcliffe Highway murders and the man, John Williams, convicted of those crimes, followed by his suicide in Coldbath prison. Williams's body would be buried at an East End crossroads – where the junction of Cannon Street Road and Cable Street now stands – his head removed and displayed at a local pub. If nothing else, this narrative became part of a topology regarding East End crime that blurs distinctions between fact, urban legend and fiction.

A century later, the Radcliffe Highway murders would be investigated by crime writer P.D. **James** in *The Maul and the Pear Tree* (1972). James would return to the same geographical territory in later novels such as *Children of Men* (1992) and *Original Sin* (1995), both of them, in turn, situated within spitting distance of where Peter **Ackroyd**'s *Dan Leno and the Limehouse Golem* (1994) takes place, not all that far from the stomping ground of the Kray twins and Jack the Ripper.

Sometimes all London crime, fact as well as fiction, seems related, linked by the city's labyrinthine streets, shadows and stories. To this day, one can still walk across Charles Booth's 1889 map of the economic texture of London and, within minutes, find a similar smattering of social classes and ethnic groups. Although gentrification and rising property values have driven out the old and brought in the new, there remains an evermore varied and eccentric mix. From the watchful eye of the Peelers to CCTV surveillance, every Londoner is a potential criminal, while perambulating crowds can, as De Quincey once noted, sometimes look like 'a masque of maniacs, a pageant of phantoms'.

Perhaps London really is no more than a well-tended garden of crime, from the personal to the political, cultivated in the name of both poverty and wealth. If so, no wonder Ackroyd's *London: A Biography* could be read as one long crime narrative, with chapters and subheadings sounding like titles of crime novels: *Crime and Punishment, Pestilence and Flame, Night and Day, Violent Delights, A Plague upon You, A Newgate Ballad, A Note on Suicide, A Rogue's Gallery, Horrible Murder, Thereby Hangs a Tale, Mobocracy, Night in the City, Dark Thames, Wild Things.* On the other hand, all London crime novels might, in turn, be interpreted as one long alternative history of London, whose participants have been driven to extremes by the corrosive elements of urban life. Whether prompted by Regency rookeries and Victorian poverty, post-war *spiv* culture, gangs, trickle-down economics, drug cartels or corporate greed, London has always been, and remains, crime-ridden and crime obsessed.

Twenty thousand streets it might be, but, for protection, or out of economic necessity, London has always been a city of villages. Andrew **Taylor** notes this in his 2003 Regency London crime novel *The American Boy*: 'London may be the greatest city the world has ever known, but it is also a cluster of villages – flung together by the currents of history and geography, but each retaining its individual character. Even in newly built neighbourhoods, the pattern reasserts itself: mankind is drawn to the villages and fears the metropolis.'

Martin Fido's *Murder Guide to London* (1986) recounts that more than half the murders in Britain occur in the capital. Likewise, Fido, in reprinted articles from the past, shows the extent to which geography and economic status have influenced the depiction of murders. A 100-year-old murder in Brixton is apt to be described as *brutal*, while an article about a Camberwell killing at the same time is likely to include the word *respectable*. Not so different from what one finds today. Not only in periodicals but in fiction, which divides itself between middle-class crime narratives, whether Sherlock **Holmes** or Agatha **Christie**, and its more hardcore counterpart.

Although the London of Dickens, Collins or Sherlock Holmes is hardly the London of Mark **Timlin**, Derek **Raymond** and Elizabeth George, the geographical contours, regardless of local, national and global concerns, remain largely intact. These days, London has become more diverse and complicated than ever. Middle England, as illustrated in the work of Frank Kippax (b.1945) (*Fear of Night and Darkness*, 1993) has become just another commute, making London, whatever its historical resonances or position in the league table of British murders, no longer the sole domain of crime as it might have been in the days of Dickens, Conan Doyle, Edgar **Wallace** and Dorothy L. **Sayers**.

Yet connections remain. Fido points to Islington behind Upper Street and City Road as a location notorious for murders. It is where, in 1795, Charles Lamb's sister killed her mother, close to where Crippen and Seddon committed their early-twentieth-century crimes, only yards from where Joe Orton would be murdered in 1967. While in central London, who knows how many crimes have been perpetrated by property developers at addresses such as the fictional 347 Piccadilly in Bram Stoker's *Dracula* (1897), or 144 Piccadilly, the site of the squat in American film director Samuel Fuller's 1971 novel of that name. Meanwhile, Cable Street, site of the Radcliffe Murders, would become the location of 1930s battles between anti-fascists and Mosleyites depicted in, amongst others, *Jew Boy* (1935) by Simon Blumenfeld (1907–2005) and, in the 1970s, where confrontations between the Anti-Nazi League and the National Front took place, as well as the setting for fictional narratives by authors ranging from Arthur Morrison (1863–1945) and Arthur La Bern (1909–1990) (*It Always Rains on Sundays*) to Peter Ackroyd.

Moreover, the criminal London that Dickens, Gissing and Conan Doyle wrote about was miniscule compared to the space depicted in later novels. Soho, long synonymous with London crime, has featured in numerous novels, including *The Strange Case of Dr Jekyll and Mr Hyde* (1896) by Stevenson, *Secret Agent* (1907) by Joseph **Conrad**, *Night and the City* (1938) by Kersh, *Wide Boys Never Work* (1937) by Robert Westerby, *Low Company* (1936) by Mark Benney and *Stand On Me* (1959) by Frank Norman, as well as, more recently, *The Long Firm* (1999) by Jake **Arnott** and *Robinson* (1993) by Chris **Petit**. Victoria pubs, Shepard's Bush and that forgotten slum area of west London, Notting Dale are the site of James **Curtis**'s *The Gilt Kid* (1936), *They Drive By Night* (1938) and *There Ain't No Justice* (1939). Patrick Hamilton sets *Craven House* (1926) in Chiswick and Kew, *The Midnight Bell* (1929) in a pub on the edge of Fitzrovia and *Hangover Square* (1941) in Earl's Court while Gissing's *New Grub Street* (1891) moves across northwest London, from the British Museum and Tottenham Court Road to Clerkenwell and City Road. London underground, specifically the Circle Line, forms the central metaphor in Graham **Greene**'s *It's a Battleground* (1934), in which Greene compares the tube map to the rings in Dante's hell, while telling the story of a communist bus driver sentenced to hang for killing a policeman at a Hyde Park demonstration.

Describing some of the same territory in which Gissing's *New Grub Street* takes place, Ruth **Rendell**'s *The Keys to the Street* (1997) portrays a 1980s frontier zone where affluence and indigence exist in close proximity. Rendell centres on areas in and around Regent's Park, the topography of which determines the fate of her characters. As in Gissing's novel, *The Keys to the Street* combines descriptions of Nash terraces, shabby streets, dark passageways and churchyards, to produce a strong gothic element. In Thatcherite London, topographical paradox – 'paths seldom led where you thought they would' – is everything. London crime fiction may have altered economically and demographically, but its narrative influence remains no less emphatic.

How, then, does the representation of fictional London crime compare to its reality? Franco Moretti's literary maps of Dickens's and Sherlock Holmes's London illustrate some early, but important, differences. He shows that crimes depicted in the Holmes stories are clustered in the City and points out that Holmes travels to the East End only once in fifty-six stories. This is despite the fact that his stories were written at roughly the same time that Jack the Ripper was active in the East End. Interestingly, Holmes tends to avoid working-class areas, although as his investigations move from his base, the crimes he investigates become bloodier. Back in the real world, Booth's 1889 'Descriptive Map of London Poverty' shows that a majority of London crime was committed near the Tower, then east, between Bethnal Green and Whitechapel, in areas of the greatest urban misery. In other words, Conan Doyle was presenting 'fictional crime in a London of relative wealth, while real crime was taking place in a London of extreme poverty'. Of course, Conan Doyle was creating escapist literature rather than a realistic portrait of London. He preferred deploying signifiers now considered cliché ridden: gentlemen's clubs, fog, the river, expensive hotels, banks, great parks and diplomatic secrets. Nevertheless, he was attentive enough to attribute the success of later Holmes stories to placing his protagonist in the correct geographical setting.

If Dickens, writing some fifty years prior to the first Holmes stories, was not the first to strive for verisimilitude, he was, according to Moretti, instrumental in unifying a conceptual London, bringing together east (poverty), west (wealth) and mid-London, as well as the middle class (Islington, the City, Soho). The point is that Dickens was responsible for a more nuanced, if not realistic, view of crime. Incorporating the entire social spectrum, he was able to include London villages just as later crime writers would incorporate outlying boroughs and suburbs.

An updated map of London crime fiction, were one to appear, would show narratives moving away from central London in accordance with economic changes and fears, often media driven, about a rising crime rate. While some novelists address these anxieties, others prefer to write about London as though it were a static entity unaffected by local, national and international events. It is a perspective that has become increasingly difficult to sustain. At the other extreme, there are also those who purport to replicate reality, courting voyeurism in their insistence that readers vicariously experience places they would otherwise fear to tread, whether a deprived housing estate, dodgy pub, specialist brothel or a bus stop in an unfamiliar borough after midnight. Nevertheless, there has always been an anthropological element to a certain type of crime fiction regardless of its setting. And despite the clichés about the city's fog, its architecture, the murder of prostitutes or its detectives who deploy deductive reasoning to solve any case that comes their way, London crime fiction remains popular, growing more so in direct proportion to the increased middle-class insularity.

If one writer has reinvigorated the modern London crime novel, it is Derek **Raymond**. In the 1960s, under his real name, Robin Cook, he penned a series of novels set in Chelsea and Soho, populated by wide boys, con artists and chancers.

An old Etonian, Cook knew his way around the capital, having worked as a front for London conman Charles Da Silva, then as a mini-cab driver. His harrowing *Factory* novels – the first of which, *He Died With His Eyes Open*, appeared in 1984, and the last of which, *Dead Man Upright*, appeared in 1993 – centre on a Poland Street police station and a harrowing world in which only the victims and murderers are named.

Regarding their geography and ambiance, Raymond's *Factory* series recalls Gerald **Kersh**'s *Prelude to an Uncertain Midnight* (1947) and the aforementioned *Night and the City* (1938). The latter is a Hogarthian depiction of London low-life, comparable perhaps only to a Greene's *A Gun for Sale* (1936). It centres on small-time grifter Harry Fabian, who lives by his wits as he scrambles from one clip joint, gym, pub and all-night cafe to another, wheeling and dealing as if his life depended on it. While *Prelude to an Uncertain Midnight*, a multi-voice narrative that concerns the hunt for a child-murderer, picks up on post-war anxieties and a world in which 'one murder makes many'. One of the more prolific authors of the era, Kersh published other London-set novels, including *Fowler's End* (1957), set in suburban Enfield. Not a crime novel, it centres on a cinema, and, if nothing else, show that London noir could function outside central London.

The equal of Raymond and Kersh, Patrick Hamilton portrays the lives of Londoners before and after the war. Invariably his characters consume too much alcohol, obsessively pursue the wrong women, have diminishing funds, kill time in afternoon cinemas and make tragic fools of themselves. Published in 1942, the stylish *Hangover Square: or, The Man With Two Minds: the Story of Darkest Earl's Court in the Year 1939*, centres on anti-hero George Harvey Bone who imagines himself smashing a Mosleyite to death with a golf club, drowning an inconvenient woman and escaping to Maidenhead, but spends most of his time perusing north London, haunting Fitzrovia pubs, hanging-out with fascists, as well as Great Portland Street car salesmen, prostitutes, actresses, professional bores and bullies.

Numerous recent writers have made London a major component, if not main character, in their fiction. None more so than the writers Mark Timlin and Martina **Cole**. While Timlin's terrain is south London, Cole's books are set in Essex. Both write pacy thrillers, although Cole is arguably the more important of the two. Emulating past pulpists, Timlin could be described as a Raymond protégé, although he has less of the latter's poetic vision and tragic demeanour. Capable of being both tough and tender, he, along with his protagonist, Nick Sharman, covers some of the same terrain as Raymond and his nameless detective. At least Sharman and Timlin's characters in his more substantial *Answers from the Grave* (2004) are out on the street, exposing themselves to the vicissitudes of London life. Unlike the likes of P.D. James's Dalgliesh, who views the less salubrious areas of London from behind the windscreen of his expensive automobile.

Cole's characters are similarly exposed, too. The product of an Essex council estate, Cole, beginning with her *Dangerous Lady* (1992), writes gritty page-turners. Most of her characters, caught in a world of violence and crime, come from a similar background as her own. Veering between realism and sensationalism, Cole has put paid to the notion that the genre is the province of male writers, or writing crime fiction a middle-class preoccupation. More importantly, Cole never over-romanticises her subject, nor shows any trace of cynicism or condescension.

Neither should one fail to mention P.B. **Yuill**'s (the writing team of Gordon Williams and football manager Terry Venables) *Hazell* novels from the 1970s. Adapted for television, they were, at the time, instrumental in reinvigorating the London crime novel, as well as spawning a series of small-screen wisecracking, hard-boiled East End detectives. More recently, Chris Petit's *Robinson* (1993) takes place mostly in Soho, while his *The Hard Shoulder* (2001) is situated in Kilburn. Both could be homage to Raymond/Cook. Nor would any discussion of current London crime fiction be complete without mentioning Iain **Sinclair**, whose early proto-noir novels begin in Hackney and move in a south-easterly direction, taking into account Jack the Ripper and an assortment of criminals and outsiders. Peter Ackroyd's historical crime fiction, such as *Hawksmoor*, takes place in the East End and Clerkenwell, where past and present collide to create new meanings.

One might also cite such writers as Laura **Wilson**, who also writes about Soho; Simon **Kernick**, who concentrates on Clerkenwell, Islington and Kings Cross; Andrew Taylor, particularly in *The American Boy*, a novel set in the late Regency period and mostly taking place in the mansions of Mayfair, Russell Square, Stoke Newington and the slums of St Giles and Seven Dials. Also set in London are novels by Mark **Billingham**, John **Milne**, Cathi Unsworth, Anne **Perry**, Christopher **Fowler** and Mo **Hayder**. And that is only the tip of the iceberg that constitutes recent London crime fiction.

In fact, these days, there are so many chronicling the city that one might say that any thriller in which there is a protagonist who has retained their links with the capital could be called a London crime novel. No matter that they live in the suburbs, the Homes Counties or, with the internationalisation of crime, another country. But then London crime fiction has to be able to adapt to the world as it *is* rather than simply respond to how it *was*. Besides, there is only so much mileage to be derived from tales of serial killers, East End and Soho criminal gangs, the Krays and Jack the Ripper. Has it not always been the case that the writers who best document the city have been those unafraid to pursue their own eccentric investigations, or redefine what crimes are worthy of analysis, and who are unyielding in their attempts show disparities in wealth, corruption in high places or the obsessive pursuit of power? Ideally, London crime fiction should be as varied as its many streets. Only then could one declare with any assurance that to be tired of London crime fiction is to be tired of London itself. *See also* The Shires: Rural England and Regional Crime Fiction.

Further Reading
Ackroyd, Peter. 2000. *London: The Biography*. Vintage.
Fido, Martin. 1994. *The Murder Guide to London*. Weidenfeld.
Glinert, Ed. 2003. *The London Compendium*. Penguin.
Moretti, Franco. 1998. *Atlas of the European Novel, 1800–1900*. Verso.
Sinclair, Iain. 1997. *Lights Out for the Territory*. Granta.
Worpole, Ken. 1983. *Dockers and Detectives*. Verso.

Woody Haut

London Mystery Magazine, The

The London Mystery Magazine (*LMM*) ran for 132 issues from Summer 1949 to March 1982, with a name change to *London Mystery Selection* (*LMS*) from March 1958 (issue 36). It was edited by Michael Hall until issue 15 (Spring 1952), when it ceased publication, but was revived by Norman Kark the following year. It was published in the standard digest form until issue 86 (1970) when it switched to pocketbook size. *LMM*, Britain's longest-running crime fiction magazine, also ran stories of the supernatural and macabre.

58. Cover of *The London Mystery Magazine*, 1950.

At the outset, the publisher (Hulton Press) was allowed to use Sherlock **Holmes**'s address, 221b Baker Street, as its editorial address, which generated sufficient interest to place *LMM* on the map. It was liberally illustrated throughout, the first issue alone boasting artists Mervyn Peake (1911–1968), Eric Fraser (1902–1983), Ronald Searle (b.1920) and Austin Osman Spare (1886–1956), with Pauline Baynes (1922–2008) a regular from the second issue.

Hall wanted the magazine to present a diverse interpretation of 'mystery'. The first issue included both traditional detective stories (Mary Fitt) and rather more villainous crimes (Jack Trevor Story (1917–1991)), plus unusual mysteries by Christopher Morley (1890–1957) and Lewis Spence (1874–1955) and the outright supernatural from H. Burgess Drake (1894–1963) and Algernon Blackwood (1869–1951). The same diversity flavoured the non-fiction as well. Hannen Swaffer recalled his days as a journalist and the part he played in the arrest of Dr Crippen, whilst Lillian de la Torre provided a historical crime reconstruction. There were articles on the identity of Shakespeare, how humans communicate with horses and the sense of direction of homing pigeons, the last two pushing the definition of 'mystery' a little too far and they were not repeated.

Sales were good, and the lifting of paper rationing at the start of 1950 allowed the magazine to appear bimonthly, which encouraged Hall to develop several regular contributors and series, all of them highly original. Perhaps the best known was that featuring Sollius, the Slave Detective by Wallace Nichols (1888–1967), the longest-running series in *LMM*. Set in the Roman Empire in the second century AD, the stories relate the investigations of Sollius – slave of the senator Titius Sabinus – who becomes renowned for his ability to solve crimes. Country doctor Liliane Clopet (1901–1987) contributed a series of fantasy detective stories for children, featuring Shipshape Shilling, a sailor made of glass who lives on a ship in a bottle and helps a young boy solve problems. Another series, initially anonymous, was 'Clorinda'. Through her diary, the fashion-conscious Clorinda reveals secrets of her days in Intelligence and as a private detective. From issue 8, the stories were credited to Charles Franklin, the pseudonym of Frank Usher (1909–1976). Mary Fitt penned a series about solicitor Mr Pitt, who is helped in his investigations by his Siamese cat. From issue 7, Fitt started a new series featuring a country doctor with a sharp eye. Fitt was a pseudonym of classicist Kathleen Freeman (1897–1959), who under her own name presented three legal cases from ancient Greece starting with 'Murder in Athens' (issue 6).

Other regular contributors, mostly with weird tales, were H. Burgess Drake, W. Stanley Moss (1921–1965), who was just then establishing a reputation with his wartime thriller *Ill Met by Moonlight* (1950) and Russell Kirk. Robert Aickman (1914–1981), little known at that time, contributed a piece about his memories of Harry Price (1881–1948) (issue 5, 1950). Brett Halliday, creator of Mike Shayne, wrote a story especially for *LMM*, 'You Killed Elizabeth' (issue 8, 1951). John Dickson **Carr** adapted a 1948 radio play as 'Flight from Fleet Street' (issue 14, 1952), but a planned series by Carr never eventuated.

This diversity may have worked against the magazine as sales were not sufficient to counter the rapid rise in the price of paper and printing. After issue 15 in April–May 1952 the magazine went into receivership and the title was offered for sale. It was acquired by the enterprising South African publisher of *Courier*, Norman Kark (1898–2000), who revived the magazine as a quarterly in February 1953. It was edited by his son, Austen Kark (1926–2002), who acquired material by several new names later to become well known. His first issue included Peter Antony, a name hiding the identity of twin brothers Peter and Anthony Shaffer. Their story, 'Before and After', featured Mr Verity, who helped the police in their more unusual cases. Both Peter and Anthony Shaffer contributed separately to the magazine and from issue 25 (June 1955), Anthony became the magazine's resident book reviewer.

Other contributors destined to become better known were Gerald **Kersh**, whose 'The Brighton Monster' (issue 16, 1953) has become something of a classic; Brian Moore (1921–1999), who had just one story in the magazine 'Fly Away Finger, Fly Away Thumb' (issue 17, 1953), and Brian Cleeve (1921–2003), whose 'Death' (issue 17) may have been his first story sale. Nina Bawden's (b.1925) 'The Madames' (issue 17) was her first sale. She assisted on the magazine and married Austen Kark in 1954. Edmund Cooper (1926–1982) became a regular contributor starting with the spy story 'Appointment in Bermuda' (issue 17), whilst Michael Harrison (1907–1991) had a Victorian occult mystery, 'At the Heart of It', in issue 19 (1953). A more surprising name in that issue was Barbara Cartland (1901–2000) with the rather grim 'Murder by Mouth'.

During 1954 Austen Kark went to work for the BBC and thereafter Norman Kark edited the issues directly. Although he continued to run weird tales it was under his editorship that the magazine shifted towards more traditional crime stories, often with an unusual twist. Whilst he ran stories by a wide range of writers, including Denys Val Baker (1917–1984), Muriel Spark (1918–2006), Francis Grierson (1888–1972), Celia **Fremlin**, Derek Stanford (b.1918), Barry Perowne (1908–1985) and

Philip Youngman Carter (1904–1969), he relied on a smaller coterie of regular contributors which included (in addition to Wallace Nicholls) Rosemary Timperley (1920–1988), L.P. Davies (b.1914) (the magazine's most prolific contributor), Jeffrey Scott (also as Shaun Usher, b.1937), John Taverner (with a series about Detective Superintendent Logan of Scotland Yard) and Guy N. Smith (b.1939). There was also a long-running series by Derwent Vale, featuring Toni Blake who in 'Target–Paris' (issue 81, June 1969) becomes an intelligence agent, a blend between Modesty Blaise and the Girl from U.N.C.L.E..

Towards the end *LMS* lacked the vitality and diversity of its early years. The stories, with many by new or lesser known writers, became predictable or unchallenging. Norman Kark was by then in his eighties and beset by health problems and the loss of his wife. When the lease on his premises expired at the end of 1981 Kark chose not to renew. The magazine's circulation was at 12,000 and dropping, and rising costs had made it unprofitable. He had hoped to find a buyer for the magazine but there was no one he believed could continue it as he wished. When it folded with issue 132 in March 1982, it was the last surviving regular British market for crime and mystery fiction. *See also* Magazines.

Further Reading
Indexed in Cook, Michael L. 1982. *Monthly Murders*. Greenwood Press.

Mike Ashley

Long Good Friday, The (film, 1980)

John Mackenzie, director

Written by Barrie Keeffe (b.1945) (author of the trilogy, *Barbarians*, 1977) and made in 1979, at the dawn of Thatcherism – the film's release was delayed by two years when the original financiers (ITC) were spooked by its terrorist theme and sold the completed picture on to HandMade. *The Long Good Friday* offers an amazingly prescient look into the 1980s as hustling, wannabe legit gangster Harold Shand (Bob Hoskins) tries to set up a dodgy development in London Docklands to ride the city's inevitable ascension to become the capital of Europe (though the presumption that London would host the 1988 Olympics is a bit off). The sharp-suited, bumptiously cheerful, eager-to-please kingpin and his cool, canny upper-class second wife Victoria (Helen Mirren) set out to spend the Easter weekend giving a smooth presentation to a mafia investor (Eddie Constantine) and his fastidiously non-criminal lawyer (Stephen Davies). Mysterious forces assault Shand's crime empire and attendant legitimate enterprises, murder his best friend (Paul Freeman) at a swimming bath, set off a car bomb in the Rolls Royce waiting to chauffeur his mum from church and blow up the pub where he is about to host a lunch for his leery American mafia investors. Attacked on all sides and unsure who to trust, Harold loses his jovial veneer and turns into the torturing, snarling, throat-slitting bastard who got to the top in the first place, accompanied by his unforgettable enforcer Razors (P.H. Moriarty) and educated right-hand man Jeff (Derek Thompson). Most gangster films follow *Macbeth* and are rise-and-fall stories, but this is closer to *King Lear* – the tragedy of a ruler who loses everything through trusting the wrong people, torn between nostalgia for a cockney past and greed for a monied future, blind to the threat that comes from a fanatical, political force he cannot buy or kill. Barrie Keeffe's original screenplay was called *The Paddy Factor*, which director John McKenzie changed on the grounds that it gave away the nature of Harold's unknown enemy – an IRA who also want to move into London and reorganise its criminal world, albeit on an even more brutal, pragmatic model (their front is a demolition derby) than Harold's dreamed-of high-class casinos, airports, hotels and restaurants. Keeffe's dialogue, which required a glossary for the US release, is delivered superbly by Hoskins, who gives a definitive gangland performance, but the film also knows when to shut up as in a long, remarkable, wordless last shot as Shand is driven away for execution by an IRA hit man (a young Pierce Brosnan) and complex emotions ripple across his face while Francis Monkman's pulsing theme plays out on the soundtrack. It is a rare British film that uses the gangster as American movies often do – as a representative of the nation, encapsulating undoubted virtues as well as self-deluding vices and a reduced-to-ferality capitalism that some audiences find perversely appealing. By denying Harold his hail of onscreen bullets, and telling a story of losing rather than gaining everything, *The Long Good Friday* suggests a bleak view of Britain in the late twentieth century. *See also* Film and Crime: Page to Screen.

Kim Newman

Longrigg, Roger (1929–2000)

Roger Erskine Longrigg, born in Edinburgh on 1 May 1929 was the author of more than fifty distinguished books. Most of these novels were published under a number of pseudonyms, eight at the last count. Whether Longrigg wrote under any other names is yet to be ascertained.

One of Longrigg's first creations was the single-minded Rosalind Erskine, who appeared in the novel *The Passion-Flower Hotel* (1962). The novel was a success and generated considerable interest from lesbian readers, who felt that this 'female' author had caught a woman's feelings so well in this tale of a group of schoolgirls who turn their school into a brothel. Longrigg's male gender was revealed, and Erskine soon after was laid to rest.

Subsequently, a steady flow of novels appeared. Longrigg wrote historical romance under the pen-name of Laura Black and crime/suspense thrillers as Ivor Drummond and Frank Parrish. Other novels were written as Grania Beckford, Megan Barker and Domini Taylor as well as under his own name.

With the advent of Domini Taylor, Longrigg created one of his most commercially successful novels: *Mother Love* (1983). It is a persuasive study of obsession and jealousy. The book was adapted for the television by Andrew Davies and starred Diana Rigg in the principal role of Helena, a woman who feels thwarted at every corner but is outraged when she finds that she has been the victim of an ambitious subterfuge (even involving her son) for many years. The six-part series was televised in 1989, for which serial Rigg won the British Academy Award in 1990.

Longrigg then went on to write eight more Domini Taylor novels. The second in this series, *Gemini* (1984), is a chilling novel about the innocent (or not-so-innocent) twins who wreak havoc. *Suffer Little Children* (1987) followed with *Praying Mantis* (1988). The narrative here involves an utterly ruthless woman who has way, whatever the cost. *Siege* (1989) is a powerful, claustrophobic novel following the fate of a family in France under threat from a malevolent force.

Domini's last four novels moved to another publisher in order to bring more highly impressive novels from Longrigg's pen. *Not Fair* (1992) is a rich, dark fable about obsession. *The Eye behind the Curtain* (1993), again a commercial success, shows Longrigg at his strongest and most subversive. Burglaries are destabilising the charming town of Conyngham Smedley; someone within the community is informing a gang of thieves when a house is empty. Throughout this clever novel, Longrigg shifts suspicion from one member of the community to another. *The Tiffany Lamp* (1994) followed, and Longrigg's last novel as Domini Taylor was *Pig in the Middle* (1996), the disturbing tale of a protagonist excluded by siblings and family and had grown to resent the exclusion. This was a thread that ran through the Domini Taylor books. All nine were certainly very different from each other (and notably different from his early works), but Longrigg had made a niche for himself with such dark, shocking tales of what could be done for the sake of love, or rather the lack of it.

Longrigg married Jane Chichester in 1957 and had three daughters during their long marriage. Roger Longrigg died in February 2000. *See also* Feminist Readings in British Crime Fiction *and* Gay and Lesbian Crime Fiction.

Selected Works by the Author

As Ivor Drummond
The Priests of the Abomination (1970)
The Jaws of the Watchdog (1973)
The Diamonds of Loretta (1980)

As Frank Parrish
Fire in the Barley (1977)
Sting of the Honeybee (1978)
Bait in the Hook (1983)
Face at the Window (1984)
Caught in the Birdlime (1987)
Voices from the Dark (1993)

As Domini Taylor
Mother Love (1983)
Suffer Little Children (1987)
Siege (1989)
Pig in the Middle (1996)

Chris Simmons

Lorac, E[dith] C[aroline] R[ivett] (1894–1958)

Although she did not rival Sayers, Christie, Marsh and Allingham, Lorac – who at one time even Dorothy L. **Sayers** was persuaded into believing was a man – was one of many talented women detective-story writers who enriched the Golden Age. Her writing had perhaps less distinction than her plotting, and this may explain why she is so much less read now than she was at one time. Her first novel, *Murder on the Burrows*, was published in 1931; in the twenty-seven years from 1931 to her death, she published seventy-one novels, twenty-three of them under her pseudonym, Carol Carnac, plus several short stories, one half-hour radio play (1948) and a contribution to a Detection Club co-operative, *No Flowers by Request* (1953).

Lorac/Carnac concentrated entirely on police detectives. The debut for Chief Inspector Rivers was in *Double for Detection* (1945), though perhaps the most accomplished novel was *Upstairs Downstairs* (1950), with a plot concerning a cleverly planned murder of a clerk in a medical research centre. Carnac's earlier sleuth was Inspector Ryvet (!), who made his bow in *The Case of the First-Class Carriage* (1936).

The forty-eight novels under the Lorac by-line (and also the radio play) all feature Chief Inspector Robert Macdonald, a Scot by birth but a Metropolitan Police officer, shrewd and not unkindly, who sometimes, as in *Murder in St John's Wood* (1953), is assigned a case on home territory but more usually seems to be given more rural investigations. Two of them, *Murder in the Mill Race* (1952) and *Fire in the Thatch* (1946; the then petrol rationing is an important factor), are set in Devon; two others, *Crook O'Lune* (1953) and *Fell Murder* (1944), find Macdonald in north-west England. By and large, the later Macdonald novels are the better ones, although all are worth seeking out, especially by those for whom the puzzle element, always adroitly handled by this author, is a key factor.

Selected Works by the Author
The Murder on the Burrows (1931)
Murder in St John's Wood (1934)
Bats in the Belfry (1937)
Fell Murder (1944)
Fire in the Thatch (1946)
The Dog it Was That Died (1952)
Murder in the Mill Race (1952; also published in the United States as *Speak Justly of the Dead*)
Crook O'Lune (1953; also published in the United States as *Shepherd's Crook*)
Dishonour among Thieves (1959)

As Carol Carnac
The Case of the First-Class Carriage (1939)
A Double for Detection (1945)
Upstairs Downstairs (1950)
A Policeman at the Door (1953)
Death of a Lady Killer (1959)

Philip Scowcroft

Lovesey, Peter (b.1936)

Peter Lovesey is both prolific and ingenious. His crime novels range from Victorian mysteries to modern-day **police procedurals**, all presented in clear, crisp prose with engaging dialogue.

He began his writing career by winning a publisher's contest in 1970, the prize being £1000. His first novel, *Wobble to Death*, was published in 1970, featuring his Victorian policeman Sergeant Cribb. He went on to write another eight of the Cribb mysteries, each one focusing on one, usually quirky, aspect of Victorian life – from bare-knuckle boxing (*The Detective Wore Silk Drawers*, 1971) to spiritualism (*A Case of Spirits*, 1975). The books were turned into a television series by Granada Television.

After Cribb, Lovesey spread his wings a little and tried other characters and time periods. There was *The False Inspector Dew* (1982), set on an Atlantic liner in 1921, which won the **Crime Writers' Association** (CWA) Gold Dagger; *Keystone* (1983), set in the early film industry; and then his brief series of three novels and two short stories featuring Bertie, the Prince of Wales and future Edward VII. While Bertie behaved outrageously, he also solved a number of crimes. Lovesey was to have great fun with the character and period, involving other famous personages of the time in the plots, including Sarah Bernhardt and Toulouse-Lautrec, who, in *Bertie and the Crime of Passion* (1993), help to investigate a murder committed in the Moulin Rouge.

59. Peter Lovesey.

While most of Lovesey's work has been written under his own name, he did write three novels under the pen-name Peter Lear, including the best-selling *Goldengirl* (1977), in which a neo-Nazi doctor tries to make a superwoman of his daughter who has been specially fed, exercised and conditioned since she was a child, in order to run in the Olympics. It was made into a successful movie in 1979.

Lovesey did not write a contemporary mystery using his own name until he created his charismatic and single-minded (and some might say, belligerent) police detective Peter Diamond, placing him in the beautiful city of Bath. Diamond first appeared in *The Last Detective* (1991), in which he is forced to resign from the force because of his frustration with the new methods of policing; in the second entry in the series, *Diamond Solitaire* (1992), he is working as a private detective. However, he returns to the police fold in the third novel of the series, *The Summons* (1995). The following Diamond episode, *Bloodhounds* (1996), was awarded the CWA Silver Dagger. The series continues and is currently being developed for television. With the right treatment and cast, this could be the new Morse.

Lovesey has also written several stand alone novels – *On the Edge* (1989; filmed as *Dead Gorgeous*), *The Reaper* (2000) and *The Circle* (2005) – as well as numerous short stories, including the ingenious 'Youdunnit' (1989), in which he very cleverly proves that the reader is the murderer.

Lovesey can always be relied upon to come up with the goods. His plots are clever and challenging, his characters solid and believable, and his narratives often permeated with a dry sense of humour. The CWA awarded him the Diamond Dagger in 2000 for his excellent oeuvre. *See also* Historical Crime.

Selected Works by the Author
Wobble to Death (1970)
The Detective Wore Silk Drawers (1971)
Waxwork (1978)
The False Inspector Dew (1982)
Keystone (1983)
The Last Detective (1991)
Upon a Dark Night (1997)
Diamond Dust (2002)
The Secret Hangman (2007)

David Stuart Davies

Lyall, Gavin (1932–2003)

Gavin Lyall's first novels in the adventure and espionage field were published
to considerable acclaim in the 1960s and are influenced (like those of other thriller
writers of his generation) by his experience in National Service and of the Cold War.
He took several career breaks but came back twice to writing, first with the Major
Maxim series in the 1980s, in which he pits a man of action against the bureaucrats
of Whitehall, and then in the 1990s with the historical Honour series.

Lyall was born and educated in Birmingham, served as a pilot in the Royal Air
Force (RAF) and then read English literature at Cambridge. He worked in film
industry and journalism before embarking on full-time writing. He won the **Crime
Writers' Association** Silver Dagger in 1965 and chaired the association during
1967–1968. His first few novels feature cynical but warm-hearted men who use their
training and experience in the army or RAF in more or less legal ways. They know
their way around Europe and are at ease with guns and planes. Many of them –
or their colleagues or quarry – battle with alcoholism.

The love interest in these novels is generally provided by beautiful women who are
cleverer, richer or more aristocratic than the hero, and long-term happiness is never
a likely outcome. The tone is laconic but perceptive, with a nice line in fantastical
irony. One of the best is *Blame the Dead* (1972), in which James Card, a retired major,
fails to prevent the killing of his current client, a senior insurance underwriter
from Lloyds of London. The action moves between London and Bergen, and the
characterisation is more developed than in some of the other titles. The last of this
group of novels is *Judas Country* (1975).

Lyall moved on with a quartet featuring Major Harry Maxim, a Special Air Service
officer who has missed his chance of promotion and been assigned to Number 10
Downing Street as a security adviser with an unspecified brief. The first, *The Secret
Servant* (1980), was filmed by the BBC with Charles Dance as Major Maxim. These
novels are quieter than the earlier thrillers and take their tone from the death
of Maxim's wife in an aeroplane blown up in front of him, after which he 'wanted
to get out and drive and shoot – particularly shoot'. The superior woman in this
series is Agnes Algar, a spy, who works as a liaison officer between MI5 and
Number 10, tries to control Maxim and fails to find a way to love him. Among
the other attractive characters are Maxim's schoolboy son and his boss, George
Harbinger, a fat intelligent drinker with an aristocratic wife.

Another quartet concluded Lyall's work. This is set before the First World War and features disgraced gentleman spy Matthew Ranklin. Like the earlier novels, these were well reviewed, but they never gained as large a readership as the Maxim series.

Selected Works by the Author
The Wrong Side of the Sky (1961)
Midnight Plus One (1964)
Venus with Pistol (1969)
Blame the Dead (1972)
The Secret Servant (1980)
The Conduct of Major Maxim (1982)
Spy's Honour (1993)

Natasha Cooper

M

McAuley, Paul (b.1955)

Paul McAuley initially became known as an award-winning science fiction writer but has recently colonised the crime/thriller genre with equal panache.

McAuley was originally a research biologist at various universities, including Oxford and UCLA and, for six years, was a lecturer in botany at St Andrews University. The first short story he ever finished was accepted by the American magazine *Worlds of If*, but the magazine folded before publishing it and he took this as a hint to concentrate on an academic career instead. McAuley started writing again during a period as a resident alien in Los Angeles and became a full-time writer in 1996.

His first novel, *Four Hundred Billion Stars* (1988), won the Philip K. Dick Memorial Award, and the fifth, *Fairyland* (1995), won both the 1995 Arthur C. Clarke and the John W. Campbell awards.

McAuley's assault on the thriller genre was inaugurated with *White Devils* (2004), *Mind's Eye* (2005) and *Players* (2008). The first of these thrillers, *White Devils*, is a complex, multi-stranded mix of Conrad's *Heart of Darkness*, Mary Shelley's *Frankenstein* and H.G. Wells's *The Island of Dr Moreau* – updated for the cyberpunk age. It combines contemporary concerns about genetic manipulation, globalisation of economics and environmental issues becoming a thought-provoking mesh of ideas, in a style not dissimilar to that of Michael Crichton. *Mind's Eye* has a very different emphasis. The core of the story is a hunt for the meaning of bizarre graffiti imagery that may date to an ancient cult and is linked to an evil that is as sinister as it is covert – one which dates to ancient Iraq. The **police procedural** *Players* (2007) is simultaneously McAuley's most accomplished and conventional work in terms of the crime-thriller genre, with a real-world hunt for the murderer of a girl in an Oregon forest. McAuley's novels have been described as future noir, and his work compared to that of Michael **Marshall** [Smith], but he has his own very distinctive voice and finely tuned imagination. The transition from the science fiction to the techno-thriller genre is a parlous process, but McAuley has demonstrated that he is a master of both genres. *See also* Thrillers: Novels of Action.

60. Paul McAuley.

Selected Works by the Author
The Secret of Life (2001)
Whole Wide World (2001)
White Devils (2004)
Mind's Eye (2005)
Cowboy Angels (2007)
Players (2007)
Second Skin (2007)

Website
www.omegacom.demon.co.uk/

Ali Karim

McCall Smith, Alexander

See Smith, Alexander McCall

McClure, James (1939–2006)

James McClure's detective novels cast a fascinating light on South African society in the era of apartheid. Born and educated in South Africa, the son of Scots parents, McClure worked as a photographer and teacher before becoming a crime reporter. In 1965, he emigrated to Britain to work in journalism, first for *The Daily Mail* in Scotland and later for *The Oxford Times*, where he became deputy editor – the editor being **espionage** novelist Anthony **Price**. McClure's first novel, *The Steam Pig* (1971), boasted all the virtues of a crime novel, including crisp writing from the first paragraph about a sad undertaker to the last, downbeat sentence; a gripping story (with sober insight into the nature of racism); and a fascinating detective team in the Afrikaaner Lieutenant Tromp Kramer and his Bantu sergeant, Mickey Zondi of the Trekkersburg Murder Squad. It is small wonder that the book earned McClure a **Crime Writers' Association** (CWA) Gold Dagger. He followed it up with the less-celebrated *Four and Twenty Virgins* (1972) but returned to Kramer and Zondi, and top form, with *The Caterpillar Cop* (1972), which opens with the brutal death of a young boy, strangled by wire and mutilated. McClure never shirked the dark areas of human behaviour, yet his work is illuminated by shafts of wit and benefits from unsentimental compassion. The relationship between his two detectives, divided by racial barriers but united in a commitment to the investigative cause, is superbly accomplished. Because he avoided preaching, his critique of apartheid is all the more convincing.

McClure's non-series work was varied. *Rogue Eagle* (1976), awarded the CWA Silver Dagger, was a political thriller in which he drew on the exploits of his father, an intelligence officer during the Second World War. *Spike Island* (1980) was a compelling account of police work in Merseyside while *Copworld* (1984) studied crime investigation in San Diego, California. Yet, after *The Artful Egg* appeared in 1984, he published only one more novel, albeit of high merit: *The Song Dog* (1991) moves back in time to recount the first meeting between Kramer and Zondi. Later, McClure concentrated on journalism and, after a spell as editor at *The Oxford Times*, took a similar appointment at *The Oxford Mail*. Following his retirement, he started work on a new novel set in Oxford and even began a blog, but McClure's last years were blighted by illness. Inevitably, his failure to produce more than a single novel during the last twenty-two years of his life meant that he had slipped out of the public eye by the time of his death. Nevertheless, the quality of his writing, especially in the Kramer and Zondi series, is such that his reputation is secure. Few authors have exploited the potential of the crime genre for **social** comment to such powerful effect.

Selected Works by the Author
The Steam Pig (1971)
The Caterpillar Cop (1972)
Four and Twenty Virgins (1973)
The Gooseberry Fool (1974)
Snake (1975)
Rogue Eagle (1976)
The Sunday Hangman (1977)
The Blood of an Englishman (1980)
The Artful Egg (1984)
The Song Dog (1991)

Martin Edwards

McClure, Ken (b.1942)

Ken McClure (also known as Ken Begg) writes novels that have often been compared to those of Michael Crichton. His effective science-based thrillers explore different areas in which medicine can turn malignant, ranging from plague, Scrapie, Gulf War syndrome, the Ebola virus and bird flu.

Begg was born and bred in Edinburgh; he became a very junior laboratory technician at Edinburgh's City Hospital, which was to lead him to study for his PhD in molecular genetics. Ken's thesis went on to win the Difco Triennial Prize for research in microbiology in 1980. Working with the Medical Research Council of Great Britain, he was on a research trip to the University of Tel-Aviv in Israel when he conceived the idea and wrote notes, what would become his second book, *The Scorpion's Advance* (1986), concerning a medical researcher following a trail which leads him to Israel. After four books under his own name, he adopted the Ken McClure nom de plume when a local newspaper reported on the novel, and he began getting phone calls from people who had looked him up in the phone book wanting medical advice rather than to comment on his books.

As McClure, he created the popular character Dr Steven Dunbar, whose background is very similar to that of McClure's own: a medical researcher and trained scientific medical specialist. Dunbar is ex-Para and recruited by Sci-Med to investigate crimes, the consequence of which is that he often takes a decision which may not be legally or morally correct but which matches his apprehension of what constitutes 'the right thing'. Dunbar was introduced in *Donor* (1998), where he investigates Medic Ecosse, a state-of-the-art new private hospital, where all is not as it appears to be. There are further titles addressing different medical/scientific aspects: *Deception* (2001) deals with genetically modified crops; *Wildcard* (2002) is about the Ebola virus; *The Gulf Conspiracy* (2004) explores the governments denial of existence of Gulf War syndrome; *The Eye of the Raven* (2005) questions DNA profiling; and in *The Lazarus Strain* (2007), Dunbar investigates the death of a scientist and the possibility that it is connected to terrorism and biological warfare.

Although McClure turned to full-time writing in 2000, he keeps *au fait* with modern medicine, and his later novels utilise his research into little-known medical/scientific facts; this technique of merging real-life scenarios with fiction adds to the thriller elements in his books which had led to comments that his novels were being prophetic. Scrapie is a mutation of a little-known sheep's-brain disease, and *Crisis* (1993) deals with the mutation which causes brain disease in humans – mad-cow disease. In the 1990s, the public became aware of the flesh-eating bacteria known as fasciitis necroticans, discussed in McClure's prescient thriller, *Chameleon* (1994). McClure ensures that his novels are grounded in verifiable scientific truth and then shored up with strong characters and kinetic action sequences. *See also* True Crime.

Selected Works by the Author
The Scorpion's Advance as Ken Begg (1986)
Chameleon (1994)
Donor (1998)
The Lazarus Strain (2007)

Mike Stotter

McCutchan, Philip (1920–1996)

Philip Donald McCutchan's lifelong love of all things naval – reflected in his sweeping espionage thrillers – can be traced back to a childhood growing up amidst the hustle and bustle of Portsmouth Dockyard, one of the largest Royal Navy bases in the United Kingdom.

Having served on several British warships during the Second World War, McCutchan turned to writing at the age of forty with *Gibraltar Road* (1960), the first in a long-running series centring on the James Bond–style exploits of one Commander Esmonde Shaw of Naval Intelligence. In his first adventure, a breakneck dash across Spain leads to a climactic nuclear countdown in which only he and his glamorous girlfriend Debonnair Delacroix can avert wholesale destruction. More stories followed in a broadly similar vein – publicised as 'Commander Shaw Counterspy Novels' – with the emphasis very much on action and sex.

Alongside these, McCutchan indulged his fascination with military history in a series of novels featuring clean-shaven hero James Ogilvy, subaltern with the 114th Highlanders in late Victorian India. Written under the pseudonym Duncan MacNeil, these were fairly glamorised accounts of the British Army's experiences on the Northwest Frontier in the 1890s; they began with *Drums along the Khyber* (1969, also known as *The First Command*) and continued for a further fourteen instalments.

Other maritime characters included St Vincent Halfhyde (sixteen books), Donald Cameron (fourteen), James Mason Kemp (six) and Tom Chatto (three). Land-based espionage was represented by Cold War secret agent Simon Shard in titles such as *A Very Big Bang* (1975) and *The Executioners* (1986).

Selected Works by the Author
Gibralter Road (1960)
The Man from Moscow (1963)
The Screaming Dead Balloons (1968)
Call for Simon Shard (1973)
Cameron's Convoy (1982)

Mark Campbell

McDermid, Val (b.1955)

As a crime writer, Val McDermid pulls no punches. Her writing is vivid and unstintingly graphic in a fashion that forces the reader to smell the blood and taste the fear, and in recent years, she has become one of the most popular and successful female writers in the genre.

McDermid was born in Kirkcaldy in Scotland, read English at St Hilda's College, Oxford, and then trained as a journalist – she was nominated the National Trainee Journalist of the Year in 1977. Attention to detail and sense of place, which are essential requisites of newspaper work, are strong elements of her fiction. She turned to full-time writing in 1991, and her first three novels, featuring a Scottish journalist, Lindsay Gordon, met with great acclaim. It is interesting to note McDermid's progression from these early books which, in many ways, followed the formula of the standard whodunit. For instance, her first novel, *Report for Murder* (1987), is set in a girls' public school where a body is discovered locked in a cupboard. Where McDermid deviated from the format was in the creation of her female sleuth, Gordon, who was a hard-drinking, socialist lesbian feminist – about as far away from Miss Marple as possible. By the time McDermid came to write the third novel, *Final Edition* (1991), she was not only dealing with murder but also exploring social issues, thus adding more depth to her narrative, in this instance, an intelligence cover-up in a women's protest camp and the unpleasant consequences that result.

61. Val McDermid.

She next created Kate Brannigan, a feisty, red-headed PI working in Manchester. She could easily have been Sara Paretsky's V.I. Warshawski's British sister. McDermid was really getting into her stride now. The plots grew more cunning and more violent. Brannigan takes on cases which initially seemed straightforward such as car sales fraud in *Crackdown* (1994) and art theft in *Clean Break* (1995), but she then finds herself drawn in into dark, dangerous and nasty worlds. These novels allowed McDermid to explore the violent criminal underbelly of Manchester. *Crackdown*, which led Brannigan into the realms of child pornography and drug trafficking, was shortlisted for the **Crime Writers' Association** (CWA) Gold Dagger and the Anthony Award.

McDermid's third series featured clinical psychologist and profiler, Tony Hill, who has sexual demons of his own to contend with. It is interesting (and significant) to note that while McDermid's work features many strong dominant leading female characters, Hill, her only male star, is impotent. In his first outing, a taut and gripping psychological thriller, *The Mermaids Singing* (which won the CWA Gold Dagger for 1995), Hill is employed to help track down a gay serial killer who has a gruesome and stomach-turning modus operandi. Because Hill has the facility to get inside the heads of these violent criminals, the novel turns into an exciting duel of wits between the killer and the psychologist. Hill returned in **Wire in the Blood** (1997) in which he is now head of a National Profiling Task Force. He is joined by a colleague from the previous book, DCI Carol Jordan, in the cat-and-mouse game with the killer who has murdered one of their own team.

McDermid kept fans waiting five years for the next book in the Hill series, *The Last Temptation* (2002), in which a twisted killer is targeting criminal psychologists in Europe. The solution to the mystery has its roots in Nazi atrocities. This novel was followed by *The Torment of Others* (2004), which involves a series of killings that replicate the crimes of a murderer who is already in prison. The latest Hill title appeared in 2007: *Beneath the Bleeding* sets Tony Hill and Carol Jordan at odds with each other as they have never been before, forcing them to ask questions of themselves they would never have imagined possible. A series of bizarre poisonings and a bomb blast in a crowded football stadium test their skills to the limit.

The books were turned into the television series *Wire in the Blood*, with Robson Green as Hill and Hermione Norris as Jordan. Starting in 2002 and running until 2006, there have been four seasons which were as gritty and visceral as the novels.

In between the Hill thrillers, McDermid has created several stand-alone novels. In 1999, she wrote what is possibly her greatest work so far, *A Place of Execution*. The early part of this multi-layered novel is set in 1963 in the north of England, the time and location of the Brady and Hindley murders. A child goes missing and is assumed dead. A young policeman investigates, attempting to make some sense of this dark puzzle, but it is two decades later before the shocking truth is revealed. Nothing is quite what it seems, and through her writing, McDermid creates not only a haunting and emotionally draining work but, as one reviewer called it, 'A Greek tragedy in modern England'.

Killing the Shadows (2000) has a kind of knowing satirical edge to it as it concerns a serial killer whose victims are famous crime novelists. The climax is suitably melodramatic.

McDermid presented another mystery that spans the years in *The Distant Echo* (2003). In 1978, four male students find the body of Rosie Duff half-buried in the snow, and their lives are variously damaged by the suspicion that falls on them when the murder is never solved; a quarter of a century later, the case is reopened, and suddenly, the quartet are killed one after the other. With cunning and sleight-of-hand misdirection, McDermid keeps the reader guessing right to the end.

In *The Grave Tattoo* (2006), a modern-day murder has its roots in the eighteenth century and the mutiny on the *Bounty*. Both Fletcher Christian and his friend William Wordsworth are entwined in this 200-year-old mystery. McDermid's heroine, a Wordsworth scholar, in searching for a long-lost poem, finds that death dogs her heels and the past threatens the present in a very real and dangerous way.

McDermid's considerable output is impressively unsparing and ambitious in its reach. *See also* Women Crime Writers.

Selected Works by the Author

Lindsay Gordon Series
Report for Murder (1987)
Final Edition (1991)

Tony Hill Series
The Mermaids Singing (1995)
Wire in the Blood (1997)
Beneath the Bleeding (2007)

Non-Series Novels
Place of Execution (1999)
The Distant Echo (2003)
The Grave Tattoo (2006)
A Darker Domain (2008)

David Stuart Davies

MacDonald, Philip (1900–1980)

Philip MacDonald (who also wrote as Oliver Fleming, Anthony Lawless, Martin Porlock and Warren Stuart) is a revered name in the field of crime writing. The key to MacDonald's enduring reputation among crime fiction fans lies in his ability to write an entirely different type of book each time, both in subject matter and in narrative technique. Add to this a flair for the macabre and the capacity to create vivid characters whose fate you care about, and you have a potent mixture.

MacDonald was the grandson of the author George MacDonald and a cavalry officer in the First World War. In 1931, his most productive year (in which he published eight novels, including the first book as Martin Porlock, his well-known pseudonym), he moved to Hollywood to work as a scriptwriter. Here he worked with Alfred Hitchcock and on the Charlie Chan and Mr Moto films. In 1953 he won the Edgar Award for the best short-story collection, *Something to Hide* (1952), and he won the award again in 1956 for the year's best short story, 'Dream No More' (*EQMM*, November 1955).

His writing style varied from the normal first- or third-person narrations to more experimental ways. *Rynox* (1930) begins with an epilogue, ends with a prologue and has authorial comments on the action throughout. *Persons Unknown* (1931) is told entirely through police witness statements.

The best known of MacDonald's creations is the suave Colonel Anthony Gethryn, an 'adviser' to Scotland Yard, who makes his debut in *The Rasp* (1924), a conventional country-house mystery. The author's versatility is soon apparent; in the subsequent eleven books featuring him, Gethryn becomes involved in a locked-room mystery, thrillers, severely intellectual problems and attempts to save a condemned man from the gallows. His masterpiece is *The Nursemaid Who Disappeared* (1938), where an overheard snatch of conversation puts him on the trail of an unknown criminal, plotting the kidnapping of an unknown victim. In the Edgar-nominated *The List of Adrian Messenger* (1959), he tackles a labyrinthine five-year-old murder plot (the book was the subject of a bizarre but enjoyable John Huston film, with American actor George C. Scott – complete with impeccable English accent – as Gethryn).

Of the non-series novels, MacDonald's first masterpiece is *Murder Gone Mad* (1931). Superintendent Pike, Gethryn's colleague, takes charge in this gripping and still shocking story of a small town stalked by a serial killer. The second is the Porlock novel *X v Rex* (1933), which takes us, in part, into the mind of a serial killer who targets only policemen. Other titles of interest include *The Dark Wheel* (1948), written with A. Boyd Correll, and *Guest in the House* (1955). Both these books are character studies of men pushed to very different extremes.

In his work, MacDonald furthered the boundaries of what could be done within the confines of a mainstream detective novel, raising his readers' expectations and challenging his contemporaries. *See also* Film and Crime: Page to Screen.

Selected Works by the Author
The White Crow (1928)
The Link (1930)
The Nursemaid Who Disappeared (1938; also published in the United States as *Warrant for X*)
The Man Out of the Rain (1955)
The List of Adrian Messenger (1959)
Death and Chicanery (1962)

Further Reading
Donaldson, Norman. 1969. 'Philip MacDonald: Gethryn and Others'. *The Armchair Detective*, volume 3.
Kimber, Nick. 2005. 'Philip MacDonald's Mr Anthony Gethryn'. *CADS* 47: 31–36.
Medawar, Tony. 2007. 'Serendip's Detections XII: The Gladiator'. *CADS* 52: 26.

Nick Kimber

McDowall, Iain

Iain McDowall's detective novels featuring DCI Frank Jacobson and set in the fictional English town of Crowby show both realism and humour, and, in avoiding the conventional clichés of crime writing, they offer something very distinctive.

Born in Scotland but residing in the English West Midlands – though footloose and given to disappearing for months with his wife on extensive travels – McDowall, previously a philosophy lecturer and a computer software specialist, began writing crime fiction in the mid-1990s. His novels gave routine **police procedurals** a harder edge. The town of Crowby, too, was portrayed as hard, but this unsympathetic and unforgiving viewpoint was softened by McDowall's injections of dark **humour**. In a review by the author Andrew **Taylor**, the fictional Crowby was described as less a town than 'a state of mind'. It appears real, has its own consistency, but is based on no particular real-life locale – though it is clearly within commuting distance of Birmingham. Crowby is modern and reasonably thriving, but although the town is technologically advanced, its residents remain emphatically and satisfyingly basic in their attitudes. Thus, rather than serve as a mere background to the stories, Crowby the town appears in each book with as much personality as do its inhabitants. One cannot avoid the feeling that McDowall intends his fictional town to stand as a metaphor for the increasingly amoral and uncaring attitudes often promoted and praised in modern British life.

His first book, *A Study in Death*, though published in 2000, was written and set five years earlier. (It took him almost five years to get it published.) Later books in the series are contemporaneous with when they were written, and they are longer than the first, giving that volume the air of a first-time novelist's try out – more telegrammic in style, more curt. McDowall's style is also unusual in that many scenes are seen through the eyes and perceived through the thoughts of specific, though different, characters – both law abiding or law breaking. The crimes he writes about are equally untraditional: McDowall features a 'family annihilator' in *Perfectly Dead* (2003), twenty-first century arms dealers in *Making a Killing* (2002) and far-right racist killers in his fourth book *Killing for England* (2005). Conventional serial killers and gang lords appear rarely in his territory. Realism rules in his books. Some readers complain that the series hero, DCI Frank Jacobson, is bleak and unsympathetically drawn, though to McDowall's fans, it is Jacobson's dark take on life and the man's black humour that appeal. In common with other fictional cop heroes, Jacobson has a failed marriage behind him, a daughter to stir his guilt and a readiness to take a drink. (He prefers beer to spirits.) Jacobson stands out from other cops in the books – indeed, from cops in many other writers' books – in that his politics, though kept in the background, are clearly left-wing, and his relationship with criminals is less automatically censorious. It is not difficult to detect the guiding hand of a left-wing author in these novels, but fortunately, McDowall is an author who lets preaching, politics nor 'message' interrupt his story. *See also* Conventions *and* Humour and Crime Fiction.

Selected Works by the Author
Perfectly Dead (2003)
Killing for England (2005)
Cut Her Dead (2007)

Russell James

McGown, Jill (1948–2007)

Jill McGown, who died aged fifty-nine in 2007 after a long illness, was one among the generation of British crime writers who shifted the genre firmly into the modern world. Although she held fast to the traditional skill of well-crafted plots, she brought a contemporary perspective to characters and situations, creating a series of thoughtful and engaging **police procedurals**.

Her Latin teacher at Corby Grammar School in Northamptonshire was Colin **Dexter**, the later creator of the **Inspector Morse** novels. By strange coincidence, they were both subsequently signed up by the same editor at Macmillan.

Although McGown also wrote five stand-alone suspense thrillers primarily from the viewpoint of the victims, she will be best remembered for the thirteen novels featuring Chief Inspector Danny Lloyd and Sergeant Judy Hill. Theirs was a relationship that encompassed the personal as well as the professional, and McGown's deft handling of its development was one of the keynote elements of the books.

Selected Works by the Author
A Perfect Match (1983)
The Stalking Horse (1987)
Redemption (1988; also published in the United States as *Murder at the Old Vicarage*)
Death of a Dancer (1989; also published in the United States as *Gone to her Death*)
The Murders of Mrs Austin and Mrs Beale (1991)
The Other Woman (1992)
Verdict Unsafe (1997)
Scene of Crime (2001)
Births, Deaths and Marriages (2002)

Website
www.jillmcgown.com

Val McDermid

McIlvanney, William (b.1936)

The success of *Laidlaw* (1977), which won the **Crime Writers' Association** Silver Dagger, thrust William McIlvanney into the forefront of UK crime writers, but he was already a prominent novelist in Scotland, having won the Geoffrey Faber prize for his first novel, *Remedy Is None* (1966), and the Scottish Arts Council book award for each of his next two, *A Gift from Nessus* (1968) and *Docherty* (1975). Although they are not crime novels, like most of his 'mainstream' fiction, they deal with issues of violence and masculinity within a particularly gritty Scottish setting. *Docherty*, which also won the Whitbread Prize, is set among Scottish miners during the Depression and tangentially related to crime novels in much the same way as *On the Waterfront* (1954). His mainstream work has often been described as 'Scottish socialist realism', but as he progressed, his Glasgow took on increasingly metaphoric depths, and his concern with the nature of personal development during his lifetime became more evident.

Laidlaw's success arose from the same concerns; DI Jack Laidlaw is a child of this violent society, and his attitude towards the crimes he investigates is understanding to the point of sympathy. *Laidlaw* is influenced somewhat by American hard-boiled fiction, particularly in its wise-cracking dialogue(this influence is reflected in Ian **Rankin**'s Rebus, even though Rebus prowls the more outwardly genteel mean streets of Edinburgh).

McIlvanney was born in Kilmarnock, the son of a miner, in 1936. His brother Hugh is arguably the best British sportswriter of his generation. After Glasgow University, McIlvanney taught until 1975 and has continued to teach creative writing at the University of Strathclyde. His early work included collections of poetry – *The Longships in Harbour* (1970) and *Landscapes and Figures* (1973); his later collections *These Words* (1984), *In through the Head* (1988) and *Surviving the Shipwreck* (1991) also include critical essays.

Jack Laidlaw appeared in two more novels: *The Papers of Tony Veitch* (1983), which also won the Silver Dagger, and *Strange Loyalties* (1991), in which McIlvanney switched to first-person narration as Laidlaw looked into the death of his brother. Although it won no awards, it may be the most intriguing of the trilogy – marking a move deeper into a reflection of McIlvanney's own experience – and a confluence of his crime novels with his mainstream fiction, as elements of *The Big Man* (1985) reappear in *Strange Loyalties*. *The Big Man* became a successful film with Liam Neeson playing the eponymous bare-knuckled fighter. McIlvanney's short story 'Dreaming', which appeared in the collection *Walking Wounded* (1989) was filmed by BBC Scotland and won a BAFTA Award.

Self-reference became more evident in *The Kiln* (1996), whose protagonist, Tom Docherty, is the son of Conn from *Docherty*; Tom, like McIlvanney, becomes a writer, where Conn followed his father Tam into the pits. His most recent novel, *Weekend* (2006), is a departure of sorts, in that it chronicles self-discovery among a group of students. Although it is tempting to include much of McIlvanney's mainstream work among his crime fictions, the three Laidlaw novels stand by themselves as one of the most impressive bodies of work in British detective fiction. *See also* Realism and Crime Fiction.

Selected Works by the Author
Remedy Is None (1966)
A Gift from Nessus (1968)
Docherty (1975)
Laidlaw (1977)
The Papers of Tony Veitch (1983)
These Words (1984)
The Big Man (1985)
Walking Wounded (1989)
Strange Loyalties (1991)
Surviving the Shipwreck (1991)
Weekend (2006)

Michael Carlson

MacKill's Mystery Magazine

MacKill's was a British digest **magazine** that ran monthly for twenty-two issues
from September 1952 to June 1954, though the last four issues were undated. It was
published by Todd Publishing Group, which had hitherto published a number of small
paperback books by Peter **Cheyney**, Dorothy L. **Sayers** and Nigel **Morland**. No
editor was credited on the magazine, but it is likely to have been Morland, who also
had stories in six of the issues and contributed a regular column, 'Background
to Murder', to the last eight issues.

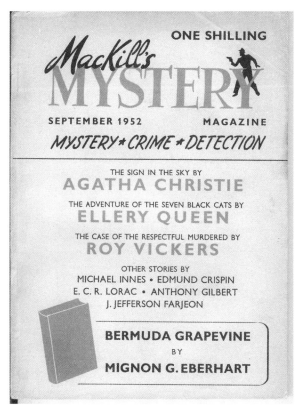

62. Cover of *MacKill's* Mystery Magazine in September 1952.

MacKill's was predominantly reprint, though for the most part it selected stories
of recent vintage, some of which had appeared only in the United States and so would
not have been that familiar to British readers. Each issue ran seven or eight **short
stories** and a few non-fiction pieces plus a substantial novella. These were all reprints,
mostly but not all by American writers, and included some significant works by
Raymond **Chandler**, Erle Stanley Gardner, Rex Stout, Georges Simenon and Agatha
Christie. From the June 1953 issue, it began a specific reprint slot on 'The Great
Detectives', with stories featuring Father Brown, Lord Peter **Wimsey**, Dr John
Thorndyke, Max Carrados and others.

It only ran a few new stories, usually one or rarely two per issue. Among these were
several stories by Michael **Innes**, plus some new *Department of Dead Ends* tales by
Roy **Vickers**, though even some of these had previously appeared in *Ellery Queen's*

Mystery Magazine in America. This source ceased when a separate British edition of *Ellery Queen's* was issued by Mellifont Press starting in February 1953. *MacKill's* turned to other sources, predominantly British, and reprinted stories by Agatha Christie, Margery **Allingham**, Freeman Wills **Crofts** and Ronald **Knox**.

For readers at the time, *MacKill's* was an excellent source of good quality stories, not all of which were otherwise readily available, but it was a minor market for new fiction. Unfortunately, Todd Publishing Group ceased operations during the overhaul of paperback publishers in the mid-1950s and *MacKill's* folded. It remains a fine and highly readable magazine that is becoming increasingly rare. *See also* Magazines.

Further Reading
Cook, Michael L. 1982. *Monthly Murders*. Greenwood Press.

Mike Ashley

McLaren, John (b.1951)

John McLaren is an author who has achieved success in a variety of genres – no doubt due to energy levels that many of his peers would envy. Along with turning out highly successful crime novels such as *Black Cabs* (1999), McLaren has made a mark as a diplomat, a venture capitalist, classical music entrepreneur and director of two major investment banks, not to mention being chairman of the Barchester Group.

63. John McLaren.

Black Cabs has the unique premise of three **London** cabbies as its protagonists; they take a high risk and utilise the knowledge one of them has overheard about a clandestine corporate takeover – and soon live to regret it, as violent retribution is only one of the banking magnates' weapons.

Running Rings (2001) is a typically gritty McLaren entry, about a crime family who have hit hard times. Their latest drug operations have been beached on the south coast, and the restaurants and clubs that the ring runs as fronts are haemorrhaging cash. The head of the villainous dynasty vows to turn things around – with, finally, disastrous consequences.

For his plausibly authentic naval thriller *Blind Eye* (2004), McLaren hobnobbed with the upper echelons of the naval establishment, who (no doubt aware of the good PR possibilities) readily gave their co-operation in his research for the book.

Selected Works by the Author
Press Send (1997)
Seventh Sense (1998)
Black Cabs (1999)
Running Rings (2001)
Blind Eye (2004)

Barry Forshaw

MacLean, Alistair (1922–1987)

A best-selling author in his time, Alistair MacLean's forte was the construction of unpretentious adventure yarns, usually with a nautical theme, that inevitably pitted a single man – occasionally a team – against seemingly insurmountable odds.

MacLean was born Alistair Stuart MacLean in Shettleston, a slum area of Glasgow, and his father (also Alistair MacLean) was a Church of Scotland minister. The family spoke Gaelic as their first language, the younger MacLean not learning English until he was seven. He spent much of his childhood in the picturesque village of Daviot in Aberdeenshire, where his father had bought a farm, before returning to his birthplace after his father's death in 1936.

He was educated at Hillhead High School, Glasgow, and at the age of eighteen, he joined the Royal Navy, where he rose in rank from ordinary seaman to leading torpedo operator. Initially assigned to a converted paddle steamer, *Bournemouth Queen*, he later served on HMS *Royalist*, escorting Russian convey ships in the Arctic Circle, followed by wartime operations in the Mediterranean and South East Asia.

He returned to his studies in 1946, obtaining a degree in English literature at the University of Glasgow. This enabled him to take the post of English and history master at Gallowflat School in Rutherglen, a suburb in the south-east of Glasgow. A year later, in 1954, he won £100 in a competition for his short story 'The Dileas', while his first professional sale, 'The Cruise of the Golden Girl', appeared in the September 1954 issue of the renowned *Blackwood's Magazine*.

Encouraged by the Glasgow-based publisher Collins, MacLean began work on a novel based on his wartime experiences in the North Atlantic, and this was published the following year as *HMS Ulysses* (1955). The semi-autobiographical novel recounted the nightmarish conditions on board a naval vessel escorting merchant ships in the Arctic, in which the frighteningly inhospitable weather conditions were every bit as dangerous as the German warships. Fans of MacLean's later books may be surprised by the unremittingly bleak and plotless nature of the storyline, which arguably serves as one of the most intense depictions of the realities of war since Erich Maria Remarque's *All Quiet on the Western Front* (1929).

MacLean's next book could not have been more different. Although still a wartime sea adventure story, *The Guns of Navarone* (1957) was a gung-ho adventure story about a group of hand-picked Allied servicemen sent to destroy two huge Nazi guns in a heavily fortified base on a Greek island. While it retained all the authentic detail of his debut novel, the style and tone was much lighter and the plot significantly more far-fetched. It was filmed to great effect in 1961 with an all-star cast headed by Gregory Peck, David Niven and Anthony Quinn.

The success of these two novels prompted MacLean to resign his teaching post and move to the tax-free haven of Switzerland with his wife, Gisela Heinrichsen (whom he had met in 1949), and their young son, Lachlan. His third novel, *South by Java Head* (1958), concerned the Japanese invasion of Singapore and continued the successful formula established in *The Guns of Navarone*.

Settling down to roughly one novel per year (despite his claims that he spent only thirty-five days on each one), MacLean's next major success was *Ice Station Zebra* in 1960. A secret mission to a desolate weather station at the polar ice cap formed the basis for a fantastically tense adventure tale that combined an old-fashioned 'locked-room' whodunit with a Cold War thriller utilising the very latest technological advances. Its hero, American secret agent Carpenter, kept his motivations closely guarded, always retaining some vital titbit until the next chapter (a clever conceit considering the first-person narrative), thus making the storyline at times almost unbearably tense. In 1969, it was loosely adapted into a movie version by John Sturges, starring Rock Hudson and Patrick McGoohan.

In 1963, following two novels written under the pseudonym Ian Stuart (*The Dark Crusader*, 1961, and *The Satan Bug*, 1962), MacLean briefly retired from writing to manage four English hotels from his home in Geneva. But three years later, he was back at the typewriter, with *When Eight Bells Toll* appearing in 1966. His only novel set primarily in Scotland, it moved away from his familiar wartime setting to tell a contemporary crime story involving a gold-bullion robbery.

Where Eagles Dare (1967) was a virtual retread of *The Guns of Navarone*, and marked the start of a gradual downturn in the author's writing style. Although it was made into another hugely successful film in 1968, starring Clint Eastwood and Richard Burton, it never quite recaptured the quality of MacLean's earlier works. With the exception of another straightforward crime story, *Puppet on a Chain* (1969), the author's output from this point on become increasingly erratic. In 1968, MacLean's only sequel, *Force Ten from Navarone*, was published, eventually being adapted into a 1979 movie starring Robert Shaw and Harrison Ford.

Various personal problems (he divorced Gisela in 1972 and married actress Marcelle Georgius) formed the troubled backdrop to many of the author's less-than-satisfactory 1970s offerings, of which perhaps *Breakheart Pass* (1974) is the best remembered. Plots became increasingly unbelievable, characters correspondingly shallower and description virtually non-existent. Although his 1980s books continued the downward trend, his 1985 collection *The Lonely Sea* (which included his first short story, 'The Dileas') reminded loyal readers of what he could be capable.

After a series of strokes, MacLean died of a heart attack on 2 February 1987 in Munich and was buried in Celigny in Switzerland. He left behind various story outlines for a mooted American film series featuring the exploits of UNACO, a fictional United Nations crime organisation. These were subsequently turned into workmanlike novels by a variety of authors. *See also* Film and Crime: Page to Screen.

Selected Works by the Author
HMS Ulysses (1955)
Ice Station Zebra (1960)
Night without End (1960)
Fear Is the Key (1961)
The Satan Bug (1962)
When Eight Bells Toll (1966)
Where Eagles Dare (1967)
Force Ten from Navarone (1968)

Mark Campbell

McNab, Andy (b.1959)

Formerly a serving officer in Britain's highly secretive SAS, Andy McNab achieved huge popularity with his first military adventure *Bravo Two Zero* (1993). A highly credible account of recognisable and recent areas of operation, it was also notable in being written in McNab's 'other ranks' language, the real-life speech of a 'grunt', a man who had worked in the field.

Biographical data on McNab is hard to come by, as both the SAS and his publishers emphasise the need to keep his identity secret. (McNab is a pseudonym.) But this much is known: he joined the infantry in 1976 as a boy soldier and in 1984 joined 22 SAS Regiment, where he served for nine years on covert and overt operations, including anti-terrorist and anti-drug operations in the Middle and Far East, South and Central America and Northern Ireland. His training included VIP protection, prime target elimination, demolitions, weapons and tactics, and covert surveillance in hostile environments. Particularly helpful to his subsequent writing career was his work with police forces, prison services, anti-drug forces and western-backed guerrilla movements. His achievements were recognised when he was awarded both the Distinguished Conduct Medal and the Military Medal. When he finally left the SAS in February 1993, McNab was the British Army's most highly decorated serving soldier.

His first book, *Bravo Two Zero*, became one of the best-selling war book of all time, selling a million and a half copies in the United Kingdom alone. The all-adventure story was narrated by the man who subsequently became McNab's series hero, an ex-SAS awkward man, Nick **Stone**, working as a deniable agent for British Intelligence – and hooked into the scheme by a predictably gorgeous top woman spy. The surprise for most readers was not the story itself, which was gripping throughout, but the fact that an ex-SAS operative could write so effectively. *Bravo Two Zero* was not only a page-turner but also clammily credible – by no means exclusively to male readers. The extended stake-out sequence, in which Stone camps out in the branches of a tree overlooking his target building, is a masterpiece of both clear exposition (after which many red-blooded men fancied they now knew how to do this) and extended suspense.

Although his subsequent thrillers could not match the sales of *Bravo Two Zero*, they notched up figures to make most authors turn khaki with envy, each book selling over half a million copies in the United Kingdom. *Remote Control* (1997) was followed by *Crisis Four* (1999), *Firewall* (2000), etc., though after the excellent *Deep Black* (2004) on Iraq, the series tired. *Recoil* (2006) in the Congo seemed just another outing. Although, like many popular successes, McNab is often dismissed by those who have not read him, he remains one of the few British writers to match top Americans for bravura action and suspense.

Selected Works by the Author
Bravo Two Zero (1993)
Immediate Action (autobiography, 1995)
Deep Black (2004)

Russell James

Magazines

Unlike in the United States, where crime and mystery fiction pulps flourished, and where the first ever specialised fiction **pulp**, *Detective Story Magazine*, appeared in October 1915, Britain had no appreciable history of crime fiction magazines. The first specialised title was *The Detective Magazine* from Amalgamated Press, which appeared fortnightly from 24 November 1922 and ran for sixty-five issues, but it relied heavily on reprints as well as a substantial quota of non-fiction. *Mystery-Story Magazine* followed from Hutchinson, but this relied even more heavily on reprints from the American pulps.

In Britain, crime and detective fiction was always regarded as a key feature of the general fiction magazines, especially since the popularity of Sherlock **Holmes** in *The Strand* where his adventures began in July 1891. Crime fiction had been popular for generations before in magazines. *Bentley's Miscellany*, for instance, serialised both Charles **Dickens**'s *Oliver Twist* (1837–1839) and Harrison Ainsworth's *Jack Sheppard* (1839–1840), which drew heavily on the imagery of the criminal underworld, while Wilkie **Collins**'s seminal detective novel, *The Moonstone*, was serialised in *All the Year Round* in 1868.

Popular though these novels were, they did not become the selling point of the magazine until the success of Sherlock Holmes had both *The Strand* and its rival magazines clamouring for more in that vein. *Ludgate Monthly* was one of the first, with a series about female detective Loveday Brooke by C.L. Pirkis running from February to July 1893. *The Strand* began its own successor with Arthur Morrison's stories about Martin Hewitt (from March 1894). The new *Windsor Magazine* soon lured Morrison and Hewitt to its pages but found it had an even greater hit on its hands with the character of Dr Nikola created by Guy Boothby in the serial 'A Bid for Fortune' (began January 1895). *The Strand* fought back with not one but several series by the infinitely adaptable L.T. Meade such as 'The Adventures of a Man of Science' (July 1896–February 1897) with Clifford Halifax and 'The Brotherhood of the Seven Kings' (January–October 1898) with Robert Eustace.

The Royal found success with Baroness Orczy's series about 'The Old Man in the Corner' (May–October 1901). *The Lady's Home Magazine* ran the stories of Addington Peace (August 1904–January 1905) by Arthur **Conan Doyle**'s friend B. Fletcher Robinson. *Pearson's Magazine* introduced R. Austin **Freeman**'s scientific detective, Dr John Thorndyke, in 1908, while *The Story-teller* proudly presented G.K. **Chesterton**'s Father Brown in 1910.

These magazines paid top rates and had large circulations and there were more than enough of them to cater for a demanding readership. Crime fiction was a major

64. Cover of a war-time issue of *The Strand Magazine*.

selling point of these magazines meaning that there was little need for the big writers
to work for any specialist magazines at what would be much lower wordage rates.
As a result, all the major writers, especially in the 1920s, sold to the leading popular
weeklies and monthlies. Agatha **Christie**'s Poirot **short stories** first appeared
in *The Sketch* in 1923 and she also sold to *The Grand* and *The Novel*. Dorothy Sayers
introduced Lord Peter **Wimsey** in *Pearson's Magazine* in 1925 and also sold to *The
Passing Show* and *20-Story Magazine*.

There was also an attitude that the specialist magazines catered for a more juvenile
readership. In America, the pulps had emerged from the dime novels. *Detective Story
Magazine*, for instance, had been a continuation and revamping of the long-running
Nick Carter Stories which had begun life as the *Nick Carter Library* in August 1891.
There were similar British series. The Aldine Publishing Company reprinted many
American dime novel series, sometimes augmenting them with home-grown material,
and among them was *Aldine Detective Tales*, which ran from 1889 to 1906 and was
revived again in 1922. These were to some extent outgrowths of the notorious penny
dreadfuls of the mid-Victorian era, and it was in retaliation to those that Alfred
Harmsworth began his cheaper but more morally upright halfpenny series. It was
in the *Halfpenny Marvel* story paper that the first stories featuring Sexton **Blake**
and Nelson Lee appeared in 1893 and 1894. Blake became a regular feature in the
Union Jack juvenile paper and in due course generated the *The Sexton Blake Library*
in 1915 alongside the *Nelson Lee Library*, started the same year. The *Union Jack* was
eventually revamped as *Detective Weekly* in 1933, the emphasis not only remaining

on Sexton Blake, but also featuring the work of Leslie **Charteris**. Charteris's stories of Simon Templar, the Saint, had taken shape in the pages of another weekly series, *The Thriller*, which ran from 1929 to 1940.

Regardless of anything of quality that appeared in these specialist magazines, they tended to be regarded as downmarket and few of the major writers contributed to them, though their work was reprinted there. Moreover, many of the American pulps were distributed in Britain, some with British editions, which further encroached on any remaining market for specialist magazines. As a consequence, most of them flourished briefly and then faded. *The Detective Magazine* ran for less than three years; *Mystery-Story Magazine* for just over four. *Hush*, a rather shoddy-looking pulp published by Collins for the Detective Story Club, and again relying heavily on reprints, survived just one year (June 1930–June 1931). *Mystery Stories* (1936–1942) had only twenty-five issues in six years. All these pulp magazines fell in the gap between the juvenile weeklies and the prestigious top monthlies which, in the 1920s and 1930s, could offer all new work by Christie, Sayers, Chesterton, John **Buchan**, Sax **Rohmer**, the Reggie Fortune stories by H.C. Bailey, the baffling impossible crime stories of Vincent Cornier, and much more.

65. Cover of the first issue of *Mystery Stories* in 1936.

It was not until the Second World War, when the general fiction magazines died away, that the specialist crime fiction magazine was allowed some room. The grandfather of these magazines was the ***London Mystery Magazine***, which also outlived all its rivals, running from 1949 to 1982, the longest surviving of any such

British title. It also ran predominantly new material, so was Britain's premier market during those years. Other titles that appeared at this time – which included *MacKill's Mystery Magazine* (1952–1954), *The Saint Mystery Magazine* (1953–1967), *Creasey Mystery Magazine* (1956–1965), *Suspense* (1958–1961) and *Edgar Wallace Mystery Magazine* (1964–1970) – relied heavily on reprints and provided little space for new stories by either beginners or established names. They also found it difficult to compete with the rise in paperbacks, which provided more than enough reading material, plus the advent of television, so that by the 1970s the crime fiction magazine, especially in Britain, was becoming an anomaly. For new fiction, they have generally been superseded by the anthology market, with occasional series such as *Winter's Crimes* (1969–1992) and *Fresh Blood* (1996–1999).

There have been few magazines published since the 1970s, and those that do appear have usually been from small presses or specialist publishers. *Sherlock* (edited by David Stuart **Davies**), with the obvious emphasis on the world of Sherlock Holmes, ran from 1991 to 2005; *A Shot in the Dark*, later retitled *Shots* (edited by Mike Stotter), ran from 1994 to 2001 before converting as a webzine, while *Crime Time* (edited by Barry Forshaw) began in 1995 and continues today as both magazine and webzine. All these three magazines ran occasional fiction but focused primarily on reviews and articles covering the field. There have been many magazines produced over the years by devotees of the field that concentrate on the study of crime fiction, the best known currently active is **CADS** (edited by Geoff Bradley), which has been running since July 1985 with just two or three issues per year.

Magazines that do opt to publish short fiction have converted to webzines, and most of these are American-based. One British webzine, which shows the healthy state of crime fiction in Scotland, is *Crime Scene Scotland*, which began in April 2003 and is run by Russel D. McLean (http://www.crimescenescotland.com) though even this magazine has stopped running fiction and switched to reviews only. The future of short fiction may well rest on webzines and occasional anthologies as the magazine market in Britain has otherwise virtually ceased.

Further Reading
Cook, Michael L. 1983. *Mystery, Detective, and Espionage Magazines*. Greenwood Press.

Mike Ashley

Male Crime Writers

To the uncritical eye, crime fiction seems the most straightforwardly masculine of genres, dominated as it is by both male writers and protagonists. The act of detection itself is traditionally seen as a male occupation, an 'unsuitable job for a woman' to quote the title of P.D. **James**'s 1972 novel. Yet this is not to say that the genre casts an uncritical eye on male experience. Crime fiction has always reflected the values and concerns of the society in which it was produced, and as the position of men has changed over the course of the twentieth century, crime fiction too has evolved, with authors interrogating dominant myths of masculinity and offering new insights into the problems facing men.

The year 1887 witnessed the birth of a crime fiction legend when Arthur Conan **Doyle** published *A Study in Scarlet*, the first Sherlock **Holmes** novella. The figure of Holmes, accompanied by his trusty sidekick Dr John Watson, immediately struck a chord with Victorian readers. With his cool, detached rationality and scientific approach to his cases, Holmes seems to serve as a classic exemplar of straight-laced Victorian masculinity. Yet other less-conventional aspects of his character, such as his penchant for cocaine, reflected the more bohemian spirit of turn-of-the-century **London**. To the reader, Holmes appears as a quasi-divine figure, blessed as he is with intimidating powers of deduction and boundless egotism. Holmes's success where the state mechanisms of law and order repeatedly fail confers upon him an omnipotence that is rarely undermined (though, of course, Irene Adler does inflict a notable defeat in the 1891 story 'A Scandal in Bohemia'). Despite the popularity of his fictional creation, Conan Doyle was soon tired of crime writing and, eager to turn his literary talents elsewhere, attempted to kill Holmes off. In 'The Final Problem' (1893), Holmes and his nemesis, Professor Moriarty, plunge into Reichenbach Falls. However, not even death could stop the great **detective** for long and following a journey back into Holmes's past in *The Hound of the Baskervilles* (1902), Doyle succumbed to market forces and resurrected his hero in the 1905 story collection *The Return of Sherlock Holmes*.

In the early years of the twentieth century, Doyle's successors largely adhered to the model of detective as superhero. In *The Four Just Men* (1906), the incredibly prolific Edgar **Wallace** went even further, creating not merely one seemingly unstoppable hero but four self-appointed champions of law and order, feared internationally for their tenacious pursuit of the corrupt and criminal. In 1907, R. Austin **Freeman** published *The Red Thumb Mask*, in which he introduced his serial protagonist Dr Thorndyke, a scientist and lawyer, whose precision and pedantry owned much to Holmes. G.K. **Chesterton**, however, chose to step away from the Holmesian archetype with his detective, Father Brown. First published in 1910, Chesterton's priest employs a different approach to his cases, relying upon attributes usually typified as feminine, such as intuition and the ability to read people. Agatha **Christie** would later endow Hercule **Poirot** with similar characteristics.

When considering **Golden Age** crime fiction of the interwar years, the writers who immediately spring to mind are all female – Agatha Christie, Dorothy L. **Sayers** and Margery **Allingham**. Given that they were writing at a time of catastrophic global violence and lasting economic depression, it is unsurprising that these authors created male detectives who deviated from the superhero script. Christie's Poirot, for example, is a Belgian refugee who is fastidious about his appearance and a man of thought rather than action. Sayers's hero, Lord Peter **Wimsey**, shares Poirot's affinity for all things dapper and is further estranged from traditional male heroism by frequent bouts of shell shock. To a population traumatised by the First World War, Poirot's attention to domestic detail and Wimsey's vulnerability represented a fictional respite from the reality of male militarism. Of course, many male writers also utilised the Golden Age clue–puzzle format. E.C. **Bentley** (whose 1913 novel *Trent's Last Case* is actually cited by some as the first Golden Age text), Freeman Wills **Crofts**, Anthony Berkeley Cox and Ronald **Knox** were all popular throughout the 1920s and 1930s. Writing slightly later were John Innes Mackintosh Stewart (under the pen-name Michael **Innes**) and Robert Bruce Montgomery (again, employing a pseudonym – Edmund **Crispin**). However, none of these authors has enjoyed the longevity of their female counterparts. Standing in marked contrast to the fiction of the Golden Age is the hard-boiled school of crime writing. Although hard-boiled crime fiction is usually associated with American writers such as Dashiell Hammett and Raymond **Chandler**, the style was occasionally embraced by British authors. A notable example is *No Orchids for Miss Blandish*, written by René Raymond and published in 1939 under the tougher sounding pseudonym James Hadley **Chase**. Set in the American south, *No Orchids* is a hard-boiled text par excellence, featuring the kind of brutal violence usually absent from British crime writing of the time.

The years following the Second World War saw a movement away from fiction featuring private detectives as the **police procedural** became the dominant form. Two early and influential procedural writers were the British novelist John **Creasey** and the American novelist Ed McBain, creator of the *87th Precinct* series. In 1955, Creasey, writing as J.J. Marric, introduced Commander George Gideon of Scotland Yard. In his Gideon novels, Creasey strove for realism, depicting the routine nature of modern policing and the negative impact a career in law enforcement can have upon family life. Other, more exotic procedural writers include H.R.F. **Keating**, who wrote about Inspector Ghote of the Bombay CID, while Nicolas **Freeling** used Amsterdam as the setting for his Van der Valk novels.

The 1970s witnessed the emergence of two major procedural writers – Reginald **Hill** and Colin **Dexter**. Both are notable not only because of the strong regional detail that appears in their novels (Hill's are set in Yorkshire and Dexter's in Oxford) but also because their books hinge upon unlikely male bonding. In 1970, Hill published *A Clubbable Woman*, introducing the detectives Dalziel and Pascoe. Dalziel is a lewd glutton, resolutely lowbrow and proud of it. He is an old-fashioned copper, while Pascoe, the younger and more junior of the two, is emblematic of a more modern masculine identity. He has been to university and is capable of a tact and diplomacy that escapes the plain-speaking Dalziel. During the series, Pascoe also marries Ellie, whose feminist sensibilities cause further tension between her husband and his boss. Yet, despite their differences, Dalziel and Pascoe form an efficient team. The same can be said of Dexter's protagonists – the gloomy, crossword-loving, real-ale aficionado Inspector Morse, and Lewis, his long-suffering side-kick. First featured in *Last Bus to Woodstock* (1975), Morse initially displays nothing but contempt for his grammatically challenged junior officer. However, as the series progresses, it becomes clear that there is a deep, if unspoken, bond between the two. This becomes particularly obvious in *Death Is Now My Neighbour* (1997), in which Morse is hospitalised because of diabetes – it is a hallmark of the great detective that he is incapable of taking good care of himself. A visit from Lewis leaves Morse feeling 'unmanned' by gratitude. Rather than expressing his feelings of camaraderie to Lewis's face, Morse sends him an affectionate postcard when he has recovered. One less palatable aspect of Dexter's novels is Morse's sexism. Downplayed in the television adaptation, in which Morse is depicted as a sensitive and slightly ascetic intellectual, the novels are replete with examples of Morse acting like a dirty old man. Dalziel, too, is notable for his less-than-enlightened attitude towards women; but this is counterbalanced by the more equitable Pascoe. One writer who shunned the procedural format is Dick **Francis**. A former jockey, Francis published his first crime novel, *Dead Cert*, in 1962, setting it against the backdrop of the horse-racing world. Since then he has written almost forty novels yet rarely employs the same protagonist from one text to another.

In recent years, British crime fiction has been dominated by authors from Scotland, with writers such as Christopher **Brookmyre**, Paul **Johnston**, Philip **Kerr** and William **McIlvanney** proving both critically and commercially popular. Both Kerr and Johnston have set novels in the not-too-distant future. Kerr's *A Philosophical Investigation* (1992) is a particularly interesting text. In Kerr's vision of the future, it has become possible to identify criminals before they perpetrate their crimes, and he considers the implications of this in a compelling story that is only slightly compromised by its unconvincing hard-boiled heroine.

A writer whose work is resolutely based in the here and now is Ian **Rankin**, the leading exponent of what has been dubbed 'Tartan Noir'. Between 1987 and 2007, Rankin published seventeen novels and two short-story collections featuring the Edinburgh-based policeman John **Rebus**. Rebus is in many ways the typical contemporary detective hero – estranged from his family and sustained by a combination of hard work and harder drinking. With little regard for his career, Rebus demonstrates pathological insubordination and a burning need to uncover the truth no matter how potentially compromising. In this respect, Rebus's character-isation owes much to the American hard-boiled formula. The violence to which Rankin subjects his protagonist also echoes the hard-boiled model. The mid-series novels *Black and Blue* (1997) and *The Hanging Garden* (1998) are particularly notable for the litany of physical and mental abuse endured by Rebus, which includes repeated beatings, the death of his best friend and a near-fatal accident involving his daughter. This capacity to endure is a key facet of Rebus's characterisation – his masculinity is contingent upon a masochistic willingness to embrace any form of suffering. A hard man who has turned his aggression inwards (although at times he is also happy to vent it on others), Rebus is representative of a dying breed; a man of independent thought and action who is being sidelined by the increasing feminisation of modern policing, with its emphasis on networking, press liaison skills and bureaucracy. Perhaps it is no surprise then that Rebus's metaphorical successor is therefore a woman – Siobhan Clarke. If the police force is becoming too feminised for a real man such as Rebus, then it makes sense that a woman might be on safer ground. Rankin being one of the few contemporary male crime writers to convinc-ingly portray a female character, it remains to be seen whether he will return to Siobhan Clarke now that Rebus has officially retired. Aside from the character of Rebus, Rankin's novels are of interest because of their political agenda. A range of international and domestic issues appear in Rankin's work, from immigration and third-world poverty to Scottish devolution. In contrast to the socially conscious work of Rankin is that of Alexander McCall **Smith**, one of Scotland's other top-selling crime writers. Smith writes gentle, escapist fables, set in Botswana and featuring the amateur detective Mma Precious Ramotswe. As such, Smith's popularity is something of an anomaly within the framework of contemporary **Scottish crime fiction**.

It remains the case that British crime writers, men perhaps more than women, struggle to keep up with American counterparts. The American continent is kind to crime writers. It is vast. Within striking distance of any American, no matter how urbanised, lie great tracts of unoccupied lonely countryside; many small towns are isolated; the police and justice systems are fragmented and corruptible; many people, especially single men, live transient lives – and above all, Americans carry guns. Britain's women writers, if they are affected by America at all, follow the Patricia Cornwell lead and make their heroines forensic scientists, psychologists or profilers – though these women writers keep their British hero in a British milieu. Many male writers – certainly most of the successful – do the same. But a number follow the lead of wartime quasi-Americans like Peter Cheyney and James Hadley Chase, setting their tough guy heroes against armed hoodlums in Britain's mean city streets. These stories struggle to be credible. No one pretends Britain does not have its mean streets, nor that we do not have armed hoodlums, but to rival America on this ground is like setting Manchester United against a team from the Corinthian League: both teams play football, but between them there is no contest. If British men want to write such stories they would be advised go to America, as did John Connolly and above all, Lee Child. For the rest, the great majority of extremely able British writers who stay here, the best will always be those who exploit not just their masculinity but their Britishness. *See also* Academe, Death in; Clerical Crime; Feminist Readings in British Crime Fiction; Gay and Lesbian Crime Fiction; The Great Detectives: Sherlock Holmes, Hercule Poirot, Lord Peter Wimsey; Pulp; Sexuality in British Crime Fiction; Thrillers: Novels of Action; *and* Women Crime Writers.

Susan Massey

Mann, Jessica (b.1937)

Now in her fourth decade of crime writing, Jessica Mann has a wide range of subjects and characters. Her only real series characters have been the archaeologist-cum-amateur detective Tamara Hoyland (first encountered in *Funeral Sites*, 1981), who appeared in half a dozen books, and the more recent Dr Fidelis Berlin, a psychiatrist who debuted in *A Private Inquiry* (1996). Mann has written numerous fine stand-alone crime novels as well as works of non-fiction. Despite her large output, she has several other lives, as a broadcaster, a critic, a planning inspector, chairperson of various public committees and an advisor to the National Health Service.

66. Jessica Mann.

Mann's active life beyond writing informs and enriches her crime fiction. She is an active member of groups such as PEN, the **Crime Writers' Association**, the Detection Club, the Society of Authors, Forum UK, Hypatia Trust and **Mystery**

Women. She holds two university degrees: one in archaeology from Cambridge and another in law from Leicester University. She has novels set in Edinburgh and others at the opposite end of the country in Cornwall, both being places where she lived for some years. Other books are set in **London**. Her knowledge of university life and of the world of archaeology is put to frequent and skilled use.

Mann's first book was *A Charitable End* (1971), which surprised some with its far from charitable exposé of goings-on inside a Scottish charity. She followed this with another non-series book, *Mrs Knox's Profession* (1972), before presaging her Tamara Hoyland series with *The Only Security* (1973), a book which introduced Tamara's tutor, Thea Crawford, recently appointed professor of archaeology at Edinburgh. Crawford might have inspired a series in her own right, but in the event, there were only two Crawford books, and Tamara herself did not branch out in her own story until 1981 with *Funeral Sites*. Crawford, though, was the initiator of Tamara's second adventure in the follow-up, *No Man's Island* (1983), an adventure indeed, with the plucky Hoyland despatched to a remote British island as an undercover agent in a murky dispute between islanders and the government for the island's oil. The archaeological slant continued through titles such as *A Kind of Healthy Grave* (1986) and *Death beyond the Nile* (1988).

Mann may be happier outside the series straightjacket. Stories such as *The Sting of Death* (1978) and *Funeral Sites* allowed her to explore the tensions in provincial towns. Recent books have explored Cornwall, her new home, and her penetrating study of five British fe**male crime writers**, *Deadlier than the Male* (1981), remains of interest. Her book *The Mystery Writer* (2005), despite its title, is a work of fiction. Another good example of her non-series work can be found in *Out of Harm's Way* (2005), telling of the wartime evacuation of children out of London. *See also* Women Crime Writers.

Selected Works by the Author

Thea Crawford Series
Captive Audience (1975)

Tamara Hoyland Series
Funeral Sites (1981)
Faith, Hope and Homicide (1991)

Fidelis Berlin Series
The Voice from the Grave (2005)

Non-Series Novels
Mrs Knox's Profession (1972)
The Sting of Death (1978)
Out of Harm's Way (2005)

Russell James

Markstein, George (1929–1987)

The author of several adroitly written (and moderately successful) spy thrillers, George Markstein's chiefly contributed to the **espionage** genre as co-creator of the cult ITC television series *The Prisoner* (1967).

Markstein was born in Berlin in 1929, and his family emigrated to England shortly before the Second World War. He became a crime reporter in the early 1950s, later serving as a military correspondent in Europe with links to British Intelligence. It was here that he discovered a remote 'safe haven' for retired secret agents – Inverlair Lodge in Scotland – which formed the basis for both the television series *The Prisoner* and his 1974 novel *The Cooler*.

While acting as script consultant on the final two episodes of the literate and intelligent espionage series *Danger Man* (1960–1968), Markstein mentioned the lodge to the series' star, Patrick McGoohan, who thought it would make an excellent premise for a new show. Quitting *Danger Man* after only two colour episodes were made of what would have been its fourth season, McGoohan set Markstein up as co-creator and story editor of *Danger Man*'s loose sequel, *The Prisoner*. The Scottish prison-cum-retirement home became The Village, an unknown location (although by the final episode it appeared to be just off the A20 in Kent), while the shadowy figure of its leader, No. 1, would remain cryptic until the very end.

Markstein had the honour of appearing in almost every episode of the series as the bald, bespectacled man to whom McGoohan throws down his resignation letter at the start of the programme's title sequence. However, after eleven episodes, Markstein quit the show, citing creative differences with the increasingly egocentric McGoohan. Following his departure, the series descended into evermore bizarre storylines culminating in a deliberately inconclusive finale, which the author later described as 'an absurd pantomime'.

For his first novel, *The Cooler* (1974), Markstein presented a fictionalised account of Inverlair, here renamed Inverloch, setting his story in the run-up to D-Day and featuring the undercover activities of the Special Operations Executive, a covert organisation that ran the real-life Inverlair during the Second World War; a later novel, *Ferret* (1983), hinted at American and Russian equivalents.

Other novels included *Tara Kane* (1978), a lively adventure set during the American gold rush of the 1890s, and the Cold War KGB thriller *Traitor for a Cause* (1979). Markstein also worked on the television series *Special Branch* (1969–1974) and *Callan* (1967–1972) and co-wrote screenplays for the films *Robbery* (1967), a gritty dramatisation of the Great Train Robbery, and *The Odessa File* (1974), based on the book by Frederick **Forsyth**.

He died on 15 January 1987.

Selected Works by the Author
The Cooler (1974)
Tara Kane (1978)
Traitor for a Cause (1979)
Ferret (1983)

Mark Campbell

Marlowe, Derek (1938–1996)

In the Golden Age of English **espionage fiction**, which began with Ian **Fleming**'s *Casino Royale* (1953) and bloomed in the 1960s with Len **Deighton** and John **le Carré**, there are some maverick figures whose stars burned brightly for a time before dimming or altogether disappearing. One of these is Derek Marlowe.

He was born in 1938 and educated at London University. He was a playwright, adapting Gorky for the Royal Shakespeare Company, and later a scriptwriter, with novel writing occupying the space between. In the mid-1970s, Marlowe moved to Los Angeles and concentrated more on film and television work than on prose fiction. He died in California in 1996.

Marlowe's best-known and most successful novel was his first, *A Dandy in Aspic* (1966). Alexander Eberlin, the dandy of the title, is a Russian plant working for British Intelligence. He is given the task of disposing of a top Soviet assassin called Krasnevin, in reality himself. The hall-of-mirrors consequences were already familiar from *The Spy Who Came in from the Cold* (1963) and *The Ipcress File* (1962), to which *Dandy* makes a couple of knowing references; however, whereas le Carré and Deighton aimed for gritty realism and hip realism, respectively, Marlowe turned the spy game into baroque absurdity. Hypocrisy and double-crossing are less important than Eberlin's suits and his Wildean witticisms. *A Dandy in Aspic*, which was filmed with the reliably cold Laurence Harvey in the lead in 1968, is possibly the only spy novel of the period in which the anti-hero is trying to get over the Berlin Wall in the wrong direction, west to east.

The elevation of the hit man into a contemporary Everyman continued in *Echoes of Celandine* (1970), republished as *The Disappearance* in 1977. The story of an assassin who is engaged on a multiple search for his wife, his paymaster and an elusive target, *Echoes of Celandine* is a study of identity and ambiguity rather than a traditional thriller with an ending which blurs things more than it clarifies. Another homage was made in *Somebody's Sister* (1974), although this time to Raymond **Chandler** instead of the spy thriller. Failing private eye Walter Brackett investigates the death of a young girl in a car crash on the Golden Gate Bridge and uncovers suspects who include the girl's middle-aged lover as well as his partner, a pensioned-off detective in a Rest Home. It is characteristic of Marlowe's subversion of form that the novel is set in San Francisco rather than Los Angeles and that Brackett should be English and not an American.

Marlowe was a consciously intellectual writer, and there is a literary strain to his work. One of his best books is *A Single Summer with L.B.* (1969), a re-creation of the moment when Lord Byron was holidaying with Shelley and other friends on the shores of Lake Geneva, and another non-genre work is the characteristically languorous *Do You Remember England?* (1972). Sometimes disdainful of the constraints of the thriller or suspense format, Derek Marlowe produced material that was mannered, flamboyant and idiosyncratic. He does not deserve to be forgotten. *See also* Literature and Crime Fiction.

Selected Works by the Author
A Dandy in Aspic (1966)
A Single Summer with L.B. (1969)
Echoes of Celandine (1970; later reissued under the title *The Disappearance*)
Do You Remember England? (1972)
Somebody's Sister (1974)

Philip Gooden

Marple, Jane

The quintessential, cosy English spinster, village sleuth Miss Jane Marple was the brainchild of Agatha **Christie** in 1927 – her fourth detective series following Poirot in 1920, Tommy and Tuppence Beresford in 1921, and the stories of Harley Quinn in 1924. Miss Marple's popularity equalled, if not eclipsed, that of the famous Belgian policeman, despite featuring in far fewer stories.

Aimed squarely at a female readership, Marple was inspired by a number of sources. First, the character of Caroline Sheppard in *The Murder of Roger Ackroyd* (1926), 'an acidulated spinster, full of curiosity, knowing everything, hearing everything – the complete detective in the home'. Secondly, Miss Amelia Butterworth, the spinster detective created by Anna Katharine Green (1846–1935) and introduced in *That Affair Next Door* (1897). Thirdly, a composite of her grandmother, who always saw the worst side of human nature, and her 'Ealing cronies' – old ladies she met in many different villages she visited as a child. In her autobiography, Christie says, 'Miss Marple was born at the age of sixty-five to seventy – which, as with Poirot, proved unfortunate because she was going to have to last a long time in my life.'

Miss Marple first appeared in a series of stories called 'The Tuesday Night Club' in *The Royal Magazine* during 1927–1928, and these formed the basis of the collection *The Thirteen Problems* (1932). Her first book appearance was in *The Murder at the Vicarage* (1930), although her presence is not really felt until the end. Described by her friend Dolly Bantry as 'the typical old maid of fiction' (*The Thirteen Problems*), Marple was an elderly spinster who lived most of her life in St Mary Mead, a village about 25 miles from London. She is first described as wearing 'a black brocade dress…black lace mittens, and a black lace cap [which] surmounted the piled-up masses of her snowy hair' (*The Thirteen Problems*). Her later appearance is toned down to a less-stern 'white-haired old lady with a gentle, appealing manner' (*The Murder at the Vicarage*, 1930).

67. Joan Hickson as Miss Marple in *A Pocketful of Rye* (BBC Television, 1985).

From the vantage point of her much-loved garden, Marple can see everything that goes on around her and considers herself an amateur sleuth of some distinction – although prior to her first murder case, she has only solved mundane puzzles, among them the disappearance of a gill of pickled shrimps and the theft of the Church Boys' outing money by the organist! But she is confident that she can solve more serious mysteries by extrapolating on her experience of village life. To this end, she quotes a saying of her Great Aunt Fanny: 'The young people think the old people are fools; but the old people *know* the young people are fools!' Although Radfordshire's Chief Constable Melchet has a different view: 'I really believe that wizened-up old maid thinks she knows everything there is to know. And hardly been out of this village all her life. Preposterous. What can she know of life?' (*The Murder at the Vicarage*).

When Marple solves her first case, she is quite happy that the honour goes to the abrasive Inspector Slack – like Sherlock **Holmes**, her place is behind the scenes. Sir Henry Clithering, ex-commissioner of Scotland Yard, says of her: 'She's just the finest detective God ever made. Natural genius cultivated in a suitable soil'. She is also a tough nut – of a murderer she declares, 'I feel quite pleased to think of [him] being hanged' (*The Body in the Library*, 1942). Concerning her unerring ability to be in the thick of things, she admits, 'I have never read books on criminology as a subject or really been interested in such a thing. No, it has just happened that I have found myself in the vicinity of murder rather more often than would seem normal.'

As to her age, when she investigates a murder on a train for her friend Mrs McGillicuddy (*4.50 From Paddington*, 1957), she claims to be nearly ninety, but despite this decrepitude, she slips 'with incredible swiftness' from a villain's grasp. In a later case, *The Mirror Crack'd from Side to Side* (1962), she has suffered a fall and is taking things easy – until a murder occurs. By this time, she is too elderly to do anything in her garden other than 'a little light pruning' and remembers fondly when her eyesight was good and she could keep an eye on the village goings-on.

Marple is much perkier on a Caribbean holiday paid for by her nephew, the writer Raymond West (*A Caribbean Mystery*, 1964). Even at her advanced age, she gets round easily and thinks nothing of sneaking through a flowerbed to eavesdrop on a suspect. Another trip, to an old-fashioned London hotel (*At Bertram's Hotel*, 1965), seems to rejuvenate her even more, and by the time of her penultimate case (*Nemesis*, 1971), she has apparently discovered the elixir of life, as she is now 'seventy if she is a day – nearer eighty perhaps' – a decade younger than in 1957!

Marple's final recorded case (*Sleeping Murder*, 1976) has all the hallmarks of being a flashback to the 1940s. The years have rolled away, and she is described as 'an attractive old lady, tall and thin, with pink cheeks and blues eyes and a gentle, rather fussy manner'. Once she has successfully closed the case, we can imagine this more youthful Jane Marple going on to solve many more puzzling mysteries.

Her life beyond the confines of the written word has been largely dominated by two actresses: Margaret Rutherford (1892–1972) and Joan Hickson (1906–1998). In four black-and-white films made by MGM, rotund comedy actress Rutherford was arguably miscast as a dotty version of Miss Marple in stories that played down the 'whodunit' element of the novels and upped the humorous content. *Murder She Said* (1961) was a loose version of *4.50 From Paddington*, while *Murder Ahoy!* (1964) was a weak comedy that has the distinction of being the only television programme or film to date that is *not* based on an original Christie work. *Murder at the Gallop* (1963) and *Murder Most Foul* (1964) were, bizarrely, based on Poirot novels *After the Funeral* (1953) and *Mrs McGinty's Dead* (1952), respectively.

It was not until 1984 that fans were treated to a far more authentic piece of casting, with the BBC's sumptuous adaptations of all twelve Marple novels (although not in chronological order) starring the redoubtable Joan Hickson. Seventy-eight years old in her first outing, *The Body in the Library* (1984), Hickson was immediately hailed as the ideal Marple by many viewers. (Indeed, in 1946, while appearing in Christie's play *Appointment with Death*, the author had sent Hickson a note saying that she hoped the actress would one day play her 'dear Miss Marple'.) Filmed on location in a variety of authentic English villages and country houses and featuring a gamut of excellent actors and actresses, the series was an enormous success and is still considered by many to be a benchmark for future adaptations. The production team even decamped to Barbados to provide an authentic backdrop for *A Caribbean Mystery* in 1989.

American actress Helen Hayes portrayed the character in two workmanlike 1980s films, while the recent ITV series *Marple* (2004–present) features Geraldine McEwan as a rather mannered detective with unwonted lesbian undertones in a series that attempted to modernise Christie's storytelling but ended up being panned mercilessly by the critics. *See also* The Detective in British Fiction; Feminist Readings in British Crime Fiction; Gay and Lesbian Crime Fiction; The Shires: Rural England and Regional Crime Fiction; *and* Women Crime Writers.

Further Reading
Hart, Anne. 1985. *The Life and Times of Miss Jane Marple*. Dodd, Mead.

Mark Campbell

Marsh, Ngaio (1895–1982)

A superb practitioner of classic country-house (or theatre) mysteries, Ngaio Marsh produced, in her long career, a fascinating range of work with gentlemen detectives and monstrous divas, all struggling to come to terms with modernity.

68. Ngaio Marsh (right) and Agatha Christie (left) meet at a party at the Savoy Hotel, June 1960.

Born in New Zealand of British descent, Marsh had an extraordinary dual career in twentieth-century arts. In her native country, she is remembered as an important pioneer in the theatre, whereas in England she is known as an enthusiast for upper-class living and author of **Golden Age** detective fiction. With Agatha **Christie**, Dorothy L. **Sayers** and Margery **Allingham**, Marsh is sometimes known as one of the four queens of crime. Like the other three, her work is more complex and socially ambivalent than suggested by the simple allegation of conservatism.

In the first place, some of Marsh's most startling fictions bring the two parts of her life together: they are set either in the theatre or among actors outside it. Novels such as *Opening Night* (1951), *False Scent* (1960) and *Death at the Dolphin* (1967) present identity itself as theatrical and mutable. It does not really require the outrageous performances of the Lamprey family in *Surfeit of Lampreys* (1941) to show that with all the fascination with the glamour of class, Marsh is also showing its capacity for hollowness and deceit as the family manipulate their secret codes to obstruct the law.

Perhaps we should look to Marsh's series detective, Chief Inspector Roderick Alleyn, for a true gauge of her attitude towards the leisured class whose decline she maps with regret. Alleyn has a fortunate heritage. With a name derived from Shakespeare's famous actor, he is the second son of a baronet. Looking like a cross between a monk and a grandee, Alleyn rarely acts. A characteristic of the books is a series of interviews of suspects. Alleyn is fastidious and apart, refusing to compromise his self. He embodies frail motif underpinning the social order with metaphysical value. His unshakeable relationship with his lower-class subordinate, Inspector Fox, is a metonym for solidarity between the classes, while all about them is the chaos of murder. At a mythical level, Marsh's plots call upon Alleyn and Fox to turn the chaos of violence and desire into a blood sacrifice to the status quo. Like Christie's novels, the success of this narrative form is often symbolised by a romance among the suspects. While this is reversion to myth in an attempt to resist social change, Alleyn, Fox and Alleyn's wife, Agatha Troy, are distinguished by their social responsibilities beyond their own class. It is Alleyn's conception of his *job* that is a key ingredient of his metaphysical qualities. A close look at Marsh's reveals that the gentry are in decline unless they take up the professions.

The most naked version of the conversion of murder into a ritual purging of disruptive desires is *Off with His Head* (1957). Here, a mummer's play, described as a pagan pre-Christian fertility rite, becomes both the means of murder and its detection. Aged William Anderson and his five sons regularly perform the 'Dance of the Five Sons', at the dead of winter in a village stubbornly clinging to a semi-feudal past. Modernity threatens the social order, partly because the sons want to turn old William's forge into a garage and because William's long-lost granddaughter, Camilla, is beloved by the Squire's heir, Ralph Mardian. Old William stands implacably opposed to modernity in both forms. Marsh, on the other hand, is prepared to suggest that an over-investment in the past can be lethal. In the play, the old man is beheaded and rises again. But this time he does not rise again, for the beheading was real. However, Alleyn decides to complete the ritual, on the one hand to discover the killer, and on the other hand, to symbolically incorporate the dead man into a sacrifice to ensure the fertility of the present. So Alleyn fulfils his namesake by re-staging the ritual. When a figure rises from 'death', the killer is discovered and the resurgence of life ensured. Indeed, the culprit was the one who refused to *respect* the past in grasping for social change. The still deferential sons will get their garage, and Camilla is free to marry Ralph.

Marsh is also noted for her treatment of colonial identity and of sexuality, particularly in relation to 'acting the part'. Several of Marsh's works take Alleyn to New Zealand, especially during the Second World War. A novel that unites the theme of the female colonial with the exploration of sexuality in almost explicitly Freudian terms is *Opening Night* (1951). Marsh mentions Freud in several novels. Here, a New Zealander with a gender-ambiguous name, Martyn Tarne, is destitute in London. She is taken on as a dresser by the Dolphin theatre where her resemblance to the leading man, Adam Poole, is so striking that many believe her to be his child. Eventually, she admits to being both his cousin and an actress. She gains the crucial role of a perverted version of Adam himself in the current production. Murder fractures Martyn's progress towards self-hood in the *mirror* of Adam, the pool. However, in the end, it is as Adam's lover, not daughter, that she will forge an erotic attachment to adult identity in her world.

Martyn resembles all of Marsh's women who are successful in love. She has intelligence, sensibility, a reticence about sexuality and a job. The ur-type of these figures is Alleyn's wife who shuns Alleyn's passion for several novels. There is a counter-type, a diva, who is greedy for lovers and is frequently punished by death. Marsh's stories support professional women but tend to punish the overtly sexual. *See also* Sexuality in British Crime Fiction.

Selected Works by the Author
A Man Lay Dead (1934)
Enter a Murderer (1935)
Artists in Crime (1938)
Death in a White Tie (1938)
Death at the Bar (1940)
Surfeit of Lampreys (1941; also published in the United States as *Death of a Peer*)
Death and the Dancing Footman (1942)
Off with His Head (1957; also published in the United States as *Death of a Fool*)
Photo-Finish (1980)

Further Reading
Acheson, Carole. 1985. 'Cultural Ambivalence: Ngaio Marsh's New Zealand Detective Fiction'. *Journal of Popular Culture* 19/2: 159–174.
Lewis, Margaret. 1991. *Ngaio Marsh: A Life*. Chatto & Windus.
Rahn, B.J. 1995. 'Ngaio Marsh: The Detective Novelist of Manners'. *The Armchair Detective* 28/2: 140–147.
Reilly, John M., ed. 1980. *Twentieth-Century Crime and Mystery Writers*. Macmillan.
Rowland, Susan. 2001. *From Agatha Christie to Ruth Rendell*. Palgrave.

Susan Rowland

Marshall, Michael (b.1965)

Michael Marshall's output as a highly successful thriller writer is only half the story; under his full name of Michael Marshall Smith, he has also penned award-winning science fiction novels and many horror/fantasy short stories.

Michael Marshall Smith was born on 3 May 1965 in the small Cheshire town of Knutsford. His early childhood was spent in America, South Africa and Australia, before his family moved back to England in 1973. He read philosophy and social and political science at King's College, Cambridge, where he also became involved with the famous Cambridge Footlights revue show, touring the United Kingdom in 1987 and America the following year. Under the name 'Michael Rutger', he was a writer-performer on BBC Radio 4 comedy *And Now in Colour* (1990–1991), as part of a group originally called 'The Throbbs'.

While working as a graphic designer in the early 1990s, Smith discovered Stephen King and began writing horror and fantasy stories, most of them with a noir twist, and was three times winner of the coveted British Fantasy Award for Best Short Story. His first novel, *Only Forward* (1994), a freewheeling satire on futuristic city life, won the August Derleth Award for Best Novel and later the Philip K. Dick Award in 2000. His short stories have since appeared in numerous horror anthologies.

Citing James Lee Burke and Jim Thompson as literary influences, Smith's fifth novel, *The Straw Men* (2001), marked a change in genre from fantasy to crime, although still with a surreal bent. Dropping his last name, partly to avoid confusion with a similarly titled book by a similarly named author, Smith successfully broke into the crime market on both sides of the Atlantic with an elaborate thriller that combined a hunt for a vicious serial killer with an *X Files*-style conspiracy plot of global proportions.

A sequel, *The Lonely Dead*, appeared three years later. Ward Hopkins and other surviving characters from *The Straw Men* reappeared, as did the titular mysterious organisation at the centre of Smith's conspiracy. This time, events revolved around a serial killer called the Upright Man with further revelations trickling through about the Straw Men manifesto and its effect on mankind.

The trilogy was completed in 2005 with *Blood of Angels*. Hopkins and his ally John Zandt returned, along with the Upright Man, in a story that once more hinged on corruption and conspiracy deep within the heart of the American government.

Characteristic of all three books is a subject close to Smith's heart: the nature of evil and how it impinges on everybody, no matter how 'normal' their upbringing. Violent scenes are therefore de rigueur, although his sharply crafted psychological horror is often more frightening. He lives in North London and continues to divide his writings into mainstream modern thrillers and morbid tales of esoteric horror. *See also* Tartan Noir *and* Pulp.

Selected Works by the Author

As Michael Marshall
The Straw Men (2001)
The Lonely Dead (2004, also published in the United States as *The Upright Man*)
Blood of Angels (2005)
The Intruders (2007)

As Michael Marshall Smith
Only Forward (1994)
Spares (1996)
One of Us (1997)

Website
www.michaelmarshallsmith.com

Mark Campbell

Marston, Edward (b.1940)

Edward Marston is the best-known pseudonym of the talented Welsh-born author Keith Miles, second only to Paul **Doherty** as the most prolific writer of historical crime novels.

After earning a BA with honours at Oxford University in 1962 (and an MA in 1964), Miles became a lecturer in modern history. He also served as a drama lecturer at Winsom Green Prison before becoming a full-time author and playwright in 1965. He contributed to the television series *Crime Buster* in 1968 about an investigative sports journalist. During the 1970s, he wrote many plays for BBC Radio including a series featuring Bow Street Runner Ben Spiggott. None of these plays has been published, though the first story, which later became a play, was included in his story collection *Murder Ancient and Modern* (2005).

Miles's earliest books covered a variety of subjects from the popular British radio soap opera *The Archers* to various sports; he also wrote a series of children's books. His first crime novel, *Bullet Hole* (1986) as Keith Miles, was also sport-related and featured a professional golfer, Alan Saxon, who encounters murder at St Andrews. The series ran to six books in total, the last two not appearing until 2002 and 2003. Another book was reworked as *Stone Dead* (1991) to feature Don Hawker, an athlete turned reporter who also encounters sporting crimes. This book and its sequel, *Touch Play* (1991), appeared under the pseudonym Martin Inigo.

Miles continued to produce a remarkable stream of books – including ones for children featuring sporting crimes – and plays, but he eventually brought together his fascination for theatre and history with the Nicholas Bracewell series which began with *The Queen's Head* (1988) and marked the first appearance of the Marston byline. Bracewell is a former sailor who now manages one of the leading theatre companies in Elizabethan England, Lord Westfield's Men. Far from a quiet life, the company is frequently menaced by rivals, political intrigue or even internal sabotage and it is invariably left to Bracewell to resolve the problems. The series has reached sixteen volumes as of 2007. The seventh book, *The Roaring Boy* (1995), was shortlisted for the Edgar Award.

For his next series, Miles went back to the years following the Norman Conquest when King William, determined to tax England thoroughly, ordered a complete survey of all land and property – the *Domesday Book*. Starting with *The Wolves of Savernake* (1993), Marston chronicles the work of Norman soldier Ralph Delchard and the Breton-Saxon lawyer Gervase Bret as they work their way across England, following up irregularities identified by the survey and inevitably encountering resistance and all manner of crimes. The series reached its eleventh volume with *The Elephants of Norwich* (2000).

Miles's third historical series was set during the restoration of the monarchy under Charles II in the 1660s. *The King's Evil* (1999) introduces Christopher Redmayne, a young architect with royalist sympathies, who has returned to England after the Great Fire of London to help rebuild the city. He befriends a local constable, Jonathan Bale, whose Puritan views have him convinced that the fire was a purge to cleanse London of its corruption. Unfortunately, as Redmayne's work discovers, corruption is still rife. The series reached its sixth book with *The Painted Lady* (2007).

Not content with three concurrent series, Miles began three more. Under the pseudonym Conrad Allen, he commenced a series featuring murders upon famous ships in the years of the great liners starting with *Murder on the Lusitania* (2000). They feature American George Dillman, a former actor who works as a private detective for the Cunard and other shipping lines. In the first novel, Dillman encounters a young English woman Genevieve Masefield who ends up becoming his partner. The eighth book in the series is *Murder on the Celtic* (2007).

The next series has so far seen only two titles, *Murder in Perspective* (1997) and *Saint's Rest* (1999). They feature Welsh architect Merlin Richards who, inspired by Frank Lloyd Wright, travels to America to fulfil his dreams, but murder soon intrudes upon his designs. Miles's most recent series began with *The Railway Detective* (2004). It is set at the dawn of the railway age in the 1850s and features former barrister turned police detective Inspector Robert Colbeck. *The Iron Horse* (2007) is the fourth book in the series.

In all of these series, Miles shows a remarkable creativity, with an eye for detail, and is able to bring authenticity to each period together with a degree of satirical introspection and light-hearted farce when needed. As J. Kingston Pierce observed in *January Magazine*, 'Keith Miles is one of the most consistently enjoyable and innovative historical mystery writers working today.'

Selected Works by the Author
The Queen's Head (1988)
The Lions of the North (1996)
The Fair Maid of Bohemia (1997)
The Amorous Nightingale (2000)
Murder on the Mauretania (as Conrad Allen, 2001)
The Excursion Train (2005)

Further Reading
Pierce, J. Kingston. 1999. 'The Many Roles of Keith Miles'. *January Magazine*, http://januarymagazine.com/profiles/miles.html.
Stotter, Mike. 'Keith Miles, Is He Going off the Rails'. *Shots Magazine*, www.shotsmag.co.uk/interviews2005/keith_miles/kmiles.html.

Website
www.edwardmarston.com/

Mike Ashley

Martin, Andrew (b.1962)

Andrew Martin's first novel, *Bilton* (1998), was a satire on lifestyle journalism set in the near future and quite unlike his subsequent work. He turned to crime with his second book, *The Bobby Dazzlers* (2001), which concerned a gang of young burglars getting up to various sordid activities against the beautiful medieval backdrop of Martin's native city, York. In 2002, he began the series of period-set thrillers which established his signature style. These were set on the railways in Edwardian times with a vivid evocation of period and locale.

The Necropolis Railway (2002) had a factual basis in that there really had been a line of that name, along which dead bodies were carried from London to Brookwood cemetery in Surrey. The carriages were pulled slowly through the vast Necropolis, the dead being deposited at stations within the cemetery according to religious denomination. Martin inserted into this strangest of all railway operations a young, decent, gauche, aspirant railwayman from the north of England, Jim Stringer. The book was very well received and commended as outstandingly atmospheric. Martin followed this up with the equally adroit *The Blackpool Highflyer* (2004), in which Stringer is firing engines carrying holiday makers from the mill towns of West Yorkshire to the garish seaside resort of Blackpool. In *The Lost Luggage Porter* (2006), Stringer has become a railway policeman based at York station. He infiltrates a gang of safecrackers, operating at night (and usually in the rain) in the vast railway territories that once surrounded York. With the formula satisfyingly established, Martin's *Murder at Deviation Junction* (2007) tackled the mystery of the disappearance of a whole carriage-load of prosperous men.

Jim Stringer grows up during the series but retains his decency and his occasional naivety. As a detective, he does his best, but he is not always able to wrap things up neatly. A strength of the books, atmosphere aside, is the characterisation, especially that of Jim and his ambitious wife, generally referred to, in the north of England manner, simply as 'the wife'. It should be emphasised that the books are about people rather than trains, and more than one reviewer has pointed that you do not need to be a railway aficionado to enjoy them. *See also* Historical Crime.

Selected Works by the Author
Bilton (1998)
The Bobby Dazzlers (2001)
The Necropolis Railway (2002)
The Blackpool Highflyer (2004)
The Lost Luggage Porter (2006)
Murder at Deviation Junction (2007)
Death on a Branch Line (2008)

Barry Forshaw

Mason, A[lfred] E[dward] W[oodley] (1865–1948)

An outstandingly popular writer of his day, Mason wrote historical fiction, adventure, espionage, thrillers and crime fiction featuring Inspector Gabriel Hanaud of the Paris Sûreté.

Towards the end of his life, he quoted Peter Pan, saying that 'to die will be an awfully big adventure'. However that notion turned out for him, it cannot be doubted that adventure played a big part in his life. At different times, he was an actor with a travelling company, a member of parliament and, in the Great War, a secret agent; he was a crack shot, keen mountaineer, yachtsman and clubman and a great traveller. His literary output reflects this love of adventure. Some of his adventure novels are historical, including the spy story *Fire over England* (1937), set in Elizabethan times, while others, such as the popular *The Four Feathers* (1902), are not, and it seems clear that his crime fiction is but an extension of his adventurousness. Not all these are classic detective stories: *A Romance of Wastdale* (1895), set in the Lake District; *Running Water* (1907), his mountaineering thriller; *The Witness for the Defence* (1912), originally a play; *The Summons* (1920), which in part relives Mason's secret service; *The Dean's Elbow* (1929), Mason's yachting novel and marginally 'crime'; *The Sapphire* (1933); and most notably, *No Other Tiger* (1927), one of the finest thrillers in the English language, which moves swiftly from Burma to London and ends in the south of France.

Mason's series detective, Inspector Gabriel Hanaud, does not figure largely in any of these, although he nearly made his debut in *Running Water* and does make a sparkling cameo appearance in *The Sapphire* (his sidekick, the dilettante retired tea merchant Julius Ricardo, also appears in *No Other Tiger*). Hanaud's recorded cases comprise two short stories and five novels published between 1910 and 1946. Despite this long span – and the action of the last of them, *The House in Lordship*

Lane (1946), is stated to be pre-1939 – he never seems to age or, despite his flair and ability, be promoted; maybe his employers found him too independent a spirit and frowned on his encouraging the culprit in *The Prisoner in the Opal* (1928) to commit suicide.

Mason has told how he took elements from two real cases to assist the plot of Hanaud's first recorded case, *At the Villa Rose* (1910), set in Aix in the Savoy Alps. A wealthy widow is murdered, her young (English) companion is missing and a trusted servant is found bound and chloroformed. Has the companion committed the murder? An admirer says no, and he persuades Hanaud, who is on holiday, to take up the case, which moves to Geneva for the dénouement. The whodunit is a surprise; another surprise is that his revelation comes little more than halfway through the book, thus affording a much-expanded 'clearing-up' section, well-handled by Mason, though one is glad he did not repeat the experiment. Hanaud, despite a moment of carelessness when he allows a key witness to be murdered under his nose, is splendid – police routine allied to (French) flair. His gentle, or less gentle, mocking of his 'Watson', Ricardo, provides lighter moments.

Not until 1924 did Hanaud reappear, in *The House of the Arrow* – one of the finest of all detective novels. The scene is Dijon, and again the victim is an elderly widow. Her brother-in-law, who clearly has an eye to the main chance, accuses the victim's (English) niece and adopted daughter of murder. Hanaud is called in by the local police and solves the murder and a troublesome case of anonymous letters. Ricardo is absent and Hanaud's sidekick is a London solicitor acting for the niece, a Mason look-alike as he has climbed Mont Blanc five times. This eminently re-readable book is notable for its rich interplay of character, its romantic interest, its depiction of a French provincial town and its clock alibi. Hanaud again takes risks to secure hard evidence against the culprits.

Ricardo returns in *The Prisoner in the Opal*, set in the Bordeaux area at the time of the wine harvest. Again, there are two strands of evil – devil worship and murder (of one of the devil worshippers), the former handled unusually convincingly. Advisedly 'evil', as Mason, in his old-fashioned way, felt that villains should be wicked and some of his women are particularly so. As with Hanaud's previous two cases, the climax is the timely rescue of the heroine, a charming American girl; an interesting touch is the way the devil worshippers are pinpointed by mustard gas varnish painted on a gate – an incident borrowed from Mason's wartime secret-service experience.

The setting of *They Wouldn't Be Chessmen* (1935) is the lower Seine valley in Normandy. Mason never wrote the same novel twice, even if certain details recur from time to time (here the dénouement is yet again the rescue of an imprisoned heroine). The form of the story may be seen as 'partially inverted'; we know there is a conspiracy to steal some priceless pearls and more or less who the conspirators are, but not their modus operandi. Mason turns this to his advantage, as the conspirators do not stick to the script (hence the title) but do their own thing. Again Hanaud is in great form and again takes risks. Ricardo, sometimes the object of ridicule (and not just from Hanaud), again shows perceptive observation – one of the best Watsons in the business.

The House in Lordship Lane was Mason's last completed novel. It begins in France – Brittany this time – but after one chapter, it moves to England, where Hanaud announces his intention to stay with Ricardo at his Grosvenor Square home. Ricardo hastens there by yacht in a storm-tossed Channel crossing, which by outrageous coincidence (not the novel's last) yields an incident of relevance to the eventual case, which involves murder (of a City magnate), kidnapping and drug-running in Egypt, three strands that are less well fused than in earlier Hanaud cases – a matter of trying to force too much material into one book. *The Sapphire*, although an enjoyable read, is another example; *The Summons* still another.

Mason had not made this misjudgement with *No Other Tiger*, which, although it does not involve Hanaud, is worth discussion. It begins atmospherically with the hero, Colonel Strickland (surely the most focused of all Mason look-alikes – of many in his fiction), in a Burmese forest clearing, hoping to shoot a man-eating tiger. The beast is frightened away by a devilish man, fresh from committing murder, so that 'no other tiger passed that way that night'. The tiger-man reappears in London and seems to pose a threat to Strickland's friend Lady Ariadne Ferne, said to be based on Lady Diana Cooper, whom Mason knew well. Tension is sustained brilliantly, and, yes, again the heroine is rescued in the nick of time, but by Strickland, not Hanaud, this time. Incidentally, Strickland 'gets the girl', whereas most of Mason's look-alikes do not (like Mason himself, who never married).

Mason, a supreme storyteller, is less popular than he was; perhaps his spirit of adventure is outdated these days. But his work, and particularly his detective novels, has an elegance and depth of characterisation and background that few, if any, **Golden Age** authors matched. His principal detective has a penetrating intelligence (he is said to be based on a real Sûreté chief, or a mixture of two of them, but he also has much of his creator) and also flashes of humour and endearing difficulties with English idioms, rarely overdone, though they are more apparent in later books. Above all, he is human, no mere thinking machine, and not above making mistakes. For all that, he should have climbed higher than Inspector. As for Mason, perhaps his very diversity has worked against his reputation with a readership bent on pigeonholing authors.

Selected Works by the Author
A Romance of Wastdale (1895)
The Four Feathers (1902)
Running Water (1907)
The Witness for the Defence (1912)
The Summons (1920)
No Other Tiger (1927)
The Dean's Elbow (1929)
The Sapphire (1933)
Fire over England (1937)

Hanaud Novels
At the Villa Rose (1910)
The Affair at the Semiramis Hotel (short story, 1917)
The House of the Arrow (1924)
The Prisoner in the Opal (1928)
They Wouldn't Be Chessmen (1935)
The Ginger King (short story, 1940)
The House in Lordship Lane (1946)

Further Reading
Green, Roger Lancelyn. 1952. *A E W Mason*. Max Parrish.
Jakubowski, Maxim, ed. 1991. *100 Great Detectives: Or the Detective Directory*. Xanadu.

Philip Scowcroft

Masters, Brian (b.1939)

Already an accomplished biographer, Brian Masters entered the **true crime** genre with his award-winning study of killer Dennis Nilsen, *Killing for Company*, in 1985.

Masters, who had published on subjects as diverse as dukedoms and French literature, was living in London when he became intrigued by the motivation of local serial killer Dennis Nilsen. He wrote to the killer at Brixton Prison and received a letter which opened with the words 'I pass the burden of my life on to your shoulders'. In time, the former civil servant provided the writer with over fifty notebooks detailing his thoughts and deeds. The resultant book was a poignant study of alienation, of an unloved boy whose most enduring childhood memory was of seeing his beloved grandfather in his coffin. As an adult, he killed his young male visitors when they wanted to leave.

Masters examined his own motives for writing about Nilsen, motives he again questioned when he adopted a disturbed teenage boy, Gary. The eponymous book which followed was a sensitive portrayal of violence and vulnerability.

He brought equal depth to *The Shrine of Jeffrey Dahmer* (1993), travelling to Milwaukee to meet Dahmer's parents and attempting to view the world through the killer's eyes. But his US publisher said that Americans did not want to understand the cannibalistic Dahmer, and the contract was broken by mutual consent. It later became a widely praised bestseller in the United Kingdom. His collection of essays, *On Murder* (1994), exploring every type of homicide from serial to spree killing, was equally well received.

While attending Rose West's trial, Masters became convinced that, on the basis of the evidence available, she should have been acquitted. He concluded that she was convicted because no one believed that her husband could have carried out the murders in the family home without her having been aware of it, hence his ironic title, *She Must Have Known* (1996). That same year, he published his treatise on moral philosophy, *The Evil That Men Do* (1996), showing how often gross behaviour is encouraged or condoned by authority. But he also included numerous examples of goodness and forbearance, citing, as one example, his mother's uncomplaining approach towards her lifelong illness. Meanwhile, he retained his interest in a wide variety of subjects, producing books about great hostesses, the mistresses of Charles II, wealthy ideologue John Aspinall, Rabelais, Camus and the life of Victorian writer E.F. Benson while penning superior journalistic pieces for everyone from *The Spectator* to *Vanity Fair*.

At the start of the millennium, Masters turned his biographer's eye upon himself and produced the memoir *Getting Personal* (2002), in which he wrote of discovering his sexuality, the choice of subjects for his writing and his search for goodness in people, in literature and in art.

In a true crime genre which often dwells on murderous deeds and ignores motive, Masters explores – in impressive depth – why killers commit their unconscionable acts.

Selected Works by the Author
Killing for Company (1985)
Gary (1990)
The Shrine of Jeffrey Dahmer (1993)
On Murder (1994)
She Must Have Known (1996)

The Evil That Men Do (1996)
Getting Personal (2002)

Carol Anne Davis

Masters, Priscilla (b.1952)

Although she has written some stand-alone novels, Priscilla Masters is known mainly
for two series. The first is set in the moorlands of Staffordshire and the small real-life
town of Leek. It comprises contemporary **police procedurals** featuring Detective
Inspector Joanna Piercy, a decidedly un-masculine feminist who likes cycling,
and her pathologist boyfriend, Dr Matthew Levin, who unfortunately is married
to someone else. The other series tells of Martha Gunn, the Shrewsbury coroner.

Though she sells enough books and is borrowed from libraries in sufficient numbers
to frequently earn out her full dues under the Public Lending Right, Masters does not
write full time. She is married to a doctor and works as a GP attached nurse working
with the sick and mentally ill. Despite this respectable background, she has an air
of natural bohemianism and hurry. As a child, she first started reading detective
stories, she says, in her Romany caravan, deep in the heart of a Welsh mining valley.
She is one of seven multi-racial children adopted by an orthopaedic surgeon and his
classics graduate wife, and the caravan – in which Masters as a child preferred to live –
was acquired for her by her adoptive father, and it stood in their garden for years.

Masters introduced Joanna Piercy with her first book, *Winding up the Serpent*
in 1992, though it was four years before the second Piercy book, *Catch the Fallen
Sparrow*, was published. (The non-series *A Wreath from My Sister* was published
in 1977.) The Piercy and non-Piercy books then continued in roughly equal numbers
at the rate of one book a year. There are echoes of the author in Joanna Piercy.
Disorganised but committed, forever on the go, Piercy charges full tilt at her cases.
Faced with the sexism common to many crime stories with female leads, Piercy's
approach is usually to ignore it. She does at least have the comfort of being supported
by Detective Mike Korpanski, a half-Polish body-building fan, and together they set
about reducing the number of homicides in the Staffordshire moorlands. *Scaring
Crows* (1999), fifth in the Piercy series, casts an interesting light on the uneasy
coexistence of town and country people, incomers and locals, in rural Staffordshire.

Martha Gunn, as befits a coroner, has a more measured approach to her casebook,
and the Gunn series is generally more mature and reflective than the Piercy.
It is noticeable that Masters's non-writing profession encourages her to introduce
professional women as lead characters – Dr Harriet Lamont in *Disturbing Ground*
(2002) and the psychiatrist Dr Claire Roget, who works in and out of a secure
psychiatric unit, in *A Plea of Insanity* (2004). Masters has a finer grasp of psychiatric
subjects than have most crime writers, and *Disturbing Ground* is a good example,
dealing with the blurred line between sanity and insanity, and painting a haunting
picture of what once were the Welsh mining valleys. *See also* Feminist Readings
in British Crime Fiction; The Shires: Rural England and Regional Crime Fiction;
and Women Crime Writers.

Selected Works by the Author
Catch the Falling Sparrow (1996)
Scaring Crows (1999)

Disturbing Ground (2002)
A Plea of Insanity (2004)
Slipknot (2007)

Russell James

Maugham, W. Somerset (1874–1965)

Although not usually seen as a 'crime' writer, several of Maugham's classic short stories display a knowledge, and love, of the crime and spy genre, while his intelligent, cliché-free prose blurs the distinction between literature and mainstream fiction.

One of the most popular and influential writers of his generation, William Somerset Maugham was born on British soil, albeit at the British Embassy in Paris, on 25 January 1874. His parents died when he was a child – his mother of tuberculosis and his father of cancer – and he was sent to England to be looked after by his uncle Henry, a vicar at Whitstable in Kent. A private but curious boy, Maugham disliked the repressive atmosphere at the vicarage, and coupled with the strict regime of his Canterbury boarding school, he became very depressed, developing a stammer that was to remain with him for the rest of his life.

At sixteen, he gratefully left The King's School to study philosophy and literature at Heidelberg University. On returning to England, he spent five years as a medical student at St Thomas Hospital, training to be an obstetric clerk in the Lambeth slums. He used this experience when writing his first novel, *Liza of Lambeth* (1897), a documentary-style examination of the social conditions of London's working class, centring on the tragic life of young factory-worker Liza Kemp. The book, later turned into a short-lived musical in 1976, was successful enough for Maugham to abandon his medical training and become a full-time author.

By the outbreak of the First World War, Maugham had had ten plays produced and ten novels in print. Along with Ernest Hemingway and E.E. Cummings, he joined the so-called literary ambulance drivers employed by the Red Cross in France. In 1917, the British SIS (later MI6) co-opted him to work undercover in Russia in a last-ditch effort to keep the country's provisional government in power and avert revolution. He failed, but, like his work in Lambeth, he later used his experiences to inform a fictional recreation: *Ashenden: Or the British Agent* (1928).

In these six stories, set against the backdrop of Europe during the Great War, Maugham had as his protagonist a civilised British agent who exhibited all the chemistry and charm of a young James Bond. Indeed, it has been said that Ian **Fleming** was inspired by these stories when he created his famous character two decades later.

Although Rudyard Kipling and Erskine **Childers** had written about spies in the early years of the century, in comparison, Maugham's John Ashenden tales were fresh and contemporary and filled with all the details we now take for granted in the genre (Hitchcock's 1936 film, *Secret Agent*, was based on two of the stories). From John **le Carré** to Eric **Ambler**, it is not an overstatement to say that *Ashenden* was a template for many future spy writers, especially those with literary leanings.

Of Maugham's other novels, *Of Human Bondage* (1914) and *The Razor's Edge* (1944) both deal with extremes of human behaviour and damaged psyches with a psychological acuity not often found in crime fictional treatments of similar themes. *The Magician* (1908), Maugham's quasi-occult mystery novel based on the life of Aleister Crowley, moved into territory that was not customary for Maugham, but with intriguing results. *See also* Film and Crime: Page to Screen.

Selected Works by the Author
Of Human Bondage (1914)
Ashenden: Or the British Agent (1927)
The Razor's Edge (1944)

Mark Campbell

Melville, James (b.1931)

James Melville (born Roy Peter Martin) also wrote as Charles Hampton and made his mark in the field of complex, foreign-set crime mysteries that utilised his background as a British Council officer in the 1970s. As a diplomat, Melville secured important appointments in the Middle East and other countries, parleying his personal knowledge into an impressive series of novels featuring the Japanese chief of police, Deputy Superintendent Tetsuo Otani.

After a career in education, Melville undertook educational roles in countries such as Hungary and Indonesia. But his tenure as head of the British Council in Japan in the late 1970s provided him with a particularly useful grist for the crime-writing mill he was setting his sights on. *The Wages of Zen* (1979) inaugurated his new career and introduced his wily copper, confronting both crime and governmental duplicity in the city of Kobe. While the theme of the honest policeman at odds with both his superiors and a rapidly changing society is now something of a cliché, Melville remained an important progenitor in this field, and his books provided a vivid and multi-stranded portrait of Japanese society, caught between its traditional (and often hidebound) past and the exigencies of modern life. Throughout such diverse and entertaining novels as *The Chrysanthemum Chain* (1980), *The Ninth Netsuke* (1982) and *The Death Ceremony* (1985), Melville utilised Otani's relentless investigations as a way of stripping bare a society that the author knew well and regarded in an affectionate but clear-eyed fashion. The final book in the series, *The Body Wore Brocade* (1992), has a suitably valedictory air, with Melville's detective giving the reader the narrative after he has taken his pension. It was a fittingly diverting finale to a most accomplished series. Melville also wrote a series of novels featuring the spy Ben Lazenby, which also drew on the author's experience in countries such as Hungary, and he also tackled historical fiction. He made a contribution to the revival of the Miss Seeton series (originally written by Heron Carvic), though the latter remains a footnote to a career distinguished by its series of challenging and ingenious books. *See also* Espionage Fiction.

Selected Works by the Author
The Wages of Zen (1979)
The Chrysanthemum Chain (1980)
The Ninth Netsuke (1982)
The Death Ceremony (1985)
The Body Wore Brocade (1992)
Diplomatic Baggage (1995)
The Reluctant Spy (1995)

Barry Forshaw

Melville, Jennie

See Butler, Gwendoline

Milne, John (b.1952)

Bermondsey-born John Milne is probably best known for his television writing, but he is also an award-winning novelist and the creator of hard-boiled private eye Jimmy Jenner.

Milne originally wanted to be an artist and became a writer by chance. After leaving art college, lack of funds led him to a job at the post office where he began writing his first novel, *Tyro*, during his breaks. This novel, about the army experiences and turmoil of a young man, was published in 1982 by the first publisher who read it. *London Fields*, a literary novel about London's criminal underclass, followed a year later. Milne wrote one more novel, *Out of the Blue* (1985), which won the John Llewelyn Rhys award, before creating disabled private eye Jimmy Jenner. Jenner is an ex–metropolitan policeman who lost part of his leg and hearing in one ear after surviving a bomb blast. By having his hero thus restricted, the series is more character than action driven and filled with sharp observation and wry humour; the novels do not suffer because of this.

The first Jenner novel, *Dead Birds* (1986), is a typical hard-boiled detective novel with Jenner being framed for murder and for tangling with violent gangsters and ambitious coppers. This was followed in 1987 by *Shadow Play* (also known as *The Moody Man*), with Jenner helping a long-lost friend when a dead woman is left in his flat. Jenner is soon embroiled in events beyond his control, dealing with Special Branch and the British secret service. With a complex plot, *Shadow Play* has as much intrigue and betrayal as any good spy novel. In *Daddy's Girl* (1988), Jenner is hired to find an egocentric actor/author's daughter who has gone missing in France. He finds that she is involved with the death of an Italian politician. Jenner has to deal with tough French police, retired drug lords and mafia hit man as well as a prospective member or parliament with a past he wants kept in the closet. After falling out with his publishers, Milne concentrated on television scriptwriting. He started writing episodes for *Bergerac* in the late 1980s, and this was followed by work on *EastEnders*, ***The Bill*** and the BAFTA-nominated *Futurecast* among others. In 1998, Milne received the Mystery Writers of America's Edgar Award for the *Silent Witness* episode, 'Blood, Sweat, and Tears'. After a ten-year hiatus, Jenner returned in *Alive and Kicking* (1998), after Milne was persuaded to write another novel by No Exit Press publisher, Ion Mills. In *Alive and Kicking*, the past comes back with a vengeance when associates of a notorious gangster – Tommy Slaughter, who was gunned down in 1968 – are being murdered. It becomes clear that Jenner is a catalyst in these events and that they are linked to the death of Jenner's elder brother. Milne is currently dividing his energies between lecturing and television work.

Although not a prolific crime writer, John Milne is much respected, and in Jimmy Jenner, he has arguably created one of only a few convincing British private eyes. *See also* Conventions *and* Police Procedurals.

Selected Works by the Author
Tyro (1982)
London Fields (1983)
Out of the Blue (1985)
Dead Birds (1986)
Shadow Play (1987; also published in the United States as *The Moody Man*)
Daddy's Girl (1988)
Alive and Kicking (1998)

Terry Fountain

Mina, Denise (b.1966)

One of the foremost exponents of the so-called school of Tartan Noir, Denise Mina's Glaswegian crime stories are dark and harrowing affairs brought to life by the author's intimate association with the area and her deep insight into criminal psychology.

Born in 1966 in East Kilbride, near Glasgow, her father's career as a North Sea oil engineer meant an itinerant childhood travelling from one European country to another. In total, Mina moved twenty-one times in just eighteen years. Unsurprisingly, her potted educational background discouraged her from further study and she left school at sixteen, initially working in a variety of poorly paid jobs – including kitchen porter and meat factory worker – before becoming an auxiliary nurse for geriatric and terminal care patients.

At twenty-one, the author retook her exams and finally entered Glasgow University to study law. While supposedly researching for her PhD thesis on female offenders, she succumbed to the lure of writing fiction – and her debut novel, *Garnethill* (1998), won the **Crime Writers' Association** John Creasey Memorial Award for best first novel. Set in a bleak residential area of Glasgow, it introduced sexual abuse victim Maureen O'Donnell, accused by the local police of slitting the throat of her psychiatrist lover Douglas Brady. Her determination to prove her innocence leads to the disturbing discovery of sexual malpractice at a psychiatric hospital and the certainty of Douglas's killer coming after her. The novel dealt graphically with sexual abuse and its consequences, with its chief strength being its unflinching portrayal of an abused woman who is strong enough to rise above her perceived status of victim. Also of note was Mina's stark depiction of working-class Glasgow, uncompromisingly downbeat but at the same time luridly colourful and laced with wry humour.

The Garnethill trilogy continued in two further books, *Exile* (2001) and *Resolution* (2001). *Exile* saw O'Donnell heading off to London to investigate the brutal murder of a client from a Glaswegian shelter for battered women, while in *Resolution*, things come to a head with the trial of Duncan's murderer from *Garnethill* forming a grim backdrop to nasty goings-on at a seemingly respectable chain of health clubs.

Mina's second trilogy introduced young journalist Patricia 'Paddy' Meehan. Set in an acutely realistic 1980s Glasgow during the deprivations of the Thatcher era, the first in the series, *The Field of Blood* (2005), concentrated as much on the central character as it did on the crime itself, in this case, the shocking murder of a three-year-old by a minor. To make matters worse, the child culprit is the cousin of Paddy's fiancé, Sean.

Besides short stories and radio plays, Mina also wrote the stand-alone novel *Sanctum* (2002), two stories for *Hellblazer* comic, and a graphic novel entitled *A Sickness in the Family* (2007). Her first stage play, *Ida Tamson*, debuted at Glasgow's performing arts venue Òran Mór in April 2006.

Selected Works by the Author
Garnethill (1998)
Exile (2000)
Resolution (2001)
Sanctum (2002; also published in the United States as *Deception*)
The Field of Blood (2005)
The Dead Hour (2006)
The Last Breath (2007)
Slip of the Knife (2008)

Website
www.denisemina.co.uk

Mark Campbell

Mitchell, Dreda Say (b.1965)

Accolades such as 'poetic', 'original' and 'distinctive' have been lavished on Dreda Say Mitchell's highly individual brand of urban noir.

Her work focuses on London's underworld, with the police given a back seat in her novels. Mitchell first hit the crime-writing scene in 2004 with her debut novel *Running Hot* (2004), the first in a trilogy about three characters who live on an imaginary housing estate in East **London**. It was awarded the Crime Writer's Association John **Creasey** Memorial Dagger. The protagonist, Elijah 'Schoolboy' Campbell, a small-time drug dealer, decides he wants to escape from the underworld. This chase thriller perfectly illustrates Mitchell's ability to utilise the crime genre as a springboard for exploring key contemporary social issues. Schoolboy, in many respects, represents the lives of some of the young men Mitchell grew up with on a tough East End housing estate.

Her second novel, *Killer Tune* (2007), is much more epic in scope; the narrative shifts between contemporary London and the capital in 1976. Once again, Mitchell shifts the crime novel into an area not usually explored – that of radical politics and the police's relationship with the black community. The structure of the book is unusual, eschewing a chapter for a 'double album' structure.

Her third book, *Geezer Girls* (2009), once again revisits a character on her imaginary estate in East London: Jackie Jarvis, the fearless matriarch of a housing block. This is the story of four fifteen-year-old girls who end up in the care system and find themselves forced to work for a well-known underworld 'Face'.

Mitchell is also a regular reviewer of crime films and television on Radio 4's arts programme *Front Row*. *See also* Conventions *and* Literature and Crime Fiction.

Selected Works by the Author
Running Hot (2004)
Killer Tune (2007)
Geezer Girls (2009)

Barry Forshaw

Mitchell, Gladys (1901–1983)

Gladys Mitchell's early novels were some of the strongest in her career – often extremely eccentric and tackling issues such as transvestism and nudism. Mitchell never wrote books that were straightforward (her plots sometimes became too convoluted). However, it was Mitchell's taste for the strange and unusual (as well as the vibrancy of her writing) that has made her a firm favourite from the **Golden Age** of crime writing.

Gladys Maude Winifred Mitchell was born in Oxfordshire in April 1901. Her early years were spent in Oxfordshire and Hampshire, but in 1909, her family moved to Middlesex, where she was educated in Brentford and Isleworth. Mitchell became a teacher of English, history and games, and though she found success as a writer, she remained in the teaching profession until her first retirement in 1950. Mitchell's first novel, *Speedy Death*, which introduced Mrs Beatrice Bradley, was published in 1929, closely followed by *The Mystery of a Butcher's Shop* (1929), which is now regarded as a classic Bradley mystery. From the famous *Death at the Opera* (1935) onwards, Mitchell published a novel a year, sometimes bringing out two in the same year, until her death in 1983 (leaving three to be published posthumously).

Among her early novels, *Brazen Tongue* (1940) is notable for Mitchell's own description of it as 'that horrible book'. *Printer's Error* (1939) is another entertaining novel about the publication of a controversial book which leads to a number of murders. Mitchell's novel (which includes both Nazism and nudism) is a particularly piquant mix from a British novelist as the country was just about to enter the Second World War.

During this period, Mitchell continued teaching at different schools. She specialised in history and athletics, and her love of the latter sometimes impinged on her crime novels, most notably in the late-period *A Javelin for Jonah* (1974), which took place at a school for students excelling in the world of sports. It was this love of athletics that gained Mitchell membership in the British Olympic Association.

After three years of retirement, Mitchell was offered a teaching post which she accepted. Mitchell finally retired from teaching in 1961 at the age of sixty. On her retirement, she moved to Corfe Mullen in Dorset.

Mitchell's most famous series featured the tenacious and enquiring Mrs Bradley, but the author also wrote other books besides the Bradley novels. In the 1930s, she penned five **historical** adventure titles under the name Stephen Hockley and published nine children's books between 1936 and 1959. Another foray into the world of crime fiction came under the name Malcolm Torrie. These six novels featured Timothy Herring as the protagonist (the first, *Heavy as Lead*, was published in 1966). The series stalled with the sixth in 1971, with Mitchell candidly explaining that it was of lack of sales that had done for Mr Torrie. Some thirty or so stories appeared in newspapers during the 1930s to 1950s and most remain uncollected, though a number were assembled for the first time in *Sleuth's Academy* in 2005.

After her first showing in *Speedy Death*, Mrs Bradley appeared in sixty-five more detective novels, Mitchell reaching her zenith during the 1940s and 1950s with titles such as *The Dancing Druids* (1948), an excellent mystery dealing with the disappearance of men at nine-year intervals, mixing in art fraud and smuggling; *Groaning Spinney* (1950), a Christmas mystery; *Merlin's Furlong* (1953), one of her most famous novels; *The Twenty-Third Man* (1957), one of Mitchell's best, with the Grand Dame on the island of Hombres Muertos; and *The Man Who Grew Tomatoes* (1959), which deals with suspicious deaths in East Anglia.

As the novels progressed and Mitchell aged, her writing lost a little of the complexity of her earlier work, although she could still produce gems in her later years, such as the marvellous *Nest of Vipers* (1979) which again utilises a witchcraft theme. Her last book (published posthumously) was *The Crozier Pharoahs* (1984, a stylish, tidy little mystery to bring Dame Beatrice's illustrious career to a close). *See also* Sexuality in British Crime Fiction.

Selected Works by the Author

Mrs Bradley Mysteries
Speedy Death (1929)
Printer's Error (1939)
Laurels Are Poison (1942)
The Dancing Druids (1948)
Tom Brown's Body (1949)
The Man Who Grew Tomatoes (1959)
A Javelin for Jonah (1974)
Nest of Vipers (1979)
The Crozier Pharoahs (1984)

As Malcolm Torrie
Heavy as Lead (1966)
Late and Cold (1967)
Your Secret Friend (1968)
Churchyard Salad (1969)
Shades of Darkness (1970)
Bismarck Herrings (1971)

Website
www.gladysmitchell.com

Chris Simmons

Mitchell, James (also known as James Munro) (1926–2002)

James Mitchell was an immensely versatile and professional writer, successfully forging three distinctive and individual fictional franchises: the book and television **espionage** series *Callan*; a drama concerning a northern shipyard trade unionist, *When the Boat Comes In*; and as James Munro, penning one of the most inventive riffs on the James Bond books with his series featuring tough secret agent John Craig.

Mitchell was born in Tyneside in 1926 and was the son of a union activist father who moved from working in the shipyards to becoming the city's mayor. After studying at Oxford and King's College, Newcastle, Mitchell tried to make his mark in repertory theatre before undertaking a wide variety of career options (including the civil service and the teaching profession). During most of these non-vocational choices, Mitchell was always an assiduous writer of fiction, and his first professional work was as a playwright, with a play performed in a modest drama group in his native South Shields. Mitchell's real métier, however, was the novel, and after a short struggle to be published, he wrote many, both under his own name and under the pseudonym James Munro. His low-key, unglamorous secret agent Callan first appeared in a one-off television drama (for ITV's *Armchair Theatre*) in 1967, entitled 'A Magnum for Schneider'. This immediately established the bolshie anti-establishment protagonist (not a million miles away from Len **Deighton**'s unnamed protagonist in *The Ipcress File*), and so striking was the character that it was hardly a surprise that a series followed, which ran from 1967 to 1972. Edward Woodward perfectly incarnated Mitchell's surly hit man, and while the series was occasionally dismissed as Deighton/le Carré-lite, it was immensely popular and regarded dispassionately in the twenty-first century; it still wears well. Novels such as *A Magnum for Schneider* (1969, the Callan television premier), *Russian Roulette* (1973) and *Death in Bright Water* (1974) were books written with an unassuming craftsmanship and skill, creating a queasy moral universe in which Mitchell's undercover hero is frequently obliged to choose between pragmatism and altruism; the resolutions were usually bleak.

Writing as James Munro, Mitchell delivered surprisingly adept results in what was clearly a commercial enterprise: feeding the public's insatiable appetite in the 1960s for Fleming-style sybaritic espionage adventure. John Craig, the best of the would-be Bonds, was a tenacious and rootless British agent reporting to Department K in British Intelligence. Carefully synthesising the elements that Fleming had burnished to perfection, Mitchell upped the ante in terms of violent action and soon located his protagonist in a more realistic world than other, similar entries in the ersatz-Bond field. Books such as *The Man Who Sold Death* (1964) incorporated jaw-dropping outrageous plotting into an eminently readable narrative, guaranteeing a succession of sequels (notably the very fast-moving *Die Rich, Die Happy*, 1965, and the more gritty *The Innocent Bystanders*, 1969). In all the books, protagonist John Craig takes the kind of beatings that were de rigueur for Marlon Brando in his contemporaneous films, but the narratives were always delivered with great brio. Mitchell's literary credentials may rest on the more worthy success of *When the Boat Comes In* (with its still-resonant political underpinnings), but crime and thriller readers remember the more eventful oeuvres of James Mitchell and James Munro with much affection. *See also* Espionage Fiction *and* Film and Crime: Page to Screen.

Selected Works by the Author

As James Mitchell
A Magnum for Schneider (1969)
Russian Roulette (1973)
Death in Bright Water (1974)

As James Munro
The Man Who Sold Death (1964)
Die Rich, Die Happy (1965)
The Innocent Bystanders (1969)

Barry Forshaw

Mona Lisa (film, 1986)

Neil Jordan, director

A crippling limitation of British cinema is the tyranny of realism over romance – outside of fantastical genres like horror or the musical, magic is rarely found in British national cinema. Neil Jordan is a writer-director who is an exception to the rule. In *Mona Lisa*, he draws the plot from a newspaper item about an ex-convict up on a GBH charge, who claimed in his defence to be protecting prostitutes from their violent pimp, and spins out a multi-layered fairytale gloss on the British crime movie. Emotionally clueless ex-con George (Bob Hoskins) is an ultimate romantic, who sacrifices everything for an ideal. Warned away from his old family home, George seeks work from Mortwell (Michael Caine), the crime boss he went to jail for, and becomes the driver for Simone (Cathy Tyson), 'a tall, thin, black tart' – ferrying her from upscale hotel to private residence, always outside while she conducts her business with various well-heeled degenerates. The odd couple are initially antagonistic, but become dependent on each other: she buys him clothes which help him fit in and shows a crack of humour and charm that wins him over, and he takes on her private crusade to find an underage girl (Kate Hardie) she wants to save from the seamier, more dangerous end of her profession. Just as George once took a fall for Mortwell, he finds himself on the run when his loyalty to Simone overrides any duty he feels to his criminal masters – though his inarticulate, romantic yearnings for the woman (or, as she says of her clients, the woman he thinks she is) are cruelly rebuffed when he realises what Simone's overriding obsession is. After his turn as the brutal, bumptious, broken bottle-wielding mob boss Harold Shand in **The Long Good Friday** and the frustrated, doomed fantasist Arthur Parker in the television version of *Pennies From Heaven*, Hoskins was a familiar face in the world of *Mona Lisa* – but his George is a fresh, heartbreaking character, amusing in the early stretches (he calls in a gangland debt by delivering an enigmatic rabbit), an aghast outsider as he trawls the vice-ridden streets and clip joints where Simone's friend is lost (spurning overpriced champagne in a hooker bar, he asks a girl for a cup of tea and is told to piss off) and ultimately a lovelorn hero of Cyrano or Quasimodo proportions. 'Don't you ever need someone?' Simone asks, justifying her exploitation of George's feelings for her, only to be told – in one of the best line-readings in the movies – 'all the time'. Like *Taxi Driver* (1976), it is a film about drifting in a cage of a car through a sordid night-time city, with eruptions of violence (in the form of a razor-wielding pimp) and battered waifs (Sammi Davis as a fifteen-year-old prostitute who gets George to buy her ice cream) pressing in on the protagonist – but Jordan is more of an optimist than Martin Scorsese or Paul Schrader, and George does eventually find a path to daylight, focusing at last on the one girl he can help, his near-estranged but cheerful daughter (Zoe Nathenson).

Kim Newman

Moody, Susan (b.1940)

The creator of two series characters, Penny Wanawake and Cassie Swann, and the author of several stand-alone crime novels, Susan Moody writes both crime and non-crime novels. She has married into the Danish royal family.

In her twenties, Oxford-born Moody lived in racially torn Tennessee, and it was her experience there that in part inspired the creation of her first series character, the rich, black and empowered Penny Wanawake, daughter to an English Lady married to an African UN ambassador. Penny is less a sleuth than a principled con artist, and her first escapade in *Penny Black* (1984) sees her set up a modern Robin Hood scam (literally, a robbing hood) to steal from the rich and give to the Third World poor.

Later in the series, we see her rescuing or investigating the death of sundry friends. In these brightly told tales, Penny is a cheerful companion.

Moody's next series heroine, Cassie Swann, appeared after the Penny series ended and was very different to Miss Wanawake (though the writing remained cheerful). Mild-mannered, overweight and a bridge expert – she teaches and plays the game – Cassie brings her vulnerability to the fore in a series of pleasant puzzle mysteries, carefully arranged to suit a potentially large audience of intelligent but sedentary types who play bridge and enjoy mysteries. Cassie is no mere game player, untouched by reality. Despite the light tone, her cases are grimmer than were Penny's pranks: she investigates real murders and, in *King of Hearts* (1995), even has to investigate the mysterious death of her father. In *Dummy Hand* (1998), she is herself the victim of a hit-and-run 'accident'.

Moody's non-series crime novels – darker, more serious – began when the Penny Wanawake series ended and before Cassie Swann started, starting with *Playing with Fire* (1990) and continuing through the fine *Hush-a-Bye* (1991, which told of the aftermath when a baby was kidnapped), *House of Moons* (1993, set today but looking back to the Spanish Civil War), *The Italian Garden* (1994, in which a mother discovers her daughter's death may not have been the suicide everyone thought), and *Falling Angel* (1998, in which a lone woman probed into her sister's unexplained murder).

Moody's non-crime novels include a romantic pot-boiler written to extend the life of a television advertising campaign for a coffee company: *Love over Gold* (1993, writing as Susannah James), *Misselthwaite* (1995, a sequel to Frances Hodgson Burnett's *The Secret Garden*), and two novels written as Susan Madison: *The Colour of Hope* (2000) and *Touching the Sky* (2003).

Suitably for a lightweight series, all the Wanawake titles have a Penny in them. Similarly, the Cassie Swann titles will be recognised by bridge lovers.

Selected Works by the Author

Penny Wanawake Series
Penny Black (1984)
Penny Royal (1986)
Penny Saving (1990)

Cassie Swann Series
Takeout Double (1993; also published in the United States as *Death Takes a Hand*)
Grand Slam (1994)
Doubled in Spades (1996)

Non-Series Novels
Playing with Fire (1990; also published in the United States as *Mosaic*)
Hush-a-Bye (1991)
House of Moons (1993)
The Italian Garden (1994)
Falling Angels (1998)

Russell James

Morland, Nigel (1905–1986)

Nigel Morland was a novelist, short-story writer, criminologist and magazine editor, today best known for his stories and novels about Mrs Pym.

Morland was a compulsive writer, selling a poem when he was only eight and soon writing stories and essays. His mother was friends with Edgar **Wallace**, and Morland grew up devoted to the man and his work, modelling himself on the master. When he assembled *How to Write Detective Novels* (1936), he cited Wallace as a primary example of dedication and hard work, and to some extent, Morland inherited Wallace's mantle, at least in the 1930s.

Morland lived in Shanghai from 1919 to 1925, and it was here that his earliest books were published, starting with *The Sibilant Whisper* in 1923. Unfortunately, all his early papers were destroyed and no record survives of these sales, which also included many stories to magazines. Perhaps Morland's most enduring achievement while in China was to save the life of the young Mao Tse Tung during a police investigation.

When Morland returned to England, he discussed his work with Edgar Wallace, who regarded his early writings as 'dreadful'. He advised Morland to take time out to mature. Morland continued to work as a journalist and wrote several children's books but did not return to novel-length fiction until *The Phantom Gunman* (1935). This was the first of his books featuring Mrs Palmyra Pym, a widow who had become a policewoman in Shanghai but returned to England and rose to the rank of Assistant Commissioner of CID at Scotland Yard. Mrs Pym was no Miss Marple. She was tough, not averse to swinging her fists, eccentric in her attire but ever determined to resolve difficult cases. The early stories were in the thriller vogue, but Morland soon tamed the action in later volumes and increased the puzzle factor. In *The Corpse on the Flying Trapeze* (1941), a trapeze artist is decapitated in mid-air with no visible assailant. Morland continued to write about Mrs Pym even after he had ceased writing all other fiction, producing twenty-two novels, ending with *The Dear, Dead Girls* (1961), and nearly fifty short stories.

During the late 1930s, he was producing three or four books a year. It is claimed he wrote over 300 novels and as many reference books, though this figure is difficult to support. His total recorded output is around 100 books under his own name and six known pseudonyms, though there is doubtless much more in old magazines. As Roger Garnett and Neal Shepherd, he wrote fairly traditional **police procedurals**. He also wrote as Hugh Kimberley and Vincent McCall, and once passed off his work as by a woman, Mary Dane. But the works which perhaps come closest to the real Nigel Morland are those under the pseudonyms Norman Forrest and John Donavan. As Forrest, he wrote two books featuring John Finnegan, head of the Department of Forensic Medicine and, as Donavan, five books featuring the police detective Sergeant Lamb, who had been trained as a pathologist and brought scientific analysis to his investigations. Morland had a keen interest in science as an aid to detection and wrote several books on the subject. These include *Finger Prints: An Introduction to Scientific Criminology* (1936), *The Conquest of Crime* (1937), *An Outline of Scientific Criminology* (1950) and *Science in Crime Detection* (1958). Other such books include *Crime against Children* (1939) and *An Outline of Sexual Criminology* (1966). He also wrote detailed studies of several murderers including Florence Maybrick in *This Friendless Lady* (1957) and Madeleine Smith in *That Nice Miss Smith* (1958). Morland ceased writing fiction in 1965 as he was tired of it and concentrated on reference books.

Morland has edited many magazines and journals including the British **Edgar Wallace Mystery Magazine** (1964–1967) and was founding editor of *Crime & Detection* from 1966 (retitled *The Criminologist* in 1967), *Forensic and Medico-Legal Photography* from 1972 and *Current Crime* from 1972. Morland also compiled a *Who's Who in Crime Fiction* but the only manuscript copy was lost prior to submission and no amount of forensic research recovered it. *See also* Short Stories *and* Magazines.

Selected Works by the Author
The Clue of the Bricklayer's Aunt (1936)
Death Took a Publisher as Norman Forrest (1936)
The Case of the Rusted Room as John Donavan (1937)
Death Flies Low as Neal Shepherd (1938)
Mrs Pym and Other Stories (stories, 1976)

Further Reading
Aldrich, Pearl G. 1980. 'Nigel Morland–Fifty Years of Crime Writing'. *The Armchair Detective* 13/3: 194–198.

Mike Ashley

Morris, R[oger] N[orman] (b.1960)

Purloining a character from one of the masterpieces of world literature for his entrée into historical crime fiction certainly signalled R.N. Morris's audacity, if not recklessness, as a writer. The character in question was Porfiry Petrovich, the wily, psychologically astute investigator from Dostoyevsky's *Crime and Punishment*. It was never Morris's intention to set himself up as another Dostoyevsky, but to take on Porfiry Petrovich for his own, wholly different purposes. In *A Gentle Axe* (2007), he has created an intricately plotted, atmospheric and entertaining sleuthing yarn.

At times lurid, macabre and even grisly, Morris's twisting narratives reveal an imagination fascinated by the extremes of human experience and suffering, by wealth and poverty, brutality and gentility, good and evil. Morris's writing is both visual and literate, and a particular strength is the creation of individual scenes and set pieces. Morris is on record as saying that the idea came to him from a misleading blurb, which described *Crime and Punishment* as one of the first detective novels. In a sense, he has simply written the book promised by that expectation. Themes, characters and milieu are consistent with Morris's source of inspiration, so that at times the work reads as though Dostoyevsky had been persuaded to collaborate on a work of **pulp** noir and has thoroughly enjoyed himself in the process. As entertaining as the book is, its spiritual, philosophical, moral, and even political preoccupations justify Morris's appropriation. One critic remarked that whereas *Crime and Punishment* was concerned with the metaphysics of murder, *A Gentle Axe* is about the metaphysics of investigation; to that extent, at least, it can be considered a companion piece. In the eyes of literary purists, Morris has perhaps compounded his original offence by writing a second Porfiry Petrovich crime novel, *A Vengeful Longing* (2008). There is every indication that he intends to continue the series. Writing as Roger Morris, the author has published a work of contemporary urban fiction, the literary thriller *Taking Comfort* (2006). The book is the story of a man driven to take souvenirs from scenes of tragedy and disaster; the novel is a lyrical exploration of the consolations and dangers of consumerism, as well as a dark journey into obsession and criminality, itself not free from the influence of Dostoyevsky. *See also* Literature and Crime Fiction; Realism and Crime Fiction; *and* True Crime.

Morris, R[oger] N[orman]

Selected Works by the Author
Taking Comfort (2006)
A Gentle Axe (2007)
A Vengeful Longing (2008)

Barry Forshaw

Morse, Inspector

See Dexter, Colin and *Inspector Morse*

Morson, Ian (b.1947)

British, but now resident in Cyprus, Ian Morson is noted for his historical mysteries. A former librarian, with an interest in amateur dramatics, he turned to writing with *Falconer's Crusade* (1994), which introduced Regent Master William Falconer, a progressive, forthright teacher at the fledgling Oxford University in the mid-thirteenth century. His mentor is the even more renegade Roger Bacon. Falconer adopts Bacon's empirical approach and uses scientific methods in his investigations of crimes, which appear to be plentiful. Falconer's age was a turbulent time in British history with rebellion from Simon de Montfort against the king, Henry III, and his young son, the future Edward I. Morson has undertaken a great deal of research to ensure the historical accuracy of his series and to develop different and original ideas. There is murder at a mystery play in *Falconer and the Face of God* (1996), an early bibliomystery in *A Psalm for Falconer* (1997) while in *Falconer and the Great Beast* (1999), the most original of the series – Falconer has to face the Tartars. This volume was shortlisted for the Ellis Peters Historical Dagger. The research for this book laid the groundwork for Morson's new series set in the Mongol Empire in the thirteenth century, which began with *City of the Dead* (2008). The strength of the series is the resourcefulness of Falconer at a time when the scientific method was still locked in beliefs of magic and alchemy.

Morson is a member of the group known as the Medieval Murderers who give talks and readings and have collaborated on a series of episodic novels starting with *The Tainted Relic* (2005), which contains a new Falconer novella. *See also* Historical Crime.

Selected Works by the Author
Falconer's Crusade (1994)
Falconer and the Face of God (1996)
A Psalm for Falconer (1997)
Falconer and the Great Beast (1999)
City of the Dead (2008)

Website
http://www.ianmorson.co.uk

Mike Ashley

Murder on the Orient Express (film, 1974)

Sidney Lumet, director

This now-classic adaptation was the breakthrough for Agatha **Christie**'s novels on the screen. Prior to *Murder on the Orient Express*, despite heading best-seller lists for half a century, Christie seemed doomed to be a cinema footnote. Austin Trevor played Hercule **Poirot** in three films in the early 1930s and Margaret Rutherford was Miss Marple in a run of camp, tongue-in-cheek 1960s films, but Tony Randall's peculiar Poirot in *The Alphabet Murders* (1965) suggested Christie's world was hopelessly outdated in screen terms.

Murder on the Orient Express changed all that The movie was a major commercial success (securing a Best Supporting Actress Oscar for Ingrid Bergman) that established a manner of presenting Christie to contemporary audiences, which has been followed in subsequent films and television series. Directed by the usually heavyweight Sidney Lumet – who showed in *Twelve Angry Men* that he could film lengthy explanations without descending into tedium – and waspishly scripted by Paul Dehn and an unbilled Anthony Shaffer (who add real wit), this uses Christie's contrived plot as an excuse for a nostalgic wallow in the bygone luxuries of the eponymous railway train, with gorgeously costumed, hugely famous, slyly overacting movie stars swanning through hordes of Turkish beggars (the all-star casting is an echo of the most successful earlier Christie film, Rene Clair's *And Then There Were None*). Richard Rodney Bennett's swishy score accompanies the elegant locomotive as it ploughs into a snowdrift, and attention is paid to odd little props like Poirot's moustache-waxing contrivance and a 1930s hatbox used to decipher an important clue. When a nasty millionaire (Richard Widmark), who has profited from a Lindbergh-like child kidnapping and murder, turns up stabbed twelve times, Poirot – an unrecognisable Albert Finney, also unbending after a more serious career – finds practically everyone in the carriage has a motive for avenging this foul deed. Christie's novel shuffles quickly through its contrivances to get to its gimmick explanation, but the film takes a leisurely pace through its many interrogations, after each of which a railway official (Martin Balsam) is eager to pin the crime on the latest suspect. All the cast gets 'turns': Sean Connery's bristling British officer makes Poirot swear 'on your word as a foreigner', Anthony Perkins riffs on Norman Bates as a twitchy secretary, John Gielgud stands ramrod-straight as a haughty butler, Lauren Bacall chatters as an obnoxiously much-married American (Christie's anti-American snobbery is faithfully reproduced, almost until the last moment), Bergman does hilarious Swedishised English, Michael York and Jacqueline Bisset look lovely and Wendy Hiller channels the Queen of Spades as a veiled Russian aristocrat, while even the non-star actors (Rachel Roberts, Dennis Quilley, George Couloris, Colin Blakely) get funny bits of business. Finney and Lumet felt once was enough, but producers John Brabourne and Richard Goodwin brought in Peter Ustinov, John Guillermin and Guy Hamilton for broader, laxer follow-ups (*Death on the Nile, Evil under the Sun*). David Suchet would become a definitive *Poirot* in an ITV series from 1989, but he did not tackle this case again; that was left to Alfred Molina in a needlessly modernised 2001 television remake in which technophobe Poirot accesses the internet for clues. *See also* The Great Detectives: The Mass Appeal of Holmes, Poirot and Wimsey; TV Detectives: Small-Screen Adaptations; *and* Women Crime Writers.

Kim Newman

Murphy, Margaret (b.1959)

Margaret Murphy's psychological thrillers are noted, above all, for their variety.

After studying environmental biology at Liverpool University, Murphy began a teaching career as a biology teacher and later became head of a dyslexia unit at an independent school. At the age of thirty, after a serious illness, the desire to write, which had dominated her youth, resurfaced. Her debut novel, *Goodnight My Angel* (1996), was shortlisted for the First Blood Award. This novel set the tone for her future work, which often explores the experience of the alienated in a voiceless society. Murphy handles the claustrophobia of evil in an intelligent and absorbing fashion.

While building her writing career, Murphy also continued her university studies, gaining an MA in writing at Liverpool John Moores University, where she now tutors students on the same course.

In her second novel, *Desire of the Moth* (1997), Murphy tackled the difficult subject of child abuse. **The Times** referred to the book's mood as 'terrific menace and tension'. Murphy turned up the psychological suspense even further in *Caging the Tiger* (1998), in which the heroine, Helen, finds herself the prime suspect for the murder of her thoroughly unpleasant husband. The twist is that Helen herself is not sure if she is responsible for his death.

By the time she had written her fifth novel, *Darkness Falls* (2002), which introduced the barrister Clara Pascal, Murphy was receiving an excellent batch of reviews.

69. Margaret Murphy.

Val **McDermid** said: '*Darkness Falls* is a model of what the modern suspense thriller should be – tense, scary, page-turning and stomach-churning – because we care most of all about what happens to the characters.'

Clara Pascal featured in Murphy's next novel, *Weaving Shadows* (2003), where again the barrister finds her professional life invading her personal one with terrifying consequences.

Murphy subsequently took her writing career into a different direction, working with a wider canvas with *The Dispossessed* (2004), which focuses on the distressing and often murky world of asylum seekers. It introduced a police-procedural element with new series characters Chief Inspector Rickman and Detective Sergeant Foster. The series, set in Liverpool, continues with *Now You See Me* (2005), a fast-paced thriller centring on internet crime. The *Guardian* said of it, 'The truly exciting ending is a triumph of inventiveness, in which Megan uses her technical expertise to extract a confession from a seriously bad man in an altogether original way'.

Murphy is the founder of Murder Squad, a touring collective of crime writers, and she travels widely giving talks on her novels and research. She was shortlisted for the **Crime Writers' Association** Dagger in the Library in 2006.

Selected Works by the Author
Goodnight My Angel (1996)
Desire of the Moth (1997)
Caging the Tiger (1998)
Darkness Falls (2002)
The Dispossessed (2002)
Now You See Me (2005)

David Stuart Davies

Mystery Women (author group)

Mystery Women is a UK-based group set up by Michelle **Spring** and Kate **Charles** in August 1997. The impetus for setting up the group was inspired by the fact that lesser-known female crime writers were not being given the support and help with publicity that they should be. The main aim of the group is to raise the awareness and profile of female crime writers, as well as to provide a forum for the discussion of crime fiction by enthusiastic crime fiction addicts. The group also furnishes a lively friendly atmosphere in which authors and readers can meet and exchange ideas and enthusiasms. Even though Mystery Women was set up to support female crime writers, male members are always welcome to join – provided they support the aims of the group. Mystery Women is very loosely based on the concept of the American group Sisters in Crime. The group produces a newsletter, which covers any event that has been organised and taken place, forthcoming events and book reviews. Periodically, a reading list is produced, drawn from books read over the past year by members. This list caters for all areas of the genre and is distributed widely. Members of the group are not solely based in the United Kingdom but all over the world. A meeting is held at St Hilda's College, Oxford, every August, which coincides with the annual Crime and Mystery Conference. *See also* Conventions *and* Feminist Readings in British Crime Fiction.

Website
www.mysterywomen.co.uk

Ayo Onatade

N

Nabb, Magdalen (1947–2007)

The city of Florence and its surroundings provide the rich backgrounds for Magdalen Nabb's evocative crime novels featuring Marshal Salvatore Guarnaccia of the Carabinieri. In her late twenties, Nabb settled in Florence. Here she turned to writing after a career as a potter; her vision of the city is more astringent than any comfortable tourist's view.

The area Guarnaccia polices would be familiar to visitors to the city, as he commands the station at the Pitti Palace. His living quarters are above it – with a magnificent view over the Boboli gardens. For him, crossing the Ponte Vecchio is a common occurrence. Even so, he cannot understand why tourists want to visit Florence in the gruelling heat and smog of July and August.

Guarnaccia is Sicilian by birth. Initially, his wife and two young sons cannot join him, but when they do, his normal, stable family background is a foil to the cases he investigates. He has a good relationship with his second in command and is kind to young subordinates, some of whom are conscripts completing their national service. When two of his officers die in the course of investigations, he is heartbroken. He has a large and solid stature and has to wear sunglasses, as he is allergic to sunlight. He believes he is lacking in brains and energy. His technique is to visit people and places and then retire into his thoughts, when he is oblivious to everyone. This stolidity is often considered stupidity, but his superior, Captain Maestrangelo, knows better. When Guarnaccia is diffident about his ability to deal with a case, Maestrangelo persuades the prosecutors in charge to trust him. Prosecutors are a constant source of irritation, if they are of the type who want to interfere in the case. Guarnaccia's knowledge of people and their habits is one of his great strengths in solving crimes. Besides local residents, craftsmen and tradespeople, he knows about the eccentric old ladies, the prostitutes and the criminal community in his area. In this he resembles Simenon's Maigret, who is also slow-moving and grumpy and has a similar intuitive knowledge of human behaviour. Both are notable for their compassion, not only to victims of crime but often to criminals.

Two of the Marshal's cases are set in mountainous country outside Florence. Here he is helped by local marshals to deal with the population of Sardinian shepherds, who occasionally augment their income from ewes' milk cheese with the proceeds of kidnapping. Guarnaccia's two kidnapping cases are different. One is a disastrous amateur affair involving a young student. The other (in *Property of Blood*, 1999) deals with the kidnapping of a business woman by professional criminals. This book includes one of the author's recurring themes – discord and even hatred in families, especially aristocratic ones, where greed and jealousy can lead to death. So, too, does the shortage of accommodation in Florence. The Marshal solves the mysteries, but the endings are often far from happy.

Nabb was a skilled storyteller, as also shows in her books for children (in particular the 'Josie Smith' series). Georges Simenon admired (and inspired) her writing and became a lifelong friend. *See also* Historical Crime.

Selected Works by the Author
Death of an Englishman (1981)
The Marshal and the Madwoman (1988)
The Marshal Makes His Report (1991)
The Marshal at the Villa Torrini (1993)
Property of Blood (1999)
The Innocent (2005)

Christine Simpson

Nadel, Barbara

A love for the country she has been visiting since the 1970s and a belief that modern Turkey is under-represented in crime literature led Barbara Nadel to set her primary series of police detective novels in Istanbul.

70. Barbara Nadel.

Nadel was born in the East End of London and initially pursued a career in the mental health services with a brief sidestep into training as an actress. She worked as a patients' advocate in a psychiatric hospital and then went on to become a publicist for mental health charities and (subsequently) the patron of a day-centre project in Shrewsbury. She first went to Turkey for a holiday, later visiting a relative working there, and fell in love with Istanbul at first sight. She says that she is 'fascinated by every tiny back street, all of which have their – often very strange – tales to tell'.

Belshazzar's Daughter (1999) introduced the unkempt but canny Inspector Cetin Ikmen of the Istanbul Police Department and his young, relatively innocent, by-the-book sergeant, Mehmet Suleyman. Ikmen has a long-suffering wife, Fatma, a large brood of children and a difficult elderly father. He is prone to drinking a fair bit of brandy and chain-smoking his way through the day. His obsession with work often means he neglects his family, but the patient Fatma knows he would eventually come home. Suleyman has an overbearing mother who wants to marry him off, so he spends a lot of time in the office. After a brief marriage to his hapless cousin Zuleika (*A Chemical Prison*, 2000), he eventually breaks away and marries an Irish-Turkish doctor (*Petrified*, 2004), and his numerous love affairs provide a sexy foil to Ikmen's family-man status. Readers are first allowed to observe them on the case when they investigate the gruesome murder of an elderly man whose wall is daubed with a swastika – the title, *Belshazzar's Daughter*, refers to the Biblical king who saw the famous writing on the wall. Those involved include a lovesick Englishman, a sexy Russian girl and her terrifyingly haughty grandmother who has many secrets.

Nadel often draws on the history of the Ottoman empire – *A Chemical Prison* has Ikmen working on a case involving a dead man found locked in a room in a state of suspended youth, and Suleyman, who is descended from a noble Ottoman family, discloses that when the eldest son of a Sultan took power, it was the custom to kill all his other brothers to eliminate any problems of rival claims. Later Sultans would imprison their brothers instead, letting them live a life of luxury in a golden cage of a room within the palace. In *Harem* (2003), a young woman is found in a cistern dressed in an old Ottoman court dress, having been subjected to a violent rape.

In *Arabesk* (2001), the diligent Suleyman is promoted as Inspector, with his own case to solve – albeit with the help of his mentor Ikmen – involving the death of the wife of a celebrity Arabesk singer. *Deep Waters* (2002) gets Ikmen involved in an Albanian blood feud for which he has to consult his cousin Samsun. With numerous bodies piling up in *Petrified*, Suleyman and Dr Zelma produce a son and Ikmen uses his sixth sense, an inner voice inherited from his Albanian mother. The youth of Istanbul start acting strangely in *A Deadly Web* (2005) when there is evidence of bizarre sexual practices and two teenage victims seem to have stabbed themselves in the heart. Ikmen and Suleyman are forced to visit Goth nightclubs. The only time Ikmen leaves Istanbul for a case is in *Dance with Death* (2006) in which he travels to the barren landscape of Cappadocia and digs among a rural community to solve the murder of a woman found in a cave, having died of gunshot wounds twenty years ago. A more recent Ikmen novel is *A Passion for Killing* (2007), in which the inspectors come up against a serial killer and a carpet that used to belong to Lawrence of Arabia.

Nadel's alternative series is very different to the Ikmen oeuvre. The first is *Last Rights* (2005). Francis Hancock is a half-Indian running his late father's undertaker business in the East End of **London** during the Second World War. His shell shock from the first war renders him incapable when the sirens wail, so his local community considers him a bit 'barmy'. To complicate matters further, he is in love with a Jewish prostitute. But he is a good, trustworthy man, as Pearl Dooley finds out when she is arrested for the murder of her husband, a man Francis finds has been stabbed with a hatpin. Francis looks after Pearl's daughter Velma, endures threats and beatings from her nasty in-laws and investigates through the rubble to bring the real murderer to justice. In his second outing, *After the Mourning* (2006), Francis is summoned to Wanstead Flats, near Epping Forest, to collect the body of a young gypsy girl, who had had a vision at her sister's recent wake. The gypsy camp becomes a home to all sorts of fugitives from justice, including a Nazi spy. Romany mythology and superstition is effectively used throughout.

Nadel says that Istanbul is 'a mixture of the familiar and the exotic', a feature reflected in the Ikmen series – the sultry climes of Turkey alongside the regular banter and diligence of the police procedural. Francis's East End is convincingly rubble-strewn and on edge. The main characters are decent men who fight for the underdog, determined in their quest for the truth, not just dashing heroes (though Suleyman is very handsome). They exude penetrating, intuitive intelligence rather than physical strength and impress us as men with feeling and compassion amid the horrors happening around them. A dark humour throughout the books counterbalances intricate, brutal and cruel plots interwoven like the delicate interlacings of Islamic art. *See also* Historical Crime *and* Police Procedurals.

Selected Works by the Author

Cetin Ikmen Series
Belshazzar's Daughter (1999)
A Chemical Prison (2000; also published in the United States as *The Ottoman Cage*)
Arabesk (2001)
Deep Waters (2002)
Harem (2003)
Petrified (2004)
Deadly Web (2005)
Dance with Death (2006)
A Passion for Killing (2007)

Francis Hancock Series
Last Rights (2005)
After the Mourning (2006)

Thalia Proctor

Neel, Janet (b.1940)

With a glittering career in the legal profession, the city and government, Janet Neel has had plenty of real-life experience to draw upon for the mystery novels she has written to date: seven of which feature civil servant Francesca Wilson and DCI John McLeish and two of which she wrote under her married name Janet Cohen.

Of the Francesca Wilson novels, *Death's Bright Angel* (1988) won the John Creasey Award for best first crime novel and *Death of a Partner* (1991) and *Death among the Dons* (1993) received **Crime Writers' Association** Gold Dagger nominations.

At the start of the series, Francisca has domestic as well as professional challenges, having four younger brothers to take care of. Over the first three books, her relationship with DCI John McLeish blossoms into marriage, but marriage brings its own difficulties to surmount, including the demands of motherhood.

Neel's novels cover a wide range of social and political issues, including the textile industry in Thatcherite Britain in *Death's Bright Angel*, academia in *Death among the Dons*, domestic violence and drugs in *A Timely Death* (1997) and human trafficking in her latest novel, *Ticket to Ride* (2005) – in which solicitor Jules Carlisle helps an illegal immigrant who claims that his brother was one of eight men found in a mass grave on a beach near Kings Lynn. It is a case that leads Jules to face the moral dilemma of following legal protocol or doing what her sense of compassion tells her.

Beginning her career as a solicitor, following a degree in law from Cambridge, Neel moved into industrial relations with the Department of Trade and Industry, where she rose to Assistant Secretary. She has also been a director of several public companies, including the London Stock Exchange and BPP Holdings. She retains her interest in the public sector and was a governor of the BBC from 1994 to 1999 and of the Sheffield Development Corporation from 1993 to 1997. In 1995, she was awarded the honorary degree of Doctor of Letters (D.Litt.) by Humberside University. In 2000, she received a life peerage, joining Ruth **Rendell** and P.D. **James** in the House of Lords as Baroness Cohen of Pimlico. And in 2008, she was installed as president of the BPP College of Professional Studies, the first for-profit entity group to be granted degree-awarding powers. She is active in the House of Lords on two European Union committees and chairs The Parliament Choir. She is also the chairperson of the Cambridge Arts Theatre. *See also* Academe, Death in.

Selected Works by the Author

Francesca Wilson Series
Death's Bright Angel (1988)
Death on Site (1989)
Death of a Partner (1991)
Death among the Dons (1993)
A Timely Death (1997)
To Die For (1999)
O Gentle Death (2001)

As Janet Cohen
The Highest Bidder (1992)
Children of a Harsh Winter (1994)

Julian Maynard-Smith

Newman, G.F. (b.1946)

G.F. Newman's reputation as a hard-nosed crime writer started in 1970 with the publication of *Sir, You Bastard*, a no-holds-barred look at police corruption and brutality.

Gordon Frank Newman was born on 22 May 1946. After leaving school, he became fascinated by the less-salubrious side of the UK legal system and wrote his first novel, *Sir, You Bastard*, as a way of lifting the lid on the seething corruption he saw at the heart of Britain's police force. Nominated for an Edgar Award and featuring bent copper Terry Sneed – the forerunner of *The Sweeney*'s Jack Regan – it sold 20,000 copies and prompted two sequels: *You Nice Bastard* (1972) and *The Price* (1974). The original novel was later transplanted to the mean streets of America for a 1974 film version entitled *The Take*, starring a young Billy Dee Williams as Sneed.

With the popularity of 'cops on the box' in the 1970s, Newman's next venture – after an unsuccessful attempt to write for *Z Cars* – was as creator of *Law and Order* (1978), a series of four hard-hitting television plays showing different aspects of Britain's criminal justice system in a far from flattering light. Not to be confused with the glossy American series of the same name, the story featured Derek Martin as crooked copper DI Fred Pyle framing gangster Jack Lynn (Peter Dean) for a crime he did not commit. Each week the same plot was seen from four different perspectives, namely *A Detective's Tale*, *A Villain's Tale*, *A Brief's Tale* and *A Prisoner's Tale*. Questions were raised in the House of Commons and the series was heavily criticised by the police and prison services.

Newman courted more controversy with his one-off play *Nineteen 96* (1989) about sexual abuse in a Welsh orphanage, while in *Black and Blue* (1991), the portrayal of a black West Country policeman working undercover in a London council estate touched on further corruption within the force, this time concerning the Met's secret killing of drug dealers.

In 1991, he was awarded the BAFTA writers' award (now the Dennis Potter Award). His most recent television work, *Judge John Deed* (2001–2007), starred ex-*Professionals* actor Martin Shaw as a high court judge unafraid to show his real feelings. Although softer in approach to his previous dramas, Newman's supplementary role as producer, and sometimes director, allowed him free reign to focus on such cutting edge issues as he had made his name with in the 1970s and 1980s. *See also* Police Procedurals *and* TV Detectives: Small-Screen Adaptations.

Selected Works by the Author
Sir, You Bastard (1970; also published in the United States as *Rogue Cop*)
You Nice Bastard (1972)
The Abduction (1972)
Player and the Guest (1972)
Three Professional Ladies (1973)
The Split (1973)
The Price (1974; later reissued as *You Flash Bastard*)
The Streetfighter as Gordon Newman (1975)
A Detective's Tale (1977)
A Villain's Tale (1977)
The Obsession as Gordon Newman (1980)
The Men with the Guns (1982)
The Nation's Health (1983)
The Testing Ground (1987)
Circle of Poison (1995)

Mark Campbell

Newman, Kim (b.1959)

One of the quirkiest and most individual literary talents in the United Kingdom, Kim Newman has a body of work that could hardly be described as conforming to any tenet of the crime genre (or, for that matter, any one genre), but his often surrealistic multi verse synthesises a dizzying variety of elements from many aspects of the crime field. There is a particular stress on lovingly rendered vintage elements, referenced in a massively ingenious series of genre pastiches.

However, the term 'pastiche' does not do justice to Newman's achievement – implying (as it does to many readers) an element of parody: Newman's encyclopaedic knowledge of everything concerning British fictional crime protagonists in their literary, cinematic and televisual incarnations always celebrates as opposed to guying his subjects (Newman is as renowned a film and television critic as he is a novelist).

Newman was born in London and educated in Somerset and at the University of Sussex. His first short story appeared in *Interzone* (1984), while his first non-fiction books were *Nightmare Movies* (also 1984) and *Ghastly Beyond Belief* (1985), the latter with Neil Gaiman (b.1960).

Newman's particular specialty – which he does with more panache than other writers who have trawled the same waters – is the reinvention of durable literary characters (drawn from Doyle, Haggard, Fleming, Stoker and others) and their inculcation into fantastic narratives, bristling with invention and strip-mined with an astringent commentary on period (and contemporary) mores.

The list of subjects in Newman's oeuvre is ambitious: *The Night Mayor* (1989) is a film noir/science fiction hybrid, set in a computer-generated world derived from 1940s thrillers; *Anno Dracula* (1992) – perhaps his most accomplished novel – evokes the Jack the Ripper murders; *The Quorum* (1994) boasts a heroine, a female private detective (Sally Rhodes, who has featured in Newman's short stories). And writing as Jack Yeovil, Newman produced *Beasts in Velvet* (1994), which riffs on notions of Dirty Harry versus a serial killer in a fantasy setting (some of his other Yeovil stories have crime/detective elements, notably 'No Gold in the Gray Mountains').

Particular favourites of Newman aficionados are *The Man from the Diogenes Club* (2006) and *The Secret Files of the Diogenes Club* (2007) – exuberant occult mystery stories featuring **psychic detectives** (sharing elements with many of Newman's stories, notably the ones that have been gathered together as *Seven Stars*, 2000). Other diverting entries in the Newman canon include the stories 'Pitbull Brittan' (1991), with a bizarre retooling of Sapper's Bulldog Drummond; 'Clubland Heroes' (2006), a 1920s murder mystery set among **pulp** heroes; and the 'The Original Dr Shade' (1990), a brilliant spin on a newspaper cartoon-strip vigilante hero.

Newman has a particular affinity for Conan Doyle's world of Victorian mystery. The series of Newman's Professor Moriarty stories (including 'A Shambles in Belgravia', 'Volume in Vermillion', 'The Red Planet League' and 'The Hound of the d'Urbervilles') afford a variety of arcane pleasures.

Newman is a contributor to *The BFI Companion to Crime* and a regular columnist in **Crime Time** magazine. He scripted *A Study in Sherlock* (2005), a BBC4 documentary about the denizen of 221b Baker Street. He has also directed a short crime film, *Missing Girl* (2001). *See also* Pulp, Science Fiction and Crime Fiction, Short Stories, *and* Thrillers: Novels of Action.

Selected Works by the Author
The Night Mayor (1989)
Beasts in Velvet as Jack Yeovil (1994)
The Quorum (1994)
Seven Stars (2000)
The Man from the Diogenes Club (2006)
The Secret Files of the Diogenes Club (2007)

Barry Forshaw

Night and the City (film, 1950)

Jules Dassin, director

Directed by exile-from-the-blacklist Jules Dassin, *Night and the City* re-imagines Gerald
Kersh's pre-war novel as a post-war story about the archetypal spiv. Harry Fabian
(Richard Widmark) – a Yank doubtless left behind in London after the war ended –
touts for low-rent nightclubs while cadging loans from his 'hostess' girlfriend (Gene
Tierney) to finance sports schemes which never pan out (a football pool, a greyhound
stadium). Harry sees an opportunity when he overhears an argument between
Gregorius the Great (Stanislaus Sbyszko), a former world champion wrestler, and his
son Kristo (Herbert Lom), who promotes a crass, laughing-stock version of the sport
starring the dim-witted Strangler (Mike Mazurki). Posing as a devotee of the Graeco-
Roman game, Harry schemes to have 'control of all wrestling in **London** in the palm
of my hand' by banking on monopolist Kristo's inability to shut down a competitor who
has his father as a partner. Harry wheedles Helen (Googie Withers), wife of bloated
club-owner Phil Nosseros (Francis L. Sullivan), to secure start-up capital, which
prompts Nosseros to take a terrible, reluctant revenge. The Strangler does not take
kindly to being needled and gets in the ring with Gregorius for an uneven bout (without
paying customers present) that the old man wins at a terrible cost. Widmark goes
to squirming extremes as always-on-the-run Harry, flashing a smugly triumphant grin
when he thinks he is on the way up but quivering in babyish frustration when it falls
apart. Hugh Marlowe is the token decent, normal fellow, available to pick up the
heroine at the end, but is completely marginalised and cannot even make spaghetti.
The film accords dignity even to its worst villain – Lom has a moving moment with the
father he knows he disappoints but loves fiercely, and Sullivan and Withers play an
unforgettable scene in which the fat man begs his wife not to walk out but cannot bring
himself to tell her why he knows she will come back. Dassin uses real locations in the
Naked City–style and offers a wealth of insider detail about how rackets are worked,
exploring a side of London rarely seen in the cinema, visiting the clubs, gyms and
beggars' hideouts of the night-time city and running towards a climax in the misty
dawn by Blackfriars Bridge. The film exists in two distinct versions, an American cut
scored by Franz Waxman and a British cut scored by Benjamin Frankel. Scenes were
deleted, retaken or rearranged to shorten a longer British version into the director-
approved American cut, but it is a toss-up as to which release is superior. Frankel's
score, which knows when to shut up and let footsteps and heavy breathing do the work,
plays better than Waxman's effective but melodramatic work, but the UK cut has more
of Marlowe and Tierney's second-best romance than we really need, including an upbeat
final shot which is not as resonant as the American film's sign-off (Lom walking coldly
away). However, other scenes in the British film deepen the Harry–Helen–Nosseros
triangle and point up some of the sleazier, crime-can-be-made-to-pay elements.

Kim Newman

Noir

See Pulp

No Orchids for Miss Blandish (film, 1948)

St. John Legh Clowes, director

The various film versions of one of the most celebrated (and reviled) of gangster novels have all caused a stir, but it was the original British film adaptation that caused howls of outrage from contemporary moral guardians – much as the original book had done. It might be said, in fact, that even the original film brought little novelty to the powerful mix of elements in the book. To discuss the impact of the film, it is necessary to focus on the novel.

Chase wrote his first book, *No Orchids for Miss Blandish*. Using maps, encyclopaedias and a dictionary of slang, he based the story firmly in Midwest America – despite never having set foot there. The reason Chase wrote it came from his association with the book wholesaler and distributor Simpkin Marshall. In charge of their retail and 'tuppenny' lending library divisions, he noticed how frequently hard-boiled American crime titles were bought or borrowed, as opposed to their English counterparts. Putting it down to the staid style of storytelling found in home-grown works, he decided to ape the overseas versions himself, as typified by notorious titles such as *The Postman Always Rings Twice* (1934) by James McCain and *Sanctuary* (1931) by William Faulkner, whose plot it closely resembles.

No Orchids for Miss Blandish is the story of a rich young heiress, Miss Blandish, who is kidnapped by a mob of depraved killers. Despite – or possibly because of – the violence she sees all around her, she falls in love with one of the kidnappers, Slim. She is subsequently treated as a sex slave in the full purview of his mother, Ma Grisson, the sinister matriarchal figure who runs the gang. In due course, tough private eye Dave Fenner shoots the bad guys and rescues the girl – but the final ending is far from happy.

The story was based on the real-life exploits of Ma Baker, whose involvement with her son's gangster mob in the 1920s and 1930s made her infamous in America (although her contribution has since been downsized). Written in simple, graphic prose, Chase's short novel still delivers an enormous punch. The many acts of violence are unflinchingly described ('Miss Blandish heard the bone go, quite distinctly, like the sharp note of breaking wood'), while the misogynistic qualities of the male Grisson gang are lovingly described in as much detail as 1930s censors would allow.

Unsurprisingly, on its publication in 1939, *No Orchids* was an immediate bestseller. Fuelled by a huge public outcry over its content as much as by the content itself, the book sold in its thousands – it was the most widely read novel among servicemen and women in the Second World War, for instance – and kick-started the author's long and prolific career penning hard-boiled American gangster stories.

The novel's notoriety was further enhanced by George Orwell's essay 'Raffles and Miss Blandish' in the October 1944 issue of literary periodical *Horizon*. Comparing it with the pre-war escapades of Raffles, he was quick to praise its vivid prose style yet berated it for its sadism and willingness to embrace all that was base about humankind.

Sadly, in 1942, Chase decided to water down his text, omitting some of the more contentious passages and attempting to correct occasional dialogue errors. Both versions are still available, although the original is by far the preferred choice for those seeking their thrills in unexpurgated form.

A stage play of the same name premiered in 1942, co-written by the author and Robert Nesbitt, with additional dialogue by Val Guest, while a freer adaptation by Robert David MacDonald appeared in 1988. Linden Travers played Miss Blandish in the original stage version, a role she repeated in the controversial 1948 film.

Adapted and directed by St John Legh Clowes, the film adaptation was – like the novel – a peculiar English concoction designed to mimic a uniquely American genre. A Tudor-Alliance production, filmed in Middlesex, it featured a mix of British and American actors, as well as a youthful (and hilariously miscast) Sid James, and was much criticised at the time for its (now quaint) brutality. It was given an 'A' (for Adult) rating in the United Kingdom, which allowed children to see it if accompanied by an adult, but was actually banned by several local councils and branded 'disgusting' by prominent film critic Dilys Powell. In passing the film uncut, British Board of Film Classification President Sidney Harris later issued a grovelling apology for having failed to protect the public (who, of course, flocked to see the film in their droves).

In 1971, director Robert Aldrich – now widely celebrated as an *auteur* – upped the violence ante considerably when he remade the story as *The Grissom Gang*. Dismissed as an exploitative shocker as often as it was applauded as typically astringent Aldrich fare, the blood-red violence did not create as much of a furore as its black-and-white predecessor – perhaps unsurprisingly, when one considers it was up against such controversial cinematic offerings as *A Clockwork Orange*, *Straw Dogs* and *The Devils*. *See also* Film and Crime: Page to Screen.

Mark Campbell

O

O'Brien, Martin (b.1951)

Martin O'Brien is the author of the accomplished series of novels set in the south of France featuring the attractive, pony-tailed, anti-establishment, ex-French National Rugby Squad player Chief Inspector Daniel Jacquot.

Born as the only child of a headmistress and a naval officer, O'Brien was educated at the Oratory School and Hertford College, Oxford. Formerly travel editor for *Vogue* and editorial director for UPL Films, London, he quit journalism to co-write screenplays and start a film production company.

O'Brien's first book, *Jacquot and the Waterman* (2005), introduced readers to his urbane copper Jacquot, who has a sharp eye for detail but is also a lover of blues, good food and wine. Set in the sunlit port of Marseille, Chief Inspector Jacquot finds himself investigating a series of disturbing killings where the bodies of the female victims are always found submerged in water. However, it is not only the brutal murders that Jacquot has to cope with but also the intervention of a master criminal, the importation of drugs and the blackmail of various officials. The book is told from multiple points of view, including that of Jacquot, the killer, the blackmail victims and some of the murder victims. The multiplicity of viewpoints (and criminal activities) on offer make for a pithy narrative.

The second book in the series, *Jacquot and the Angel* (2005), takes place over fifty years after the Second World War has ended and focuses on the brutal murder of three generations of a German family residing in Provence. The secret that Jacquot exposes goes back more than half a century. *Jacquot and the Master* (2007), the third book, centres on Villotte, the last of the great 'Masters', a contemporary of Picasso and Dali. Jacquot investigates the disappearance of a high-class call girl who had been persuading Villotte to relinquish some of his treasures. With a huge cast and a complex backstory, the final revelations here are perhaps a little arbitrary.

The fourth book, *Jacquot and the Fifteen* (2007), has Jacquot reluctantly attending the twentieth-anniversary reunion of his team and runs into murder. This highly adroit French police procedural series is a boon for Francophiles. O'Brien's series is full of warmth and wit.

Selected Works by the Author
Jacquot and the Waterman (2005)
Jacquot and the Angel (2005)
Jacquot and the Master (2007)
Jacquot and the Fifteen (2007)

Ayo Onatade

O'Donnell, Peter (b.1920)

Peter O'Donnell is primarily known for his series of novels featuring the iconic heroine Modesty Blaise and her wisecracking sidekick Willie Garvin. A genuinely revolutionary and original creation, Modesty Blaise's status as the ultimate fictional action heroine is still unchallenged. Her cool brain, honed combat skills and loving yet platonic relationship with the adoring Willie Garvin are the highlights of the novels, while O'Donnell's tight plotting and superb style have been much imitated but never equalled.

London-born and bred, O'Donnell served in the Second World War and was stationed in the Middle East in 1942, where he had a brief encounter with a young refugee girl whose courage and self-possession so powerfully impressed him that, twenty years later, she served as the model for Modesty Blaise. O'Donnell, a comic-strip writer, was given carte blanche by the strip cartoon editor of the *Express* to create 'the strip he wanted to write'. O'Donnell imagined a past for his orphaned refugee: having fled the war-torn Balkans, she evolved her survival skills in the harshest of nomadic existences. His aim was to create a heroine who, though feminine, would have action skills to rival or surpass male opponents (in this he was partnered by one of the consummate masters of comic-strip design in Britain, the late Jim Holdaway).

This female survivalist theme was clearly central, as he also explored it in his novels written under the pseudonym Madeleine Brent. Adventure stories featuring young heroines placed in extreme and challenging situations, the nine novels, from *Tregaron's Daughter* (1971) to *Golden Urchin* (1986), expertly blend romance and action with skilfully described exotic locations over the last century or two. Like Modesty Blaise, the Madeleine Brent heroines are changelings in foreign countries far from their

71. Cover of the Modesty Blaise novel, *A Taste for Death* (1969).

families, thrown into terrifying situations and discovering a core strength of character that enables them to survive. And, like Modesty Blaise, they form their own support network from an eccentric circle of friends who teach them skills essential in their new environments. O'Donnell's research renders every detail of these abilities – from Aboriginal foraging to flying trapeze to deep-sea diving – wholly convincing.

In the Modesty Blaise series, however, O'Donnell polished and refined this theme. The first novel (following the immense success of the strip) – *Modesty Blaise* (1965) – was a novelisation of the screenplay for the eponymous Joseph Losey film (1966), with Monica Vitti and Terence Stamp both utterly miscast as Modesty and Willie. After many rewrites, the film, which bears very little relation to O'Donnell's original screenplay (and is a source of dismal memories for the author), is a minor example of 1960s camp action films such as *Our Man Flint* (1966). Treating its heroine as a Barbarella-esque sex object, it ignores O'Donnell's groundbreaking concept of a woman as an action figure on a par with James Bond. The novel, however, was another matter: assured, brilliantly plotted and characterised, it was the harbinger for a most remarkable series.

The thirteen Modesty Blaise novels revolve around Blaise, Willie and the ambiguous father figure of Sir Gerald Tarrant, head of British Intelligence, who entices Blaise and Willie out of the retirement they have taken after amassing a fortune by successfully running the international criminal organisation known as 'The Network'. The series ends decisively with *Cobra Trap* (1996), the second collection of short stories, the first being *Pieces of Modesty* (1972). In the eponymous story, O'Donnell, with customary confidence and panache, takes the unusual step of giving both the main characters a definitive ending which underlines both his psychological understanding of his creation and his consummate skill as a writer. *See also* Short Stories.

Selected Works by the Author
Modesty Blaise (1965)
I, Lucifer (1967)
Pieces of Modesty (stories, 1972)
The Silver Mistress (1973)
Last Day in Limbo (1976)
Cobra Trap (stories, 1996)

Further Reading
Blackmore, Lawrence. 2006. *The Modesty Blaise Companion.* Book Palace Books.

Website
http://www.modestyblaiseltd.com/index.html

Lauren Mine Henderson

O'Neill, Gilda (b.1951)

Gilda O'Neill has used her East End origins to great effect in her work, both in her **London**-based crime novels and in her best-selling twentieth-century histories of working-class Londoners. She is a novelist, non-fiction writer and journalist.

O'Neill was born and reared in the East End of London, and although she left school at fifteen, she later returned to education as a mature student to take three university degrees. She has published novels and non-fiction works alongside short stories, articles and reviews and is a founding member of Material Girls, a network of women writers. She is married with two grown-up children and still lives in the East End.

72. Gilda O'Neill.

Her first book was a work of non-fiction, an account of hop-picking entitled *Pull No More Bines* (1990). The novel that followed this, *The Cockney Girl* (1992), was not a crime novel as such but told of family troubles and ill-starred romance during the hop-picking season. Several East End dramas followed. Unsentimental as they were, it was inevitable that crime would creep into these stories. In *Getting There* (2001), a young girl becomes embroiled with London's 1960s underworld; her thuggish boyfriend is murdered, and she becomes a suspect. *Sins of the Fathers* (2002), which followed, was the first of a gangland trilogy about the O'Donnell family, beginning in the 1960s, when the violent O'Donnell family ruled the East End, and coming forward to the time when their children reaped the consequences, either as gang leaders themselves or as interested parties in prison. *Make Us Traitors* (2003) and *Of Woman Born* (2005) completed the trilogy. The books are not always comfortable reading, as the O'Donnell family trade includes gambling, prostitution and Mafia-style protection. O'Neill's 2006 novel, *Rough Justice*, returns to the East End family theme, but is this time set in the 1930s, with Britain in the grip of the Great Depression. The story follows the battles of three families living on the top floor of a crumbling Victorian tenement in the East End. When a nineteen-year-old boy takes revenge for an act of family violence on a neighbour, he starts a chain of terrible repercussions.

O'Neill has had four non-fiction books published, including the highly acclaimed *Sunday Times* bestseller, *My East End: A History of Cockney London* (1990) and *Our Street: East End Life in the Second World War* (2003). These followed *Pull No More Bines* and *A Night Out with the Girls: Women Having a Good Time* (1993). Earlier East End saga novels include *The Cockney Girl*, *Whitechapel Girl* (1993) about Jack the Ripper, *The Bells of Bow* (1994), *Just around the Corner* (1995), *Cissie Flowers* (1996), *Dream On* (1997) and *The Lights of London* (1998) a follow-up to *Whitechapel Girl*. *The Good Old Days: Crime, Murder and Mayhem in Victorian London* appeared in 2006. *See also* London in Crime Fiction.

Selected Works by the Author
Getting There (2001)
Sins of the Fathers (2002)
Make Us Traitors (2003)
Of Woman Born (2005)
Rough Justice (2006)

Russell James

Oppenheim, Edward Phillips (1866–1946)

The astonishingly prolific Oppenheim was a writer of thrillers, primarily of international intrigue, but including many crime and mystery stories.

Though born in London, Oppenheim was raised in Leicester where his father was a leather merchant. He was privately educated but ended his schooling early and worked in his father's business from the age of sixteen. A secretive boy, Oppenheim had worked at a novel when at school, *Expiation*, which he succeeded in getting published in 1887. This attracted the attention of local newspapers, and he found openings to sell stories and serials, all written in such spare hours as he had. It was seven years before his next book appeared, *A Monk of Cruta* (1894), by which time he was married with a young daughter. Despite the demands of work and family, Oppenheim continued to write and met success with *The Mysterious Mr Sabin* (1898), the first of his novels of international intrigue. Sabin is the alias for a French agent who wishes to restore the French monarchy but whose plans threaten to destabilise Western Europe and give Germany a chance to gain control. Oppenheim was one of a number of writers concerned with the growing strength of Germany, and as this feeling gained momentum in the public's mind so it added to the popularity of his novels. Ironically, at this time, Oppenheim's books were popular in Germany, but in later years, especially during the First World War, when Oppenheim gave full vent to his anti-German feelings, his name was purportedly added to the list of those to be executed after a German victory.

The majority of Oppenheim's books – of which there are 114 novels and 39 story collections (most of which are series stories which work as episodic novels) – fall into the category of secret diplomacy and international **espionage**, usually conducted by aristocrats in the rich playgrounds of the world. Oppenheim eventually earned enough money from his books to adopt the lifestyle of his characters, living for many years on the French Riviera until driven out by German forces in 1940. Another home that he had in Guernsey was taken over by the Nazis as the headquarters for the Luftwaffe. So in some ways, Oppenheim's life almost followed his fiction. Unfortunately, most of his spy stories seem tame today and read like naïve boys' adventures, relying too heavily on coincidence and unlikely opportunity rather than on forethought and planning. Nevertheless, they were enjoyed immensely in his day, earning him the epithet of the 'Prince of Story-tellers'. His most popular were *The Kingdom of the Blind* (1917), *Mr Lessingham Goes Home* (1919) and *The Great Impersonation* (1920).

Few of Oppenheim's novels are classifiable as straight crime or detective stories, but he did explore this field more in his short stories, many of which form connected series. One of the best is *The Long Arm of Mannister* (1908), which was held in high regard by Rudyard Kipling (it was also the first of his books to be filmed in 1910). It chronicles the various forms of revenge exacted by Mannister upon those who had wronged him. Generally, though, Oppenheim showed little originality in his stories, mostly because of his prolific production. In later years, he was rumoured to dictate two novels at once and leave it to his secretaries to polish the final draft. Volumes such as *The Honorable Algernon Knox, Detective* (1920), *Nicholas Goade, Detective* (1927), *Slane's Long Shots* (1930) and *The Ex-Detective* (1933) follow traditional though entertaining forms of superior detectives resolving baffling crimes – in Goade's case, while he is on holiday from Scotland Yard. Despite its title, *The Cinema Murder* (1917) is a romantic adventure as is *The Mystery Road* (1923), which Oppenheim novelised from his own screenplay. Another of Oppenheim's screenplays was the unlikely *The Midnight Club* (1933) in which a master criminal secures people's doubles to provide them with alibis for their crimes. Of more interest is *The Curious Happenings to the Rooke Legatees* (1937), in which the beneficiaries of a will join forces to solve the testator's death, and the exploits of hotel 'armchair-detective' Louis the Manager and his colleague Major Lyson collected in *A Pulpit in the Grill Room* (1938) and *The Milan Grill Room* (1940).

Oppenheim's huge and rather formulaic output has overlaid the fact that he was one of the early popularisers of the spy novel. He wrote so much that there will always be something, especially among his story collections, to interest the devotee of classic British crime fiction. His daughter established the Oppenheim-John Downes Memorial Trust, still administered by the Arts Council for deserving British artists. *See also* Espionage Fiction.

Selected Works by the Author
The Mysterious Mr Sabin (1898)
The Long Arm of Mannister (stories, 1908)
The Kingdom of the Blind (1917)
Nicholas Goade, Detective (stories, 1927)
The Curious Happenings to the Rooke Legatees (stories, 1937)
A Pulpit in the Grill Room (stories, 1938)
The Pool of Memory (autobiography, 1941)
Secrets & Sovereigns (stories, 2004)

Further Reading
Gilbey, Liz. 2004. 'E. Phillips Oppenheim: The World's Most Prolific Author?' *CADS* 45: 39–42.
Morrison, Daniel Paul. 2004. Introduction to *Secrets & Sovereigns*. Star House Press.
Snow, E.E. 1985. *E. Phillips Oppenheim Storyteller, 1866 to 1946*. Evington Press.
Standish, Robert. 1957. *The Prince of Story-Tellers*. Davies.

Website
www.geocities.com/ephillipsoppenheim/

Mike Ashley

Origins of British Crime Fiction

Crime fiction, like any form of popular fiction, has its roots in many soils, and British crime fiction betrays its influences from a diversity of sources.

It is perhaps pertinent to distinguish between crime fiction and fiction about crime. Crime fiction concentrates on the crime, its effects upon those involved and, usually, upon its detection. General fiction may include crime, because crime is part and parcel of life, but its solution is not central to the plot. Most early fiction where crime features falls into this second category. For example, there is much violence, rape and theft in 'The Reeve's Prologue's Tale' in Geoffrey Chaucer's *Canterbury Tales* (written in 1380) and crimes uncounted in the plays of William Shakespeare, Christopher Marlowe and John Webster, to mention just a handful.

A more direct interest in crime and the life of criminals emerged with the publication of *The Tyburn Calendar* or *Malefactor's Bloody Register* in 1705, which was the forerunner of the notorious *Newgate Calendar*, which appeared in the 1770s. Daniel Defoe (c.1660–1731), who spent several days in Newgate because of his pamphleteering in 1703, was fascinated by the lives of criminals and wrote an account, *The History of the Remarkable Life of John Sheppard*, in 1724. He also set part of his novel *Moll Flanders* (1722) in Newgate and follows the life of Moll with her connivance, trickery and thievery.

Henry Fielding (1707–1754), best known as the author of *Tom Jones* (1749), also drew upon the Newgate records for *The Life of Jonathan Wild the Great* (1743), using the story of the notorious thief, who masqueraded as a thief-taker (an early form of fee-paid policeman), as a satire on the Prime Minister Robert Walpole. Fielding was London's chief magistrate and set up the Bow Street Runners, London's first formalised police force in 1749.

Defoe and Fielding pioneered the novels about crime and criminals, but they featured little in the way of detection. Even during the great flowering of the Gothic novel at the end of the eighteenth century and into the nineteenth, the interest remained in mysteries and villains with little care for the solving of crimes. The only real exception was the novel *Caleb Williams* (1794) by William Godwin (1756–1836). Godwin, who is chiefly remembered today as the father of Mary Shelley, the author of *Frankenstein* (1818), wrote one Gothic Rosicrucian novel, *St. Leon* (1799), but also wrote what is usually regarded as the first novel where detection is crucial to the story. *Things as They Are* or *The Adventures of Caleb Williams*, better known simply as *Caleb Williams*, is not a detective story but is a book about a crime and how its real perpetrator is unmasked. It is Williams who does the investigating only to discover that his master, the 'honourable' Ferdinando Falkland, had murdered a local bully. Two innocents were convicted of the crime and hanged. When Falkland realises that Williams knows the truth, he has him banished and pursued until he ends up in prison. Though right triumphs in the end, Williams only feels guilty for having ruined his master, and at one point confesses, 'My offence had merely been a mistaken thirst of knowledge'. Mistaken or not, it is that thirst of knowledge that has been behind all good detective fiction.

This book was the exception rather than the rule. The public taste remained for lurid tales of criminals. This was much the same in France where the Brigade de la Sûrete, employed several ex-criminals to act as spies on their former fellows. Head of the unit was François Vidocq, himself a poacher turned gamekeeper, and the story of his life was told in *Mémoires de Vidocq* (1828–1829). This book, which doubtless embellished the truth with vigorous literary licence, was a bestseller not only in France but also in England, where the first volume was translated in 1828 before the French ink was dry. This was just after an account of the work of a Bow Street Runner was published in 1827 as *Richmond: Or, Scenes in the Life of a Bow Street Runner*. Though this may be a fabrication, it is generally recognised as one of the first compilations of detective tales, but it was tame compared to Vidocq's sensational activities.

Books about criminals continued to appear and gave rise to the notorious Newgate novel which fictionalised and often glorified the adventures of known felons. The most popular of these works included *Eugene Aram* (1832) by Edward Bulwer (1803–1873), which tried to exonerate the eponymous convicted murderer; *Rookwood* (1834) by W. Harrison Ainsworth (1805–1882), which gave us the legend of highwayman Dick Turpin that we all remember; and *Jack Sheppard* (1840), also by Ainsworth, which shows how an impressionable young lad can easily fall into a life of crime. It was against this background that Charles **Dickens** wrote *Oliver Twist* (1838). To this list can be added *The String of Pearls* (1846), the most notorious of all the penny dreadfuls, generally attributed to Thomas Peckett Prest (1810–1859), and which told the story of Sweeney Todd, the Demon Barber.

Gradually, though, the sensational tales of criminals gave way to revelations of how they were caught. Robert Peel, who had set up the Metropolitan Police Force in 1829, established a detective division in 1842. Dickens became fascinated by their work. In 1844, he created in *Martin Chuzzlewit* one of the first private investigators in English fiction in the form of Mr Nadgett, who identifies, through observation and consideration, the murderer of the swindler Montague Tigg. The only earlier example is the story 'The Secret Cell' by William Burton (1804–1860), published in *Gentleman's Magazine* in 1837 and which features not only a professional detective, who is trying to trace a kidnapped girl, but also the first female detective, as the original detective involves his wife in the investigation and, when she succeeds where he failed, shares his fee with her.

Dickens spent some time with the new detective agency, writing his experiences in a series of articles for his new magazine, *Household Words*, in 1850. Dickens's contact in the police force had been Inspector Field, and he used him as the model for Inspector Bucket in the intensely interwoven novel *Bleak House* (1853). Bucket was the first significant police detective in fiction. He has considerable experience, knows his territory and understands human nature, and what is more, the criminals know him. Bucket knew his job and did it well. Dickens's interest moved the police detective in fiction ahead by a considerable margin.

At the same time, William Russell (1807–1877) began a series of stories under the pseudonym Thomas Waters for *Chambers's Edinburgh Journal*, purporting to be first-person accounts of a London detective. The series ran between July 1849 and September 1853, and the early episodes were pirated in America as *The Recollections of a Policeman* in 1852, eventually appearing in Britain as *Recollections of a Detective Police-Officer* in 1856. These were very popular, particularly in America, where the image of the detective, especially the private detective, was being enhanced by the creation of the first private detective agency in 1850 by Allan Pinkerton (1819–1884), who was Scottish.

The Americans paid Dickens handsomely for a detective story, 'Hunted Down', which was serialised in *The New York Ledger* from 20 August to 3 September 1859. The story centres upon a girl whose life is insured but then mysteriously dies. One of the employees of the insurance company, Mr Meltham, looks into her death and tracks down the real criminal.

Dickens's friend and erstwhile collaborator, Wilkie **Collins**, also delighted in the detective story. In 1858, he wrote 'Who Is the Thief?' (*Atlantic Monthly*, April 1858), which was incorporated into his novel *The Queen of Hearts* (1859) as the episode 'The Biter Bit'. It is a fairly light-hearted piece telling, by a series of extracts from police memoranda, how the police eventually identified the villain. But it was another ten years before Collins produced his masterpiece of detective literature, *The Moonstone* (1868). It introduces Sergeant Cuff who is brought in to find a stolen Indian jewel. Cuff is solid, reliable and thorough and solves the case through rational and meticulous means.

By the time *The Moonstone* appeared, the detective was rapidly becoming established in fiction. In *The Experiences of a Lady Detective* (1861), the all-but-unknown William S. Hayward introduced the first policewoman. The book was so popular that it spawned a sequel *Revelations of a Lady Detective* (1864). Andrew Forrester, Jr., who had already compiled *The Revelations of a Private Detective* (1863) also featured a female detective, 'Mrs G.' in *The Female Detective* (1864). Mary E. Braddon included a barrister detective in her classic melodrama of murder and bigamy, *Lady Audley's Secret* (1862), one of the most successful of all Victorian novels. In *The Notting Hill Mystery* (serialised in *Once a Week* during 1862–1863), Charles Felix introduced maps, letters, reports and other paraphernalia as part of the evidence in trying to establish whether a husband had murdered his wife, not directly, but by hypnotising her to take poison.

Even excluding popular novels in France and the United States which were published in Britain, all the basics were in place long before Fergus Hume wrote his bestseller *The Mystery of a Hansom Cab* (1886) or Conan Doyle his first Sherlock **Holmes** adventure, *A Study in Scarlet* (1887). At this same time Robert Louis Stevenson

(1850–1894) wrote his groundbreaking novel of personality disorder featuring the sociopathic Mr Hyde in *Dr Jekyll and Mr Hyde* (1886).

The crime novel emerged with the public's fascination in criminals, and the detective novel appeared once the public became fascinated in catching them. *See also* The Detective in British Crime Fiction; Godfathers of British Crime Fiction; *and* Literature and Crime Fiction.

Further Reading
Kayman, Martin A. 1992. *From Bow Street to Baker Street*. Macmillan.
Murch, A.E. 1958. *The Development of the Detective Novel*. Peter Owen.
Ousby, Ian. 1976. *Bloodhounds of Heaven: The Detective in English Fiction from Godwin to Doyle*. Harvard University Press.
Symons, Julian. 1972. *Bloody Murder*. Faber.

Mike Ashley

P

Palliser, Charles (b.1949)

Charles Palliser's main claim to fame continues to be his first novel, *The Quincunx* (1989), a massive and labyrinthine mystery set in, and written in the style of, the early nineteenth century.

The very British Charles Palliser was born in New England and is an American citizen. He has lived in the United Kingdom since the age of ten. He went up to

73. Charles Palliser.

Oxford in 1967 to read English Language and Literature and took a First in June 1970. He was awarded the B.Lit. in 1975 for a dissertation on Virginia Woolf. From 1974 until 1990, he was a lecturer in the Department of English at Strathclyde University. He was the first deputy editor of *The Literary Review* when it was founded in 1978. He taught creative writing during the Spring semester of 1986 at the University of Rutgers, NJ. In 1990, he gave up his university post to become a full-time writer. He has published four novels, which have been translated into a dozen languages, and has also written for the theatre, radio and television. His stage play, *Week Nothing*, toured Scotland in 1980. His ninety-minute radio play, *The Journal of Simon Owen*, was commissioned by the BBC and broadcast on Radio 4 in June 1982. His short television film, *Obsessions: Writing*, was broadcast by the BBC and published by BBC Publications in 1991. His short radio play, *Artist with Designs*, was broadcast on BBC Radio 3 on 21 February 2004. He teaches occasionally for the Arvon Foundation, the Skyros Institute, London University and Middlesex University. He was Writer in Residence at Poitiers University in 1997.

As a very clever synthesis of Charles **Dickens** and Wilkie **Collins**, Palliser's labyrinthine magnum opus *The Quincunx* (1989) is carried off with supreme *élan*. But although all the tropes of historical mystery developed by the masters of an earlier century are reactivated with great skill, it is the infusing of a modern sensibility with these dark deeds of the past that makes this arm-straining volume so distinctive. John Huffam and his mother have been leading clandestine lives for as long as he can remember. John's potential inheritance is formidable, but there are many people laying claim to this wealth. The proof of John's right to his estate lies in a missing will – and the search for this proof in the dark corners of a cathedral town is the engine for the vast, baffling narrative which is often as redolent of Mervyn Peake as it is of Dickens (though neither author raked so many carefully orchestrated suspense sequences in which John Huffam's life is under serious threat). While characterisation is writ large, the naïve hero is particularly well honed – though it is the fustian period atmosphere that claims the attention. In 1991, *The Quincunx* was awarded the Sue Kaufman Prize for First Fiction by the American Academy and Institute of Arts and Letters. Subsequent novels have been less ambitious in scope but have gleaned a host of new admirers, notably the disturbing *The Unburied* in 1999, a wonderfully complex Russian-doll of a novel which explores the multi-layered connections between events and crimes. Aficionados of *The Quincunx*, however, live in hope that Palliser will again tackle something on the same massive scale as his breakthrough novel. *See also* Godfathers of British Crime Fiction.

Selected Works by the Author
The Quincunx (1989)
The Sensationist (1991)
Betrayals (1993)
The Unburied (1999)

Barry Forshaw

Pargeter, Edith

See Peters, Ellis

Pawson, Stuart (b.1940)

Formerly an artist, Stuart Pawson is the author of a series of detective novels featuring Charlie Priest, an art-school graduate.

Early in his writing career, *Crime Time* magazine described Pawson as 'Yorkshire's best kept secret'. It was a sobriquet he was anxious to leave behind. After several nominations, longlists and shortlists for awards, he has never managed to be first past the post, but he likes to think that the news is finally out. Redundancy from his job as an electrical engineer gave him the necessary free time to pursue his first love – painting – but he soon discovered that while friends and relatives were happy to have a Pawson on their walls, few people (basically, none) were ready to pay their hard-earned money for one. He decided to attempt a discipline he had tried before, writing a full-length crime novel. The result was *The Picasso Scam* (1995). Charlie Priest, the detective inspector who features in Pawson's work, had a long gestation period. He is an art-school graduate, and Pawson now does all his painting vicariously, via Priest. The intention was to make him a zany character who always did the right thing for the wrong reasons. Unfortunately, it is difficult to maintain a syndrome such as this, and Charlie soon became his own man and developed his own unique personality. When creating a new detective protagonist, it is difficult not to fall into certain traps. Charlie, unique among fictional detectives, has a good relationship with his senior officers (he does the dirty work and gets results) and even believes in doing the paperwork ('Paperwork catches crooks', he tells his troops), although he has been known to break this rule himself. Pawson enjoys relating the locker-room banter that leavens the grimness of the main storylines. *The Mushroom Man* (1995) overcame the 'difficult second book' hurdle and became a success in a very short time. By the twelfth book in the series, *Grief Encounters* (2007), reviewers held the Pawson books in high esteem. The author lives in Yorkshire, and although he

74. Stuart Pawson.

tries to avoid the Professional Yorkshireman syndrome, he enjoys using the landscape as a background to his stories. He fell-walks every week with a group of retired detectives and gleans some of his best lines from them.

Selected Works by the Author
The Picasso Scam (1995)
The Mushroom Man (1995)
The Judas Sheep (1996)
Some by Fire (1999)
Chill Factor (2001)
Over the Edge (2004)
Shooting Elvis (2006)
Grief Encounters (2007)

Website
www.meanstreets.co.uk

Barry Forshaw

Peace, David (b.1967)

With his Red Riding Quartet, Ossett-born yet Tokyo-based David Peace created an entirely new sub-genre of crime fiction known as Yorkshire noir. *Nineteen Seventy Four* (1999) kick-started the series with a pair of blood-spattered steel-toecapped boots. Having buried his father and gotten his girlfriend pregnant, Edward Dunford would have enough on his plate for an average Hampstead novel, but as North of England Crime Correspondent for the *Yorkshire Post*, he finds himself reporting on the disappearance of a ten-year-old girl. When the missing-person case becomes a murder enquiry, Eddie finds himself sidelined; responsibility for the main story is handed to his rival, Crime Reporter of the Year Jack Whitehead. Eddie pursues his own lines of journalistic enquiry, which soon drag him into a deadly vortex of intimidation, violence and police brutality. As the backstory of blackmail, greed and deep-seated corruption begins to take shape, the plot becomes Chandleresque in its complexity, but Peace's fast, brutally pared-down prose, with its abrupt sentences and deliberate repetition of names and titles, verbal tics and catchphrases, is utterly compelling. Ultra-basic for the most part, the language is allowed occasional flashes of poetry and melodrama.

The Red Riding Quartet is not so much about the Yorkshire Ripper as about the Yorkshire of the Ripper. It is about that part of the world, and the particular time in life, in which Peace grew up, his childhood overshadowed by a notorious series of terrible murders. Peace believes very strongly that crime novelists have a responsibility to the victims of crime. 'Crime is brutal, harrowing and devastating for everyone involved', he writes in **Crime Time**, 'and crime fiction should be every bit as brutal, harrowing and devastating as the violence of the reality it seeks to document. Anything less at best sanitises crime and its effects, at worst trivialises it. Anything more exploits other people's misery as purely vicarious entertainment.'

Peace's fifth novel, *GB84* (2004), is a story of the miners' strike that took place in Britain in 1984. The indefinite article is deliberate. It does not purport to be *the* story of the miners' strike, though in large part it is. The fictional embroidery is the icing on the cake, which is just the kind of mixed metaphor Stephen Sweet, also known as the Jew, would savour. 'This mole of yours is certainly a busy bee' is one of his best. Clichés and proverbs pepper his speech: 'chop chop', 'idle hands'. 'I am her eyes and her ears,' he confides to his driver, Neil Fontaine, referring to the prime minister, who has put him in charge of breaking the strike. With his aviator shades, strokable moustache and white tux, he is in sharp contrast to his adversary, the unnamed president of the national union of mineworkers. But it is Neil Fontaine who is the most dashing and chilling, the most Machiavellian agent in this gripping tale of cross and double cross, this bloke-and-dagger political thriller.

In *The Damned United* (2006), Peace again writes fiction based on fact, in this case, the brief period in 1974 when Brian Clough was manager of Leeds United Football Club.

Selected Works by the Author
Nineteen Seventy Four (1999)
Nineteen Seventy Seven (2000)
Nineteen Eighty (2001)
Nineteen Eighty Three (2002)
GB84 (2004)
The Damned United (2006)

Nicholas Royle

Pearce, Michael (b.1933)

Michael Pearce is the author of three different – and distinctive – series of novels set variously in Egypt under the British rule between 1908 and the First World War, 1890s Tsarist Russia and British embassies and consulates in Europe in the early 1900s.

Born in 1933, Pearce grew up in what was at the time Anglo-Egyptian Sudan, a country he later returned to in order to teach. He currently lives in London.

The most celebrated of the three series by Pearce is the Mamur Zapt series. The first book, *The Mamur Zapt and the Return of the Carpet* (1988), introduced readers to Welshman Captain Gareth Owen, head of Cairo's secret police. Set in 1908, during the tail end of indirect British Rule, there are tensions abounding with the attempted assassination of a politician raising the prospect of a major terrorist attack during a major religious event. It falls to the Mamur Zapt to avert a disaster. Elegantly and wittily written, this is a series from a writer who clearly loves Egypt and who skilfully brings to life the city and surrounding political turmoil with a dry sense of humour. In *Mamur Zapt and the Spoils of Egypt* (1992), during the First World War, the Mamur Zapt is tasked with finding some missing rifles and rounding up enemy aliens. This novel received the **Crime Writers' Association** Last Laugh Award (for funniest crime novel of the year). Both *Death of an Effendi* (1999) and *A Cold Touch of Ice* (2000) have been shortlisted for the Ellis Peters Historical Dagger Award. A more recent novel in the series *The Point in the Market* (2005) was equally well received. All the books in the series are entertaining, droll and irresistible reads.

Pearce's second series is set during the period of Tsarist Russia, during which the legal system is undergoing a series of reforms. This sequence features Dimitri Kameron, a lawyer of Scottish/Russian descent. In the first book, *Dimitri and the Milk-Drinkers* (1997), Kameron finds himself investigating the mysterious disappearance of a beautiful and well-connected young woman. The second entry in the series is *Dimitri and the One-Legged Lady* (1999).

Seymour of Special Branch is the third sequence produced by Pearce. Set in various embassies and consulates in Europe, the inaugural book in the series, *A Dead Man in Trieste* (2004), sees Seymour trying to track down the missing British Counsel as well as protecting Britain's commercial interests. The fourth entry, striking and individual, is *A Dead Man in Tangiers* (2006).

No matter which series by Pearce the readers dips into, they will find themselves drawn to the entertaining and dry wit of the author, one of the most piquant features of his writing. *See also* Historical Crime.

Selected Works by the Author
The Mamur Zapt and the Return of the Carpet (1988)
The Mamur Zapt and the Donkey-Vous (1990)
The Mingrelian Conspiracy (1995)
Dimitri and the Milk-Drinkers (1997)
The Fig Tree Murder (1997)
A Dead Man in Trieste (2004)
The Point in the Market (2005)
A Dead Man in Athens (2007)

Ayo Onatade

Pears, Iain (b.1955)

Iain Pears is first and foremost a literary novelist, whose best work is undoubtedly the outstanding historical mystery *An Instance of the Fingerpost* (1997). But he has also created an entertaining niche of his own with a series of seven detective stories based around art crime and featuring English art historian Jonathan Argyll.

Pears was born in Coventry, educated at Wadham College, Oxford, winning the Getty scholarship to Yale, and he went on to take a doctorate in art history before working as a journalist for both television and press.

He worked for the BBC, Channel 4 and Germany's ZDF television before becoming a correspondent for Reuters news agency working in France, Italy, Britain and the United States from 1982 to 1990 when he began to devote himself to full-time writing.

His first book was a serious work of art history, *The Discovery of Painting: The Growth of Interest in the Arts in England 1680–1788*. The publication of this scholarly tome in 1988 inspired Pears to experiment with crime fiction based around the art world which led to *The Raphael Affair* (1990), which was to be the first of a successful series that established his name in a wholly different genre.

Building on Pears's experiences in Rome, it featured General Bottando of the Italian Art Theft Squad and his glamorous assistant Flavia di Stefano. But the real hero of the series is the (loosely autobiographical) Jonathan Argyll, apprehended for breaking into a church, apparently trying to prove a genuine Raphael is concealed beneath a lesser painting. The painting, however, has vanished only to turn up, revealed in its true glory, in England. Vandalism and murder follow, and Argyll proves his mettle, and worth, to Bottando.

This was followed by *The Titian Committee* (1991), again involving the same trio, and *The Bernini Bust* (1992), with Argyll now romantically linked to Di Stefano. By now, Pears had established a familiar but intriguing routine of stories that involve fraud, forgery and theft in a world which allowed the author to use his specialist knowledge to both intrigue and enlighten his readers.

The Last Judgement (1994) mercifully broke away from the Ludlumesque formulaic titles, to be followed by *Giotto's Hand* (1994), *Death and Restoration* (1996) and *The Immaculate Deception* (2000) in which the pun excuses an apparent return to the Ludlum formula.

In the meantime, however, Pears's life and output had been completely transformed by a book which had nothing to do with the successful little series that had established a career as a niche genre detective writer.

An Instance of the Fingerpost is a magnificent, sprawling yet tightly interwoven tale set in Oxford, where Pears had made his home, in the immediate aftermath of the Restoration that followed the English Civil War and Cromwellian Commonwealth.

At its heart is the death of an Oxford don and the trial of a young woman for witchcraft, but this is approached only gradually, through a series of concentric ellipses as the story is told in turn by a variety of narrators whose reliability is left to the reader to judge. We are immersed in a world where science and witchcraft do not so much conflict and overlap, where treason is a matter of opinion and corruption endemic.

Despite its seventeenth-century setting, *Fingerpost* qualifies both as a detective story and as a literary novel of inspirational brilliance that amuses, shocks, intrigues and uplifts right to its unexpected quirky and quasi-mystical end. An absolute masterpiece.

Sadly, the same cannot be said for *The Dream of Scipio* (2002), a literary novel of immense ambition that fused philosophy, history and human emotion, set in three time periods, but unfortunately suffocated under the weight of its own unwieldiness.

The Portrait (2005), a short novel exploring why an artist abandoned his work at the height of his fame, almost seems an autobiographical coda.

Whether Pears will (or should) return to the Argyll series is anyone's guess. For the moment, it seems his much-loved early creation may be the final victim of one remarkable novel's overwhelming success. *See also* Realism and Crime Fiction *and* Science Fiction and Crime Fiction.

Selected Works by the Author
The Raphael Affair (1990)
The Bernini Bust (1992)
An Instance of the Fingerpost (1997)
The Immaculate Deception (2000)
The Dream of Scipio (2002)
The Portrait (2005)

Peter Millar

Pearson, John (b.1930)

John Pearson is the eclectic British writer who was commissioned to write the biography of the notorious British gangsters The Krays.

Pearson graduated from Peterhouse Cambridge with a double first in history and then worked on the Economist Intelligence Unit. He became a trainee producer for the BBC before being offered a job as Ian **Fleming**'s assistant on *The Sunday Times* 'Atticus' column. Pearson started work on Fleming's biography in 1965 when the novelist had been dead for less than a year. The resultant *The Life of Ian Fleming* was published to great acclaim in 1966. (It was republished with a new author's introduction in 2003.)

In 1967, Pearson was living in Rome when a London publisher commissioned him to write the authorised biography of East End gangsters Ron Kray and Reg Kray. He returned to Britain and spent months with the violent twins and their henchmen, and they told him everything except where the bodies of their enemies were hidden – he would later speculate that they were disposed of at sea.

By the time Pearson finished researching the book, the Krays were serving life sentences and the original publisher got cold feet. Another publisher declined to bring out the book because it uncovered a scandal involving Ron Kray and the peer Lord Boothby. But when *The Profession of Violence* (1969) was published, it became an international bestseller, was nominated for the Edgar as one of the year's best fact crime books and became the most popular book in British prisons after the Bible. It is still regarded a landmark in true crime publishing.

In 2002, Pearson produced a sequel to his Krays biography, *The Cult of Violence*. By now, the gangsters and many of their cohorts were dead, and he was able to write more openly about their exploits in a chilling look at how high-profile criminals become celebrities.

Pearson has also written fiction, winning the Author's Club Award for best first novel with *Gone to Timbuctoo* (1962) and having follow-up success with the novel *The Kindness of Dr Avicenna* (1982).

In 2005, he profiled Lord Lucan and four of his stylish, risk-taking friends in an entertaining book called *The Gamblers* (2005). One interviewee told him that Lucan had been smuggled abroad after trying to kill his wife but mistakenly killing his children's nanny. His confidante said that Lucan had later wanted to return to Britain to be with his children, but had been killed by the man who had helped him emigrate because he knew too much and was buried in Switzerland. Some armchair detectives immediately dismissed this theory, but others found it totally convincing.

Apart from his diverse topics, Pearson's work is notable for its detail, intelligence and humour. His subjects open up to him which makes for fascinating, if sometimes uncomfortable, biography.

Selected Works by the Author
Gone to Timbuctoo (1962)
Bluebird and the Dead Lake (1965)
The Life of Ian Fleming (1966)
The Profession of Violence (1969)
One of the Family: The Englishman and the Mafia (2003)
The Cult of Violence (2003)
The Gamblers (2005)

Carol Ann Davis

Performance (film, 1970)

Donald Cammell and Nicolas Roeg, directors

The writer Jorge Luis Borges often essayed bizarre spins on the crime genre, but perhaps his greatest influence in the medium of film is in the ultimate cult British crime movie, which takes some of his ideas and plays with them. Smooth South London criminal Chas Devlin (James Fox), fleeing a gangland reversal, takes refuge in the bizarre mansion of Turner (Mick Jagger), a long-haired and louche ex-rock star, and shares with his two mistresses, the womanly Pherber (Anita Pallenberg) and the androgynous waif Lucy (Michele Breton). While hiding out, Chas is sucked into Turner's world of drugs and kinky sex – and perhaps melds his identity with that of his alter ego. 'The only performance that makes it, that makes it all the way', claims a strung-out but intense Jagger, 'is the one that achieves madness. Am I right? Eh?' Financed by Warner Brothers in the hope of getting a youth-appeal musical with hot-name Jagger, this is the Siamese-twin directorial debut of then-cinematographer Nicolas Roeg, who went on to greater heights in the later 1970s, and Donald Cammell, who made a few interesting films but never fulfilled his promise. Aptly, given that it is now impossible to watch the film without wondering which ideas or effects belong to which director, it is an exchange-of-personality piece as a Krayish wide boy and an agoraphobic pop star clash ('You're a comical little geezer', Fox tells Jagger, 'you'll look funny when you're fifty') and merge. The opening reels are not all that far from ***Get Carter***, with Fox – usually cast in plummier toff roles – adopting a feral cockney snarl and hard-man stare, physically and verbally assaulting or menacing various unfortunate souls who cross him. However, he is cast out of the inner circle almost on a whim as allegiances change. With familiar Britfilm faces (Stanley Meadows, Anthony Valentine, Allan Cuthbertson and Ken Colley) and aptly cast non-actors (John Bindon, a Kray associate whose acting career was cut short by a murder charge), this presents an unusual but credible version of British gangland hanging on during the youth explosion of the 1960s, outmoded but still dangerous. Chas loses himself in Turner's psychedelic *The Old Dark House*, sucked out of his tidy crime-movie persona into an acid-tinged, exhilarating but terrifying freak-out of malleable personality, orgiastic behaviour and incredible coups de cinema. However, the fragmented, impressionist vision of the gangster's everyday world of punishment beatings and vandalism (acid poured on a Rolls and a head-shaved chauffeur) shows the cracks that widen in the mushroom-fuelled wonderland – most notably, the hints of sexual ambiguity that broaden as Chas (who claims to be a juggler) is absorbed into Turner's collapsing happening even as the girly pop star adopts a sharp suit and slicked hair to deliver the film's only real song ('Memo From T'). One of those movies which puzzles on first acquaintance but rewards repeated viewings, *Performance* has some of the psychedelic clutter expected of its era, plus an air of grotty sexual decadence, but its cinematic sensibilities were calculated to outlast its moment. Though it has the fashions, music and faces of 1968, it is as fresh and disturbing now as it ever was, and moments – like the zoom through a bullet hole (and a flash image of Jorge Luis Borges) into a pulsing brain – remain unmatchably astonishing. *See also* Film and Crime: Page to Screen.

Kim Newman

Perry, Anne (b.1938)

Anne Perry is the author of historical mysteries, set either in the Victorian era or against the background of the First World War. She is also one of those rare writers whose real life is more fascinating than the fictional world she has created.

The daughter of mathematical physicist Dr Henry Hulme and clergyman's daughter Hilda Reavley, Perry was born Juliet Marion Hulme on 28 October 1938 in Blackheath, south-east London. Earlier that year, her father had become Chief Assistant of the Royal Observatory at Greenwich and the family lived there for a number of years. However, Juliet's continued problems with tuberculosis required that she be sent abroad for the good of her health, eventually being consigned to a sanatorium in New Zealand at the age of ten. A few months later, in mid-1948, Dr Hulme and his wife joined her, along with their four-year-old son; Hulme had been made Rector of the prestigious University of New Zealand in Christchurch – a post he would be forced to resign six years later due to conflicts with senior figures at the school.

After a brief but unpleasant time at a boarding school, Juliet was reunited with her family in 1950 and two years later met Pauline Parker, a kindred spirit who suffered from the bone disease osteomyelitis. Quickly forming a close bond, the teenagers concocted a fantastical plot to murder Pauline's mother, Honora Rieper, who was in the throes of splitting up with her partner and leaving for South Africa. On 22 June 1954, the girls lured Rieper to a deserted path where they killed her in cold blood using a brick wrapped in a stocking. The murder was slow, bloody and brutal – the coroner recorded forty-five separate blows.

Less than two months later, the girls – who never attempted to cover up their crime – were sentenced to five years' imprisonment, being too young for the death penalty. The judge forbade them to ever meet again, and on her release, Juliet travelled to England where she took up residence with her mother and stepfather. Taking the surname of her stepfather, she changed her name by deed poll to 'Anne Perry' and began rebuilding her life. Various jobs followed, including a short period as a flight attendant, but her natural desire to become a writer eventually bore fruit, and in 1979, her first novel was published.

The Cater Street Hangman (1979) was a rich, evocative murder story set in Victorian London, and the first book to feature the diligent Inspector Pitt. Investigating the murder of a housemaid, the working-class policeman soon finds himself falling in love with society lady Charlotte Ellison. Rebelling against the conventions of the age, the couple swiftly marry, with Pitt making good use of Charlotte's aristocratic connections to penetrate areas of Victorian society to which he would never normally be given access.

A second novel followed in 1980 – *Callandar Square* – in which even the upper echelons of society are not immune to a spot of first-degree murder. Since then, a further twenty-three novels have appeared, each as carefully researched as the previous one, each exploring the dark hypocrisies that characterised the world of the class-bound Victorian era. Perry's *Buckingham Palace Gardens* (2008), is set in the rarefied environs of the royal palace.

In 1990, Perry created a second Victorian sleuth, William Monk. Monk was a police officer who lost his memory in a terrible coach accident and was forever trying to piece his past life back together again. Aided by Crimean War nurse Hester Latterly, every new case brought with it a fresh clue to his past existence, and over the course of many books (fifteen at the last count), Monk and Hester eventually grew close enough to marry.

In 1994, Perry's identity as a criminal was revealed to the world at large due to the imminent opening of Peter Jackson's *Heavenly Creatures*, a generally faithful film adaptation of the infamous 1954 murder case, starring Kate Winslett as Juliet. Understandably, Perry was upset and embarrassed by the media attention towards this previously secret aspect of her childhood and accused the film-makers of sensationalising much of the story, specifically denying any lesbian relationship between herself and Pauline (now living under a new name in Kent, England).

This century, Perry has embarked on a new series of crime stories set against the doomladen backdrop of the First World War: *No Graves as Yet* (2003) was the first, set in 1914. Four others followed, tracing the war years until 1918. Stand-alone books have included the mystical *Tathea* (1999), a revised version of her very first attempt at a novel in the 1960s (a sequel, *Armageddon*, following in 2001); *The One Thing More* (2000), a French Revolution murder story; and various popular Christmas-themed novellas from 2003 onwards.

The author now lives with her brother Jonathan in a restored stone barn in Portmanhomack on the east coast of Scotland. A committed Mormon since a visit to Salt Lake City in the 1970s, she has had a remarkably prolific career, often penning two books each year. She enjoys enormous popularity in the United States, probably more so than in the United Kingdom, where her quintessentially English mysteries are always well received by critics and readers alike.

Selected Works by the Author

Thomas and Charlotte Pitt Series
The Cater Street Hangman (1979)
Resurrection Row (1981)
Silence in Hanover Close (1988)
Bethlehem Road (1990)
Traitor's Gate (1995)

William Monk Series
The Face of a Stranger (1990)
Sins of the Wolf (1994)
A Funeral in Blue (2001)

Further Reading
Glamuzina, Julie & Laurie, Alison J. 1991. *Parker & Hulme: A Lesbian View*. New Woman's Press.

Mark Campbell

Peters, Ellis (1913–1995)

Ellis Peters is the pseudonym of Edith Mary Pargeter, a prolific author who single-handedly revitalised, if not reinvented the genre of historical crime fiction through her creation Brother Cadfael, the twelfth-century Benedictine monk and detective.

Pargeter was born in Horsehay, Shropshire, as the daughter of a clerk at a local ironworks. She was educated in local schools and lived in Shropshire for almost all her life. Her love for the countryside and its history is evident in much of her writing. She began writing novels while she was working as a chemist's assistant, a job which provided her with information about medicines which would later be useful in her crime fiction. During the Second World War, she had an administrative post with the Women's Royal Navy Service in Liverpool, duties for which she was awarded the British Empire Medal. She continued to produce novels during this period, including *She Goes to War* (1942), which was based on her wartime experiences, but it was not until the end of the war that she was able to devote all her time to writing.

She made her publishing debut with *Hortensius, Friend of Nero* (1936), which was not particularly well received, but she had more success with some of the historical novels which followed. Between 1938 and 1940, she also wrote several now-forgotten books under the names John Redfern, Jolyon Carr and Peter Benedict.

In 1947, Pargeter attended an international summer school in Czechoslovakia and began an affectionate and long-lasting relationship with the country and its people. She wrote three books about Czechoslovakia in this period. Her feelings for the country are clearly expressed in *The Fair Young Phoenix* (1948), an emotional love story, which was followed by another more-restrained novel and a travel book. She taught herself the Czech language and subsequently translated several books by the country's leading writers, including Jan Neruda, Bohumil Hrabal and Josef Skvorecky, for which she was recognised by the award of the Czechoslovak Society for International Relations' Gold Medal for services to Czech literature.

It was not until 1951 that Pargeter's first crime novel appeared. *Fallen into the Pit* introduced Detective Sergeant George Felse, as well as his teenage son, Dominic, who was to play an increasingly large role in future books. The mystery, vivid characterisation and depiction of the Shropshire countryside showed that this was a writer capable of standing alongside the best crime writers of the period. Felse did not, however, make another appearance for ten years, during which time Edith wrote several stand-alone crime novels. As her crime writing career developed, she chose to distinguish this from her other work, and decided to use another name, Ellis (for her brother) and Peters (for Petra, a Czech friend).

During this period, she also continued to write historical fiction and produced the first real impact of any of her work with her *The Heaven Tree Trilogy* (1989). This stirring saga, set against the background of the English/Welsh borderlands during the thirteenth century, spanned thirty-four years. The eponymous first book came out in 1960 and told the story of a mediaeval mason, Harry Talvace. The story of Harry's son and his legacy is followed in the second volume, *The Green Branch* (1962), and *The Scarlet Seed* (1963) completed a work of which she was justly proud.

Felse returned in *Death and the Joyful Woman* (1961), which was awarded an Edgar for best novel when it was published in America two years later. He was promoted to detective chief inspector and featured in a further eleven books between 1964 – *Flight of a Witch* – and 1978 – *Rainbow's End*. While Felse's part in the stories varies in importance, he maintains a critical presence, and the books demonstrate Pargeter's skill at creating rounded, wholly believable characters, as well as producing an intriguing mystery.

But it is for the creation of Brother Cadfael that she will be best remembered, and it is a formidable achievement. Until Cadfael's appearance, the historical whodunnit scarcely existed. There were a few light-hearted books by an American, Lillian de la Torre, the first of which appeared in the 1940s, featuring Dr Johnson and Boswell as investigators, and John Dickson **Carr** produced *The Bride of Newgate* (1950). The most successful example was Robert van Gulik's series, published between 1949 and 1968, in which the investigations were conducted by a real historical figure, the seventh-century Judge Dee. Ellis Peters and Brother Cadfael created a new genre of crime fiction which was eventually, from about 1990 onwards, taken up, with varying degrees of success, by many other authors.

The introduction of Cadfael and his growing popularity marked the disappearance of Pargeter's name from new fiction. Henceforth, she would be mainly remembered as Ellis Peters, though some of her earlier work, especially *The Heaven Tree*, and *The Brothers of Gwynedd Quartet*, which was published between 1974 and 1977, retained its loyal fans, some of them newly attracted to it by their enjoyment of the chronicles of Cadfael.

The chronicles of Cadfael, twenty novels in all, plus a collection of short stories cover the period from about 1135 to 1145, a stormy time which saw almost continuous war between the two rivals for the English throne, King Stephen and the Empress Matilda. Their see-sawing battle for supremacy affected much of the country, and a city's loyalty to one or other side often had severe consequences.

Although we learn more about Cadfael in the later books, he appears from the first as a fully developed character and one who stands out immediately from his fellow monks. A former soldier, sailor and veteran of the first Crusade, he is nearing sixty and has belonged to the Benedictine Abbey of Saint Peter and Saint Paul at Shrewsbury for some seventeen years when he tackles his first investigation. Cadfael ap Meilyr ap Dafydd is a Welshman and proud of his heritage – as was his creator, who also had Welsh blood – and several of the books are based partly in Wales, which shared its border with Shrewsbury. He is content with his life as the abbey's herbalist, responsible for tending the garden and preparing concoctions from its plants to provide medicines for the abbey as well as the townspeople. He is not, however, a submissive member of the community, and we see him occasionally breaking the rules and disobeying orders when he feels it imperative to do so to save a life or to right a wrong.

His decision to join the abbey is not explained until the appearance of a collection of short stories published under the title of *A Rare Benedictine* (1988). In her introduction, Pargeter says that Cadfael's experience on the road to Woodstock, while returning from abroad, is not a conversion but simply the acceptance of a revelation, because he has always been a believer.

Cadfael made his debut in *A Morbid Taste for Bones* (1977). He has been sent with a group from the abbey to a Welsh village to acquire the bones of an obscure saint, Winifred, which they hope will cure one of their sick brethren. His role is to act as interpreter, but when the leader of the villagers who object to the removal of their saint is murdered, it is Cadfael who reveals the guilty party. The story shows not only a budding sleuth but a first glimpse of the personality of one of the recurring characters in the series, the abbey's second in command, Prior Robert. The proud, arrogant Robert wants the bones not simply to cure an ailing brother but to fulfil his ambition to equal, if not outdo, the reputation of another abbey which has recently acquired its own holy relic. Robert is habitually accompanied by his sycophantic sidekick, the odious Brother Jerome, a sneak and a troublemaker who shows particular animosity towards Cadfael.

In the second book, *One Corpse Too Many* (1979), Shrewsbury Castle falls in the battle between the rivals for the throne, and its ninety-four defenders are hanged as traitors, but when Brother Cadfael administers the last rites to the dead, he discovers ninety-five corpses. His investigation leads him to suspect one of two engaging young men as the villain – a recurring theme – and the outcome is decided in a trial by single combat, the result of which will be accepted as God's judgement. The victor is Hugh Beringar, who will have an important role to play in all the books that follow.

Monk's Hood (1980), which was awarded the **Crime Writers' Association** (CWA) Silver Dagger, reveals more about Cadfael's early life. A wealthy man falls ill while a guest of the abbey, and Cadfael is sent to minister to him but cannot save him from what turns out to be a lethal poison, monk's hood oil stolen from Cadfael. When he meets the dead man's wife, he realises that she is Richildis, the woman to whom he was betrothed before he left for the Crusades. Once again there are two young men as possible murderers, but Cadfael is convinced that Richildis's son, prime suspect in the eyes of the sheriff's officers, is not guilty. The sheriff's men are not investigators but merely on hand to hunt down, and beat up, likely suspects. Cadfael, on the other hand, shows some skill when it comes to examining a corpse and making deductions based on evidence found at the scene of a crime. His investigation proves that Richildis's son is innocent and identifies the real killer. It is also clear that Cadfael feels that the Welsh law of inheritance, a crucial factor behind the crime, is superior to the English, though he is too discreet to express his opinion.

By the time we reach the fourth chronicle, *Saint Peter's Fair* (1981), the main characters have been well defined. Hugh Beringar is now deputy sheriff. The elderly Abbot Heribert has been retired by the Bishop, and Prior Robert's ambition to succeed him has been frustrated by the appointment of an outsider. The new Abbot, Radulfus clearly has the qualities required of a chief executive. He assumes command smoothly, recognising the talents and the shortcomings of the brothers and has no hesitation in using Cadfael's experience of the outside world and his special gifts for investigation when the occasion arises.

Like all chief executives, Radulfus is capable of making mistakes, as he shows in *The Raven in the Foregate* (1986), when he appoints a new priest to a vacant living. The newcomer is a clever scholar, but he is soon revealed as a self-righteous zealot, whose rigid adherence to his own narrow interpretation of his duties and lack of humanity antagonise his parishioners. When his body is found drowned in the mill-pool, Cadfael is once again called on to investigate.

The Virgin in the Ice (1982) introduces the character of Olivier de Bretagne. It is not long before Cadfael realises that this resourceful young knight must be his son and that, unknown to him, Mariam, the Muslim woman with whom he lived in Antioch during his time as a crusader, had been pregnant when he returned home. Cadfael rejoices in seeing that his union with Mariam – 'a woman worth the loving' – has produced such a brave and chivalrous young man, but he chooses to keep their relationship secret.

The relationship between Cadfael and Hugh Beringar, despite the many years of difference in their ages, is not that of father and son, nor does Hugh play the part of a Watson to Cadfael's Holmes. Even before Hugh is promoted to sheriff, in *The Raven in the Foregate* (1986), theirs is a friendship between equals, based on mutual respect and an ever-growing affection which allows Cadfael, godfather to Hugh's son, to feel that he is part of the Beringar family.

The popularity of the series led to adaptations of some of the books for television, with Derek Jacobi as a charismatic, though distinctly un-Welsh, Cadfael and with the inevitable changes to the plots required by the different medium. There were also several radio dramatisations starring Philip Madoc (a genuine Welshman).

Cadfael's place in the genre is assured, as is the author's, although admittedly, the books are somewhat formulaic: there is a murder, a suspect whom Cadfael must prove innocent and a pair of lovers who need Cadfael's help to come together. The mystery is often enjoyably hard to solve, but it is the characters that make the books so successful. They are always vividly realised; there is a wealth of fascinating historical detail which illuminates without overwhelming the stories; and the narratives, written in Edith's flowing (and occasionally overflowing) prose, are well paced. Cadfael cannot be claimed as one of the great fictional detectives. Given the period in which he lived, his methods of detection are inevitably limited and intuition plays a large part in the process. He does not approach his investigations as an intellectual pursuit, like Sherlock **Holmes**, and he has perhaps more in common with Miss Marple, with whom he shares an endearing nosiness and an understanding of human nature. Above all he is concerned with discovering the truth and protecting the innocent, while remaining non-judgemental and true to his faith.

In 1993, Pargeter was awarded the CWA Diamond Dagger, to mark a lifetime's achievement in crime writing. Her obituary in *The Times* accurately described her as 'a deeply sensitive and perceptive woman…an intensely private and modest person'. The chronicles of Cadfael show her love for the countryside in which she lived for almost all her life, and it seems fitting that, two years after her death, a new stained glass window depicting St. Benedict was installed in Shrewsbury Abbey and dedicated to her memory. *See also* The Shires: Rural England and Regional Crime Fiction.

Selected Works by the Author
Death and the Joyful Woman (1961)
*A Morbid Taste for Bone*s (1977)
One Corpse Too Many (1979)
Monk's Hood (1980)
The Virgin in the Ice (1982)
The Rose Rent (1986)
A Rare Benedictine (stories, 1988)
The Potter's Field (1990)
The Holy Thief (1992)

Further Reading
Hagemann, Susanne et al. 1997. Murderous Intersections: Genre, Time, Place and Gender in Ellis Peters's Cadfael Mysteries. *Cuadernos de Literatura Inglesa y Norteamericana*, www.fask. uni-mainz.de/inst/iaa/peters.html.
Lewis, Margaret. 1994. *Edith Pargeter: Ellis Peters*. Seren.
Whiteman, Robin. 1995. *The Cadfael Companion: The World of Brother Cadfael*. Introduction by Ellis Peters. Little, Brown.

Susanna Yager

Petit, Chris (b.1949)

One-time film editor of *Time Out*, Chris Petit broke into directing with his cult black-and-white road movie *Radio On*, which was followed by more features, before he turned to writing fiction. *Robinson* (1993), his first novel, focused on the relationship between the narrator and a shadowy, charismatic Soho character called Robinson. Together they work in the porn industry and hang out in Soho pubs, but the novel is perhaps of interest to crime aficionados mainly for its portrait of Cookie, a housemate of the narrator's who is clearly based on crime writer Robin Cook, also known as Derek **Raymond**, whom Petit knew well.

Petit's second novel, *The Psalm Killer* (1996) is an ambitious political thriller/police procedural set in and around a gloomy mid-1980s Belfast: Petit obviously spent as much time tramping the Crumlin Road as previously he had hung around the archway at the end of Manette Street that was his narrator's gateway to Soho in *Robinson*. A serial killer is at large in Northern Ireland, working across the sectarian divide, but his criteria for victim selection are far from indiscriminate. In charge of the police case, Cross and Westerby, whose relationship is always destined to burgeon outside the barracks despite his being married to Deidre and her engagement to Martin, are complex, sympathetic characters – sympathetic not because they are particularly likeable, but because they are so well rendered that they come to life.

The story of the killer's apprenticeship includes flashback sequences covering a lot of ground in the history of the Troubles; much of the backstory involves real people and events in Ulster's turbulent past (there is even a glossary). This is a thriller that more than fills its end of the bargain: its grip tightens almost unbearably as we approach the horrifying conclusion, but Petit never loses sight of the serious issues behind his story. He does not let his killer off the hook, but there is no mistaking who he thinks are the real villains of the piece.

Back from the Dead (1999) is a mystery. When past-it rock star McMahon starts receiving letters from a dead girl, he hires Youselli, a tough cop up for a bit of moonlighting. As the letters keep coming, containing information only the dead girl could know, the mystery deepens, and Youselli gets in too deep. It is when the background shifts from the music business to the film industry that the narrative becomes most compelling. Youselli finds himself drawn down parallel trails of movieland investigation – porn and art house – until he loses it himself. *Back from the Dead* takes risks with form, structure and narrative, and all its gambles pay off. It is strong, dark, brilliant stuff.

If *The Hard Shoulder* (2001), set among the Irish community of north-west London, picked up a little closer to where *Robinson* left off, Petit moved less ambiguously into the territory of the intelligent thriller with Nazi legacy suspenser *The Human Pool* (2002) and white-knuckle ride *The Passenger* (2006), which kicks off over Lockerbie.

Selected Works by the Author
Robinson (1993)
The Psalm Killer (1996)
Back From the Dead (1999)
The Hard Shoulder (2001)
The Human Pool (2002)
The Passenger (2006)

Nicholas Royle

Phillips, Mike (also known as Joe Canzius) (b.1946)

Mike Phillips is a one-off. Black writers have tackled the urban crime scene before – and often with conspicuous success. But this Guyana-born practitioner of the thriller, while *au fait* with most aspects of black culture in both the United States and the United Kingdom, is quintessentially British, and the author's own clear-eyed vision is refracted through this heady mixture to create a remarkable series of books. Phillips's principal character, the crime-involved journalist Sam Dean, is a conduit for the reader to venture into a world rich and strange for many a white crime aficionado. And Phillips's invigorating, often brutal prose never attitudinises – we are allowed to make up our minds about the characters (black or white, honourable or callous) we encounter. There is a sharp social intelligence and analysis at work in Mike Phillips's novels – but never at the expense of a cracking crime plot. Phillips first came to Britain in 1956 and, after attaining a degree in English and politics, took a variety of jobs that afforded a very wide experience of society – factory and garage work, community activism and the running of a hostel for homeless black youths in Notting Hill. As a journalist, he stored up the savvy that would be so crucial to his tough-but-honest journo hero, and with the first Sam Dean novel, *Blood Rights* (1989), it was immediately clear that a striking new voice had arrived on the British crime-writing scene. A less-than-successful BBC Television adaptation of the novel did not lessen the steadily growing impact that successive Sam Dean novels, such as *Point of Darkness* (1994), began to make. As Joe Canzius, he writes even tougher urban thrillers such as *Fast Road to Nowhere* (1996), in which the reader is forced to root for an amoral petty thief hero in a dangerous city landscape.

It has often been pointed out that Phillips's writing has more in common with American urban crime writers than with most British middle-class authors – despite the fact that his protagonist, Dean, is very English. In the final analysis, of course, Phillips himself is an English writer, even though he has noted that he is most engaged by the same themes as classic American crime writers: urban alienation, political corruption, the way that individuals cope with the difficulties of modern life and the consequences of industrialisation. But if this makes his writing sound worthy, it should be pointed out that it is actually anything but: a sardonic sense of humour and a careful attention to the exigencies of keeping the crime plot on the move ensures that any sense of point-making is kept at bay. In terms of plotting, Phillips has no interest whatsoever in the Christie-style classic mystery plot in which various elements of the puzzle are slotted into place; his is a messy, chaotic universe, with the author only just managing to pull everything together, creating a rough kind of closure. Phillips is aware of the perception that his Joe Canzius books are more squarely aimed at a black readership, but (he has said) this is not really the case. His first published book – a collection of short stories – was aimed at a black readership, but after that he decided that he wanted to write for whoever chose to pick up his books. Certainly, Sam Dean is a relatively easy character for white readers to identify with – while he is scathing about racism, he is often in as much danger from black villains as from prejudiced whites. And, of course, he is the ideological firm centre of the books – tough, but a very moral character. The author's avowed intent is never (he has said) to idealise the black experience in his books. He clearly has a deep distrust of particular groups claiming that their perception is more valid than any other. When quizzed about his responsibility in dealing with the black criminal class, Phillips is clear as to his position – he has always been true to his own instincts; his criminals may be black or white, but in the final analysis he has to be the judge of what they can or cannot say, and issues of political correctness cannot enter into it. Phillips clearly bears in mind that some people who do not know him will assume that he is stigmatising black or mixed-race people in his books, which clearly is not so. One of the most intriguing things about Mike Phillips, however, is in the range of influences he adduces: Graham **Greene** and even Umberto Eco (perhaps because the puzzle element he so dislikes in Agatha **Christie** is handled in Eco's *The Name of the Rose* in such an exemplary fashion).

Selected Works by the Author
Blood Rights (1989)
Point of Darkness (1994)
The Dancing Face (1997)

As Joe Canzius
Fast Road to Nowhere (1996)

Barry Forshaw

Pirie, David (b.1953)

David Pirie, a specialist in classical romantic literature and its influence on classic horror cinema, has carved out an alternative career by mining the antecedents of Sherlock **Holmes** in a series of highly accomplished novels.

The macabre and sinister world of Conan Doyle's master detective is dear to most of our hearts. From the bloodstained fangs of *The Hound of the Baskervilles* (1902) to the many grisly and bizarre methods of murder that Holmes exposes, it is an incomparable influence that is spread across most literary fields, even as far as science fiction (Isaac Asimov co-edited an anthology that took Holmes through time and space). Pirie was once celebrated as perhaps the finest of all writers on horror cinema. His *A Heritage of Horror* (1973) was quite simply the most influential book written on English horror cinema, and the book did much to confer a gravity and seriousness on a genre that had all too often been dismissed as meretricious audience fodder. Pirie was particularly noted for bringing about a revaluation of the greatness of Hammer films; before his books, these marvellous examples of British cinema had been loftily dismissed by most serious critics. Pirie's later book *The Vampire Cinema* (1997) performed a similar function on a similarly undervalued blood-boltered genre. Again, his treatment of many classic movies has never been surpassed. More recently, Pirie became known as a first-rate screenwriter, and his BBC adaptation of Wilkie **Collins**'s *The Woman in White* was a model of its kind (even if its director could hardly be said to have done service to Pirie's screenplay). He subsequently created for television a fascinating picture of the genesis of fiction's greatest detective, with Conan Doyle himself featured as Watson to the Sherlock Holmes of the remarkable doctor Joseph Bell, on whom Doyle is said to model Baker Street's most famous citizen when Doyle studied with Bell. *The Patient's Eyes: The Dark Beginnings of Sherlock Holmes* (2001) was the first book in an intriguing series that boasted all the gothic frissons and fascination of Doyle's most atmospheric work, and it created an anticipatory excitement for further books in the series. These have not disappointed, maintaining the achievement of the debut book, notably *The Dark Water* (2005), which was the most complex and ambitious of the series. This impressive series does not read as a clone of the Conan Doyle template, rather as something allied but different. *See also* The Great Detectives *and* Literature and Crime Fiction.

Selected Works by the Author
The Patient's Eyes (2001)
The Night Calls (2002)
The Dark Water (2005)

Barry Forshaw

Poirot, Hercule

When Agatha **Christie** came to invent her first, and most long-running, detective, she recalled a colony of Belgian war refugees that had lived in her hometown of Torquay in the early 1900s. She imagined one of them as a retired Belgian police officer, and since she envisioned him as being 'a tidy little man', the name of Hercules – the strongman of Greek mythology – seemed amusingly ironic.

Although Christie grew up on the stories of Sherlock **Holmes**, she envisaged *her* detective as being quite dissimilar. However, certain traits are clearly common to both – not least their vanity and obsessive attention to minutia. Various other influences are often cited, including Marie Lowndes's Hercules Popeau, a retired French detective, but he first appeared in *The Lonely House*, published two months after the first Poirot novel was being serialised in the *Times Weekly* in 1920, so any similarities are coincidental. Lowndes later used Popeau in two stories, 'Popeau Intervenes' (1926) and 'A Labour of Hercules' (1929) as pastiches of Poirot, rather than the other way round. Another suggested source is Monsieur Poiret, known as 'Old Pawray', a French detective living in retirement in England. He was created by Frank

75. Portrait of Hercule Poirot by Smithson Broadhead, published in *The Sketch* in 1923.

Howel Evans (1867–1931) for a series of stories in *The New Magazine* in 1909, which Christie might well have read, but it remains supposition.

When we first meet Poirot in *The Mysterious Affair at Styles* (1920), he is in his late sixties (and never seems to grow older), having retired from the Belgian police force as one of its most celebrated heroes. He is living a sedentary life in the village of Styles St Mary, together with a number of other Belgian refugees, and investigates the death of wealthy heiress Emily Inglethorp only because she had shown hospitality to several of his countrymen.

His first appearance is described thus: 'He was hardly more than five feet, four inches, but carried himself with great dignity. His head was exactly the shape of an egg, and he always perched it a little on one side. His moustache was very stiff and military. The neatness of his attire was almost incredible; I believe a speck of dust would have caused him more pain than a bullet wound.' He is said to limp badly, but a little later, when inspecting Mrs Inglethorp's room, he darts around, 'with the agility of a grasshopper'. Appearances can be deceptive, though: 'His faultless evening clothes, the exquisite set of his white tie, the exact symmetry of his hair parting, the sheen of pomade on his hair, and the tortured splendour of his famous moustaches – all combined to paint the perfect picture of an inveterate dandy. It was hard, at these moments, to take the little man seriously.'

It was at Styles Court that Poirot bumps into his old friend Captain Arthur Hastings, an officer in the First World War who was wounded in the Somme ('The Affair at the Victory Ball', the first Poirot short story, *The Sketch*, 7 March 1923) and invalided out of the army. Hastings marries Dulcie Duveen in *Murder on the Links* (1923), and they emigrate to Argentina. But he periodically returns to England to visit his old friend Poirot, leaving his wife at home on their ranch.

After *The ABC Murders* (1936), a gap of many years follows – in which his place is filled by the efficient Miss Lemon, formerly Parker Pyne's secretary – before he returns to help Poirot one final time in *Curtain: Poirot's Last Case* (1975).

Poirot has moved to the village of King's Abbot in *The Murder of Roger Ackroyd* (1926), but by the time of *The ABC Murders*, he is residing at central London's swanky Whitehaven Mansions, an apartment block he admires for its 'most pleasing symmetry'. The name of these apartments changes twice, whether by accident or design is unsure, to Whitehouse Mansions in *Cat among the Pigeons* (1959) and Whitefriars Mansions in Christie's penultimate book, *Elephants Can Remember* (1972).

Poirot sanctifies mother-love but is cynical about romantic attachments: 'Women are never kind, though they can sometimes be tender,' he states in *After the Funeral* (1953). The one exception to this self-imposed rule is the flamboyant Russian aristocrat Vera Rossakoff from *The Big Four* (1927) – she is often in his thoughts, and he cannot help but unfavourably compare London girls with her. He seems generally uninterested in sex, but can be moved by great beauty, be it male or female. In *Hallowe'en Party* (1969), he observes a young man 'of an unusual beauty…[he] was tall, slender, with features of great perfection such as a classical sculptor might have produced'.

His over-riding characteristic is egotism. 'I admit freely and without hypocrisy that I am a great man,' he proclaims in *The Mysterious Affair at Styles*. He is proud of his intellectual capabilities – those famous 'little grey cells' – and always maintains that, 'every fact that I know is in your possession. You can draw your own deductions from them.' In the short story 'The Kidnapped Prime Minister' (*Poirot Investigates*,

1924), he taps his forehead knowingly and exclaims, 'The true clues are within – *here!*' He sneers at the Sherlock Holmes–type detective who rushes around the lawn measuring wet footprints in the grass – even though he is known to do the same thing himself.

The only failure in his illustrious career occurred during his early days in the Belgian police force in which he neglected the significance of a blue lid on a pink box. 'My grey cells, they functioned not at all,' Poirot admits in 'The Chocolate Box' (*Poirot Investigates*). From then on, he asks Hastings to murmur 'chocolate box' in his ear (akin to 'Norbury' in Arthur Conan **Doyle**'s *The Adventure of the Yellow Face*) should he ever become conceited about his abilities.

In many early cases, the detective says he has retired to grow vegetable marrows, but apart from the one that he throws over the fence (accidentally) at his neighbour Dr Sheppard (*The Mysterious Affair at Styles*), we see little evidence of this pastime. He also says that he would make a good pickpocket, a claim we should perhaps take with rather a large pinch of salt.

A man of leisure, he treats himself to many holidays. He travels abroad, occasionally accompanied by his manservant George. He has visited such exotic locales as the Holy Land (*Appointment With Death*, 1938) and the Nile (*Death on the Nile*, 1937) and can sometimes be found staying at The Ritz (*Three Act Tragedy*, 1935). But there are also times when he mixes business with pleasure. He passes through Hassanieh, the dig site in Mesopotamia, on his way to Baghdad after 'disentangling some military scandal in Syria' for the French government in *Murder in Mesopotamia* (1936). When he returns home on the *Orient Express*, he uncovers another scandal that he must resolve before the train reaches its destination (***Murder on the Orient Express***, 1934).

His fame as a detective goes before him. M Fournier of the French Sûreté (*Death in the Clouds*, 1935) has heard of his reputation from M Giraud (*Murder on the Links*, 1923), and he arrives speedily at the scene of a Yuletide murder because he has been staying nearby with the chief constable of the fictitious Middleshire (*Hercule Poirot's Christmas*, 1938). On another occasion, his presence at a suspected poisoning in *Sad Cypress* (1940) is because Dr John Stillingfleet from the short story 'The Dream' (*Saturday Evening Post*, 23 October 1937) recommended him to Dr Peter Lord. But he realises that as he gets older, fewer and fewer people will have heard of him. He stops himself saying, 'Most people have heard of me', when he realises that those people are probably now in their graves (*Elephants Can Remember*).

Poirot's idea of the perfect crime, as discussed in *The ABC Murders*, would have 'no complications' – in other words, no emotional entanglements, just a simple puzzle to solve. Such a case might involve four people in a closed room playing bridge while a fifth is murdered in full view of them; a prescient comment considering the exact same situation occurs soon after. Chief Inspector James Japp, the ferret-faced policeman he sometimes works alongside, says he will end up detecting his own death, something Poirot does indeed do in *Curtain: Poirot's Last Case*.

He enjoys children's verse, albeit reluctantly ('A jingle ran through Poirot's head. He repressed it. He must *not* always be thinking of nursery rhymes'), with his recollection of 'Rub a Dub Dub' helping to locate a missing girl in the *Third Girl* (1966). He knows 'Hickory Dickory Dock' and can quote easily from Lewis Carroll. As for 'serious' literature, he has a sound knowledge of English poetry, especially Tennyson (*The Hollow*, 1946), but misquotes Shakespeare (*Taken at the Flood*, 1948). Berating his lack of classical education, he indulges in a crash course on ancient legends and then proclaims grandly that he will only solve cases if they conform to the twelve labours of his namesake Hercules (*The Labours of Hercules*, 1947). He forgets this promise soon after, thank goodness!

With regard to more contemporary reading matter, he recommends the following (real) murder mysteries: *The Leavenworth Case* (1878) by Anna Katherine Green, *The Adventures of Arsène Lupin* by Maurice Leblanc and *The Mystery of the Yellow Room* (1908) by Gaston Leroux. But he criticises the techniques of (fictional) crime writers Cyril Quain, Garry Gregson and Ariadne Oliver (a best-selling crime writer invented by Christie as a semi-autobiographical figure who would go on to star in several novels of her own). Concerning Arthur Conan Doyle's *The Adventures of Sherlock Holmes* (1892), he is content with the simple exclamation, 'Maître!' He is so well versed on the subject of detective fiction, in fact, that he publishes a critique in *Third Girl*, in which he writes scathingly of Edgar Allan Poe and Wilkie **Collins**. He is typically proud of his book, despite the 'really incredible number of printer's errors' contained in it.

As for culinary tastes, he considers himself a gourmet – he dines alone at a favourite Soho restaurant (*Mrs McGinty's Dead*, 1952) and is known to enjoy a breakfast of brioche and hot chocolate (*Third Girl*). And he is certainly interested in the eating habits of others, especially when they lead to murder (Four and Twenty Blackbirds, *Collier's*, 9 November 1940).

He admits that his oft-repeated remarks about retiring bear more than a passing resemblance to 'the prima donna who makes positively that farewell performance'. But the moment does indeed arrive when he makes his very last curtain call. Confined to a wheelchair, his thin face lined and wrinkled and sporting a dyed moustache and wig (*Curtain: Poirot's Last Case*), the incredibly aged Poirot admits that 'This, Hastings, will be my last case'. *See also* The Great Detectives: The Mass Appeal of Holmes, Poirot and Wimsey; The Police in Golden Age Crime Fiction; *and* Police Procedurals.

Further Reading
Hart, Anne. 1990. *The Life and Times of Hercule Poirot*. Pavilion Books.

Mark Campbell

The Police in Golden Age Crime Fiction

The police play a double role in the traditional British crime fiction of the **Golden Age**, which flourished in the 1920s and 1930s. On the one hand, they put the resources of the state at the disposal of the principal detective, typically a genteel amateur whose forensic brilliance by far outshines that of the professionals. On the other hand, their deferential attitude both to the principal detective and to other members of the upper and middle classes soothes the political anxieties and social insecurities of the genre's readers.

Earlier fictional policemen tended to be formidable figures – examples include Inspector Bucket in Charles **Dickens**'s *Bleak House* (1853) and Sergeant Cuff in Wilkie **Collins**'s *The Moonstone* (1868). The arrival of Sherlock **Holmes** and his followers in the late nineteenth century changed this trend. An omniscient 'consulting detective' could not reasonably be expected to co-exist with competent police officers capable of mounting effective criminal investigations all by themselves.

In the early twentieth century, the consequences of the First World War transformed the world and Britain's place in it. Popular culture reflected this, and it is no accident that the Golden Age detective is so often a gentlemanly (or ladylike) amateur. The middle classes needed to feel that their values were still important in a changing world. Hence the fact that the professional police were so often portrayed as not only intellectually inferior to the detective but socially inferior as well. But police officers still had their uses. Even the grandest of sleuths had to have some contact with the unglamorous machinery of the law.

Agatha **Christie** is not the best example of the syndrome. When police officers appear in her novels, they are not exactly realistic, but on the whole, they are not sneered at either.

Dorothy L. **Sayers** took a different approach. With Lord Peter **Wimsey** and Inspector Parker, she created the classic relationship between gentleman sleuth and police officer. Parker's face is described as 'plain, though pleasant' in *Strong Poison* (1930); his origins are lowly; he has a comical if inexplicable taste for the theology of the early church. In *Whose Body* (1923), Wimsey has to leave London. He summons Parker and gives him a string of orders, culminating with 'Don't march in there blowing about murders and police warrants, or you may find yourself in Queer Street...'. Parker improves his social position over time, largely because of the elevating influence of Wimsey's friendship, and he eventually marries Wimsey's sister; but even when gentrified, he remains properly conscious of his station in life.

Margery **Allingham**'s first Campion novels are set in a similar mould, for Campion's family is even grander than Wimsey's. But in her portraits of Chief Inspector Oates and Superintendent Luke, Allingham does not place such stress as Sayers does on the social divide separating the professional from the amateur sleuth; and the gap between them steadily decreases as the series progresses.

Some Golden Age crime novels had a professional sleuth, a police officer, on centre stage. This was less of a departure than it might appear. Many of these novels are no more than dramatised puzzles, like those of Freeman Wills **Crofts** whose Inspector French is little more than a pipe-smoking brain attached to a digestive system. Others simply allow the gentleman sleuth with a private income to masquerade as a police officer.

Ngaio **Marsh**'s novels provide a case in point. One scene is regularly repeated in her books – a character's surprise at meeting Inspector Alleyn for the first time. In *Overture to Death* (1939), Alleyn is talking to the squire, and the squire's son Henry comes to rescue his father. Henry fears that the policeman 'will carry his bowler in with him and his boots will be intolerable.... A mammoth of officialdom!' Imagine his surprise when he finds someone who looks like one of his father's friends – 'an extremely tall man, thin and wearing good clothes, with an air of vague distinction...' who reminds Henry of a 'grandee turned monk'.

Alleyn's brother is a baronet, and in many ways, the inspector is indistinguishable from Wimsey or Campion: he too has a good tailor, a degree from Oxbridge, a flat in the West End and a manservant. And he also has his lower-class sidekicks. Chief among them is Inspector Fox, usually referred to with relentless whimsy as 'Brer Fox'. Even Alleyn's murder cases seem made to measure. In *The Nursing Home Murder* (1935), for example, the Home Secretary dies under suspicious circumstances.

Naturally, it is Alleyn who is called in. After all, he was at school with the Home Secretary's brother-in-law.

Michael **Innes**'s John Appleby is the donnish variant of the gentleman sleuth masquerading as a police officer. In *Hamlet, Revenge* (1937), the Lord Chancellor is murdered during amateur theatricals at a ducal house party. Later that evening, when Inspector Appleby saunters back to his London flat from the ballet, he finds the Prime Minister and the Commissioner of Metropolitan Police waiting eagerly for his return. Only Appleby, it seems, has the requisite forensic, social and literary-critical skills for a case of this gravity. There is even a fire engine parked outside Appleby's flat to whisk him to the scene of the crime – because, rather endearingly, the Prime Minister thinks fire engines have nicer sirens than police cars and earn more respect from the travelling public.

Josephine **Tey**'s detective, Inspector Alan Grant, is a transitional figure. In the earliest of her novels, *The Man in the Queue* (1929), his debt to the gentleman sleuth is most evident – he has private means, 'good manners' and handmade shoes. But Grant evolves steadily into a flawed and fascinating character. By Tey's last book, *The Singing Sands* (1952), he has left the Golden Age behind and moved into the post-war era.

In its attitude to the police, crime fiction often reveals more than its authors ever intended about contemporary attitudes to society. The attitude of the Golden Age is no exception. *See also* Police Procedurals.

Further Reading

Ousby, Ian. 1997. *The Crime and Mystery Book*. Thames & Hudson.
Symons, Julian. 1985. *Bloody Murder*, rev. ed. Viking.
Watson, Colin. 1979. *Snobbery with Violence*, rev. ed. Methuen.

Andrew Taylor

Police Procedurals

Given that most crimes are investigated by the police, it seems odd that the crimes in so many crime stories are investigated by private detectives especially in the early days of the genre. Nothing more clearly underlines the fact that the stories we choose to read are fiction. The police are the true professionals; they have greater resources, greater manpower and greater experience. Private detectives in real life solve few murders and practically no robberies. The casebook of the British private detective today comprises missing persons (a few sad episodes), adultery (less than fifty years ago), credit reference and debt collection. However effective we think the police are at solving crime, they are in real terms all we have got.

Early crime stories reflected this. Leaving aside the earliest, from Japan and China where the crimes were solved by 'magistrates' who were, in effect, investigating officers, the earliest Western tales were French, and in those, the investigators were the police. The two most famous, Vidocq and Lecoq, were officers of the Sûreté, and the fictional detectives who followed tended to be police officers too. Exceptions prove the rule. Poe's Auguste Dupin was sensational because he *was not* a policeman: he broke new ground. Sherlock **Holmes** became a prototype. Before him, Britain's early detectives were policemen such as Inspector Bucket and Sergeant Cuff, though unlike their French counterparts, they were not the heroes of their books. Vidocq's memoirs were boastful, supposedly factual, while Lecoq grew into his books, being introduced warily in his first case, because for most people then, as his creator Gaboriau made clear, the police and therefore police detectives were feared and detested. Here, perhaps, is the clue we seek as to why police detectives failed for so long to achieve the popular success of amateur rivals: law-abiding citizens need the police but do not like them. (We have always preferred to imagine ourselves rescued by heroes, knights in armour or fairy godmothers than by unromantic but legitimate authorities.)

76. James Ellis and Arthur Slater star in *Z Cars* (BBC Television).

When the charismatic (if fantastical) Sherlock Holmes arrived to kick detective fiction into a new playing field, readers and writers abandoned the uneasy relationship they had had with police heroes and welcomed the amateur instead. Here was a hero untainted by the prying and intrusive state, one unfettered by legal niceties, one who could set his own rules to ensure that fairness and justice rather than mere law prevailed. Yet, meanwhile, out in the real world, the police were transforming themselves to be independent from political paymasters, instead to be impartial upholders of law and order and seekers of truth. They made increased and effective use of technology – fingerprints, ballistics, chemical analyses and forensic jurisprudence – and raised their skills far above those that could be practised by an amateur. In fiction, during the amateur detective boom, policemen (they were always men) plodded about in awe of those brilliant civilians and touched their forelocks to wealthy witnesses. They were without a clue. Reality was different, so it was inevitable that the unreal world must eventually catch up with the real.

It would be wrong to say that, in the early twentieth century, there were no fictional police detectives or that they were entirely eclipsed by amateurs. Nor was it true that they always had second billing. Considerable sales were achieved by stout policemen such as A.E.W. **Mason**'s Inspector Hanaud (who was certainly stout, and French – he too worked for the Sûreté) who appeared first in 1910 (*At the Villa Rose*). In 1920, Freeman Wills **Crofts** introduced Inspector Burnley (*The Cask*), a less interesting character than Hanaud but arguably the first realistic police detective – so realistic that the modern reader finds him dull. Burnley was a policeman, working as a policeman would, relying on no flashes of astounding intuition but instead carefully piecing together snippets of evidence and building a case. All this he did on the page, sharing the process with the reader. Crofts replaced Burnley (perhaps even Crofts found Burnley dull) with three other short-lived police detectives before settling on his equally realistic Inspector French, a contentedly married, well-balanced officer who went on to appear in over thirty books. Being stories, his cases were not ones an officer met every day: they relied on complicated alibis based, more often than not, on Crofts's personal delight: railway timetables. (He had been an engineer on the Belfast and Northern Counties Railway.) In the wake of Inspector French came other officers, interesting in their day but now forgotten despite the length of their series, including G.D.H. Cole's Henry Wilson (twenty-five books, 1923–1943), J.J. Connington's Chief Constable Sir Clinton Driffield (seventeen books, 1927–1947), John Bude's Inspector Meredith (twenty-five books lasting till 1957) and Cyril **Hare**'s Inspector Mallet (less titles, only seven, but a successful series, the last and most famous being *He Should Have Died Hereafter* in 1958). None of these, good as they were, carried the acrid whiff of reality one sniffed from France, where the splendid Maigret books of George Simenon revealed the most believable policeman of them all.

Few of these books were real police procedurals. They were crime stories in which the detective was a policeman. After Simenon, Crofts came closest, but his timetable obsession became more important to him than did police procedure. With all these writers, greater authenticity lay in their having policemen rather than amateurs as detectives, but the actual detection in their books was almost as removed from reality as were the solutions teased out by plain-clothed rivals. The books were in competition with **Golden Age** detective stories, stories in which reality was neither attempted nor called for by readers. All this would change.

The Second World War brought greater changes in crime fiction than did the First. (The Golden Age began before the First World War and continued barely different after.) If class structures were shaken by the First World War, they were shattered by the next. The millions – literally millions – reading light fiction in the war came out hard-eyed and rational. They knew the world; they knew violence. They had stared death in the face and were done with whimsy.

Old-style authors had to change. Lord Peter **Wimsey** did not survive the war. Albert **Campion** sloughed off his irritating toffish mannerisms and took a back seat in stories only nominally written about him. Strangeways, Nicholas **Blake**'s sleuth, clung on, as did Inspector Alleyn, but they seemed increasingly anachronistic. Christie's detectives had never been real: one did not read her for reality, so she survived, as she survives today, through the brilliance of her puzzles. Readers seeking something new could turn to American-style British tough-guy writers such as Peter **Cheyney** and James Hadley **Chase**, but they were as unreal, in their different way, as the Golden Age retainers. Real crime was nasty, and it was not solved by Golden Age detectives or pseudo-Yanks carrying guns; it was solved, as readers knew, by everyday policemen. There was Maigret, but he was French.

The nineteenth century was long past, and few post-war readers remembered a time when the police had been hated agents of the state. Now they were seen as necessary and reliable – men doing their duty: everyone could identify with that. Crime films (mostly American) had swung towards reality; gangster films had been a mainstay of 'B' movies since the 1930s and against the gangster was the cop. Cop shows began to appear on American television. *Dragnet* came on radio. But with books, it was several years after the war ended before this new wave beached and the police procedural could be added to the existing genre of crime novels. America, inevitably, claims to have produced the first such novel, *V as in Victim* (1945) by Lawrence Treat, and although its claim for precedence will never be absolutely settled, it seems secure enough. A British author, Maurice Procter (1906–1973), followed close behind. His *No Proud Chivalry* (1946) benefited from his twenty years in the force and featured PC Pierce Rogan of 'Otherburn Borough' Police. In 1951, he introduced DS Philip Hunter of 'Yoreborough' in *The Chief Inspector's Statement* and in 1954 came his more famous DCI Harry Martineau, in **Hell Is a City**. It was closely followed by one of the most prolific crime writers of all time: J.J. Marric, a pseudonym of John **Creasey**, who with *Gideon's Day* (1955) launched Britain's first major police procedural series.

The time was right. In 1954, BBC Television launched its ground-breaking *Fabian of Scotland Yard*, starring Bruce Seton as Fabian, with episodes based on the real-life Detective Inspector Robert Fabian, recently of the Flying Squad, and known to the public for his newspaper column and best-selling autobiography. (He had led Britain's largest ever murder hunt following the gunning down of an innocent garage-owner, Alec de Antiquis. Shortly after the killing, a photojournalist snapped what was to become the best-known crime photo of the 1940s – of Antiquis lying at the kerb on the corner of Soho's Charlotte Street, attended by two plain-clothes detectives.) *Fabian of Scotland Yard* showed how exciting police work could be, and although on-screen Fabian was played by Seton, each episode ended with Fabian delivering an epilogue. The series was a huge success, even in America, and the lesson was not lost on British crime writers.

Procter's Harry Martineau worked in the fictional northern city of Granchester. Procter used his considerable experience to create realistic officers, warts and all, tackling realistic crimes perpetrated by believable criminals. Marric set his policeman in London, as a detective superintendent at New Scotland Yard, and from his first appearance (in *Gideon's Day*, 1955), Marric introduced a narrative technique used widely since (most notably by the American author Ed McBain with his eighty-seventh Precinct series, launched a year later) of having his hero investigate several cases simultaneously. Here again was a technique entirely credible when telling of the hectic life of a busy police officer, but less so for a private or amateur detective. No longer need a single case be spun out beyond its natural length; the police detective could step aside whenever the author chose to deal with a parallel case or one unconnected to the main investigation. More often than not, certainly in Marric's tales, the main strands would eventually come together, giving the reader greater satisfaction when not one but several mysteries reached solution. Martineau and Gideon starred in over twenty books each.

The 'several strands' approach highlighted another advantage of police procedurals over detective novels: where the Great Detective is restricted in the crimes, he is hired to investigate – albeit a reasonably fruitful field of murder, disappearance, blackmail or robbery – the police detective can handle all these plus any number of more ordinary and perhaps more human crimes, such as rape, arson, fraud, prostitution, drugs or illegal immigration. (No one employs a private detective to investigate these.) The policeman, too, can deploy an army of specialist assistants – profilers, forensic scientists and armed officers – and has access to a powerful array of state-funded databases and surveillance tools.

Specialists were less in evidence in the early years. In the first decade of police procedurals, authors found they had enough material in the wealth of crimes investigated and from the expansion beyond tales with a single leading officer into tales where the reader met a team of investigators, each of whom could make their own small or significant contribution. Readers learned the difficulty of building a case against a suspect, the problems added by government regulations or inter-departmental rivalry and the conflicts between police work and private life. Other authors capitalised on geography, as in the Sergeant Cluff novels set in Yorkshire, written by Gil North (1916–1988), and the Thane & Moss series set in Glasgow, by Bill Knox (1928–1999). Nevertheless, in their reconstructed reality, these early police procedurals ran the risk of becoming as dull and humdrum as real police work. Real investigations require boundless patience: knocking on doors, interviewing at length, sending samples for analysis and waiting for results – none of which makes for exciting fiction. Before the genre became too settled, it needed another shot in the arm.

Television had continued to gain high viewing figures from police dramas. *Fabian* had been followed by successful series such as *Dixon of Dock Green* (1955), *Colonel March of Scotland Yard* (1956), *Murder Bag* (1957; later *No Hiding Place*), *Dial 999* (1958), *Nick of the River* (1959) – even as a slight variation, *The Man from Interpol* (also 1959). But television is a restless medium, always seeking change. In 1960, BBC Television launched the superbly photographed, tightly performed *Maigret* starring Rupert Davies. For a while, it seemed the future might lie with the lone police detective solving crime largely on his own. But it was not to be. In 1962, the BBC shattered every conception of how the police behaved (in drama, at least) with a complex police procedural that from its very first episode provoked headlines in the newspapers – over little more, one feels when looking back at the fuss, than the fact that officers on duty were shown in shirt sleeves in Panda Cars *smoking cigarettes*! The real shock, though, was that this gritty northern series, *Z Cars*, had policemen who bullied, were racist, drank too much, smoked and gambled – in one case, a policeman beat his wife – yet remained dedicated to their sweaty unpleasant job. If some viewers were shocked, most loved the series. High-ups within the police feared the programme would have a detrimental effect on the public's image of the force, so help from police consultants was withdrawn. (Many serving officers, though, welcomed the realism.) Long before the first series ended, it seemed obvious that this was the future for police procedurals. By the time Marric's Gideon appeared on screen, in *Gideon's Way* (1965), he seemed hopelessly old-fashioned.

That same year, a *Z Cars* scriptwriter, Allan Prior (1922–2006), brought out *The Interrogators*, a new-wave police procedural novel in which an unscrupulous senior officer broke the rules and guidelines to clear his case. The year 1965 also saw the first of John **Wainwright**'s new-style Yorkshire-based procedurals, *Death in a Sleeping City*, again with a tough uncompromising leading officer and an unglamourised police force. Wainwright's many books (some eighty) are very much 'precinct' novels in which different characters take the leads. But onto the same ground strode surprisingly few other British writers, leaving aside Jonathan Ross (b.1916), whose *The Blood Running Cold* began a series in 1968, and Roger Busby (b.1941), starting with *Robbery Blue* in 1969. Even Reginald **Hill**, whose first Dalziel and Pascoe novel, *A Clubbable Woman* came out in 1970, spun his plots around the two detectives, rather than their colleagues. The police procedural thrived in America but remained a minor thread in Britain. British writers wrote police detective stories in which, as with Inspector Alleyn and others from decades before, a police detective rather than a department starred; examples include Nicolas **Freeling** (Van der Valk), Ruth **Rendell**

Police Procedurals

(Inspector **Wexford**), P.D. **James** (Adam **Dalgliesh**) and W.J. **Burley** (Wycliffe). Fine as they are, they are not police procedurals.

In the 1970s, television moved from *Z Cars* to its continuations, *Softly, Softly* and *Barlow at Large*, followed by *The Sweeney* in 1975, but largely preferred detective dramas. *Juliet Bravo* revived the procedural in 1980, but again stood alone until television's truest police procedural ***The Bill*** began in 1984. In 1991, ***Prime Suspect***, though it centred on Jane Tennison, showed the whole of her department with its feuds and rivalries but, like the television shows that followed, hesitated to move away from its powerful central character. ***Cracker*** (1993) and *Silent Witness* (1996) expanded from the police themselves to the specialists working beside them, but most series stuck with one strong central character: think of Inspector **Frost**, Hamish Macbeth, Inspector Lynley, Inspector **Morse** and John **Rebus**.

The same pattern was seen in crime books. The last five names above join a squad of best-selling police detectives. Adam Dalgliesh solves crimes practically on his own. Though he usually works in East Anglia, he hails from the anonymous Scotland Yard; we know little about his team. Ruth Rendell's Wexford, on the other hand, has a strongly drawn right-hand man, Mike Burden, but although he gets input from Kingsmarkham colleagues, we learn little of consequence about them. **Wingfield**'s Inspector Frost is a loner, unlikely to fit comfortably anywhere, though his cantankerousness does help us get to know a little of his reluctant colleagues and the ins and outs of their routine. John Rebus, too, another loner, battles as much with his colleagues as with villains, but those colleagues, Siobhan apart, remain shadowy figures. We know as much about Rebus's early life as about those who share his life today. We learn more about Edinburgh than about them, rather as, in the Morse books, we learn more about Oxford than about that city's police. Sergeant Lewis apart, Morse's fellow officers are mere furniture. The stories are mysteries – intricate and teasing mysteries – but not police procedurals.

But if none of these police series from our leading crime writers can be described as police procedurals – any more than can those of Mark **Billingham**, John **Harvey**, Bill **James** or Stephen **Booth** – we are forced to ask to what extent procedurals exist in print away from the television screen. In a few seconds the camera reveals a roomful of officers, each immediately identifiable and each employed in different ways. A line or two, a flick of the eye, and the camera shows us all we need to know of their interrelationships, tensions and doubts, their strengths and weaknesses, successes and mistakes. We see the office, the machinery they use, which officers wear uniform, which cars they drive. We see, behind the action, all the detail that takes pages to describe. There are books that do describe all this; one remembers the 1950s novels of Maurice Procter, the 1960s of John **Wainwright** and Peter N. Walker, the 'P' Division stories of Peter Turnbull – even the chaotic Aberdeen novels of Stuart MacBride – but good as they are, they remain (in sales terms) outside the first division. None achieve the success of American authors such as Ed McBain. Britain awaits its first top-selling precinct novel. Until it comes we must settle for lesser-known authors or sit in front of television and watch *The Bill*. *See also* The Police in Golden Age Crime Fiction *and* TV Detectives: Small-Screen Adaptations.

Russell James

Porter, Henry (b.1953)

Reading the novels of Henry Porter, it is immediately obvious that he knows the world of **espionage** and the people who inhabit this shady underworld. He has quickly carved out a reputation for accuracy and labyrinthine plotting, which have made his novels worldwide bestsellers.

The son of a career soldier, Porter was educated at Wellington and Manchester University studying art. He is a former reporter and journalist and has written for *The Guardian*, *The Daily Telegraph* and *The Sunday Telegraph* and the defunct *London Evening Standard*. He became the London editor of *Vanity Fair* magazine in 1992 and shares the honour with Ian **Fleming** for once being the editor of the 'Atticus' column on the *Sunday Times*.

He turned to writing a novel when he had the idea of terrorists being able to detonate bombs remotely by telephone (critics were harsh on the book's technical exposition). *Remembrance Day* (1999) is a briskly told story of a race against the clock to stop further atrocities. While the Troubles of a post–Northern Ireland timeframe is essential to the plotting, the story is driven by an absorbing set of characters. The novel sticks fairly close to the standard conventions for a thriller but there is no denying that Porter had a flair for storytelling. With the collapse of the Soviet Bloc and end of the Cold War, spy novelists had to look elsewhere for inspiration and Porter looked at the world of global terrorism for his next two books. *A Spy's Life* (2001) is the story of ex-spy Robert Harland who survives the crash of a sabotaged UN plane. Harland is now working for the Red Cross but is targeted by someone out to kill him. To add further pressure, a young Czech boy shows up, claiming to be his son. Harland's life is turned upside down as he gets caught up in a multi-government dragnet intended to plug intelligence leaks and in the tracking down of a brutal Bosnian war criminal who he had thought was dead but is being protected by Western powers. *Empire State* (2003) deals with Islamist terrorists from the training grounds of Afghanistan and Bosnia and their plan to carry out an audacious attack against the West. The novel opens with an assassination near Heathrow, witnessed by Isis Herrick, daughter of a long-standing SIS operative; she knows the spy game and now is pitted against the ex-mujahedeen terrorist.

Brandenburg (2005) won the Ian Fleming **Crime Writers' Association** Steel Dagger as the best thriller of 2005. The genesis of the story had been with the author since he witnessed the fall of the Berlin Wall in 1989, and the book is set in the dark and intriguing days of the Cold War just eight weeks before the event. Rudi Rosenharte is the unlikely hero, an East German art historian who is lured back into East Germany by an ex-lover working for the Stasi and finds himself caught in a web of deceit from Western secret agents from the British SIS, the American CIA and the Russian KGB. It is a complex thriller that, among other themes, explores the evil within the then Communist regime, the underlying paranoia of East German society and Rosenharte's conflict of loyalty.

Most of us are attracted to the notion that there is an unseen hand at work in most important endeavours. In Henry Porter's books, the characters are responding pragmatically to such a duplicitous world, and due to the nature of this secret world that they inhabit, they are open to infinite manipulation. *See also* Espionage Fiction.

Porter, Henry

Selected Works by the Author
Remembrance Day (1999)
A Spy's Life (2001)
Empire State (2003)
Brandenberg (2005)

Mike Stotter

Porter, Joyce (1924–1990)

Despite cornering the market in humorous, cleverly written detective stories for a number of years, Joyce Porter now remains a footnote in the annals of crime fiction, with none of her titles currently in print.

Porter was born in Cheshire on 8 March 1924 and educated at King's College London, whose alumni include Thomas Hardy, Susan **Hill** and Anita Brookner. For a while, she served in the Women's Royal Air Force before penning her first novel, *Dover One*, in 1964. The title character was one Chief Inspector Wilfred Dover, New Scotland Yard's laziest and most incompetent policeman, who is packed off to farthest Creedshire – as far away from the rest of his colleagues as possible, in fact – to investigate the disappearance of a young housemaid under mysterious circumstances. In a later book, *Dover & the Claret Tappers* (1976), Doven's long-suffering partner Sgt MacGregor thinks he has seen the last of him, only to have Dover's kidnappers swiftly return him when their ransom demands are refused. The portly Dover returned for a further nine cases, as well as several short stories for *Ellery Queen Mystery Magazine* (collected in 1995).

Sour Cream with Everything (1966) was the first of four books featuring another similarly light-hearted character: Edmund 'Eddie' Brown, the world's most unlikely spy. In 1970, the Honourable Constance Ethel Morrison-Burke made the first of five appearances, beginning with *Rather a Common Sort of Crime*, a tongue-in-cheek spoof of the amateur sleuth genre popularised by Miss Jane **Marple** and others. Known to all as 'the Hon Con', this delightfully eccentric spinster waded in where angels (and police detectives) feared to tread, solving a potpourri of crimes with a mix of feminine intuition and good old-fashioned pluck. *See also* Humour and Crime Fiction.

Selected Works by the Author
Dover One (1964)
A Meddler and Her Murder (1972)
It's Murder with Dover (1973)
Dover & the Claret Tappers (1974)

Mark Campbell

Price, Anthony (b.1928)

Anthony Price is a conservative romantic, whose output represents the apotheosis of the **espionage** tale as a puzzle/mystery to be resolved, with its resolution depending on understanding some conundrum from the past.

Price studied history at Oxford and thereafter worked in the literary world as a journalist and editor for the Westminster Press. In the 1960s, he was crime fiction reviewer for the *Oxford Mail* and a judge for the Crime Writers Association's annual awards, the Gold and Silver Daggers. Remarkably, he received the latter for his first book, *The Labyrinth Makers* (1970), and not long after received the highest award for a crime novel with *Other Paths to Glory* (1974). Price's romantic preoccupation with the past, and with the broad canvas of history, is the deeper subject matter behind the specific problem or task of each investigation. His historical puzzles range from archaeology and the ancient world through to the English Civil War, American Civil War and especially the two world wars. His conservative espionage thrillers are clever, rather cerebral defences of Great Britain under threat from the Soviet Union.

The main recurring character is Dr David Audley, a slightly eccentric classicist who once worked the Middle East desk and is blessed with perhaps the subtlest mind in modern espionage fiction. Along with the retired soldier, Colonel Jack Butler, he engages their Russian adversaries in stratagems of counter-espionage. Although each book is a self-contained mystery, the author develops an over-arching timescale from Audley and Butler's meeting during the war (*The '44 Vintage*, 1978) through several episodes set in the 1950s or 1960s through to the 1970s. Audley emphasises the need for clear thinking and honour, while Butler reminds us that discipline is another important personal and corporate asset. They both work as intelligence officers in an establishment called R&D, but it is comparatively rare for them to be engaged as field agents on dangerous assignments. Younger members such as Elizabeth Loftus and Paul Mitchell undertake fieldwork. Most of the characters are well educated, but the appeal is broadened by having them think and behave differently, and Butler is a working-class Lancashire lad.

Many of Price's best novels are about things that happened long ago under the haze of war. *The Labyrinth Makers* boasts a brilliant opening in which the RAF find a crashed plane that was not missing; the mystery unfolds around the Dakota that may or may not have been ferreting rocks or buried treasure from bombed-out Berlin. The book is partly a detective story, asking what happened and why, and partly espionage suspense, as competing intelligence services vie with each through deception and misinformation.

In Anthony Price's spy world, Britain finds itself in a struggle with the USSR where unpleasant deeds take place elsewhere, and tact, diplomacy (read deception) and guile are the tools of trade. It can resemble a master chessboard game – but a better analogy would be snakes and ladders – where progress actually depends on skill *and* chance – going back and forth can be more stimulating.

Selected Works by the Author
The Labyrinth Makers (1970)
The Alamut Ambush (1971)
Colonel Butler's Wolf (1972)
Other Paths to Glory (1974)
War Game (1976)
The '44 Vintage (1978)
Tomorrow's Ghost (1979)
The Hour of the Donkey (1980)
Soldier No More (1981)

Michael Johnson

Priestley, J[ohn] B[oynton] (1894–1984)

J.B. Priestley, Yorkshire-born (though latterly he lived away from the county), excelled as a novelist, a dramatist, an essayist, a scriptwriter and a broadcaster. One does not readily think of him in connection with crime fiction, but he did write an essay on reading detective stories in bed and frequently tried his hand at writing crime fiction of his own, in various genres. He even introduced 'crime' elements into two mainstream novels, *They Walk in the City* (1936) and, his own favourite novel, *Bright Day* (1946) – in both cases as an apparent afterthought and (it might be argued) not convincingly.

Other Priestley books are more obviously crime fiction, though most share his sometimes quirky prejudices, political and otherwise. The earliest is *Benighted* (1927), an updated gothic horror thriller, twice filmed. *The Doomsday Men* (1938) is an early example of a nuclear cliffhanger (predating Hiroshima by seven years), fast-moving with strong characterisation and nicely described scenes in England, the French Riviera and (mostly) America. Priestley returned to a nuclear thriller in 1961 for *Saturn over the Water*, another kinetic and exciting tale, its action again covering much of the world.

Blackout in Gretley (1942), a 'story of – and for – wartime', incorporates counter-espionage and the black market and is set in a depressing north Midlands town; the hero, an MI5 man, shares Priestley's idealism and left-wing predilections. *The Shapes of Sleep* (1962), in which a missing document is chased all over Europe, is another thriller that moves with exciting fluency. *Salt Is Leaving* (1966) is, like *Blackout in Gretley*, set in a Midlands town. Here, two people, a bookseller and a sex-obsessed young woman, disappear. Salt, a general practitioner (the latter victim was his patient), is convinced that they were murdered; he investigates with a Maigret-like blend of energy and apparent lethargy, despite his desire to leave town. He solves the mystery and acquires a (second) wife.

Priestley's plays often feature criminal elements. His first such was *Dangerous Corner* (1932) in which a group of people reveal facts about themselves which gradually reveal the true nature of events related to a friend's death. Priestley was fascinated by the idea of 'serial time', as proposed by J.W. Dunne, and he used the idea again in possibly his best known play, *An Inspector Calls* (first performed 1945; 1947). Here a police inspector calls upon a family to investigate a local girl's suicide and unravels how all contributed towards her fate. The play's twist ending jolts the conscience. His other plays also dwell on deception and surprise. The hero of *Laburnum Grove* (first performed 1933; 1934), an apparently dull suburban resident, turns out to be a forger of international notoriety. In *Mystery at Greenfingers* (1937), subtitled *A Comedy of Detection*, the reality of the lives of the staff at a hotel are revealed with subtle surprise, whilst *Bright Shadow* (1950), again set in a lonely old house, is the nearest Priestley came to an orthodox detective case.

Generally speaking, Priestley's crime fiction is worth investigation as much for readability as for ingenuity – but one has to be patient with his proselytising.

Selected Works by the Author
Benighted (1927; published in the United States as *The Old Dark House*)
The Doomsday Men (1938)
Blackout in Gretley (1942)
Saturn over the Water (1961)
The Shapes of Sleep (1962)
Salt Is Leaving (1966)

Further Reading
Scowcroft, Philip L. 'A Good Companion of Crime Fiction'. *CADS* 10: 8–11.

Philip Scowcroft

Prime Suspect (television series, 1991–2006)

Lauded by the critics and avidly followed by the viewing public on both sides of the Atlantic, this landmark, multi-award-winning television crime drama established a new paradigm for small-screen British **police procedurals** when it was first aired in 1991.

Commissioned by ITV, *Prime Suspect* was the brainchild of the Liverpool-born former R.S.C. actress-turned-writer, Lynda **La Plante** (b.1946) who had previously made a name for herself as the creator of the successful 1980s ITV mini-series, *Widows*. With *Prime Suspect*, La Plante defied tradition and made middle-aged high-ranking copper Detective Chief Inspector (DCI) Jane Tennison (peerlessly portrayed by Helen Mirren) the police drama's central protagonist (at the time the series debuted, there were reported to be only four female DCIs operating in the United Kingdom's police force). With a feature-length running time of just over three hours and shown over two consecutive nights, *Prime Suspect* was an immediate hit and established a format that rapidly became the norm for ambitious, large-scale television dramas on British terrestrial channels. A raft of awards followed (including a clutch of BAFTAs), prompting a second instalment (*Prime Suspect 2*), which was transmitted a year later in 1992. Further sequels followed in 1993 (*Prime Suspect 3*), 1995 (*Prime Suspect 4*) and 1996 (*Prime Suspect 5: Errors of Judgement*). After a seven-year hiatus, the series returned in 2003 with *Prime Suspect 6: The Last Wilderness*, and more recently, in 2006, it reached a climactic finale with the valedictory episode, *Prime Suspect: The Final Act*.

The inaugural episode of the 1991 series focused on the brutal slaying of a young girl, who turned out to be the victim of a serial killer. Tennison takes over the case from DCI John Shefford, who is incapacitated by a heart attack. Her controversial appointment provokes much hostility among male colleagues and ultimately exposes the police force as one of the last bastions of deeply entrenched male chauvinism. Gritty and uncompromisingly graphic in equal measure, the programme's drama derives not only from the 'whodunit' sense of suspense generated by a murder enquiry but the internal police politics that threaten to curtail Tennison's career. Ultimately, though, as a result of her determination, obstinacy and sheer ruthlessness, Tennison succeeds in her quest, bringing the murderer to book and gaining the respect (albeit grudgingly) of her male colleagues in the process. However, there is a price to pay for her success, which takes its toll on her private life – both her romantic and family relationships suffer, and she relies overmuch on alcohol for recreational relief (this is explored in later episodes).

With 1992s *Prime Suspect 2*, Allan Cubitt took on the role of screenplay writer, fleshing out La Plante's original story outline about a badly decomposed body of a girl that is found buried in a garden in a predominantly Afro-Caribbean London neighbourhood which is deeply suspicious of the police and beset by racial tension. The plot is labyrinthine and littered with many red herrings and, significantly, examines the thorny subject of racism in the police force (the fact that Tennison has an affair with a junior black officer further complicates matters). Though not as gripping as its predecessor, this second instalment nevertheless garnered its fare share of awards including an Emmy and Edgar Allan Poe Award as well as a second successive BAFTA for Mirren.

La Plante returned to the helm for 1993s *Prime Suspect 3*, which finds Tennison transferred to take charge of a vice team tackling Soho's rent-boy problem. However, the murder of a young male prostitute leads the feisty detective into a murky, tenebrous underworld of transsexuals and, worst of all, predatory paedophiles. Tautly plotted and consummately acted, *Prime Suspect 3* scooped an Emmy for Outstanding Mini-Series while Helen Mirren picked up her third BAFTA Best Actress award for the series.

Four-and-a-half hours long, *Prime Suspect 4* (1995) represented a departure in the series' format and comprised three markedly different but equally compelling self-contained stories – 'The Lost Child', 'Inner Circles' and 'The Scent of Darkness'. The 1996s *Prime Suspect 5: Errors of Judgement* witnessed a return to the original single-story format and found Tennison transferred to Manchester where she investigated the shooting of a drug dealer. After this, Helen Mirren elected to quit her celebrated role on the grounds that it could lead to typecasting.

Almost a decade elapsed before Mirren was persuaded to reprise her role as Jane Tennison when she appeared in *Prime Suspect 6: The Last Wilderness* in 2003. It proved to be one of the best stories in the series, with the indefatigable policewoman – now promoted to a Detective Superintendent – testing her nerve, wit and resolve to the limit as she turns her attention to murder victims of a fugitive East European war criminal who is masquerading as an optician.

Three years on, *Prime Suspect 7: The Final Act* brought the curtain down on Jane Tennison's stellar police career. Although Tennison is beleaguered by personal problems – her father is dying and she is having difficulty acknowledging her alcohol addiction – she is focused on tracking down the killer of a schoolgirl in a high-profile case that puts her under intense scrutiny. Urged by colleagues to retire, Tennison confronts her demons, attends an Alcoholics Anonymous meeting (where she makes up with an old adversary) and eventually solves the case.

Compelling storylines, brilliant acting and edge-of-the-seat drama aside, *Prime Suspect* offers a valuable insight into the sacrifices high-ranking police women must make to succeed in their profession. The central drama at the core of *Prime Suspect* is Tennison's struggles to strike the right balance between career and private life, which she is patently unable to do. She has sacrificed romance, friendship, even motherhood – she had a terminated pregnancy in *Prime Suspect 3* – and family life to succeed in her profession. But it has left her bruised, obsessive, lonely, unpopular and an alcoholic, though she ultimately achieves redemption in the concluding episode. While it made an international star of Helen Mirren, the series proved profoundly influential; its authenticity, realism and examination of difficult moral issues undoubtedly raised the bar for UK television crime dramas. *See also* Conventions; Police Procedurals; *and* TV Detectives: Small-Screen Adaptations.

Television Series
Prime Suspect (1991)
Prime Suspect 2 (1992)

Prime Suspect 3 (1993)
Prime Suspect 4 (1995)
Prime Suspect 5: Errors of Judgement (1996)
Prime Suspect 6: The Last Wilderness (2003)
Prime Suspect 7: The Final Act (2006)

Charles Waring

Pryce, Malcolm (b.1960)

Malcolm Pryce is the author of a series of highly individual crime novels set in
the Welsh town of Aberystwyth. Comic and clever parodies of American noir in the
unlikeliest of settings, they have achieved cult status.

Pryce, born in Shrewsbury, went to school in Aberystwyth. He read German
at the universities of Warwick and Freiburg before graduating in 1984 and then
travelled wildly, juggling an assortment of odd and colourful jobs in hotels, factories,
aluminium sales and advertising. He ended up in the Far East, where after work in
Singapore, he wrote the first draft of *Aberystwyth Mon Amour* (2001) on a banana boat
bound for Guyana. He now lives in Bangkok and has no wish to return to the United
Kingdom, until both the weather and the trains improve.

The Aberystwyth saga, which has now reached four volumes, is a unique series
which both parodies the private-eye genre and pays gentle homage to it. Critics first
greeted it as an unholy mix of Raymond **Chandler**/*Chinatown* and *Monty Python*, as
the adventures of Louie Knight, Aberystwyth's only private detective, regularly take
a most bizarre turn into the absurd, although without ever losing their pathos and
convoluted plot lines. At times, the reader will feel as if he has entered a twilight
zone, a fourth dimension in which the Welsh army once invaded Patagonia and
fought a bloody, bitter war with echoes of Vietnam and the local mafia are, of course,
Druids, and the tough private detective prefers ice cream to hard liquor. But, beyond
the decidedly comic aspects of the novels, there is also at the heart of the stories
a wonderful appreciation and love of the detective genre allied with a sentimental
soft core and genuine affection for its colourful characters: the fragile-hearted Louie
Knight, his schoolgirl cohort and apprentice sleuth calamity Jane, night-club singer
Myfanwy Montez and a wondrous gallery of nasties, allies and bizarres whose fates
are strangely intertwined, beyond the ghosts of the Patagonian past and legends
of derring-do and damaged souls.

Aberystwyth Mon Amour introduces the melancholy Louie, when schoolboys are
disappearing all over Aberystwyth. He is soon joined by a precocious schoolgirl and is
assisted by his father, who walks donkeys across the seafront promenade, and Sospan,
the philosopher cum ice-cream seller to whom he goes for advice when times are
tough. Louie is in love with torch singer Myfanwy, who sings like an angel in a night-
club owned by the nefarious druids. As the plot unfolds, we learn about the ill-fated
Patagonian expedition and its remaining influence on the town and the mystery
of famous guerrilla leader Gwenno Guevara. Pryce plots his book with a cross-stitch
precision with all the talent of Chandler and other classic authors, and the frantic
pace encapsulates every private eye cliché possible together with touching stories
of love, friendship and the inevitable opposing policeman with a strong dislike

for amateur sleuths. The finale is packed with twists and turns and a cinematic struggle between goodies and baddies in a plane about to bomb Aberystwyth to smithereens.

Most of Pryce's surviving characters reappear in *Last Tango in Aberystwyth* (2003). On this occasion, Louie plunges deep into Aberystwyth's notorious bed and breakfast ghetto, a dark labyrinth of Druid speakeasies and toffee-apple dens when a local academic disappears after receiving a mysterious suitcase intended for a ruthless assassin. Louie becomes entangled with local porn performer Judy Juice, a star of the town's 'What the Butler Saw' industry. The suitcase plot is an homage to Aldrich's film of Spillane's *Kiss Me Deadly*, but with the necessary added surrealist touch of clowns, donkeys, a brain in a box and whelk stalls. However, again, the combination works to great effect, and the ending of the book adds ironic layers of tenderness to Louie's travails.

In *The Unbearable Lightness of Being in Aberystwyth* (2004), Myfanwy has lost her mind after being drugged with raspberry ripple and vegetates in a care home, and Louie is now inconsolable, while his new partner Calamity Jane assumes more responsibilities for the sleuthing. In a bow to hard-boiled tradition, the novel begins with a barrel-organ man walking into Louie's office. He wants a murder investigated but has, as you would, lost his memory. And his monkey is a former astronaut. The crazy plot soon evokes a labyrinth of intrigue populated with mad nuns, gangsters and waifs, the cloning of Jesus, buried skulls and the obligatory bursts of gunfire. The novel bathes in a strong melancholy mood, as Louie pines for his lost love and confirms his status as the Philip Marlowe of the West Wales coast.

Don't Cry for Me Aberystwyth (2007) is the latest instalment to date in Louie Knight's topsy-turvy adventures. It is Christmas in Aberystwyth, and in a filthy alley in Chinatown, Father Christmas lies dead in a pool of his own blood, not only knifed but also cruelly mutilated. Louie and Calamity Jane soon discover the connection between the dead body and the Patagonian War as the story unfolds, with a nod to John **le Carré**'s Cold War thrillers and an erstwhile spy who is trying to come in from the cold. Add to this the mystery of the fate of Butch Cassidy and the Sundance Kid's after their supposed death, the enigma of an angel who appeared to Welsh combatants before a pivotal battle of the war in South America and the intervention of the Queen of Norway. Many of Louie's past foes and allies return for a last hurrah as the frenetic plot delves into every bizarre corner and tension rises between Louie and his new associate. Somehow, all the strands are wrapped up in the end, with appropriate twists and surprises and some hope that Louie and Myfanwy's love affair has a future.

The Aberystwyth series is more than just Welsh noir. It is also a clever bow to hard-boiled tropes and a bizarre world with its own logical rules and practices where characters very much of flesh and blood love and suffer against an absurdist horizon that has no equal in contemporary crime fiction. *See also* Tartan Noir *and* Pulp.

Selected Works by the Author
Aberystwyth Mon Amour (2001)
Last Tango in Aberystwyth (2003)
The Unbearable Lightness of Being in Aberystwyth (2004)
Don't Cry For Me Aberystwyth (2007)

Maxim Jakubowski

Psychic Detectives

In *The Sign of Four*, Sherlock **Holmes** famously suggests 'when you have eliminated the impossible, whatever remains, however improbable, must be the truth'. For detectives like William Hope Hodgson's Carnacki the Ghost Finder or Algernon Blackwood's John Silence – Physician Extraordinary, eliminating the impossible is, itself, impossible – their specific domain is the impossible, and they are called in to deal with hauntings, curses, monsters, psychic attacks and the like, just as more rational sleuths are called in to cope with murderers, blackmailers, racketeers and so forth (which is not to say that human villains are not frequently exposed during their investigations). The eighth of S.S. Van Dine's 'twenty rules for writing detective stories' is that 'the problem of the crime must be solved by strictly naturalistic means. Such methods for learning the truth as slate-writing, ouija-boards, mind-reading, spiritualistic séances, crystal-gazing, and the like, are taboo. A reader has a chance when matching his wits with a rationalistic detective, but if he must compete with the world of spirits and go chasing about the fourth dimension of metaphysics, he is defeated *ab initio*.' Again, some sleuths ignore this – and go to work using occult means (they are the literal 'psychic detectives', rather than just occult investigators).

The prototype of these characters might well be the historical philosopher Apollonius of Tyana, who features (briefly) in John Keats's poem *Lamia* (1819) and tries to determine the nature of the vampire-like creature who has ensnared the young hero Lycius (who, at the end, is unhappy to be 'saved' from the magical creature by the aged, annoying rationalist). Joseph Sheridan Le Fanu's Dr Martin Hesselius, who is at once a character in some of the stories collected in *In a Glass Darkly* (1972) and their supposed editor, follows Apollonius – he takes an interest in the supernatural and is consulted in several strange cases, but he rarely seems to help anyone (most of his patients die). As the detective story developed, so did the tradition of the seemingly inexplicable mystery which turns out to have a rational explanation – the most famous of these stories is *The Hound of the Baskervilles* (1902), in which Sherlock Holmes investigates an apparent haunting and discerns a would-be heir who is passing off a phosphor-painted mastiff as the spectral dog which persecutes the Baskerville family. This tradition, formalised in the various incarnations of the television cartoon *Scooby-Doo, Where Are You?*, is not truly that of the psychic detective, for the initial assumption is that all ghosts and monsters will turn out to be smugglers dressed up in luminous outfits. Holmes even rationalised away 'The Adventure of the Sussex Vampire'.

In *Dracula* (1897), Dr Van Helsing is essentially a physician detective (like Drs Hesselius and Silence), called in to attend a patient and deduce what manner of supernatural ill afflicts her – his initial patient (Lucy) dies too and has to be staked and beheaded when she rises as a vampire, but Van Helsing lays out the plan which leads to the defeat of Dracula. Van Helsing is an archetype of supernatural detective – though the version played by Peter Cushing in several Hammer films is a more active and engaged investigator than Stoker's broken-English-spouting Dutchman. Flaxman Low, created by E. and H. Heron for a series of stories which ran in *Pearson's Magazine* in 1898, is an investigator of hauntings, after the manner of the Victorian Society for Psychical Research. Blackwood's Dr Silence and Hodgson's Carnacki, who appeared in single books of collected stories, are Holmesian private investigators who use scientific (or pseudo-scientific) occult methods – cannily,

Psychic Detectives

Hodgson has solved some of the mysteries Carnacki looks into by exposing the bogus supernatural (the villain of 'The Horse of the Invisible' is pulling a Baskerville stunt by impersonating the family ghost and is punished when the real ghost kills him). The Silence and Carnacki stories are not reckoned among their authors' best works, and H.P. Lovecraft (among other critics) suggested that the air of 'professional' occultism and detective story plotting worked against the chills that come from a good ghost-story. The various academics who investigate or stumble over hauntings in M.R. James stories do not count as 'psychic detectives' because they tend to solve the mystery only by being driven mad or murdered by the culprit – which, admittedly, makes for a scarier story.

There has been a trickle of British short-story series and one-off novels using psychic detective heroes – Alice and Claude Askew's Aylmer Vance, 'real-life' ghost-hunter Elliott O'Donnell's Damon Vance, Dion Fortune's Dr Taverner, Sax **Rohmer**'s Morris Klaw (*The Dream-Detective*, 1920), A.M. Burrage's Francis Chard and Derek Scarfe, Jack Mann's Gregory George Gordon (also known as Gees), Dennis **Wheatley**'s Duc de Richlieu (notably in *The Devil Rides Out*, 1934) and Neils Orsen, Jessie Douglas Kerruish's Luna Bartendale (*The Undying Monster*, 1936), Margery Lawrence's Miles Penoyer (*Number Seven Queer Street*, 1945), John Rackham's Dr K.N. Wilson, Peter Saxon's The Guardians (*Through the Dark Curtain*, 1968), Brian Lumley's Titus Crow, R. Chetwynd-Hayes's Francis St. Clare and Frederica Masters, Guy N. Smith's Mark Sabat (an ex-priest SAS veteran), Brian Mooney's Reuben Calloway, Mike Chinn's Damian Paladin, Robert Holdstock's Lee Kline (*Necromancer*, 1978), James Herbert's David Ash (*Haunted*, 1988), Clive Barker's Harry D'Amour, Paul **McAuley**'s Mr Carlyle, and Kim **Newman**'s Sally Rhodes (*The Quorum*) and Richard Jeperson (*The Man From the Diogenes Club*, 2005). Collections of psychic detective stories (mixing British and American essays in the sub-genre) include Michel Parry's *The Supernatural Solution* (1976), Peter **Haining**'s *Supernatural Sleuths* (1986), Charles G. Waugh and Martin H. Greenberg's *Supernatural Sleuths* (1996) and Stephen Jones's *Dark Detectives* (1999). UK television-series characters like Doctor Who and John Steed have occasionally turned their attention to the supernatural, and there are even haunted-house or witch-cult episodes of *Taggart*, *Paul Temple* or *Bergerac*; a few British shows have tackled parapsychology as a primary subject (*The Omega Factor*, *Sea of Souls*, *Afterlife*) and Donald Pleasence made a fine Carnacki in an adaptation of 'The Horse of the Invisible' on *The Rivals of Sherlock Holmes* (1971). *See also* The Great Detectives: The Mass Appeal of Holmes, Poirot and Wimsey.

Kim Newman

Pulp

British noir was the illegitimate offspring of American hard-boiled fiction. It was fathered by Dashiell Hammett, Raymond **Chandler** and W.R. Burnett and fostered through the ominous days before and after the Second World War. Like the pulps in America, it was full of solitary heroes, femme fatales, crime and murder that often brought together high society and the low life of the harsh city streets. It was here that violence and death were always just a heartbeat away in the midst of the urban nightmare. Both British and American noir also captured the anxieties, preoccupations and grim moral code of the times in which they were written.

William Roland Daniel (1880–1969) deserves the credit for writing the first British noir novels – although he had actually been born in America, his name was for years thought to be a pseudonym, and for much of his life he lived in seclusion in Devon. The son of a wealthy Florida fruit plantation owner, he was sent to England for his education, but he remained to become an itinerant actor before turning his hand to thriller writing in the late 1920s. A chance of reading Burnett's *Little Caesar* was the inspiration for his success and to launch the home-grown hard-boiled novel *The Gangster* in 1932. The book's lurid cover (a hard man brandishing a gun at a terrified blonde) would soon prove to be the archetype for Roland Daniel covers – and for many of his successors, too. Compared in a rather over-blown blurb to the best of Dashiell Hammett's work, the title sold well enough to justify a sequel, *The Gangster's Last Shot* (1939), and put the author on a treadmill of production that would see him amass over 200 novels with titles such as *The Murphy Gang* (1934), *The Slayer* (1936) and *Big Squeal* (1940), all carrying the claim, 'If you want to be thrilled read Roland Daniel.' Sadly when this man who had helped to pioneer English hard-boiled fiction died, only one local newspaper reported his death at the age of eighty-eight in Torquay Hospital.

The first British author to write about underworld characters and crime in London was Hugh Desmond Clevely (1898–1964), who introduced *The Crime Smasher* in 1937. John Martinson is a battle-scarred tough guy with close-cropped red hair and a pugnacious square jaw, who decides to take on the London crime barons after he and his girl friend, the beautiful Sylvia, are victims of one of the toughest gangsters, Al Tortoni. After putting the Italian thug behind bars, Martinson and Sylvia take on various other undesirables in *The Gang Smasher Again* (1938), *Gang Law* (1939) – which involved Benito Moroni, a Chicago mobster with plans to muscle in on London – and *The Gang Smasher Calling* (1940). Clevely was almost as unlikely a character to have written noir as Roland Daniel, being the son of a Bristol clergyman. During the war, he served in the RAF and rose to the rank of wing commander. He wrote less hard-boiled fiction in the 1950s and died mysteriously when his bloodstained body was found face down in a weir on the river Stour in Dorset in May 1964. The coroner recorded an open verdict.

Richard Goyne (1902–1957) was just beginning to build a reputation for hard-boiled fiction when he was called up into the army in 1940 and served as a commando throughout the war, later describing his experiences in *Destination Unknown* (1945). Goyne was the son of a London schoolteacher and overcame infantile paralysis as a child to lead a very active life as a writer and soldier. He began his career as a reporter on the *Hornsey Journal* before producing crime and mystery stories for the D.C. Thompson group. For a time, he wrote semi-pornographic novels under the pen name Paul Renin with evocative titles such as *Lonely Wives* (1932), *Wild Oats* (1936) and *Good Times Girls* (1940). His facility for noir became evident in *Lady of Leicester Square* (1939) about small-time crook Frank Stanley who becomes a prostitute killer and *London Night Haunts* (1940) with its graphic picture of the city's gangland in operation under the shadow of war. After his army service, Goyne wrote a series featuring a hardman private eye, Peter Parker, of which *Harvest of Hate* (1952) is notable. Like many others writing paperback fiction at this time, Goyne received little credit in the handful of obituaries that appeared after his death.

Obscurity was also the fate of William J(ames) Elliott (1886–c.1947) of whom no death notices have been found. He wrote prolifically throughout the 1930s and 1940s and was popular with wartime readers for his escapist tales of 'English Ed' Gunning, 'one of the most ruthless and dangerous gunmen ever' who proves to be the nemesis of the criminals and scheming women to be found in *Freak Racket* (1941), *Snatched Dame* (1942) and *Kissed Corpse* (1946). Like Roland Daniel before him, Elliott was an actor before becoming a scriptwriter in the 1920s and wrote fourteen of the first series of Sherlock **Holmes** movies starring Eille Norwood. He is believed to have acted in one of the pictures and later directed several silent short dramas. Elliott's novel-writing career began in the 1930s when he was living in the small Hertfordshire village of Bedmond where he became a familiar figure striding over the area wearing a battered cape as if he had just stepped out of one of the Sherlock Holmes's films. Few of his neighbours, though, were aware of the entertainment that he provided for thousands of people sheltering from German bombs with his tales of blood and gore.

The first British writer to make an enduring reputation for writing noir was Peter **Cheyney** (1896–1951), whose major character, Lemmy Caution, complete with slouch hat and machine gun tucked under his arm, has been acknowledged as the precursor of Mickey Spillane's Mike Hammer. Katherine Gunn has written of the author, 'He was the King of the "Hard Nosed" Thriller – British variety', and there is no doubt about the immediate impact his book *This Man Is Dangerous* (1936) had on the public. It would prove to be the first of a long-running series about Caution who, despite his name, was always inclined to punch or shoot first when dealing with the criminals who pedalled drugs and sex in the London underworld. Although the reviews of his early titles condemned Cheyney for his excessive use of violence and brutality, the books were soon selling by the million and their author has the distinction of being the first UK author to take hard-boiled fiction back across the Atlantic when his books were successfully republished in the United States. Reginald Southouse Cheyney was born in London's East End where his father ran a stall selling jellied eels. While employed as a clerk in a firm of solicitors, he began to write comic sketches for the theatre and then spent the years of the First World War employed in the Labour Corps Records Office. For several years, he served as a special constable in the Metropolitan Police, which provided him with first-hand experience of the brutal city streets. In 1932, he formed 'Cheyney Research and Investigations' which undertook a number of cases and even retrieved some stolen property for one client. He enjoyed more success, though, when he ghosted the memoirs of ex-DI Harold Brust in *I Guarded Kings: The Memoirs of a Political Police Officer* (1935). A year later, he became an international bestseller when he exchanged fact for fiction and introduced Lemmy Caution, dropping his Christian names for the more masculine Peter. Ten books followed about the redoubtable Caution, during which time he also created a private eye, Slim Callaghan, in *The Urgent Hangman* (1938), after a friend had challenged him that he 'could only write Yank gangster stories'. Cheyney worked hard on the promotion of his books and ended his days a wealthy man from sales and the eight films of Lemmy Caution cases starring the formidable US tough guy actor, Eddie Constantine.

Overnight success was also achieved by arguably the most famous British author of noir, James Hadley **Chase**, whose first novel, ***No Orchids for Miss Blandish*** (1939), is among the most iconic titles in crime fiction and has never been out of print in over sixty years. Based loosely on a news story about the kidnapping of an American heiress and her brutal treatment at the hands of her captors which turned her mind, the publication of the book provoked widespread accusations that it was degenerate and immoral – and guaranteed sales in millions. Chase, whose real name was Rene Lodge Brabazon Raymond, was the son of an army medical officer and, after quarrelling with his authoritarian father, was forced to earn his living from the age of seventeen as a door-to-door salesman of children's encyclopaedias. Convinced he was never going to make much money from this and seeing the success being enjoyed by writers such as Hammett, Chandler and, particularly, Peter Cheyney, he decided to write his hard-boiled story. It took just six weeks – the title struck him while he was having a bath. George Orwell was among the severest critics, describing reading it as 'taking a header into a cesspool'. Orwell thought the only explanation for its success was 'the mingled boredom and brutality of the war'. Nonetheless, the mixture of eight murders, an uncountable number of killings and woundings, the torture of a woman with lighted cigarettes and the graphic flogging of Miss Blandish, not to mention other elements of cruelty and sexual perversion, made it a landmark in crime fiction and the author notorious. Chase's later string of eighty sexy and violent bestsellers – most of which were set in America, though he never visited the country and relied on atlases, guides and dictionaries of slang for his background information – enabled him to live in luxury in Switzerland, where he remained as reclusive as Cheyney had been self-promoting, although ultimately praised by other critics as 'the Faulkner of the masses' for the harsh realism of his stories. For a time, Chase was so prolific that a number of his books were issued under the pen-name Raymond Marshall. He was also published in America where some of his more risqué titles such as *Twelve Chinks and a Woman* (1940) were adapted to the less racially provocative 'Chinamen' – although others such as *The Dead Stay Dumb* (1940) inexplicably became *Kiss My Fist*. In 1942, while serving in the RAF, where he rose to the rank of squadron leader, Chase and his publishers were charged at the Central Criminal Court in London with 'publishing an obscene libel' in the shape of *Miss Callaghan Comes to Grief*. Though the case was vigorously defended – in particular that the police had cited extracts from the story out of context – a verdict of guilty was returned by the jury and the publishers and Chase were each fined £100. Chase was not to be the last British writer of noir who would find himself in trouble with the law.

Michael Storme (1918–1979) was another RAF officer who took advantage of his off-duty hours to cater to the insatiable demand for escapist fiction, and the books which flowed from his versatile pen would earn him the praise of Steve Holland as being 'amongst the most popular gangster writers of the time'. Storme was the pseudonym of George Dawson, a former newspaperman who had joined the RAF in 1939 and saw service in Egypt, Sudan and Italy, where he got the inspiration for his private eye, Nick Cranley, in what became the Make Mine series. At Bari airfield, he met an American sergeant who had been a private eye in America in the 1930s and regaled the Englishman with stories of his exploits. Cranley was modelled on the sergeant and featured in two dozen noir paperbacks, including *Make Mine a Shroud* (1948), *Make Mine Beautiful* (1949) and *Make Mine a Redhead* (1952).

'If You're Nervy – Don't Read Hervey' was splashed on the hard-boiled novels of Michael Hervey (1920–c.1978), who was born in London in 1920 and spent his early career at sea, narrowly missing being interned as a spy when returning home at the outbreak of the war. It was while he was working as a drama critic for *The Observer* that Hervey started writing short stories and novels, proving hugely prolific and earning an entry in the *Guinness Book of Records* for the record number of short stories: over 3,500. His hard-boiled private eye, Mike Munroe, made his debut in *Murder Thy Neighbour* (1944). Before Hervey emigrated to Australia in 1951, he wrote a staggering sixty crime and mystery titles, selling over four million copies.

Such paperback sales figures pale into insignificance, though, when considering the phenomenon that was Hank **Janson**, the alter ego of Stephen Daniel Frances (1917–1989), the favourite gangster writer of the 1940s and 1950s, whose novels of the tough-talking, hard-hitting journalist and crime fighter Janson were required reading and playground 'trade' for a whole generation of schoolboys. Francis, who was born in Lambeth, South London, grew up in poverty in a tenement block and learned about the harsh street life of the city first-hand. A conscientious-objector during the war, Francis got word in 1946 that a paperback distributor was looking for books to satisfy the demand for hard-boiled fiction and introduced Janson in *When Dames Get Tough*, leaning heavily on the works of Chase and James M. Cain as well as film noir. Such was the impact of the character – whom Francis set out to 'make like a living person' by devising a biography of exotic experiences – that Janson was credited as the author in type as big as the titles: his Christian name having been deliberately chosen because it sounded like 'Yank'. The books were further enhanced by the stunning artwork of leggy beauties with impossible breasts drawn by Reginald Heade. Sales were such that Janson soon had a trademark and a fan club and was the hero of a song 'Hank Janson Blues' by a popular female singer of the day, Anne Shelton. By the early 1950s, Hank Janson had become a byword for hard-boiled fiction in the United Kingdom and Francis sold the rights to the series and moved to Spain. He was living there in 1953, when the police seized seven of the titles, *Accused*, *Amok*, *Auctioned*, *Killer*, *Pursuit*, *Persian Pride* and *Vengeance*, and the publishers were charged with 'selling obscene titles'. Described by the Chief Justice, Lord Goddard, as 'grossly and bestially obscene', the directors of the company were sentenced to jail. Francis returned from Spain to prove that he had not written the books in question, but his reputation never recovered, and although he continued to write potboilers for the next thirty years, he died in his adopted country almost penniless. His reputation has been somewhat resurrected in recent years, thanks to the efforts of a number of people who were young men at the time and never forgot the pleasure they got from his unique brand of noir, notably Steve Holland with his biography, *The Trials of Hank Janson* (1991).

No such posthumous recognition has been given to two other writers who made significant contributions to the genre in those years. Former London advertising agency copywriter, Frank Dubrez Fawcett (1891–1968), under the pen-name Ben Sarto, took the classic American song, 'Miss Otis Regrets' by Cole Porter, as the inspiration for Mabie Otis, a tough dame with a luscious figure and heavy-lidded blue eyes who proved more than a match for the gangsters and playboys who inhabited her world in fifteen very successful books from *Miss Otis Comes to Piccadilly* (1946) to *Miss Otis Says Yes* in 1954. Dail Ambler (1919–1974), whose real name was Betty Williams, was one of the very few female English writers of hard-boiled fiction. Initially a journalist, she wrote for films and television before turning to crime fiction in the 1950s. A strikingly attractive blonde, Dail was photographed on the back of her books in a low cut evening dress, beguiling readers to meet her tough guy investigator Danny Spade who last appeared in *Danny Spade Sees Red* in 1954. He bowed out a decade later after having his fan club – which offered members signed studio portraits of the pretty author who occasionally modelled for the covers – and being translated into French. Dail continued writing under other pseudonyms but never again enjoyed the success she had as the most high-profile female writer of British noir. *See also* Tartan Noir.

Peter Haining

Q

Quigley, Sheila (b.1946)

Sheila Quigley became a best-selling author of crime novels in the most spectacular way. She was living on benefits in an estate near Sunderland, having been told her council house was due to be demolished, when her love of writing saved her. Throughout her numerous jobs, including market trader, machinist and double-glazing saleswoman, she was a voracious reader and was always writing bits and pieces that she sent to women's magazines. But when her youngest child was a teenager, she started to write in earnest and eventually sent a screenplay to agent Darley Anderson, who also represents Martina **Cole**. Spotting talent, he asked Quigley to write a novel and then whipped up a life-changing bidding war among publishers for the Detective Inspector (DI) Lorraine Hunt series, set in the North East of England. This instant fame was featured in a BBC documentary about writing as part of the Alan Yentob *Imagine* series.

Quigley has lived in Houghton-le-Spring for thirty years, and all her novels are set there, in a fictitious estate called The Seahills. Many of the families on the estate are recurring characters, and her website is named after it: www.theseahills.co.uk. Quigley is divorced with three daughters, one son, eight grandchildren and two dogs. She is a huge football fan, supporting Sunderland and her grandchildren's youth teams.

Run for Home (2004) introduces DI Lorraine Hunt who teams up with sixteen-year-old Kerry Lumsdon to find Kerry's missing sister – the fourth girl to have been kidnapped in a recent string of abductions. But Kerry, distrusting the police, sets out on her own – and comes across links to a 1985 murder of a man by a woman they call the Head Hunter. Hunt's sidekick is Detective Sergeant Luke Daniels, with whom she has a will-they–won't-they relationship after she divorces her husband John. This is later complicated by the arrival of a teenage daughter Luke did not know he had. The second book, *Living on a Prayer* (2005), is set at Christmas. DI Hunt thinks a group of teenagers know more than they are telling about their friend's supposed suicide – especially when they start disappearing. During *Bad Moon Rising* (2006), Hunt has to contend with a serial killer stalking women, while the Feast – a fair/festival bringing much celebration and mayhem – is in town, bringing a load of suspects for her to sift through. In the most recent novel, *Every Breath You Take* (2007), the case is more personal as Luke Daniels' daughter Selina is targeted by the White Rose Killer, and soon he turns his murderous attentions to Lorraine.

Quigley is overjoyed by her success after years of 'scribbling'. She says her characters literally present themselves to her – 'I could go and sit on a park bench and within five minutes someone would be sitting beside me and I'd get their life story.' She now spreads the word by talking at libraries and writing events.

Selected Works by the Author
Run for Home (2004)
Living on a Prayer (2005)
Bad Moon Rising (2006)
Every Breath You Take (2007)

Thalia Proctor

R

Raine, Jerry (b.1955)

Jerry Raine's speciality is suburban hard-boiled crime, and although his bibliography may be brief, it disguises a fascinating life story.

Raine was born in Chapeltown, Yorkshire, on 5 July 1955, the son of a detective inspector in the CID. He spent his early years in Somalia, East Africa, before returning to England in 1961. Educated in Surrey, he left for Australia on a £20 immigration scheme in 1971 where he worked as a farmhand and a caravan fitter before making his folk-singing debut in Sydney, having learnt to play the guitar at sixteen. (Later gigs included the Cambridge Folk Festival and a solo performance at the Shepherds Bush Empire.)

Coming back to England again, he did a variety of odd jobs, including gardening and forklift truck driving, before rising to the dizzy heights of manager at London's specialist crime bookstore Murder One.

Although Raine attended a creative-writing class in Dorking in the mid-1970s, it was not until 1986 – when he won a *Mail on Sunday* fiction prize – that he was prompted to try his hand at a novel. Describing *Smalltime* (1996) as his 'attempt to write an Elmore Leonard novel set in England', it told the story of an off-licence worker who is mugged one night, only to pursue his attacker and become embroiled in the murky goings-on of the suburban London crime scene. Rejected by nine publishers, he consigned the manuscript to his bottom drawer for eight years until it finally saw the light of day in 1996. A follow-up, *Small Change*, appeared five years later.

Raine's second novel, *Frankie Bosser Comes Home* (1999), displayed echoes of Ted **Lewis**'s 1970 novel *Jack's Return Home* (filmed as **Get Carter** in 1971) with its story of a criminal hiding out in Italy who comes back to England for the funeral of his father – only to find his father had been murdered.

Frankie Bosser, a hard-boiled crime novel set in Surrey, proved so popular that Raine reused two characters for his next book, the memorably entitled *Slaphead Chameleon* (2000). A heavily fictionalised account of the author's own 1998 tour with American singer/songwriter Iris DeMent, it was deliberately more humorous than previous works in its depiction of psychotic ex-con Teddy Peppers hunting down musician Jason Campbell on a road tour around Britain. Drugs, sex and rock 'n' roll had never been so disarming.

A five-year gap came to an end in 2006 with *Some Like It Cold*. In this fallow period, Raine had worked as manager for London's only gambling bookstore, High Stakes. His fascination for blackjack and poker were obvious influences for this high-powered tale of a former nightclub bouncer turned Atlantic City card sharp who falls in love with a Russian waitress with Mafia connections. Although moving away from his earlier territory of dystopic suburbia, the seedy gambling background, the believable cast of wastrels and wannabes and the grimy London backdrop were all quintessentially Raine.

Selected Works by the Author
Smalltime (1996)
Frankie Bosser Comes Home (1999)
Slaphead Chameleon (2000)
Small Change (2001)
Some Like It Cold (2006)

Mark Campbell

Rankin, Ian (b.1960)

Ian Rankin is the United Kingdom's top-selling crime novelist. A recent estimate put his sales at 10 percent of all UK crime fiction, and his novels have been translated into twenty-six languages. His most famous creation is the Edinburgh police inspector John Rebus, the star of sixteen novels to date, from *Knots and Crosses* (1987) to *The Naming of the Dead* (2006). Rebus is aging in real time; since he was born in 1947, he has reached retirement age. Rankin has said that *Exit Music* (2007) will be the last Rebus book but that he will do at least one book starring DS Siobhan Clarke (a character who has been moving progressively centre stage in recent novels), with Rebus in the background.

Rankin's first published book was a stand-alone called *The Flood* (1986), a rite-of-passage novel about a young man from Fife dreaming of moving to Edinburgh. His first ever book, a black comedy called *Summer Rites* and set in a Highlands hotel, remains unpublished – even though his wife says it is his best book. He has written two other stand-alones as Ian Rankin and three thrillers under the pseudonym Jack Harvey, 'Jack' being his first son's name and 'Harvey' being his wife's maiden name. Rankin has described his Harvey novels as 'big, fat airport-type thrillers', but their action-packed Jack **Higgins**-style plots involving assassins and ex-SAS heroes proved popular with readers and critics alike. They also gave Rankin an outlet for experimenting with ideas and forms outside the Rebus novels, such as a female assassin (*Witch Hunt*, 1993) and a sympathetic first-person narrator who happens to be the bad guy (*Bleeding Hearts*, 1994), but he felt that the Harvey novels had come to a natural end as the Rebus books grew in length and complexity. Recent editions of the Harvey novels have been published under the name Ian Rankin.

The first Rebus novel, *Knots and Crosses* (1987), was about child abduction. Rankin himself briefly became a suspect for a real-life abduction case, when he innocently went to a police station in Leith to ask the police about how an investigation into child abductions would be conducted. *Knots and Crosses* introduced characters who

77. Ian Rankin.

would appear in several novels: Rebus's daughter Samantha, with whom he has a fractious relationship, and Gill Templar – Rebus's boss, lover then ex-lover, but always a counterfoil to Rebus in her by-the-book approach to police work. Another mainstay character is Rebus's nemesis, the career criminal Big Ger Cafferty.

Rebus is provocative, nearly alcoholic, rarely plays by the rules and is not averse to fraternising with criminals to solve crimes. There are echoes, particularly in the earlier Rebus novels, of the American hard-boiled tradition. In fact, James Ellroy, one of Rankin's favourite authors, dubbed Rankin 'the king of tartan noir'. Since then, the label **Tartan Noir** has been applied to crime fiction influenced by Scottish literature that explores themes such as the darkness of human nature and redemption versus damnation, themes explored in two of Rankin's major influences, Robert Louis Stevenson's *The Strange Case of Dr Jekyll and Mr Hyde* (1886) and James Hogg's *Confessions of a Justified Sinner* (1824). Other influences that Rankin has cited include Muriel Spark (about whom he started – but did not complete – a PhD thesis), Ruth **Rendell**, Raymond **Chandler** and Lawrence Block.

The macabre darkness of Jekyll and Hyde runs through much of the Rebus canon. Rankin himself has stated that Rebus simultaneously has a dark and light side and that Edinburgh itself is split between the 'Dr Jekyll' New Town (structured and rational) and the 'Mr Hyde' Old Town (badly designed and strange) – a city full of dark secrets and repressed by its Calvinist, Presbyterian past. He has also said that *Knots and Crosses* was a deliberate attempt to write a modern-day parallel of Jekyll and Hyde, with Rebus haunted by a former friend who tries to destroy him. Rankin was appalled that people thought he had written a whodunit and used to move copies of his book off the **Crime Fiction** shelves of bookshops onto the Scottish Fiction shelves. In *Resurrection Men* (2002), Rebus and other disgraced officers are on a retraining programme to 'resurrect' their careers, but the novel's title echoes the name given to grave robbers during the time of Burke and Hare. And *Set in Darkness* (2006) finds inspiration from the grisly true-life story of a servant who was spit-roasted and eaten in the building that is now the new Scottish Parliament.

Rankin has received great critical acclaim for his portrayals of Edinburgh, in which the city almost becomes a character in its own right. Rankin has so popularised Edinburgh that there are now Rebustours: organised walks in the spirit of the Bloomsday celebrations of James Joyce's Dublin, visiting Rebus's haunts.

The novel that brought Rankin international acclaim was *Black and Blue* (1997), winning the **Crime Writers' Association** (CWA) Macallan Gold Dagger and being shortlisted for the Mystery Writers of America Edgar Award. It is also one of the most brutal novels in the series, Rankin admitting that he used Rebus as a punch bag when he discovered that his younger son, Kit, had the neurological disorder Angelman syndrome. *The Hanging Garden* (1998), in which Rebus's daughter Samantha is the victim of a hit-and-run from which she never fully recovers, was written at the time that Rankin discovered his son would never walk.

During his acceptance speech for the 2005 CWA Diamond Dagger for lifetime's achievement in crime writing, Rankin gave a good summary of the punishments he has inflicted on his inspector: 'Through the course of his life, he has been knocked about, shot, pushed out of helicopters, tortured, walked out on by a host of girlfriends, fallen out with his family, seen friends and colleagues murdered in cold blood, and been haunted by ghosts. He's tackled terrorists and serial killers, racists and bigots, pimps and dealers and gangsters.'

As the Rebus series has progressed, the novels have grown increasingly complex, with multiple plotlines and an expanded exploration of the political and social landscape of contemporary Scotland. *Fleshmarket Close* (2004) was like a modern-day Dickens novel in highlighting the shocking conditions in which children of asylum seekers were being detained – which resulted in the authorities removing children from the notorious Dungavel detention centre. The novel also questioned Scottish identity and whether Scotland is a racist country. *The Naming of the Dead* widened the politics to the G8 Summit at Gleneagles and the Live8 concert and enabled Rankin to explore issues that he felt the Live8 crowds had not. In fact, Rankin has stated that one of the strengths of contemporary crime fiction is its willingness to confront big moral questions and contemporary society's fears, such as terrorism, religious intolerance and asylum seekers – as opposed to the contemporary novel, which he sees as being more about the individual.

Rankin has explained that his inspector's name came from John Shaft (hero in the 1970s blaxploitation movie *Shaft*) and 'rebus' as in a picture puzzle – a signifier of the crime novel as a game played with the reader. He says that he now regrets the name (devised when he was 'a smart-arse PhD student who was doing lots of semiotics and deconstruction') and was relieved when he finally encountered a real person with the surname Rebus who, in a coincidence that would not be believed if it were in a novel, lives on Rankin Drive.

Nevertheless, the name-as-puzzle is appropriate for Rebus himself, an endless enigma who feels compelled to provoke both his estranged family and his colleagues and bosses and who has a chaotic private life and yet is relentless in the pursuit of his criminal quarries.

Most of the Rebus novels are set in and around Edinburgh, where Rankin has lived for most of his adult life, and Rebus often recalls his childhood in Rankin's own childhood town of Cardenden, where there is now an Ian Rankin Court. In fact, there are many significant parallels between Rankin and his fictional creation, described in the autobiographical work *Rebus's Scotland: A Personal Journey* (2005). Later novels took Rebus further afield in Scotland, even as far as the Shetlands.

The only novel set outside Scotland is *Tooth and Nail* (original title *Wolfman*, 1992), set in London where Rankin lived for four years. He also lived in rural France for six years, where he wrote the early Rebus novels and where his two sons were born. Rankin's hometown of Cardenden is a coalmining town in Fife, some 20 miles from Edinburgh, which was blighted by the closure of the Scottish coal mines and nicknamed 'Car-dead-end'. As a young boy, Rankin escaped the town's sense of hopelessness through his imagination, creating comic books featuring the fictional music group Kaput, for whom he even wrote lyrics. In 2007, he returned to this early passion for comic books when he started writing scripts for John Constantine, a supernatural detective in *Hellblazer*, a comic published by an imprint of DC Comics called Vertigo. He had been introduced to DC Comics by fellow Scottish crime novelist Denise **Mina**, who had written a number of issues.

He went to Edinburgh University (the first of his family to go to university), where he studied English Literature and Language, graduating in 1982. From 1983 to 1986, he worked on a PhD on Muriel Spark, but started writing his own fiction. He finally abandoned his PhD when, 'One story raged out of control and became my first novel, *The Flood*.' It was a wise move not only commercially but also academically, as his fiction has earned him four honorary doctorates from the universities of Abertay Dundee (1999), St Andrews (2001), Edinburgh (2003) and the Open University (2005). In addition, he was Edinburgh University's Alumnus of the Year in 1999, won the Chandler-Fulbright Award in 1992 and was elected a Hawthornden Fellow in 1998.

The CWA has awarded Rankin not only the Macallan Gold Dagger for *Black and Blue* but also two Short Story Daggers for 'A Deep Hole' in 1994 and 'Herbert in Motion' in 1996, a Gold Dagger nomination for *Dead Souls* in 1999 and, in 2005, a Cartier Diamond Dagger for a lifetime's achievement in crime writing. In 2004, *Resurrection Men* won the top crime fiction prizes in the United States (the Mystery Writers of America Edgar Award) and Germany (Deutscher Krimipreis); in 2005, he won a British Book Award ('Nibbie') for Crime Thriller of the Year for *Fleshmarket Close*; and in 2007, he won the same award again for *The Naming of the Dead*. He has also won prizes in Denmark (Palle Rosencrantz Prize, 2000), France (Grand Prix du Roman Noir, 2003) and Finland (Whodunnit Prize, 2003).

He received an OBE in 2002 for services to literature. In 2007, he received two honours from the city of Edinburgh: in March, he became the first ever recipient of the Edinburgh Award and, in April, he was appointed Deputy Lieutenant of Edinburgh, an award that dates back to the time of Henry VIII.

Rankin has said that if he had not become a writer he would have liked to be a musician, and music has often appeared in his life and writings. Among his eclectic selection of early jobs (chicken factory worker, swineherd, grape-picker, alcohol researcher, tax collector, secretary at the National Folktale Centre and English lecturer), he was also the editor of a hi-fi magazine, and for around six months, he was the vocalist with The Dancing Pigs, 'Fife's Second Greatest Punk Ensemble'. The Dancing Pigs were hugely successful – at least fictionally – in the Rebus novel *Black and Blue*, where they were an REM or U2 style of band performing in a Greenpeace concert. Fact and fiction also overlapped when real-life singer/songwriter Jackie Leven found himself mentioned in the Rebus novel *Resurrection Men* – which led to *Jackie Leven Said* (2005), a short story written and narrated by Ian Rankin, with music written and performed by Jackie Leven. Furthermore, Rankin has written lyrics for the Scottish band Saint Jude's Infirmary.

The novel title *Black and Blue* is itself a musical reference, being the name of a Rolling Stones album. Several other novel titles reflect Rankin's (and, in a number of cases, Rebus's) own musical tastes, including *Let It Bleed* (1995) (The Rolling Stones), *The Hanging Garden* (The Cure) and *Dead Souls* (Joy Division). And in 2006, Rankin hosted *Music to Die For*, a three-part radio series on BBC Radio 4 in which he talked to fellow novelists about their love of music and its use in fiction. In 2007, he wrote the libretto for a fifteen-minute opera with music by Craig Armstrong and collaborated with Aidan Moffat on a project called *Ballads of the Book*, an album that pairs Scottish writers with Scottish musicians.

A number of the Rebus novels have been televised. John Hannah was the original Rebus, in adaptations of *Black and Blue*, *The Hanging Garden* and *Dead Souls*. A fourth adaptation, *Mortal Causes* (1994), dealt with terrorism and was scheduled for broadcast in September 2001. Following 9/11, its broadcast was delayed by a month and moved to the digital-only channel ITV3. Ken Stott took over in early 2006 and has played Rebus in all subsequent television adaptations, which to date have included *The Black Book* (1993), *A Question of Blood* (2003), *Strip Jack* (1992), *Let It Bleed*, *Fleshmarket Close* and *The Falls* (2001).

Rankin himself has appeared on television. He has played one of Rebus's colleagues, but without a speaking part. He regularly appears on BBC2's arts programme *Newsnight Review* and was the presenter for *Ian Rankin's Evil Thoughts* (2002), a three-part documentary about the nature of evil, in which he met historians, philosophers and theologians, neurologists and psychiatrists, criminals and victims. His two favourite events were receiving an exorcism from the chief exorcist in the diocese of Rome and talking to a prisoner who had been on death row in Texas for fifteen years. Another episode examined the case of SS conscripts who were offered the chance to step down from massacring entire villages but failed to do so. This historical event inspired Rankin's next Rebus novel, *A Question of Blood*, which was about a high-school shooting and which raised issues of moral accountability.

In the BBC4 documentary *Rankin on the Staircase* (2005), Rankin explored the dangers of blurring **true crime** and crime fiction. The documentary was a prologue to Jean-Xavier Lestrade's eight-part documentary *Death on the Staircase*, about the Michael Peterson murder investigation. Peterson was a novelist whose wife was found dead in a pool of blood by the ambulance crew who had arrived a mere five minutes after he had dialled 911.

In June 2007, BBC4 broadcast *Ian Rankin Investigates: Dr Jekyll and Mr Hyde*, in which Rankin explored the influences that inspired Robert Louis Stevenson's creation: from the seventeenth-century warlock Major Thomas Weir who was burned at the stake with his sister to Burke and Hare who went beyond grave-robbing to murder, to serve a medical profession desperate for corpses to dissect; to the duality of Edinburgh itself, with its vice-ridden old town where the young Stevenson went to drink and consort with prostitutes. Rankin observed in the programme that Rebus is his own alter ego. Future plans include a script for a television documentary series on modern methods of detection.

Rankin has also written two black comedies for Radio 4, set in Edinburgh in the 1790s, featuring a man called 'Cullender'. Rankin chose the name, a Scots word for 'colander', because he visualised the character as a moral sieve. He has said that he would love to write a book about this character and era, since many Parisian aristocrats fled to Edinburgh to escape the guillotine and the city was a hotbed of vice at the time.

In 2007, celebrated the twentieth anniversary of Rebus with a 'final' novel, *Exit Music*. *See also* Historical Crime *and* TV Detectives: Small-Screen Adaptations.

Selected Works by the Author

Inspector Rebus Series
Knots and Crosses (1987)
Hide and Seek (1991)
Strip Jack (1992)
The Black Book (1993)
The Falls (2001)
Resurrection Men (2002)
The Naming of the Dead (2006)
Exit Music (2007)

As Jack Harvey
Witch Hunt (1993)
Bleeding Hearts (1994)
Blood Hunt (1995)

Website
www.ianrankin.net

Julian Maynard-Smith

Rathbone, Julian (1935–2008)

Julian Rathbone wrote both crime and non-crime books and has had two of his non-crime novels shortlisted for the Booker Prize. From 1967, his output had approached one book every year. The non-crime books tended to be historical, in a uniquely Rathbone style.

Born into a book-loving Blackheath household, his father was the cousin of Basil Rathbone (the notable screen Sherlock **Holmes**), he graduated from Cambridge in 1958. Rathbone was for a few years an English teacher in Turkey and, on his return in 1962, continued with teaching. His first novels (including the now rare *Diamonds Bid* from 1967 and *Trip Trap* from 1972) were based on first-hand experience of Turkish politics at their most ferocious; he said that he honed his writing skills on Graham **Greene** and Eric **Ambler**. He became a full-time writer in 1973.

In his wide-ranging books, Rathbone included a three-book political thriller series starting with *The Euro-Killers* (1979) in which the conventional and incorruptible Commissioner Jan Argand struggled to maintain his civilised beliefs in the face of mounting challenge and temptation. If the first in the series can be called an eco-thriller, a later Argand, *Watching the Detectives* (1983), warned of dangers from Europe's new political right. *Nasty, Very* in 1984 repeated the anti-right warning, this time in Thatcher's model Britain. Other thrillers followed, perhaps the best being *A Spy of the Old School* (1982), followed by the equally splendid *Lying in State* (1985); the oddly named *Zdt* (1986), also known as *Greenfinger*, told partly from a feminine point of view; and *Sand Blind* (1993), about the moral duplicity at the heart of Gulf War One. Two further thrillers, *Accidents Will Happen* (1995) and the curious Spanish-based *Intimacy* (1996), good as they were, failed to sell, and he turned back to historical novels, producing one of his finest books, *The Last English King* (1997), a delayed sequel to an earlier historical novel *Joseph* (1979) about Wellington's Peninsular War.

The success of this title encouraged him to follow with other non-crime novels: *Blame Hitler*, *Trajectories* and *Kings of Albion* (1997–2000), together with another eco-thriller, *Brandenburg Concerto* (1998). In *A Very English Agent* (2002), running from the battle of Waterloo to the death of Wellington in 1852, Rathbone continued the literary style and themes he established in *The Last English King*, with nineteenth-century prose recast as today's and the text decorated with allusions, anachronisms and even references to his own family. (If one looks hard in other Rathbone books, one can often find minor characters reappearing as major ones or vice versa. He liked hidden jokes.)

Rathbone created one private investigator. The Bournemouth-based Chris Shovelin first appeared in *Homage* (2001) and reappeared in *As Bad as It Gets* (2003), a splendid old-style 'smuggle this out for me' adventure mystery set in parts of Kenya you would not wish to visit on safari. Rathbone died in 2008. *See also* Thrillers: Novels of Action.

Selected Works by the Author
A Spy of the Old School (1982)
Nasty, Very (1984)
Lying in State (1985)
As Bad as It Gets (2003)

Russell James

Raymond, Derek (also known as Robin Cook) (1931–1994)

Sometimes called the 'Godfather of British noir', Derek Raymond is remembered mainly for his 'factory' novels, lurid and violent books which still have the power to shock.

His real name was Robin Cook. He was born in London on 12 June 1931 – the scion of a wealthy family of textile merchants – and educated at Eton, from which he made many attempted escapes. Upon leaving at age sixteen, he unleashed the gypsy in his soul and began the travels which would eventually lead him from England to France, Morocco, Turkey and the United States, calling all these destinations (at one time or another) home. On his first return to the United Kingdom, he was called up for national service, but instead of becoming an officer and a gentleman, he preferred to join the ranks, where he rose to the great heights of, as he termed it, 'a shithouse corporal'. His nickname was 'The Baron' as he was the only conscript in his hut to own a cheque book from which he would draw out 10 shillings (50 pence) at a time to pay for drinks for him and his mates. When he left the service, he drifted into 1950s Soho where he became part of the bohemian scene concentrated around The Coach and Horses, The French Pub and The Colony Room drinking club. Alcohol was always Cookie's (as he came to be known) drug of choice, and sadly, it was eventually to be his downfall, although he never considered it thus. During this period, the author became involved with the West End underworld where he participated in illegal gambling and was employed as a 'shill', laundering the profits from long firm confidence tricks (selling non-existent properties in Spain and other criminal enterprises) because of his impeccable accent and manner, which fooled many a bank manager. He also spent time behind the counter of a porno emporium. All these ventures gave him material for his later fiction, as well as his other experiences: when money was tight, he drove a mini-cab at night so that he could write during the day.

His first novel, the semi-autobiographical *The Crust on Its Uppers*, was published in 1962 under his real name and is not only a great crime novel but also a great London book. There followed five more books in the 1960s and 1970s, and then a hiatus for thirteen years as Cook moved to France where he worked at manual jobs and drank copious amounts of red wine. Cook loved France and France loved Cook, where he was made a *Chevalier des Arts et Des Lettres* in 1991, an honour he rarely referred to, but was proud to receive, and where two of his books were filmed (*On Ne Meurt Que Deux Fois*, directed by Jacques Deray in 1985, adapted from *How the Dead Live*, 1986, and *Les Mois d'Avril Sont Meurtriers*, directed by Laurent Heynemann in 1987, adapted from *The Devil's Home on Leave*, 1985). Then the author made his comeback. After thirteen years without a new book in England, Cook returned as Derek **Raymond** (another Robin Cook had found fame as a writer of medical thrillers, so Cook took the Christian names of two of his uncles as a nom de plume). The first of the so-called factory novels featured an unnamed metropolitan police detective sergeant who investigates cases other coppers ignore, based at the Department of Unexplained Deaths at a police station in Poland Street, Soho (The Factory). These books are a blast of fetid air through the soft underbelly of English society which earned Raymond the title of the Godfather of British noir. Harsh, uncompromising and in-your-face, some people find them impossible to read, as Raymond enters parts of the human psyche that are normally better left alone. During this later period, he wrote his black masterpiece *I Was Dora Suarez* (1990), a work so grim and macabre that it is rumoured it made one editor physically sick. It is the story of a young prostitute hacked to death by a crazed axeman, and Raymond spares none of the details. The Factory series was optioned for television by the BBC (the late Tom Bell was Cook's actor of choice for the part of the detective sergeant), but perhaps proved too contentious to ever be made.

Robin Cook was a charming and generous man with time for everyone, and his nature (which was at such odds with his later work) earned him love and respect from everyone, from old Sohoites to younger generations, which was illustrated in 1993 when James Johnston and Terry Edwards from the indie rock band Gallon Drunk released a CD of original music (and Chopin) called *Dora Suarez*, with readings from the novel by the author himself.

Robin William Cook died in London on 30 July 1994. During his last months, he became a gypsy again, moving from flat to hospital to flat, sometimes staying with friends, and his final days were spent with family, close companions and colleagues nearby. But even at the end, he lost none of his innate charm which was illustrated by his last words to the nurse who tended him at night as he told her: 'Your husband is a lucky man.' His funeral was standing room only. He married four times and is survived by a son and daughter.

Cook's novels have been published and republished many times over the years under both his writing names, which can be confusing. His renaissance has been promised several times, but sadly never quite arrived. Though, as he would often say at the end of an evening's drinking, 'Darling, there's still plenty of time.'

But even now, the Cook machine rolls on. In 2006, Serpent's Tail published a translation of a 1988 French novel *Nightmare in the Street* (its first appearance in English) in tandem with a reprint of *He Died with His Eyes Open* (1984). Cook, the author, is gone but not forgotten (several of the Robin Cook novels have been republished under the name of Derek Raymond). *See also* Pulp.

Selected Works by the Author

As Robin Cook
The Crust on Its Uppers (1962)
Bombe Surprise (1963)
The Legacy of the Stiff Upper Lip (1966)
Public Parts and Private Places (1967; also published in the United States as *Private Parts in Public Places*)
The State of Denmark (1970)
The Tenants of Dirt Street (1971)

As Derek Raymond
He Died with His Eyes Open (1984)
The Devil's Home on Leave (1985)
How the Dead Live (1986)
I Was Dora Suarez (1990)
The Hidden Files: An Autobiography (1992)
Dead Man Upright (1993)
Not Till the Red Fog Rises (1994)
Nightmare in the Street (2006)

Mark Timlin

Realism and Crime Fiction

Crime is a manifestation of something wrong within a person, the person's circumstances or society. It is unsurprising, then, that crime novels are often like a stethoscope pressed to the chest of society, listening for its ailments.

Widening the scope to world-wide ills, spy novels and thrillers are particularly good litmus papers for revealing the political colours of the age's perceived enemies, be they the USSR, the IRA, Islamic fundamentalists – or even big business, a topic that John **le Carré** explored in *The Constant Gardener* (2001). Crime writers have also created dystopias to explore how society could go wrong in the future: examples include Philip **Kerr**'s *A Philosophical Investigation* (1992) and George Orwell's *Nineteen Eighty Four* (1949). And, yes, why should not we consider Orwell as a crime novelist? Or Graham **Greene** with his exploration of gang culture in ***Brighton Rock*** (1938)? As Ian **Rankin** has observed, one of the strengths of crime fiction is its capacity to confront questions of morality, and social and political issues.

Society at large inspired William Godwin's *Caleb Williams* (1794), which Julian **Symons** – in his influential critique of crime fiction, *Bloody Murder* (1972) – argued should be considered the first crime novel. It examined the injustices of 1790s Britain, when the French Revolution had sent ripples of paranoia across the Channel to England. Similarly, the detective novel followed in society's wake, specifically the introduction of a police force. Early examples include Inspector Bucket in Charles **Dickens**'s *Bleak House* (1853) and Sergeant Cuff in Wilkie **Collins**'s *The Moonstone* (1868).

Realism and Crime Fiction

Economics as well as politics encouraged crime fiction's development, cheap printing leading to a mass distribution and large readership. A notable beneficiary was Sir Arthur **Conan Doyle**, whose Sherlock **Holmes** stories were serialised *The Strand Magazine*. Holmes was, of course, the supreme rationalist – an embodiment of Victorian optimism held aloft on Empire, industrialisation and the triumph of reason, before Freud and Modernism upset everything by introducing the unconscious and irrationality.

Nevertheless, even during the interwar years, often called the **Golden Age** of crime fiction, the British crime novel still reflected a rational, ordered world. There was no equivalent of American noir, perhaps because Britain did not have prohibition and the mob. Crimes, such as the theft of jewellery or murders motivated by inheritance, were rational rather than the by-products of a crazed mind. The murderer and often the victim were unlikeable; why else would they kill or be killed?

It was an era obsessed with social order and class, when the 'lower classes' were not deemed interesting enough to have more than walk-on parts. No working-class heroes or people suffering economic hardships were seen trampling across the lawns of privilege, despite the fact that the interwar years were a time of great privation for many. Perhaps the novels satisfied a need for escapism, just as a couple of decades later *Casino Royale* (1953) and subsequent Bond novels would provide a fantasy world far from the realities of post-war austerity.

Besides the class-ridden attitudes of the time, what strikes many contemporary readers of certain Golden Age novels are racist undercurrents. A number of critics have commented on the anti-Semitism of writers such as Dorothy L. **Sayers**, particularly in *Whose Body?* (1923). Other low points include the 'yellow peril' of Sax **Rohmer**'s Fu Manchu novels, and the title of Agatha **Christie**'s *Ten Little Niggers* (1939) – hastily renamed as *And Then There Were None* (1940) but later bizarrely given another title with racist overtones, *Ten Little Indians* (1965). There were exceptions; the New Zealand novelist Ngaio **Marsh** wrote about Maoris with respect, albeit somewhat from the outside.

The Second World War marked a turning away from the upper-class world of the Golden Age, which seemed ever more anachronistic as Europe lay in smoking ruins, both physical and psychological. As Simon **Brett** observed in an article entitled 'The Long Shadow of Agatha Christie', not only did 'the breezy attitude to unnatural death' begin to feel distasteful to a nation in which many families had lost a relative, but also the large country estates began to disappear, and whodunit writers began to realise that all the good puzzle storylines had already been done. The crime novel had to adapt or die.

Fortunately it adapted, by deepening characterisation and exploring the causes and effects of crime. After all, if the argument 'Society is good, so crime must be by bad people' is no longer tenable, the argument naturally shifts to 'Society is flawed, so it produces flawed people.' This shift was abetted in the 1950s by a questioning of authority, reflected in satirical comedy shows such as *The Goon Show* and *Beyond the Fringe*. In 1960, the obscenity trial against *Lady Chatterley's Lover* (1928) showed how much attitudes towards what was acceptable in fiction had changed, the prosecutor Mervyn Griffith-Jones being ridiculed when he asked, 'Is it a book you would wish your wife or servants to read?' The 1960s saw further dramatic changes to society, including the abolition of the death penalty in 1965, and the decriminalisation of homosexuality and the Summer of Love in 1967.

If the English cosy can be accused of a lack of realism, so too can American noir, with its trench-coated heroes and damsels in distress. What distinguishes the contemporary crime novel is not the level or graphicness of violence, 'mean streets' versus country houses, but realism rather than stylisation. There are exceptions: the fetishisation of gangsters in certain current true-crime biographies and the 'gangster chic' of comedy capers such as the film *Lock, Stock and Two Smoking Barrels* (1998) can be stylisation bordering on parody. But generally, the 'mean streets' of modern Britain – for example, Val **McDermid**'s Bradfield or Ian Rankin's Edinburgh – are not populated by femmes fatales and square-jawed loners, but by everyday people with ordinary, unglamorous jobs, by people inhabiting a range of socio-economic milieus.

Rather than reinforcing stereotypes (women as femmes fatales, the xenophobia of Fu Manchu and so on), contemporary crime novels often subvert them or show them as undesirable. Although gender portrayals are covered in depth in a separate entry, they are worth touching on here. Even in the mid-1960s, assumptions about sexual orientation were so fixed that Ruth **Rendell** was able to use them to provide the big twist in her first novel *From Doon with Death* (1964). But now there are many instances of gay and lesbian protagonists such as Jake **Arnott**'s Harry Starks and Val **McDermid**'s Lindsay Gordon; and tough female characters such as Zoë **Sharp**'s Charlie Fox, a bodyguard and expert shot.

Even amateur sleuths have to be juggling a job and (particularly in novels by female writers) the obligations of families – for example, Natasha **Cooper**'s barrister Trish Maguire. After all, what victim of crime nowadays would seek help from an aristocrat rather than the police? The 'village greens and cream teas' world can now exist only in rather sentimental confections such as the television series *Midsomer Murders* and *Rosemary and Thyme*.

Contemporary authors also often use crime themes to shine a torch into the darkest corners of social ills and contemporary obsessions, such as prejudices against outsiders, religious intolerance and political protests. Ian Rankin's *Fleshmarket Close* (2004) dealt with attitudes towards asylum seekers, and *The Naming of the Dead* (2006) dealt with the G8 Summit at Gleneagles and the Live8 concert. Jake **Arnott** has used the social history of London from the 1960s to the 1990s as an integral part of all four of his novels to date; in particular, hindsight and changing political climates have enabled him to explore homosexuality in the 1960s to an extent that writers at the time would have been unable to do, for the simple reason that male homosexuality was illegal until 1967.

The modern emphasis on realism manifests itself in a number of other ways. First, there is a shift from the village to the city, and a rise in regionalism. In the Golden Age, novels tended to be set in London or quaint country villages in the south of England, but not the industrialised cities in the rest of the country. Now authors are eager to explore urban landscapes and their role in fostering crime: examples include John **Harvey**'s Nottingham and Denise **Mina**'s Glasgow. Locations and even buildings can be loaded with symbolism. In P.D. **James**'s *Devices and Desires* (1989), the ruins of a Benedictine abbey share the same headland as a symbol of the potency of science, a nuclear power station. And even those novels set in villages often portray a bleaker and darker world, a good example being the fictional Derbyshire village in Val McDermid's *A Place of Execution* (1999), a story that touches on the Moors murderers.

Which brings us to another area in which modern crime fiction differs from its Golden Age antecedents: its frequent willingness to deal with sexual taboos such as paedophilia and incest, and the psychology of abusers. Examples include Minette **Walters**'s *The Dark Room* (1995) and *Acid Row* (2001) and Laura **Wilson**'s *A Thousand Lies* (2006). Family dysfunction also has a corollary in non-fiction, with the great popularity of 'mis lit' or 'triumph over tragedy' biographies.

Frequently, novels exploring family dysfunction are examples of what Lee Horsley in *Twentieth-Century Crime Fiction* (2005) refers to as the 'non-investigative crime novel', namely one centred on transgressors or victims rather than on the detection of a crime. Freeing a novel from the need for detection and concentrating purely on characterisation can produce masterful studies of claustrophobia, repression and dysfunctional co-dependencies: many of Ruth Rendell's novels (particularly those she has written as Barbara Vine) and Morag **Joss**'s *Half Broken Things* (2003) provide excellent examples.

Similarly, contemporary writers have often taken an unflinching look at racism. In Ruth Rendell's *Simisola* (1994), a young black woman is held as a slave by an outwardly respectable white, affluent family. Furthermore, black crime writers are achieving critical and commercial success with black perspectives on crime in Britain. Mike Phillips has written four novels featuring black journalist Sam Dean, of which *The Late Candidate* (1990) won a **Crime Writers' Association** (CWA) Silver Dagger. More recently, Dreda Say **Mitchell** explored black gangland culture in *Running Hot* (2004), becoming the first black woman to win the CWA John Creasey Dagger.

There is also a growing interest in specialised scientific skills, such as forensic pathology and forensic anthropology, although these fields – popularised by writers such as Patricia Cornwell and Kathy Reichs and the various CSI television series – are still much more an American phenomenon than a British one. One science that is universally popular, however, is psychological profiling, as exemplified by Val McDermid's Tony Hill and the television series *Cracker*. This interest is notable in the **true crime** genre as well, with books by authors such as the criminal profiler Paul Britton – whose *The Jigsaw Man* (1997) won a CWA Macallan Gold Dagger for non-fiction – and Carol Anne **Davis**, a crime novelist with an MA in criminology.

Deep characterisations, social history, moral ambiguities, all the complexities of human relationships – the contemporary crime novel has encroached on all the areas that traditionally segregated 'literature' from 'lesser' forms of fiction such as the crime novel. And yet when Booker prizewinner John **Banville** chose to write a crime novel, *Christine Falls* (2006) – one he intends as the start of a series, no less – he hid (admittedly, transparently) behind a pseudonym, Benjamin Black. Many crime writers and readers feel it is time for the best crime fiction to be stacked alongside literature. *See also* Feminist Readings in British Crime Fiction; Gay and Lesbian Crime Fiction; Golden Age Crime Fiction; *and* Origins of British Crime Fiction.

Further Reading
Brett, Simon. 'The Long Shadow of Agatha Christie: An Overview of British Crime Fiction'. British Council Arts website, http://www.britishcouncil.org/arts-literature-matters-state-brett.htm.
Horsley, Lee. 2005. *Twentieth-Century Crime Fiction*. Oxford University Press.
Symons, Julian. 1972. *Bloody Murder: From the Detective Story to the Crime Novel*. Warner Books.

Julian Maynard-Smith

Rebus, Inspector

Detective Inspector John Rebus is the main series character of Fife-born writer Ian **Rankin**. Bearing the weight of the world on his shoulders – something he counteracts with copious amounts of alcohol – Rebus is usually called in to investigate the grimmest, most sordid cases on his native stamping ground of Edinburgh, a fact that has led some to refer to his books as '**Tartan Noir**'.

His name is Latin for a pictogram or a word puzzle made up of pictures: the perfect appellation for a man who solves clues for a living. First appearing in *Knots and Crosses* (1987), written when Rankin was a postgraduate student at the University of Edinburgh, John Rebus is described as having brown hair, green eyes and a generally unkempt appearance. Born in 1947, the son of a Polish stage hypnotist, he served in Northern Ireland and the SAS before joining the Lothian and Border police force. He is divorced, with an ex-wife, Rhona, and a young daughter called Samantha who grows into adulthood as the books progress. When we first meet him, he is a Detective Sergeant, but by the time of the second book, *Hide and Seek* (1991), published four years later, he has become Detective Inspector, a position he maintains for the rest of the series.

A combination of strong characterisation and vivid prose is key to the series' success, but Rankin also allows the readers' imagination to do some of the work by leaving certain details tantalisingly blank. It is this aspect that presumably led to the misguided casting of young actor John Hannah in the title role for a 2000–2001 television series. His clean-cut matinee idol looks were replaced by the more appropriately dishevelled form of actor Ken Stott for later episodes, which adapted all the books prior to *Exit Music* (2007), the alleged final book in the series. *See also* TV Detectives: Small-Screen Adaptations.

Selected Works
Knots and Crosses (1987)
Strip Jack (1992)
Mortal Causes (1994)
Resurrection Men (2002)
Fleshmarket Close (2004; also published in the United States as *Fleshmarket Alley*)

Mark Campbell

Rejt, Maria

One of the most significant (and best-liked) editors working in the crime fiction (and other) fields, Maria Rejt has been in publishing for over twenty years, with a hands-on commitment to her crime authors that is much admired. She is currently Publishing Director of several important imprints, including Macmillan, Pan, Picador and Macmillan New Writing. She has also made appearances on the influential book slot on the British television chat show hosted by Richard Madeley and Judy Finnigan and took part in the initiative to encourage debut novelists for the extremely successful 'How to Be Published' competition, which attracted 44,000 entries.

As editor, her extensive curriculum vitae includes such crime fiction luminaries as Colin **Dexter**, Minette **Walters**, Kathy Reichs and Scott Turow; an impressive enough roster, but Rejt's appetite for new discoveries is forever unslaked, and other finds include Daniel Mason's literary debut *The Piano Tuner* (2002), which has sold more than 250,000 copies. A particular specialty for Rejt is the much-acclaimed historical crime novelist C.J. **Sansom**, whose hefty, award-winning books have now sold close to a million copies in the United Kingdom. She was also behind Kate Morton's number-one bestseller *The House at Riverton* (2007), which gleaned the Summer Read 2007. Rejt has also worked with such established and upcoming talents as Chelsea Cain, Donna Leon, David Baldacci and Martin Cruz Smith (whose Russian-set Renko novels are one of the glories of modern crime writing). When time allows, she teaches creative writing at West Dean College in West Sussex.

Barry Forshaw

Rendell, Ruth (also known as Barbara Vine) (b.1930)

One of the unquestioned queens of British crime fiction, Ruth Rendell is a distinguished crime novelist important for her experimentation with the genre and for trenchant social criticism. Indeed, so profound are her radical treatments of form and cultural politics that her works often reinvent the **Gothic** origins of crime fiction.

Ruth Rendell is three crime authors in one writer. In the mode of detective fiction, her Chief Inspector **Wexford** novels, set in the fictional town of Kingsmarkham, progressively explore the possibilities for the 'good' detective to solve the mystery and heal social divisions. Always alongside the Wexfords, Rendell produced stand-alone crime thrillers, in which there is no central detective as a rational force to stem the chaos of criminal desire. In 1986, Rendell's novels embarked on another incarnation with the publication of the first work under the name of Barbara Vine. *A Dark-Adapted Eye* (1986) offered the most daring revision yet, in concentrating on a murder in which there was no doubt of guilt in the usual sense of the hand wielding the blade. It was the triumph of this and later Vines to show that 'guilt' might lie morally elsewhere, in the cruelties of class consciousness. Moreover, in a plot that makes maternity undecidable, Vine takes up Rendell's theme of the ultimate mystery of human passion, particularly that of families or of parents' intense love for children. Rendell/Vine is an author whose range of works, from the apparently conventional Wexfords to the experimentation of Vine, find in genre fiction a way of expressing the collision of psychology and social constraint. By subverting the genre, Rendell/Vine discovers new means of representing the extremities of the human spirit.

Chief Inspector Wexford does not work alone. Like other inhabitants of detective fiction, he has a subordinate companion of contrasting temperament. Inspector Mike Burden is a naturally conservative man who tends to the reactionary in his attitudes. Wexford, on the other hand, is liberal, imaginative and literary. Devoted to his wife, Dora, and two daughters, he is minded to think deeply and often positively about the social changes that impinge on the crimes of this Middle England town. Indeed, Wexford's character represents an ideal police force that cannot fully exist in the current social reality, as he acknowledges. It is not surprising that when Wexford makes a serious error, he quotes Tennyson's dying King Arthur on his way out of British society to Avalon to heal his grievous wound, in *Simisola* (1995).

More pervasive is the way Wexford and Burden represent political dynamics in the detective fiction form. Traditionally, the detective functions to stabilise the society depicted in the story. 'He' (and it is *formally* a he since the detective descends from the masculine hero myth) arrives like a *deus ex machina* to solve the crime that is usually murder, the greatest sin against human society. By identifying the criminal and removing him or her, the detective purges the social order of its intolerable sin. In restoring order, the detective replaces social values back where they were: 'he' is a conservative device. Rendell seeks in her Wexford novels to expose the political interests of this drive in the genre. For it is Burden who is the detective determined to restore the past. Wexford, his superior, is interested in a model of justice divorced from social convention. Consequently, Wexford always discovers something more than the formal author of the crime. He and the reader discover that the roots of criminal violence always exceed the capacity of social laws to contain them: either because these laws are politically unjust due to class, sexism, racism, etc. or because human desire and imagination is more mysterious than conventional thinking can comprehend.

So, in Rendell's very first novel, *From Doon with Death* (1964), love proves stranger and more terrible than the usual police enquiries can understand. *Simisola* exposes not only the racism behind murder but also the racism blinding the investigation of the murder. Class distinction is more often discovered to be class distortion of the human psyche into hate and cruelty, in all of Rendell/Vine's work. This distortion fatally combines with misogyny in novels such as *The Veiled One* (1988). Rendell also refuses to be sentimental about the young. Those who grow up deprived of love may conceal implacable coldness or murderous ambition. So in *An Unkindness of Ravens* (1985), a teenage daughter who first appears as victim of her father's bigamy is later revealed as a killer.

An Unkindness of Ravens is a good example of Wexford's preoccupation with social change as something both desired and feared. ARRIA is a radical feminist group of young women who claim to be reacting to attacks in the streets. Yet, there are dark rumours that they have an initiation ritual requiring the killing of a man. One man is found dead, others wounded, while the chief murder victim proves to have a history of exploiting young women. Meanwhile, conservative Burden is subjected to the irony that his pregnant wife is violently distraught at the news that she is carrying a girl. Jenny Burden was once the feminist. Now her conservative husband tries to teach her to value girls equally. Rendell presents progressive social change as necessary yet painful. There are deep psychic roots to a millennia of inequality of all kinds. She also distinguishes between being a victim of oppression and consciously exploiting this status to conceal a mercenary motive for murder.

Conservative Burden values his professionalism, a kind of detachment, above all in his approach to police work. The Wexford novels constantly hold this attitude up to scrutiny. Wexford is aware of what Burden is not, that his so-called neutral detachment is as politically and socially interested as his, Wexford's, risky imaginative involvement with other people. Indeed, Burden's correctness can become so correct that it slides into madness. When in *The Veiled One*, Burden decides that likely murder suspect Cliff *must* be guilty, he just lets him talk for hours, only to abruptly dismiss him as new evidence clears him. Unfortunately, Cliff will not go away. He starts to stalk Burden. Cliff's psychoanalyst explains that Cliff has made a transference. Finally, Burden and Wexford are at the former's home when they hear a rapping at the door. A bloody hand forces its way through the letterbox. Burden refuses to see Cliff because he was not a murderer. So Cliff embodies himself into the image of Burden's desire; a bloody crime is constellated by the very act of policing crime.

Yet, Wexford's imaginative empathy is no sure guide to truth either. For passion distorts the mirrors we find in our own souls. In particular, Wexford finds his love for his daughters is both illuminating for his quest and a source of illusion. For example, in *Harm Done* (1999), daughter Sylvia's work with abused women is directly helpful to the case. However, it is Wexford's greater love for his other daughter, Sheila, a partiality he regrets, that draws him into psychic and even literal danger. In *The Veiled One*, actress Sheila is playing the part of a guilty adulterous woman. So when Wexford is blown up in Sheila's car, it is assumed that hatred of bad women is the likely motive. As Wexford reflects in his hospital bed on those who take acting for reality, he acquires a sense of the masquerade of gender that enables him to penetrate the reverse simulation, a guilty woman acting the innocent victim. On the other hand, love for Sheila proves more muddling in *Kissing the Gunner's Daughter* (1992). Here is an example of Rendell's use of fairytales as lenses by which passion is shaped into plots. Daisy is a young girl found crawling in her own blood among the corpses of her family in their beautiful house in the middle of a wood. Wexford is irresistibly tempted to see her as suffering daughter and fairytale victim. This time, it is the loss of police procedure that is the serious mistake. Fairytales are a valuable guide in Rendell's world, but only if recognised as a map of the darker places in human desire. Fairytales are usually where Rendell's works enfold Gothic elements of sublime mysteries of terror and horror.

Of course, terror and horror are distributed differently in plots where there is no detective to reassure the reader at the end. Wexford is always able to show *what* happened, even if *why* remains mysterious and true *guilt* proves to stick to the social fabric. Rendell's crime thrillers without detectives unsettle the reader because there is no one true guide. No doubt that is the intention. One of the most famous is *A Judgement in Stone* (1977). The opening sentence breaks many of the conventions of crime fiction: 'Eunice Parchman killed the Coverdale family because she could not read and write'. In identifying the murderer, the motive and the victims, the novel is designed to highlight the *matter*, the aspects of the story that the genre relies upon, yet may not value sufficiently. Indeed, the 'matter' is like Eunice Parchman herself, servant to the surface polish of the Coverdale family, yet without which neither the crime genre nor the middle-class lifestyle of the Coverdales could function.

A Judgement in Stone shows how social deprivation (Eunice) and social privilege (the Coverdales) combine to precipitate a violent explosion. Eunice's illiteracy is both a sign and a partial cause of her unsocialised condition. Described as a Stone Age woman, as Miss Frankenstein, the absence of love in her poverty-stricken childhood meant she could not learn. Now without learning she is unable to love, to acquire that empathy with others that reading bestows. Taking a live-in servant job with the Coverdales, she discovers a kindly, bookish family who cut corners with her references because they wanted a cheap servant. The family is caring enough to perceive something strange in Eunice and to want to help her, yet they are not caring enough to penetrate what she regards as a horrific secret. When Eunice makes a friend of a local woman with a religious mania who has access to guns, nothing can stop her wrath. The death of the Coverdales is a Gothic kind of birth for Eunice, for she enters the world of police and courts, named and recognised by the state at last.

Eunice's lack of reading increases her lack of humanity. Money as the bedrock of class is crucial in this novel, and yet it does not provide a straightforward motive for crime. Indeed, true guilt and innocence are nowhere comfortably assigned. The careless Coverdales do not deserve to die, yet their selfish pursuit of class privilege is their undoing. Eunice Parchman's deprivation is so great that her evil propensities are inextricable from her suffering. Crime does not pay, yet to do nothing is to augment the criminal treatment of those around you. Hence the creation of a serial killer in *The Rottweiler* (2003) and the terrifying revenge of a raped woman in *The Crocodile Bird* (1993).

The inability to read or the dangers of reading badly is a topos that unites the three writers who are Ruth Rendell/Barbara Vine. Her very first story, *From Doon with Death* (1964), has Wexford puzzling over vital clues in love letters from the unknown 'Doon'. Reading is even more significant in the Barbara Vine novels as events lost in the past have to be pieced together by reading and re-reading old records. Significantly, it is no longer the police who seek to uncover the truth of a crime. In Vine novels, a single interested person, usually a family member, needs to delve into a family secret. This may involve a criminal offence such as Vera's murder of Eden explored by their niece, Faith, in *A Dark-Adapted Eye*, or Elizabeth waiting for killer Bell in *The House of Stairs* (1988). More often, the pursuit of a family mystery appears at first to contain no crime but rather a disturbing fact or event not covered by the law. These might include why a loving father appears to have invented himself in *The Chimney Sweeper's Boy* (1998) or why the cold Victorian, Henry Nanther married the sister of his first fiancée (*The Blood Doctor*, 2002), and crucially, who were the biological parents of Swanny (*Asta's Book*, 1993)? Now dead, she was the favourite child of Asta, whose early twentieth-century diaries as a Danish immigrant were published to great acclaim.

The Vine novels are about families and how the most inhuman crimes and greatest acts of love are to be found within them. The novels show how such forms of truth that come from great passion not only cannot be comprehended by the law but cannot be fully represented in the forms of fiction as well. Crime genres have traditionally claimed to be able to account for domestic and small-scale social murder, as opposed to historical large-scale atrocity. Barbara Vine demonstrates that the most terrible crimes in a domestic setting evade recognition, punishment, knowability and even representation. For what has provoked the extinction of one identity in *The Chimney Sweeper's Boy* is a loving act of incest. In *The Blood Doctor*, Henry Nanther's crime is to inflict a painful death upon his own child. Yet, the law would find it difficult to get a conviction for murder. As a researcher into haemophilia, Henry deliberately married a female carrier in an attempt to produce a son with the then terminal disease. Henry's obsession with inheritance, with 'blood' and with his own fame as a great scientist is shown to harbour murderous desires.

Set during the 1999 reforms of the House of Lords, Henry's legal criminality has a big effect on his descendent and would be biographer, Lord Martin Nanther. As a liberal minded man, Martin supports the aims behind the Lords reform. On the other hand, he is charmed by the centuries of tradition and deeply regrets the loss of his own position as a peer with all the ancient rituals and duties. At the same time, as Martin is re-reading the Nanther papers, his quest for the truth is accompanied by his wife Jude's attempt to conceive. Eventually, Henry Nanther's behaviour reveals that inheritance and tradition are not enough: the inheritance of privilege in the Lords must go and even Martin and Jude discover that their 'blood' or genetics will not let them make a child together. Henry meddled with reproduction out of lack of humanity. Jude and Martin will do so out of love; sperm donation proves to be the other factor that would make them both parents. *The Blood Doctor* begins in the expectation that a book will be written, Martin's biography of Henry, and with a miscarriage. It ends with babies about to be born and no book. The 'truth' that Martin discovers is too strange, horrifying and personal to be communicated. If the challenge to conventions of all kinds, social, psychological and literary, is common to all three of Rendell/Vine's types of crime fiction, then Vine is her most daring, attempting to suggest that the truth is what you create as well as what you find.

Asta's Book is an extraordinary Vine novel that interleaves the diary of Asta, Danish settler, and the tale of modern Ann, Asta's descendant and heir. Ann is summoned by an old friend to help with research into the sensational unsolved murder in early twentieth-century London of Lizzie Roper and her mother. Asta lived nearby, yet she wrote surprisingly little on the topic. Between powerful Asta – surviving a disappointing marriage and engaging in a platonic relationship with the war friend of her dead son – and cool Ann is Swanny. Living the privileged life of the beautiful woman, Swanny had nothing to trouble her until in late middle age when she was sent an anonymous letter alleging that she was not her parents' child. Her mother, still vigorous in old age, refused to tell her the truth. Such is the potency of a story of origins, *Asta's Book* suggests, that Swanny's eviction from family history disturbs her personality. When old herself, she behaves as she imagines a lower-class woman might. Ann realises that she believes herself to be the small child who disappeared from the Roper house at the time of the killings. So, research into the murders and into Swanny's past converges. The truth about Swanny's parents is recovered, but retrieving events serves to deepen the mysteries of a mother's desire for a child and Swanny's desperation for an identity. Asta, once united with the girl baby that her maid has brought her, writes down her unspeakable passion. Then she destroys those pages of the diary. The real truth of human motivation is unreadable.

Ruth Rendell/Barbara Vine is an important writer because she uses experiments in genre to empower her social criticism. Although her works thereby offer an insightful social record on changing Britain from the 1960s to the new century, they do more. Rendell/Vine uses form to challenge conventions of cultural practice, of literary tradition and of truth. She remakes detective fiction to explore the contradictions of a figure whose role is to identify the truth. Most originally, she turns detective fiction into a socially progressive form by making the paradise that the detective 'restores' an impossible future-oriented desire, not the society of now or of the past. Rendell's crime thrillers are radical because they explode the notion that guilt and innocence are simple alternatives. Here the law punishes, it cannot enact justice, for the roots of responsibility for crime go deep into the social fabric. Finally, Barbara Vine novels question the very definition of 'crime' and 'truth'. Vine novels are revolutionary because they argue that what is important about human beings is what is most obscure to themselves and others. Rendell/Vine makes crime fiction into Gothic literature: she shows the value of genre, in that by challenging it, important art emerges in the renewal of form. *See also* Literature and Crime Fiction; Realism and Crime Fiction; *and* Police Procedurals.

Selected Works by the Author

Wexford Series
From Doon with Death (1964)
A New Lease of Death (1967; also published in the United States as *Sins of the Fathers*)
A Sleeping Life (1978)
Put On by Cunning (1981; also published in the United States as *Death Notes*)
The Speaker of Mandarin (1983)
An Unkindness of Ravens (1985)
Harm Done (1999)
End in Tears (2005)

Stand-Alones
To Fear a Painted Devil (1965)
A Demon in My View (1976)
A Judgement in Stone (1977)
The Lake of Darkness (1980)
Live Flesh (1986)
A Sight for Sore Eyes (1998)
The Rottweiler (2004)

As Barbara Vine
A Dark-Adapted Eye (1986)
A Fatal Inversion (1987)
Asta's Book (1993; also published in the United States as *Anna's Book*)
The Chimney Sweeper's Boy (1998)
The Blood Doctor (2002)

Further Reading
Clark, Susan L. 1989. 'A Fearful Symmetry: An Interview with Ruth Rendell'. *Armchair Detective* 22.3: 228–235.
Knight, Stephen. 2004. *Crime Fiction 1800–2000: Detection, Death, Diversity*. Palgrave.
McDermid, Val. 'Ruth Rendell' for the Crime Writers' Association, http://www.twbooks.co.uk/cwa/mcdermidonrendell.html.
Moggach, Lottie. 1997. 'How I Write: An Interview with Ruth Rendell'. *Times* 13 September, 3.
Rader, Barbara A., and Howard G. Settler. 1988. *The Sleuth and the Scholar: Origins, Evolution and Current Trends in Detective Fiction*. Greenwood Press.
Rendell, Ruth with P.D. James. 1987. *Writers in Conversation*. Institute of Contemporary Arts, London video series.
Rowland, Susan. 2001. *From Agatha Christie to Ruth Rendell*. Palgrave.
Tallett, Dennis. 1995. *The Ruth Rendell Companion*. Companion Books.

Susan Rowland

Rhea, Nicholas (b.1936)

Nicholas Rhea is the best-known pseudonym of Peter N. Walker, a prolific crime writer who has (under various names) written some ninety novels. Under that name, he wrote the 'Constable' series which was later to achieve huge television success as *Heartbeat*, as well as some Montague Pluke novels, various other crime novels and some non-fiction about his home county of Yorkshire. Under his own name, he wrote the 'Carnaby' series and other crime novels and non-fiction books. He wrote yet more crime novels under the names Christopher Coram, Tom Ferris and Andrew Arncliffe, and he contributed some *Emmerdale* stories as James Ferguson. He also writes rural articles for Yorkshire newspapers. He was Chairman of the **Crime Writers' Association** during 1995–1996 and remained for many years the unofficial but active chairman of their 'northern chapter'.

Rhea became a police cadet at the age of sixteen and joined the North Yorkshire police force in 1956 to begin as a beat bobby in the seaside port of Whitby. His first short story was published in the *Police Review*. But it was his posting to Oswaldkirk, 20 miles north of York, and his position there as village bobby that inspired his most successful stories. The Carnaby series began first, with *Carnaby and the Hijackers*, his first novel, appearing in 1967. The same setting, a Yorkshire village in the 1960s, served for his 'Constable' series which ran to over thirty books. These were followed by his series on Detective Inspector Montague Pluke, beginning in 1997 with *Omens of Death*. Rhea combined writing with his police career until 1982 when he retired as Inspector. Thirty years of experience in the force provides his books with unmatchable detail and accuracy, even if it occasionally tempts him into producing plots which seem little more than case notes. This occasional fault must be set against Rhea's undeniable success in building a loyal and faithful readership. He does not often achieve plaudits from top critics in the national press (he is seldom noticed by them) but for Middle England, in an idealised version of which many of his tales are set; he and his books are sought out and savoured.

Few will doubt the accuracy of Rhea's police settings, and back in 1986, his book *Murder after the Holiday*, written under the pseudonym Andrew Arncliffe, won the first Police Review Award as the book which best portrayed police work and procedure. Four of his non-fiction books are crime-related and of particular note are *The Courts of Law* (1971) and *Punishment: An Illustrated History* (1972). But it is for his long backlist of comfortable **police procedurals** that this popular author will be remembered. *See also* Police Procedurals *and* TV Detectives: Small-Screen Adaptations.

Selected Works by the Author

Carnaby Series
Carnaby and the Hijackers (1967)
Carnaby and the Campaigners (1984)

Constable Series
Constable on the Hill (1979)
Constable on the Coast (2006)

Montague Pluke Series
Omens of Death (1997)

Russell James

Richardson, Robert (b.1940)

A journalist by profession, Robert Richardson moved from writing whodunits featuring an amateur sleuth to novels of psychological suspense. His first crime novel, *The Latimer Mercy* (1985), won the John Creasey Memorial Award for the best debut of the year. Firmly in the classic detective-story tradition, it benefited from a cathedral setting (in Vercaster, a fictionalised St Albans), a detective who rejoiced in the name of Augustus Maltravers and a confection of arresting incidents, including the theft of a rare bible – the eponymous Mercy – the vanishing of a beautiful actress and the nailing of a severed hand to a canon's front door. Maltravers, a playwright with an actress girlfriend called Tess, is an intelligent and likeable character, but three years passed before the couple returned and the mood in *Bellringer Street* (1988) is bleaker than in the first book. The disappearance of a skeleton from the cellars of Edenbridge Hall is followed by the brutal killing of the Pembury heir, yet the storytelling retains a characteristic verve. *The Book of the Dead* (1989), set in Cumbria, contains a lengthy – and well-wrought – Sherlockian pastiche. Memories of 'Silver Blaze' and the dog that did not bark in the night-time point Maltravers towards the solution to a murder mystery and help to prevent another killing. Maltravers appeared in three more novels, with varied settings in London, Devon and Cornwall, and each offers a combination of wit and ingenuity that is no less agreeable because it is reminiscent of an earlier generation of crime writing.

78. Robert Richardson.

It became increasingly clear, however, that Richardson was itching to experiment with the conventions of the traditional whodunit. He finally broke free of them with conspicuous success. *The Hand of Strange Children* (1993), a book nominated for the **Crime Writers' Association** (CWA) Gold Dagger, is an example of the 'whowasdunin'. In this type of crime novel, first popularised by the American Patricia McGerr, the identities of the murder victims described at the beginning of the book are as uncertain as the identity of their killer. Richardson blends extracts from news agency reports detailing the discovery of two bodies in a wealthy banker's house with flashbacks so as to build considerable tension. *Significant Others* (1995), in which Richardson makes use of his knowledge of the newspaper industry, and *Victims* (1997) are also entertaining stand-alone novels. In recent years, perhaps disenchanted by the vagaries of publishing fashion, Richardson has produced no more mystery novels. This is a shame, for his readability, humour and skilful plot-construction mark him as an author of considerable merit as well as range. He remains active in the British crime-writing community and has, uniquely, served two distinct terms as chairman of the CWA.

Selected Works by the Author
The Latimer Mercy (1985)
Bellringer Street (1988)
The Book of the Dead (1989)
The Dying of the Light (1990)
Sleeping in the Blood (1991)
The Hand of Strange Children (1993)
Significant Others (1995)
Victims (1997)

Martin Edwards

Rickman, Phil

Phil Rickman is a writer, journalist and broadcaster, best-known for his mystical detective series featuring Merrily Watkins.

Rickman's early novels were primarily supernatural in content and include *Candlenight* (1991), *Crybbe* (1993), *December* (1994), *The Man in the Moss* (1994) and *The Chalice* (1997), some of which share common characters and settings and have links with the Watkins books. The Watkins series began with *The Wine of Angels* (1998), which introduces Merrily, the new female vicar of a village in Herefordshire, where Rickman himself lives. Watkins is no straightforward vicar. She is the Church's 'Deliverance Consultant', the new term for exorcist, and each book finds her involved in some apparent supernatural event. Yet, the books themselves are genuine crime stories with no supernatural element and with cases investigated by the police with all the scientific regalia of modern police work. The storylines thus juxtapose earthly cravings with the unearthly or the analytical with the inexplicable. Because of Watkins's involvement, the two threads inevitably entwine, adding a darker side to the crimes. Several of the books include Rickman's own fascination with leys, New Age beliefs and local folklore. The series also includes many literary and artistic connections crucial to the plot, including Conan Doyle's Baskerville family in *The Prayer of the Night Shepherd* (2004), Aleister Crowley in *The Lamp of the Wicked* (2002), Sir Edward Elgar in *Remains of an Altar* (2006) and M.R. James in *The Fabric of Sin* (2007).

The same blend of the occult and the analytical appear in two series by Rickman, written under pseudonyms. As Will Kingdom, starting with *The Cold Calling* (1998), he created Detective Inspector Bobby Maiden who has developed, as a result of a near-death experience, an open mind to what he would previously have regarded as crackpots and a more intuitive understanding of the criminal mind. With *Marco's Pendulum* (2006), written as Thom Madley, Rickman started a new series about a young boy, with a talent for dowsing, who becomes involved in mystical and political events in Glastonbury.

79. Phil Rickman.

Rickman likes his mysteries firmly rooted in the landscape, not just the physical but the legendary: the myths and folklore that invoke the spirit of a place. In Rickman's books, the place, its people, its past and its memories are everything. They are the fertile soil in which his plots flourish and which drive the action. The characters may be strong, but they are at the mercy of the world about them. *See also* Science Fiction and Crime Fiction.

Selected Works by the Author
The Wine of Angels (1998)
Midwinter of the Spirit (1999)
The Cure of Souls (2001)
The Lamp of the Wicked (2002)
The Smile of a Ghost (2005)
Remains of an Altar (2006)
The Fabric of Sin (2007)
To Dream of the Dead (2008)

Website
Infinity Plus website, 'An Interview with Phil Rickman', http://www.infinityplus.co.uk/nonfiction/intrick.htm
www.philrickman.co.uk

Mike Ashley

Ridpath, Michael (b.1961)

A novelist of great talent and individuality, Michael Ridpath has made the world of banking and bond-dealing exciting, writing 'intelligent, fast-moving financial thrillers' (*Sunday Times*).

Growing up in Yorkshire, he went to Millfield School in Somerset and then Merton College, Oxford, before joining Saudi International Bank in London. Beginning as a credit analyst, before long, he was 'a bond trader, managing one of the largest junk bond portfolios in Europe'. In 1991, he joined Apax Partners, a venture capital firm, and while employed, he wrote his first novel, *Free to Trade* (1995). The success of this book gave him the confidence to stop working in the city and devote his energies to writing full time.

80. Michael Ridpath.

Free to Trade was written while he was still employed in venture capital. It was an exercise, he says, designed to distract him from the dealings he worked on every day, a means of giving him a different focus. At first, he wrote for his own amusement; when he showed his efforts to family and friends, their criticism made him set it aside for some months. But when he did return to his work, he saw the validity of their comments. He rewrote it, concentrating on plot and characterisation.

The book tells the story of Paul Murray, a junior bond trader. Ambitious, bright and hard working, he is set to make his mark in the City of **London**, when one of his colleagues, Debbie, suddenly dies. She worked in the company's compliance office, and Murray is convinced that she did not die by accident. This sets off an investigation by Murray into some of the dealings of his company and some of their business partners.

It is a perfect example of a novel written by an insider who understands his location, its strengths and weaknesses. He can explain the intricate workings of the money markets, how people relate within their own companies and with clients. To any one who knows nothing about the City of London, this would seem a dry theme for a thriller, but Ridpath is a natural storyteller and weaves a modern crime-thriller plot with the skill of a professional. He has made the environment his own and makes the reader see the markets from a banker's perspective: an exciting, dangerous bear pit where only the strong, determined and competitive can last the distance. Those who survive make their fortunes and earn the jealousy of their peers who fail, a theme he returned to in *The Predator* (2001).

Subsequent books have sealed his position as one of the United Kingdom's foremost thriller writers and, surely, the top writer of financial stories: 'Thrillers… [that] never fail to deliver satisfaction and excitement' (*Daily Mail*). *See also* London in Crime Fiction *and* Thrillers: Novels of Action.

Selected Works by the Author
Free to Trade (1995)
Trading Reality (1996)
The Marketmaker (1998)
Final Venture (2000)
The Predator (2001)
Fatal Error (2003)
On the Edge (2005)
See No Evil (2006)

Website
www.michaelridpath.com

Michael Jecks

Rigbey, Elizabeth

Elizabeth Rigbey is a British writer of intelligent psychological crime fiction often set outside the United Kingdom, in particular the United States and Russia, where she has lived.

Originally, she worked as a journalist and then as producer and presenter for the BBC, specialising in farming matters and gardening. After spoofing the world's longest-running drama serial, *The Archers*, she landed at a job as its editor. Four years later, she left to write her own books and to work on humanitarian aid projects with writers and actors in Russia, Afghanistan and Africa.

Her first novel, *Total Eclipse*, appeared in 1995 (as by Liz Rigbey) and was acclaimed as a major debut in the field. It stands out for its uncommon setting and left-of-field subject matter. Set in America, where Rigbey spent much of her childhood, the book was actually written while Rigbey was living in Russia. The action of this slightly askew love story takes place in an observatory in Northern California, and most of the principal characters are physicians and astronomers. Circumstantial evidence against the main protagonist, Julia, is so damning that even her attorney advises her to plead guilty to having killed her husband and stepdaughter. However, the investigating Sheriff is convinced that she has committed the perfect murder. Quantum physics, the nature of conscious reality and the labyrinths of the heart blend and collide, forming a puzzling mystery where things are not always what they seem. Few writers in the field have used scientists to such great effect as characters, and the claustrophobic and bland world of the observatory makes for a most different background.

Six years and two children later, she published *Summertime* (2004). Written after Rigbey left Russia, the novel is steeped in the motherland. The fact that the family at the centre of the intrigue is exiled and living in San Francisco and the Russia they knew no longer exists just intensifies their experience, as the author reveals: 'when I wrote it I went back again in my mind to those cold, hostile Moscow streets and the intensity of the love which awaits you when you find the right door and open it.'

Lucy Schaffer's sane, safe life – an existence she has built to escape a painful past – suddenly falls apart when she learns of the death of her father. Authorities in California say her beloved father was probably murdered, and his body dumped into the sea. In this rude, unsettling homecoming, she must dive into the deep waters of her past to make sense of the present and the murder. But what she remembers is foggy, incomplete and contradictory, a situation familiar to many of Rigbey's sharply drawn characters. As she uncovers the deceptions surrounding her family's legacy of madness and crime, Lucy has to confront the chilling memories of her childhood: her mother's insanity, her baby brother's drowning and the loss of her own son. Rigbey again weaves a hypnotic web in which her hapless characters struggle to confront reality, something of a trademark for her.

The Hunting Season (2006) saw the author use her full name, Elizabeth Rigbey, for the first time. Again set in America (she is married to an American and now divides her time between Italy and the UK countryside), her third novel is a further exploration of family dynamics peopled by nightmares and monsters from the past, and it confirms her forte as a writer who has an unerring ear for the disconnections in everyday life and how personal secrets can shape and deform the quietness of existence. The main character of the book is a medical doctor coming to grips with the moral ambivalence of the world that surrounds him.

As a British crime writer, Rigbey stands apart, a product of uncommon influences (America, Russia and rural areas) and a remarkable painter of damaged characters.

Selected Works by the Author
Total Eclipse (1995)
Summertime (2004)
The Hunting Season (2006)

Maxim Jakubowski

Rimington, Stella (b.1935)

Dame Stella Rimington is the former Director General of MI5, the British Secret Service, who has used her experience after retirement to write **espionage fiction**.

Many other authors of espionage fiction, from John **le Carré** to Ian **Fleming**, had inside knowledge of the workings of Her Majesty's Intelligence services, but Rimington was the most highly placed and least plausible candidate to become a spy writer. Her appointment as the domestic intelligence service's first female director general (DG) in 1991 would be the inspiration for the eventual casting of actress Judi Dench to play 'M' (Fleming's fictional head of MI6/SIS) in the later James Bond films.

During her years in service, she headed a drive to encourage a relative degree of openness concerning services that the British government had previously declined to admit or deny of having existed. Not only the first woman in the job, she was also the first 'DG' to be named or have her photograph appear in the press.

When she stepped down in 1996, she took up public positions with public companies including Marks and Spencer's (dealing as she said, with underwear sizes rather than international terrorism) and BG (formerly British Gas) and shattered all precedent by publishing her memoirs. *Open Secret: The Autobiography of the Former Director-General of MI5* (2001) caused a stir in the media and Whitehall, even though it had been carefully edited and approved.

Encouraged by her success, Rimington decided that she could make money out of her name and insider knowledge by producing fiction that showed the 'true' story of intelligence work.

At Risk (2004) introduced her plucky young female protagonist Liz Carlyle, who may have been intended to be loosely autobiographical but was a somewhat workaday addition to the huge existing body of espionage fiction rather than offering any fresh insights. Carlyle is blessed with innate courage, compassion and good dress sense and beset by male prejudice, public-school clichés and plodding police work. Rimington acknowledged a large amount of 'help' provided by *The Guardian* journalist and ballet critic Luke Jennings, widely rumoured to be her ghost writer.

Secret Asset (2006), Carlyle's second outing, provided more of the same, procedural, quick-paced but workaday capers involving Islamic fundamentalists, albeit with a throw-back reference to the IRA terrorists who were the actual enemy during Rimington's own time at the helm. *Illegal Action* (2007) continues her efficient, business-like work.

As an agent of the intelligence services, Rimington broke new ground and did stalwart work in shattering a veneer that had in any case become paper-thin. As an author of espionage fiction, however, she remains a curiosity. *See also* Women Crime Writers.

Selected Works by the Author
Open Secret (2001)
At Risk (2004)
Secret Asset (2006)
Illegal Action (2007)

Peter Millar

Ripley, Mike (b.1952)

Labelled 'England's funniest crime writer' by *The* **Times**, Mike Ripley is almost as well known for his long-running series of books featuring musician-cum-taxi driver Fitzroy Maclean Angel as he is for his myriad magazine columns and newspaper reviews.

Michael David Ripley was born in Yorkshire in 1952. A voracious reader of crime fiction from an early age (John D. MacDonald was a favourite), he utilised his great knowledge of the genre to become one of the most respected crime fiction critics of his generation, writing for *The Guardian*, *The Daily Telegraph*, *The Times*, *The Good Book Guide* and *The Birmingham Post*. In 1993, he was a scriptwriter on Series Five of the BBC's light-hearted crime series *Lovejoy* starring Ian McShane, but it is for his similarly light-hearted crime novels that he is most celebrated.

81. Mike Ripley.

Fitzroy Maclean Angel first appeared in Ripley's debut novel, *Just Another Angel* (1988). Set in the then-contemporary world of Thatcherism, women's peace camps and über-capitalism, Angel is a Hackney-resident jazz trumpet player who pays his bills (when he can) by driving a de-licensed black taxicab. A likeable rogue in the style of Lovejoy, he owns a cat called Springsteen and is happiest supping a beer in the company of a beautiful blonde – happier still if she pays the bar tab. But when such a woman asks for his help in recovering some stolen jewellery, he finds himself caught between a psychotic London gangster and the policeman out to get him, a situation not helped by a tenacious tax inspector hot on his heels. It is an action-packed ride, but Ripley's jovial writing style and Angel's quick succession of pithy one-liners ensure the rough and tumble never gets too unpleasant.

Angel Touch followed in 1989. Here, the itinerant trumpeter falls for the charms of another sexy femme fatale, this time, a financial analyst going by the name of Salome (named after Ripley's secretary of the time), who inveigles him into the cut-throat world of the London Stock Exchange and an inside trading scam involving young City wheeler-dealers bent on making a personal fortune – at all costs. The book won Ripley the coveted **Crime Writers' Association** Last Laugh Dagger for best comic crime novel (as did his 1991 novel, *Angels in Arms*).

Further Angel novels continued through the 1990s, featuring such diverse plot elements as animal rights activists, religious cults, the fashion industry and big-budget movie making, each marked with Ripley's characteristically irreverent humour. He also co-edited (with Maxim **Jakubowski**) three *Fresh Blood* anthologies (1996, 1997 and 1999), which highlighted the early careers of Stella **Duffy**, Denise **Mina** and Christopher **Brookmyre**.

In 2000, Ripley began working as a field archaeologist, digging up Roman sites in north Essex. But in 2003, he suffered a stroke that left him paralysed and temporarily unable to work. After spending a year recovering, he eventually wrote a self-help guide, *Surviving a Stroke* (2006), aiming to demystify the condition in his usual humorous style. In recent years, impressive historical novels have supplemented his ongoing Angel series, and he now teaches a course in crime fiction appreciation and creative writing for Cambridge University. In the crime-writing community, Mike Ripley is something of a treasure. *See also* Humour and Crime Fiction *and* London in Crime Writing,

Selected Works by the Author
Just another Angel (1988)
Angel Touch (1989)
Angels in Arms (1991)
Bootlegged Angel (1999)
Lights, Camera, Angel (2001)
Angel's Share (2006)
Angels Unaware (2008)

Mark Campbell

Roberts, David (b.1944)

David Roberts, one of the most stylish and elegant of British crime fiction practitioners, was educated at Eton College and McGill University, Montreal. He was a publisher for thirty years, becoming editorial director of Weidenfeld and Nicolson and, subsequently, partner with Michael O'Mara in O'Mara Books.

In 2000, he gave up publishing and became a full-time writer. The first of his Lord Edward Corinth/Verity Browne series – *Sweet Poison*, set in 1935 – was published in 2001. *Something Wicked*, published in 2007, is the eighth of what will be a ten-book sequence of novels.

Owing something to the **Golden Age** detective stories of Agatha **Christie** and Dorothy L. **Sayers**, Roberts books are firmly based in the second half of what W.H. Auden famously called 'a low, dishonest, decade'. His detective, Lord Edward Corinth, is, like Lord Peter **Wimsey**, the second son of a duke, but his 'Harriet Vane' is Verity Browne, a young, Communist foreign correspondent. Verity is closely involved with the left's fight against Fascism, which was to end with the outbreak of war in 1939; she gladly jettisons bourgeois preoccupations with marriage and babies and refuses to consider submission to a husband.

At odds with one another in many respects, Edward and Verity share a conviction that truth must be made to prevail and that, even when there is mass murder, it is still worth discovering who is behind the death of an individual. Despite their differing backgrounds and political views, Verity and Edward find they can work together to solve murders and find in each other similar virtues of integrity and respect for the truth.

Roberts peoples his novels with real **historical** figures such as Winston Churchill and Lord Mountbatten and many others, such as Lord Weaver – Verity's employer and the proprietor of the *New Gazette* – who are to some extent based on real people, in Weaver's case, Lord Beaverbrook, the owner of the *Daily Express*.

Roberts often uses a sporting event, such as the Henley Royal Regatta or the village cricket match, as the setting for his murders; he also utilises historical events like the Jarrow March or the Cable Street riots when Oswald Mosley was prevented

82. David Roberts.

from parading through the East End of London at the head of his British Union of Fascists. The Spanish Civil War is one of the main threads of the series. Two of the books are partly set in Spain. The Spanish Civil War was the Vietnam War of the period that fiercely divided people in Britain as a matter of conscience. Combining traditional puzzles with a well-researched historical background, Roberts provides old-fashioned tea-and-biscuits comfort with hard-nosed history – a recipe that makes for highly beguiling reading.

Selected Works by the Author
Bones of the Buried (2002)
Hollow Crown (2003)
Sweet Poison (2004)
Dangerous Sea (2004)
The More Deceived (2005)
A Grave Man (2006)
Something Wicked (2007)
The Quality of Mercy (2007)

Barry Forshaw

Roberts, Michael Symmons (b.1963)

As a poet, Michael Symmons Roberts has won the Whitbread Poetry Award and has been shortlisted for the T.S. Eliot Prize. Neither his four poetry collections nor his work as a librettist, broadcaster and dramatist would have prepared readers for his first novel, the edgy and compelling *Patrick's Alphabet* (2006), a crime novel set in the suburban industrial hinterland of London.

Roberts has said that he was wary of producing a poet's novel, which he feared would be a cliché, its story obscured by too much metaphor and description. It is in a different and less predictable way that the novel reveals its author's background as a poet: the novel benefits from an elliptical quality. In a new scene, it may be hard to discern any connection between it and the previous scene, but that connection eventually becomes clear. Thus, the story emerges bit by bit, as inserts are dropped in to illuminate a character or motivation, and the overall effect is not unlike that of a poem in which narrative may be present yet hidden beneath the surface. Having said this, the novel possesses strong narrative pull-through. The reader is hooked from the opening page and compelled to read on. The voice, which is laconic and familiar, that of a first-person narrator who takes you readily into his confidence, is part of what achieves this. Equally important is the story, which begins with the discovery, by the narrator, photographer Perry Scholes, of two bodies in a car with a shattered windscreen. Victims not of an accident but of a deliberate shooting, the bodies are then shot a second time – by Scholes with his camera. Scholes's hero is Weegee, the nickname given to American photographer Arthur Fellig to reflect his uncanny ability to be the first on the scene of a crime. Scholes drives around with his radio tuned to the police channel to pick up news of incidents so that he might be first on the scene, like his hero, and get the shots that he will then sell to the papers. 'But I'm quick too. Especially on my home turf. M4 corridor, M25 west side, suburbs and dormitory towns; I know every inch. Unless you die in bed the chances are I'll take the last shots of you.'

The influence of Roberts's dramatic work shows in the interaction between characters, where relationship dynamics are to the fore. He is good on the power of charisma, as well as the charisma of power. His interest in a particular kind of industrialised suburbia, which he calls 'the edgelands' – 'I like to say I live on the edge of the edgelands,' says Scholes – deepens the appeal of this classy fiction, which some have regarded as a crime novel, even if that does not reflect the author's intentions. 'I didn't set out to be a crime writer and I'll probably come out of it as quickly,' he revealed in an interview, in which he also said that it was his first-hand experience of the Hungerford Massacre, which he covered as a junior reporter for a local paper, that provided the inspiration for *Patrick's Alphabet*.

Subsequently, *Breath* (2008) and *Half-Healed* (2008) have further developed Roberts's remarkable gifts.

Selected Works by the Author
Patrick's Alphabet (2006)
Breath (2008)
Half-Healed (2008)

Nicholas Royle

Robinson, Peter (b.1950)

Creator of the Alan Banks detective series (seventeen by 2008), Peter Robinson's emigration to Canada at the age of thirty has not stopped him from writing about his beloved Yorkshire in vivid detail.

Robinson, Peter

Born in the working-class village of Castleford, Yorkshire, in 1950, Robinson studied for a BA honours degree in English literature at the University of Leeds. There he saw a poster advertising an MA course in English and creative writing at Ontario's University of Windsor and promptly moved out to Canada where he has stayed, by and large, ever since.

Having studied under American novelist Joyce Carol Oates, Robinson thought he could try his hand at a novel and so took a crash course in crime fiction: 'People like Chandler and Simenon...everything I could get my hands on'. After three unpublished attempts, he found success with *Gallows View* (1987), the story of DCI Alan Banks who, together with his wife Sandra, moves to the sleepy Yorkshire village of Eastvale to escape their stressful life in London. The novel's intertwining storylines and the cultured opera-loving protagonist may have contained echoes of R.D. **Wingfield** or Colin **Dexter**, but Robinson's authentic description of the villages and dales of his birthplace proved a unique selling point.

Finding that the self-imposed distance gave him greater freedom of imagination, the author stuck to Yorkshire as his locale, rather than Canada, and made Banks a series character. The second book – *A Dedicated Man* (1988), involving the death of local historian Harry Steadman – offered a similarly well-plotted storyline as the first book, with a plethora of twists that belied its relatively short length.

Robinson's gift for realistic characterisation is matched by his authentically realised geography; the landscape of Yorkshire is arguably the star of the Alan Banks books. He has won many awards for the series over the years, including the Arthur Ellis Award for Best Crime Novel for *Past Reason Hated* (1990) and the Anthony Award for *In a Dry Season* (1999).

Robinson has also authored two stand-alone novels. *Caedmon's Song* (1990, later issued in the United States as *The First Cut*) was originally written in the early 1980s and finally published after the author's success with Banks. A psychological **thriller** from a female perspective, its twin plots met with general praise although some of the detail appeared dated. *No Cure for Love* (1995) was a more successful tale about British actress Sarah Broughton who is transplanted to sunny Hollywood for a role in the cop show *Good Cop, Bad Cop*. Despite the exotic locale, her life is put in danger by a stalker who appears to know more about her past than she does. Robinson has also written many **short stories**, some of which are included in the collection *Not Safe After Dark* (1998). *See also* Feminist Readings in British Crime Fiction.

Selected Works by the Author
Gallows View (1987)
A Dedicated Man (1988)
Wednesday's Child (1994)
Innocent Graves (1996)
Not Safe After Dark (1998)
In a Dry Season (1999)
Cold is the Grave (2000)
Piece of My Heart (2006)

Website
www.inspectorbanks.com

Mark Campbell

Rohmer, Sax (1883–1959)

Arthur Henry Sarsfield Ward – who wrote under the pseudonym Sax Rohmer, which he claimed was Anglo-Saxon for 'freelance' – was the creator of the hugely popular villain Dr Fu-Manchu.

Rohmer was not, however, responsible for coining the term 'yellow peril' or even introducing the theme of the threat of the Orient into popular culture (M.P. Shiel published *The Yellow Danger* in 1898). Master villains had featured in fiction before Dr Fu-Manchu, notably Guy Boothby's Dr Nikola and Conan Doyle's Professor Moriarty. However, Rohmer's creation epitomised a style of villainy, taken up by movie serial and comic book master-fiends and carried to the present day in the forms of James Bond's nemeses (Dr No is an avowed imitation of Dr Fu-Manchu) and the press images of real-world bogeymen like Osama bin Laden.

The insidious Dr Fu-Manchu first clashed with stalwart British policeman Sir Denis Nayland Smith in 'The Zayat Kiss', published in *The Story-Teller* magazine in October 1912. This was the first of a series of run-together episodes which became *The Mystery of Dr Fu-Manchu* (1913). A Chinese mandarin 'with a brow like Shakespeare and a face like Satan', the doctor is 'the yellow peril incarnate in one man' and rules an empire of crime from the Far and Near East to London's Limehouse. He is addicted to peculiar methods of murder (one of his many nicknames is 'the Lord of Strange Deaths'), which involve deadly creepy-crawlies or poison flora delivered with the morning post to strike down respectable Britons in their own snug libraries. He also has a long-lived marmoset (the first recipient of the serum which has granted him apparent immortality) as his closest companion. His intention seems to be to bring down the British Empire and establish himself as a ruler in the East, though initially he is but one agent of the larger Si-Fan organisation (who are not always best pleased with him).

After further fix-up novels, *The Devil Doctor* (1916) and *The Si-Fan Mysteries* (1917), the doctor took a break while Rohmer pursued other interests, which included occult horror (*Brood of the Witch-Queen*, 1914, and a series of stories featuring psychic detective Morris Klaw), straighter adventure-detective fiction (often featuring dapper Parisian sleuth M. Gaston Max, detective Paul Harley or Scotland Yard's Inspector Kerry) and plays for the stage and radio. In 1931, Fu Manchu returned (without his former hyphen) in *Daughter of Fu Manchu* – perhaps because the talkie rights had just been sold. From then on, Rohmer delivered regular instalments – *The Mask of Fu Manchu* (1932), *Fu Manchu's Bride* (1933), *The Trail of Fu Manchu* (1934), *President Fu Manchu* (1936), *The Drums of Fu Manchu* (1939) and *The Island of Fu Manchu* (1941). With the Second World War – which Fu Manchu ought to have averted by murdering German dictator 'Rudolph Adlon' in *Drums* – things were a little quiet on the fictional criminal mastermind front, but Rohmer made two further attempts at reviving the franchise, with the post-war *Shadow of Fu Manchu* (1949) and a final blip of *Re-Enter Fu Manchu* (1957) and *Emperor Fu Manchu* (1959).

The Fu Manchu books keep up a hectic pace, with two- or three-page chapters that plunge headlong from peril to peril, and the villain's objectives become more interesting in the 1930s – especially when he engages with stand-ins for real-life characters like Hitler or (in *President Fu Manchu*) Huey Long. The Devil Doctor's greatest flaw seems to be in placing his trust in oriental seductresses (including his own daughter, Fah Lo Suee) who have a habit of falling in love with Sir Denis's manly young assistants (the books' narrators) and scuppering his ingenious schemes. For a few books, the possibility was raised that he was not even properly Chinese, and might be an Egyptian pharaoh dosed with immortality serum (Rohmer also wrote a lot about Egyptian curses) – but in the last novels, he is back in his homeland, clashing with the communists.

Even outside the Fu Manchu saga, Rohmer was a busy writer. *Nude in Mink* (1950, also known as *Sins of Sumuru*) introduced a female master-villain who schemed through several sexier thrillers in the 1950s (and was later played by Shirley Eaton in films), while Rohmer also ran to more 'realistic' crime fiction (*Yu'an Hee See Laughs*, 1932, and *White Velvet*, 1936) and John Dickson **Carr**-style murder mysteries (*Hangover House*, 1949, and *The Moon is Red*, 1954).

Fu Manchu first appeared in movies in a British series of silent shorts *The Mystery of Dr Fu-Manchu* (1923), a fifteen-part series starring Harry Agar Lyons, who returned insidiously in *The Further Mysteries of Dr Fu-Manchu* (1924). Warner Oland took over for *The Mysterious Dr Fu Manchu* (1929), *The Return of Dr Fu Manchu* (1931), *Daughter of the Dragon* (1931, with Anna May Wong), and a comedy cameo in *Paramount on Parade* (1930), in which he kills Sherlock **Holmes** (Clive Brook) and Philo Vance (William Powell)! Boris Karloff's camp line readings in *The Mask of Fu Manchu* (1932), with Myrna Loy as the 'sadistic nymphomaniac' daughter, make him the movies' greatest Fu Manchu, but Christopher Lee played the part more often than any other actor (*The Face of Fu Manchu*, 1965; *Brides of Fu Manchu*, 1966; *The Vengeance of Fu Manchu*, 1967; *Castle of Fu Manchu*, 1968; and *The Blood of Fu Manchu*, 1968). Other film and television Fu Manchus include Henry Brandon (the serial *The Drums of Fu Manchu*, 1940), John Carradine (a 1954 television pilot), Glenn Gordon (an ensuing series, *The Adventures of Fu Manchu*, 1956), Peter Sellers (*The Fiendish Plot of Dr Fu Manchu*, 1980) and Paul Naschy (*La hija de Fu Manchu*, 1990).

Cay Van Ash, Rohmer's biographer, produced two good 'further adventures': *Ten Years beyond Baker Street* (1984), in which Sherlock Holmes meets Fu Manchu, and *The Fires of Fu Manchu* (1987). Besides movies, Fu Manchu was also franchised to radio, comics (Marvel's *Shang-Chi, Master of Kung Fu*, expanded Rohmer's epic into the 1970s and beyond), novelty records ('Don't Fool with Fu Manchu!' by The Rockin' Ramrods) and sweet-shops (Fu Man Chews). *See also* Film and Crime: Page to Screen.

Selected Works by the Author
The Mystery of Dr Fu-Manchu (1913)
The Devil Doctor (1916; also published in the United States as *The Return of Dr Fu-Manchu*)
The Si-Fan Mysteries (1917; also published in the United States as *The Hand of Fu Manchu*)
The Mask of Fu Manchu (1932)
Fu Manchu's Bride (1933; also published in the United States as *The Bride of Fu Manchu*)
Emperor Fu Manchu (1959)

Further Reading
Rossman, Douglas A., and Robert E. Briney, eds. 1968–1981. *The Rohmer Review*. 18 issues.
Van Ash, Cay, with Elizabeth Rohmer. 1972. *Master of Villainy*. Stacey.

Website
Knapp, Lawrence, and Robert E. Briney, 'The Page of Fu Manchu', http://www.njedge.net/~knapp/FuFrames.htm.

Kim Newman

Roughead, William (1870–1952)

William Roughead 'excelled in that peculiarly Scottish province of the kingdom of letters, the recounting of criminal trials, not as a criminologist, still less as a sociologist but, like Robert Louis Stevenson, as a "tusitala", a teller of tales' (L.W. Blake, 'William Roughead', *Oxford DNB*). As the diligent attender at, and chronicler of, criminal trials in Edinburgh from 1889 to 1949, Roughead became 'the murderer's albatross' (Whittington-Egan 1991). In time he earned the reputation of being 'the greatest living exponent of the Calvinist attitude to evil' (James Bridie, 'Preface' to Roughead, *Classic Crimes*, 1951). On several occasions, his writings led directly to legal reforms. In his book *Trial of Oscar Slater* (1910), he publicised the most notorious miscarriage of justice of his day and kept it rankling with the Scottish legal system for nearly twenty years. It was this book, first published during the long imprisonment (1909–1928) of the reprieved, but wrongly convicted German Jew, Oscar Slater (1872–1948), which eventually led to the creation of the Scottish Court of Criminal Appeal. Roughead himself gave evidence at that newly created court when, in July 1928, it quashed Slater's murder conviction.

Roughead was born and educated in Edinburgh and qualified as a 'writer to the signet' (i.e. a Scottish lawyer) in 1893. His father, a prosperous draper and outfitter, had died at sea 1887, and Roughead was able to live on the proceeds of the sale of the family business. He never needed to practice as a lawyer. Endowed in his own patrimony, he was free to indulge his inclination to be a man of letters and to develop his pre-eminent talent as the stormy petrel of crime.

The first murder trial he attended was that of the 'baby-farmer' Jessie King in February 1889, though his recollection of that trial, *My First Murder*, did not appear until 1932, when the essay was included in *In Queer Street*. In November 1889, he witnessed the trial of John Watson Laurie for the 'Aran murder', though again there was a long wait – forty-three years – before the volume was published (in the *Notable British Trials* [NBT] series), this time because Laurie's relatives objected to an earlier publication in 1905. This was a blow to Roughead, not least because Harry Hodge (1872–1947), the publisher of the NBT series, had intended to make Roughead's edition of Laurie's trial the first volume in his series. Instead, Hodge commissioned Roughead to edit (and to write the introduction to) the *Trial of Dr Pritchard* (1906), a sometime naval surgeon who had poisoned his wife and her mother. (In 1865, he had been the last man to be publicly executed in Glasgow.) The format of this volume would be followed in all the future trials recorded in, or historically reconstructed for, the NBT series. The verbatim transcript of each trial (including, most valuably for law students, the cross-examination of witnesses, which, after the passing of the Criminal Evidence Act 1898, often included the defendant) made readers feel that they were sitting as members of the jury. But the separate introduction (which could be read before or afterwards) contained matters of background and opinion which no juror would have been permitted to read. In the case of his introduction to the *Trial of Dr Pritchard*, Roughead afterwards felt that he had been too sparing in his condemnation of that man. 'I didn't let myself go. Oo, a brute, a bad man' (Whittington-Egan 1991). Roughead went on to edit nine further volumes in NBT series, including three trials which he had personally witnessed: John Watson Laurie (1889, published in 1932), Oscar Slater (1909, editions published in 1910, 1915, 1929 and 1950) and John Donald Merrett (1927, published in 1929).

But Roughead's favourite volume (which he called 'my Jessie') was the *Trial of Jessie M'Lachlan* (1862, published in 1911). That trial may be taken as an object lesson in the dangers of a defendant accusing another person of being the perpetrator of the crime. Many people (Roughead amongst them) believed that Mrs M'Lachlan was telling the truth when (at a time when she could not give evidence on oath) she accused the principal prosecution witness of committing the murder she was being tried for. But the jury seems to have inverted the burden of proof and convicted the defendant because she could not prove her allegation. Although reprieved from the death penalty, she spent fifteen years in prison because of the murder of a fellow servant girl at 17 Sandyford Place, Glasgow. (Hence Roughead's description of the case as *The Sandyford Mystery* in his anthology *Classic Crimes*).

In addition to his volumes in the NBT series, and his book *Twelve Scots Trials* (1913), Roughead published a total of seventy-five essays in the *Juridical Review* during the years 1913–1941 and one essay in the *Scottish Historical Review* (July 1917). Collections of his essays appeared regularly until his death, and a posthumous anthology (*Tales of the Criminous*) was published in 1956. American compendia were also published in 1938, 1939, 1941, 1943 and 1946. In his foreword to the 1941 US volume (*The Murderer's Companion*), Alexander Woollcott reported that Roughead's work appeared on 'the President's Shelf' – a selection of books chosen by the Library of Congress to be kept outside President Roosevelt's study in the White House.

Roughead also chillingly predicted the consequences of a miscarriage of justice (in the opposite sense to the usual one) when he reviewed the case of John Donald Merrett, who was tried for the murder of his mother in 1927. That overindulged son unconvincingly explained his mother's death as suicide and escaped a conviction for murder with the Scottish verdict of 'Not Proven' and a sentence of twelve months' imprisonment for forging his mother's cheques. Returning to the case in *Knave's Looking Glass* (1935), Roughead predicted that, although the public had not heard from Merrett for several years, 'we may do so yet'. In 1954, Merrett (using the alias Chesney) murdered his wife and her mother and committed suicide. It is a mark of the effectiveness as a writer and of the wintry irony with which he castigated miscarriages of justice, that his introduction to the transcript in the *Trial of Oscar Slater* was torn out of the volume before Slater was allowed to borrow it from the prison library.

Roughead, who seldom travelled farther than the Isle of Arran and never went abroad, was a considerate correspondent and helpmate to writers seeking the benefit of his researches and his insights. But he was hurt by any unattributed reliance of his work and he was convinced that Lillian Hellman had made use of one of his essays published in *Bad Companions* (1930) for her play *The Children's Hour* (1934).

James Bridie described Roughead as 'a student of the bad whose subjects would be "nane the waur o a hangin"…[But] he has no indignation against his specimens. They are damned and cannot help it' ('Preface' to Roughead, *Classic Crimes*).

English criminal law failed to produce any similar consistent chronicler of famous trials until, in the 1960s and 1970s, a different medium (radio) popularised the work of Edgar Lustgarten (1907–1979). Between them, for eighty years, they inspired – and continue to inspire – law students and students of crime, wherever the Anglo-American method of trial, with all its faults and all its virtues, continues to hold sway. *See also* Scottish Crime Fiction *and* True Crime.

Selected Works by the Author
Dr Pritchard (NBT series, 1906)
Oscar Slater (NBT series, 1910, 1915, 1929 and 1950)
Jessie M'Lachlan (NBT series, 1911)
Burke and Hare (NBT series, 1921)
Twelve Scots Trials (essay collection, 1913)
Malice Domestic (essay collection, 1928)
In Queer Street (essay collection, 1932)
Knave's Looking Glass (essay collection, 1935)
Classic Crimes (essay collection, 1951)

Further Reading
Whittington-Egan, R. 1991. *William Roughead's Chronicles of Murder*. Lochar Publishing.

Leslie William Blake

Rowe, Rosemary (b.1942)

Rosemary Rowe is the writer of Cornish historical romances and of a historical crime series set in Roman Britain.

Rowe was born in Cornwall but was raised and educated in Australia and New Zealand, where she spent four years as a teacher before returning to England in 1967. She became a senior lecturer and, subsequently, examiner and moderator in English language and received the English Language Society price in 1978. Her profound knowledge of English has been shared in the teaching aids *Make Up Your Mind* (1979), *Teaching Tenses* (1992) and *Writing a Novel* (2004).

83. Rosemary Rowe.

Rowe turned to writing when an accident curtailed her lecturing career. Initially, she wrote romance stories for women's magazines under her married name, Rosemary

Aitken, and as Bessie Reynolds. Although divorced in 1972, she retained the name Aitken for her Cornish saga series set in Penvarris at the turn of the nineteenth century and also used the name on the first of her stories featuring Libertus, 'Mosaic' (1996). She has since developed the character for a series of novels all published under her maiden name.

Libertus was a Celtic slave but has earned his freedom and makes a living as a pavement-maker and mosaicist in Glevum (Gloucester) in Roman Britain in the second century AD. Libertus has a mind for puzzles, piecing together the clues just as he does a mosaic, looking for patterns. The first in the series, *The Germanicus Mosaic* (1999), sets the tone for the series. It focuses on the plight of the slaves and their treatment at the hands of the vicious Germanicus, so when he is murdered, his slaves are the first suspect. Under Roman law, if one slave is found guilty of murdering his master, then all of the slaves are put to death. Libertus, who has his own slave but one who operates more as an apprentice who will one day gain his freedom, is called in to help by Marcus, his patron and the local imperial administrator. A continuing thread throughout the books is the search by Libertus for his wife from whom he was separated when captured and who was also treated as a slave.

Libertus's investigations are not restricted to Gloucester. He travels to London in *The Chariots of Calyx* (2002) and into Wales in *Enemies of the Empire* (2005), where resentment against Rome still simmers.

The Roman background is thoroughly researched and the investigations are methodically unravelled with plenty of red herrings. Rowe has developed a feature of a surprise ending that propels the reader into the next volume. Being a native Briton, Libertus provides his own views on the Romans and their way of life, which adds an extra dimension to the growing number of Roman historical mysteries. *See also* Historical Crime.

Selected Works by the Author
The Germanicus Mosaic (1999)
A Pattern of Blood (2000)
Murder in the Forum (2001)
The Chariots of Calyx (2002)

Website
www.raitken.wyenet.co.uk

Mike Ashley

Rowlands, Betty (b.1923)

In her two series of Cotswold-based female detectives, Betty Rowlands's first concern is Melissa Craig, crime novelist-cum-amateur-investigator, and the second is Sukey Reynolds, crime-scene investigator.

Rowlands spent much of her professional life as a teacher but moved to the Cotswolds in later life to a small village perched above the plain of Gloucester, a village which resembles that in which Melissa Craig lives, although Rowlands has stressed that the real-life and the fictional villages are not the same. Given the number of homicides she sets around the area, her neighbours must be relieved.

An amateur detective can seem credible in a stand-alone novel but becomes unlikely in a series. Rowlands overcomes this by making Melissa Craig a working crime novelist, naturally attracted to scenes of crime. Even so, Craig needs friends to lead her towards local crimes, such as a journalist boyfriend, a friendly police contact and a nearby doctor. The Cotswold settings and the titles of her books make them sound more cosy, even spinsterly, than they are, but the rural idyll is disturbed by drug smugglers, murderers and thieves, and the sleepy village is only a short drive from the bustling city of Gloucester which, though not metropolitan, was home to Fred and Rosemary West. In the first book, *A Little Gentle Sleuthing* (1990), Melissa arrives in the village in the hope that little will disturb her writing – but before long, she is receiving a succession of mysterious telephone calls. And she has not quite escaped her previous, over-protective boyfriend. Settling in to her new environment in *Finishing Touch* (1991), Melissa takes a part-time job teaching creative writing – but someone has been too creative, and the department secretary is found with her throat slashed. By the seventh, *Deadly Legacy* (1995), Melissa's familiarity with murder makes her the obvious choice to complete the manuscript of a recently murdered crime novelist. When she reads it, however, she thinks it might hold the clue to a series of local sex murders. Then there are those recent burglaries. Could they be linked? By the time we reach *No Laughing Matter* (2003), even Melissa's mother is not safe. In her nursing home, two residents have been poisoned.

Sukey Reynolds first appears as a Scenes of Crime Officer in *An Inconsiderate Death* (1997) on a case where a businessman's wife has been strangled, and in later books, the nasty deaths continue. *Deadly Obsession* (2004) produces a corpse with a broken neck found below a garden staircase, and in *Party to Murder* (2005), a pregnant estate manager is found strangled with her necklace. Her employer made her pregnant, but did he kill her? Sukey's work makes her more mobile than Melissa, and in later books, she leaves the Gloucester area for Bristol; in *Alpha, Beta, Gamma...Dead* (2007), she achieves her ambition of joining the CID. Now anything can happen! *See also* The Shires: Rural England and Regional Crime Fiction.

Selected Works by the Author
A Little Gentle Sleuthing (Melissa Craig Series, 1990)
Alpha, Beta, Gamma...Dead (Sukey Reynolds Series, 2007)

Russell James

Royle, Nicholas (b.1963)

Nicholas Royle is an unsettling author whose crime novels deal with European culture, art cinema and disturbed states of mind. He is an idiosyncratic novelist and short-story writer whose work revolves around certain themes: the landscape of **London** and other European cities, obsession and other psychological disorders, the auteur theory of cinema and the human body as an artistic medium. Crime plays a part in much of his writing, especially in two novels that explore links between film-making and madness: *The Director's Cut* (2000) and its sequel *Antwerp* (2004).

Royle's first novel, *Counterparts* (1993), is a dark metaphysical thriller that explores the theme of divided identity. Two disturbed individuals who may be facets of the

84. Nicholas Royle.

same person come together as the Berlin Wall is falling, and the uncertain nature of their shared identity prefigures the uncertainties of Europe. *Counterparts* is not primarily a crime novel, but its dense atmosphere of nocturnal trains, sleepless nights and distorted memories will appeal to readers of noir fiction.

After two slightly lighter novels, Royle returned to the theme of madness in a richly textured noir novel, *The Director's Cut*. The discovery in a derelict London building of a human body, mummified in film stock, fuels rumours of a lost amateur film from the 1980s that recorded a real suicide. The narrative follows the lives of the four men who made the film. When one of them is found dead on a barge floating down the Thames, cremated by burning celluloid, a murder mystery develops whose solution lies in a web of secret identities.

Antwerp follows Frank, a character from *The Director's Cut*, to the Belgian city where an art-film director is using prostitutes to recreate nude scenes from Delvaux paintings. In Antwerp's red-light district, erotic art and cinema are linked to 'reality porn' and brutal abuse. On the edge of this shadowy world is a loner with his own ideas about women as the raw material for art. When Frank's girlfriend is abducted, he is forced to confront the darkness behind the cinema screen.

Royle's short stories often explore violence rooted in artistic or sexual impulses. His collection *Mortality* (2006) includes 'The Inland Waterways Association', in which a psychopath creates a sequence of murders to externalise the pattern in his mind, and 'Skin Deep', in which a husband gives his wife's lover a grim proof of the gap between surface and inner realities. Elsewhere, 'Standard Gauge' is Royle's most disturbing portrayal of psychotic crime.

For Nicholas Royle, the compulsions that drive serial killers and sex offenders are not easily separated from those inspiring cinema, music and romance. Although stark and challenging, his work deals sensitively with difficult ethical issues. The clarity of his prose and the taut suspense of his narratives ensure that his books entertain and satisfy – but the issues they raise, like the bleak images he constructs, remain in the mind long afterwards.

Selected Works by the Author
Counterparts (1993)
The Director's Cut (2000)
'Standard Gauge' in *Thirteen* (2002)
Antwerp (2004)
Mortality (stories, 2006)

Joel Lane

Ryan, Chris (b.1961)

The pseudonymous Chris Ryan, like Andy **McNab**, is a soldier who has used his personal experiences to create action-packed thrillers strong on authentic detail.

Ryan was born in the North East of England in 1961. He joined the Special Air Service (SAS) in 1984 and left in 1993. His first novel, *The One That Got Away* (1995), describes some of his real experiences in the Bravo Two Zero mission behind Iraqi lines in the first Gulf War. (His colleague and former SAS man on the same mission, Andy McNab, also turned novelist with his book *Bravo Two Zero*, 1993.) *The One That Got Away* was also adapted for television in 1996, with Ryan credited as a co-writer with Paul Greengrass, who directed the film. During his ten years with the SAS, Ryan was involved in overt and covert operations and was also Sniper Team Commander of the anti-terrorist team. During the Gulf War, Ryan was the only member of an eight-man team to escape from Iraq; three colleagues were killed and four captured. It was the longest escape and evasion of capture in the history of the SAS. For this, Ryan was awarded the Military Medal.

On returning to the United Kingdom, Ryan was involved with the SAS in selecting and training potential recruits. After leaving the service, he forged his career as a successful writer of adult action novels which display his inside knowledge of covert military operations. (Most notable is his Geordie Sharp series, inaugurated with *Stand By, Stand By* in 1996, about an SAS sergeant who returns home after being wounded in the Gulf War, only to encounter a personal crisis which sends him to Belfast. Back in action in Northern Ireland, he finds himself a target of the Provisional IRA.) In the 'Geordie Sharp' series, the character of Sharp suggests (as in his other books) a Ryan surrogate. Ryan also produced novels which feature plots freighting in the war on terror, bio-weapons, weapons of mass destruction, Middle Eastern terrorism, assassins, gold and diamond smuggling and the like; most feature the SAS embroiled in a global plot of some description. The writing is workmanlike, the results page-turning – emphatically not Booker Prize Longlist material, but the books have gleaned a dedicated fan base and are extremely readable thrillers. Ryan has also created a popular series of juvenile SAS adventures called *Alpha Force* for the youth market; the first was 2002s *Survival*, and the tenth, *Untouchable*, released in 2005. Ryan started a fresh series entitled *Code Red* in 2006 with *Flash Flood*, and the third, *Outbreak*, published in 2007.

Ryan is a prolific writer who incorporates a sharp authentic edge into his work. Between writing novels, he has worked for the BBC with a three-episode series

Hunting Chris Ryan, as well as co-creating *Ultimate Force* for ITV. He is also much employed as a motivational speaker.

Selected Works by the Author
The One That Got Away: My SAS Mission behind Iraqi Lines (non-fiction, 1995)
The Hit List (2000)
The Watchman (2001)
Land of Fire (2002)
Greed (2003)
The Increment (2004)
Blackout (2005)
Ultimate Weapon (2006)
Strike Back (2007)

Ali Karim

Ryan, Denise (b.1966)

Denise Ryan's hard-hitting urban thrillers have often been likened to those of Martina **Cole**, especially in her use of tough female protagonists who give as good as they get.

Born in the market town of Ormskirk in West Lancashire, Ryan moved to Liverpool in the late 1970s where she studied English Literature and Law. She then travelled widely throughout Europe, at one point, working as a translator and speechwriter for the British Embassy in The Hague.

Ryan's debut, *The Hit*, was published in 1999. Set in her native Liverpool, lawyer Shannon Flinder sets herself up as a vigilante to avenge the rape and murder of a local girl by her head teacher – who also happens to be Flinder's father-in-law. No one will believe Flinder's accusations, including her husband, a CID officer, so she has no choice but to step outside the law and deliver her own kind of justice. *The Hit* was a tough, take-no-prisoners read, rightfully compared with Martina Cole's early works, and told its story using a strong female lead whose intelligence and resourcefulness were more than a match for the opposition.

Having found a ready-made market, her next novel, *Dead Keen* (2000), followed a similar format. This time it was soon-to-be married Justine who found herself on the wrong side of the law when she went up against a crazed stalker who fantasised that she was in love with him. Arguably more accomplished than *The Hit*, this second book upped the ante by providing far more plot threads and characters than the first.

With the plot of a protective wife tasked with clearing her missing husband's name, *Betrayed* (2002) covered new ground with its tense scenes set inside the real-life Devil's Kingdom, a series of labyrinthine tunnels deep beneath Liverpool's Edge Hill district. The story saw the emphasis shift towards a more multi-layered and sympathetic protagonist, although the gritty storytelling techniques readers had grown accustomed to were still very much in evidence.

Her fourth book returned to the character of Shannon Flinder, protagonist of *The Hit*. *Backlash* (2003) saw the past revisiting her in the form of a terrifying killer who seems to know more about her than even she does. Ryan's latest, *Cold Blood* (2005), continued Flinder's journey into even murkier waters with her best friend murdered and an escaped killer out for her blood.

The author divides her time between Ormskirk and Holland and cites Emily Brontë, Margaret Atwood and Olivia Goldsmith as literary influences.

Selected Works by the Author
The Hit (1999)
Betrayed (2002)
Cold Blood (2005)

Website
www.deniseryan.co.uk

Mark Campbell

S

The Saint on Television

Simon Templar, also known as the Saint, a semi-reformed crook and gentleman adventurer, made his literary debut in Leslie **Charteris**'s novel *Meet the Tiger* (1928) and enjoyed a lengthy career in further books, a radio show (for which Charteris devised the character's signature whistled theme, reprised with credit in many later Saint efforts), a film series with Louis Hayward, George Sanders and others, comic strips, and other merchandise.

In 1961, British producers Robert S. Baker and Monty Berman persuaded Charteris to let them pick up the rights to the still-popular character for a television series that eventually developed under the aegis of Lew Grade's ATV. They cast Roger Moore, who had done series leads in *Ivanhoe* (1958–1959) and *Maverick* (1959–1961), as a youngish Templar and at first drew stories from Charteris's extensive backlist (though the author sniped at the production team with many memos of disapproval when details were changed). Moore's hero opened each episode with a snatch of voice-over narration, usually establishing his high-flying, cosmopolitan and international world. When a secondary character recognises 'the famous Simon Templar', Moore pauses and dips his head, allowing a halo to appear above him. The opening credits (accompanied by Edwin Astley's memorable expansion of Charteris's tune) feature the haloed stick figure familiar from Saint book jackets. The show ran from 1962 to 1969, turning out 118 episodes, shifting from black and white to colour half-way through; two theatrical features, *Vendetta for the Saint* and *The Fiction Makers*, were cobbled together in 1968.

A peripatetic adventurer, often found in Elstree backlots representing far-flung locations, the Saint had few regular supporting characters, though Ivor Dean appeared quite often as the outclassed and befuddled Inspector Teal ('Claud Eustace') of Scotland Yard and a few other coppers also recurred (Arnold Diamond as Colonel Latignant, Robert Cawdron as Sergeant Luduc). Moore's ironic turn and knack for enjoying his adventures was far better suited to Charteris's rogue than his later turn as Ian **Fleming**'s nastier Bond, and he seemed to relish the opportunity to come to grips with sultry starlets and diabolical villains. Mostly confining his activities to damsels in distress, international crooks and the odd Nazi war criminal, the Saint once or twice strayed into weirder territory (fighting giant ants in 'The House on Dragon's Rock', 1968) better left to *The Avengers*.

The show was influential enough to be imitated – by *The Baron* (1966), which was not above remaking *Saint* scripts, and the Moore vehicle *The Persuaders* (1971), which spun off from the *Saint* episode 'The Ex-King of Diamonds' (1969) – before its inevitable revival as *The Return of the Saint* (1978), with an aptly cast Ian Ogilvy and more genuine locations, but slightly naff clothes (e.g. safari jackets) and a sense that the champagne had gone flat. Andrew Clarke was Templar in *The Saint in Manhattan* (1979), a series pilot which did not sell, and Simon Dutton took the role in six feature-length adventures broadcast in 1989; the relative failure of all post-Moore Saint projects, including the 1997 Val Kilmer feature film, suggests that he still owns the halo. *See also* Film and Crime: Page to Screen *and* TV Detectives: Small-Screen Adaptations.

Kim Newman

Saint Mystery Magazine

The original *Saint Mystery Magazine* (entitled *The Saint Detective Magazine* until October 1958) was published in the United States and ran for 141 issues from Spring 1953 to October 1967, with a break during 1960/1961 due to a change in publisher. The British edition, as it was labelled (although the magazine was published in Australia

85. Cover of the magazine when it was still called *The Saint Detective Magazine*.

until December 1959), ran from November 1954 to November 1966, notching up 153 issues, 12 more than its parent, because it did not suffer the hiatus in 1960. It was published in Britain from January 1960 by Atlas Publishing, who had previously acted as distributor. The issues were edited and assembled in New York by an American editor: Sam Merwin until 1959 and Hans Stefan Santesson thereafter.

The British edition only ever ran to 112 pages, whereas the US edition was always larger, meaning that the British edition never ran complete copies of the original issues. However, the British edition usually ran more words per page, and this allowed the editor to juggle stories around as suited. There were over 200 stories that appeared in the British edition prior to appearing in the US edition, sometimes by as much as a couple of years, and there were occasions when the story never made it to the US edition. Unfortunately, this did not benefit British writers, as all stories were sold through the New York office, and there was not a single instance of a British author appearing in the British edition only; only John Brunner's 'The Nailed Hand' made it to the British edition (May 1965) before appearing in the US edition (July 1965).

Each issue ran a saint story by Charteris, most of which were reprints, and the bulk of the material was by US writers. The magazine relied generally on traditional fiction, and for much of its existence, it tried to emulate *Ellery Queen's Mystery Magazine*, even on aspects such as the number of reprints it ran. Under Santesson, it did run some more unusual fiction, including some science fiction and weird tales, and he encouraged more contributions by British writers. Julian **Symons**, Barry Perowne, Josephine **Bell**, Margery **Allingham** and Nigel **Morland** all made sales in the magazine's final years, but all via the US edition. The magazine was never a first-run British market. *See also* Magazines *and* Short Stories.

Further Reading
Indexed in Cook, Michael L. 1982. *Monthly Murders*. Greenwood Press.

Mike Ashley

Sampson, Kevin (b.1963)

More often thought of as a zeitgeist-oriented novelist of youth culture, Kevin Sampson has nevertheless engaged with criminal activities of various sorts, and in *Outlaws* (2001), he produced a novel that can be firmly placed in the crime genre. Sampson's origins in the music business (as a journalist for the music press and as manager of the influential dance-rock act 'The Farm') show in the northern, music-influenced realism of his books.

His debut novel *Awaydays* (1999) coincided with a small boom in football hooligan books that were marketed as the alternative to Nick Hornby. The narrative hinged on protagonist Carter's bid to make a name for himself with Tranmere Rovers's blade-wielding 'pack' of marauding fans, even while musical preferences and class distinctions made him an outsider. *Awaydays* showcased Sampson's talent for dialogue and regional accents while ultimately conveying the message that the hooliganism of the 1980s was a mug's game. (Simultaneously, the decline of Tranmere 'face' Elvis presented heroin as an entirely destructive influence.)

Billed as 'An Everyday Story of Rock 'n' Roll Folk', *Powder* (1999) contains clinical, borderline instructional descriptions of prostitution and recreational drug deals. Likewise, *Leisure* (2000) shows the mechanics of an ecstasy buy in exquisite detail. It took *Outlaws* (2001) to establish Sampson as a recognisable crime writer, drawing on key traits of his earlier novels by showing how young scallies evolved into forty-something gangsters, assisted by football and drugs. The novel begins on a familiar cinematic trope – 'one last job' – but this is a plot device for exploring the friendships and loyalties that bind Ged, Ratter and Moby – the Brennan boys – in the build-up to a Christmas robbery, amid competition from younger, nastier gangs. (The police are mainly restricted to the role of mere props, fronting gang leader Ged's charity work and golf.) Heroin remains the moral dividing line between respectable and irredeemable criminals. More than even *Awaydays*, the local subculture of backslang and nicknames is made pivotal to the delivery of the plot itself.

After *Outlaws*, Sampson returned to youthful, rites-of-passage novels with *Clubland* (2003) and *Freshers* (2004). While these were not crime novels as such, participation in the specific youth subcultures described involved casual contact with the criminal fraternity. Contemporary trends make way for post-punk music in 1970s Wirral in the recent *Stars Are Stars* (2006), whose artistic and fashion-conscious protagonist is a streetwise dreamer. He finds the Anti-Nazi League repugnant, splits with his girlfriend and descends into heroin addiction and petty crime. According to Sampson, life 'on the rob' in riot-torn Liverpool 8 is no life at all.

A career spent combining themes of music, regional identity and petty crime makes Sampson an extremely versatile writer who always creates the vivid impression that a soundtrack underpins his works. *See also* Realism and Crime Fiction.

Selected Works by the Author
Awaydays (1999)
Powder (1999)
Leisure (2000)
Outlaws (2001)
Clubland (2003)
Freshers (2004)
Stars Are Stars (2006)

Further Reading
Field, William. 1998. 'Highbrow Hoolies'. *Offence* 3.

Graham Barnfield

Sansom, C.J. (b.1952)

Christopher Sansom is responsible for some of the most ambitious, richly textured **historical crime** novels ever produced. His hunch-backed lawyer Matthew Shardlake, plying his trade in the turbulent reign of Henry VIII, is one of the most distinctive protagonists in the field.

Sansom was educated at Birmingham University, where he took a BA and then a PhD in history. After working in a variety of jobs, he retrained as a solicitor and practised in Sussex, before becoming a full-time writer. He lives in Sussex, a very private individual, only reluctantly taking part in the mechanism of publicity and crime author events (on the rare occasions when he does – receiving the Ellis Peters Historical Dagger in 2005 for *Dark Fire*, for instance – his distinctive height makes it difficult for him to avoid the public interaction he so dislikes).

The first Shardlake book, *Dissolution* (2003), immediately established Sansom's authority in the field, with its massively plausible historical detail affording particular pleasure (even though, as Sansom cheerfully admits, much of this detail was made up). The book's successors, *Dark Fire* (2004), *Sovereign* (2006) and *Revelation* (2008), consolidated this success, with the last being a notably accomplished entry in the series.

Winter in Madrid (2006), set in the 1940s, marked a striking departure for the author. It is always a risky strategy for an author to change horses midstream. After all, if you have enjoyed the kind of critical (and commercial) success that Sansom has had with his elegantly written Tudor-era crime novels, why test the loyalty of your readership by abandoning this fertile ground, and delivering a literary saga set in Spain at the end of the Civil War? However, Sansom rapidly established that he is as much a master of this era as he is of Henry VIII.

Harry Brett is a damaged ex-public school boy recovering from the horrors of Dunkirk. After meeting some genteel Whitehall spymasters, he finds himself reluctantly despatched to the turbulent city of Madrid, where the population is starving. Hitler is moving inexorably over Europe, and Harry has been commissioned to ingratiate himself with an old acquaintance, Sandy Forsyth, who is engaged in various suspect transactions in Madrid. Simultaneously, Sandy's lover Barbara Clare (who has worked as a nurse for the Red Cross) has her own clandestine agenda: she is engaged in a search for her ex-lover, the charismatic Bernie Piper. Bernie is introduced to the reader in a grim prologue, fighting – and seemingly dying – for the Communist International Brigade. But Barbara believes that he is still alive and hooks up with some very dangerous people to track him down.

But while all of this may suggest literary **espionage** in the le Carré vein, that is not quite what we get here. Sansom deploys a fractured time scheme, moving (sometimes jarringly) between past and present: we are back in Harry's loveless childhood, then in the murky world of 1940s Madrid, where betrayal is the order of the day, or in the public school environment where Harry and the opportunistic Sandy first meet. Similarly, the reader is catapulted from Barbara's relationships with her very different lovers, Sandy and Bernie, to the humiliations of her childhood, where her unhappiness over her own unprepossessing appearance is to mark her for life. But as *Winter in Madrid* progresses, Sansom adroitly draws the disparate strands of his ambitious saga together, and his nonpareil evocations of time and place anchor his characters with satisfying precision.

Does it matter that various literary ghosts haunt the shadows of this novel? If an Englishman adrift in a foreign city were not sufficient homage to Graham **Greene**, then there are many other touches reminiscent of Greene, such as the threatening eruptions of the brutal, anti-English Falangists, after the fashion of the Tontons Macoute in Greene's *The Comedians* (1966). Hemingway's in here too, in the terse, economical prose. But Sansom transfigures his sources into a moral universe that is very much his own, and the orchestration of sexual and moral equivocation between his characters is handled with cool assurance.

A Shardlake novel published in 2008, *Revelation*, demonstrated an audacious skill at marrying the contemporary serial killer theme with the exigencies of the historical novel, utilising elements from the *Book of Revelation*. The author admitted that he had not traced any accounts of genuine serial killers in the sixteenth century, but such is the skill of Sansom's writing that the reader has no problem in accepting the scenario.

Sansom, C.J.

Selected Works by the Author

Matthew Shardlake Series
Dissolution (2003)
Dark Fire (2004)
Sovereign (2006)
Revelation (2008)

Non-Series Novels
Winter in Madrid (2006)

Barry Forshaw

Sayers, Dorothy L. (1893–1957)

One of the great British **women crime writers** of the **Golden Age** (along with Agatha **Christie** and Margery **Allingham**), Dorothy L. Sayers published only twelve novels and a handful of **short stories** between 1923 and 1937, but she has exercised a strong influence over the genre. She has two main series characters: Lord Peter **Wimsey**, the apotheosis of the aristocratic amateur sleuth, and Harriet Vane, a much more serious proposition and a forerunner of many later feminist detectives. The novels, which are saturated with a love of language and garlanded with quotations from a wide range of literary sources, are very much of their time, but they have remained in print and still offer many pleasures.

The last is the highly accomplished *Busman's Honeymoon* (1937), in which Harriet and Peter marry. Sayers embarked on one more, *Thrones, Dominations*, then abandoned it and turned instead to plays for radio and the stage, as well as a critically acclaimed verse translation of Dante's *Divine Comedy*, which remained uncompleted at her death in 1957. Her friend Dr Barbara Reynolds took over the translation of the last part, the *Paradiso*. Later still, in 1998, Jill Paton Walsh completed *Thrones, Dominations* and created a full-length novel, *A Presumption of Death*, around letters from the Wimsey family, which Sayers had written for *The Spectator* during the Second World War, and some short stories.

She was born in 1893 in Oxford, where her father, the Rev. Henry Sayers, was headmaster of the cathedral choir school. Her love of the place remained, and many years later, she wrote in *Gaudy Night* (1935) of how Harriet Vane 'climbed up Shotover and sat looking over the spires of the city, deep-down, fathom-drowned, striking from the round bowl of the river-basin, improbably remote and lovely as the towers of Tir-nan-Og beneath the green sea-rollers'.

Her first exile from the city occurred when her father was sent to the parish of Bluntisham-cum-Earith in Huntingdonshire at the southern edge of the Fens. Life in the Fens was isolating for the young Dorothy, who had no siblings, although she made excellent literary use of this landscape later. The bleak countryside, with its ever-present threat of flooding and incongruously magnificent parish churches, forms the background to one of her best-loved books, the brilliantly ingenious *The Nine Tailors* (1934).

Dorothy was educated at home until the age of fifteen, when she was sent to the Godolphin School in Salisbury. Imaginative, clever, and already much more widely read than her contemporaries but socially inexperienced, she found mixing with them hard. Illness caused most of her hair to fall out, as it was to do in moments of stress for the rest of her life, and that made her the butt of teasing. In 1912, after some kind of crisis, she was allowed to return home to study, and in due course, she went up to Somerville College, Oxford, with a scholarship.

The university proved a much happier place for her, as she makes clear throughout *Gaudy Night* (generally considered to be one of her greatest novels) and in an unpublished autobiographical novel, *Cat O'Mary*. She published two volumes of poetry during her undergraduate years, made friends, indulged in her taste for playfulness and her love of the theatre, and further developed both an intellectual interest and a belief in Christianity. She passed her final exams with ease and would have received a first-class degree if degrees had been permitted to women at the time.

She taught modern languages in Hull for a while but missed Oxford; she returned to Oxford in 1917 to work for the publisher Basil Blackwell. When their arrangement broke down, she did some coaching in French language and literature and wrote a column for the *Oxford Chronicle*, until Eric Whelpton offered her a job as his assistant at a school in northern France. He had had polio and had been invalided out of the army. Sayers described him in a letter to her cousin, Ivy Shrimpton, as subject to faints, shivering fits and heart murmurs. The two of them flirted and confided in each other, misunderstood each other's intentions and eventually parted.

In 1920, Sayers returned alone to London, determined to make her living by writing. Oxford University had decided at last to confer degrees on the women who had successfully studied there, and Sayers took both her Bachelor of Arts (BA) and Master of Arts (MA) on 14 October that year. She moved to Bloomsbury and wrote her first novel, *Whose Body?*. The protagonist, Lord Peter Wimsey, was to bring her celebrity and money.

There has been much speculation about which of her friends and heroes was the inspiration for Wimsey, but it seems clear that he was an amalgam of many figures, both literary and real. Some commentators believe he owes a lot to E.C. Bentley's Trent, of the celebrated *Trent's Last Case* (1913). Others see something of P.G. Wodehouse's Bertie Wooster in Wimsey's earliest manifestations. His shell shock and agues may have been modelled on Eric Whelpton's, but there were plenty of other young men who had returned from the First World War with such symptoms. Among other figures who have been mentioned in this context is Roy Ridley, the chaplain of Balliol College, Oxford. Sayers herself told Muriel St. Clair Byrne in a letter dated 6 March 1935 (quoted in James Brabazon's biography) that he would be the ideal man to take the part of Wimsey on stage, but the character had existed in print for several years by the time she encountered this supposed model.

Before the first Wimsey novel was published, Sayers took a job as copywriter at Benson's advertising agency, which was to give her the background for the entertaining *Murder Must Advertise* (1933). Another romantic relationship foundered on her refusal to have sex without marriage, but she later became pregnant by Bill White and gave birth to her only child, John Antony. After three weeks, she left him in Ivy Shrimpton's care, pretending she was no more than a charitable friend of the baby's mother, who would pay for his care. In 1926, she married Oswald Atherton Fleming, and although the partnership was difficult, remained with him until his death. Aspects of all these unhappy relationships can be found in her novels, which they greatly enrich.

The first, *Whose Body?* (1923), is a straightforward puzzle story, but it contains many of the skills that mark her out from the general run of detective novelists of her day. Her playfulness emerges right at the start with the description of the body: it is found lying naked, beautifully groomed and decorated only with a pair of delicate gold-rimmed *pince-nez* spectacles, in the bath of a respectable, timid, suburban architect. A rich financier has gone missing and the police believe the corpse could be his; but when Wimsey inspects it, he sees at once that it bears many marks of poverty, in spite of the perfect grooming, and he knows it cannot possibly be that of a successful man.

Over the course of the novel, Wimsey is transformed from a Woosterish cartoon character of huge wealth and silliness into a generous, sensitive, shell-shock victim with an intriguing mixture of ruthless determination to get to the truth and awareness of its destructive power. As Sayers puts it, at the moment when he has worked out who committed the murder: 'He remembered quite suddenly how, years ago, he had stood before the breakfast table at Denver Castle – a small, peaky boy in blue knickers, with a thunderously beating heart.... He seized the tablecloth in a firm grip and pulled his hardest – he could feel now the delicate and awful thrill as the urn and the coffee machine and the whole of a Sevres breakfast service had crashed down in one stupendous ruin...'.

Clouds of Witness (1926) further develops Wimsey's character and introduces the first in a series of unhappy women: Wimsey's sister, Lady Mary, who has fallen in love with George Goyles, a romantic but unsound man. The plot deals with the death of another of her suitors, with suspicion falling first on her elder brother, the Duke of Denver, then on Goyles himself. Amongst all the high life, Sayers also introduces a subplot about serious domestic violence in a bleak agricultural setting, which is a topic that recurs in later novels.

After *Clouds of Witness* came *Unnatural Death* (1927) and then *The Unpleasantness at the Bellona Club* (1928), both of which have traditional plots concerning murder committed for the sake of an inheritance. *The Unpleasantness at the Bellona Club* also introduces two more unhappy women: one, the wife of an angry, difficult man who suffers severely from shell shock and detests her superior earning power; the other, plain solid Miss Dorland, who has been manipulated and exploited by a rotter. In order to get her out of his life, he accuses her of being, 'the gibbering sort that hangs round church doors for curates.... It's a lie. He did – he did – pretend to – want me and all that. The beast!...I can't tell you the things he said...and I've made such a fool of myself...'. Whether or not Miss Dorland has anything in common with Sayers herself, she is very like Violet Cattermole, a minor character in *Gaudy Night*, the much later novel that belongs to Harriet Vane.

Sayers introduced Harriet in *Strong Poison* (1930), standing in the dock at the Old Bailey as she faces a death sentence for the murder of her lover, Philip Boyes. She is innocent, of course, and deeply ashamed of having fallen for his lie that he wanted sex without marriage only because he had a fundamental principle against the institution.

With the arrival of Harriet in Peter Wimsey's life, he becomes steadily more credible and the novels more interesting. Seeing her imprisoned in the dock awakens him to the trap he has made of his own life and, as he proceeds to woo her, he gradually strips off all the disguises and many of the luxuries he has assumed to protect his vulnerabilty.

The first novel in which he and Harriet share the detection is *Have His Carcase* (1932). Set in a south-coast resort, the story opens with Harriet's discovery of a man's corpse. Sayers's new seriousness is signalled by the fact that the description of the body is horrific rather than amusing. The man's throat has been cut and blood flows freely, soaking his clothes. The plot is unnecessarily complex and the novel over-long, but Wimsey is allowed to lose his temper, another sign of increasing reality.

Much more satisfactory is *Gaudy Night*, in which Harriet returns to the fictional Shrewsbury College in Oxford, where she had been an undergraduate, to help the dons deal with a malicious and apparently dangerous campaign of intimidation by an unidentified villain. Sayers has often been accused of snobbery, particularly over this novel. In fact, her very choice of Peter Wimsey's name and family motto ('As my whimsy takes me') suggests she never impressed herself with his noble lineage. And her portrait of his delectable mother, the Dowager Duchess of Denver, is designedly funny.

There are many scenes in Sayers's work that jar in the twenty-first century, but she wrote at a time when the people she knew behaved and spoke and thought as her characters did. The gravamen of the charge in relation to *Gaudy Night* is that she makes her villain one of the college servants and suggests that anyone with brains, social standing and education is more valuable a human being than anyone without. This seems a misreading of the text.

In fact the message that comes across loudest from the novel is that Sayers believed all human beings should use their particular talents and live according to their own principles. As Harriet Vane puts it, 'one should do one's own job, however trivial, and not persuade one's self into doing somebody else's, however noble'. She also believed one should never sacrifice one's principles, even to make someone else feel better, harking back to Harriet's shame at having allowed Philip Boyes to overcome her own principles. In *Gaudy Night*, it is the villain's absolute acceptance of wrongdoing in someone else *because she loved him* that marks her out as less than the other women involved in the case, who refuse to allow any personal considerations to deflect them from doing what they believe to be right.

At the end of the novel, Harriet reaches the point of being able to contemplate accepting Peter's endlessly reiterated offer of marriage, because he has at last made her see that he does not consider himself in any way superior to her. With his great wealth, social sophistication, ten-year seniority and the way he saved her from the gallows, he has made her feel, according to his uncle, 'a humiliating inferiority complex'. Now, however, he allows her to risk her life without protest or patronising offers of protection, and when it comes to the final proposal, they are shown to be equal, dressed exactly alike in the gown and mortar board of the Oxonian MA. Wimsey bares his head in submission and asks in Latin whether it would please her to accept him.

Their married life begins in *Busman's Honeymoon*, in which they discover the previous owner of the house they have just bought lying dead in the cellar, with his head stove in. Sayers herself introduces the novel with a semi-Shakespearian apology, 'If there is but a ha'porth of detection to an intolerable deal of saccharine, let the occasion be the excuse', but for those who are interested in her ideas about relationships, it is illuminating.

Peter makes it clear from the start that he respects Harriet's work and will always ensure she has equal status, and also that she will be her own woman. As he says, 'for God's sake let's take the word "possess" and put a brick round its neck and drown it. I will not use it or hear it used – not even in the crudest physical sense. It's meaningless. We can't possess one another. We can only give and hazard all we have...'.

She, in turn, has to show she will never crowd him or try to make him act against his principles or force him to share those things he wishes to keep to himself, particularly his weaknesses. At the end of the novel, when his detective brilliance has sent a man to be hanged at eight o'clock in the morning, Peter plans to deal with his emotional turmoil alone. Harriet waits in agony until, at last, he comes to kneel at her feet and allow himself to show everything he has hidden for so long. 'Quite suddenly, he said, "Oh, damn", and began to cry – in an awkward, unpractised way at first, and then more easily. So she held him, crouched at her knees, against her breast, huddling his head in her arms that he might not hear eight o'clock strike.'

The freedom to express emotion and to live as and for one's self was clearly of immense importance to Sayers. Among her short stories is 'The Incredible Elopement of Lord Peter Wimsey', which shows the absolute antithesis of the ideal marriage represented by Harriet and Peter. Published in a collection entitled *Hangman's Holiday* in 1933, this story deals with a young orphan rescued from congenital cretinism by a specialist in thyroid deficiency. When she reaches her twenties, beautiful and accomplished, the specialist marries her, only to become savagely jealous when she appears to respond to another man. Her husband takes her to an isolated village in the Pyrenees and slowly starves her of the thyroid extract she needs to remain healthy, reducing her to a shuffling, whimpering figure, with a fat sloppy body, vacant eyes, dribbling mouth, and only a few strands of hair dangling from her bald scalp. She cannot use knives and forks, speak intelligibly, read or participate in normal life. In order to prolong her punishment and his gratification, the specialist sometimes gives her enough thyroid extract to bring her back, tells her what he is doing, and then slowly starves her of it again, enjoying her panic and degeneration. This truly chilling idea expresses an absolute terror of being overtaken and reduced to nothing by an overwhelming relationship.

Sayers did not always write about such unhappiness and cruelty. *Murder Must Advertise*, which is set after Peter took up with Harriet but does not feature her except in one tiny sidelong remark, is a piece of pure entertainment. Peter takes a job in an advertising agency in order to find out for the managing director precisely what is going on behind the scenes. Naturally he fulfils his task with his usual debonair aplomb, and he also takes part in a staff cricket match, which is one of the funniest descriptions of any sporting event in the genre.

Sayers also created a second detective in Montague Egg, a commercial traveller in wines and spirits, who appears in several of her short stories. Admirers of the pure puzzle type of detective stories enjoy these, but such stories do not allow her other gifts to show as well as the full-length novels.

Her wit and theatricality, which colour all her work, informed the initiation ceremony she devised for the Detection Club, an organisation originally presided over by G.K. Chesterton and of which she served as president from 1949 to 1958. Some of her assumptions and prejudices mean that her work has become dated, but she brought a new seriousness to the genre and, at her best, could write superb prose. She was a towering figure in crime writing and she will not be forgotten, either by her successors in the Detection Club or by her readers. She was also a discerning editor and compiled a series of anthologies, starting with *Great Short Stories of Mystery, Detection and Horror* (1928), which educated many in the provenance of the mystery story. *See also* The Great Detectives: The Mass Appeal of Holmes, Poirot and Wimsey; The Police in Golden Age Crime Fiction; *and* The Shires: Rural England and Regional Crime Fiction.

Selected Works by the Author
Whose Body? (1923)
Clouds of Witness (1926)
Unnatural Death (1927; also published in the United States as *The Dawson Pedigree*)
Lord Peter Views the Body (1928)
The Unpleasantness at the Bellona Club (1928)
The Documents in the Case (with Robert Eustace, 1930)
Strong Poison (1930)
The Five Red Herrings (1931; also published in the United States as *Suspicious Characters*)
Have His Carcase (1932)
Hangman's Holiday (1933)
Murder Must Advertise (1933)
The Nine Tailors (1934)
Gaudy Night (1935)
Busman's Honeymoon (with M. St. Clare Byrne, 1937)

Further Reading
Brabazon, James. 1988. *Dorothy L. Sayers: A Biography*. Gollancz.
Heilbrun, Carolyn. 1972. Sayers, Lord Peter, and God, introduction to *Lord Peter*.
Hitchman, Janet. 1975. *Such a Strange Lady*. New English Library.
Reynolds, Barbara. 1993. *Dorothy L. Sayers Her Life and Soul*. St Martins Press.
Reynolds, Barbara, ed. 1996–2000. *The Letters of Dorothy L. Sayers*. 4 vols. Hodder/Dorothy L. Sayers Society.

Website
Dorothy L. Sayers Society, http://www.sayers.org.uk/
Dorothy L. Sayers Archive, http://www.idir.net/~nedblake/sayers_0.html

Natasha Cooper

Science Fiction and Crime Fiction

The origins of science fiction are multiple, but the origins of the science-fiction story are essentially threefold: the exploration of the brave new world, the arrival of the stranger, and the incredible invention story. Science crime fiction is predominantly rooted in the 'incredible invention' story, which in the crime genre mutated into the 'howdunnit'. Interestingly, this form of crime fiction is relatively rare, because for a howdunnit to be effective, the reader must have access to the same technological information as the criminal. In science fiction, unless the author can find a way to present the technological limits of the world (as the US author Isaac Asimov did with his Laws of Robotics), it is just too easy for the author to cheat. Criticism too is rare, though there are two excellent articles in John Clute and Peter Nicholls's *The Encyclopedia of Science Fiction* (1993) (by Brian Stableford and Peter Nicholls, respectively), and Dave Mead has explored the interaction and conflicts between the demands of science fiction and the demands of crime fiction.

The invention story, as it was first conceived, presents a revolutionary invention which has enormous consequences for society. One route for the author's response is the 'gosh wow' for which science fiction is noted, but a common thread that runs across such stories is that the disruption caused by the new invention itself becomes criminal. The classic British rendition of this is Alexander Mackendrick's film, *The Man in the White Suit* (1951). The marvellous suit (stain-proof, crease-proof) will ruin the economy of the poor who make the suits, wash the suits and iron the suits.

Jeff Noon's *Vurt* (1993) is a generation-X exploration of a drug epidemic in the city of Manchester.

More common, however, is the thriller structure in which the invention becomes an object of desire, a secret power which must be obtained at all cost for the 'right' side. This gave rise to the notorious 'mad scientist' scenario where an inventor creates a fiendish weapon and threatens to take over the world – or destroy it. Jules Verne had established the template for this with his characters Captain Nemo in *Twenty Thousand Leagues Under the Sea* (1870) and Robur in *Robur the Conqueror* (1886). British equivalents included the eponymous villain in *Hartman the Anarchist* (1893) by E. Douglas Fawcett (1866–1960) or the Nemo-like inventor in *The Iron Pirate* (1893) by Max Pemberton (1853–1950), while the air-borne equivalent appeared in *The Terror of the Air* (1920) by William **Le Queux**. Other novels hoped the invention might bring peace, such as the sleep-gas in *Ultimatum* (1924; also published in the United States as *The Ark of the Covenant*) by Victor MacClure (1887–1963). Mad scientists do not have to be inherently evil, but the invention may release the evil within us as happened to Dr Hyde in *Strange Case of Dr Jekyll and Mr Hyde* (1886) by Robert Louis Stevenson (1850–1894) or Mr Griffin in *The Invisible Man* (1897) by H.G. Wells (1866–1946). All these stories, and many like them, are set out as crime or mystery thrillers first, built upon a brand new invention.

Peter Hamilton has used this trope in a number of his novels: they are distinguished from 'futuristic thrillers' by their pace, which lacks the 'running out of time' structure of the conventional thriller, and because science fiction is aware that multiple invention is not only possible, but likely. In science fiction, chasing after secrets may be replaced by trying – by experimental techniques – to replicate secrets, as in Gwyneth Jones's *Life* (2004), in which revolutionary discoveries about genetics are buried not deliberately but through casual prejudice.

Modern British science crime fiction is more often a whydunnit, although the motivations are rarely psychological in the classic sense, but more usually related to the futuristic polity of the world created. Brian Stableford, for example, has produced fiction in which competition with (and among) immortals provides an incentive for murder. Paul **McAuley**'s *Whole Wide World* (2001) makes knowledge itself both the incentive and the prize. In *Dervish Is Digital* (2001), Pat Cadigan's cyberspace becomes a place to stalk and copyright theft extends to personal identity. The structure of the novels in each case emphasises the role of place in the crime narrative: each crime becomes a facilitator, an excuse to explore the created world. This is particularly true in M. John Harrison's ironic crime novels, *Light* (2002) and *Nova Swing* (2006). In the first, Kearney thinks the crimes he commits hold off a supernatural threat, but in terms of the narrative structure, it is the crimes he commits that force him to keep moving until he reaches the Kefahuchi tract, a place of transformative liminality. In the sequel, *Nova Swing*, the detective Aschemann's constant search for a crime which has not actually been committed takes the reader in and out of constructed realities.

Comedy crime fiction is particularly popular in British science fiction. Both Jasper **Fforde**'s *Eyre Affair* (2001) (and its sequels) and the work of Michael **Marshall** (Smith) are often rooted in a form of screwball comedy in which an invention unleashes a trail of consequences. Both of these writers make use of named detectives, but the detective form is less common in science fiction than one might expect, perhaps because the presence of a singular detective demands of science fiction writers that they construct a wider social context for the protagonist than is sometimes preferred in the field. A notable exception is Jon Courtenay **Grimwood**, whose Arabesk series is driven along one strand by the curiosity of one man, but even here, it is the polity of the created world (an ongoing Ottoman Empire in a universe where the First World War was never fought) that drives the crimes.

If there is a type of British crime science fiction that stands apart from the American examples, it is the type that involves big crimes: Jon Courtenay Grimwood's domestic crimes frequently prove to be only a curtain drawn over a much bigger crime of moral responsibility, as in *Effendi* (2002) (In this case: who is responsible for the crimes committed by child soldiers?). Iain M. Banks's *Culture* novels are not usually understood in this frame, but at the heart of each one is a major war crime, whether an attempted genocide or merely ruthless oppression. Both *Consider Phlebas* (1987) and *Use of Weapons* (1990) hinge on the way the immoral is justified. *See also* Realism and Crime Fiction.

Selected Works

Fiction

Banks, Iain M. 1987. *Consider Phlebas*. Orbit.
Banks, Iain M. 1990. *Use of Weapons*. Orbit.
Cadigan, Pat. 2001. *Dervish Is Digital*. Tor.
Fforde, Jasper. 2001. *The Eyre Affair*. Viking.
Grimwood, Jon Courtenay. 2002. *Effendi*. Simon & Schuster.
Harrison, M. John. 2002. *Light*. Gollancz.
Jones, Gwyneth. 2004. *Life*. Aqueduct Press.
McAuley, Paul. 2001. *Whole Wide World*. Tor.
Smith, Michael Marshall. 1994. *Only Forward*. HarperCollins.
Stableford, Brian. 1999. *Architects of Emortality*. Tor.

Further Reading

Clute, John, and Peter Nichols. 1993. *The Encyclopedia of Science Fiction*. Orbit.
Gerlach, Neil. 2002. 'Criminal Biology: Genetic Crime Thrillers and the Future of Social Control'. In *Biotechnological and Medical Themes in Science Fiction*. Edited by Domna Pastourmatzi. University Studio Press.
Gerlach, Neil. 2003. 'Criminal Predisposition: Futuristic Genetic Crime Thrillers and Biogovernance'. In *Fantastic Odysseys: Selected Essays from the Twenty-Second International Conference on the Fantastic in the Arts*. Edited by Mary Pharr. Greenwood.
Mead, David G. 1987. 'Signs of Crime: Aspects of Structure in Science Fiction Detective Stories'. *Extrapolation* 28.2: 140–147.
Reed, Joseph W. 1989. 'Public Enemies, Space Slime, Yellow Peril, and Crime'. In *American Scenarios: The Uses of Film Genre*. Edited by Joseph W. Reed. Wesleyan University Press.

Farah Mendlesohn

Scorpion Magazine

Scorpion was a glossy A4 bi-annual magazine that appeared in the early 1990s. It was available on subscription at £4 for the year and was devoted to broadening and deepening interest in crime fiction, particularly among collectors.

The magazine was the brainchild of Michael Johnson of Scorpion Press. He had been a dealer in modern first editions with a specialist interest in crime and American thrillers. In 1991, he launched Scorpion Press, as the United Kingdom's sole publisher specialising in crime, thrillers and adventure novels in fine bindings. Each book was signed/numbered and leather bound, with marble-papered sides over boards, and contained other features of interest to the collector such as an appreciation of the author by a writer of note. Besides publishing still-popular favourites such as Colin **Dexter**, Len **Deighton**, Dick **Francis**, Reginald **Hill** and Ruth **Rendell**, the small press developed a particular interest in a stream of new writers such as Lindsey **Davis** and Minette **Walters**. The magazine was launched in Spring 1993 as an adjunct to this book publishing enterprise, and part of its mission was to educate its readers about the qualities of the new writers.

This was achieved not by reviews of new books but through the examination of trends and themes from across the whole of the genre – hard-boiled, **espionage**, **historical** mystery, continental crime, whodunits, etc. The articles were 2,000 words or more and written by well-known authors, editors from publishing houses, enthusiasts and sometimes by the editor himself. The work of individual writers was also considered at length – not so much with reference to the 'box' of crime, but as contributions to English literature. Some of the authors examined were Patricia Cornwell, Ruth Rendell, Len Deighton, Andrew **Taylor**, Minette Walters and Lindsey **Davis**. Generally, featured authors were praised, but negative criticism was given when justified. Some articles had additional notes, with first-edition values and points for collectors.

The *Scorpion* magazine also carried discussion articles on popular and/or innovative British television crime series (e.g. *Anna Lee, Cadfael,* **Cracker**, *Between the Lines*). A police officer and a critic discussed the latter, and the subsequent issue contained a response from the series creator, J.C. Wilsher. Another aspect that helped to broaden interest in the variety of different types of crime fiction was the occasional piece on relatively unknown foreign writers in translation. Issue 2 contained a detailed look at the genre in South America, Europe and Russia, under the heading 'Global Differences of La Novela Negra'.

Scorpion was an innovative mix, a kind of low-brow *Literary Review* for crime buffs with more popular appeal, even though it had tongue-in-cheek debates on 'seriousness' and titbits for collectors (the core market of the publisher). It also had a decent following with public libraries and members of the **Crime Writers' Association**, many of whom were subscribers and/or contributed pieces. Sadly, only four issues appeared. *See also* Magazines *and* Short Stories.

Michael Johnson

Scott, Manda (b.1962)

Scott writes both crime and non-genre novels, mainly historical, and in 1997, she was shortlisted for the Orange Prize for *Hen's Teeth* (1966). Her crime novels are dark and brooding, painfully intense and unlike almost any other in the field.

Scott initially practised as a vet (part-time, to allow more time for writing), specialising in acupuncture on small and exotic animals. She became a full-time writer in 1999. She had trained at Glasgow Veterinary School, and in 1986, had moved to Newmarket to work with horses, her passion since the age of twelve, when she had saved enough to buy her own pony – which she could have, her parents insisted, only if she contributed to its upkeep and got up daily at 6.30 to deliver milk to the local farmer. Before writing her first novel, Scott wrote for television, with scripts based around animals and veterinary practice, including contributions to the successful television series *Animal House*.

Hen's Teeth, a paperback from the Women's Press, was a critical success even before its submission for the Orange Prize. Scott was hailed by Fay Weldon as 'a new voice for a new world'. The story introduces Kellen Stewart, a doctor-turned-therapist whose former lover dies, apparently from an insulin overdose that is traced to her brother's hens. The brother also dies. Behind their deaths lies the bioengineering of hens to lay eggs laden with insulin and, ultimately, the marketable drug 'Hen's Teeth'. Kellen Stewart reappears in Scott's next book *Night Mares* (1998), after which came *Stronger Than Death* (1999) and *No Good Deed* (2001), stand-alone thrillers marking out the territory Scott was making her own. *No Good Deed* is deeply atmospheric, dark to the point of opacity, and establishes its bleak tone from the start. A child awakes in a filthy, darkened room littered with bottles and syringes and hears a woman whispering urgently that the men – who are they? – will soon come back and hurt them again. Again? Little is explained. The atmosphere is one of absolute darkness. At first, like the boy, the reader is a mute observer with no idea what is happening, to whom and why. Gradually we learn that the woman is part of an undercover unit in Special Branch whose quarry is an elusive Glasgow drug baron who has ruthlessly eliminated his competition. But is there a mole in the Special Branch team sent to rescue them?

From 2003 to 2006, Scott put crime writing aside to concentrate on her epic four-volume *Boudica*, fictionalising the early English rebel queen. The year 2007 saw her back with a contemporary thriller, *The Crystal Skull*, albeit with another historical thread. Legend has it that there are thirteen Mayan Crystal Skulls which, if brought together, will avert the End of Time – scheduled, according to Mayan prophesy, for 21 December 2012. But where are the skulls, now that we need them?

Selected Works by the Author

Kellen Stewart Series
Hen's Teeth (1996)
Night Mares (1998)

Stand-Alones
Stronger Than Death (1999)
No Good Deed (2001)
The Crystal Skull (2007)

Russell James

Scottish Crime Fiction

There is a case to be made that Scotland was the cradle of crime fiction, certainly in **magazine** form. *Blackwood's Magazine*, founded in Edinburgh in 1817, showed more than a cursory interest in the macabre and the morbid. Thomas De Quincey contributed 'On Murder Considered as One of the Fine Arts' as early as the February 1827 issue. Others who contributed macabre pieces included William Mudford, William Maginn and notably Samuel Warren (1807–1877), whose series later collected as *Passages from the Diary of a Late Physician* (1833) may be regarded as the progenitor of all investigative doctor stories. Scottish magazines encouraged the careers of many writers. Arthur Conan **Doyle**'s first sale, 'The Mystery of Sasassa Valley' was to Edinburgh's *Chambers's Journal* in 1879, while *Blackwood's* bought the first stories from John **Buchan**.

The genesis of crime and thriller fiction in Scotland owes much to the innovations of John Buchan. All three of Buchan's series heroes featured in novels set in Scotland: Dickson MacCunn in *Huntingtower* (1922), Sir Edward Leithen in *John MacNab* (1925), and Richard Hannay. The latter appears in *Mr Standfast* (1919), in which the country is a locale, as it is in *The Island of Sheep* (1936), and, most famously, in *The Thirty-Nine Steps* (1915), whose most hectic action takes place in Buchan's own beloved Border country. Despite the brevity of this novel and the obvious haste with which it was written, it remains one of Buchan's most vivid pieces of writing.

But how successfully do the classic detective writers utilise a Scottish ambience? Wilkie **Collins**'s novelette 'A Marriage Tragedy' (*Harper's New Monthly Magazine*, February 1858) briefly visits Northern Scotland; a private enquiry agent named Dark, engaged by a lady to track down her absconded husband, finds the natives willing to give him information so long as he praises the view from Arthur's Seat in Edinburgh. But Sherlock **Holmes** appears to never have had a recorded case north of the Border – surprisingly so, as Conan **Doyle** took his degree at Edinburgh University – neither did Dr Thorndyke, Reggie Fortune, Father Brown, Philip Trent, Hercule **Poirot** or Miss **Marple**. It is otherwise with the hardworking police detectives of Freeman Wills **Crofts**. *The Groote Park Murder* (1924) begins in South Africa but ends, excitingly, in Scotland, near Crianlarich in the Western Highlands. The detective is not Inspector French but a Scots officer named Ross. However, French did visit Scotland, while investigating *Sir John Magill's Last Journey* (1930), whose locale is basically in Northern Ireland, but the murder turns out to have been committed in Galloway, not too far from the area Richard Hannay travelled through in *The Thirty-Nine Steps*.

Another Galloway detective story, one clearly inspired by Crofts's 'railway alibi' type of detective novel, is Dorothy L. **Sayers**'s *The Five Red Herrings* (1931). Sayers and her husband enjoyed holidays at the Anworth Hotel in Gatehouse-of-Fleet around that period, and the focus of this tale shifts between Gatehouse and Kirkcudbright. The railway alibi involves the Portpatrick and Wigtownshire Railway (which features in both Buchan's and Crofts's books) and the Glasgow and South-Western Railway's Stranraer–Ayr–Glasgow line. Sayers, a much livelier writer than Crofts, gives us, as he does, much fascinating railway detail (mostly correct), and there is a good deal of attractive general description of that beautiful part of Scotland. Kirkcudbright is, and was, the centre of an artists' community; the victim is a painter and the six suspects suggested by the title are also painters, and necessarily so, as the painting found near the body is proved to have been faked. Suspicion is divided fairly evenly among the six, to the extent that five policemen who have been assigned to the enquiries put five different theories to the procurator fiscal involving all six artists. Lord Peter **Wimsey**, arbitrating between them, hugs himself with glee, says they are all wrong and proceeds to prove his case in an elaborate reconstruction. This Sayers plot delights in its ingenuity, its well-evoked Galloway setting and its sense of relaxed fun, underlining the fact that Lord Peter Wimsey is on holiday, even if it does turn out to be of the busman's variety.

John Dickson **Carr**'s Gideon Fell, although he is a resident of Lincolnshire as we are told in *Hag's Nook* (1933), the first novel to feature him, is rarely to be seen even as far north as that, let alone in Scotland, but an exception is *The Case of the Constant Suicides* (1941); Carr was of Scots descent after all. The brooding Glencoe, where one of the 'suicides' takes place, is an appropriate backdrop for a Carr: 'On either side rose the lines of mountain ridges, granite grey and dull purple, looking as smooth as stone. No edge of kindliness had touched them; it was as though nature had dried up and even sullenness had long petrified to hostility.' A man dies by falling from a tower room. It looks like suicide, but if so, the dependants cannot 'clean up' on the life insurance. If it is murder, it is one of Carr's 'impossible' ones. Is there a ghostly agency at work? Another obvious suicide/'impossible' murder takes place (in Glencoe), and then another that is nearly successful, before Fell reveals all. There is much slapstick humour in Carr's typical manner, yet the wartime atmosphere is also well captured. The difficulties of railway travel, the blackout and the Home Guard (recently renamed in September 1940) all have a part to play.

Josephine **Tey**, otherwise Elizabeth MacIntosh, was a native of Inverness, although she liked England quite as much as, if not more than, she did Scotland. The first and last of her crime novels are set, if only partly, in Scotland. In *The Man in the Queue* (1929, written as Gordon Daviot), a suspect bolts from London to Scotland, much as Hannay had done in *The Thirty-Nine Steps*. Indeed, there is more than a feel of Buchan about the chapters, the best in the book, in which Inspector Grant pursues and captures the suspect. The scene is 'Carninnish', which is clearly on the north-west coast, reachable by the Kyle railway line from Inverness and then by road. In *The Singing Sands* (posthumously published, 1952), Grant, recovering from a nervous breakdown, goes north by train to his cousin's farmhouse near Perth, called 'Scoone' in the book. A man dies on the train and his body is seen briefly by Grant as he arrives at Scoone. Not his problem, he thankfully muses, but in spite of himself, he becomes interested (the police, satisfied that the death was accidental, are not) and investigates locally at first, then on the Outer Hebridean island of 'Cladda', which could be Barra. (The Hebrides in winter, with rain and wind rampant, is quite brilliantly portrayed.) Grant's excursion to Cladda contributes nothing to his main inquiry, the solution to which he later finds in London, but it does finally cure his claustrophobia.

Another classic crime writer, if an uneven one, is Monsignor Ronald **Knox**, with his books about the insurance assessor Miles Bredon. Knox's last two detective novels *Still Dead* (1934) and *Double Cross Purposes* (1937) are both set in the Highlands (Knox often visited the Inverness area). In the former, a man runs down a child while driving 'under the influence'; he leaves the area and his return is signalled by the finding of his dead body. The body then disappears, only to be found again in the same place a couple of days later. Are supernatural agencies involved? Bredon elucidates capably. The latter book has some pleasant descriptions of Highland scenery, but the tale is implausible in the extreme.

Some musically oriented novels should also be noted. In *Dead Man's Riddle* (1957), Mary **Kelly**'s first series detective, Inspector Brett Nightingale of Scotland Yard, is in Edinburgh to hear his wife, a professional singer, perform in concert at the university where Conan Doyle (and Dr Watson) studied. She is abducted by the murderer, but her husband, aided by a song in Schubert's *Die Winterreise*, which furnishes a clue to a coded letter, discovers the truth in time. Jessica **Mann**'s *The Sticking Place* (1974) is a striking novel of suspense, whose major character is a semi-professional contralto who sings in a performance of Bach's *Magnificat* in the Scottish Border country in wintry weather.

In Jennifer Bland's (b.1925) *Death in Waiting* (1975), the narrator/heroine is a (not too successful) concert pianist who becomes the music organiser for a Scottish region. She also becomes involved in a series of deaths that at first raise supernatural fears, but these fears are dispelled when the murderers, two of them with four killings between them, are unmasked.

As the Scots gave the game of golf to the world, mention must be made of *Murder at the Open* (1965) by Angus McVicar (1908–2001); this kinetically written novel is set in the city of St Andrews, historic in its golfing, among other, associations and pleasantly evoked here. Curiously, most golfing detection stories – and there are many – are set outside Scotland, though the Gatehouse golf course figures in passing in Sayers's *The Five Red Herrings*, its secretary being one of the 'herrings'. Wimsey plays the game well. Another, more recent golfing novel is Barry Cork's *Unnatural Hazard* (1989), placed on a Hebridean island beyond Skye. Again the golf is not overdone – the policeman/narrator is himself a player.

Scotland can claim its own solid contribution to the police procedural novel in the many books from 1957 onwards authored by Bill Knox (1928–1999) and featuring Chief Inspector (later Superintendent) Colin Thane of the Glasgow force; but from time to time, since 1964, Knox has written thrillers, set in the Islands, whose hero is First Officer Webb Carrick of the Fishery Protection Service.

There are, of course, numerous mountains in Scotland, including the highest one in the British Isles. The two major mountaineering novelists in the detective field are Glyn Carr (1908–2005) and Gwen Moffat (b.1924). Carr's Abercrombie Lewker has not climbed or detected in the Grampians or indeed anywhere north of the Border, preferring Cumbria to Caledonia; the reverse is true of Gwen Moffat's Melinda Pink, middle-aged and formidable, for all her creator has born in Brighton. Moffat's Scottish titles, set on the West Coast and in the Islands, are *Miss Pink at the Edge of the World* (1975) and *Over the Sea to Death* (1976).

Simon **Brett**'s many books about his seedy, randy, bibulous, late-middle-aged actor-detective Charles Paris include one where Paris is seen at the Edinburgh International Festival, sniffing out a murder and incidentally putting on a show of his own devising in the festival fringe. *So Much Blood* (1976) is appropriately a quote from what is euphemistically known in the theatre as 'The Scottish Play'. Paris carries everything off pretty well in the resolution and it is salutary that he is glimpsed north of the Border in view of the gallons of Scotch (Bell's, usually) that he puts away in the course of his detective (and other) activities. Antonia **Fraser**'s series detective Jemima Shore, a youngish and attractive television investigative journalist, has an approach similar to that of Charles Paris in that both are intuitive rather than logical investigators, and spend much of the time barking up the wrong tree, or trees. Jemima has twice been in Scotland on cases, both in the Highlands; in *The Wild Island* (1978), which is menacing in its atmosphere but implausible and melodramatic in its plot, with crackpot royalists, an MP and a princess among the dramatis personae, and in the short story 'The Case of the Parr Children' (1979), a nice little domestic murder, reprinted in *Jemima Shore's First Case and Other Stories* (1986).

It is common for terrorists to hijack aircraft; much less frequently do they take over buses and trains. In Philip **McCutchan**'s thrillers, they have done both. *Coach North* (1975) is an example of the former, which occurs on a holiday coach tour of Scotland.

Tense and well written, *Coach North* has enough violent action to satisfy the most sanguinary reader – more violent action than John Buchan, for all his sense of adventure, would have cared to give us.

These days, Scotland is dominated by a particularly gritty form of crime novel that has been aptly coined '**Tartan Noir**' by *LA Confidential* author James Ellroy. Taking place far from the country's picturesque highlands and islands, these stories concentrate on grim Glaswegian tenement buildings or ancient alleyways in deepest, darkest Edinburgh. The chief proponents of this burgeoning genre include Ian **Rankin**, Val **McDermid**, Louise **Welsh** and Christopher **Brookmyre**.

Since 1987, Ian Rankin's hard-bitten detective John **Rebus** has patrolled the streets of Edinburgh – usually at night and usually in the rain – in some of the most talked-about (and critically acclaimed) crime novels of the past two decades. *Mortal Causes* (1994) saw him investigate the brutal murder of a man in Edinburgh's so-called 'buried city', a collection of preserved seventeenth-century alleyways beneath the City Chambers on the famous Royal Mile – now a popular tourist attraction. In *Set in Darkness* (2000), Queensbury House, site of the New Scottish Assembly, is at the centre of a political tragedy when a prospective Labour Party candidate is murdered on the eve of Scotland's first devolved parliament for almost 300 years. Blending historical tales of torture and depravity with a contemporary thriller involving a gangster crime lord, the novel's dark terrain is a perfect summation of Rankin's best work.

Former spin-doctor Quintin **Jardine** ploughs a similar furrow with his series featuring taciturn Edinburgh CID boss Bob Skinner, who first appeared on the scene in 1993's *Skinner's Rules*, in which a savage killer prowled the Royal Mile in search of victims. *Skinner's Round* (1995) saw members of the prestigious Royal and Ancient Golf Club of St Andrews being slain under cover of a sixteenth-century witch's curse. Later entries in this long-running series have seen increasingly far-fetched storylines vie with Skinner's very complicated family life, leading to criticism in some quarters that the books are veering towards soap opera.

Born in Kirkaldy, Val McDermid has risen to a supreme position insofar as intelligent Scottish crime fiction is concerned. Her breakthrough series featuring lesbian journalist Lindsay Gordon won her many admirers, while the continuing cases of the sexually dysfunctional psychologist Tony Hill – *Beneath the Bleeding* was published to great acclaim in 2007 – is a brave and unorthodox attempt at opening out the genre. The series has been adapted for television as ***Wire in the Blood*** (2002–present).

Louise Welsh's first novel, *The Cutting Room* (2002), was a powerful evocation of Glasgow's criminal underworld; it won her the **Crime Writers' Association** John Creasey Dagger and launched her into the spotlight as a young talent to watch. However, her other books have ventured far from Scotland, so her inclusion in the 'Tartan Noir' circle must be purely honorary.

A more straightforward member is Glaswegian author Christopher Brookmyre, whose iconoclastic journalist Jack Parlabane first appeared in *Quite Ugly One Morning* (1996), a novel that successfully combined satirical black humour with the down-to-earth business of telling a rattling good detective yarn. Further novels followed in the same vein, all set in and around the author's home turf.

Alex Gray, Denise **Mina** and Stuart MacBride are more recent pretenders to the paisley-covered throne of 'Tartan Noir', their books characterised by urban decay, blood-soaked murders and characters that dredge the very depths of psychological torment. *See also* Espionage Fiction, Godfathers of British Crime Fiction, Women Crime Writers *and* Sexuality in British Crime Fiction. *See also* Humour and Crime Fiction *and* The Great Detectives: The Mass Appeal of Holmes, Poirot and Wimsey.

Philip Scowcroft and Mark Campbell

Sexuality in British Crime Fiction

Sexuality, crime, violence and death are inextricably linked motifs in the crime and mystery fiction genre, whether the literary beginnings are located as far back as Greek drama (Oedipus's transgressive desire for his mother and his unwitting murder of his father), or more recently in the nineteenth century, with Edgar Allan Poe's set of short stories featuring Auguste Dupin, who saves at least one important royal personage from sexual scandal. A more particularly English cultural fascination with popular stories motivated by sexual intrigue reaches back to the eighteenth-century Newgate Calendar; continues through the sexual preoccupations of the nineteenth-century sensation fiction of Mary Elizabeth Braddon (1835–1915) and others; and arrives at the '20th century crime thriller...[with] its sensational, and often shockingly frank, depictions of sex and violent death' (Scaggs 2005, 107). The treatment of sexuality (its expression and consequences) in British crime fiction since the middle of the nineteenth century reflects changing anxieties and attitudes in the larger social order and is often a source of social and moral commentary.

Changing cultural anxieties about homosexuality, for instance, can be traced back to the absence of the subject in most nineteenth-century crime and mystery. By the 1920s and 1930s, **Golden Age** fiction produced a range of minor characters whose closeted gay or lesbian sexuality is generally constructed in coded stereotypes, ranging from the flamboyant (gay) theatre designer to the tweedy (lesbian) companion. As social mores and attitudes changed following the sexual revolution of the 1960s and 1970s, more positive images of gay and lesbian sexualities began to surface in the work of British writers. For example, one of Reginald **Hill**'s police characters, Sergeant Wield, is revealed as homosexual in *A Killing Kindness* (1981); he comes out of the closet in the 1987 *Child's Play*. Many other writers, such as Robert **Barnard**, Simon **Brett**, P.D. **James**, Ruth **Rendell**, Ian **Rankin** and John **Harvey**, have dealt sympathetically with a range of gay and lesbian characters and themes throughout the last three decades. Writers such as Stella **Duffy**, Manda **Scott**, Val **McDermid** and Dan **Kavanagh** have produced detective figures and friends and associates whose open sexuality as gay, lesbian or bi-sexual is only one aspect of their subjectivity. The genre thus clearly demonstrates a capacity to reflect, and perhaps influence, changing social attitudes about aspects of sexuality.

Sexuality is dealt with in a number of ways by crime and mystery writers: as characterisation, theme, motive for murder, transgression. Further, the motif of sexuality often intersects with constructs of class, race and gender. An examination of any period of the genre will reveal novels which seem to inscribe fixed categories of the social order (such as class, race, gender or sexuality) and writers whose work can be read as more transgressive of the insistent codes of, for example, heterosexual norms or class hierarchies. Wilkie **Collins**, for example, in *The Moonstone* (1868), an early prototype of the 'whodunit' formula, exposes the hypocrisies of mid-Victorian attitudes towards class difference and the stereotype of the 'fallen woman' through the stories of Rosanna and Godfrey Ablewhite. Perceptions of what is normative, and what transgresses, in terms of sexual characteristics and behaviour, and perceptions of how to present these aspects, do seem to change with the times.

By the turn of the twentieth century, sexuality as part of the detective's subjectivity, for instance, seems more conspicuous by its absence than its presence. The celibate figure of the male detective, embodied in Sherlock **Holmes**, predominates; sexuality by omission allows the detective to keep the world at arm's length. Sex and gender roles, and therefore expressions of sexuality, are fixed and remain largely unchallenged well into the Golden Age. The critical mass of women writers in this period (1920s and 1930s) does little to change dominant paradigms of masculinity, femininity and sexual behaviours. Aberrant sexual expression (which could include homo-eroticism, bi-sexuality, transvestism, sado-masochism, sexual fetishism, voyeurism, child abuse) might be located in villains and victims, but not in the detective. Golden Age authors Margery **Allingham**, Dorothy **Sayers** and Ngaio **Marsh**, whose famous male detectives initially exist in a state of sexual semi-suspension, all eventually provide their sleuths with wives who have careers and wits of their own. Unusually, Dorothy Sayers even allows Harriet Vane to be sexually active as a single woman before she marries Lord Peter **Wimsey**. Unconventional as these spouses might be, they still function to anchor the detectives within the confines of a 'normal' heterosexual romance, and therefore within the sex and gender roles endorsed by the social order of the period.

As crime and mystery fiction moved out of rural English villages and into the modern city, the work of later twentieth century and twenty-first century writers brought new perspectives to bear as social norms changed. By the 1950s, Julian **Symons** notes, crime and mystery writers are noticeably more interested in abnormal psychology and violence, and are using 'the sexual motive in a way from which Golden Age writers would have flinched' [1972 (1992 ed.), 147]. Even so, Symons points out, Nicolas Freeling's first Van der Valk novel, *Love in Amsterdam* (1962), was rejected by several English publishers because 'it was thought to be too sexually outspoken' (149). More recently, Liza **Cody**'s 1990s series featuring Eva Wylie, 'The London Lassassin', reveals the instabilities of supposedly fixed categories of class, while also interrogating the norms of heterosexuality and clichéd constructions of both masculinity and femininity.

Female sexuality in particular is consistently the source of mystery and anxiety in mystery fiction, resulting in a limited range of roles and characterisations for women characters. Female characters, almost by definition, play secondary roles in a genre that is defined by the masculinity and sexual attractiveness of the detective, as well as by power structures that privilege the male subject. The genre is marked with constructs of the sexually dangerous woman; seducer, betrayer, killer, victim. As John Cawelti observes, in his discussion of the formulas of popular fiction, 'the intense masculinity of the [hard-boiled] detective is in part a symbolic denial and protective coloration against complex sexual and status anxieties focusing on women' (1976, 154). The American hard-boiled tradition gave the genre one of its staples in the figure of the femme fatale, the sexually predatory and unreliable woman. The treacherous femme fatale, the woman who is not what she appears to be, also permeates the pre- and post-war British spy thriller tradition, circulating throughout Ian **Fleming**'s James Bond novels, for example.

Sexuality in British Crime Fiction

Another predictable construct of female sexuality is the woman as victim of sexual violence. While contemporary women characters are allowed a wider range of sexual behaviours and desires than in earlier periods, the idea of female sexuality as disturbing and in need of control is still firmly embedded; voyeuristic images of sexually mutilated female corpses are a marked feature of crime fiction, then and now. The recent, increasingly commonplace, figures of the male serial killer (there are occasional variations, e.g. Chelsea Cain's 2006 novel *Heartsick* featured a female serial killer) and the forensic pathologist with his/her focus on the violated body are both testimony to directions in which the genre is being pushed to achieve shock value and produce the effect of horror. However, the focus on sadistic violence, usually driven by male sexual obsession and culminating in graphic physical expressions of a fear of and disgust for women, can also be read as confirmation of the genre's typical uneasiness about what it is to be male or female. Further, this focus underscores violence as predominantly a male province. A recent critical discussion of Patricia Cornwell's work points to 'the connection between urban anxieties and female victimization on which the crime novel commonly relies' (Messent in Chernaik et al. 2000, 127).

In response to this historical reliance on such typification of the female, explicitly feminist writers such as Sarah **Dunant**, Michelle **Spring**, Joan **Smith** and Helen Zahavi tend to be more interested in constructing a female subjectivity by exploring gender roles and sexual politics, as Smith, for example, does in *A Masculine Ending* (1987), and Zahavi does in her 1992 novel *Dirty Weekend*, a satirical parody of noir conventions. When engaging with sexual violence, as Dunant does in *Transgressions* (1997) and Spring does in *Nights in White Satin* (1999), the subjectivity of the female victim is foregrounded, which arguably functions in opposition to the genre's historical reliance on the typification of the female as sexual object.

Historically then, the genre has brought taboo subject matter into the open, affording a space to explore cultural and social anxieties about sex and death, and the paradoxical attractions and fears we attach to such subjects. Safe within a literary construct that both entertains and shocks, the genre addresses a wide range of recurring concerns and fascinations about the power and mystery of sexual characteristics and impulses. As the crime and mystery novel moves further into the twenty-first century, with readers and writers more alert to issues of discrimination based on gender and sexuality, and more sensitive to the relationships between gender, sexuality and sexual politics, perhaps the voices and stories that so far continue to speak from the margins on the complex subject of sexuality and its repercussions will move closer to the centre. *See also* Gay and Lesbian Crime Fiction.

Further Reading

Cawelti, John G. 1976. *Adventure, Mystery, and Romance, Formula Stories as Art and Popular Culture*. The University of Chicago Press.
Messent, Peter. 2000. 'Authority, Social Anxiety and the Body in Crime Fiction: Patricia Cornwell's Unnatural Exposure'. Pp.124–137 in *The Art of Detective Fiction*. Edited by Warren Chernaik, Martin Swales and Robert Vilain. Macmillan Press.
Scaggs, John. 2005. *Crime Fiction*. Routledge.
Symons, Julian. 1972. *Bloody Murder, from the Detective Story to the Crime Novel: A History*. 1992 edition. Pan Macmillan.

Margaret Kinsman

Sexy Beast (film, 2000)

Jonathan Glazer, director

Among the most distinctive of the many post–**Lock, Stock and Two Smoking Barrels** (1998) British gangster films, *Sexy Beast* is a character piece blessed with a dark streak of humour that makes it more convincingly hard-boiled than the jumped-up wannabes. Gary 'Gal' Dove (Ray Winstone) sits broiling in the sun by his Spanish swimming pool, shacked up with his ex-porn starlet girlfriend DeeDee (Amanda Redman), enjoying his retirement. However, one day, he is nearly crushed by a boulder that rolls down his hill into his pool, and his best friend Aitch (Cavan Kendall) shows up, terrified, to say another old comrade, Don Logan (Ben Kingsley), is on the way to visit. Don needs Gal to come in as a footsoldier on a heist planned by the smooth mastermind Teddy Bass (Ian McShane): the breaking of a London safe deposit vault (tunnelled into from another swimming pool).

The point is the effect of Don Logan on all concerned. Kingsley does his best screen work as an anti-Gandhi, constantly playing violent word games in profane conversation (he cops one neologism from Harold Pinter, 'insinuendo') or even talking to himself, freezing all the other characters in utter fear (the role was aptly referenced when Kingsley cameoed as himself on *The Sopranos*). Even when Logan gets killed, shot by DeeDee, he has power over his former friends, with Gal having to take part in the robbery – for which he gets an insulting tenner from Bass (who makes him break a twenty for change), though he pockets some jewel earrings – to cover up the death. Much of the film is blankly enigmatic, with the heist plan relayed as several near-identical conversations along a chain of flashbacks, and a horned, furry cowboy creature turning up from Gal's nightmares. Directed by debuting commercials man Jonathan Glazer, who sometimes gets tricksy (a POV shot of a rolling boulder), *Sexy Beast* yet again stresses the gay feel endemic to Brit gang flicks, as represented by the hero's unmanly name, his relationship with a Spanish boy who does odd jobs, and weird currents between Gal and Logan which undermine the aggressively hetero dialogue. *See also* Film and Crime: Page to Screen.

Kim Newman

Seymour, Gerald (b.1941)

Gerald Seymour began his career as a newsman and never really abandoned it, making hard-nosed actuality the basis for a flourishing career in writing thrillers with a strong sense of both history and current affairs.

Born in Surrey and educated at Tavistock and University College, London, he joined ITN in 1963 and became a frontline foreign correspondent covering Northern Ireland, the Middle East, Vietnam and Europe for most of the next fifteen years.

He reported to camera on the kidnapping crisis at the Munich Olympics in 1972 and the massacre of Israeli athletes, and not only contributed to the Oscar-winning television documentary *One Day in September* (1999), but ended up appearing in a cameo role on television footage in Steven Spielberg's *Munich* (2005).

But it was his experiences in the Northern Ireland conflict, including his presence on the streets of Londonderry during the 'Bloody Sunday' riots, that formed the background for his first novel, *Harry's Game*, published in 1975 to immediate critical acclaim.

The story revolved around the assassination of a British cabinet minister and the tracking down of his killer by an undercover agent who eventually dies. The book was credited with introducing the world to the equivocal, if much abused, phrase 'One man's terrorist is another man's freedom fighter.'

It was three years after the success of his first novel that Seymour finally decided to give up his day job and make writing his full-time occupation. He approached his new career with a remarkably methodical attitude, setting himself the goal of a book each year, and twenty chapters to each. As soon as one book was delivered to his agent, he would begin research on the next, always painstakingly and invariably visiting most of his locations.

For the subsequent quarter-century, he has maintained that output, establishing a firm fanbase in the process even if he has at times faced criticism that his work has a journeyman feel to it rather than real star quality.

A modest man, Seymour has rated his output in football terms as 'mid-ranking championship rather than the premier league'. Dedicated Seymour fans would counter by defending his characterisation and the almost educational benefit of the research that forms each book's background.

The topics he has covered have been as widespread as the news bulletins of the last twenty-five years, including Israeli snipers in Lebanon (*At Close Quarters*, 1987), the hunt for war criminals in former Yugoslavia (*The Heart of Danger*, 1995), Saddam Hussein's annexation of Kuwait (*Condition Black*, 1991), escape from East Germany in the final days of the Cold War (*The Waiting Time*, 1998) and suicide bombers in Britain (*The Walking Dead*, 2007).

'If you don't understand history,' said Seymour in an interview, 'then you simply have no comprehension of anything at all.'

He has never been afraid to broach controversial issues from 'shoot-to-kill' policies in Ulster to the morality of tactics used by US drugs enforcement agencies. Overall, however, Seymour is primarily a middle-aged British man writing hard-nosed, serious, politics-based adventure novels for other middle-aged British men. He admits to never being expert at depicting two significant species in the thriller writer's world: Americans and women.

At times, his meticulous research means his books do not just reflect what has actually happened in the realm of **espionage** or warfare, but may even pre-empt them. His KGB interrogator in *Traitor's Kiss* (2003) was based on an interview with ex-KGB officer Alexander Litvinenko, who was later killed by polonium poisoning in London in an operation alleged to have been planned in the Kremlin.

Significantly, however, Seymour has never developed a single leading character to develop into a series, a factor that may have prevented his sales from reaching the heights he might otherwise have reached. In part, this is because his books have remained so tied to the news agenda, and because he has relished a completely new field of research for each novel.

He has not been afraid to focus on the villain, notably in *The Untouchable* (2001), where the main character Albert Packer is a magnificent incarnation of a traditional London mob leader whose mastery of his 'manor' is so complete that he feels justifiably invulnerable from the short arms of British justice.

It is a classic Seymour plot, therefore, to take him out of context, send him on his quest to cut out the middle man in a heroin trafficking operation to the lethal streets of Sarajevo in war-torn Bosnia, and have him pursued by an unprepossessing junior customs and excise archivist. A diversion from Seymour's more customary action heroes, the customs man nonetheless proves the nemesis for the hard villain in a book that seduces the reader into sympathy for the tragedy of the Balkan conflict and the lethal chaos wrought by indiscriminate landmines. Several readers bought *The Untouchable* on the mistaken premise that it was a crime story, only to be disappointed by the international current affairs element, which is exactly what makes it such classic Seymour.

An honest, honourable player in the British thriller tradition, Seymour has for decades offered intelligent, well-crafted and fact-based adventure stories without playing clever games. His work may eventually come to seem dated but only because it – like his style – is so firmly rooted in its own geopolitical context.

Selected Works by the Author
Harry's Game (1975)
A Song in the Morning (1986)
Condition Black (1991)
The Waiting Time (1998)
A Line in the Sand (1999)
The Unknown Soldier (2004)

Peter Millar

Sharman (television series, 1995–1996)

Actor Clive Owen was coming into prominence in the mid-1990s, following his appearance in the television series *Chancer*, when he was cast as the tough South London PI Nick Sharman (World Productions for Carlton/ITV) – the series was based on the gritty novels by Mark **Timlin**. As a character, Sharman has his share of problems: a former police officer whose career was derailed due to drink and drugs, which also cost him his marriage, he lives on the edge as a private eye scratching a living in the alleyways of South London. He has a daughter, Judith, to support as well as a string of girlfriends and low lifes who are forever troubling him. The youthful Clive Owen was perfectly cast as Sharman, with the bad-boy good looks and a contemptuous sneer that breathes life into his portrayal. Most importantly, his eyes show the pain and the void in his soul brought about by his hard life.

The first of the Nick Sharman television adventures was the feature-length 'The Turnaround' (1995) based on the book of that name, adapted by writer Tony Hoare and directed by Suri Krishnamma. The adaptation follows the novel's plot closely. Sharman is hired by James Webb (Bill Paterson) to find the men who murdered his sister and her family. The case goes seriously off the rails and Sharman becomes the principal suspect in the murders and is attempting to clear his name. Timlin himself makes a very brief cameo appearance. This pilot episode for the Sharman series attracted ten million viewers and was the only episode released on VHS.

It was not until 1996 that Owen returned as Sharman in 'Take the A-Train' (the official Episode 1), with actress Samantha Janus playing a nude model. Sharman investigates the (apparent) suicide of a former police colleague who appears to have thrown himself off a tower block. Sharman's investigation devolves on a gang war in the neon world of clubland. 'Hearts of Stone' (Episode 2) is probably the most accomplished of the series, with writer Paul Abbott (b.1960) following the novel's story trajectory closely. Sharman is in pursuit of a couple of heavy-handed debt collectors when he gets roped in by former colleagues from the police drugs squad to infiltrate a dope smuggling operation. It is an assignment he cannot refuse, as the alternative offered is fifteen years on the wrong side of prison bars. The episode features a manic Keith Allen playing to the actor's customary form. 'A Good Year for the Rose' (Episode 3) is based on Nick Sharman's actual debut in print and features a strong performance from Ray Winstone. Sharman is hired as a minder for a lesbian dancing duo when Winstone (playing hard-man George Bright) hires Sharman to track down his missing eighteen-year-old daughter. The case takes a turn for the worse when Sharman finds Bright's daughter dead, overdosed in a squalid squat. 'Sharman' (Episode 4) – the last in the series – was an original screenplay, but does feature a scene from Timlin's novel *Pretend We're Dead* (1994). The cyclical furore about violence on television was in one of its periodic ascendancies, following the aftermath of the Dunblane shootings, and Carlton/ITV cancelled *Sharman* just as the series was finding its feet. It has never been repeated on terrestrial television, but has had some digital showings and is certainly overdue for a DVD release.

Although Nick Sharman is British, his roots from Timlin's novels are pure Raymond **Chandler**, as the cynical vision he deploys comes from the American PI tradition. Timlin will always be remembered for Nick Sharman, as Chandler is always associated with Philip Marlowe, and those with long memories will always associate Clive Owen with Sharman, despite whatever the actor does under the shadow of Hollywood's famous hills. Ironically, Owen is adding Philip Marlowe to his CV, in the form of television adaptations. *See also* TV Detectives: Small-Screen Adaptations.

Selected Episodes
'The Turnaround' (5 April 1995). Suri Krishnamma, director; Tony Hoare, writer.
'Take the A-Train' (4 November 1996). Robert Bierman, director; Guy Jenkin, writer.
'Hearts of Stone' (11 November 1996). Robert Bierman, director; Paul Abbott, writer.
'A Good Year for the Roses' (18 November 1996). Matthew Evans, director; Dusty Hughes, writer.
'Sharman' (25 November 1996). Matthew Evans, director; Mick Ford, writer.

Website
Mark Timlin website, www.nicksharman.co.uk
ThrillerUK, Nick Sharman special, www.thrilleruk.fsnet.co.uk/latest.htm
Crime Time, 'The Rise and Fall of Nick Sharman', www.crimetime.co.uk/features/marktimlin.php

Ali Karim

Sharp, Zoë (b.1966)

Zoë Sharp is the author of a series of thrillers featuring an ex-special forces-turned-bodyguard heroine, Charlie Fox.

Sharp was born in Nottinghamshire, the daughter of a magazine editor and granddaughter of an actress. In fact, it was her grandmother who started Sharp's lifelong love of crime fiction by giving her an original copy of one of *The Saint*

86. Zoë Sharp.

books, which she still has today. Her early life was as colourful as her novels. She spent most of her formative years living on a catamaran on the north-west coast of England. After a promising start at a private girls' school, she opted out of mainstream education at the age of twelve in favour of correspondence courses at home. She was accepted for membership of Mensa and wrote her first novel at fifteen. Sharp became a freelance photojournalist in 1988, and this has been her day job ever since.

The idea for the first book in the series to feature Charlie Fox came about after Sharp received death threats during the course of her work. The resultant book, *Killer Instinct*, was published in the United Kingdom in 2001. Since then, she has written a further six titles in the Charlie Fox series, which have received critical acclaim. *First Drop* (2004) was nominated for a Barry award in the United States for Best British Crime Novel. The latest title in the series, *Second Shot*, was published in the United Kingdom in September 2007.

In her creator's own words, 'Charlie Fox is a tough, self-sufficient heroine who doesn't suffer fools gladly and can take care of herself.' Charlie never stays in one place or one job for long. She seems to stray into where danger and crime are lurking. We find her in a different situation in each novel. For example, in the first book in the series, she is a self-defence instructor with a slightly shady military background and a painful past, but by book number 2, *Riot Act* (2002), she has moved on to working in a gym where she comes face to face with a spectre from her military past, Sean Myer. It is Sean who asks Charlie to go undercover to a bodyguard training school in Germany, where the next novel, *Hard Knocks* (2003), takes place. By the time we get to *First Drop* (2004), Charlie is working for Sean's close protection agency on her first assignment in Florida. However, wherever this gutsy girl goes, we can guarantee that she will be tearing around on a high-powered motorbike – another passion of the author.

Sharp's books are regularly praised for their authenticity, and Charlie Fox has been described by best-selling thriller author Lee **Child** as 'today's best action heroine' and by Ken Bruen (b.1951) as 'the must-read heroine of mystery'.

Sharp is currently at work on the first in a new series set in the English Lake District, where Sharp and her husband have recently self-built their own house. *See also* The Shires: Rural England and Regional Crime Fiction *and* Thrillers: Novels of Action.

Selected Works by the Author
Killer Instinct (2001)
Riot Act (2002)
Hard Knocks (2003)
First Drop (2004)
Road Kill (2005)
Second Shot (2007)
Third Strike (2008)

David Stuart Davies

Sherlock Magazine

Sherlock began life in 1991 as *The Sherlock Holmes Gazette*, a sepia-coloured magazine that attempted to capture the air of Victoriana redolent in the Holmes stories. At first, the magazine recorded the latest happenings in the Sherlock world, especially the doings of the Sherlock Holmes Society of London. It was the brainchild of journalist Liz Wiggins, who from the early issues employed the services of David Stuart **Davies**, a writer and Sherlockian expert. Davies's contributions grew over time, and when Wiggins sold the magazine to Robert Godfrey, a newspaper publisher on the Channel Islands, Davies was retained as the main contributor. At the time, in the early 1990s, the Sherlock world was buoyant, stimulated to a large extent by the success of the Granada television series featuring the charismatic Jeremy Brett, which ran from 1984 to the mid-1990s.

Robert Godfrey died suddenly and the magazine was left in limbo until it was purchased by Peter Harkness, who was the publisher of a number of professional medical journals. He installed Eddie Bissell, an old journalist friend, as editor, but once again Davies was employed to give the magazine Sherlockian accuracy. When Bissell left suddenly to work abroad, Davies was appointed editor on Issue 17 and the magazine became *Sherlock Holmes – The Detective Magazine*. Davies believed that for the publication to succeed on a commercial level, it had to broaden its scope, and so he set about doing just that by introducing articles and regular features which concerned other aspects of detective fiction. He brought in new writers, including some of his colleagues from the **Crime Writers' Association** (CWA) such as Mike **Ripley** and Martin **Edwards**. While Sherlock **Holmes** was still the focus of the publication, the character was now presented within the context of the broader world of crime fiction. As well as Holmes pastiches, Davies introduced other detective stories written by such writers as Peter **Lovesey**, Peter **Guttridge**, June **Thomson** and Danuta Reah, whose story, 'No Flies on Frank' (2004), won the CWA Short Story Dagger in 2005. The magazine also introduced the Sherlock Awards for writers and actors. Recipients included John **Harvey**, Colin **Dexter**, Mark **Billingham**, P.D. **James**, John Thaw and Ian Richardson.

As Peter Harkness's empire grew, the magazine became increasingly the Cinderella publication, and in 2001 he sold it. It was purchased by Mark Coleman, a Holmes enthusiast, who set up Atlas Publishing especially for the magazine. Once again Davies was employed as editor. All started well, but after a year, the lack of Atlas's success in marketing the product began to tell, and the magazine became somewhat irregular in its appearance. Things came to a head in the spring of 2005 when Davies was removed from his editor's chair and replaced by Teddy Hayes, an American writer who was prepared to invest in the magazine. After one disastrous issue, Hayes left. Following a six-month hiatus, Davies was asked to return, and the magazine was re-launched in a smarter colour format, but this time, Atlas wanted to focus solely on Sherlock Holmes. It lasted two issues. It would seem that there was not a large enough audience for Holmes alone. Davies still believes that given the appropriate promotion and support, a bright and lively crime fiction magazine with a broad scope would succeed. '*Sherlock* is not dead', he says, 'it is just sleeping.' *See also* Anthologies *and* Short Stories.

Brian Ritterspak

The Shires: Rural England and Regional Crime Fiction

Introduction

It is obvious that Britain's major cities – not just London but Manchester, Birmingham, Bristol, Leeds and others – have formed the settings for much crime fiction. But a marked feature of British crime writers is their contrasting partiality to provincial locations. Choosing to avoid the metropolis, many crime writers have based their stories in provincial England. This article cannot cover them all, but in taking five areas of which crime writers have been especially fond – the South-Eastern Counties, the Lake District and the Peak District, Yorkshire, the South and East Midlands, and 'Wessex' – it seeks to sketch out something of the tradition.

As was the case of, for example, Thomas Hardy and his Wessex or D.H. Lawrence's Nottinghamshire, crime authors tend to set their tales in areas they know well through birth, residence in later life or frequent visits. It must be noted, however, that many of the great detectives of fiction were well travelled. Sherlock **Holmes**, of course; Freeman Wills **Crofts**'s Inspector French, who (like Josephine **Tey**'s Inspector Grant), although a Metropolitan Police officer, rarely seems to have a case in London, and French visits with enjoyment Northern Ireland (where Crofts once worked), Surrey (where he later lived), Devon and other places. There is also Dorothy L. **Sayers**'s Lord Peter **Wimsey**. Sayers's best-described locales, apart from London, were those she knew best, including the Fenlands of eastern England, Galloway (south-west Scotland), where she spent holidays, and Oxford, her alma mater – far enough apart in a geographical sense.

The Shires: Rural England and Regional Crime Fiction

Agatha **Christie**'s locales are as far flung as any writer's (more so than most), with four of her novels – and some short stories – set in the Middle East and others in Europe. Many of her English locations are vaguer than those of several of her contemporaries, but there are seventeen of her books that feature – at least in part – her native Devon: *The Man in the Brown Suit* (1924), *The Murder of Roger Ackroyd* (perhaps) (1926), *Partners in Crime* (1929), *The Sittaford Mystery* (1931, also known as *Murder at Hazelmoor*), *Peril at End House* (1932), *The ABC Murders* (1936), *Ten Little Niggers* (1939, also known as *And Then There Were None*), *The Regatta Mystery* (1939), *Evil under the Sun* (1941), *The Body in the Library* (1942), *The Moving Finger* (1942), *Towards Zero* (1944), *Mrs McGinty's Dead* (1952), *Dead Man's Folly* (1956), *Ordeal by Innocence* (1958), *Postern of Fate* (1973) and *Sleeping Murder* (1976). In some of these, the Devonshire locations are specific, while others are disguised or vaguely general (Torquay, her birthplace, appears in Christie's work under its own name and at least three aliases). Most are in the southern half of the county. But even if all the above titles are accepted as Devonshire, they represent only about a fifth of all of Christie's output.

It is a similar situation with Christie's contemporary Margery **Allingham**, who lived in Essex for much of her life: a fair proportion of her oeuvre is set in that county or over the border in Suffolk – but still not enough to identify her as a regional crime novelist.

In more recent years, however, crime authors have concentrated less on the pure puzzle element, and have taken more trouble with things such as characterisation and backgrounds. Often, this background reflects, as may be seen with **Golden Age** authors such as Crofts, Sayers, Allingham and Christie, the author's own experience. It is natural, for instance, for Martin **Edwards**, a practising Liverpool solicitor, to make his earlier detective hero, Harry Devlin, also a Liverpool solicitor. In recent years, however, Edwards has changed course (and detectives) and has set books in the Lake District.

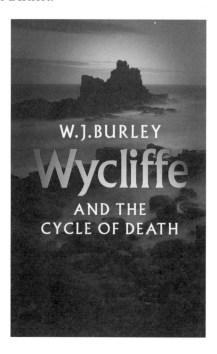

87. Cover of *Wycliffe and the Cycle of Death* (1990), one of W.J. Burley's novels set in Cornwall.

Where an author utilises a policeman or policewoman as his or her series sleuth, it is more natural for their books to become regionally orientated. There is Robert **Barnard**'s Charlie Peace books (and others) set in Yorkshire where Barnard lives, Ruth **Rendell**'s Wexford series (Sussex), Ann **Cleeves**'s police novels from North-East England (though she does not confine herself to that area), W.J. **Burley**'s Wycliffe series featuring Cornwall and parts of Devon, and Reginald **Hill**'s Dalziel and Pascoe saga, based in Yorkshire, although Hill's topography is not easy to pinpoint therein (he now lives in the Lake District, but for many years, he lectured at a college in Doncaster, South Yorkshire). Judith **Cutler** has written inter alia two series – one police focused (Kate Power, a policewoman), the other (Sophie Rivers) not particularly – but both are set in Birmingham.

Not that one needs a police sleuth or sleuths to establish a regional series. There is Val **McDermid**'s Manchester PI Kate Brannigan, Cath **Staincliffe**'s Sal Kilkenny, also from Manchester, and two series based in the Cotswolds, by John Penn and by M.C. **Beaton** (the Agatha Raisin saga). The list below is, of necessity, selective – to do justice to all the regions of the United Kingdom would require considerably more space than is available here.

South-Eastern Counties

The three counties to be covered here are Surrey, Sussex and Kent. Their proximity to London does pose problems: firstly as to where London ends and the adjacent county begins, and secondly, where a novel is set obviously somewhere near the metropolis but the topography is vague. So many crime novels set just outside London are indeterminate in this way, and the problem seems to become greater nearer to London. But it is hopefully possible to erect some meaningful signposts.

The three counties have produced or afforded residences for many crime writers over the years. Sussex, county of Kipling, Sheila Kaye-Smith (who was associated particularly with the Weald), Hilaire Belloc, Harrison Ainsworth, William Blake, Robert Bridges and others, can claim the following crime writers as natives: Joan **Aiken** (Rye; she lived in Petworth); Patrick **Hamilton**, author of the plays *Rope* and *Gaslight*; thriller writer John Burke (also Rye); Hammond **Innes** (Horsham); Gwen Moffat (Brighton, b.1924); and Harry Keating (St Leonard's-on-Sea). Simon **Brett** lives in Arundel, Jocelyn Davey (1908–1994) lived in Hove, Leonard Gribble (1908–1985) in Worthing, Lawrence Meynell (1899–1989) lived in Brighton, John Rhode (1884–1965) lived in Seaford, Lord **Gorell** lived latterly at Burpham, and Kipling himself, author of *Kim* (1901), one of the finest of spy stories, lived at Hassocks. 'Mark **Hebden**' (John Harris) and Christopher Bush (1885–1973) also lived in Sussex. A.A. Milne's (1882–1956) Sussex estate figures in the Winnie-the-Pooh books, but not in *The Red House Mystery* (1922).

Surrey is even more favoured: Caryl **Brahms**, Simon Brett (Worcester Park), John **Creasey**, William **Haggard**, Colin **Watson** (the latter two at Croydon), Henry **Wade**, Cyril **Hare** (Mickleham) and Margaret **Yorke** (Compton) were all born in the county. Sussex residents are or were Josephine **Bell**; Gwendolyn Butler, creator of Inspector Coffin; David **Williams**, creator of Mark Treasure (Virginia Water); William Haggard (Camberley); Tim **Heald** (Richmond); Patricia **Wentworth**; R.C. Sherriff (1896–1975), whose crime plays *Home at Seven* (1948) and *A Shred of Evidence* (1960) are both set in the 'stockbroker belt'; Cyril Hare; and Freeman Wills Crofts. The latter two we shall come back to.

The Shires: Rural England and Regional Crime Fiction

Kent's natives include 'Leo Bruce' (Rupert Croft-Cooke, 1903–1979), creator of Sergeant Beef and schoolteacher detective Carolus Deene, whose school might well be in Kent also (Bruce was born in Edenbridge); H.G. Wells (remember, among other crime stories by him, *The Invisible Man*, 1897); and Elleston **Trevor**, author of many thrillers including *The V.I.P.* (1959). Both Wells and Trevor were born in Bromley. Kentish residents in this field are also a distinguished group, which includes Charles **Dickens** (Rochester), Michael **Gilbert** (Luddesdown), Roderic Jeffries (Romney Marsh; b.1926), Mary Stewart (Sevenoaks; b.1916), Julian **Symons** (Deal), Ted Willis (1918–1992), creator of *Dixon of Dock Green* (Chislehurst), Catherine **Aird** (Sturry, near Canterbury; though her 'Calleshire' should not be regarded as having too much of Kent in it), Basil **Copper** (Sevenoaks – several of his Solar Pons stories are set in Kent), R. Austin **Freeman** (Gravesend), Amy Myers (Lenham; b.1938), Dorothy **Simpson** (Maidstone) and Russell Thorndike (1885–1972; Romney Marsh, the setting for his Dr Sin stories).

A more detailed survey of Kent is of interest. Charles Dickens has already been mentioned. Here is Rochester, which, thinly disguised as 'Cloisterham', is the scene of *Edwin Drood* (1870):

> A monotonous, silent city, deriving an earthy flavour throughout from its Cathedral crypt.... A drowsy city, whose inhabitants seem to suppose...that all its changes lie behind it and that there are no more to come...the streets of Cloisterham city are little more than one narrow street...the rest being mostly disappointing yards with pumps in them and no thoroughfare.... In a word, a city of another and a bygone time...with its hoarse Cathedral-bell, its hoarse rooks hovering about the Cathedral tower. (Chapter 3)

Drood is the *ne plus ultra* in mystery novels, as it was left unfinished when Dickens died. Scholars and others have argued over it for upwards of a century; answers to the questions, Is Drood dead? and Who is the obviously disguised Mr Datchery?, must remain speculative. Dickens's *Great Expectations* (1861, which is a crime novel of a sort, with its themes of mystery, convicts and crime) is also a Kent novel, set not far from Rochester on the south bank of the Thames.

Sherlock **Holmes** had a large number of cases in this area, which are listed here county by county. His visits to Kent were in 'The Golden Pince Nez' ('Yoxley Old Place', near Chatham) and 'The Abbey Grange' ('Marsham', near Chislehurst), while he and Watson changed trains smartly at Canterbury to throw off Dr Moriarty's pursuit in 'The Final Problem'. Kent was even more popular with R. Austin Freeman's medico-legal prodigy Dr Thorndyke. No fewer than four of seven Thorndyke short stories figure in *The Puzzle Lock* (1925) collection: 'The Green Check Jacket' (Gravesend, near which town a Kentish dene-hole reveals a body), 'A Mystery of the Sand-Hills' (Sandwich), 'The Apparition of Burling Court' (a fictitious resort, on the coast) and 'The Mysterious Visitor' (Whitstable). One of Thorndyke's most anthologised cases, 'The Blue Sequin', takes him to 'Woldhurst', stated to be in Kent (Wadhurst is in Sussex). 'The Case of the White Footprints' finds him in Margate in a boarding house situated in 'a quiet suburban street which abounded in similar establishments...undergoing a spring-cleaning and renovation...for the approaching season', while in 'The Funeral Pyre', from the same collection (*Dr Thorndyke's Case Book*, 1923), he investigates a body found in a burnt-out hayrick near Dartford. *The Penrose Mystery* (1936) has him dig up a long barrow near Chilham and find a body of much more recent origin. *When Rogues Fall Out* (1932) sees the demise of Thorndyke's police acquaintance, Inspector Badger, murdered in Greenhithe Tunnel on the Dartford–Strood railway line. But Thorndyke avenges him by careful observation. *The Mystery of Angelina Frood* (1925) is set at Rochester, as befits a variation of *Edwin Drood*.

When Rogues Fall Out and 'The Blue Sequin' are two of many railway detective tales placed in Kent from pre-*Edwin Drood* days up to the present. In Andrew Forrester's 'Arrested on Suspicion', from *Revelations of a Private Detective* (1863), a map in the South Eastern Railway Guide affords the narrator a clue to enable him to track down a jewel thief at Margate and so clear his falsely accused sister. Miles Burton's *Death in the Tunnel* (1936) is not only one of his best, but is one of the finest of all railway detective stories ever written and is set in commuter Kent. In Freeman Wills Crofts's short story 'The Landing Ticket', an absconding accountant disappears on a cross-channel ferry from Dover: 175 landing tickets are issued; 174 are collected. Suicide? It appears so to the local police, but the reader has been informed that the fugitive has received two tickets but given up only one. Inspector French solves the case after investigations on the boat train. Gerald Sinstadt's *Whisper in a Lonely Place* (1966) is a counter-espionage tale which ends with the hero hijacking a locomotive to evade pursuit and being killed when its boiler explodes. Michael Crichton's (b.1942) *The Great Train Robbery* (1975) is a semi-fictitious reconstruction of a real railway bullion robbery perpetrated in 1855 on the London Bridge–Folkestone route.

Kent's Channel ferries figure again in J.S. Fletcher's (1863–1935) *The Passenger to Folkestone* (1927) and Andrew **Garve**'s *The Long Short Cut* (1968). (Fletcher, Yorkshire-born, has also provided us with at least one Sussex mystery in *The Great Brighton Mystery*, 1925, and a Surrey mystery in *The Box Hill Murder*, 1931.) Kent's eastern tip, Thanet, is the scene of the dénouement of John **Buchan**'s classic thriller *The Thirty Nine Steps* (1915), as 'Bradgate' is clearly Broadstairs in all essentials. Mollie Hardwick's (1916–2003) series featuring antique dealer Doran Fairweather and her parson husband, Rodney Chelmarsh, which began with *Malice Domestic* (1986), is set in and around 'Eastgate', and is obviously the same area with its profusion of '-gates'. These pleasantly written books show a canny awareness of the traditions of detective fiction.

Returning to those traditions, mention must be made of the best of Christianna **Brand**'s detective novels, the famed *Green for Danger* (1945), set in a wartime military hospital where the victim dies on the operating table in view of seven people.

Agatha Christie did not often favour Kent. The quiet heroine of *The Mystery of the Blue Train* (1928), Katherine Grey, lives in 'St Mary Mead', which is clearly stated to be in Kent. Does this mean that Miss Marple, a long-time resident of a village called St Mary Mead, also lives in Kent? On the whole, as Miss Marple's village seems to be further west and further north than Kent, one is forced to the conclusion that there are (at least) two St Mary Meads. Christie's play *Spider's Web* (1954), such a hit for Margaret Lockwood, is specifically set in a house in Kent.

Dorothy L. Sayers only occasionally visited Kent in her fiction. One of her worst criminals is incarcerated in Maidstone Gaol in *The Nine Tailors* (1934), and in the same novel, a body is discovered down a dene-hole near Dartford. Lord Peter Wimsey's personal man and resourceful assistant detective, Mervyn Bunter, was brought up in Kent, near Maidstone. Josephine Tey's *A Shilling for Candles* (1936) tells of the murder of a female film star on the beach at 'Westover', which might be identified as Folkestone (i.e. a harbour town west of Dover and within easy reach of Canterbury). The Kentish background is nicely sketched. 'Westover' reappears in Tey's *Brat Farrar* (1949), a delightful mystery with its attractive evocation of horse riding on the 'downs' – clearly, the Kentish North Downs – and an agricultural show. John Dickson **Carr** was another Golden Age writer who did well by Kent. *The Crooked Hinge* (1938) is one of his finest novels; while the historical *The Witch of the Low Tide* (1961), idiomatically set in the Edwardian period, tells of an 'impossible' murder in a bathing hut at a fictitious resort on the Kent coast, though perhaps 'Fairfield' is Broadstairs again. John Rhode's *Death in the Hop Fields* (1937) sounds like a Kentish murder for Dr Priestley. Heron Carvic (1913–1980) lived at Bearsted, near Maidstone, though his Miss Seeton lives in a village near Rye, and Helen Robertson's (real name Helen Edmiston) (1913–1987) *The Chinese Goose* (1960) is set in an atmospherically described marshy country around Gravesend and Rochester where Miss Robertson lived. David Frome's *Mr Pinkerton and the Old Angel* (1939) takes place in 'the rosy-roofed little hilltop town' of Rye. Pinkerton is delighted with it.

Mentioning Rye represents a move to Sussex, a county that saw Sherlock Holmes a number of times: *The Valley of Fear* (1914), in 'The Five Orange Pips' (Horsham); 'The Musgrave Ritual'; and 'The Sussex Vampire' ('Lamberley', south of Horsham). Holmes liked Sussex well enough to retire there, where he keeps bees and solves the problem of 'The Lion's Mane'. Even before Holmes's day, an important episode in Willie Collins's *The Moonstone* (1868) takes place in Brighton. Brighton is popular with authors in the crime field. Three good evocations of it are David Frome's (1898–1983), *The Guilt Is Plain* (1938), featuring the Pavilion in particular (complete with plan; Evan Pilkington finds a body in the Music Room); Douglas G. Browne's (1884–1963), *Death in Perpetuity* (1950), a reconstruction of the Wallace Case; and Peter **Lovesey**'s *Mad Hatter's Holiday*, set in Victorian times. If my reading experience is any guide, however, specifically Sussex locales are rather less common than Kentish ones. The 'Weald', which straddles both counties, is the setting of Georgette **Heyer**'s *Why*

88. Cover of P.D. James's *A Shroud for a Nightingale* (1971), set on the Sussex-Hampshire border.

Shoot a Butler? (1933). Agatha Christie only occasionally set her mysteries in Sussex. Tommy and Tuppence Beresford have one (rather unsuccessful) case, 'The Case of the Missing Lady', in *Partners in Crime* (1929), which takes them to 'Maldon' (fictitious in a Sussex sense), while the 'B' murder in *The ABC Murders* (1936) is at Bexhill, though the skimpy description Christie vouchsafes of it makes one wonder if she ever visited the place. A.E.W. **Mason**, though, loved the county and more than once took a lease of a large house there. Much of *The Summons* (1920), though not the spy episodes that really qualify this book for inclusion here, happens in a Sussex country house; *The Witness for the Defense* (1913), derived from a play, begins (on Bignor Hill, delightfully imagined) and finishes in Sussex. Dorothy L. Sayers, by contrast, ignores the county, apart from casual mentions of Eastbourne, Brighton, Worthing and Lewes and some suggestive place names in *Unnatural Death* (1927), which book, however, may be claimed for Hampshire. G.K. **Chesterton**'s Father Brown locales almost always are shadowy, but 'The Quick One' from *The Scandal of Father Brown* (1929) is explicitly said to take place on the Sussex coast.

Freeman Wills Crofts provided *Mystery in the Channel* (1931). A Newhaven–Dieppe ferry steamer encounters a yacht in mid-channel with two corpses on board. Is it suicide or murder? And what has happened to the crew? Inspector French is summoned from the Yard and makes enquiries at Newhaven:

> On the east side the river is fronted by the usual vertical walled quay, on which, a little lower down, is the Harbour Station and the berths of the Dieppe boats. On the west side there is no wharf in the ordinary sense, the river bank being an ordinary stone-pitched slope. Connexion with shipping on this side is obtained by means of a row of separate gangways projecting out from the bank like a series of miniature pierheads: spidery erections of timber piles. (Chapter 5)

Christie may not have been to Bexhill, but the meticulous Crofts was familiar with Newhaven. French later enjoys a trip in a motor boat along the coast past Peacehaven and Rottingdean to Brighton, and back, to obtain some necessary timings, and he visits France before he arrives at the solution. From roughly the same period is John Bude's (1901–1957) the *Sussex Downs Murder* (1936), with an inland Sussex setting. Sussex has, like Kent, its commuter railway mystery in the shape of *The Corpse Now Arriving* (1983) by Margaret Hinxman. A middle-aged woman who is drunk falls to her death from a commuter train as it approaches its South Coast terminus, just after she has told a fellow passenger that somebody was going to kill her. Was it an accident or murder? The police opt for the former, but the fellow passenger noses around and makes some startling, not to say risky (to her), discoveries. The characterisation is good, and there are interesting sidelights on commuter travel on the southern region in the 1980s. P.D. **James**'s *Shroud for a Nightingale* (1971) has a hospital setting, on the border between Hampshire and Sussex.

As suggested previously, much of Surrey has now become part of London's suburbia. It, however, is possible to point to a few genuine Surrey titles. Sherlock Holmes, whose London stretched far less than London does now, had several assignments in the county, including some of his most noteworthy cases: 'The Speckled Band' ('Stoke Moran' is in West Surrey, near Leatherhead), 'The Beryl Coronet' (Streatham), 'The Reigate Squires', 'The Naval Treaty' (Woking), 'The Solitary Cyclist' (Farnham), 'The Cardboard Box' (Croydon), 'Wisteria Lodge' (Esher) and 'The Illustrious Client' (Kingston-on-Thames). Lord Peter Wimsey visits a curious villa near Dorking to solve the pleasant, if somewhat over-cerebral, problem of 'Uncle Meleager's Will', and Wimbledon is the title story of *In the Teeth of the Evidence* (1939). Croydon's airport, so famous in the inter-war period, was familiar to him. It also figures in Agatha Christie's *Death in the Clouds* (1935) and in Freeman Wills Crofts's *12.30 from Croydon* (1934). The house in 'The Hollow', a scene of Christie's novel of that name (1946), was modelled on the Haslemere home of the actor Francis L. Sullivan. Crofts himself, as recorded earlier, settled in Surrey, near Guildford, and no fewer than three stories written in the 1930s are set in his home territory: *The Hog's Back Mystery* (1933), one of the best-plotted Inspector French books; *Crime at Guildford* (1935); and *Golden Ashes* (1940). Cyril Hare, a Surrey native, as we saw, also lived there for much of his life, sitting locally as a County Court judge. He died in Dorking in 1958. 'Markhampton' figures in several of his books and short stories and this has much in common with Guildford, including a cathedral. It appears first in *Tragedy at Law* (1942) as the first stage of the Assize Circuit which turns out to be so full of incident. *When the Wind Blows* (1949) features the Markhampton Orchestral Society, considerably affected by the murder of a visiting soloist; it is not too fanciful to see this in reality as the Guildford Philharmonic Orchestra, then basically an amateur body but later a fully professional outfit. In *That Yew Tree's Shade* (1954), as in the previous two Hare titles quoted here, we meet barrister Francis Pettigrew, who in this novel becomes (like his creator) a County Court judge, though only temporarily. Pettigrew has now acquired a cottage overlooking 'Yew Hill', which needs little semantic progression to turn into Box Hill, where J.S. Fletcher also set a murder mystery. Hare describes it so: 'The hill lies in the parish of Yewbury, a village tucked snugly away in the valley and nearly a mile distant.... Agents are wont to advertise [nearby] houses as "commanding unrivalled views of Yew Hill". If Pettigrew's experience was anything to go upon, it was in fact the view that commanded them' (Chapter 1). The view from Pettigrew's window becomes important when murder is committed on the hill shortly afterwards. He is still living at Yewbury when he makes his final appearance in *He Should Have Died Hereafter* (1978), but the action of this book takes place elsewhere. Box Hill brings to mind a scene in Jane Austen's *Emma* (1816) which has been described as a mystery story before its time.

Of these three south-eastern counties, it is Kent that has most opportunities to project itself distinctively, although Sussex and Surrey have their moments. Between the three of them, they have been satisfyingly utilised by luminaries of the English detective genre.

The Lake District and the Peak District

It is commonplace to note that many notable figures in English literature have lived in or been inspired by the Lake District: Wordsworth, Coleridge, Hugh Walpole, Beatrix Potter and Arthur Ransome, to name but five. But when examining the field of English crime fiction, it is clear that there are relatively few authors who follow a similar path.

Much of the action of Wilkie Collins's classic thriller *The Woman in White* (1860) takes place at Limmeridge House in Cumberland. (His novelette *A Marriage Tragedy*, 1858, also has a Cumberland setting.) Limmeridge House, we learn early in the novel, is on the coast and is reached by a ninety-minute drive along bad roads from the nearest railway station, which is on a branch line 'which ran in the direction of the coast' (i.e. from Carlisle). From the house, 'the distant coast of Scotland fringed the horizon with its lines of melting blue'. From these facts, it seems clear that the branch line is the Maryport and Carlisle Railway, which had been opened in 1845, four years before, and the station is probably Aspatria or, rather less likely, Wigton. This is just outside the Lake District proper, as also is the setting of Freeman Wills Crofts's short story 'The Mystery of the Sleeping Car Express'; the body is discovered as the train comes to a halt in 'the wild moorland country of the Westmorland highlands', in fact, at Shap Summit, as we learn later.

A.E.W. Mason's first novel was *A Romance of Wastdale* (1895), a sad little tale presenting a romantic triangle that culminates in one of the two men murdering the other on Scafell. This is remarkable principally for its mountain descriptions, to which Mason, himself a keen climber, was to return in two later crime novels, *Running Water* (1907) and, briefly, *The House of the Arrow* (1924), though his descriptions in these are of Alpine mountains. Mason had spent holidays in Wastdale when an undergraduate at Oxford. Gwen Moffat's much more recent *A Short Time to Live* (1976) is set in Lakeland in November – very much the close season – and features Moffat's usual sleuth, the awesome Melinda Pink, who, like her creator, is a rock climber.

Dorothy L. Sayers's Lord Peter Wimsey twice visits what is now Cumbria in the course of his investigations. He flies across the Atlantic twice with proofs of his brother's innocence of murder in *Clouds of Witness* (1926), and his plane force-lands at Whitehaven. In *The Five Red Herrings* (1931), he goes to Brough in Westmorland on the track of one of the suspect artists and eventually catches up with him in a nearby village. The artist, who is escaping from his wife rather than the police, had thought of going to 'the Lake Country [to] paint little pictures for tourists.... It's fearfully easy. You can knock off two or three in a day – hills and water and mists, you know – and idiots will give you ten bob a time, if the stuff's sentimental enough.' Instead, he plumps for painting inn signs. In the slightly earlier *Strong Poison* (1930), Wimsey sends his assistant, Miss Katherine Climpson, to 'Windle' in Westmorland to find a missing will. Obviously, Windle can be either Kendal or Windermere. Both are on the same railway line, to reach which necessitates a change at Preston (as Miss Climpson does). Wimsey says Windle has a boot factory and a rather good view. Both Kendal and Windermere might be said to enjoy a good view, but only Kendal has a boot factory. Miss Climpson tracks down the will, and although she does some bus riding, she has no time for the scenery.

There are two novels that include an exciting chase across Cumbria. In Reginald Hill's *Fell of Dark* (1971), the viewpoint character is a man whose marriage is on the point of breaking up. He takes a holiday in the Lakes with a (male) friend; a pleasant chance encounter with two young women turns sour when they are later found murdered – and he is then on the run. The topographical detail, as in Mason's book mentioned earlier, seems perfect, and there is a reference to the delightful miniature railway that runs between Ravenglass and Eskdale. 'Ravenhaven', an obvious conflation of Ravenglass and Whitehaven, figures in Macdonald Hastings's (1909–1982) *Cork on the Telly* (1966). Valuable jewels are stolen from a television studio; the elderly insurance executive Montague Cork goes in pursuit, taking a night express to Ravenhaven, the point of departure for a breathless and ultimately successful pursuit across the snowbound fells. This may not be the best of Hastings's five Cork novels, but the tale is told with an infectious zest.

More recently, Robert **Richardson**'s *The Book of the Dead* (1989) features his usual series character, writer Augustus Maltravers, a murdered solicitor, an unpublished Sherlock Holmes story and (as in Reginald Hill's story mentioned above) some very carefully delineated Lakeland scenery. In H.C. Bailey's (1878–1961) short story 'The Dead Leaves' from *Clue for Mr Fortune* (1936), a visit to the Lakes, here charmingly evoked, is necessary for the voluble Reggie to solve the murder of a woman whose body was found in Richmond Park – Buttermere, Crummock Water and, by association, Ullswater figure prominently. Melvyn Bragg (b.1939) explored a real-life historical murder in *The Maid of Buttermere* (1987). Ullswater also features in the more recent *A Christmas Visitor* (2006), by Anne **Perry**. And John Bude's *The Lake District Murder* (1935) is one of a series of topographical mysteries by this author, who also covers Sussex, Cornwall and other picturesque areas.

Climbing in the Lake District is the background for Joanna Cannan's (1898–1961) *The Body in the Beck* (1952). And Martin **Edwards** has recently deserted his Liverpool settings for the Lakes, which he describes idiomatically and evocatively, in a series of well-plotted mysteries starting with *The Coffin Trail* (2004) and continuing with *The Cipher Garden* (2005) and *The Arsenic Labyrinth* (2007).

Shifting the remit a touch, it is possible to include a setting in Lunesdale in North Lancashire, stretching from Morecambe Bay to just east of Kendal. In E.C.R. **Lorac**'s *Fell Murder* (1944), Chief Inspector Macdonald of Scotland Yard is presented with a case in that area and likes it so much that he fancies buying a farm there for his retirement. In *Crook O'Lune* (1953), he is in Lunesdale again, negotiating for the purchase of the farm, but is diverted by another murder. He finally achieves his aim at the end of his last recorded case, *Dishonour among Thieves* (1959).

The Peak District, an area not dissimilar in size and beauty of scenery to the Lakes, and also a national park, has less in the way of a general literary tradition than the Lake District. There is the playwright L. du Garde Peach (1890–1974), writer of over 400 plays, many of them of local interest, and there are some literary associations of the area with Jane Austen and Charlotte Brontë. The 'straight' novels of Robert Murray Gilchrist (1868–1917) and the 132 racing novels of Nat Gould (1857–1922), both men Peak-born, are now forgotten, though not the children's books of Alison Uttley.

The first fictional murder in the area was that of the unfortunate German master Herr Heidegger, in Conan Doyle's Sherlock Holmes tale 'The Priory School'. The school is said to be situated in the 'cold bracing atmosphere of the Peak County' (in the story it is only mid-May), which Holmes finds 'invigorating and pleasant'. It is apparently 'near Mackleton', which could be either Macclesfield or Congleton, either of which could then be reached by train from Euston, from which London terminus Holmes and Watson set out; Macclesfield is more probable than Congleton, as it is rather nearer the Peak. Doyle's topography is typically vague, with only two real place names being mentioned: Chesterfield, where the murderer was apprehended, and Hallamshire, in which 'Holdernesse Hall' is supposedly situated – which is that part of South Yorkshire around Sheffield and immediately adjacent to the Derbyshire border. In no way can we match Macclesfield and the real Hallamshire with the respective positions of the Priory School and the Hall as shown on Doyle's sketch map, so for a seeker after geographical precision, some mental adjustments and allowances are necessary. For all that, the story is ingenious and exciting, one of Doyle's best.

John Buxton Hilton (1921–1986) set several of his detective novels in the Peak District, unsurprisingly so as he was born in the spa town that furnishes his middle name. One of these novels is *Passion in the Peak* (1985), whose setting is a projected musical production of the Passion of Christ – a kind of updated Oberammergau – in the village of Peak Low, the 'least heard of the triple villages of Peak Dale, Peak Forest and Peak Low' (it is the 'least heard' because it is fictitious; the other two are real), which may possibly be the real Doveholes. At first, the trouble consists of minor hassles aimed at the show's successive Mary Magdalenes, but then the dissolute superannuated rock singer playing Christ is done away with. Police and private detectives combine uneasily to unearth the real culprit. There is not much scenery, and the show never achieves a public performance, but there are plenty of odd characters. Other novels by Hilton set in North Derbyshire are *The Anathema Stone* (1980) – which, like *Passion in the Peak*, features Superintendent (or ex-Superintendent) Kenworthy – and the historical detective novels *Gamekeeper's Gallows* (1977), *Rescue from the Rose* (1976), *Dead Nettle* (1977), *Mr Fred* (1983), *The Quiet Stranger* (1985) and *Slickensides* (1987), all featuring Inspector Brunt, a late Victorian officer of the Derbyshire Constabulary. *Some Run Crocked* (1978), a Kenworthy novel, has a modern setting but involves consideration of 'historical' Peakland murders. Hilton was an uneven writer, but his Derbyshire books ranked among his best.

Ivon Baker's (b.1928) *Peak Performance* (1976) is a rather unfocused tale of Second World War prisoners of war, murder and inheritance. Gwen Moffat's (b.1924) *Deviant Death* (1973), an early pre–Miss Pink effort, is set in the Derbyshire Dales – near enough to the Peak. *The Broken Jigsaw* (1961) by Paul Somers, otherwise Andrew **Garve** (and whose real name was Paul Winterton), involves one of the great reservoirs of the Peak, Ladybower or Derwent. A murderer, an unscrupulous former police officer, disposes of a body, safely as he thinks, by burying it under the reservoir bed, but a drought causes the water levels to recede dramatically – as happened at Ladybower and Derwent during the hot summer of 1959 and in the equally halcyon one of 1989 – and thus reveal evidence of the disposal. The jigsaw of the title relates, of course, to the patterns of a dried-up reservoir bed. In Somers's earlier *The Shivering Mountain* (1959), whose hero is a young journalist, the 'shivering mountain' is Mam Tor. There is also John Sherwood's (1913–2002) *Green Trigger Fingers* (1984), for although its basic setting is in the Home Counties, Sherwood's series investigator Celia Grant visits 'Melsingham Hall' in Derbyshire as part of her botanical researches. Melsingham may be Chatsworth House in disguise.

More recent titles include Michael O'Donnell's *The Long Walk Home* (1988), which tells of an MoD scientist, suffering from amnesia, 'on the run' in the area. Others include Aline Templeton's *Shades of Death* (2001); *Night Angels* (2001) by Danuta Reah, which visits the (real) Snake Pass; and Val McDermid's *A Place of Execution* (1999). Since his debut with *Black Dog* (2000), Stephen **Booth** has made the Peak District (and maybe the adjoining areas of Yorkshire moorland) his own in titles such as *One Last Breath* (2004) and *Dancing with the Virgins* (2001).

Yorkshire

Crime fiction stimulatingly reflects the infinite variety of Yorkshire: its industrial cities, country towns and villages, its people, sometimes grim but often warm-hearted, its pastimes, even its weather. Not all the classic detectives of fiction penetrated so far north, but the county has inspired writers from the mid-nineteenth century onwards. Charles Dickens's *Nicholas Nickleby* (1839) ranks as a mystery, if not quite as a crime novel, and no one will need reminding that the infamous Dotheboys Hall was in Yorkshire, near Greta Bridge. And there is of course Bram Stoker's *Dracula* (1897), greatest of vampire thrillers, set in Whitby.

The Shires: Rural England and Regional Crime Fiction

Yorkshire is the largest county in England with, so it is said, more acres than there are words in the Bible. Whatever the truth of this assertion, Yorkshire contains plenty of acreage in which to commit crime, a fact exploited by many crime writers from the time of Charles Dickens and Wilkie Collins onwards. Well over half of Collins's classic novel *The Moonstone* (1868) takes place in the county: 'Our house is high up on the Yorkshire coast, and close by the sea. We have got beautiful walks all round us, in every direction but one [which]…leads for a quarter of a mile through a melancholy plantation of firs and brings you out between low cliffs on the loneliest and ugliest little bay on all our coast.' 'Frizinghall', the nearby town, could be Scarborough. As for the local fishing village, 'Cobb's Hole', this sounds a little like Robin Hood's Bay – but Cayton Bay would be nearer Scarborough and is within walking distance of it as 'Frizinghall' is of the Verinders's house. The stormy weather so common on the Yorkshire coast is exemplified in the novel, which, though not perhaps the first English detective novel as has been asserted, is surely the first 'country house' English detective novel. In his earlier novel, *No Name* (1862), Collins had briefly but effectively recalled the bustle of the old, pre-1877 railway station at York.

Wilkie Collins was not born in Yorkshire, but a considerable number of crime writers were: Catherine Aird (Huddersfield), Phyllis Bentley (Halifax, 1894–1977; for her short stories featuring the elderly spinster Miss Phipps), John **Bingham** (York), Jocelyn Davey (Middlesbrough, 1908–1994), Lionel **Davidson** (Hull, b.1922), Francis Durbridge (also Hull, 1912–1998), J.S. Fletcher (Halifax), Reg **Gadney** (Cross Hills), Stanley Hyland (Shipley, 1914–1997), Mark **Hebden** (Rotherham), E.W. **Hornung** (Middlesbrough), Michael Kenyon (Huddersfield, b.1931), C.H.B. Kitchin (Harrogate, 1895–1967), Duncan Kyle (Bradford), Gil North (Skipton, 1916–1988), J.B. **Priestley** (Bradford, 1894–1984), Angus Ross (Dewsbury, b.1927), John **Wainwright** (Leeds, 1921–1995), Arthur Wise (York, 1923–1983) and Sara Woods (Bradford, 1922–1985). Few of these lived, or live, in the county during their adult lives, though some of them at least went to school in Yorkshire, and the writings, crime and non-crime, of at least three – Fletcher, Priestley and Woods – often featured Yorkshire backgrounds. Against that, two present-day crime authors – Robert **Barnard** and Reginald Hill, neither of them Yorkshire born – have lived for substantial periods in the county (Barnard in Leeds and Hill in Doncaster between 1967 and 1988, where he was for many years a lecturer at the College of Education, though he has now moved to Cumbria). Other authors with Yorkshire associations are Patricia **Hall**, born and educated in the county, and Stephen Murray, who until recently lived in Knaresborough. The former's *Poison Pool* (1991), her first novel, has a Yorkshire locale.

An archetypal Yorkshire writer was, notably, Phyllis Bentley. It is worth recalling that her industrial saga *Inheritance* (1931) began with the murder, in 1812, by Luddites of a mill owner – an incident mirrored in real life. Bentley created a Miss Marple-type sleuth, Marian Phipps, but she appeared only in short stories.

Returning to the classic detective writers, it is clear that not many of these often visited Yorkshire in their writings. Conan Doyle's Sherlock Holmes, for all that William Baring-Gould's 'biography' credited him with a North Riding birthplace, gets no nearer to it than the mention of Hallamshire in 'The Adventure of the Priory School', and, also in *The Return of Sherlock Holmes* (1905), a reference to Doncaster race course grandstand in 'The Six Napoleons'. Dr Thorndyke, Dr Reggie Fortune and Father Brown did not manage even that, nor, despite the Yorkshire provenance of his creator, did Raffles. Father Brown, however, solved the mystery of 'The

Oracle of the Dog', from *The Incredulity of Father Brown* (1926), which happened at a fictitious place on the Yorkshire coast, from a distance. Agatha Christie's one and only Yorkshire locale is again Doncaster, for a few chapters of *The ABC Murders* (1936) in which the St Leger is alluded to, but the descriptions of the town are sadly unidiomatic. Audrey Williamson's (1913–1986) *Death of a Theatre Filly* (1980) also reaches its climax at the St Leger meeting, but Miss Williamson should have known that by 1980, the St Leger had long since ceased to be run on a Wednesday.

John Dickson Carr's Gideon Fell is said in *Hag's Nook* (1933) to live in the neighbouring county of Lincolnshire, but he is rarely seen so far north in subsequent books, and Sir Henry Merrivale never is. 'Fairacres', near Doncaster, is fleetingly mentioned near the end of Carr's mid-Victorian novel *Scandal at High Chimneys* (1959), but it is difficult to identify Fairacres as a district or village on a real map of the area. Freeman Wills Crofts twice used Yorkshire as a setting: the first is the moorland country near 'Thirsby' (which sounds like Thirsk, but since French leaves London from St Pancras and changes at Hellifield, it cannot be) in *Inspector French and the Starvel Tragedy* (1927), the Scotland Yard man's third recorded case, and the second is Hull and the Humber estuary in *The Pit-Prop Syndicate* (1922), one of Crofts's finest efforts – it is pre-French, of course, but Inspector Willis is just as tenacious and thorough as his more famous successor.

Dorothy L. Sayers taught in Hull for a year or so in 1916/1917. Her Yorkshire residence emerged in one short story, 'Suspicion' (an engaging domestic poisoning tale set indeed in Hull, written in 1933 and collected in book form in *In the Teeth of the Evidence*, 1939), and one novel, *Clouds of Witness* (1926). The murder (for which Wimsey's brother is tried in the House of Lords) takes place in 'Riddlesdale', which is probably either Wensleydale or Swaledale – more likely the latter – with Riddlesdale village being Reeth. But Sayers's descriptions do not evoke the Yorkshire Dales particularly well. York is visited briefly as the duke is held there awaiting trial and Lord Peter has to dodge into the minster to avoid a press reporter, but he has to go to Paris and New York for his solution.

Returning to native Yorkshire crime writers, Catherine Aird's 'Calleshire', a composite county, owes only a little to Yorkshire, while none of the books of John Bingham, Jocelyn Davey or Lionel **Davidson** have a Yorkshire setting. Francis Durbridge was at least educated in the county, at Bradford Grammar School, and his books and radio plays featuring Paul Temple and others are so legion that somewhere or other, Yorkshire must get a mention; *The World of Tim Frazer* (1962) features the county while *Paul Temple and the Curzon Case* (1971) is certainly set near Whitby at 'Dulworth Bay' (perhaps Robin Hood's Bay, though Durbridge's topography and his railway history are both rather flexible).

J.S. Fletcher is strong in Yorkshire allusions; although he left Yorkshire to live in southern England later in life, he kept in touch with his roots. Crime stories set in the county include *Scarhaven Keep* (1920; 'Scarhaven' is Scarborough and figures in other Fletcher stories), *False Scent* (1924), *The Yorkshire Moorland Murder* (1930), *The House in Tuesday Market* (1930; whose location is Beverley) and many of the short stories. Perhaps the best of Fletcher's series detectives is Archer Dawe, an elderly Yorkshireman who dresses in 'an antique frock-coat and trousers made too short to reach the top of his shoes'. Reg **Gadney**'s **espionage** thrillers and Mark **Hebden**'s detective stories featuring Inspector Pel do not inhabit a Yorkshire ambience (Pel is French, of course), but the second of Stanley Hyland's unusual and very literate detective novels, *Green Grow the Tresses-O* (1965), is set in the county against a background of textile manufacture.

Michael Kenyon visits Yorkshire only occasionally, and J.B. Priestley's most overt crime works, *Blackout in Gretley* (1942) and *Salt Is Leaving* (1966), both have vaguely North Midland urban, rather than specifically Yorkshire, settings. It is, however, otherwise with the works of John Wainwright, Gil North and Angus Ross. Many of Wainwright's often starkly realistic and inelegantly written novels – and there are over sixty – are set in northern cities (Wainwright served in the West Riding Constabulary for over twenty years) or in adjacent county areas. One of his series police investigators, Charles Ripley, has an archetypal Yorkshire surname. Gil North's Sergeant Cluff books are basically rural in setting ('Gunnershaw' is fictitious but may be Skipton where North was born and where, after colonial service, he returned to live). Angus Ross specialises in espionage novels, and it is pleasing to see that some of them are set in Yorkshire rather than the more exotic climes so often used as spy backgrounds. Examples are *The Huddersfield Job* (1971), *The Bradford Business* (1974) and *The Leeds Fiasco* (1975); at least three others have North Country settings.

Sara Woods's long series of detective stories with a legal background contain many references to her native county, although she did not begin writing until she emigrated to Canada well after the Second World War. Antony Maitland, her barrister series detective, was involved in counter-espionage activity in Yorkshire during the war. He has a friend, a farmer in the Dales, whom he visits from time to time, notably in *They Love Not Poison* (1972), set in snowbound, austerity-ridden 1947 with overtones of witchcraft, Civil War history and buried treasure. Other Maitland cases happen in the Yorkshire mill city of 'Arkenshaw' (perhaps a cross between Woods's native Bradford and nearby Leeds) – for example *And Shame the Devil* (1967), *Serpent's Tooth* (1971), *A Show of Violence* (1975) and *Murder's Out of Tune* (1984) – or in the nearby village of 'Burton Cecil', like *Done to Death* (1964) and *Nor Live So Long* (1986), which gives a new twist to the expression 'sex murderer'.

Reginald Hill's Dalziel/Pascoe novels have an undoubted Yorkshire flavour and are perhaps set in the south east of the county near its borders with Lincolnshire and Nottinghamshire. This would suggest Doncaster, where Hill lived and taught for so many years, but there is no strong topographical detail that would confirm this identification. *Bones and Silence* (1990) introduces a 'Mid-Yorkshire' Mystery Play (Wakefield and York have real Mystery Play cycles). Its predecessor, *Under World* (1988), had the miners' strike of 1984–1985 as a backdrop. *On Beulah Heights* (1998) visited the Mid-Yorkshire Dales Summer Music Festival – there are several real music festivals in the dales.

Robert **Barnard** has set several of his novels in Yorkshire, of which *Blood Brotherhood* (1977), set in an Anglican community on the Yorkshire moors, was the first. More recent examples include *A Fatal Attachment* (1992), *A Gathering of Vultures* (1993), *No Place of Safety* (1997), *The Corpse at the Haworth Tandoori* (1998), *Unholy Dying* (2000; set in a Leeds religious community), *The Bones in the Attic* (2001) and *The Mistress of Alderley* (2003; with its operatic background, doubtless inspired by the real-life achievements of Opera North). Barnard's Perry Trethowan book, *The Missing Brontë* (1983), is an entertaining read with several quirky characters, mostly academics. The thought of a 'missing' Brontë manuscript is about as heady as a 'lost' Shakespeare manuscript, which has formed the basis for at least one detective novel (Edmund **Crispin**'s *Love Lies Bleeding*, 1948). Even better is *The Disposal of the Living*

(1985), set in a Yorkshire country town, 'Hexton-on-Weir', which may have something in common with Richmond and seen from the standpoint of the vicarage. Unlike a classic Golden Age whodunit, the social undercurrents are observed with sharp brilliance. There are mentions of cricket and choral music, two things Yorkshiremen like to think they are good at. *Political Suicide* (1986) mostly takes place in a (rather sleazy) South Yorkshire parliamentary constituency during a by-election. Is the death of the previous MP (in London) suicide or murder, and, if it is the latter, is one of the by-election candidates guilty? A police officer on the brink of retirement carries out the investigation, but the dénouement is inconclusive. Latterly, Barnard has given considerable exposure to Charlie Peace, a Yorkshire detective officer, most recently in *A Fall from Grace* (2007). A snap comparison of Hill and Barnard suggests that the former is more realistic, the latter the more entertaining.

Also realistic is the work of Maurice Procter (1903–1973), who was born in Lancashire, but served for some twenty years in the one-time Halifax Borough Police. With his DCI Harry Martineau novels, Procter may be the earliest British exponent of the 'police procedural' – but the Yorkshire milieu of the Martineau novels is not definitely established ('Grantchester' could well be Manchester), though the 'Yoreborough' of his Superintendent Hunter tales, *The Chief Inspector's Statement* (1951) and *I Will Speak Daggers* (1956), may perhaps be York. Another crime writer who was born in Lancashire but made her living in Yorkshire (as a journalist of the *Yorkshire Evening Press*) was Osmington Mills (1922–2003), whose *Stairway to Murder* (1959) is set in a snowbound Pennine hotel. Alan Sewart (1928–1998) was a Lancashire man but his *Drink! For Once Dead* (1983) has a Yorkshire setting.

Three sporting titles deserve mention. Douglas Clark's (1919–1982) novels featuring the Scotland Yard team led by Detective Chief Superintendent George Masters mostly take place in the south of England, though two (***Performance***, 1985, and *Plain Sailing*, 1987) are set in Northumbria and *The Libertines* (1978) has as its background a club cricket festival in the Yorkshire Dales; it is as readable as any of Clark's carefully plotted volumes. Nancy Spain's (1917–1964) *Death before Wicket* (1945), another novel with a cricket theme, takes place in a girls' private school in Yorkshire; the bitchy gym mistress is the victim. Brian Ball's *Death of a Low-Handicap Man* (1974) is set in a South Yorkshire golf club; the murder is, unlike those in Douglas Clark's books, investigated by the local force with a police constable member of the club prominent.

In Ivon Baker's *Death and Variations* (1977), the undercover hero, who is guarding the teenage daughter of a US politician against a feared kidnap attempt, lands from America with his charge at Royal Air Force Finningley, which was near Doncaster and just, if only just, in Yorkshire; his later adventures, nothing to do with his primary task, take place further south. Still another novel set in the Dales country is *A Dedicated Man* (1988) by Peter **Robinson**, born in Yorkshire, but now living in Canada; the venue is 'Helmthorpe', whose name argues for a location in the area north east of York, though such semantic arguments are, as we have seen, often unsafe. Dan Lees's *The Rainbow Conspiracy* (1972) is a PI tale built around two Yorkshire murders tied in with the Great Train Robbery. *Murderous Justice* (1991), television producer Steve Haywood's debut book, is largely set on the Yorkshire moors.

The moors, which are not always clearly defined, are popular among authors: those who have visited them include Jeremy Dronfield (*The Locust Farm*, 1998), Maureen

The Shires: Rural England and Regional Crime Fiction

Peters (*Goodbye Holly Jane*, 2001), Sally Spencer (*Death of an Innocent*, 2002), Alison Taylor (*Unsafe Convictions*, 1999) and Gillian **Linscott** (*Dead Man's Music*, 1996). Some of these were doubtless inspired by real-life tragedies in that area. The North York Moors are – understandably, in view of their dramatic scenery – also favourites with authors and readers: Graham Thomas's *Malice on the Moors* (1999) and Peter Robinson's seven police novels featuring DCI Alan Banks – *Caedmon's Song* is set around Whitby, as of course are Nicholas **Rhea**'s books based on television's police/soap opera hybrid *Heartbeat*.

Joan **Aiken**'s rather **Gothic** brand of crime story is perhaps not unsuited to a Yorkshire rural setting, and we may point to two such: her first crime novel, *The Silence of Herondale* (1965), and the later *The Embroidered Sunset* (1970). In the former, 'Herondale' is remote, reached by a branch line train from Leeds and then a country bus; the weather is very cold! The latter features a pianist heroine and allusions to the Brontës; the setting veers between the moorland village of 'Appleby-under-Scar' and a fishing village which sounds a little like Staithes, though the topography hardly seems very precise. Curiously, as in Sayers's *Clouds of Witness*, York Minster's famous window is mistakenly called the Seven Sisters, but the minster scaffolding mentioned here was real enough in 1970. John Trench's *Docken Dead* (1953), the first appearance of archaeologist detective Martin Cotterell, is another Yorkshire story – the first of Trench's four detective stories, this has all the zest and freshness of a first novel. John Freeman Fairfax-Blakeborough (1883–1978), a Yorkshireman, wrote mainly about horse-racing, but his few crime novels include *The Disappearance of Cropton* (1933) set in the Thirsk/Ripon area. Alan Plater's humorous story *The Biederbecke Connection* (1992) also has a Yorkshire setting.

Mention must also be made of John Greenwood's six Mr Mosley books published between 1983 and 1987: *Murder, Mr Mosley*; *Mosley by Moonlight*; *Mosley Went to Mow*; *Mists Over Mosley*; *The Mind of Mr Mosley*; and *What Me, Mr Mosley?* Mr Mosley is a detective inspector, stationed in the moorland country on the Yorkshire–Lancashire border, an unorthodox officer, who causes headaches for his superiors but who gets results. Greenwood was John Buxton Hilton's pseudonym, many of whose novels under his own name were set in the present day or during the last century, in the adjacent county, Derbyshire, where he was born. The Greenwood novels afford a genuine, well-observed Yorkshire atmosphere and have an engaging humour.

Andrew **Garve** was catholic in the settings of his highly readable crime thrillers, and it took him a while to get round to Yorkshire, but he finally did so in *Counterstroke* (1978), set in the Pennines. A woman is kidnapped, against the liberation of a villain 'doing time'. An actor, made up to look like him and carefully coached in the part, is duly exchanged, but how can he survive for more than a few minutes before the gang discovers the imposture? Luck and some typically fierce and stormy Pennine weather come to his assistance.

J.R.L. Anderson's *Death in the North Sea* (1975) features Lincolnshire and a North Sea oil rig, apparently threatened with sabotage by a terrorist organisation, rather than Yorkshire, but Anderson's resourceful soldier/policeman Colonel Blair, in the course of his inquiries, visits 'Seathorpe', a fictitious, unattractive new town on the coast half-way between Hull and Bridlington, and also goes to Bridlington itself, where he buys an old Yorkshire coble which plays a part in the exciting dénouement.

York is popular as a setting with crime writers, whether their mysteries are historical ones like Barbara Whitehead's (b.1930) *The Killing at Barley Hall* (1995) and Paul **Doherty**'s *Satan's Fire* (1995) or more modern ones such as Whitehead's *Sweet Death Come Softly* (1992), whose background is one of those sweet and chocolate factories that once abounded in the city; David Bowker, *The Death Prayer* (1995); Peter Turnbull (b.1950), *Embracing Skeletons* (1996), *Treasure Trove* (2003) and *Chill Factor* (2005); and John **Baker** (b.1942), *Poet in the Gutter* (1995) and *King of the Streets* (1998). Whitehead, Bowker and Baker (at least) were York residents and not always did they focus on York's heritage and tourist aspects. Barbara Whitehead, born in Sheffield, wrote *Playing God* (1988), whose action takes place in York during the rehearsals and performances of that city's famous cycle of Mystery Plays. There is widespread resentment that a pop star has been chosen to play Christ and a number of accidents disrupt the rehearsals. Finally, the director is stabbed at the dress rehearsal. But why? The atmosphere of the city and the plays is well conveyed. In Whitehead's later *The Girl with Red Suspenders* (1990), also set in York, an off-duty detective inspector finds a dead girl. When murder is eventually confirmed, the case turns out to be bound up with drug distribution in the York area via the river Ouse from Goole. Again the atmosphere is well conveyed, and the climax, on a river boat, is exciting.

As previously mentioned, many of Robert **Barnard**'s books take the Leeds/ Bradford area as their inspiration. Others include Stuart **Pawson**'s police novels featuring Inspector Charlie Priest of 'Heckley' (Heckmondwike/Batley), Pauline **Bell**'s police series, Christian Thompson's *Sing No Sad Songs* (2004, Bradford), Lesley **Horton**'s *Snares of Guilt* (2002) and *On Dangerous Ground* (2003), John **Connor**'s *A Child's Game* (2006, Leeds), Richard Haley's novels which include *When Beggars Die* (1996) featuring a Bradford PI, and Patricia **Hall**'s considerable corpus of novels, from *The Poison Pool* (1991) onwards – her later books feature 'Bradfield' which is, perhaps, Bradford rather than Sheffield. Sheffield does much less well than Bradford or Leeds, though Danuta Reah's *Bleak Water*, set beside the Sheffield Canal, is an exception. However, Hull is a popular venue with authors including Barbara Deighton (*Good Intentions*, 1988), John Baker (*The Chinese Girl*, 2000, set in the docks), Danuta Reah (*Night Angels*, 2001) and Robert **Edric** (*Cradle Song*, 2001).

South and East Midlands

The South and East Midlands cover the counties of Derbyshire, Nottinghamshire, Leicestershire, Northamptonshire, Rutland, Bedfordshire, Buckinghamshire, Hertfordshire, Berkshire and Oxfordshire: a large area and, viewed as a whole, rather inchoate, even anonymous. At one end, it borders on Greater London; at the other, on the northern counties of Lancashire and Yorkshire. Many provincial English settings in fictional crime, such as E.R. Punshon's (1872–1956) 'Wychshire' (anonymous by its very title), where Bobby Owen often operates, are probably somewhere in this residual area, but there is often little to identify them more precisely. Nottinghamshire, the county of D.H. Lawrence, is particularly poorly covered, exceptions being John **Harvey**'s and Keith Wright's recent police novels set in the City of Nottingham and the novels of Stella Shepherd. Titles by John Harvey (who was a Nottingham resident) include *Lonely Hearts* (1989), *Cutting Edge* (1991), *Wasted Years* (1993) and *Living Proof* (1995), all featuring Detective Inspector Charlie Resnick. From Leicestershire there is Christine Green's *Deadly Errand* (1991), in which a Loughborough nurse is murdered, and a group of **police procedurals** set in Leicester: Frank Palmer's (1993–2000) *Testimony* (1992), *Bent Grasses* (1993),

Unfit to Plead (1992), *Blood Brother* (1993), *Night Watch* (1994), *Double Exposure* (1995) and *Dead Man's Handle* (1995), all featuring Detective Inspector 'Jacko' Jackson.

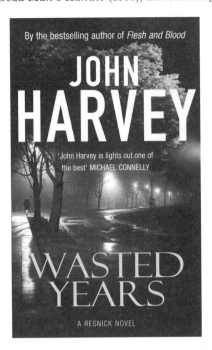

89. Cover of John Harvey's *Wasted Years* (1993), a Charlie Resnick story set in Nottingham, in the Midlands.

Further south, though, we have Oxfordshire and, specifically, the city and University of Oxford. Oxford fictional crime features even in the Middle Ages, with Ian **Morson**'s *Falconer's Crusade* (1994) and *Falconer's Judgement* (1995). Several Oxford dons have been notable writers in the crime field, including Michael **Innes** (J.I.M. Stewart), whose *Operation Pax* (1955), *Hare Sitting Up* (1959) and his debut, *Death at the President's Lodging* (1936), are all set in Oxford, more or less. (The latter is supposedly impartial in location in that the setting could be either Oxford or Cambridge, but it has more of the former.) Innes's detective creation, Sir John Appleby, is himself an Oxford graduate. G.D.H. (George Douglas Howard) Cole, another Oxford don, wrote many detective stories from 1923 onwards in collaboration with his wife Margaret – who, however, went to Cambridge University – of which *Off with Her Head* (1938) is an Oxford case for Superintendent Wilson. J.C. Masterman, sometime Provost of Worcester College and an Oxford don for sixty-four years prior to his death in 1977, penned *An Oxford Tragedy* (1933), plausible in plot and evocative in its senior common room background, and the 'diversion in pre-detection', *The Case of the Four Friends* (1951), which is indeed diverting but just a little too neat to be wholly satisfying. It is only an 'Oxford' tale because it is told in (the fictional) St Thomas' College's senior common room.

Fictional dons figure as detectives, the most truly memorable being Edmund Crispin's (Bruce Montgomery's) Gervase Fen, of 'St Christopher's' College (an English don like his Cambridge counterpart Dr Davie), who is thrice seen on home ground: in *The Case of the Gilded Fly* (1944); in that glorious romp *The Moving Toyshop* (1946); and in *Swan Song* (1947), which is set against the background of a professional production of Wagner's opera *Die Meistersinger* in the city. Anthony Lejeune's (b.1928) Professor Glowray is another don investigator. *Professor in Peril* (1987) climaxes in Oxford after stirring events in Brazil and South Carolina; *Key without a Door* (1988) is another investigation featuring him. Still another Oxford don sleuth is Jocelyn Davey's Ambrose Usher; philosophy is his subject and he is erudite yet light in touch in books such as *The Naked Villainy* (1952) and *A Touch of Stagefright* (1960). Oxford plays little part in Davey's books, though. Nor does it play a big part in Sarah **Caudwell**'s books about Professor Hilary Tamar, a legal history don of 'St George's College' and the detective protagonist of *Thus Was Adonis Murdered* (1983), *The Shortest Way to Hades* (1984) and *The Sirens Sang of Murder* (1989).

Adam Broome's (1888–1963) *The Oxford Murders* (1929) is an impartial counterweight to the same author's *The Cambridge Murders* (1936) and is possibly the first detective novel set in Oxford. Another early example is M. Doriel Hay's *Death on the Cherwell* (1935). Victor Whitechurch, later chaplain to the Bishop of Oxford, set his *Murder in the College* (1932) in 'Exbridge', a university which is clearly Oxford, albeit not strongly characterised, as there are references to 'scouts' and 'quads'. Gwendoline Butler's Inspector John Coffin visited Oxford in *Death Lives Next Door* (1960) and *Coffin in Oxford* (1962). *A Coffin for Pandora* (1973), notwithstanding the title, does not feature him but is set in the Oxford of a century ago. Katherine Farrer (1911–1972) wrote *The Missing Link* (1952), *Gownsman's Gallows* (1957) and *At Odds with Morning* (1960), all set, in whole or in part, in Oxford. Dermot Morrah's (1896–1974) *The Mummy Case Mystery* (1933) has archaeological overtones, and Robert Robinson's (b.1929) *Landscape with Dead Dons* (1956) has a pleasingly light touch. One may also point to Julian Maclaren-Ross's (1912–1964) *Until the Day She Died* (1960) and Raymond Postgate's (1896–1971) realistic *The Ledger Is Kept* (1953). Margaret Yorke's *Dead in the Morning* (1970), *Silent Witness* (1972), *Grave Matters* (1973), *Mortal Remains* (1974) and *Cast for Death* (1976) feature English literature don Patrick Grant, whose college is 'St Mark's', which 'lurked in obscurity at the end of a cobbled street'. Anthony **Price**'s (b.1928) counter-espionage thriller *Colonel Butler's Wolf* (1972) and Jonathan Gray's *Untimely Slain* (1948), another spy tale, both take place in Oxford, as does David Frome's *Body in the Turl* (1935), featuring Evan Pinkerton. *Where Scholars Fall* (1961) by Timothy Robinson (b.1934) is a pleasing take-off where the detection is done by three undergraduates of 'St Saviour's College', Janet **Neel**'s *Death among the Dons* (1993) is set in 'Gladstone College', and Robert Bernard's (b.1918) *Death Takes the Last Train* (1968) encompasses Woodstock and Blenheim as well as Oxford itself. (Robert Bernard is not to be confused with Robert **Barnard**, who has set novels in various universities at home and abroad, but not so far in Oxford; though it does figure briefly in *The Skeleton in the Grass*, 1987. Barnard's wickedly amusing short story 'The Oxford Way of Death' – collected in *Death of a Salesperson*, 1989 – is his only true venture into the university so far.)

Michael **Dibdin**'s *Dirty Tricks* (1991), set in the Oxford of the 1980s, has a very apposite title; it is told in the first person by an English teacher. Hazel Holt's (b.1928) *The Cruellest Month* (1991) tells of a death in the Bodleian Library, visits the Parks cricket ground, alludes to Dorothy L. Sayers's *Gaudy Night* (1935) and even refers to a real event of the Dorothy L. Sayers Society held in Balliol College in 1990. Antonia **Fraser**'s *Oxford Blood* (1985) has Jemima Shore, television investigator, exploring – in more ways than one – the gilded youth of Oxford and incidentally solving two murders and several attempted murders. Jemima's first full-length case, *Quiet as a Nun* (1977) is another Oxford one. Jeffrey Archer visited Oxford for *Not a Penny More, Not a Penny Less* (1976) and Veronica **Stallwood**'s *Death and the*

The Shires: Rural England and Regional Crime Fiction

Oxford Box (1993), *Oxford Exit* (1994), *Oxford Mourning* (1995) and *Oxford Fall* (1996) provide a series of fictional Oxford crime mysteries. The action of Father Ronald **Knox**'s *The Footsteps at the Lock* (1928), probably his best-known crime book, takes place on the upper reaches of the river Thames, but as one of the two canoeist cousins who are the main protagonists is an Oxford undergraduate, the city is inevitably visited in the course of the novel. G.K. Chesterton's Father Brown was in Oxford to solve 'The Crime of the Communist' from *The Scandal of Father Brown* (1935). David Williams's *Treasure in Oxford* (1988) is set in 'All Saint's' college during the long vacation and centres around the annual meeting of an architectural endowment trust. A local dealer is murdered; is this anything to do with his possession of sketches of Oxford attributed to John Constable? Merchant banker Mark Treasure, one of the trustees, elucidates with competent urbanity.

Four detectives who are Oxford graduates, and of differing ability, are Anthony Berkeley's (1893–1971) Roger Sheringham; Tim Heald's Board of Trade investigator Simon Bognor, who has an Oxford case in *Masterstroke* (1982) in his own college 'Simon Magus'; Conan Doyle's Sherlock Holmes, whose status as a one-time Oxford, rather than a Cambridge, undergraduate now seems to be generally established (and in 'The Creeping Man', 'Camford' is presumably Oxford as Holmes recalls the hostelry that he and Watson patronise); and Dorothy L. Sayers's Lord Peter Wimsey of Balliol. Lord Wimsey's Oxford investigation is *Gaudy Night* (1935): it is not a murder, but he has the satisfaction not only of solving the mystery but of persuading Harriet Vane, whom he has been pursuing for years, to marry him. Harriet, it appears, is also an Oxford graduate. Her college ('Shrewsbury') has asked her to sort out a tiresome problem, but in the end, she has to pass it on to Wimsey to deal with. Their wedding ceremony is solemnised in St Cross Church in Oxford at the start of *Busman's Honeymoon* (1937). Sayers's other series detective, wine salesman Monty Egg, also has an Oxford case in 'Murder at Pentecost' – 'Pentecost' being a college. If *Landscape with Dead Dons*, *The Moving Toyshop* and, perhaps, *Masterstroke* all take a light-hearted, even irreverent, view of Oxford, then *Gaudy Night* is much more exalted.

Colin **Dexter**'s Chief Inspector **Morse** has become very well known from John Thaw's memorable portrayal on television. As Morse is based in Oxford, all Dexter's novels are set in the city or its immediate hinterland. One of the most satisfying is the first of the series, *Last Bus to Woodstock* (1975), but its successors – including *Service of All the Dead* (1979), *The Dead of Jericho* (1981) and *The Wench Is Dead* (1989), among others – are all worth noting. The latter, a 'murder mystery in the past', is forcibly reminiscent of Josephine Tey's *The Daughter of Time* (1951), as Morse, like Tey's Inspector Grant, is convalescing in hospital. The university and its dons inevitably impinge in Dexter's work – the body of a don is pulled out of the Oxford Canal in *The Riddle of the Third Mile*, others are heavily involved in *Last Bus to Woodstock*, and so on – but by and large, Dexter's books are 'town' rather than 'gown'. So popular did Morse become that the television series ran out of Dexter novels to film. The 'concocted' television stories were on the whole less satisfying; however, the book *The Jewel That Was Ours* (1991) was originally a television script. *The Way through the Woods* (1992) is partly set at Blenheim Palace and comes complete with a map, while *The Daughters of Cain* (1994) returns to an Oxford college background. Dexter lives in Oxford, although he took his degree at Cambridge. Morse went to Oxford but failed to take a degree, rather like E.C.R. Lorac's Inspector Macdonald, who was up at Pembroke either side of the Great War.

John Penn's novels often have a Cotswold setting and involve visits to the City of Oxford, for example *Unto the Grave* (1986) and *A Feast of Death* (1989). Penn's *Outrageous Exposures* (1988) is more specifically an Oxford novel in which the disappearance of three girls is followed by murder. His *A Knife Ill-Used* (1991) has as its central character a woman principal of an Oxford college. Joan **Smith**'s *A Masculine Ending* (1987) visits Oxford (one – the less important – of its two female investigators is a don of an unspecified college), as do its sequels *Why Aren't They Screaming?* (1988) – in which most of the action takes place in the county of Oxfordshire near a fictitious US Air Force base – and *Don't Leave Me Like This* (1992). *What Men Say* (1993) is more specifically an Oxford city/university novel. Oxfordshire, the county, is the scene of most of Robert **Barnard**'s *The Skeleton in the Grass* (1987), and skulduggery and murder take place in rural Oxfordshire in Ann Granger's *A Touch of Mortality* (1996). Further back than either, Freeman Wills Crofts's *The End of Andrew Harrison* (1938) centres round a houseboat moored at Henley.

Oxfordshire is quite popular as the region in which crime writers were born or resident: Joanna Cannan, Gladys **Mitchell**, Dorothy L. Sayers and P.D. James were all born in or adjacent to Oxford, although Sayers and James soon moved eastwards. Baroness James's vision of the future *The Children of Men* (1992) is set in Oxford, but it is not a detective novel, nor even really a crime novel. (Sayers, though, was to become spiritually attached to Oxford from the time she took up her studies as an undergraduate at Somerville.) Mrs L.T. Meade (1854–1914), prolific writer of short stories, often with a medical flavour, lived in Oxford. Mitchell, born in Cowley, places her *Dead Men's Morris* (1936) in that very area, with Iffley and Stanton St John prominent, and *Late, Late in the Evening* (1976) probably draws on Mitchell's childhood holidays in the area. Graham **Greene**, writer of high-class thrillers like *Stamboul Train* (1932), was born in Berkhamsted. Dick **Francis** lived in Didcot and Anthony **Price** near Oxford, though his Dr David Audley is a Cambridge graduate. John Mortimer (b.1923), creator of Rumpole of the Bailey, is a Henley resident, and Anne Morice (1918–1989), creatrix of that highly intuitive actress detective Tessa Crichton (Price), also lived there. Sure enough, Morice's amusing *Murder in Outline* (1979) takes place at 'Waterside', a ballet and drama school on the banks of the Thames, midway between Oxford and Goring.

John Buchan latterly bought a house near Oxford, and after the Great War, as *The Three Hostages* (1924) and *The Island of Sheep* (1936) tell us, his hero Richard Hannay was also an Oxfordshire resident, at 'Fosse Manor'. Miles Tripp was born and educated in Hertfordshire, as was Ian Stuart, though his books are largely set elsewhere. Gwendoline **Butler** lives near Windsor, in Berkshire. Bedfordshire can point to Ritchie Perry (b.1942), who lives in Luton, and Edmund Crispin (Bruce Montgomery) was born in Chesham Bois, Buckinghamshire – which presumably means that the 'Long Fulton' film studio of *Frequent Hearses* (1950) is home territory for him: 'To all intents and purposes the studios had annihilated Long Fulton village…[but]…as a village there was little or nothing to be said in Long Fulton's favour; its architecture was uniformly undistinguished and its lack of historical and literary association such as to strike even the most resolute and exhaustive guide-books dumb' (Chapter 1). The film studios in Carter Dickson's *And So to Murder* (1941) are similarly set in Buckinghamshire and are likewise reached from London by train from Marylebone. John Trench (1920–2003) lived in Amersham, and Margaret Yorke in Aylesbury. Henry **Wade** was in the 1920s a justice of the peace and county alderman for Buckinghamshire, becoming High Sheriff in 1925, experience which doubtless furnished the background for *The Dying Alderman* (1930) and *The High Sheriff* (1937). Both are readable if not quite among Wade's best. The further north one goes in the region, the fewer associations can we point to, but Frances **Fyfield** was brought up near Chesterfield, while Bernard Newman, prolific producer of spy stories and, after the end of the Second World War, 'ordinary' mysteries, was born at Ibstock, in Leicestershire. Andrew Garve (Paul Winterton) was Leicester-born. Nottinghamshire and Northamptonshire at one time seemed relatively barren in this respect, though Jill **McGown** lived in Corby in the latter county for some years, and the four novels by Keith Wright – *One Oblique One* (1991), *Trace and Eliminate* (1992), *Addressed to Kill* (1993) and *Fair Means or Foul* (1995) – are police procedurals written by an officer in the Nottinghamshire City police and featuring Detective Inspector Stark of that force. *Fair Means or Foul* is set at Nottingham's historic Goose Fair. Furthermore, all the novels of Stella Shepherd, which include *Black Justice* (1988), *Murderous Remedy* (1989), *Nurse Dawes Is Dead* (1994) and *Embers of Death* (1996), each of them medically based and whose settings include a medical school, hospitals, general practices and a pharmacy, are set in the city or county of Nottingham.

If we consider the South Midlands counties, a large proportion of detective stories of the Golden Age (and later) that have a rural setting outside, but not too far away from London, are candidates, but so many authors are topographically vague, perhaps deliberately so, that they confer no special character on their locales. It may well be that J.J. Connington's (1880–1947) Sir Clinton Driffield is the Chief Constable of one of those counties and that authors like, taking two at random, Georgette **Heyer** and John Rhode/Miles Burton place a large proportion of their crime novels there or thereabouts. So, too, does E.R. Punshon, whose 'Wychshire' is the scene of many of his Bobby Owen novels of the wartime (1939–1945) era, but it is well-nigh impossible to place it more precisely. However, Punshon's Carter and Bell novel *The Cottage Murder* (1931) is specifically a Buckinghamshire one. And is A.A. Milne's Red House hereabouts?

What of Agatha Christie? In later years, she owned a house at Wallingford in Berkshire and is buried in the nearby churchyard. Chimneys, the stately home familiar from *The Secret of Chimneys* (1925) and *The Seven Dials Mystery* (1929), is surely not far away. Earlier in her life, while still married to Archibald Christie, she resided in a house – called Styles – hard by Berkshire's famous Sunningdale golf course (she was a 'golf widow'), and 'The Sunningdale Mystery', a Tommy and Tuppence Beresford 'short' from *Partners in Crime* (1929), features the course. 'Market Basing', scene of 'The Market Basing Mystery' and of *Dumb Witness* (1937), is stated in the latter to be in Berkshire. 'St Mary Mead', home of Miss Marple and hotbed of crime, including many murders, could be in Wiltshire, or, just as easily, in the Midlands – in, say, Berkshire or Oxfordshire. 'Brackhampton', in *4.50 from Paddington* (1957), where Mrs McGillicuddy glimpses a murder in a train running parallel to hers, is, in terms of journey time from Paddington on the old GWR main line, clearly Reading, which again is in Berkshire, but the action soon moves to 'Brackhampton' and such topographical details as are supplied hardly tally with Reading. Generally speaking, Christie can rarely be tied down to exact English locations, particularly away from her native county of Devon.

Among Ronald **Knox**'s output, *The Viaduct Murder* (1925) and his Miles Bredon novel *The Three Taps* (1927) both surely take place in the South Midlands, but once again, we cannot suggest an exact geographical 'fix' for either. However,

Knox's *Footsteps at the Lock* (already referred to) is, despite its fictitious place names, one of a group of novels in which the action takes place in the Thames valley, either above or below Oxford. Others are Ngaio **Marsh**'s *Clutch of Constables* (1968), Michael Gilbert's *The Body of a Girl* (1972) and *Death of a Favourite Girl* (1980); Peter Lovesey's *Swing, Swing Together* (1976), with its overtones of Jerome K. Jerome; Aline Templeton's *Past Praying For* (1996), which has a clerical background; and J.R.L. Anderson's *Death on the Thames* (1975), in which Colonel Peter Blair looks into the death of an elderly fisherman on the river's upper reaches; the Thames floods dramatically and excitingly at the end.

For Bedfordshire, it is possible to cite Reginald Hill's *Blood Sympathy* (1993) and *Killing the Lawyers* (1997), as his engaging black PI Joe Sixsmith is based in Luton. Berkshire and Buckinghamshire can each point to a few titles, besides the Christie ones just mentioned for the former: Ascot racecourse is in Berkshire and is visited briefly in Sayers's *Gaudy Night* and more fully in John **Francome**'s (b.1952) *Stone Cold* (1994). Virtually all the stories in Victor Whitechurch's *Thrilling Stories of the Railway* (1912) are in fictitious railway localities, but the most popular and ingenious of them, and a tale quite often anthologised, 'Sir Gilbert Maxwell's Picture', is an exception as it happens at a siding at Churn on the one-time Didcot, Newbury and Southampton line of the old Great Western Railway. Whitechurch loved the Berkshire Downs, and it is these downs that figure in his *Shot on the Downs* (1927). The gruesome Sherlock Holmes short story, 'The Engineer's Thumb', is set on the borders of Berkshire and Oxfordshire. C.A. Alington (1872–1955), sometime Dean of Durham, wrote the entertaining *Crime on the Kennet* (1939; the Kennet is a Berkshire river), and 'Artinswell', on its banks, is the home of Sir Walter Bullivant of John Buchan's *The Thirty-Nine Steps* (1915), where Richard Hannay finds sanctuary after his exertions in the Border country. R.A.J. Walling's (1869–1949) *A Corpse without a Clue* (1944) also has scenes here, on the GWR line between Hungerford and Newbury. The 'country' scenes (and two murders) in John Dickson Carr's mid-Victorian essay *Scandal at High Chimneys* (1959) take place at a house a few miles from Reading.

Some of the action of Macdonald Hastings's (1909–1982) *Cork and the Serpent* (1955) takes place in horsey (and historic) country on the Berkshire downs:

> It was a sunken road enclosed between two ramparts overgrown with spindle and hawthorn, scrub and wild-armed, wind-broken yew trees. The chalk bottom of the track, soft and sticky like a newly-iced cake, was stuck about with the black flints which men used to work into arrowheads and scrapers.... It was one of those tracks in the chalk trodden out by shaggy little men in the Stone Age and rutted by the chariot wheels of the Roman conqueror when the legionnaires, in the outposts of Empire, guarded the bare and rolling line of the Downs. (Chapter 7)

The point of departure of J.R.L. Anderson's *Death in the Greenhouse* (1978) is a murder in a Berkshire village, and Anderson's last novel, *Late Delivery* (1982), deals with a murder in another Berkshire village situated between Newbury and Wantage. Dick Francis's *Longshot* (1990) is also set in Berkshire, while the title of G.D.H. and Margaret Cole's *Burglars in Bucks* (1930) gives away its locale (although the American title was, curiously, *The Berkshire Mystery*). And Ngaio Marsh's *Artists in Crime* (1938), in which Alleyn gets to know – though not yet to marry – Troy, is another Buckinghamshire story and one of Marsh's best. Agatha Christie's short story 'How Does Your Garden Grow' reads a little like a trial run for *Dumb*

Witness, but, unlike the latter, it is set not in Berkshire but in 'Charman's Green', Bucks – it would seem that these two counties are interchangeable in crime fiction. But Elizabeth George's *Well Schooled in Murder* (1990) is quite definitely a Buckinghamshire tale as its locale is Stoke Poges of Gray's celebrated Elegy. And so, probably, is Deborah **Crombie**'s *Leave the Grave Green* (1996), as its setting is in the Chilterns.

Turning to Hertfordshire, the house itself in Charles Dickens's *Bleak House* (1853), home of John Jarndyce, is in that county near St Alban's, and Robert Richardson's elegantly written *The Latimer Mercy* (1985) is set at an arts festival held in a cathedral city that could well be St Alban's. Augustus Maltravers, playwright and detective, functions here as he also does in Richardson's *Bellringer Street* (1988), which seems to be placed in roughly the same area, certainly in a new town, of which Hertfordshire has several. The author admits that Hatfield provides some of the topographical background, while Hertfordshire is also the scene of Richardson's non-Maltravers *The Hand of Strange Children* (1993). The county can also claim Freeman Wills Crofts's pre-French novel *The Ponson Case* (1921), in which Inspector Tanner investigates. Northamptonshire is almost as thin in reference points as is Nottinghamshire or Leicestershire, though we can perhaps instance, for Northants, Ivon Baker's *Death and Variations* (1977), on the ground that the preserved 'Wilde Valley Railway', important in the plot as the first train on the rejuvenated line runs over the murderer as he is trying to escape, is the actual preserved Nene Valley Railway. The 'Paulborough' of E.C.R. Lorac's *Policemen in the Precinct* (1950) is perhaps Peterborough; and, recalling John Buchan's *The Island of Sheep*, it is from a school in the county that Anna Haraldsen is rescued in the nick of time, a prelude to an excitingly described chase up the Great North Road.

Dorothy L. Sayers serves Hertfordshire well. Peter Wimsey and his hard-won Harriet spend their honeymoon at 'Paggleham', which may be identified as Stanstead Abbots, and is a village near 'Pagford' (Hertford) and 'Broxford' (Broxbourne). We also learn from *Busman's Honeymoon* that Harriet was born and raised in the district. A brief return is made to Paggleham by Sayers for the late, and slight, short story 'Talboys', named after Harriet and Peter's honeymoon house, which has now become their 'country' residence. Once a farmhouse, it dates from Tudor times. Other Hertfordshire short stories by Sayers are 'Absolutely Elsewhere', placed around Welwyn and Baldock, and 'The Cat in the Bag'. This features another race up the Great North Road, but between two motorcycles this time, which tear northwards from Hatfield and into Bedfordshire, passing through Biggleswade and Tempsford before they come to a halt at Eaton Socon. One of the motorcycles is carrying, inadequately wrapped, the severed head of a woman. Sayers manages toe-holds in Buckinghamshire, as 'Lopsley', visited by the Wimseys during their eventful honeymoon, is clearly in that county and somewhere in the Chilterns, and in Berkshire also, as Wimsey is seen at Royal Ascot during *Gaudy Night*. 'Lopsley' is a better advertisement for Buckinghamshire than Crispin's 'Long Fulton' described earlier:

> An old village with a new church and a pond flanking a trim central green, all clustered at the base of a little rise.... Below and to the left was spread the pleasant English country, green and russet with well-wooded fields sloping to a stream that twinkled placidly in the October sunshine. Here and there the pale glint of stubble

showed amid the pasture; or the blue smoke drifted above the trees from the red chimneys of a farm. (*Busman's Honeymoon*, Chapter 14)

Many authors in the crime field fail to characterise their localities well enough for them to be definitely identified, and this is particularly true in the southern part of this region. Even those authors who trouble to pinpoint, more or less, their crime locations often convey little of their character. Oxford is, of course, an exception, particularly in the books of Sayers, Innes, Postgate, Frome, Crispin (however light-heartedly) and Dexter, who extends his scope to the surrounding areas of Oxfordshire. The component parts of the rest of this wide swathe of territory come to life scarcely at all, and therefore, the East and South Midlands make a relatively poor showing in crime fiction compared with some other regions in England.

Wessex

When we think of Wessex in a literary sense – and for the purposes of this essay it comprises the counties of Dorset, Hampshire, Wiltshire and Somerset – thoughts inevitably fly to Thomas Hardy. Indeed, Hardy might well properly figure herein, for *Tess of the D'Urbervilles* (1891) is a stark tale of murder. But Wessex, as we have defined it, was figuring in crime fiction even before *Tess* was written. A considerable portion of the action of Wilkie Collins's *The Woman in White* (1860) takes place at Sir Percival Glyde's country seat, Blackwater Park, in Hampshire: 'The house is situated on a dead flat and seems to be shut in – almost suffocated – by trees. One wing of it is said to be five hundred years old, it had a moat round it once, and it gets its name of Blackwater from a lake in the park.' Hampshire was a county beloved of Dr Watson (he yearns 'for the glades of the New Forest or the shingle of Southsea'), so it is perhaps not too surprising that four of Sherlock Holmes's recorded cases take him to that county: 'The Problem of Thor Bridge'; 'The Crooked Man', which has a military background and is appropriately placed in the garrison town of Aldershot; 'The Adventure of the Copper Beeches', which takes Holmes to the Winchester area; and the last pages of 'Silver Blaze', in which Holmes and Watson witness the running of the rescued Silver Blaze in the Wessex Cup, again at Winchester.

Several other classic detectives of fiction have had their associations with the region. Freeman Wills Crofts's Inspector French had one case in Hampshire in *Mystery on Southampton Water* (1934) and one in Dorset, in *Death on the Way* (1932). Dorothy L. Sayers's *Unnatural Death* (1927), featuring Lord Peter Wimsey, is her principal Wessex novel. The first murder, which has already taken place when the book begins, takes place in Hampshire, at the town of 'Leahampton', which may be identified as Basingstoke, though other observers prefer Alton. The second probably also happens in Hampshire as the same chief constable is involved, but the description of the (coastal) scene of the crime sounds more like Sussex than Hampshire or Dorset, which has also been proposed. (Wimsey does visit Salisbury briefly in *Whose Body?*, 1923, where he interviews a local solicitor and attends evensong in the Cathedral.)

The A murder in Agatha Christie's *The ABC Murders* (1936) is at Andover, so Hercule **Poirot** went to Hampshire at least once. It may be twice as 'Portlebury', near the action of *The Clocks* (1963), is obviously Portsmouth. And the 'Lymstock' of Christie's *The Moving Finger* (1942) may well be in Dorset, the 'Lym' prefix suggesting Lyme Regis. This latter is a Miss Marple, of course.

The Shires: Rural England and Regional Crime Fiction

In A.E.W. Mason's *Running Water* (1907), the best scenes of the book are the mountaineering ones, in Switzerland, but a sizeable proportion of the English part of the action takes place at a rural location in Dorset, a house near a little brook, the 'running water' of the title. (The heroine of Mason's later Hanaud novel *The House of the Arrow*, 1924, Ann Upcott, was a Dorset girl.) A character in Mason's *The House in Lordship Lane* (1946) is kidnapped and kept in a lonely farmhouse on Sedgemoor, in Somerset, later pinpointed by reference to an airline schedule.

Eden Phillpotts (1862–1960) is a writer more usually associated with Devon, but *A Voice from the Dark* (1925) and *Physician Heal Thyself* (1935) both have Dorset settings, respectively, inland and on the coast. H.C. Bailey's Reggie Fortune visits an archaeological site (or is it?) at Stoke Abbas in Dorset in 'The Long Barrow', from *Mr Fortune's Trials* (1925). And John Rhode's Dr Priestley solves *Death on the Boat Train* (1940) after visiting Southampton to check procedures between boat and train, a Southampton–Waterloo service.

Lyme Regis in Dorset, with its Cobb and nearby Golden Cap, and full of literary associations from Jane Austen to John Fowles, figures briefly at the beginning and end of Nicholas **Blake**'s Nigel Strangeways novel *The Beast Must Die* (1938). More recently, Lyme Regis is where Inspector Morse is on holiday at the starting point of Colin Dexter's *The Way through the Woods*. In Victor Bridges's (1878–1972) *Greensea Island* (1922), the island of the title is presumably Brownsea Island in Poole Harbour.

John Dickson Carr's Dr Gideon Fell tale *The Seat of the Scornful* (1942) takes place in Somerset. The murder is at the coastal town of 'Tawnish' which is said to be 'a few miles' from Taunton, the county town of Somerset, where one of the principal characters lives. The north Somerset coast is nearer Taunton than the south Devon coast, but 'Tawnish' sounds a bit like Dawlish, in South Devon, and the investigative team of police comes from Exeter, also in Devon. But no matter; the middle third of *He Who Whispers* (1946), one of Dr Fell's 'vampire' cases, is set in a house in the New Forest and is thus clearly in Wessex for our purposes.

Also from the Golden Age period, it may noted that the second of Francis **Iles**'s psychological crime novels, *Before the Fact* (1932), has a Dorset setting. So does *Not to be Taken* (1938), an enjoyable rural poisoning mystery by Iles's *alter ego* Anthony Berkeley. Lawrence Meynell's *The House on the Cliff* (1932) has a Salisbury setting. Is Agatha Christie's Miss Marple's home village of 'St Mary Mead' in Wessex? It is difficult to say: it could be in Wiltshire or Hampshire, but Oxfordshire or Berkshire is just as likely. And Edmund Crispin's Gervase Fen case *The Long Divorce* (1951) sounds like a Dorset one as the *locus criminalis* is Cotten Abbas, 'Abbas' being very much a Dorset place name suffix.

But the true Wessex detective writer of the Golden Age (and beyond) was Gladys Mitchell, who lived for many years at Corfe Mullen in Dorset. Her series detective, the reptilian-looking Mrs (later Dame) Beatrice Adela Lestrange Bradley, lives in the New Forest, also in Wessex. Many Mitchell novels are set in Hampshire or Dorset. In *The Devil at Saxon Wall* (1935), 'Saxon Wall' is a village in Hampshire. New Forest novels include *Twelve Horses and the Hangman's Noose* (1956) and *Adders on the Heath* (1963); in the latter, a man camping in the forest finds in his tent the body of a man he knows and with whom he has quarrelled. When he returns with the police, there is a different body, of a man he does not know. The other body soon re-emerges, and the camper is suspected. Fascinating stuff, and Dame Beatrice is, of course, equal to finding the true murderer. In *Death and the Maiden* (1947), Winchester is named as the setting and the River Itchen figures prominently.

Mitchell's Dorset books include *Skeleton Island* (1967), the island being Portland, more or less; *Dance to Your Daddy* (1969), set at 'Galliard Hall', a Jacobean manor house somewhere between Wareham and Weymouth; *The Dancing Druids* (1948), featuring a group of primitive stones based on the Devil's Nine Stones of Winterborne Abbas, a kind of miniature Stonehenge (Mitchell was fascinated by old folklore and pre-history and Wessex is rich in both); and *Lovers, Make Moan* (1981), which revolves round an open-air production of Shakespeare's *A Midsummer Night's Dream* staged at what seems like Compton Acres at Poole. These examples are by no means exhaustive.

A few crime writers besides Gladys Mitchell have, or had, connections with Wessex. 'Dick Donovan' (otherwise James Emerson Preston Muddock, 1842–1934), writer of many sensational spy stories and thrillers, was born in Southampton. A much later and more sophisticated purveyor of espionage fiction, John **le Carré**, was born in Poole and educated at Sherborne School, both in Dorset. Tim Heald, creator of Simon Bognor, was born in Dorchester and also went to school at Sherborne, while Barry Perowne, remembered particularly for his Raffles pastiches, was Wiltshire born. Another fine writer of spy stories, Geoffrey **Household**, was a native of Bristol. Selwyn Jepson lived latterly in Hampshire, and Victor Alonzo Whitechurch (d.1933) was a Canon of Salisbury Cathedral. Thriller writer Douglas Rutherford (1915–1988) lived in Hampshire.

As has been suggested, both Dorset and Wiltshire are rich in archaeological sites, so it is not surprising to see several archaeologically based novels set in Wessex, to add to the H.C. Bailey short story mentioned earlier. John Trench's *Dishonoured Bones* (1954) is a Martin Cotterell book, a sequel to Trench's debut effort *Docken Dead*, set in Yorkshire. The archaeological background here is within a quarrying community in Dorset on the 'Isle of Albany', otherwise the Isle of Purbeck; the dig reveals a corpse, much more recent in origin than was expected. J.R.L. Anderson's *The Nine Spoked Wheel* (1975) starts at Avebury in Wiltshire with the discovery of a corpse under one of the famous standing stones and ends with an attempt to re-enact the transport, in a replica Iron Age vessel, of the stones of Stonehenge from quarries in South Wales across a stormy Bristol Channel, an attempt which ends in tragedy and disaster. Lesley Grant-Adamson's *Patterns in the Dust* (1985) is yet another archaeological novel, a Somerset one this time. The books of Anthony Price tantalisingly link Cold War counter-espionage with military history, often far back in time. An example is *Our Man in Camelot* (1975), in which the 'history' aspect has to do with King Arthur and the famous (real) victory over the Saxons attributed to him at Mons Badonicus (AD 500). Price follows the best modern opinion in placing this battle at Liddington Hill in Wiltshire, just south-east of Swindon – although its site has long been fiercely disputed by historians.

Much of Margaret Yorke's *Grave Matters* (1973) is set in a Hampshire village near Winchester, while Joan Smith's *Don't Leave Me This Way* (1990) partly takes place around the Isle of Wight ferry port Lymington, described as 'a prosperous shopping street dominated by a rather ugly parish church'. Hampshire depends heavily on Portsmouth and its environs, which have been covered by Freeman Wills Crofts in *The Box Office Murders* (1929) and more recently in Graham **Hurley**'s police novels *Turnstone* (2000), *The Take* (2001), *Angels Passing* (2002) and *Bloody and Honey* (2006). The Isle of Wight chips in with Diana Winsor's *Red on Wight* (1972) and Christine Green's Kate Kinsella investigation in *Deadly Partners* (1979), as well as Graham Hurley's *One Under* (2007). It also figures briefly in John Penn's *A Knife Ill-Used*

(1991), and Osmington Mills set *The Case of the Flying Fifteen* (1956) on the Isle of Wight during the Cowes Regatta week.

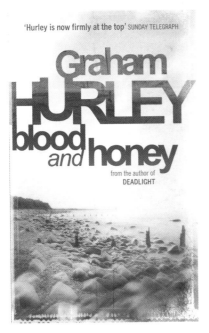

90. Cover of Graham Hurley's *Blood and Honey* (2004), set in Dorset.

Geoffrey Household's short – but gripping – thriller *A Rough Shoot* (1951) is set in a remote Dorset farming area. The book might be described (along with other Households) as 'Buchanesque'. P.D. James is an author perceived of as East Anglian once her settings strayed outside the metropolis, but two of her novels have taken place in Dorset. *The Black Tower* (1975) features an ailing Adam Dalgleish and is set on the coast; *The Skull beneath the Skin* (1982), which has a pronounced theatrical flavour, is the second recorded case of James's female private eye Cordelia Gray and is set on the fictitious 'Courcy Island'. W.J. Burley's novels mostly take place in Cornwall, Burley's county of domicile, or in Devon. *Wycliffe and the Schoolgirls* (1976) is no exception, but the murders arise out of an incident on a school journey to Dorset many years previously. The West Wessex Golf Club featured in Barry Cork's *Dead Ball* (1988) is not easy to pinpoint, but a Dorset location may be suggested here also. Terrorism and golf are stirred into the intriguing mix here.

Minette **Walters** favours Dorset, with *The Scold's Bridle* (1995), *The Break* (1998), *Festival* (2002), *Fox Evil* (2003) and *Disordered Minds* (2004) all featuring the county, mostly village settings. Other Dorset titles include David Williams's *Treasure by Post* (1992; Shaftesbury, much disguised), Neville Stead's *Tinplate* (1986; Studland, in its real persona), Susan **Moody**'s *Death Takes a Hand* (1994), John le Carré's *A Murder of Quality* (1962), Sarah Diamond's (b.1976) *Beach Road* (2000; 'Underlyme' is surely Lyme Regis), Elizabeth McGregor's *The Wrong House* (2000), Roy Hart's *Remains to be Seen* (1989), Margot Arnold's (b.1925) *Dirge for a Dorset Druid* (1994), which presents Maiden Castle near Dorchester, very thinly disguised. Older examples include Nicholas Blake's poison pen novel *The Dreadful Hollow* (1953), Anthony Berkeley's *The Piccadilly Murder* (1929) and *The Silk Stocking Murders* (1941) and, oldest of them all, J. Meade Falkner's (1858–1932) *Moonfleet* (1898), one of the best of all smuggling yarns.

Michael Gilbert's first book, the orthodox detective novel *Close Quarters* (1947), takes place in 'Melchester' cathedral close, which could be based on Salisbury, and his much later *The Black Seraphim* (1983) returns to Melchester and its cathedral. John Creasey's *Theft of Magna Carta* (1973) features 'Handsome' West investigating at Salisbury, whose cathedral owns a copy of the charter. The city features briefly in Gilbert's *Death Has Deep Roots* (1951), set mostly in London and France, and we also visit the 'washed grey uplands' of Salisbury Plain. An early depiction of Wiltshire is in W.H. Lane Crauford's (1885–1954) *The Ravenscroft Mystery* (1934); more recent appearances include Anthony Eglin's *The Blue Rose* (2004).

Douglas Clark's *Poacher's Bag* (1979) is set in rural Wiltshire, with Chief Superintendent Masters's mother-in-law asking him to investigate the death of her fiancé as she is not satisfied that the local police, who have arrested a notorious poacher, have got to the bottom of things. She proves to be right. *Dead Letter* (1984) takes place further south in Wessex, on the coast of what is now Dorset. This features 'bent' coppers, drug smuggling and the cryptic letters from DCI Green's wartime Royal Artillery comrade. As in *Poacher's Bag*, though for rather different reasons, Masters and his team start their investigations as 'poachers', i.e. without alerting the local police forces. Their deductions are brilliant indeed; but as 'Chinemouth' is quite obviously Bournemouth and the adjacent town of 'Ponde' is even more clearly Poole, one wonders why they do not appear under their real names. Even the Sandbanks car ferry, unnamed, figures in this tale.

Among stories set in Somerset, notable are Dorothy L. Sayers's short stories 'The Professor's Manuscript' (a Monty Egg investigation at Wellington) and 'The Cyprian Cat' (a supernatural mystery), both from *In the Teeth of the Evidence* (1939), and Ralph Stephenson's (b.1910) espionage thriller with musical overtones, *Spies in Concert* (1966), which has as its background the Bath Festival. Simon Brett's *Murder Unprompted* (1982) finds Charles Paris acting and detecting in Taunton, while *Mr Pinkerton Has the Clue* (1936) by David Frome sees Mr P in Bath, staying at a hotel in 'Pulteney Street'. Bath provides a setting for Catherine Aird's *After Effects* (1996); Michael Lewin's *Family Business* (1995); Christopher Lee's *The Bath Detective* (1995) and *The Killing of Sally Keemer* (1997); Lizbie Brown's *Fly Broken Star* (1992), *Turkey Tracks* (1995) and *Jacob's Ladder* (2000); Margaret Duffy's (b.1942) *Dressed to Kill* (1994), *Corpse Candle* (1995) and *Prospect of Death* (1996); and Vivien Armstrong's *Beyond the Pale* (2002). In John Dickson Carr's *The Black Spectacles* (1939), Gideon Fell is at Bath for 'the waters' and happily on hand to solve the mystery at 'Sodbury Cross' nearby.

Simon Nash's (b.1924) *Dead Woman's Ditch* (1964) has as its background a Somerset inn during early autumn, and Andrew Puckett's *Desolation Point* (1993) is set at a nuclear power station on the Somerset coast. John Bowker's *The Butcher of Glastonbury* (1997) has Chief Superintendent Laverne's efforts hampered by the obstructive behaviour of the local police force.

Finally, and briefly, to Exmoor. The peripatetic Gus Maltravers, Robert Richardson's earlier sleuth, visits Porlock and its once fearsome hill in *Sleeping in the Blood* (1991). Mention should be made of two older thrillers: Ben Bolt's (1872–1935) *The Sealed Envelope* (1931) and Victor **Canning**'s *The Kingsford Mark* (1975). And Minehead becomes 'Taviscombe' in Hazel Holt's Mrs Mallory mysteries.

Philip Scowcroft

Short Stories

The short story is as suited to the crime genre as the novel, and 'The Murders in the Rue Morgue', by Edgar Allan Poe, published in 1841, is commonly regarded as the first detective story. Fifty years passed before the full potential of the shorter form was recognised by British writers of detective fiction. The Victorian novel of sensation increasingly featured detectives, but although the likes of Wilkie **Collins** and Mary Elizabeth Braddon (1835–1915) wrote occasional short stories, their best work was (sometimes very) lengthy. Detective 'memoirs' of dubious authenticity, such as those by 'Waters' (the pseudonym of William Russell), enjoyed a vogue in the 1850s, but not until magazine circulations grew rapidly in the 1880s did circumstances arise in which the short detective story would truly flourish.

When, in the spring of 1891, Arthur Conan **Doyle** submitted 'A Scandal in Bohemia' and 'The Red-Headed League' to the recently launched *The Strand Magazine*, it was at once apparent that a worthy successor to Poe had at last been found. Writing short stories played to Conan Doyle's strengths: ingenuity marked by a fascination with the macabre and the offbeat, coupled with a straightforward style of storytelling. Holmes's eccentric yet unforgettable character was at the heart of a series of investigations that changed the course of sensational fiction forever. Among many highlights, 'The Red-Headed League' and 'The Adventure of the Copper Beeches' (1892) remain regularly cited as among the finest of all short detective stories. 'Silver Blaze' is a notable later work, famous for Holmes's cryptic reference to the curious incident of the dog that did not bark in the night-time.

'Rivals of Sherlock Holmes' (to borrow a phrase popularised by Hugh Greene's, 1910–1987, 1970s anthologies) soon emerged in countless stories, but none matched the sage of 221b Baker Street. A mistake often made by Conan Doyle's imitators was to focus on the gimmicks with which he adorned his work, rather than on the substance and subtlety of his writing. Arthur Morrison's (1863–1945) Martin Hewitt was an exception: a resolutely ordinary private investigator whose cases attained a popularity that has not lasted. The same author's unscrupulous Dorrington ('the chief matter of Dorrington's solicitude was his own interest', we are told in 'The Affair of the "Avalanche Bicycle and Tyre Co. Limited" ', 1897) was a more intriguing protagonist, but he appeared in only one collection and is now almost forgotten. E.W. **Hornung**'s A.J. Raffles, cricketer and amateur cracksman, represented more successfully the dual personality of the apparently respectable villain with a taste for solving crimes, as well as committing them. The blind Max Carrados, created by Ernest Bramah (1868–1942), was among the more memorable detectives to emerge in the early twentieth century, and in 'The Game Played in the Dark' (1913), he uses his lack of sight and the acuity of his other senses as an advantage – having extinguished the light in a room where he is outnumbered by two criminals, he warns his adversaries, 'I shoot by sound, not sight'. Victor L. Whitechurch's stories about the vegetarian hypochondriac Thorpe Hazell possess the merit of an interesting background: Hazell specialises in detecting crime associated with the railways.

G.K. **Chesterton**'s contribution to the genre was more enduring. That his most celebrated investigator, Father Brown, is a priest was not a cheap means of attracting attention, but rather a device that enabled him to explore puzzles and paradoxes of human nature. Chesterton acknowledged that 'the detective story is only a game... the reader is not really wrestling with the criminal but with the author'. He played the game skilfully and, at his best, was capable of using the form to make neat comments on society and the way people behave. 'The Invisible Man' (1911) concerns, it turns out, a 'mentally invisible man' and Father Brown muses that although 'nobody notices postmen, somehow', they 'have passions like other men, and even carry large bags where a small corpse can be stowed quite easily'. Besides Father Brown, Chesterton created other detectives, including Mr Pond, a mild-mannered civil servant not dissimilar from Edgar **Wallace**'s Mr J.G. Reeder, and Horne Fisher, 'The Man Who Knew Too Much' (a description that Alfred Hitchcock purloined for two films, owing nothing else to Chesterton). None had the staying power of the modest cleric.

Nor did Philip Trent, who featured in the first, and only noteworthy, novel by Chesterton's old school friend, E.C. **Bentley**. *Trent's Last Case* (1913) was an ironic take on the traditions of detective fiction; its success took the author by surprise, but when he brought Trent back in less subversive mood, notably in a sequence of short stories collected as *Trent Intervenes* (1938), the results were competent but conventional. Nevertheless, 'The Genuine Tabard', which first appeared in *The Strand Magazine*, January 1938, deserves mention as an enjoyable example of detective work.

R. Austin **Freeman** has two claims to fame. He hit upon the idea of the 'inverted' detective story, in which the reader first sees the criminal at work before watching the investigator trying to bring the culprit to justice and *The Singing Bone* (1912), a collection of stories structured in this way, is a landmark in the genre. In 1907, he had introduced the first notable British detective to be an expert in science (although L.T. Meade had published detective stories with a medical slant in collaboration with Clifford Halifax as early as 1894). Dr John Thorndyke, handsome but no Casanova, is a bachelor of Holmesian omniscience specialising in medical jurisprudence. Freeman was equally at home with short stories and novels, but the former have lasted better, since his economical style and focus on a single ingenious idea is sufficient to distract the reader from his limitations in terms of depicting character.

Although the decadent Prince Zaleski, created in 1895 by M.P. Shiel (1865–1947), rarely left his divan to solve his strange mysteries, the real prototype of the 'armchair detective' appeared in *The Old Man in the Corner* (1909) stories by Baroness Orczy, otherwise renowned for her books about the Scarlet Pimpernel. Sitting in a London teashop, drinking milk and untying knots in string, he solves mysteries recounted by journalist Polly Burton. There is a hint in 'The Mysterious Death in Percy Street' (1908) that he is the murderer Bill Owen, whose crime is 'one of the cleverest bits of work accomplished outside Russian diplomacy'. The title character in Orczy's collection *Lady Molly of Scotland Yard* (1910) was dismissed by the critic Julian **Symons** as 'silly' but her exploits did at least help to pave the way for more credible female detectives.

The arrival on the scene of Agatha **Christie** coincided with a decisive shift in detective fiction, from short story to novel. She led the way in demonstrating that a writer gifted at the construction of ingenious plots could sustain reader interest in a detective's unravelling of a complex whodunit mystery at novel length. In her early years, Christie was a prolific writer of short stories for magazines, but many of those involving Hercule **Poirot**, apart from the later collection *The Labours of Hercules* (1947), reveal a heavy debt to Conan Doyle. *Partners in Crime* (1929), featuring Tommy and Tuppence Beresford, parodies the work of fellow mystery writers and is an interesting historical curiosity. Stories in *The Mysterious Mr Quin* (1930) and *The Hound of Death* (1933) blend detection with the supernatural. Jane **Marple** first appeared in short stories and 'Motive v. Opportunity' is one of several neat entries gathered in *The Thirteen Problems* (1932); but it was with cases recorded in novels that Miss Marple earned her place in the pantheon of **Great Detectives**. Overall, with isolated exceptions, such as 'Witness for the Prosecution' (1925) and 'Accident' (1929), Christie's short stories were inferior to her novels. The same was true of Dorothy L. **Sayers**, although she did write a few gems and was a notable early anthologist of short mystery fiction. Her second string sleuth Montague Egg, who never made the leap from detecting in a short story to detecting in a novel, is an unimpressive figure compared with the sometimes maddening but unforgettable Lord Peter **Wimsey**. Margery **Allingham** wrote several sharp short stories, but two other major female detective novelists of the **Golden Age**, Ngaio **Marsh** and Josephine **Tey**, had little interest in short fiction, while Gladys **Mitchell**'s efforts at the form were inconsequential.

Anthony Berkeley's 'The Avenging Chance', first appeared in *Pearson's Magazine*, September 1929, remains celebrated not only for its cleverness but also because it formed the basis of an even more ingenious novel, *The Poisoned Chocolates Case* (1929). H.C. Bailey (1878–1961) was a writer much admired in his day whose reputation slumped after his death, but his short stories featuring Reggie Fortune, an early fictional expert in forensics, although an acquired taste, do not deserve to be forgotten. Roy **Vickers**, a prolific hack writer, rose to unaccustomed heights with his creation of Scotland Yard's Department of Dead Ends. The stories utilise the inverted form inaugurated by Freeman, and 'The Rubber Trumpet' (1934) has often been anthologised.

Thomas Burke's (1886–1945) 'The Hands of Mr Ottermole' appeared in *The Story-teller*, February 1929, a chilling story about a serial killer (written long before fictional serial killers became ten-a-penny), and 'The Tea Leaf' by Edgar Jepson (1863–1938) and Robert Eustace (1854–1943), first appeared in *The Strand*, October 1925, have stood the test of time. So have two stories by writers otherwise little known, 'Inquest' (*The Strand*, April 1932) by Loel Yeo and 'By Kind Permission of the Murdered Man' (*The Strand*, March 1934) by Hylton Cleaver (1891–1961). But although *The Strand* limped on until 1950, its heyday was long past leaving a distinct lack of outlets for those British crime writers who enjoyed writing the short story.

In the 1950s, from Roald Dahl's (1916–1990) acerbic *Tales of the Unexpected*, 'Lamb to the Slaughter' (1953) and 'The Way up to Heaven' (1954), first appeared in *Harper's* and *The New Yorker* respectively. Back in London, the *Evening Standard* published a large number of very short stories during the 1950s; Leo Bruce (1903–1979) and Michael **Innes** were among the writers regularly featured. But the stories, although often well crafted, were usually limited by their brevity to offering a single twist in the tale. Some of the trickiest stories were very effective – a nice example is 'Who Killed Baker?' (1952) by Edmund **Crispin** and Geoffrey Bush (1920–1998), but in time, the formula palled. British writers never had the benefit of a market to compare with America's *Ellery Queen's Mystery Magazine* (EQMM) – although EQMM's editors have long shown much generosity towards contributors from the United Kingdom – and those crime story magazines launched from time to time on a tide of optimism have seldom survived for long.

Against this background, it was small wonder that in introducing *Butcher's Dozen* (1956), the first anthology of the recently formed **Crime Writers' Association**, editors Michael **Gilbert**, Josephine **Bell** and Julian **Symons** said that, as regards the market for short stories, 'the outlook is bleak'. Gilbert also edited a posthumous collection of Cyril **Hare**'s short fiction, which provided a reminder of the talent lost by the early death of his friend and fellow lawyer. 'Name of Smith' and 'Back on the Shelf' are amongst Hare's minor classics. Christianna **Brand** was an equally adept practitioner, but it was Gilbert himself who, arguably, became the most consistently enjoyable British short story writer of the past half-century. His range was remarkable, extending from spy stories to tales of legal practice, the latter informed by his long and distinguished career as a solicitor (his clients included Raymond **Chandler**). Gilbert's elderly spies Calder and Behrens featured in two first-rate collections, while the solicitor Jonas Pickett takes centre stage in *Anything for a Quiet Life* (1990). Two books of short stories feature policeman Patrick Petrella, while tales about the parainsomniac lawyer Henry Bohun are included in both *The Man Who Hated Banks* (1997) and *Stay of Execution* (1971); the latter is possibly Gilbert's finest short story collection. 'Judith' (1993), with its atypically dark conclusion, is a reminder that his talents were not confined to light entertainment.

The short stories of Gilbert's contemporary Julian Symons changed in nature during his career. After beginning with short-shorts featuring the private detective Francis Quarles, he concentrated on more seriously conceived crime stories, such as those collected in *The Tigers of Subtopia* (1965) and *The Man Who Hated Television* (1987). Equally sophisticated is the short fiction of Ruth **Rendell**. 'The Fallen Curtain' (1974) provides an early example of her insight into character, while 'The Wrong Category' (1982) shows that she is adept at the last minute twist as the entertainers of the Golden Age. P.D. **James**'s occasional forays into short fiction, such as 'The Girl Who Loved Graveyards' (1983) and 'The Part-Time Job' (2006), are of high quality. The tireless H.R.F. **Keating** has published many enjoyable short stories, despite warning tyros in a perceptive passage in *Writing Crime Fiction* (1986) that short stories are difficult to write well and seldom remunerative. He has produced collections chronicling investigations of his principal detective, Inspector Ghote, and one recounting the exploits of a cleaning lady, Mrs Craggs. Although Mrs Craggs appears in a Keating novel, she is one of those amateur sleuths better taken in small doses. 'The Rio de Janeiro Paper' (1979) and 'On the Psychiatrist's Couch' (1997) are dazzling examples of Reginald **Hill**'s mastery of the form.

The short story presents a formidable challenge to writers. Concision demands skill; there is no room for padding. Unsurprisingly, leading novelists are apt to be the most successful writers of short mysteries. Sometimes they give their main series characters an outing in a short story – Hill's Andy Dalziel, for instance, appears in several stories including the outstanding 'The Game of Dog' (2003). Among younger crime novelists, Ian **Rankin** is a gifted short story writer whose finest work includes 'Tell Me Who to Kill' (2003), featuring DI John Rebus, and two Dagger-winning stories, 'A Deep Hole' (1994) and 'Herbert in Motion' (1996). Although much less renowned, Mat **Coward** and Jerry Sykes are versatile crime writers, unusual for having made a speciality of short fiction.

Over the past thirty years, anthologies have become a more important market for British short story writers than magazines. One-off anthologies range from the conventional to the innovative; examples of the latter include *Tart Noir* (2002), edited by Stella **Duffy** and Lauren **Henderson**, and *The Mammoth Book of Future Cops* (2003), edited by Maxim **Jakubowski** and M. Christian. Macmillan's *Winter's Crimes* series, which spanned twenty-four volumes, included much original work of high quality, while more recently, the industrious and widely read Jakubowski has produced annual gatherings of *The Best British Mysteries*. The Detection Club has published occasional collections (including two celebrating the eightieth birthdays of former Presidents Symons and Keating) whose high calibre reflect the Club's select membership. Meanwhile, Crime Writers' Association anthologies have appeared almost every year over the past fifty years; since 1996, each book has focused on a different theme – missing persons, crime in the city, crimes of identity and so on. Thematic anthologies have become increasingly popular, perhaps because there is much pleasure to be gained from the varied ways in which different authors tackle the same subject. Mike **Ashley** has virtually cornered the market in anthologising historical crime stories; his other compilations include a gathering of new Sherlock **Holmes** pastiches and *The Mammoth Book of Locked-Room Mysteries and Other Impossible Crimes* (2000).

Locked-room mysteries suit the short form. The various devices for breaching a locked room may seem outlandish, and their investigation sometimes wearisome if chronicled at novel length. This is one reason why the impossible crime story has declined in popularity since the Golden Age. But tales like Peter **Lovesey**'s 'The Amorous Corpse' (2000) illustrate that, in the hands of a craftsman, the impossible crime story still has the capacity to entertain and amuse. Stories which play with form and structure are occasionally found: examples are Lovesey's 'Youdunnit' (1989), and Martin **Edwards**'s 'InDex'. While truly successful comic crime novels are rare, humour in the short story is often effective. Coward, Robert **Barnard** and Simon **Brett** are consistently funny, while Edmund **Crispin**'s 'We Know You're Busy Writing…' (1979) is an often reprinted classic.

In an age of short attention spans, the future of the short story might seem to be bright. Yet, mainstream publishers are depressingly wary of bringing out story collections, arguing that readers much prefer novels. Sales figures support their reservations, although this may be due to a lack of adequately resourced marketing. A publisher passionate about short fiction can achieve impressive results: the American press Crippen and Landru has included in its list of 'lost classics' books containing previously uncollected stories by writers such as Berkeley, Gilbert, Symons, Brand and Ellis **Peters**.

Most crime novelists enjoy writing short stories. They offer a break from routine, the pleasure of trying something different, perhaps the chance of striking out in a new direction when the next novel is planned (Hill's Luton-based private eye Joe Sixsmith first appeared in a short story). It seems certain that British crime writers from bestsellers to beginners will continue to relish the demands of the short story and they may take the form to fresh heights in years to come, even if it is unlikely that the extraordinary commercial success enjoyed by the Holmes adventures will ever be repeated. Short stories are written for love, not money. *See also* Anthologies; Harris, Herbert; Literature and Crime Fiction; *and* Magazines.

Selected Works
Doyle, Arthur Conan: *The Adventures of Sherlock Holmes* (1891)
Chesterton, G.K.: *The Innocence of Father Brown* (1911)
Freeman, R. Austin: *The Singing Bone* (1912)
Bramah, Ernest: *The Eyes of Max Carrados* (1923)
Sayers, Dorothy L.: *Great Short Stories of Mystery, Detection and Horror* (1928)
Christie, Agatha: *The Labours of Hercules* (1949)
Crispin, Edmund: *Beware of the Trains* (1953)

Gilbert, Michael (ed.): *Best Detective Stories of Cyril Hare* (1959)
Gilbert, Michael: *Game without Rules* (1967)
Gilbert, Michael: *Stay of Execution* (1971)
Rendell, Ruth: *The Fallen Curtain* (1976)
Hill, Reginald: *Pascoe's Ghost* (1979)
Symons, Julian: *The Tigers of Subtopia* (1982)
Barnard, Robert: *Death of a Salesperson* (1989)
Lovesey, Peter: *Butchers* (1985)
Brett, Simon: *A Box of Tricks* (1985)
Rankin, Ian: *Beggar's Banquet* (2002)

Anthologies
Sayers, Dorothy L. (ed.): *Tales of Detection* (1936)
Bell, Josephine, Michael Gilbert and Julian Symons (eds): *Butcher's Dozen* (1956)
Greene, Hugh (ed.): *The Rivals of Sherlock Holmes* (1970)
Symons, Julian (ed.): *Verdict of Thirteen* (1978)
Keating, H.R.F. (ed.): *The Man Who...*(1992)
Adrian, Jack (ed.): *Detective Stories from 'The Strand'* (1991)
Ashley, Mike (ed.): *The Mammoth Book of Locked-Room Mysteries and Other Impossible Crimes* (2000)
Edwards, Martin (ed.): *Mysterious Pleasures* (2003)
Jakubowski, Maxim (ed.): *The Best British Mysteries* (2003)
Brett, Simon (ed.): *The Detection Collection* (2005)

Martin Edwards

Shots Magazine

Shots is a crime and mystery website produced by what is known as the 'Shots Collective', consisting of Mike Stotter as editor, Ali Karim as assistant editor and Donna Moore as fiction editor with other web-based support staff. It seeks to continue what had been developed by two previous hard-copy magazines, *A Shot in the Dark* and *Shots*.

A Shot in the Dark began as a free handout at the Shot-on-the-Page crime fiction convention held in Nottingham in June 1994. The 'collective', under the overall editorship of Bob Cartwright, decided to continue it as a quarterly magazine, initially produced in A5 format. Its purpose, which has remained the same throughout, was stated as, 'to provide a forum for crime/mystery enthusiasts to discuss their favourite books and a news medium for authors and publishers to publicise their crime fiction titles'. It aimed to provide a critical platform from which the enthusiasts could examine the treatment of crime fiction within the publishing and book-selling industries. These aims have meant that the magazine has tended to champion the 'underdog', those new or mid-list writers, British or American, not necessarily receiving the promotion or support from their publisher that their work demands. The emphasis in each issue, which has continued through *Shots* to the webzine, has been on articles, reviews, critical essays and interviews rather than fiction, although most issues ran some stories or extracts. Issue 12 (Summer 1997), for example, ran three items by Ed Gorman (b.1941), Julian **Rathbone** and Joel Rose.

With Issue 10 (Winter 1996/1997), *A Shot in the Dark* switched to the larger A4 format. Mike Stotter took over as editor from Issue 11 (Spring 1997) and then, after Issue 14 (Winter 1997/1998) it was revamped as *Shots*, first issue dated Spring 1998.

Despite the title change, some reformatting and returning to Volume 1, Number 1, nothing else changed, although initially there was a greater emphasis on fiction. The first issue ran stories by Margaret **Yorke**, Paula Gosling (b.1939), Russell **James**, Arthur Winfield Knight (b.1937) and Phil Lovesey (b.1963), and there were three or four stories in most issues until the last two, when there was only one. The magazine's strengths lay in its surveys of writers, articles by writers about their work and interviews. British authors who have contributed or been interviewed include Christopher **Brookmyre**, Gillian **Linscott**, Frances **Fyfield**, Lindsey **Davis**, Carol Anne **Davis**, Colin **Dexter**, Deryn **Lake**, Keith Miles and Mark **Billingham**. There have been occasional analyses of classic writers, including Dorothy L. **Sayers** and Edgar **Wallace**, but the emphasis was predominantly on the new and the up and coming.

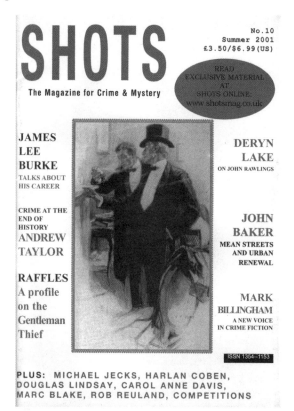

91. Cover of *Shots* magazine, Summer 2001.

The cost of producing *Shots*, which was always on high-quality paper and profusely illustrated, became prohibitive; after Issue 10 (Summer 2001), it switched to the webzine format. There have been further web issues, each similar to the hardcopy magazine with articles, interviews and reviews. However, since the website is constantly updating its contents much along the lines of the hard copy, the issue format has ceased.

Website
www.shotsmag.co.uk

Mike Ashley

Sidey, Paul (b.1943)

Paul Sidey is one of the most distinguished of British editors, whose lengthy career has allowed him to work with some of the most talented names in British fiction. After failing to get his own film company off the ground, Sidey started salaried life at Penguin in 1970 as Editorial Programme Controller (a job for which he was uniquely unqualified), later becoming a junior editor on a list for which he was totally unsuited. The subjects included geography and the environment, education, sociology and business. It was a testing period. But then came the opportunity to take charge of the revived Penguin crime list, with its distinctive green spines. There was no looking back. Julian **Symons**, author and critic, was retained as advisor. And the list ranged from Golden Agers such as Agatha **Christie**, Ngaio **Marsh**, Margery **Allingham** to Rex Stout, Ed McBain, Robert B. Parker and the still underrated Margaret Millar, wife of Ross Macdonald. P.D. **James** also took a bow, as did Antonia **Fraser**'s Jemima Shore and Peter **Lovesey**'s Sergeant Cribb. There was at least one Simenon Omnibus every year. The great and forgotten John Franklin Bardin, author of *The Deadly Percheron*, was tracked down, in true detective fashion, and republished to general acclaim. Sidey also looked after Patricia Highsmith in paperback, but (for some reason) her titles remained with orange spines.

The job grew to include hardcover responsibility, where authors included Jorge Luis Borges and John Mortimer (b.1923) (both of whom utilised crime tropes). In 1980, Sidey moved to Hutchinson, before it became part of the Random House group. There he has remained as Editorial Director through many management changes for twenty-eight years. The brief has been fairly elastic. In the early days, there was an inheritance of the romantic, tragical, historical and pastoral. Barbara Cartland (1901–2000) was still in full flow (her achievement of twenty-four novels in one year still stands in the Guinness Book of Records). At present, non-fiction amounts to probably more than 50 percent of Sidey's output. Sidey has also worked with several important thriller writers: Charles McCarry, Evelyn **Anthony**, Peter Benchley and Philip **Kerr**. And, in the crime genre, Margaret **Yorke**, Craig Russell and Carol O'Connell.

But Sidey's pivotal relationship for twenty-five years has been with one of British crime fiction's greatest figures, Ruth **Rendell**. In the twenty-first century, she continues to be one of Sidey's – and the publisher Hutchinson's – most loyal, consistent and successful authors.

Barry Forshaw

Simms, Chris (b.1969)

The tense, dark thrillers of Chris Simms combine psychological insight with set pieces that genuinely disturb and frighten.

The idea for his highly original debut novel, *Outside the White Lines* (2003), came to him one night when broken down on the hard shoulder of a motorway. Staccato chapters alternate between viewpoints of The Searcher, The Hunter and The Killer, each character roaming the roads of Britain in pursuit of his own obsessive agenda.

92. Chris Simms.

Simms followed this up with another stand-alone, *Pecking Order* (2004). Largely set on a battery farm, the plot follows the naïve but cruel Rubble who is duped into believing that he has been enrolled as an agent on a sinister government project. Partly inspired by the 1960s experiments of Stanley Milgram into man's obedience to authority, the novel also touches on such diverse issues as euthanasia and the ethics of factory farming. It does so with 'intelligence and subtlety' according to the trade journal *TheBookseller*.

Simms then changed publishers with *Killing the Beasts* (2005), inaugurating a series featuring Manchester policeman, DI Spicer. Descended from Irish immigrants who helped build the world's first industrial city, Spicer never shies away from Manchester's violent and lawless corners in his investigations. The novel is set during 2002, with the city's hosting of that year's Commonwealth Games providing a spectacular backdrop to the action. The plot revolves around a killer who, apart from sealing his victims' airways with a viscous gel, leaves them totally unscathed.

Its sequel, *Shifting Skin* (2006), sees Spicer tracking 'The Butcher of Belle Vue', a murderer who uses surgical skills to remove large swathes of his victims' flesh. The investigation ultimately leads Spicer into the city's shady escort scene and the unscrupulous end of the cosmetic surgery industry.

Third in the series is *Savage Moon* (2007). Containing multiple references to the horror classic, *An American Werewolf in London* (1981), the novel is concerned with a brutal killing that takes place on the notorious Saddleworth Moor, to the edge of the city. At first, it is assumed that a mysterious black cat that has been spotted prowling the wild terrain is responsible. But then more bodies start to appear, each one a little closer to the centre of the city itself.

Fourth in the series is *Hell's Fire* (2008), a tense and trenchant thriller that looks at the role of religion in modern day society. In it Spicer is charged with unravelling who is behind a spate of arson attacks on churches around Manchester.

Simms attracts critical acclaim for the fashion in which he combines details of Spicer's domestic life with pithy descriptions of police procedure and convincing glimpses into the minds of killers. In May 2007, Simms was selected as a 'Waterstone's Author for the Future'. He was one of twenty-five writers tipped by publishers, editors and agents 'to produce the most impressive body of work over the next quarter century'.

Selected Works by the Author
Outside the White Lines (2003)
Pecking Order (2004)
Killing the Beasts (2005)
Shifting Skin (2006)
Savage Moon (2007)
Hell's Fire (2008)

Barry Forshaw

Simpson, Dorothy (b.1933)

One of the stalwarts of British crime fiction, Dorothy Simpson wrote **police procedurals** in the classic style of the genre, with deceptively simple, skilfully plotted mysteries and a detective who represents the best traditions of the country policeman.

Dorothy Simpson worked as a French teacher and then as a marriage guidance counsellor before turning to writing full-time. She made her publishing debut with a suspense novel, *Harbingers of Fear* in 1977. Four years later, *The Night She Died* (1981), an investigation into the murder of a young housewife, introduced Detective Inspector Luke Thanet and his assistant, Detective Sergeant Mike Lineham. Thanet is a model for the traditional British police detective. Gently puffing on his pipe, he seems genial and unthreatening, but his appearance is deceptive and hides a shrewd intelligence. Unlike many of today's fictional policemen, he is happily married, with a son and daughter, and there are frequent glimpses of his comfortingly normal home life in between the details of his investigations. The investigations involve murder of course, mostly of apparently respectable men and women who have for different reasons aroused the hatred of someone in their circle of friends and acquaintances. Because these are domestic murders, not stranger killings, the suspects are to be found within a relatively small group. Thanet's beat is in Sturrenden, a small country town in Kent, and its surrounding area, where the well-to-do middle class live in quaint villages and elegant country estates. The dead girl in *Close Her Eyes* (1984), however, comes from a less-affluent family, members of a rigidly puritanical religious sect. It is a quietly moving story in which Thanet, the devoted father, is emotionally affected by the fate of the youthful victim.

The personality and behaviour of the victim is central to Simpson's mysteries, which deal with genuine human dilemmas within the often claustrophobic setting of a peaceful English town or village. Simpson does not set out deliberately to shock, but the effect is nonetheless sometimes shocking, because of the commonplace setting and the homeliness of the characters involved in the drama, which demonstrates that danger often exists within an outwardly ordinary family. These are the qualities for which she was recognised when her fifth novel, *Last Seen Alive* (1985), a clever mystery in which she is in top form, was awarded the **Crime Writers' Association** Silver Dagger. There are fifteen books in the series; the last Thanet investigation, *Dead and Gone* appeared in 1999. They are the kind of crime novels which are described, sometimes rather sniffily, as cosy, but beneath their genteel setting Simpson's stories have a hard core of realism and some of her puzzles are ingenious and hard to solve. *See also* The Shires: Rural England and Regional Crime Fiction.

Selected Works by the Author
Six Feet Under (1982)
Puppet for a Corpse (1983)
Close Her Eyes (1984)
Last Seen Alive (1985)
Dead on Arrival (1986)
Element of Doubt (1987)
Once Too Often (1998)

Susanna Yager

Simpson, Helen de Guerry (1897–1940)

Crime fiction has sported a comparatively small percentage of Australian-born, English-domiciled authors – notable in this company was Helen Simpson. She died of cancer at a relatively young age, but even had she lived, it is probable that there would have been little more crime fiction. Apart from one crime story, *Acquittal* (1925), her early output comprised plays, verse and short fairy stories; much of the 1930s was devoted to historical works, novels and 'straight' history, some of the former involving her native country, most of the latter, including biographies of Henry VIII (1934) and Mary Tudor (*The Spanish Marriage*, 1933), concerned with the sixteenth century. Also from the 1930s came a crime-cum-detective story, *The Prime Minister Is Dead* (1931), a tale blending suspense, humour and romance, involving sport and British politics, pleasantly written and characterised.

But the three novels that brought Simpson and her co-author (the playwright Clemence Dane, 1888–1965) an entrée to the Detection Club date from 1929 to 1932. In *Enter Sir John* (1929), the flamboyant actor-manager Sir John Saumarez takes up the case of a young actress accused of murder, clears her with a mixture of shrewdness and intuition and marries her at the end (she played less 'hard to get' than Lord Peter **Wimsey**'s Harriet Vane in a similar situation). Its sequel, *Printer's Devil* (1930), sees Sir John in a peripheral role, but he is back centre stage in *Re-enter Sir John* (1932). A young actor protégé is framed for cheating at cards in a club and the fall-out affects the actor's next performance. An unexplained death follows. Sir John, assisted by his wife, Lady Martella, has to play golf and attend a séance during his enquiries. After narrowly escaping being shot in the head, he extracts a confession by reconstructing the crime (à la play scene in *Hamlet*, but the reconstruction is by means of a film). The felicities of the writing may be due to Simpson or to Dane, or to both together – it is hard to anatomise the division.

Peripheral crime writings by Simpson included contributions to the Detection Club co-operatives *The Floating Admiral* (1931), *The Scoop* (not published until 1983),

Ask a Policeman (1933) and – true crime – *The Anatomy of Murder* (1937), plus a sketch of Dr Watson for *Baker Street Studies*, and, with Dorothy L. **Sayers** and others, studies in the Wimsey family history.

Her elegant, well-informed writing deserved a better fate than the neglect it has suffered. *See also* Short Stories.

Selected Works by the Author
Enter Sir John (1929)
Printer's Devil (1930)
The Prime Minister Is Dead (1931; also published in the United States as *Vantage Striker*)
Re-enter Sir John (1932)

Further Reading
Dean, Christopher. 1998. 'Helen Simpson and Clemence Dane'. *Proceedings of the Dorothy L Sayers Society 1997 Second Seminar* May: 32–37.
Scowcroft, Philip L. 1991. 'Detection, History and Australia: The Literary Experience of Helen Simpson'. *CADS* 16: 33–35.
Scowcroft, Philip L. 1996. 'Helen Simpson'. *Proceedings of the Dorothy L Sayers Society 1995 Seminar* May: 42–47.
Scowcroft, Philip L. 1998. 'Helen Simpson'. *Proceedings of the Dorothy L Sayers Society 1997 Second Seminar* May: 29–31.

Philip Scowcroft

Sinclair, Iain (b.1943)

Although few would describe Iain Sinclair as a crime writer, a fascination with crime, particularly the seedier elements of its lifestyle and the part they play in the culture of London's East End, has played an important role in his work. Nowhere is this illustrated better than in the anthology *London: City of Disappearances* (2006), which he edited, and whose entries are a mix of reminiscence of the London demi-monde to which Sinclair was drawn in the 1960s, and more straightforward tales of the ways **London** and its crime swallow up its denizens.

This is very much in keeping with the two books for which Sinclair is probably now best-known, the explorations of London, in *Lights Out for the Territory* (1997) and *London Orbital* (2002). The first, and more revealing, is a series of walks through the city, which illuminate what he terms the 'psychogeography' of the city; for example a confluence of its darker history, of mystic patterns in the design and placement of Hawksmoor's churches. This concern was set out in his early book of poetry, *Lud Heat* (1975), and formed the basis for his first novel, the excellent *White Chappell, Scarlet Tracings* (1987).

That book, which has the Ripper murders at its heart, is the one which most easily could fall into the crime category, though it works hard at, and indeed is to some extent concerned with, transcending genre boundaries. Breaking boundaries is crucial to all of Sinclair's work; he is relentless in displaying prominently its literary and theoretical roots, which are as wide as they are arcane. A stylist of considerable talent, Sinclair mixes a keen eye for setting and a keener ear for everyday dialogue with a didactic urge that often sees him appearing to channel French structuralists and Beat poets together through Hackney's alleys.

Educated at Cheltenham College, Sinclair pursued further studies at various times at Trinity College Dublin, the London Film School and the Courtauld Institute; the importance of critical theory to students of film and art is reflected in both his fiction and non-fiction writing, as well as a certain filmic formality. His film about Allen Ginsberg in London, *Ah! Sunflower* (with Robert Klinkert, 1967), was made for WDR TV (Cologne), and financed his house purchase and his early self-publishing. The book he subsequently produced about the film was called *The Kodak Mantra Diaries* (1971). He has also collaborated with Chris **Petit**, whose novels share something of Sinclair's filmic style, on several documentaries, including *The Cardinal and the Corpse* (1992) and *The Falconer* (1997).

93. Iain Sinclair.

The most powerful influences on Sinclair's early work were the east end of London (he settled in Albion Drive in Hackney well before the area was gentrified) and American poetry, the Beats and the projective verse theories of Charles Olson and his British disciples like the Cambridge don J.H. Prynne.

Olson's insistence on breath-oriented lines is an obvious marker for Sinclair's poetry, but his focus on the importance of place and 'things themselves' are evident in the potpourri of ideas, facts and places that litter all of Sinclair's work. In fact, those looking for a sensibility close to Sinclair's might settle on the little-known poet Allen Fisher, whose long poem 'Place' has a similar concern with the minutiae of his London setting, and who appears in the *London: City of Disappearances* anthology.

Sinclair worked various odd-jobs, most notably as a groundskeeper for Hackney council, and also dealt in second-hand books. The shady machinations of the rare-books business, a sort of genteel and eccentric microcosm of a pseudo-criminal underworld, underlays a number of his novels. His earliest work was poetry, published by his own Albion Village Press in limited editions which are now, ironically enough, collectors' items. *Suicide Bridge* (1979) and *Lud Heat*, in particular are remarkably inventive, and among the very best work in this British strand of projective verse, and include prose poems, essays and small stories. *Lud Heat* provides the template for the 'psychogeography' of London, and most of Sinclair's work which followed can be said to do the same.

The success of *White Chappell*, originally published by the small press Goldmark, was at least in part due to the attention paid to Peter **Ackroyd**'s novel *Hawksmoor* (1985). Ackroyd, who originally moved in many of the same poetic circles as Sinclair, had taken the impetus for his book from *Lud Heat*, and his frequent acknowledgement of such influence gave *White Chappell* an imprimatur.

The novel sets the efforts of a group of seedy book dealers to acquire a first edition of Conan Doyle's *Study in Scarlet* (1887) against the Ripper murders; it also is an essay in exploitation, as Sinclair argues against himself for glorifying the Ripper myth even as he deconstructs it.

His next novel, *Downriver* (1991), could be looked at as science fiction, since it takes place in a London blighted by the rule of The Widow, who has established a one-party state in Britain. As a satiric metaphor for the Thatcher years, it falls somewhere short of Swift, probably closer to Orwell, as well as Alan Moore's (b.1953) *V for Vendetta* (1995). *Downriver* won the James Tait Black Memorial Prize and the Encore Prize firmly establishing Sinclair as a major figure.

If his later novels proved progressively more difficult, if not mannered, the graphic novel *Slow Chocolate Autopsy* (1997), illustrated by Dave McKean (b.1963), was classic Sinclair, a series of stories and vignettes narrated by 'Norton, prisoner of London', which include Marlowe's murder at Deptford and, of course, the Ripper killings. The book was also designed to parallel his film *The Falconer* (1998).

Sinclair's essays and fragments, collected in *White Goods* (2002), can often verge into self-parody, and excerpts from his writing appeared frequently in Private Eye's Pseud's Corner column. But *Rodinsky's Room* (1999, written with Rachel Lichtenstein) was a fascinating portrait of a cabbalist scholar who disappeared from his garret which was strewn with his mystic research. Increasingly, Sinclair's concerns were with non-fiction, punctuated with rants about London's development. Indeed, his most recent novel, *Dining on Stones* (2004) details a poet's long walk up the A13, a cross between *London Orbital* and *Edge of the Orison* (2005), which told the story of John Clare's walk from a madhouse in Epping to his Northamptonshire home, and his forthcoming *Sixty Miles Out*, the final book in his trilogy of 'London walks', will start on the A13 and encompass a 60 mile circle around the capital. *See also* Literature and Crime Fiction.

Selected Works by the Author

Fiction
White Chappell, Scarlet Tracings (1987)
Downriver (1991)
Radon Daughters (1994)
Slow Chocolate Autopsy (1997)
Landor's Tower (2001)
Dining on Stones (2004)

Non-Fiction
Lights Out for the Territory (1997)
Crash (1999)
Liquid City (with Marc Atkins) (1999)
London Orbital (2002)

Michael Carlson

Smith, Alexander McCall (b.1948)

Alexander McCall Smith, born in Zimbabwe in 1948 and a professor of medical law in Edinburgh with a string of academic publications behind him, has achieved enormous success with a series of gentle and whimsical detective novels set in Botswana. Their unlikely heroine, Mma Precious Ramotswe, a 'traditionally built' African lady inordinately proud of her country and possessed of both deep intuition and sharp rationality, is the founder of the No 1 Ladies' Detective Agency, which provides the title for the first book in the series.

The small-town crimes which her agency is called upon to investigate are minor incidents by the standards of conventional crime novels: the theft of a truck, marital infidelity, the dishonest repair of a motor car. But the attraction of Smith's (so far) eight-volume series lies not in the novels' ability to shock or excite the reader, but in their depiction of Botswana as a haven of old-fashioned values and virtues, Smith's own witty, sympathetic style of writing, and perhaps above all, a remarkable cast of characters who create a soap opera of their own throughout the series. Adjectives typically applied by reviewers to the series include 'appealing', 'engaging', 'delightful' and 'affectionate'.

Mma Ramotswe herself follows a strong, simple moral code: 'We must help one another and love one another in our daily lives.' This, as she sees it, is 'the traditional African way'. She is invariably cheerful and positive, and determined to be grateful for what little she has, in spite of a rather lurid past: she was married, briefly and unhappily, to a glamorous but abusive jazz trumpeter, Note Mokoti, and they had a child, who lived only a short time. But at the beginning of the series, she is about to be married again, to Mr J.L.B. Matekoni, proprietor and chief mechanic of Tlokweng Road Speedy Motors, whose unswervable honesty, together with his nervousness about how to treat women, provides much of the comedy throughout. He also has two ne' er-do-well apprentices, who, much to the consternation of Mr J.L.B. Maketoni and Mma Ramotswe, do not always uphold the values of modest living which their employer adheres to. Mma Ramotswe's assistant at the detective agency is Mma Makutsi, economically but memorably characterised by her large glasses and her childish pride in a record-breaking 97 percent score in her final examination at the Botswana Secretarial College. In due course, she sets up her own business, the Kalahari Typing School for Men, which gives its name to the fourth book in the series. Another key character is Mma Potokwani, matron of the local 'orphan farm', who manipulates – usually for good ends – everyone around her, using a cunning blend of rich fruit cake and emotional blackmail. Early on in the series, Mr J.L.B. Matekoni and Mma Ramotswe foster two children, one in a wheelchair, from her orphanage.

The chief virtues Smith celebrates through his characters are personal integrity, good manners and tolerance. Giving others the benefit of the doubt – such as offering a job to a man who has been in jail, or encouraging a wrongdoer to make quiet amends – always reaps rewards in these novels. What rescues them from cloying piety is the sly humour which Smith, most often through Mma Ramotswe, brings to bear on human weakness and social hypocrisy. She sees the essence of detective work as close observation of human behaviour and intuitive understanding of human nature – a sort of Botswanan Miss Marple, she almost always solves her cases by close attention to gossip, to which she is addicted. Both she and Mr J.L.B. Matekoni are always referred to, and indeed refer to each other, by their full names. This can sound quaint, but when, for instance, Note Mokoti turns up unannounced and carelessly addresses Mma Ramotswe as Precious, the effect is electrifying. Smith has created this idyllic little world with absolute conviction.

Some critics, however, have questioned the appropriateness of idealising a nation and a society which in the real world has serious problems. It is not difficult to transform poverty into an enchanting anti-materialism especially attractive to western readers (nor then to share Mma Makutsi's delight in her new two-roomed house, where she will have her own tap, and may even, for the first time in her life, have a rug on the floor). Smith does allude to Botswana's horrifying AIDS crisis, but again transforms it, by presenting it as an opportunity for humane and right-thinking characters to exercise charity and compassion for the suffering and bereaved. Others have felt uncomfortable about what they see as patronage of Smith's characters' simplicity, reflected for instance in the faux-naif titles of the books. But Mma Ramotswe herself focuses on how fortunate Botswana has been – no apartheid, no civil wars, education blossoming and with it women's equality – and her lyrical patriotism is in the end both impressive and deeply enviable: Botswana is 'a country so large that the land seemed to have no limits; there was a sky so wide and free that the spirit could rise and soar...'.

As well as a number of other fictional works, including short stories and books for children, Smith has also had (lesser) success with a series of crime novels set in Edinburgh, which functions, just like Botswana in the Mma Ramotswe novels, as a bastion of old-fashioned, in this case Scottish, virtues, presided over by a sensible, unmarried, female amateur detective, Isabel Dalhousie. However, Dalhousie's particular brand of rational thought springs not from age-old traditional wisdom, like Mma Ramotswe's, but from rather undigested academic philosophy; and Edinburgh's Enlightenment virtues of prudence, good sense, financial probity and social propriety are not so attractive. The somewhat prescriptive nature of this morality is reflected in some of the books' titles. Neither is Isabel, with her penchant for fine art and fine wines, her dislike for modern music and bad manners, and her independent means and attentive housekeeper, a fully sympathetic character. *See also* Humour and Crime Fiction.

Selected Works by the Author

Mma Ramotswe Series
The No 1 Ladies' Detective Agency (1998)
Tears of the Giraffe (2000)
Morality for Beautiful Girls (2001)
The Kalahari Typing School for Men (2002)
The Full Cupboard of Life (2004)
In the Company of Cheerful Ladies (2004)
Blue Shoes and Happiness (2006)
The Good Husband of Zebra Drive (2007)

Isabel Dalhousie Series
The Sunday Philosophy Club (2004)
Friends, Lovers, Chocolate (2005)
The Right Attitude to Rain (2006)
The Correct Use of Compliments (2007)

Heather O'Donoghue

Smith, Joan (b.1953)

Joan Smith is a feminist, journalist and polemicist whose five published crime novels reflect her commitment to radical politics and broadly left-wing ideals.

94. Joan Smith.

The heroine of the five novels, Loretta Lawson, is a highly engaging figure: young, articulate, a university academic and, of course, a staunch feminist. In all the novels, she is the humorous voice of commonsense and reason, pitted against pompous, sexist, unimpressive men. Lawson is heterosexual, separated from, but in a love–hate relationship with, her patronising ex-husband (a journalist whose contacts often prove useful to her investigations) and with the cheerfully unselfconscious attitude towards casual sex, which usually characterises male characters in popular fiction. Smith's novels are dominated by their sexual politics. In the first, *A Masculine Ending* (1987), Lawson is in Paris attending an academic conference about sexism in language when she stumbles across a dead body in a borrowed flat; the title puns on the subject of the conference and the demise of a male colleague. In *Why Aren't They Screaming?* (1988), Lawson happens across murder in connection with a women's peace protest group, a smaller, fictional version of the Greenham Common camp. The victim in *Don't Leave Me This Way* (1990) is a member of a women's group Lawson used to belong to; in *What Men Say* (1993), Lawson's best friend, Oxford academic Bridget Bennett, is accused of the murder of a young woman found dead in an outhouse at Bennett's farm. The final novel, appropriately entitled *Full Stop* (1995), with its return to a grammatical pun and its suggestion of finality, is set in a rather luridly crime-ridden New York, where Lawson is plagued by obscene telephone calls and a mysterious stalker. Its dramatic dénouement ties up loose ends from earlier novels but relies on an improbable degree of coincidence. Sexism is everywhere in Smith's novels, as represented by the attitudes of all but a select few enlightened male characters; the police are particular offenders. Many of the issues Smith takes on – whether Lawson should be known as Ms, Miss or Dr, for example, or her male colleagues' almost unanimous anxiety about feminist literary criticism – now seem dated, but the novels offer very vivid evocations of the left-wing, middle-class viewpoints of their time. Smith's depiction of academic life in London and Oxford is also unusually authentic. Her characters inhabit a comfortable, cultured, educated world; they are generally well-meaning and full of talk about wine, music and fine art at dinner parties and idyllic country retreats. The various murders are a shocking intrusion into this setting, but they are largely crimes of passion, and not the product of a troubled society or endemic criminality. Smith does not create complex plots, and indeed several of the novels end abruptly or inconclusively. Lawson's investigative strengths are neither intellectual nor scientific; the truth about a killing tends to emerge through Lawson networking, empathising, and keeping an open mind. The novels succeed as light-hearted vehicles for their right-on heroine, who happens to be exactly the same age as Smith herself, and evidently shares her author's own political convictions. *See also* Feminist Readings in British Crime Fiction; Gay and Lesbian Crime Fiction; *and* Sexuality in British Crime Fiction.

Selected Works by the Author
A Masculine Ending (1987)
Why Aren't They Screaming? (1988)
Don't Leave Me This Way (1990)
What Men Say (1993)
Full Stop (1995)

Heather O'Donoghue

Social Comment in Crime Fiction

Crime readers know what they like and what a good crime book should be. But they are not of one mind. Some like puzzle mysteries, some like whodunits, some like thrillers, while others prefer **police procedurals**. Practically no one wants a social tract. Yet, our books, insist many crime writers, bring you the real world. We tell you how it is. There is a dichotomy here: crime writers want to trade in realism, but crime readers want to be distanced from its ghastliness and to visit instead a world in which people are spectacularly murdered, lose jewels of inestimable worth, are kidnapped, fooled and blackmailed, and yet do not rouse us to pity or moral outrage. We may shiver with fear, we may tense our shoulder blades, but that's about as much as we want to care.

Does this mean that crime fiction is nothing more than escapism? Not at all – there are elements of social comment freighted into some of the best work in the field. Dealing with sin and retribution as it must, does crime fiction not have a duty to display society's evils and move us to eradicate them? If that is its duty, it has always shirked it.

In the first hundred years of crime fiction (mid-nineteenth to mid-twentieth century), there was little social comment to be found anywhere in crime fiction. Far less was there a drive to change society. Sherlock **Holmes** had no interest in doing so, and neither did his rivals. They lived comfortably, in country residences or smart London flats. Holmes's rival Martin Hewitt – widely read in his day – could have been an exception: he was an ordinary man, a solicitor's clerk turned detective, and more significantly he was created by Arthur Morrison (1863–1945), an author much concerned with social issues, as in his non-crime books *Tales of Mean Streets* (1894) and *A Child of the Jago* (1896). Many of Hewitt's investigations were among ordinary folk in the ordinary parts of town, but they contained barely a whiff of social criticism. Hewitt, along with Holmes and practically every detective who tracked the footsteps of Auguste Dupin, existed in a gentle fantasy where criminals were ingenious and where mysteries baffled the mind. Few of their villains were driven to villainy by poverty, harsh upbringing or social deprivation.

The one writer who stood apart from this, who signalled a different path along which no one followed, was Charles **Dickens**. His Inspector Bucket took us into desperate lodgings, festering slums and the wretched houses of working people. He showed undeserved poverty. He showed law's injustice. He revealed the cruel social prejudices which entrapped people and squeezed out their life. If Dickens was not a crime writer, crime was a strong thread in his stories. He had several minor detectives – Bucket in *Bleak House* (1852–1853), Nadgett in *Martin Chuzzlewit* (1843–1844), Dick Datchery in *Edwin Drood* (1870), all to some extent inspired by the author's first-hand, real-life experiences with Inspector Field – but crime lay at the heart of most of his plots and was tangled by him into searing indictments of inequalities and injustices. His friend Wilkie **Collins** strayed a little way down the path, as did any number of Victorian mainstream novelists, but most crime writers of that time and since have confined themselves to a surprisingly narrow world.

The late-nineteenth-century detective – Holmes included – was well fed, well housed and comfortably well off. Adventures into the stews were expeditions into unknown lands, those of the lower class, into which the detective went like an explorer entering darkest Africa, a white man in a pith helmet. Once his quest was fulfilled, he returned to the civilised world to report quaint customs. This approach to writing crime fiction persisted long into the twentieth century. The early decades, beginning with the late Edwardians and continuing to the Second World War, have been called the **Golden Age**, and the fiction of that age was not tarnished by social realism. Outside of fiction, the real world faced the most terrible war history had seen, immediately followed by two decades of mass poverty, unemployment, the Great Depression and the ominous build-up to another world war. Crime fiction meanwhile told of country houses, toff detectives, respectable villains and policemen who knew their place. Practically no kind of social comment, one would have thought, appeared in these polite fantasies. Or did it? Perhaps this was the way Britain wanted to see itself. Perhaps, despite the turmoil and unrest, there could be a parallel dream world in which we could help ourselves to kedgeree or kidneys from the breakfast sideboard, peruse *The Times*, attend briskly to our affairs, eat lunch, have tea brought out to the lawn and never be in any doubt as to what clothes we should change into for dinner. The servants could attend to mundane necessities and one of our amusing friends would prove to be jolly clever at solving puzzles. It made for wonderfully escapist fiction.

Only when one lifted one's eyes from the page might one notice that the world was changing: beyond the book-jacket lurked a world of poverty and unemployment, alarms from Europe and a brash and sometimes baffling clamour from upstart America. Our cousins from across the Atlantic sent us loud exciting music, jazzy films and, for those who read these things, new variations in crime fiction. There were few country houses. Crime occurred in the streets, and the corpse was dragged out of the library to be dumped in the gutter where it belonged. The setting of American crime stories and films was undeniably different, as were the perpetrators and the victims.

We learned for the first time to speak of hoodlums, dicks and molls. This was a more realistic world. But for all their in-your-face grit and violence, were these tough stories any more real than their snobbish British counterparts? Did they comment on society? At times, they did. Raymond **Chandler**, for one, included wry observations on the high and low societies his hero encountered, but Chandler, Hammett and other streetwise writers were counterbalanced by S.S. Van Dine with his snobbish Philo Vance, Rex Stout with his sedentary Nero Wolfe, and the Vance-like younger Ellery Queen. For all their brash new realism these American writers still put plot before social commentary.

Came the Second World War, and in its aftermath the revolutionary Labour government, and from that maelstrom came new kinds of writers. The new wave did not immediately affect crime writing but the upheaval had its effect, and the old-fashioned 'silly ass' detective and posh amateur had to change. They took their time; they faded, they changed their coats – Sayers, Allingham, Christie, Crispin, Innes and others had dusted themselves off and carried on for decades – while they faced up to new challengers. Simenon from France they had met before. Cheyney and Hadley Chase were copycat Americans. Creasey and Gilbert were competent exponents of the new police procedural. In the immediate post-war years, these different kinds of writers lived side by side. By the time the austerity years eased in the 1950s, the world of crime fiction had accommodated these new sub-genres but there was still little sign of social criticism. Outside the crime fiction world, the world was being assaulted by the Angry Young Man, but in the crime world little changed, and tempers remained curiously imperturbable – curious because crime fiction deals with crime and violence. Yet it would not get angry. The timidity of crime fiction became even more obvious in the sizzling sixties. Revolution was in the air, the times they were a-changing, but you would not have known it from crime fiction – or not in book form. The year 1960 saw the release of a splendidly tough British crime film, *The Criminal*, and British television shocked its public with series such as *Z Cars*. In response British publishers introduced Adam **Dalgliesh** and Inspector **Wexford** – fine detectives both, but not over-concerned with incisive social comment.

In the 1980s came a new artistic imperative: to 'subvert the genre', to turn crime fiction upside down. In practice, most of the generally younger writers tempted down this path knew that to break all the rules at once would be counterproductive. (If William Burroughs ever wrote a mystery we would *never* know whodunit.) The trick, these writers thought, would be to take one founding principle and discard it, thus breathing new life into a tired old literary form. The detective, generally till now an authoritarian, right-thinking *man*, would be altered in some fundamental way – becoming instead female, or libertarian, or gay or physically handicapped, or of different ethnicity. Some of the writers who made these changes found that the fresh angle they had given themselves gave an entirely fresh approach to what they wrote. Their different detective looked at the world differently too, seeing it in a less condemnatory, less black-and-white way. The detectives, or their authors, began to comment on what they saw.

Changes in ethnicity in the late 1980s ranged from Mike **Phillips**'s Jamaican-born Samson Dean, an investigative journalist living and working in contemporary London, to Michael **Dibdin**'s Italian policeman Aurelio Zen. Samson Dean showed Britain from a black man's point of view, though compared to Americans such as Walter Mosley's Easy Rawlins or, earlier, Chester Himes's Johnson and Jones stories, Phillips's hero had a distinctly middle-class, almost white liberal point of view. The series was encouragingly reviewed but did not sell in large numbers and, significantly, no British series with a black hero has sold well since. (The excellent television series, *The Chinese Detective* (1981–1982), did not get a second outing.) Dibdin's Zen was on safer ground – Italy being more appealing territory – and his series did make it into top ten sales, encouraging other writers to set their series in that country (such as American writers Donna Leon and British writers David **Hewson** and Magdalen **Nabb**). Unexpectedly, these foreign-based novels examined the politics and geography of their setting more acutely than did most equivalent novels based in Britain, as if British writers were too close, too much a part of their environment, to see it objectively. Other British writers who have set their books abroad bear out this premise: Julian **Rathbone** with his African and European thrillers, Philip **Kerr** with his Berlin trilogy, Christopher West (b.1954) with Inspector Wang, and more recently, Barbara **Nadel**'s Turkish policeman Cetin Ikmen.

Perhaps these writers are inspired by other European writers, who comment on society more often than do British authors. When one looks for British writers who do make political or social comment a part of their work, one struggles to find them. Politics does appear, largely in the tired guise of having a corrupt politician as the (easily spotted) villain, but there is rarely a political argument. Social *conditions* feature in many crime books (they could hardly fail to) but sustained comment, exposé or agitprop is almost never seen. One can take Denise **Mina** as an exception to that, which she certainly is, but compared with Britain's one great campaigning crime writer, Dickens, she hammers her message so heavily that its cutting edge is dulled. Similarly, Peter Turnbull's (b.1950) shattering novel *Embracing Skeletons* (1996) was too unsettling for most readers. More readably, Paul **Johnston** set his Quint Dalrymple novels in the near future in an altered Britain which satirised the current state; John **Baker** had his Sam Turner as troubled by the damaged souls he worked with as would be the most caring social worker; Margaret **Murphy** writes sensitively of ordinary but overburdened folk. Inevitably, given that most criminals come from, and most crime occurs among, what the Victorians termed 'the dangerous classes', there are plenty of crime writers who do set their books within that section of society: the poor and desperate, the hardened and ostracised. By far the most successful, in sales terms at least, is Martina **Cole**, whose Essex-based gangland sagas are brutally realistic. To Cole, and to the others mentioned above can be added several who sell in far smaller numbers, such as Martyn **Waites**, Cath **Staincliffe**, Russell **James**, Lesley **Horton** and Quintin **Jardine**. But each of these – and one has to look hard to find even these examples – stands as a testimony to the *lack* of real social comment in practically any British crime writer. In place of social comment they give social realism.

Exposés, of a sort, can be found in 'bent cop' novels, just as in those with corrupt politicians. G.F. **Newman** probably heads the list here: his first books comprised what came to be known as the 'Bastard Trilogy' (*Sir, You Bastard*, 1970; *You Nice Bastard*, 1972; and *You Flash Bastard*, 1974), featuring the unscrupulous Inspector Sneed, and he went on to greater notoriety with hard-hitting factual television series *Law and Order* (1978) and *Black and Blue* (1992). Simon **Kernick**'s cop moonlighted as a part-time hit man; Mark **Timlin**'s undisciplined Sharman stole drugs and narrowly escaped being thrown out of the force (he was invalided out and set up as a private detective); Ken Bruen's Roberts and Brant were a pair of sleazy, violent vigilantes. But all of these (Newman's perhaps excepted) were nothing more than devices used to frame strong stories. A more sensitive approach might be expected from the post-1980s writers who created gay heroes (or heroines). Gay, even transvestite, heroes come from the pens of writers such as Stella **Duffy**, Val **McDermid** and Nicholas **Blincoe** – though there have been gay heroes before – remember Nancy Spain's Birdseye and Nevkorina — and welcome as their stories are, they carry no particular social message.

The inescapable conclusion is that crime fiction and social comment do not mix, or at least that few British authors will let them mix. They are probably right. In a crime story there is little room for comment of any sort: it slows the action. Paragraphs of comment are what the editor cuts. As Elmore Leonard famously said, 'I leave out the parts readers tend to skip.' No one wants paragraphs – or worse, pages – of social comment dragged in for the crime reader to stumble over, and the reader does not want to see the writer 'sounding off'. Once a reader spots such writing, the story has stopped and the author has failed. That is not to say that a social cause or argument has no place in a crime story. On the contrary, one can easily argue that social ills can be more effectively demonstrated in a crime story than in any other form of novel, but the message cannot be simply fastened onto the story. It must be integral. In the best of Dickens's novels, the entire plot is designed to demonstrate the argument, but it is a moot point whether this is a task for the modern crime story. Crime fiction may have to settle for merely reflecting society, rather than trying to change it.

Today's top-selling crime novels may – indeed often do – get out in the streets on the wrong side of town, but their stories seldom twist far from what they really are: puzzle mysteries, thrillers or police procedurals. It may disappoint ambitious writers to be so proscribed, but fans do not read them for social comment. Top writers know this, and that is why they sell. People read crime stories to be entertained, to escape their own world. They get enough reality at home.

Russell James

Spencer, John B. (1944–2002)

John B. Spencer was a musician and writer of science fiction crime who later produced four bitter and remarkable **London** noir novels. He became a respected blues and folk musician in the 1970s before writing three hard-boiled crime novels set in a future America. In 1996, the Do-Not Press published the first of the four London-based noir novels on which his reputation as a British crime writer is based. These novels depict a society in which justice is a faded dream. They represent a weary and bitter outlook, but they are rich in humour and emotion.

Quake City (1996), the last of Spencer's futuristic novels, pits his resourceful PI against a corrupt power structure in which making enemies can lead to your being stripped of your ID – thus losing the right to work, rent property or even walk the streets. Spencer blends the influences of Chandler and Philip K. Dick to deliver a fast-moving, angry pastiche.

Perhaps She'll Die! (1996) finds the same darkness in present-day London. The exclamation mark is the only false note in a novel of brooding intensity. A property developer decides to punish a man who has slept with his wife, and several lives unravel as a result. There is no one to 'catch' the criminals – only an evolving pattern of desire, loss and betrayal.

Tooth & Nail (1998) probes deeper into the property world, opening with the burning alive of an immigrant family. The narrative is a series of terse close-up scenes, often focused on the passions of lust and rage. It is the story of a vain young crook on the make, unaware of what he is dealing with. The brutal resolution is less significant than the way Spencer explores the corrosion of human values.

Stitch (1999) depicts the working and personal lives of a number of thieves, including a psychopath who sleeps with his mother in order to repay her for having him adopted. A poignant account of a musician's death from MS, and his wife's trauma of grief, raises the emotional stakes in a novel whose underlying theme is love.

The title of *Grief* (2003) refers both to the pain of loss and to more practical kinds of trouble. A criminal with a prosthetic hand falls out with an old friend; a young heroin addict robs his sister and rapes her girlfriend; a schizophrenic man falls into a mesh of deceit. *Grief* is a novel of bitter compassion, played out in a physical and spiritual wasteland. One of Spencer's property dealers remarks: 'The law only matters if you don't.' It is a suitable epigraph for a body of work that explores the affinities between criminality and Thatcherite culture. There is as much grief as cynicism in Spencer's writing. His strongest recurrent theme is the corrosion of emotional ties. In Spencer's world, a stranger is just a friend who has not betrayed you yet. *See also* Pulp.

Selected Works by the Author
A Case for Charley (1984)
Charley Gets the Picture (1985)
Quake City (1996)
Perhaps She'll Die! (1996)
Tooth and Nail (1998)
Stitch (1999)
Grief (2003)

Joel Lane

Spring, Michelle (b.1951)

Michelle Spring's distinctive series of crime novels are built around PI Laura Principal, based in modern Cambridge and **London**. Clearly influenced by the **feminist** hard-boiled novels of US writers Marcia Muller, Sue Grafton and Sara Paretsky (Spring is Canadian), the novels nevertheless offer a more collective notion of the detective than a single figure on mean streets. Laura Principal works with partners, Sonny (who is also her lover) and Stevie, an enigmatic woman of great resource. Moreover, Principal has another base for living, officially nothing to do with her work. Wildfell is a remote country cottage she and Stevie share with a close woman friend, Helen. There, Laura tells us, she finds her 'true centre of self'. This is a clue to the underlying myth of the series. Narrated in the first person (like Muller's Sharon McCone, Grafton's Kinsey, Paretsky's V.I.), Spring's series is a feminist-inflected quest for self, crucially a self understood as relational and social. For although Laura finds herself forced to turn inward in the course of her investigations, the stories very deliberately focus outwards into an England warped by inequalities and deprivation. Most often there is a root of misogyny, often of ancient origin, twisting round the crimes Laura detects. In the hard-boiled tradition, Laura uncovers more than individual criminals. She often detects a terrifying fragility within the social advances of feminism, the welfare state and even the institution of the family, to nurture the vulnerable.

95. Michelle Spring.

Even in the novel that most focuses on a single family and the tragedy of the loss of a child (which might be argued to transcend social structures), *In the Midnight Hour* (2001), Spring's incisive cultural criticism is acute. Jack and Olivia Cable have endured almost more than they can bear in the loss of their four-year-old son, Timmy. He disappeared from a Norfolk beach twelve years previously. With no body being found, Olivia persists in treating Timmy as if he were alive. The couple comes to Laura because Olivia believes she has found Timmy, now a sixteen-year-old street musician. Jack wants him investigated. A shadowy presence in the atmosphere of trauma is Catherine, Timmy's elder sister, who, even before his son's vanishing, took second place in Jack's eyes. Catherine is hurt, but fortunately, proves resilient to the inequalities of gender. Far more fascinating is the role of Jack Cable's heroism in the destruction of his family. *In the Midnight Hour* is the novel where the feminist myth of relational self comes up against the traditional masculine myth of autonomous heroism. Here the male path involves an impossible journey for treasure/discovery, bravery, saving a life, and returning to the thanks of a grateful nation. However, while Laura has to battle with a profound breach of her autonomy in a miscarriage, she slowly discovers the heavy price Jack's family paid for his heroism: an obsession to locate two lost ships in the arctic. Made sick by his refusal to rest, Jack either neglected his son until the child drowned, or may even have lashed out at the boy who was whining for his attention. In the unknowability of Timmy's exact fate lies a space where tragedy and patriarchy meet.

Selected Works by the Author
Every Breath You Take (1994)
Running for Shelter (1995)
Standing in the Shadows (1998)

Spring, Michelle

Nights in White Satin (1999)
In the Midnight Hour (2001)

Further Reading
Humm, Maggie. 1990. 'Feminist Detective Fiction'. In *Twentieth Century Suspense*. Edited by Clive Bloom. Macmillan.
Walton, Priscilla L., and Manina Jones. 1999. *Detective Agency: Women Rewriting the Hard-Boiled Tradition*. University of California Press.

Susan Rowland

Spy Fiction

See Espionage Fiction

Staincliffe, Cath (b.1956)

Cath Staincliffe is the creator of two female detectives who juggle child care with investigative work. She cites as influences the American writers Marcia Muller and Sue Grafton. Their female private eyes inspired the creation of Sal Kilkenny, based in Manchester, a single mother looking after young children, who undertakes enquiries in the classic gumshoe tradition. Sal made her first appearance in *Looking for Trouble* (1994). Originally published by a small press, it attracted attention for its brisk, no-nonsense picture of the life of a contemporary working woman. To date, seven novels featuring Sal Kilkenny have been published and the urban setting ('You can't live in Manchester and not know rain,' Sal muses in *Towers of Silence*, 2002) provides a credible, if sometimes dour, background to her cases. A notable city centre landmark, the Arndale Centre shopping mall, features regularly, and in *Towers of Silence*, the question is whether Miriam Johnstone's plunge to her death from the Centre's car park was suicide or – given that Miriam was scared of heights – murder. Staincliffe's novels include *Bitter Blue* (2003), in which Sal investigates a hate campaign against elegant Lucy Barker while trying to discover why her daughter Maddie no longer wants to go to school.

When Staincliffe departed from her series to write a stand-alone **police procedural**, at first the book failed to attract a publisher. Undaunted, she turned the storyline into a television script which won high audience ratings when screened and formed the basis for the popular ITV series *Blue Murder* (first aired 2003). Completing the circle, she revised the novel and it was published as *Blue Murder: Cry Me a River* (2004). So far it has had one successor, *Hit and Run* (2005). Both novels feature DI Janine Lewis, a cop whose struggle to cope with the work–life balance again lends the stories a touch of realism. Again the Mancunian backdrop – Janine is the city's first female Detective Chief Inspector – is integral to the appeal of the books. When first encountered, she is a single parent with three children and a fourth on the way. Her husband left her on the day she got the promotion after she found him in bed with the cleaner. The books about Janine are written in the third person, while Sal recounts her own adventures and this reflects a common distinction between the police novel and the private eye story. Staincliffe's occasional short stories include 'Death in the

96. Cath Staincliffe.

Air' featuring Sal Kilkenny, to be found in *Murder Squad* (2001), an anthology put together by the collective of Northern Crime Writers of which she was a founder member. The non-criminous *Trio* (2002) is rooted in Staincliffe's experience of being adopted and reflects her interest in family ties as well as social history. *See also* Feminist Readings in British Crime Fiction *and* Women Crime Writers.

Selected Works by the Author
Looking for Trouble (1994)
Go Not Gently (1997)
Dead Wrong (1998)
Stone Cold Red Hot (2001)
Towers of Silence (2002)
Bitter Blue (2003)
Blue Murder: Cry Me a River (2004)
Hit and Run (2005)
Missing (2007)

Martin Edwards

Stallwood, Veronica

Veronica Stallwood has made a speciality of the Oxford-set crime novel, often matching (and at time surpassing) that other specialist in crime under the Dreaming Spires, Colin **Dexter**. Her prose has a brisk, no-nonsense efficiency, and her sense of locale is always sure-footed.

Stallwood's novels feature as sleuth a thirty-something romantic novelist, Kate Ivory. Stallwood has lived in Oxford for many years, and knows both the city and its university well. Yet, she views the city with the sharp eye of an outsider and brings it to life in an unsentimental way, far removed from the chocolate-box images usually shown on television. She flings open the oaken doors of venerable colleges and shows what is really happening inside, based on her own experience of working at the Bodleian, Oxford's library, as well as in various colleges. And her sleuth, Kate Ivory, is also less than perfect – 'a flesh-and-brains heroine', as one critic put it, she enjoys white wine, chocolate biscuits and the company of unsuitable men. An ever-expanding circle of friends and lovers, not to mention her mother and her literary agent, have joined Kate over the years, developing strong characters and stories of their own.

97. Veronica Stallwood.

Born in London, Stallwood attended an American school in Athens, then a French school in the Lebanon, returning to England in her late teens. After a variety of jobs, she eventually settled in Oxford with her two children, discovering quite late in her working life that she had a talent for writing. Acceptance of her first novel, *Deathspell* (1992), was immediate, and since the mid-1990s she has been a full-time writer, using her varied life experiences to enrich her work. Stallwood's 'Oxford' novels include *Oxford Exit* (1994), *Oxford Knot* (1998) and *Oxford Letters* (2006). These ingenious novels (all of which feature the resourceful Kate Ivory) have a devoted following. Stallwood's finely turned stand-alone suspense novel, *The Rainbow Sign* (1999), based on her experience in Lebanon, demonstrated that Stallwood's adroit plotting matched that of any of her contemporaries; *Oxford Menace* (2008) showed that her city of choice is still fecund territory for her.

When she is not writing, Stallwood enjoys talking, and walking in the beautiful (though frequently muddy) Oxfordshire countryside. *See also* The Shires: Rural England and Regional Crime Fiction.

Selected Works by the Author
Deathspell (1992)
Oxford Exit (1994)
Oxford Knot (1998)

The Rainbow Sign (1999)
Oxford Letters (2006)
Oxford Menace (2008)

Barry Forshaw

Starling, Boris (b.1969)

With four novels, Boris Starling has established himself as one of the most versatile, and least predictable, of crime writers. Before he had ever published a book, Starling had already gained a different reputation in the crime field, by participating in the television programme *Mastermind*. As a contestant in 1996, he reached the semi-finals: his specialist subject: the novels of Dick **Francis**. His appearance received even more attention when Francis appeared in the studio to watch Starling perform.

Educated at Eton and Cambridge, where he took a first in history, Starling worked as a journalist and for a business called Control Risk, which consults on issues of terrorism, kidnap and political instability. This experience would be reflected particularly in his third novel, *Vodka* (2004). Interestingly for an old Etonian, his first book, *Messiah* (1999) dealt with a serial killer who cuts out his victims' tongues and replaces them with a silver spoon. Opening with a 'double-event', it drove Metropolitan Police serial killer expert Red Metcalfe and his team through an ever-grislier world of corruption and deception, climaxing in a betrayal that was foreshadowed in its title. Starling was part of the W.H. Smith 'Fresh Talent' promotion, and the book became a bestseller in both Britain and the United States. It was adapted for television by the BBC, with the ubiquitous Ken Stott as Metcalfe and Starling taking a cameo role as Bart Miller. The adaptation was later re-titled *Messiah I: The Awakening* to allow for its three sequels, on which Starling was credited as the series creator.

In print, Starling followed *Messiah* with a semi-sequel, *Storm* (2000), which brought back Kate Beauchamp from Metcalfe's team. She survives a ferry disaster in Aberdeen, after which she pursues another serial killer, while her estranged father heads the investigation into the sunken ferry. Like *Messiah*, *Storm*'s title signals a parallel, from Greek mythology. *Storm* won a W.H. Smith 'Thumping Good Read' award, and also cracked the bestseller lists. Four years later, *Vodka*, was a departure in many ways, a sprawling story with overtones of nineteenth-century epics. An American banker, Alice Liddel, is sent to privatise the Red October distillery, owned by Russian politician and mafia leader Lev, himself at war with Chechen gangsters. Russia is in chaos and Moscow is being stalked by a serial killer who preys on children. A wry reminder of Boris Yeltsin's vodka crisis, the novel's central conceit is telegraphed by Alice's name, but some critics felt Starling had over-reached himself.

Although his fourth novel, *Visibility* (2006), also dealt with the **historical** past, its story elements were more tightly intertwined, and it was an overwhelming critical success. The drowning of a scientist in Hyde Park is investigated by Herbert Smith, reassigned to Scotland Yard after being the fall guy for MI5's allowing Donald McLean to escape. Historical figures include Rosalind Franklin, Linus Pauling and a notorious Nazi war criminal; while Smith's own story parallels his investigation, as he begins a romance with a blind woman. London in 1952, choked by the Great Fog, is evoked tellingly, and Starling's coda, drawing the strands together, is perfectly judged.

Selected Works by the Author
Messiah (1999)
Storm (2000)
Vodka (2004)
Visibility (2006)

Michael Carlson

Stone, Nick (b.1966)

Nick Stone's exuberant, atmospheric *Mr Clarinet* (2006) and *King of Swords* (2007) are the first instalments in a proposed series featuring Miami cop, and later PI, Max Mingus. Besides the colourful characters, these thrillers establish Stone as a master of delirious plotting; *Mr Clarinet* derives much of its compelling atmosphere from the inclusion of voodoo, a Haitian-based black magic religion.

Born in Cambridge on Halloween 1966, Nick Stone is the son of a Scottish father (the celebrated and controversial historian Norman Stone) and a Haitian mother who descends from the Aubreys, one of Haiti's oldest families. (In the late nineteenth century Nick Stone's great-great grandfather reputedly cured the French navy in Haiti of yellow fever using voodoo medicine for which he was awarded the Légion d'honneur.) At six months, Stone was sent to live with his grandparents on the Caribbean island and, although he would return to Britain for his education in 1971, he continued to visit Haiti throughout his formative years. Following attendance at various schools, Stone followed in his father's footsteps and went to Cambridge to read History in 1986. After a thirteen-year absence Stone returned to Haiti in 1996 to work in the marketing department of a national bank for a year. His visit coincided with the presence of the United States and United Nation's peacekeeping force, and it was during this visit that Nick Stone conceived the idea for *Mr Clarinet*. He discovered that a little-publicised consequence of the 1994 US occupancy of Haiti was the repatriation of most Haitian criminals from American prisons – hundreds of murderers, rapists, gang members and drug dealers were flown back to the island and handed over to the country's authorities. As well as the chaos resulting from the convicts being released shortly after their arrival back in Haiti, another consequence was that infants of wealthy Haitians started being kidnapped. The disappearance of Haitian children had been a regular problem for years, but with the influx of the criminals it escalated.

Stone's background and knowledge of the island became invaluable when writing his first novel. In *Mr Clarinet*, former Miami policeman Max Mingus, in his forties, and just released from prison for a triple murder, is haunted by his vigilante past. He takes on a case to find Charlie, the missing child of a wealthy Haitian family. Charlie has been missing for three years, and Max's predecessors have all regretted taking on the job. At first, Max is reluctant to accept the assignment, but he is drawn in despite himself. Is the disappearance of the child related to Tonton Clarinette, the fabled voodoo spirit? Evocative descriptions of Haiti, with its poverty and corruption, form the fascinating backdrop to this novel. *Mr Clarinet* is very much Max's story, but writing it provided the inspiration for a prequel that has a multi-stranded narrative. *King of Swords* features murder, drug-running, corrupt policing, black magic – all part of the history of 1980s Miami. As well as introducing many new and compelling characters, it further reveals more of the history of those introduced in *Mr Clarinet*: Max's wife Sandra, his police partner, Detective Sergeant Joe Liston and their boss Deputy Chief Eldon Burns. Looming over *King of Swords*, though, is Solomon Boukman, a terrifying figure of mythical proportions, who becomes Max's nemesis, and goes on to haunt him when he takes on the Mr Clarinet case.

The concept for future Max Mingus novels is to focus on key moments in Miami's history through to the present day. The (working) title for the third instalment is *90 Miles*, with Miami and Cuba as locations.

Selected Works by the Author
Mr Clarinet (2006)
King of Swords (2007)
90 Miles (2009)

Adrian Muller

The Strand Magazine

The Strand is the legendary magazine that did most to popularise crime and mystery series, most notably the Sherlock **Holmes** stories by Arthur Conan **Doyle**. It ran for 710 monthly issues from January 1891 to March 1950. It was edited for forty of those years, until December 1930, by H. Greenhough Smith, who had originally proposed the idea to publisher George Newnes. What distinguished the magazine from its competitors was its use of new printing techniques to allow pictures and photographs on almost every page, in imitation of the American magazines such as *The Century* and *Scribner's*, and to offer this at the remarkably low price of sixpence, which made the magazine affordable to the mass of middle-class readers who were establishing themselves by the end of the century.

Originally, *The Strand* offered translations of European stories mixed with articles on popular subjects and interviews with celebrities, but there was little of significance in the fiction until Smith acquired from Doyle the first series of 'Adventures of Sherlock Holmes', which began in the July 1891 issue. Doyle's genius was not only in creating a formidable detective capable of solving crimes by a judicious assessment of seemingly minor clues, but also in developing unusual crimes (very few Holmes stories involve murder) and setting them in places around London well known to readers. Indeed the very gall of putting Holmes's consulting rooms at a recognisable location (221b Baker Street) but one which the public could not find added to the fascination. Watson's habit of referring to other crimes gave Holmes a past and a history and, with each successive case, built him into a believable individual. Many readers were convinced that Holmes was real, which is why it caused such an outcry when, after twenty-four stories, Doyle sent Holmes to his death in 'The Adventure of the Final Problem' (December 1893). Yet, if the introduction of Holmes had taken *The Strand* to the front-rank of magazines, with its worldwide sales rising from 100,000 at the start to 450,000 before the decade was out, the death of Holmes placed the magazine in a dilemma. It had to replace Holmes with something that would satisfy a hungry readership, and it was evident that no one

98. Cover of *The Strand Magazine* for February 1936, advertising a new story by Agatha Christie.

author or character could achieve that. As a consequence, there was a proliferation of new series characters each trying to outdo the other, either in their similarity to Holmes and his methods, or in developing mysterious and unusual plots.

The first such series in *The Strand*, rushed to fill the gap between the first and second series from July to November 1892, was 'A Romance from a Detective's Casebook' by Dick Donovan. Donovan was the writing alias of James Preston Muddock (1843–1934), but it was also the name of his Glasgow detective, whose stories had already proved popular before *The Strand* appeared and had been collected in *The Man-Hunter* in 1888. Indeed, prior to the emergence of Holmes, Donovan was probably the most popular detective in fiction. Yet, Holmes soon eclipsed him, for though the Donovan stories continued to appear in books, no more appeared in *The Strand*.

Combining the approaches of Doyle and Donovan, the Irish writer L.T. Meade (1844–1914), working with Clifford Halifax for medical advice, produced 'Stories from the Diary of a Doctor' (July 1893–June 1894) in which a doctor relates his accounts of strange cases that arise from his patients. The most direct imitation of Holmes came from Arthur Morrison (1863–1945) with 'Martin Hewitt, Investigator' (March–September 1894). Hewitt, like Holmes, is a London-based consulting detective (with offices near the Strand) and also like Holmes, he pays attention to detail and logic. To add to the Holmes image, Hewitt was illustrated by Sidney Paget, who had created the unmistakable profile of Holmes for *The Strand* (based on Paget's brother, Walter) and which has been endlessly reproduced.

However, Hewitt was soon lured away to *The Windsor Magazine*, and *The Strand* had to suffice with a second series of Meade's 'Diary of a Doctor', whilst Doyle contributed his preferred historical stories, first the Brigadier Gerard series and then the serial 'Rodney Stone'. Mrs Meade became a stalwart of the magazine, concocting various series. 'The Adventures of a Man of Science' (July 1896–February 1897), again with Clifford Halifax, relates the stories of Paul Gilchrist whose travels and research bring him into contact with conflict and mystery. Turning to new collaborator Robert Eustace, Meade then produced 'The Brotherhood of the Seven Kings' (January–October 1898), about an Italian secret society that is infiltrating Britain under the corrupt woman scientist Madame Koluchy. Koluchy proved to be the trial run for an even more evil villain, Madame Sara, who appears in 'The Sorceress of the Strand' (October 1902–March 1903). She is not simply a femme fatale but is generally regarded as the first female master-criminal in English literature.

Another stalwart of *The Strand* in the 1890s was Grant Allen (1848–1899) whose series included 'An African Millionaire' (June 1896–May 1897), which featured Colonel Clay, a confidence trickster who prefigured E.W. **Hornung**'s Raffles by two years. In 'Miss Cayley's Adventures' (March 1898–February 1899), Lois Cayley, determined to make her way in the world, thinks nothing of confronting criminals and villains. Unfortunately, Allen died before completing his next series, 'Hilda Wade' (March 1899–February 1900), where a young nurse sets out to prove her father innocent of murder, and the final episode was finished by Conan Doyle. Doyle was himself back in Dr Watson's chair with the best known of all Sherlock Holmes stories, 'The Hound of the Baskervilles' (August 1901–April 1902), which caused sales of *The Strand* to rise by another 30,000 up to 500,000. Thereafter Doyle resurrected Holmes in 'The Adventure of the Empty House' (October 1903) and continued to contribute Holmes stories over the next twenty-four years until 'The Adventure of Shoscombe Old Place' (March 1927). Smith knew that the presence of Doyle in an issue, and especially Holmes, always added to *The Strand*'s circulation more than any other contributor.

During the Edwardian decade, *The Strand* published fewer detective and mystery series, preferring the more fanciful stories by Edith Nesbit (1858–1924) and Rudyard Kipling, plus early stories by P.G. Wodehouse (1881–1975), but it did run the 'Stingaree Stories' (September 1904–April 1905) by E.W. Hornung, about an Australian bushranger, and the automobile mysteries by C.N. Williamson (1859–1920) and A.M. Williamson (1869–1933), 'The Scarlet Runner' (December 1906–November 1907). It also ran a feature article 'The Greatest Detective Agency in the World' (December 1905), about Pinkerton National Detective Agency. E. Phillips Oppenheim, who had already made a name elsewhere, and who would be a regular in *The Strand* between the wars, put in his first appearance, with several stories in 1908 including 'The Money Spider' (November 1908), which shows how fate can lead to either fortune or crime. The end of the Edwardian era saw the serialisation of A.E.W. **Mason**'s 'Murder at the Villa Rose' (December 1909–August 1910), which introduced Inspector Hanaud of the Sûreté.

Richard Marsh (1857–1915) had contributed several stories to *The Strand*, but his best remembered was the series 'Judith Lee' (August 1911–August 1912), about a lip reader who uses her skill to tackle criminals. E.C. **Bentley** had produced an instant classic with *Trent's Last Case*, published in February 1913, and *The Strand* ran two Philip Trent stories in 1914 and a third in 1916, but it was to be another twenty years before Bentley wrote any more Trent stories. Bentley's stories were a landmark in the modernisation of the detective story, away from the Holmesian clue-based deduction to a more relaxed, natural human exploration of relationships, allowing room for error. They were a forerunner of the country-house crime tales of the 1920s, though the route to them was disrupted by the First World War.

One of the main writers to emerge from the First World War was 'Sapper' (H.C. McNeile, 1888–1937) who, though he sold initially to the *Daily Mail* and *Pearson's Magazine*, began selling to *The Strand* with 'Shrapnel' (May 1916) and made the magazine his premier market in the 1930s; during this period, *The Strand* ran several of his Bulldog Drummond stories. However, *The Strand* had, by the 1920s, lost its position as the market leader. *Nash's* paid more and was the most prestigious market, while *The London* had a greater circulation, but there was a cachet attached to *The Strand* because of its status, and many writers remained loyal to the magazine. Doyle, Wodehouse, Oppenheim and Sapper dominated *The Strand* in the 1920s, and the latter three into the 1930s. They were joined by F. Britten Austin (1885–1941), Edgar **Wallace** (whose Sergeant Sir Peter stories ran during 1929–1930) and Agatha **Christie**. Christie contributed most of her short stories to *The Strand* between January 1932 and July 1944, including the *The Labours of Hercules*. Dorothy L. **Sayers** was less in evidence, though three Lord Peter **Wimsey** stories appeared between 1934 and 1938, but Margery **Allingham** was more of a regular, with fifteen Mr Campion stories between August 1936 and May 1940. At the same time, John Dickson **Carr** (initially as Carter Dickson) became a regular contributor, with fourteen stories, and E.C. Bentley at last returned with Trent's real last cases, so that the late 1930s was a brief quasi-**Golden Age** of crime fiction in *The Strand*.

Unfortunately, the paper rationing introduced during the Second World War led to *The Strand* being drastically reduced in size to a small digest format from October 1941, and it lost most of its personality, even though it was one of the few surviving fiction magazines of the period. There were a few gleams in the darkness though. C. Day-Lewis, writing as Nicholas **Blake**, contributed three stories featuring Nigel Strangeways in 1944 and 1949. Eric **Ambler** put in a brief appearance with 'The Unknown Traitor' (December 1948) and there were translations of two non-Maigret stories by Georges Simenon. But in its final days, *The Strand* was grasping at straws, and in an attempt to capture old glories, it commissioned Ronald A. Knox to write a new Sherlock Holmes story, 'The Adventure of the First Class Carriage' (February 1947), with Tom Purvis doing his best to recreate the imagery of Sidney Paget. It was a valiant effort but lacked the vital spark. *The Strand* was eventually merged with its stablemate, *Men Only*, after March 1950.

It was revived briefly as *The New Strand* from December 1961 to February 1963, edited in the latter stages by John **Creasey**, but apart from further attempts to cash in on Sherlock Holmes with a series of articles by Lord Donegall, plus two serials by Creasey himself, the magazine had little to offer the crime fan. Most recently, the name has been appropriated by an American publisher who re-launched *The Strand* in 1998 primarily as a crime and mystery magazine. It frequently runs new fiction by British writers, including H.R.F. **Keating**, Michael **Gilbert**, Peter **Lovesey**, Catherine **Aird**, Michael **Pearce** and John Mortimer, as well as several Holmes pastiches, and though clearly a modern-day copy, it has much to offer. Whilst it takes advantage of the golden memory of the original *Strand*, it cannot hope to reclaim the original atmosphere as the real fiction magazine has long since lost the battle against television.

Yet, the fact that *The Strand* lives on in name and spirit is testament to its importance and significance in the development and popularisation of the detective short story, and it is a legacy that it shall never lose.

Further Reading
Beare, Geraldine. 1982. *Index to The Strand Magazine, 1891–1950*. Greenwood Press.
Pound, Reginald. 1948. *A Maypole in the Strand*. Ernest Benn.
Pound, Reginald. 1966. *The Strand Magazine, 1891–1950*. Heinemann.

Mike Ashley

Suspense

Suspense was a pocketbook-sized magazine published by the Amalgamated Press
(Fleetway Publications from September 1959) and edited by Dorothy M. Sutherland
as a companion to the short-story magazine *Argosy*. It ran for thirty-two monthly
issues from August 1958 to April 1961, missing only August 1959.

99. Cover of *Suspense* magazine, July 1959.

As the magazine's title implied, the emphasis was on suspense, and so contents
were not restricted to crime or mystery stories but any adventure stories classifiable
as 'thrillers'. So, alongside the crime stories were westerns, science fiction and the
occasional weird tale. The first twelve issues, for example, carried new stories written
to the format of the US television series *Wagon Train* which was then being broadcast
on commercial television. Amongst the science fiction were reprints of stories by Ray
Bradbury, Philip Wylie and Fredric Brown, whilst stories by John Collier (1901–1980),

Nigel Kneale (1922–2006) and Jack Finney, amongst others, might best be classified as 'unusual' or 'strange'. Whilst these non-crime stories accounted for at most a fifth of the content, they were an important part of the flavouring of the magazine, showing its broad diversity. There were also real-life stories of suspense, with foreign legion or wartime experiences, as well as fictional stories set in combat situations. There were times when *Suspense* seemed to be trying to please several readerships, aiming as much for the men's magazine market, as exemplified by *Wide World Magazine* in Britain and *Adventure* or *Argosy* in the United States, as in the mystery magazine market.

For much of its run, at least half of each issue's contents were reprints – early issues were almost entirely reprints. Some came from early sources but most were from near-contemporary US magazines, so that stories were new to most British readers. However, the titles of some reprinted stories were changed and no indication given, which must have frustrated some readers. For instance, the first issue carried Agatha **Christie**'s 'Double Alibi', which turns out to be a reprint of 'Triangle at Rhodes', readily available in the paperback collection *Murder in the Mews*. The reprints tended to be by the major names in each issue, with stories and sometimes longer items from Dashiell Hammett, Leslie **Charteris**, Raymond **Chandler**, Edgar **Wallace**, Georges Simenon, Cornell Woolrich and John Dickson **Carr**, amongst many others.

However, *Suspense* did run advance serialisation of novels just prior to their book publication, and this gave readers a special scoop, even though most of these were abridged. Amongst them were *Hide My Eyes* (serialised in August–September 1958) by Margery **Allingham**, *World in My Pocket* (serialised in January–March 1959) by James Hadley **Chase** and 'The Happy Travellers' (October 1959–January 1960) by Manning Coles (in book form as *Crime in Concrete*). *Suspense* also ran new material by George Langelaan, Victor **Canning**, Leonard Gribble (1908–1984), Joan **Aiken** and Julian **Symons**.

Each issue of *Suspense* had puzzles and contests for the readers of which the most interesting were those in which Michael **Gilbert**, Manning Coles and Tom Tullett (1915–1991) provided stories but left the solution open for readers to solve. These stories were accompanied by picture clues and other devices. Rather curiously whilst the Coles and Tullett stories were new, Gilbert's had previously appeared in a magazine which may have given some readers an unfair advantage.

Because so many of the reprints were from American sources, and included gritty adventure stories, *Suspense* had the general feel of an American men's magazine, and the occasional traditional British detective story felt oddly out of place. These were also mixed with slick fantasies from such American magazines as *Esquire* and *Saturday Evening Post*. As issues progressed, *Suspense* grew more like its companion *Argosy*, which also reprinted many American crime, horror and adventure stories and, in due course, from May 1961, the two titles were merged. Nevertheless, *Suspense* contains much of interest for those who seek diversity and a sense of adventure in their reading.

Further Reading
Indexed in Cook, Michael L. 1982. *Monthly Murders*. Greenwood Press.

Mike Ashley

Symons, Julian (1912–1994)

Julian Symons, novelist and critic, was one of the most influential figures in British crime writing in the second half of the twentieth century. Although at first glance his background and early writings would not have suggested a taste for crime, Symons confessed in his seminal history of the genre, *Bloody Murder* (1972, revised 1985, 1992), that he was 'an addict, with a passion for crime literature that survives any rational explanation for it'. Like so many crime writers, particularly of his generation, he was caught at an early age by the Sherlock **Holmes** and Father Brown stories.

Another personal note from *Bloody Murder* reveals Julian Symons's high expectations of the genre and helps to explain the different strands which made up his writing life. He says in the preface that he hopes to convince 'new generations of readers that the best crime stories are not simply entertainments but also literature'. For Symons's background was distinctly literary in a style that has long since vanished. Born in Battersea, the youngest of five children of Russian-Jewish immigrants, Symons left school at fourteen and worked as a clerk for an engineering firm. In literary terms at least, he was essentially self-taught, under the guidance of his brother A.J.A. Symons (1900–1941). This older brother was a dandy, bibliophile and cult author whose best known book is *The Quest for Corvo* (1934), a classic about yet another cult author, Frederick Rolfe or 'Baron Corvo' (1860–1913). Julian produced his own account of A.J.A.'s brief life in *A.J.A. Symons: His Life and Speculations* (1950). This readable, affectionate biography recalls an earlier literary world haunted by echoes of Oscar Wilde and the 1890s. It is significant that Symons himself always took the long perspective in his critical and biographical work, although the decade that shaped him personally was the 1930s.

In the pre-war period, Julian Symons was a Trotskyist and a poet, a not unusual combination at the time. Interestingly, it is this politico-cultural period that he revisits in the best of his late novels, *Death's Darkest Face* (1990). Symons's outlook may have modified but he retained a mild radicalism, shown in a sceptical and satirical attitude towards authority, particularly the legal system. His first detective novel, *The Immaterial Murder Case* (1945), was intended as a parody – it featured a sleuth called Teake Wood – but its reception was warm enough to encourage Symons to produce more serious contributions to the genre, even if he never quite lost the playful, detached attitude of that early work. Symons went on to write almost thirty detective novels, ranging from the historical to the light-hearted to the sober, psychological study. His self-declared concern with 'the violence behind respectable faces' and his belief that the 'criminal can now be the most interesting character of the lot' indicate how removed Symons was from the conventions which then dominated more traditional areas of the genre. A sampling of work through several decades displays his variety and consistent quality.

In 1957, Symons won the **Crime Writers' Association** (CWA) award for the best novel of the year (later known as the Gold Dagger) with *The Colour of Murder*. The book is about John Wilkins, a respectable young clerk in the Complaints Department of an Oxford Street store. Unhappily married, prone to blackouts and bouts of rage, he is obsessed with Sheila, a librarian whom he pursues without success. The opening half of the story is Wilkins's first-person narration, leading up to the discovery of Sheila's murdered body on a Brighton beach. The clerk from Complaints is the obvious suspect even if he can remember little about the night of the murder. The second half, told from several viewpoints, examines the court case against Wilkins, who is found guilty and sentenced to death, although he is later committed to Broadmoor. The book has a traditional twist, since a more plausible murderer is revealed in the epilogue but – in defiance of convention – goes unpunished.

Symons was an adept practitioner in several styles of crime writing. One of his most sombre books, *The Players and the Game* (1972), is an effective study of a pair of psychopaths, like the relationship between Moors murderers Ian Brady and Myra Hindley. By contrast, *The Plot against Roger Rider* (1973) is a more familiar type of puzzle, although this novel too turns on a dangerously dependent relationship between two individuals. School friends Roger Rider and Geoffrey Paradine follow diverging paths in life: the first is a thriving businessman, and the second, his apparently dull employee (and failed novelist). When Rider disappears from his Spanish villa, Paradine is the obvious suspect. Symons weaves his way through a confusion and fusion of identities, with a final revelation that is also a literal unravelling when a character takes off the bandages that hide unsuccessful plastic surgery.

Two later stories, *The Blackheath Poisonings* (1978) and *Death's Darkest Face*, examine crimes committed within the family context. In the first, a Victorian murder mystery, Symons gleefully offers us the traditional elements: a repressive older generation, a rebellious or discontented younger one, an outbreak of deaths by poison, a dramatic trial scene and a postscript from the 1930s in which the final culprit reveals himself. The tortuously plotted *Death's Darkest Face* switches between the 1930s and the 1960s, as an ageing actor struggles to establish the truth about his father who may (or may not) be a cold-hearted womaniser and murderer. The general elusiveness of the past is of a piece with the ambiguity of individual guilt.

In a long writing life, Julian Symons produced several histories and biographies, such as *The Tell-Tale Heart* (1973), a life of Edgar Allan Poe, but it is as a crime writer that he is remembered. Symons's novels show a certain impatience with notions such as respectability, but it was indeed respectability and critical weight which he brought to the genre through his reviewing and books such as *Bloody Murder*. He was one of the founding members of the CWA (of which he was the chairman in 1958) and successor to Agatha **Christie** as president of the Detection Club. It is fitting that Symons was one of the earliest recipients of the Cartier Diamond Dagger, given in 1990 to mark his lifetime contribution to crime writing. *See also* The Great Detectives: The Mass Appeal of Holmes, Poirot and Wimsey; Literature and Crime Fiction; *and* Short Stories.

Selected Works by the Author
The Colour of Murder (1957)
The Progress of a Crime (1960)
The Thirties (non-fiction, 1960)
The Man Who Killed Himself (1967)
Bloody Murder (non-fiction, 1972)
The Tell-Tale Heart (non-fiction, 1973)
A Three Pipe Problem (1975)
The Blackheath Poisonings (1978)
Death's Darkest Face (1990)

Philip Gooden

T

Tallis, Frank (b.1958)

Frank Tallis is a clinical psychologist and author of atmospheric and intelligent historical crime novels and non-fiction – with the latter, most notably *Hidden Minds* (2002), a history of the unconscious, and *Lovesick* (2004), an exploration of the relationship between romantic love and mental illness.

100. Frank Tallis.

Tallis obtained a PhD after conducting research into cognitive aspects of anxiety at St George's Hospital Medical School, London, and then trained in clinical psychology at the Institute of Psychiatry, London. After qualifying, he specialised in the treatment of obsessional states and wrote the first British self-help manual for people suffering from obsessive–compulsive disorder, *Understanding Obsessions and Compulsions* (1992). Tallis's fiction is profoundly influenced by his familiarity with academic psychology and his experiences as a clinician. His first two novels, *Killing Time* (1999) and *Sensing Others* (2000), are dark, irreverent and somewhat quirky urban thrillers with counter-culture settings. In *Killing Time*, Tom – a gifted mathematics student – murders his girlfriend during a transient psychotic episode (induced by spending time in a virtual reality computer game). *Sensing Others* follows the fortunes of Nick, a struggling rock musician, who while taking part in a drug trial begins to experience disturbing memories that are not his own. In both books, a suspect first-person narrative blurs the boundary between subjective and objective realities. Although *Killing Time* and *Sensing Others* are primarily examples of crime writing, they are unusual in that they include ideas, concepts and plot devices, more frequently found in science fiction. *The Liebermann Papers*, at present consisting of four volumes, *Mortal Mischief* (2005), *Vienna Blood* (2006), *Fatal Lies* (2008) and *The Kabbalist* (2009), are more conventional in style but make even greater use of psychology – being murder mysteries set in Sigmund Freud's Vienna. Tallis's protagonist, Dr Max Liebermann, is an early acolyte of Freud and employs the new science of psychoanalysis as a forensic tool. A distinctive feature of this series is Liebermann's use of authentic psychoanalytic techniques (for example, close observation of small errors, dream interpretation and the ink blot test). Typically, plots revolve around an impossible or deeply mystifying crime, which takes place in the context of some form of closed community: in *Mortal Mischief*, a spiritualist circle; in *Vienna Blood*, a proto-Nazi secret society; and in *Fatal Lies*, a military school. Key themes include the conflict between reason and emotion, the effect of Darwinism on political ideology and the origins of National Socialism. In many respects, Tallis's vision of *fin de siecle* Vienna serves as a metaphor for his contemporary London – and many parallels can easily be drawn; however, in a post-9/11 world, the most obvious question raised is the ultimate fate of audacious experiments in multiculturalism. In 1999, Tallis received a Writers' Award from the Arts Council of Great Britain, and in 2000, he won the New London Writers' Award from the London Arts Board. He was shortlisted for the Ellis Peters Crime Writers' Association Historical Dagger in 2005.

Selected Works by the Author
Killing Time (1999)
Sensing Others (2000)
Mortal Mischief (2005)
Vienna Blood (2006)
Fatal Lies (2008)
Darkness Rising (2009)

Barry Forshaw

Tart Noir

The sub-genre tart noir, was founded by Lauren **Henderson**, who was becoming aware that she and several other female writers were in the process of creating a new sort of crime writing, featuring series heroines who were tough, wise-cracking and – though strong-minded and feminist – have none of the automatic hostility to men that characterised many of the novels with female protagonists of the previous generation. Henderson approached Sparkle Hayter, the then writer of a series of screwball mysteries featuring accidental sleuth Robin Hudson, and suggested that they bond together and name their sub-genre. On a noir panel at the Bouchercon conference held in Philadelphia in 1998, the panellists had been asked to name their own style of noir – Gary Phillips called his 'noir noir', Nicholas **Blincoe** 'vomit noir' and Henderson, wearing a T-shirt with the slogan 'Barbie Is a Slut', jokingly suggested 'slut noir'. Hayter modified this to 'tart noir', and a new sub-genre was named.

Tart noir as a sub-genre quickly expanded to include the writer Katy Munger, whose Casey Jones mystery series shared the key ingredients of the burgeoning sub-genre – a hard-nosed, funny, sexy heroine who took on dangerous cases and enjoyed as many relationships with men as the male detectives in classic noir novels did with women. With the addition of Stella **Duffy**, the author of the private investigator (PI) Saz Martin series, tart noir consisted of four writers, all of whom had started their series several years before meeting each other, but whose creative output encapsulated the Zeitgeist characterised as 'girl power'. Young women throughout the world were reinventing feminism in their own image – fun-loving, male-friendly, able to wear lipstick and stiletto heels without any sense that an overt show of femininity would compromise their empowerment.

In the mid-1990s, after years of second-wave feminism, and female writers who either created male protagonists or modelled their female protagonists on male stereotypes, this attitude was genuinely revolutionary. The writers of tart noir, despite their individual differences, were united in their desire to create heroines who were role models for a new breed of women and to examine the many ways in which female strength differed from the male version. Henderson has been quoted as saying that many previous female crime novelists wrote heroines who were 'Philip Marlowe in a dress – which is not such a successful drag act'. The tart noir writers were collectively engaged on a project to reinvent the concept of what constituted a strong heroine, using playfulness, wit and social satire as well as powerful action scenes and social commentary.

Henderson's and Duffy's books were rooted in London, with Henderson's heroine, Sam Jones, working as a metal sculptor, a profession Henderson used to satirise the excesses of the international art scene and the vogue for young British conceptual artists. Hayter's Robin Hudson was a New York City television reporter. Munger's heroine, Casey Jones (the fact that two tart noir heroines have the surname 'Jones' is complete coincidence), is a PI based in North Carolina. And Duffy's Saz Martin is also a PI. The protagonists have widely varying backgrounds and interests, and the first three women are heterosexual, while Saz Martin is lesbian. The many differences between the four writers allowed for a wide range of definition of tart noir, even as there emerged a coherent philosophy of the sub-genre and a fresh examination of what it meant to be a heroine in a crime novel.

On their website, the tart noir writers cite their literary and television heroines as Modesty Blaise, Tank Girl, Emma Peel, Roseanne and Darlene Connor from the series *Roseanne* and Patsy and Edina from the series *Absolutely Fabulous*. The fact that the first three of these characters were created by male writers was specifically embraced by tart noir in keeping with its male-friendly ethos, as a redefinition of feminism, one which did not automatically privilege women over men, or assume that only women could create strong funny female characters.

The four writers originally shared the website, which was created by Hayter and Henderson and designed by Hayter. Hayter left after a few years to work on her own projects, and to date, she has published a couple of stand-alone novels. Munger left a year afterwards. The site is now shared by Henderson and Duffy, both of whom have a wide range of writing projects. In 2001, frustrated that they were regularly asked to contribute to crime and literary anthologies whose contributors were always a majority of male writers, Henderson and Duffy decided to edit an all-female anthology that would demonstrate how many talented female writers were either currently working in the crime genre or able to turn their skills to crime writing. Called *Tart Noir*, the anthology came out in the United Kingdom and the United States in 2001 and was translated into over ten languages. Featuring stories from some of the leading lights of crime fiction, it was a widely varied collection, from hard-core thriller writers such as Val **McDermid**, Denise **Mina** and Karin Slaughter to romantic comedy writers including Jenny Colgan and Lisa Jewell. Duffy's short story for the collection, 'Martha Grace', won the prestigious **Crime Writers' Association** Short Story Dagger for 2002.

Tart noir is naturally associated with a confident, sexy style of crime writing, and has spawned many imitators, as has the anthology. Several MA and PhD theses have already been written about the phenomenon. Henderson and Duffy remain committed to the tart noir philosophy, which informs all of their creative projects, from non-fiction (Henderson's how-to dating guide, *Jane Austen's Guide to Dating*, 2005) to films (Duffy has written the screenplay of her novel *State of Happiness*, 2004). They are still actively engaged on tart noir–related work. Henderson's Scarlett Wakefield series, of which the first novel is *Kiss Me Kill Me* (2008), is Young Adult Tart Noir, while Duffy has recently published a novel in the Saz Martin series, *Mouths of Babes* (2005). They regularly speak on tart noir at writers' conferences and encourage promising upcoming writers. *See also* Feminist Readings in British Crime Fiction; Gay and Lesbian Crime Fiction; *and* Pulp.

Website
www.tartcity.com

Eve Tan Gee

Tartan Noir

See Scottish Crime Fiction

Taylor, Andrew (b.1951)

A creator of atmospheric, well-crafted mysteries, Andrew Taylor is one of a number of award-winning novelists (including Minette **Walters** and Barbara Vine/Ruth **Rendell**) who have moved the traditional crime novel on to a deeper level of psychological exploration.

Taylor grew up in Ely and was educated at Cambridge University and University College, London. After five years spent travelling and doing various odd jobs, he worked as a librarian and an editor before becoming a full-time writer in 1981. His output is prodigious – besides two series, two trilogies and several stand-alone novels, he has written books for children and adults and was, for a time, the editor of the Society of Authors' magazine.

His first novel, *Caroline Minuscule* (1982), introduced William Dougal, a charming but amoral postgraduate student who reluctantly turns a detective when he stumbles upon the garrotted corpse of his tutor and becomes embroiled in the hunt for a cache of diamonds. During the course of the seven subsequent novels, Dougal becomes a private investigator. He is, as his creator points out, 'the sort of detective who is as likely to commit murders as solve them'. In the eighth novel, *Odd Man Out* (1993), he kills an acquaintance in the course of a quarrel and, unable to turn to the police, is left with the task of disposing the body. Celia Prentiss, Dougal's girlfriend (introduced in the third novel, *Our Fathers' Lies*, 1985), who has a clear sense of right and wrong, and James Hanbury, the con man whose protégé Dougal becomes, represent either end of the moral spectrum, and Dougal constantly veers between the two.

An Air That Kills (1994) was the first book in the Lydmouth series, and there are eight titles to date. These books, which demonstrate a growing assurance and maturity as the series progresses, are set in and around the fictional town of Lydmouth, situated on the Anglo-Welsh borders, in the years after the Second World War. The use of the 'closed world' setting of the genteel provincial town, with two main characters who are outsiders (along with the multiple points of view), allows Taylor to paint a social and political portrait of 1950s Britain as well as presenting the reader with a series of engrossing puzzles. Detective Inspector Richard Thornhill comes from the Fens and journalist Jill Francis from London. Thornhill is married to a local woman, Edith, but his attraction to Jill gradually ripens into love, and she becomes his mistress. This adulterous relationship adds another layer of tension to the books, as the two protagonists, in their different ways, become involved in the murder mysteries, and the emphasis of the series is as much on the development of their characters as it is on the solving of crimes.

Taylor's preoccupation with the present consequences of past actions is much in evidence here, as it is in the *Roth Trilogy* (televised in 2007 as *Fallen Angel*), the first book of which was *The Four Last Things* (1997). Set in an ecclesiastical milieu (Taylor's father was a clergyman), the first book is set in the 1990s; the second, *The Judgement of Strangers* (1998), in 1970; and the third, *The Office of the Dead* (2000), in 1958. Taylor likens them to an archaeological dig, stripping away layers to reveal the background and motivation of a female serial killer (the author is as unsentimental about children as he is about the past – in his world, boys and girls can be lethally dangerous as well as cute and vulnerable). Although the deft structuring ensures that each novel may be enjoyed as a stand-alone, the careful handling of the overarching theme of crime and retribution means that, taken as a whole, the books form an extraordinary, and possibly unique, exploration of human beings as the flawed victims not only of their own folly but also of their misguided desire to do good.

Taylor's modern stand-alone novels are reminiscent of Barbara Vine in their emotional and psychological complexity. Again, their theme is the relationship of the past and the present. *A Stain on the Silence* (2006) is the story of a man who discovers that he has a daughter from an affair twenty-five years earlier and that she is on the run for murder. It is an exploration of the relationship of parents and children, love, loss and what might have been. *The Barred Window* (1993) is narrated by an apparently guileless man, haunted by the past, and deals with the blurry division between predators and victims. Set in Cornwall, it uses many of the conventions of the Gothic novel – imprisonment, persecution and madness. *The Raven on the Water* (1991) deals with childhood rivalries, jealousy and betrayal.

Set in 1819, the award-winning *The American Boy* (2003) is a tour de force in the style of Wilkie **Collins**, blending the conventions of the Dickensian tangled web with the conventions of modern crime writing. A many-layered mystery that is also a historical novel and a love story, it is narrated by Thomas Shield, an impoverished schoolmaster with a history of mental instability who becomes caught up in the twisted intrigues of the powerful family of one of his pupils. Set in London and rural Gloucestershire, the canvas is broader than usual, taking in both polite society and the seedy anonymity of London's poorer quarters and the divided loyalties of the Anglo-American War of 1812. The eponymous American boy, always hovering on the edge of the action, is the young Edgar Allan Poe, who never learns the significance of the part he plays, except – perhaps – at the end. *The American Boy* is the most accomplished work to date from this highly versatile writer.

Equally at home in the mind of a hormone-crazed adolescent, a shell-shocked nineteenth-century schoolmaster or a bitter 1950s divorcee, Taylor researches meticulously but resists the temptation to show it off and expertly weaves plot strands together to produce a compelling whole.

Selected Works by the Author
Caroline Minuscule (1982)
Waiting for the End of the World (1984)
Our Fathers' Lies (1985)
Blood Relation (1990)
The Mortal Sickness (1995)
The Four Last Things (1997)
The American Boy (2003)
A Stain on the Silence (2006)
Naked to the Hangman (2006)
Bleeding Heart Square (2008)

Website
www.andrew-taylor.co.uk

Laura Wilson

Tey, Josephine (1896–1952)

Josephine Tey remains the most readable and most modern of the five classic women writers of the **Golden Age**, though her reputation during her lifetime was quite different. Tey, the name chosen by Elizabeth MacKintosh for her crime-writing career, also wrote plays under the name Gordon Daviot, and, when she died, her obituaries concentrated almost exclusively on her work for the theatre. Now even the most successful of the plays, *Richard of Bordeaux* (1932), which ran for over a year and helped make the career of the young John Gielgud, has been forgotten. People remember Tey's portrait of Richard III from her novel *The Daughter of Time* (1951) and not the tragic Richard II of her celebrated play.

Tey was born in Inverness in 1896, the eldest of three daughters of Colin and Josephine MacKintosh. She was educated at the Inverness Academy and then at the Anstey College of Physical Education in Birmingham, which gave her the background for *Miss Pym Disposes* (1946). During the First World War, she served with the Voluntary Aid Detachment (VAD).

Tey worked in London for a Danish physiotherapist, before taking a variety of teaching posts and then spending several years at Tunbridge Wells High School in Kent. In 1923, her mother was diagnosed with cancer, and as the eldest and unmarried daughter, she returned home and remained there after her mother's death to look after her father. There are many intelligent, independent women in her fiction who have had to take on family responsibilities because of unexpected death or disaster. Some are happier than others. In *Miss Pym Disposes*, young Mary Innes, the star of Leys Physical Training College, undertakes as penance for the death of a rival to spend her life on good works in the stifling small town where she was born. In *Brat Farrar* (1949), the infinitely happier Bee Ashby, took over the care of her

101. Elizabeth Mackintosh,
also known as Josephine Tey,
photographed in April 1934.

young nephews and nieces and the family stud farm when her brother and his wife were killed in an air accident. And in *The Franchise Affair* (1948), the forthright Marion Sharpe, who loathes domesticity but has no career, lives with her elderly mother.

Partial escape for Tey came with an annual holiday on the Kent and Sussex border, which she had grown to love during her time at Tunbridge Wells, and through her writing. Her first foray into crime, *The Man in the Queue* (1929), was written for a competition, for which she used her Gordon Daviot pseudonym. Although she won the competition, this is the least interesting of her novels, a traditional murder mystery with red herrings and an obvious suspect who turns out to be innocent. But it introduces Inspector Alan Grant, who was to figure in almost all her novels, except *Miss Pym Disposes* and *Brat Farrar*.

Grant is a clever man, detached but affectionate, who suffers from depression and panic attacks and has a powerful interest in face-reading. He believes he can diagnose both character and criminal tendencies from features such as the shape and spacing of the eyes or the lack of lines on an adult's face. He always identifies his criminal in the end, but often makes mistakes, a realistic trait that marks him out from the sleuths created by Tey's rivals.

His interest in faces comes to the fore in *The Daughter of Time* (1951), her most famous novel. Here Grant is trapped in hospital, flat on his back and bored, when Marta Hallard, a tall, frigid, beautiful actor who features in several of the novels, brings him a batch of portrait reproductions. Each subject is connected with some famous historical mystery. Grant becomes mesmerised by the facial features and expression of Richard III and, with the help of a young visiting American researcher, delves into the mystery of whether the king killed his nephews, 'the princes in the Tower'.

Brat Farrar also deals with the reality behind the mask, in a story based on the real case of the Titchborne Claimant. Brat is a foundling, who ran from a bleak existence in England to a career with dangerous horses in the States. Returning to his home country, he is persuaded to assume the identity of Patrick Ashby, a boy who would have inherited the Latchetts stud and estate had he not disappeared at the age of eight. Brat easily insinuates himself into the family, who come to love him, and not only finds his true identity but also solves the mystery of Patrick's disappearance.

This novel displays many familiar aspects of Tey's work beyond her interest in character and identity. In Patrick's twin, Simon, she has created one the monsters of egotistical selfishness in which she specialised. Universally charming and beautiful to look at, they create havoc among those they trick, lying with a fluent ease and caring nothing for anyone else's suffering. One of the most chilling is Betty Kane in *The Franchise Affair*, another novel with a plot based on a real case, this time from the eighteenth century. Another is the Arabist and explorer Heron Lloyd in Tey's posthumously published *The Singing Sands* (1953). Only in *To Love and Be Wise* (1950) does she take her readers into the mind of such a character and give both an explanation and some sympathetic absolution. Even here, there is a yet more selfish character at the root of the beautiful liar's actions.

Many of her characters are sexually ambivalent and even those who are not display a lack of interest in heterosexual relationships she clearly shared. She kept her privacy throughout her short life, and when she died in South London in February 1952, many of the friends who came to her funeral had never met her sisters or each other. Her writing is elegant, her psychological perception acute and her novels are cherished by readers far more interested in 'why' than in 'who' or 'how'. *See also* Women Crime Writers.

Selected Works by the Author
The Man in the Queue, as Gordon Daviot (1929; also published in the United States as *Killer in the Crowd*)
A Shilling for Candles (1936)
Miss Pym Disposes (1946)
The Franchise Affair (1948)
Brat Farrar (1949; also published in the United States as *Come and Kill Me*)
To Love and Be Wise (1950)
The Daughter of Time (1951)
The Singing Sands (1953)

Further Reading
McDermid, Val. 1977. 'Queer Crime'. P.106 in *Waterstone's Guide to Crime Fiction*. Waterstone's.
Perriam, Geraldine, and Catherine Aird, eds. 2004. *Josephine Tey: A Celebration*. Festschrift.
Roy, Sandra. 1980. *Josephine Tey*. Twayne.

Natasha Cooper

Thomas, Edwin (b.1977)

The authorial equivalent of 'rags to riches' came in 2001 for Edwin Thomas when he was a runner-up in the **Crime Writers' Association** Debut Dagger for the best submission from an unpublished writer. He had submitted the first 3,000 words of his proposed novel *The Blighted Cliffs*, a historical crime romp set in 1806. It was seen by an agent, was shown to a publisher and became his first published book. More followed, including a different series under the name Tom Harper.

Though British, Thomas was born in Frankfurt and grew up in Belgium and Connecticut, United States. He came to England to study history at Lincoln College

Oxford, and when he left university, he knew he wanted to be a novelist. After three years with a local actuarial firm, he saw an advert for the Debut Dagger competition, entered the first chapter of his book and finished as a runner-up.

The Blighted Cliffs (2003) introduced Lieutenant Martin Jerrold, an insouciant adventurer and one of the few men to survive the Battle of Trafalgar without an ounce of credit to his name. Waking one morning at the foot of the Dover cliffs with a bad hangover and an unknown corpse lying beside him, Jerrold finds himself suspected of murder – and tried by a magistrate who would like him dead. Jerrold's only hope is to trawl the narrow streets of Dover in the hope he can net the real killer. He has two weeks to do so – in which time he manages to become entangled in large-scale smuggling and to find himself again at the mercy of the French navy. The follow-up, *The Chains of Albion* (2004), continues directly from *The Blighted Cliffs* with Jerrold commanding a prison-hulk filled with French captives, one of whom he loses. This, of course, is the one prisoner he should not have lost. But no one told Jerrold the man was important. Nor did they tell him why. His amusing attempts to recapture the Frenchman lead him from the Medway to the stinking marshes of Chatham and hence to the slums of London and from the wilds of Dartmoor to the newly fashionable seaside resort of Brighton. The tales are sprightly and amusingly told.

As Tom Harper, Thomas also wrote a series of historical novels set in the Byzantine empire around the time of the First Crusade, with an eleventh-century Greek hero, Demetrios Askiates, a man of many parts, at one time monk, soldier, mercenary, detective and spy. The series began with *The Mosaic of Shadows* (2004), with the army of the First Crusade at the gates of Constantinople. Among historical set pieces are the siege of Antioch and the crusade's shocking climax at Jerusalem, during which Askiates's ordeals test his strength, wits, faith and soul as he probes the violence and murder at the heart of the crusade. *See also* Historical Crime.

Selected Works by the Author

As Edwin Thomas
The Blighted Cliffs (2003)
The Chains of Albion (2004)
Treason's River (2006)

As Tom Harper
The Mosaic of Shadows (2004)
Knights of the Cross (2005)
Siege of Heaven (2006)
The Lost Temple (2007)

Russell James

Thomson, June (b.1930)

British crime fiction between the 1970s and 1990s owes much to writers like June Valerie Thomson, who brought to the genre a steady output of well-crafted, entertaining mysteries.

Thomson was born in Rettendon, Essex, and educated at Chelmsford High School. Formerly, she was a teacher. She has produced twenty-three crime novels, but she is best known for the twenty books which make up her series featuring Detective

Chief Inspector Jack Finch of Chelmsford CID, whose investigations frequently take place in the genteel rural places popular with writers of traditional English mysteries.

Finch made his first appearance in *Not One of Us* (1972), together with his assistant, the burly, broad-shouldered Sergeant Tom Boyce. Finch, at this stage yet to be promoted from inspector, is described as stocky, with the bluff, open air features of a farmer. This deceptive appearance hides a talent for intuitive detection which serves him well in solving some of the ingenious mysteries thought up for him by Thomson. He did not marry and has grown accustomed to his comfortable bachelor existence with his widowed sister, Dorothy, who keeps house for him. On several occasions, he has been attracted to women he has met during an investigation, but nothing comes of these relationships. By the time Finch's most recent case *Going Home* appeared in 2006, Thomson had embarked on another successful series. For the American editions of the books, which began with the second in the series, *Death Cap* (1973), Finch was renamed Rudd to avoid confusion with another character of that name.

In 1990, Thomson, a long-time fan of Arthur Conan **Doyle**, produced a collection of short stories entitled *The Secret Files of Sherlock Holmes*. In several of Conan Doyle's stories, Dr Watson refers to a trunk containing all his unpublishable material; this is the source which Thomson claims for her stories. Many writers have tried to produce Holmes pastiches, but none has been more authentic than Thomson, who not only reproduces the literary style with great accuracy, but remains faithful to the characters of Holmes and Watson. She also comes up with some clever mysteries which are worthy of investigation by the great man. There are perhaps too many footnotes by the purported editor of the stories, some of which do not seem to be necessary for the purpose of clarification, but they do illustrate Thomson's encyclopedic knowledge of the original works. The collection was followed by five more, all with the same qualities, though the last, *The Secret Notebooks of Sherlock Holmes* (2004), shows some signs of running out of steam with regard to both the pace and the quality of the plots.

Thomson's work is marked by meticulous plotting, vivid characterisation and human insight. Her **police procedurals** may not be the gritty, realistic investigations usually encountered today, but her cosier version of the genre continues to have a loyal following, and she will be particularly remembered for her contribution to the Sherlock **Holmes** legend.

Selected Works by the Author
The Long Revenge (1974)
A Dying Fall (1985)
The Secret Files of Sherlock Holmes (stories, 1990)
The Secret Chronicles of Sherlock Holmes (stories, 1992)
Holmes and Watson: A Study in Friendship (non-fiction, 1995)
Burden of Innocence (1996)
The Unquiet Grave (2000)

Susanna Yager

The Thriller

The Thriller was a weekly story paper, aimed at a more adult readership than most such publications of the type, published by Amalgamated Press. It ran for 589 issues, in small tabloid format, from 9 February 1929 to 18 May 1940, though its last eleven issues were retitled *War Thriller*. Each issue consisted of a long lead story plus a serial episode and occasionally a short story plus a few reader features. Although Leonard Pratt was the day-to-day editor, the brains behind it was P.M. ('Monty') Haydon, who retained the guiding hand and dealt with most of the major contributors.

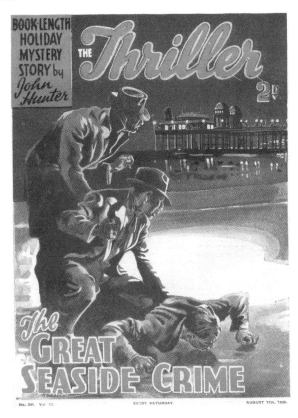

102. Cover of *The Thriller* magazine, August 1935.

The Thriller proved immensely popular and is generally regarded as the closest Britain came to producing the same atmosphere (though not format) as the American crime fiction pulps such as *Black Mask* and *Dime Detective*. During its last two years, *The Thriller* even ran versions of Walter Gibson's Shadow novels from *The Shadow* pulp, rewritten in-house to be set in London, but still published under the pseudonym Maxwell Grant.

Though Americanised in its 'gangster' formula, the stories were still typically British. *The Thriller*, as with its companion *Detective Weekly*, was a regular market for Amalgamated Press's main stable of writers including G.H. Teed (1886–1938), Edwy Searles Brooks (1898–1965), George Dilnot (1883–1951), Stacey Blake (1878–1964) and John Hunter (1891–1961), but other names also appeared from time to time, including several prominent writers. Edgar **Wallace** led the first issue with a specially commissioned J.G. Reeder novella, 'Red Aces'. Wallace contributed several further stories though later ones were reprints. *The Thriller* is perhaps best known because it was here that Leslie **Charteris** developed the character of the **Saint**. Simon Templar had appeared in one earlier novel, *Meet the Tiger* (1928), and Charteris brought him back in the novella 'The Five Kings' (4 May 1929), which included Templar with his friends. Charteris wrote several more 'Five Kings' stories, but with 'Without Warning' (24 May 1930), he began to chronicle the adventures of Templar alone and continued to contribute over the next few years, though later stories were reprints. The cover of the 6 June 1931 issue, which ran 'Black Face', was the first to feature the now-familiar haloed matchstick figure.

The grandfather of the Saint and all similar rogue heroes was E.W. **Hornung**'s gentleman thief, Raffles, and Philip Atkey (1908–1985), who wrote as Barry Perowne, became best known when he revived Raffles for a series of adventures, starting in the 28 January 1933 issue. In similar vein was the Toff by John **Creasey** who appeared in four stories in *The Thriller* starting with 'The Black Circle' (2 December 1933).

Margery **Allingham**, whose father had been one of Amalgamated Press's leading story-paper writers, had an early story 'The Mystery Man of Soho' in the 1 April 1933 issue. This was eventually reprinted as 'A Quarter of a Million' in *The Allingham Minibus* in 1973. Agatha **Christie**'s three stories in *The Thriller* were all reprints. Other contributors of note include Sydney Horler (1888–1954), Bruce **Graeme**, Roy **Vickers**, Nigel **Morland** and Peter **Cheyney**.

As the magazine's title implied, the stories were not solely mystery or crime stories but all kinds of thrills and adventures. The magazine reprinted Charles Nordhoff and James Hall's 1932 book *Mutiny on the Bounty* in 1936. Arch Whitehouse contributed a flying serial, 'Demons of the Air' (26 August to 18 November 1933), and this may have paved the way for Captain W.E. Johns to contribute several of his stories about air adventurer 'Steeley' Delaroy, starting with 'Calling All Cars' (8 August 1936). In the magazine's final days, when it was retitled *War Thriller*, Johns contributed a Biggles serial, 'Storm Troop of the Baltic Skies' (9 March to 18 May 1940).

Wartime paper rationing brought an end to *The Thriller* as it did to hundreds of other magazines. Its significance has grown over time as one of Britain's more influential and interesting crime magazines.

Further Reading
Adley, Derek J., and W.O.G. Lofts. 1990. *The Thriller*. Colne.
Holland, Steve. Indexed in 'British Juvenile Story Papers and Pocket Libraries Index'.

Mike Ashley

Thrillers: Novels of Action

The thriller has become a loose generic terms which covers a wide range of novels of suspense, adventure and intrigue. There are psychological thrillers, political thrillers and action thrillers, the latter being the more significant field with the longest history and most influence. It is, of course, possible for novels to include all three features, most notably in the field of **espionage**, owing much to the form and success of *The Thirty-Nine Steps* (1915) by John **Buchan**.

British novels of action have a long tradition of moving their narratives onto an international canvas, which suited more large-scale political machinations and espionage. This is, perhaps, a corollary of the legacy of the British empire with its relics of war and conquest. Even when the empire was in decline, British thriller fiction still utilised the international stage and reflected the flux in world politics. The nemeses may have changed from the Axis nations during the First and the Second

World Wars, and the communist nations during the Cold War, to the modern era owing to its cabals of international terrorists (principally related to the Middle East and petro-economics) as well as to the emerging trends of eco-terror.

Sir Henry Rider Haggard (1856–1925) is a key progenitor of the British adventure thriller, notably with the groundbreaking *King Solomon's Mines* (1885), *Allan Quatermain* (1887) and *She* (1887). Rider Haggard's work transported readers to the far frontiers of the British Empire. Considering the mores of the times in which he wrote; these fanciful tales are much less jingoistic than one might imagine, often deeply sympathetic towards the peoples and lands that they portray. Rider Haggard is often credited for influencing the early American **pulp** writers such as the prolific Edgar Rice Burroughs – the creator of Tarzan and John Carter. Another descendant of *Allan Quatermain* was the American writer Lester Dent's Doc Savage series written under the pseudonym Kenneth Robeson. The influence of Rider Haggard cannot be underestimated; he created the trajectory for action thrillers that travelled from Britain to the four corners of the empire, and American writers exploited this genre with alacrity, to both commercial and critical acclaim.

Rudyard Kipling (1865–1936) and Erskine **Childers** also formulated the basic tenets for the British action novel, though both *Kim* (1901) and *Riddle of the Sands* (1903) should also be considered as espionage novels. Mention must also be made of Joseph **Conrad**, who inaugurated the existential adventure tale with *Heart of Darkness* (1899), one inspiration for Francis Ford Coppola's film *Apocalypse Now* (1979).

The action thriller lent itself more to popular fiction rather than literary works, although authors like Conrad, Kipling and Buchan crossed that divide in the years before marketing genres were defined. Such commercial work was hugely popular both sides of the Atlantic, and in Britain reflected the country's position at the centre of a huge empire but one under threat from growing European powers. Many thrillers of the late nineteenth and early twentieth centuries dealt with Britain menaced by foreign powers: usually France or Germany but also Russia and as far afield as China or Japan. Such works include *The Angel of the Revolution* (1893) by George Griffith (1857–1906), *The Yellow Danger* (1898) by M.P. Shiel (1865–1947), *Mysterious Mr Sabin* (1898) by E.P. **Oppenheim**, *England's Peril* (1899) by William **Le Queux**, *The Giant's Gate* (1901) by Max Pemberton (1863–1950) and *The Aerial Burglars* (1906) by James Blyth (1864–1933). Many of these books were racist or, at the very least, established ethnic stereotypes. This was most evident with the concept of the sinister oriental or 'yellow peril', which was used profitably by Sax **Rohmer** in his series featuring Fu Manchu.

The name that would most closely be associated with the crime and action thriller, and did the most to popularise it, was Edgar **Wallace**, starting with *The Four Just Men* (1905). Wallace's name became synonymous with the thriller as did that of one of his most successful imitators, Sydney Horler (1888–1954), whose books often carried the banner, 'Horler for Excitement'.

The British adventure novel threw up a slew of durable protagonists, e.g. Sir Arthur Conan **Doyle**'s Professor George Edward Challenger and Leslie **Charteris**'s Simon Templar, also known as the Saint, before the genre as whole tale took centre stage on bestseller lists during the 1960s and 1970s when Hammond **Innes**, Alistair **MacLean**, Desmond **Bagley**, Ken **Follett**, Dick **Francis**, Jack **Higgins** and – of course – Ian **Fleming** ruled the book charts. However, MacLean and Fleming were the key figures during these two decades with their prolific output and many successful film adaptations.

Significant in the history of the genre is a mould-creating action novel by Geoffrey **Household**. *Rogue Male* (1939) is a precursor for major contemporary works such as Richard Condon's *The Manchurian Candidate* (1959), Frederick **Forsyth**'s *The Day of the Jackal* (1971) and Ken **Follett**'s *Eye of the Needle* (1978). The unnamed protagonist in Household's novel states that 'Like most Englishmen, I am not accustomed to inquire very deeply into motives.... I remember asking myself when I packed the telescopic sight what the devil I wanted it for; but I just felt that it might come in handy.' An unnamed big-game hunter enters an unnamed European state with the sole purpose to assassinate an unnamed tyrannical dictator – who, of course, is a thinly veiled Adolf Hitler. *Rogue Male* poses a variety of intriguing moral dilemmas.

Scot Alistair MacLean is sometimes dismissed as a formulaic writer, but his influence on many contemporary novelists – such as Lee **Child**, Dennis Lehane and Robert Crais – was profound; all list MacLean as a major influence. His critical work includes *The Guns of Navarone* (1957), *The Last Frontier* (1959; also published in the United States as *The Secret Ways*), *Night without End* (1960), *Fear Is the Key* (1961), *Ice Station Zebra* (1963) and *Circus* (1975) – his hugely underrated novel set against a Cold War backdrop. Ian Fleming and his immortal creation James Bond (the aristocratic British Secret Agent 007) are discussed elsewhere in this volume.

As the sun started to set on the British empire, the adventure tale became far more cynical and notably more political as writers such as Eric **Ambler**, Graham **Greene**, James Hadley **Chase**, Michael Gilbert, Victor **Canning**, Dornford Yates, Adam Hall, Len **Deighton**, Frederick **Forsyth**, Gerald **Seymour** and Stephen **Leather** took the genre into more complex (and perhaps more cerebral) territory. The British action thriller continues in the hands of ex-SAS men Andy **McNab** and Chris **Ryan** with work that may not make the Booker list, but that routinely appears on the bestselling charts. McNab has written about his experiences in the SAS in two best-selling books, *Bravo Two Zero* (1993) and *Immediate Action* (1995). *Bravo Two Zero* is the highest selling war book of all time and has sold over 1.7 million copies in the United Kingdom. To date, it has been published in seventeen countries and translated into sixteen languages. Chris Ryan published his first novel *The One That Got Away* in 1995, detailing his real-life exploits of the Bravo Two Zero mission behind Iraqi lines in the first Gulf War. Colleague and former SAS man (and novelist) on the same mission was Andy McNab.

Another highly professional writer of action thrillers is Simon **Kernick**. Since Kernick's debut crime thriller, *The Business of Dying*, was published in 2002, we have learned much about this novelist's world. And it is a dark place, indeed – best that you bring a torch along. In Kernick's world, which centres on the ganglands of north London, it is often difficult to distinguish the good guys from the bad. This is a domain bathed in the grey blur of contradictions and murky moralities; a world heavily populated by prostitutes, pimps, drug lords, hit men and cops so bent that it is a wonder they can still fit into their wardrobes. It is a world where scalding gun barrels and bruised knuckles, rather than arrest warrants and slamming jail cells, are the result of injustices being righted.

Which is not to say that Kernick's fiction cannot be fun; on the contrary, all his books so far have hinted at their author's hip sense of humour. However, it is their dramatic elements – shoot-outs in car parks, police confrontations with Colombian drug smugglers and an episode of torture that makes the abuses committed on George W. Bush's watch at Abu Ghraib prison look like tongue baths – that really propel readers through Kernick's twisted tales. Add to those strengths his sizzling dialogue,

distinctly un-PC view of modern society and characters who are fairly bursting with
flaws and credible dimensions, and you begin to understand why critics have likened
his yarns to those of American Dennis Lehane. His later work including *Relentless*
(2006) and *Severed* (2007) have taken his work away from the police procedural
territory and driven it to pure thriller territory.

One of the most popular British practitioners of the action genre is Lee Child
who sets his kinetic narratives against an American backdrop. Child's protagonist,
ex-military policeman Jack Reacher, is developed from the heroic-altruism tradition
in British crime fiction exemplified by Leslie **Charteris**'s Simon 'the Saint' Templar
and Peter **Cheyney**'s Lemmy Caution – a mysterious benefactor who arrives on the
scene to help out when the law no longer can. As this tradition evolved, the enigmatic
champion took an antiheroic turn in the hands of Dornford Yates, Hammond Innes,
Alistair MacLean and Eric Ambler. More recently, the character darkened
considerably under John **le Carré**, Adam Hall (also known as Elleston **Trevor**),
Len Deighton and Ian Fleming. Indeed, it became frequently difficult to distinguish
the heroes from their nemeses. Child's *Killing Floor* (1997) won both the Anthony
Award and the Barry Award for Best First Novel. After Child's second decade
as a writer of adventure thrillers, his popularity – like that of the British adventure
thriller genre itself – shows no sign of fading. The spirit of Rider Haggard's *Allan
Quatermain* may be utterly transmuted in its various contemporary manifestations,
but it demonstrates commendable durability.

Further Reading
Forshaw, Barry, ed. 2007. *The Rough Guide to Crime Fiction*. Penguin.
Harper, Ralph. 1969. *The World of the Thriller*.
Palmer, Jerry. 1978. *Thrillers: Genesis and Structure of a Popular Genre*.
Taylor, Phyllis. *The British Thriller: An Introduction to the British Novel*. www.yale.edu/ynhti/
curriculum/units/1981/2/81.02.09.x.html.

Ali Karim

Tiger in the Smoke (film, 1956)

Roy Ward Baker, director

Films of celebrated crime novels have an intrinsic interest (depending on the level
of expertise employed) in how much justice they do to the source material. But Roy
Ward Baker's 1956 version of one of Margery **Allingham**'s most influential novels
freights in several extra layers of rewarding material for the informed viewer:
a picture of British film-making conventions in the mid-1950s, a striking visual record
of London not available for a novelist, the compromises forced on any film-maker
in adapting a difficult novel. *Tiger in the Smoke* focuses on the activities of a group
of ex-servicemen in London and the swathe a psychotic criminal cuts through his
opponents. Allingham's narrative is reproduced by a director whose career varied
widely in terms of its achievement; some of Baker's films are lacklustre journeyman
efforts, while others seem to locate him firmly in a talented school of British auteurs –
this film inclines to the latter view. Alec Clunes's incarnation of detective Charlie
Luke makes only a fitful impression. It is left to Tony Wright as the sinister psychopath
Jack Havoc (the name, of course, possessing a Dickensian utilitarian quality) to raise

the emotional temperature of the film, particularly in the atmospheric opening.
A group of crooked Second World War veterans track down their former sergeant,
Havoc, who appears to have absconded with loot from a wartime commando raid.
Havoc has, in fact, broken out of Wormwood Scrubs and is similarly tracking down
the missing loot, but ruthlessly eliminating anyone who gets in his way (including
a luckless caretaker). *Tiger in the Smoke*, when set against other contemporary
British crime films such as *Blind Date* and *Sapphire* (both 1959), demonstrates that
the cinema of the day was attempting to engage with various social issues (such
as racism in *Sapphire*), and it addresses the issue of servicemen cast adrift after the
war and moving into criminality (other examples of this trend includes *They Made
Me a Fugitive* (1947). The moral issues here are ambiguous: what is the responsibility
of society to men who have fought for it? However, this film, like most other entries
in this subgenre, ends with the death of the crooked servicemen. The most memorable
aspect of the film today is its prescient picture of psychopathic evil as embodied
in the ruthless Havoc, who menaces a rural priest and his daughter. Tony Wright,
while patently not plumbing the depths of psychopathic menace that both earlier
and later actors had stripmined (notably, James Cagney and Robert De Niro), is still
a disturbing presence, and the film transcends the genteel qualities of many British
crime films to convey an authentic, lean toughness. *See also* Film and Crime: Page
to Screen *and* London in Crime Fiction.

Barry Forshaw

The Times Crime Fiction Supplements

During the late 1990s, *The Times* published three crime fiction supplements in
consecutive years. The project was inspired by *Vrij Nederland*, the Dutch weekly
arts and current affairs magazine, which has produced an annual supplement since
the early 1980s. This lists every author in print in the Dutch language. In 1998, the
British **Crime Writers' Association** (CWA) contacted various British newspapers
to propose a similar supplement for the United Kingdom. *The Times* responded with
enthusiasm but decided to concentrate on 100 masters of crime rather than provide
a list of all novels published that year. The CWA is prohibited from offering prefer-
ential treatment to some members over others, so it could not participate in choosing
the authors. Instead, individual members offered *The Times* their expertise. The
100 masters of crime were determined by polling prominent reviewers of crime fiction,
specialist booksellers and crime novelists with special knowledge of the genre and its
history. These included Natasha **Cooper**, Martin **Edwards**, Barry Forshaw, Adrian
Muller and Andrew **Taylor**. Together with other experts, many of those polled also
contributed by writing entries. The sixteen-page '100 Masters of Crime' supplement
proved highly influential. Besides the list of 100 crime novelists, the supplement also
included an introduction by *The Times* crime fiction reviewer, Marcel Berlins – who
would also write the preface for the subsequent editions; interviews with P.D. **James**
and Ruth **Rendell**; and essays on the various sub-genres by their most prominent
authors – hard-boiled (Val **McDermid**), historical (Edward **Marston**), new-wave
(Nicholas **Blincoe**), police procedural (Ian **Rankin**), psychological (Natasha Cooper)
and traditional (H.R.F. **Keating**). The following year, the 'Crime'99' supplement

followed the format of the Dutch guide: the twenty-four-page supplement listed every crime novel published in 1999. It also included features on the 1999 Dead on Deansgate convention and its guest authors; Andrew Taylor wrote a brief description of the genre's origins; Val **McDermid**, chairman of that year's judges for the John **Creasey** Award for Best First Crime Novel, provided a run-down of some of the year's debuts; Martin **Edwards** wrote about the art of the short crime story; Adrian Muller looked at the increasing popularity of crime on audio; and Natasha Cooper explored the reasons for the genre's popularity. In its final year, the 'Crime 2000' supplement reverted back to a sixteen-page format and, subsequently, listed only a selection of the titles published that year. There again were features on the guest authors appearing at that year's Dead on Deansgate; US bookseller Barbara Peters discussed the differences between British and American crime writing; and Andrew Taylor took over Val McDermid's duties on debut crime novels. The undisputed highlight of the 2000 supplement was a selection of the 100 best crime novels of the twentieth century, chosen by authors H.R.F. Keating and Mike **Ripley**. Both authors contributed a brief introduction in which they explained their pleasures and difficulties in compiling the prestigious list. A new version of the crime fiction supplement appeared under the supervision of *The Times*'s Erica Wagner, Richard Whitehead and Tom Gatti and its crime critic Marcel Berlins in 2008. Contributors for this updated version (built around Berlins' choices of fifty key authors) included Val McDermid, Barry Forshaw and Natasha Cooper – and even Prime Minister Gordon Brown. *See also* Magazines.

Adrian Muller

Timlin, Mark (b.1944)

Mark Timlin is the creator of South London's premier private detective Nick Sharman.

He was born in Cheltenham, Gloucestershire, on 15 June 1944 (at the local borstal requisitioned by the Royal Navy for the use of the WRNS as a maternity home), and within nine days, he was back in London with his mother and grandmother dodging V2 rockets and spending most days under the kitchen table in the family's Kilburn home. When Timlin was seven, the family relocated to Tulse Hill in South London where he was later educated at the Strand Grammar School in nearby Brixton Hill. As an adult, Timlin tried a panoply of various jobs: a forklift truck driver, mini-cab driver, skateboard manufacturer, and roadie for T-Rex and The Who (giving him a healthy sampling of the excesses of the era – which he was later to put to good fictional use). It was not until 1985, faced with another period on the dole, that Timlin decided to add 'novelist' to his expanding CV.

A Good Year for the Roses (1988) was Timlin's answer to the hard-boiled noir of 1940s America, uprooted lock, stock and barrel to the dingy back streets of 1980s South London. Nick Sharman, a down-at-heel ex-copper with a gunshot wound in his foot, is opening his private investigation business in a shopfront close to Tulse Hill station when he is hired to track down a teenage runaway named Patsy Bright.

Timlin's love of vintage cars is reflected in the vehicle that Sharman drives – a shiny E-type Jaguar, which comes to a sticky end during a particularly frenetic car chase. Combining humour with brutal violence, Timlin's breezy writing style tapped into the rich tradition of British gangster films such as ***Get Carter*** (1971) and ***The Long Good Friday*** (1980) with Sharman himself very much a modern take on the quintessentially American Philip Marlowe-style 'tec, which mirrors the author's love of Raymond **Chandler**, Ross Macdonald, Richard Stark (Donald Westlake), John D. MacDonald and others. More Sharman books followed, with *The Turnaround* (1991) being chosen to launch Sharman's television career in a one-off pilot starring Clive Owen. Alas, caught in the crossfire of media hysteria concerning screen violence following the tragic Dunblane massacre in March 1996, the series proper was eventually shunted to a late time slot, only managing four more episodes before the plug was pulled. Latterly though, it has enjoyed reshowings and a welcome reappraisal.

Other notable Sharman books include *Pretend We're Dead* (1994) and *Quick before They Catch Us* (1999) which dealt with the hot topic of racism in the Asian community, in both London and Manchester. *All the Empty Places* (2000) saw Sharman dealing with the problems of a girlfriend, when a thuggish ex-flame of hers promised violent retribution, and had the surprising plot turn of Sharman leaving the country to live on a Caribbean island. After a long break *Stay another Day* (2009) sees the return of Sharman to London when his daughter is in danger.

Answers from the Grave (2004) is a long (for Timlin) stand-alone novel about a criminal family in South London where Sharman makes a guest appearance.

Timlin's noms de plume include Jim Ballantyne, Martin Milk, Tony Williams and (most recently) Lee Martin for his more mainstream novel *Gangsters' Wives* (2007). This may have explored the female side of gangland violence, but it still offered the same copious amounts of sex and violence so prodigiously displayed in the author's previous more male-dominated offerings.

Timlin lives in Docklands, where he likes to keep a close eye on his South London roots, and is the crime critic for *The Independent on Sunday*. *See also* Pulp *and* Sexuality in British Crime Fiction.

Selected Works by the Author
A Good Year for the Roses (1988)
Take the A-Train (1991)
Zip Gun Boogie (1992)
Falls the Shadow (1993)
Paint It Black (1995)
Sharman and Other Filth (stories, 1996)
Dead Flowers (1998)
All the Empty Places (2000)
Answers from the Grave (2004)

Website
www.nicksharman.co.uk

Mark Campbell

Tope, Rebecca (b.1948)

Novelist, smallholder and small-press publisher, Rebecca Tope is the author of crime stories which include those featuring undertaker-detective Drew Slocombe, those concerning Devon police detective Den Cooper and, more recently, those chronicling the adventures of a Cotswold housesitter Thea Osborne (a profession one would have expected to produce a limited oeuvre). Tope is also Membership Secretary to the **Crime Writers' Association** and works as a ghost writer to the television series *Rosemary and Thyme*. Tope's three *Rosemary and Thyme* novelisations appeared during 2004–2006.

Tope grew up on farms, first in Cheshire, then in Devon, and now farms in Herefordshire on her own smallholding close to the Black Mountains. She also works for the Milk Marketing Board, visiting farms on their behalf. Unsurprisingly, rural issues are a prominent feature in her work.

Her first novel, *A Dirty Death* (1999), in which the obligatory corpse was found in a slurry pit, was the first of four to star the likeable policeman Den Cooper. The second Den Cooper title was *Death of a Friend* (2000) and the third *A Death to Record* (2001). In the fourth, *The Sting of Death* (2002), Tope had Cooper meet and join forces with her other early hero, Drew Slocombe. We first encounter Slocombe in *Dark Undertakings* (1999), in which he, going about his routine business as an undertaker, was not convinced that the otherwise healthy corpse in front of him met his end as the medical report suggested. The Slocombe books are informed by an earlier period in Tope's life when she worked for seven years at an undertaker's in Sussex, and the concept of an undertaker handling corpses every week who doubles as an amateur detective would seem to have had more mileage in it than the series actually delivered.

A less obviously fruitful concept seems that of the peripatetic housesitter, Thea Osborne, who in the company of her cocker spaniel Hepzibah works in a succession of Cotswold houses, in an alarming number of which foul deeds have been perpetrated. The series is set in named and identifiable Cotswold villages and begins with *A Cotswold Killing* (2004) and continues with *A Cotswold Ordeal* (2005), *Death in the Cotswolds* (2006) and *A Cotswold Mystery* (2007). They are less cosy than the titles suggest. *Death in the Cotswolds*, for example, has Thea and her detective boyfriend come to terms with yet another murder in Cold Aston – a Cotswold village – and the tale is enlivened with paganism and Freemasonry.

Tope is a reliable writer, increasingly popular with library readers who are attracted by her ability to combine a good mystery with her knowledge and passion for the nation's dying rural heritage. Her press, Praxis, concentrates on poetry, rural matters and the works of the Victorian author and polymath Sabine Baring-Gould. *See also* The Shires: Rural England and Regional Crime Fiction.

Selected Works by the Author
A Dirty Death (1999)
Dark Undertakings (1999)
Sting of Death (2002)
Death in the Cotswolds (2006)

Russell James

Tremayne, Peter (b.1943)

Peter Tremayne is the pseudonym reserved for his fiction by Celtic scholar and author Peter Berresford Ellis.

The work of Ellis/Tremayne, who also writes occasionally as Peter MacAlan, really hides three, perhaps even four, areas of interest that manifest themselves in various ways. Under his own name, Ellis is a renowned author of reference books about the Celtic world, starting with his first non-fiction, *Wales–A Nation Again!* (1968). These titles now exceed thirty volumes covering Celtic history, culture and mythology. The emphasis is on Ireland, as Ellis is Irish by birth, but also covers all Celtic cultures, with books ranging from *The Cornish Language and Its Literature* (1974) to *The Ancient World of the Celt* (1998).

Despite having degrees in Celtic studies, Ellis followed in his father's footsteps as a journalist and worked in several editorial posts before turning to full-time writing in 1975. He retains an interest in the world of writing and the creative mind, particularly of writers of boys and adventure fiction. He has written biographies of H. Rider Haggard, W.E. Johns (with Piers Williams), Talbot Mundy and Bram Stoker (with Peter **Haining**) and has written horror and fantasy books in their style, all under the pseudonym Tremayne, including *Dracula Unborn* (1977), *The Revenge of Dracula* (1978), *Dracula, My Love* (1980) and *The Vengeance of She* (1978). He also paid homage to E.W. **Hornung**'s gentleman thief by resurrecting him in *The Return of Raffles* (1981). He has also written **espionage** novels and thrillers as Peter MacAlan including *The Judas Battalion* (1983), *Airship* (1984) and *Kitchener's Gold* (1986). One of the MacAlan books, *The Confession* (1985) concerns an investigation into an apparent suicide of a Franciscan friar in a Vatican sanctuary and is more in keeping with the traditional crime novel.

Tremayne has also paid homage to the memory of Nancy Drew and the Hardy Boys in the occasional story featuring Constable Hardy Drew set during the Elizabethan and Jacobean period. No novels have yet featured Drew, but several stories appear in the collection *An Ensuing Evil* (2006).

In 1993, however, Ellis became fascinated by the idea of a female investigator in the ancient Celtic world. The seventh century was a critical period for the Christian church because of a rift that had developed between the Celtic church and the Roman. At the Synod of Whitby in AD 664, the Saxon king of Northumbria agreed to abide by the Roman rites and liturgy rather than the Celtic, which had been the one continuity of Christianity in Britain prior to the arrival of Augustine in the late sixth century. Furthermore, the Celtic church, especially under Irish rule, gave greater protection to women than any other western culture and treated them as equals. Thus, it was not unusual to find a female *dálaigh* (pronounced 'dhaulee') or advocate of Brehon laws of Ireland. Ellis created the character of Sister Fidelma, a religieuse who is also a *dálaigh*, and has the right to investigate any crime. She first appeared in several short stories, but the novels began with *Absolution by Murder* (1994), which is set at the Synod of Whitby. There Fidelma meets the Saxon monk Eadulf, and the two become partners in most of the later novels and are due to be married in *A Prayer for the Damned* (2006). Most of the investigations take place in Ireland, although the second book, *Shroud for an Archbishop* (1995), which follows on immediately from the first, takes place in Rome, *Act of Mercy* (1999) is set almost entirely on board ship and *The Haunted Abbot* (2002) takes place in Suffolk. The books are steeped in Celtic lore and tradition, all fully explained by Ellis, who uses many of the Celtic practices as intrinsic to his mysteries. They are also fixed firmly within an historical template, with a strong sense of place and time directing the greater action within the story. But Ellis has never lost his delight in the sensational and mysterious, and the crimes that Fidelma encounters are frequently unusual, such as a whole community of monks vanishing in *Smoke in the Wind* (2001) or unspeakable rites in *Badger's Moon* (2003). Ellis's blend of scholarship and sense of adventure makes the series unique in the annals of crime fiction both for its setting and period and for its special female protagonist. *See also* Feminist Readings in British Crime Fiction.

Selected Works by the Author
The Confession (as Peter MacAlan, 1985)
Absolution by Murder (1994)
Valley of the Shadow (1998)
Hemlock at Vespers (2000)
Smoke in the Wind (2001)
Whispers of the Dead (2004)
An Ensuing Evil and Others (stories, 2006)

Further Reading
Cuthbertson, Sarah. 2004. 'The Fascination for Sister Fidelma'. *Solander: The Magazine of the Historical Novel Society* 8.1: 2–6, www.historicalnovelsociety.org/solander/fidelma.htm.
Kiplinger, Christina. 1988. 'Quietly Soaring: Peter Tremayne'. Pp.135–138 in *Discovering Modern Horror Fiction II*. Edited by Darrell Schweitzer. Starmont House.

Website
International Sister Fidelma Society, www.sisterfidelma.com

Mike Ashley

Trevor, Elleston (also known as Adam Hall) (1920–1995)

A prolific writer, Elleston Trevor/Adam Hall was recognised as one of the most accomplished thriller and **espionage** writers of the Cold War.

Born Trevor Dudley Smith in Bromley, Kent, he was educated at Yardley Court Preparatory School, then Sevenoaks School from 1932 to 1938. He served in the Royal Air Force and, during the war, published a number of books under his own name. It was after the war that he first used the pseudonym Elleston Trevor for a non-mystery novel. The name was so attractive, he later took it for his own.

It was as Elleston Trevor that he wrote his first successful mass-market novel, *The Flight of the Phoenix* (1964), which was released as a film in 1965. In this beautifully constructed narrative, a plane crashes in the Libyan desert, and the passengers must battle the heat, thirst and Arab bandits before cannibalising the wreckage to fly on to safety.

Successful as this was, today the author is better known as Adam Hall, author of the much-admired *Quiller* series – 'The best of the new-style spy thrillers,' as *Life Magazine* contemporaneously described them. The first of this series was written after Trevor read (and was greatly impressed by) *The Spy Who Came In from the Cold* (1963), although his protagonist was very different from le Carré's George Smiley.

Quiller was introduced in *The Berlin Memorandum* (1965), and it was later released as a film of the same name, with the enigmatic screenplay written by Harold Pinter. Quiller was a man of the 1960s: martial artist, linguist, pilot and diver; Quiller would undertake the most dangerous of missions – always without a firearm ('I never carried a gun in peace-time').

Working for a government bureau 'not known publicly to exist', Quiller is helping to arrest war criminals, and about to return home when he is informed by his control, 'Pol', that Jones, another respected operator, has been killed. He is given his predecessor's mission: to track down a group of ex-Nazis called Phoenix.

In 1965, *The Quiller Memorandum* won him the Edgar Award from the Mystery Writers of America. In France, it won the Grand Prix de Littérature Policière. Another nineteen books in the Quiller series were to follow, the last (and most elusive for collectors) *Quiller Balalaika* being published posthumously in 1996.

Trevor lived in France from 1958 to 1973, when he moved to Phoenix, Arizona. Widowed, there he married Chaille Anne Groom, who survived him when he died of cancer in 1995, leaving a son by his first marriage.

During a prolific writing life, Trevor wrote under many pseudonyms: historical treatises as Roger Fitzalan, mystery stories as Simon Rattray and novels as Howard North, but he also used the names Mansell Black, Trevor Burgess, T. Dudley-Smith, Warwick Scott, Caesar Smith and Lesley Stone.

It is *The Quiller Memorandum* which will be remembered longest. The book was unique in its achievement and holds resonance today. The individualist who risks all has continued in popular fiction and film, from the Reacher series by Lee **Child** to the *Die Hard* films. With Quiller, Trevor/Hall left an indelible mark on the British spy thriller.

Selected Works by the Author

As Adam Hall
The Berlin Memorandum (1965; also published in the United States as *The Quiller Memorandum*)
The 9th Directive (1966)
The Striker Portfolio (1968)
The Warsaw Document (1971)

As Elleston Trevor
Squadron Airborne (1957)
The Flight of the Phoenix (1964)
Bury Him among Kings (1970)

Further Reading
Penzler, Otto. 1978. *The Great Detectives*. Little, Brown.

Website
The Unofficial Quiller Web Site, www.quiller.net.

Michael Jecks

Trow, M.J. (b.1949)

Countless Sherlock **Holmes** spin-offs have appeared over the years, but M.J. Trow's long-running Inspector Lestrade series is amongst the most entertaining.

Born in Ferndale, a coal-mining town deep in the heart of the Welsh Rhondda Valley, Meirion James Trow was a poorly child who moved home twice before the age of ten – first to Macclesfield Forest in the Pennines and then to the tiny village of Bubbenhall in Warwickshire. Trow was educated at Warwick School, an independent boys' school that dates back to the tenth century, and read History at King's College, London, from 1968, followed by a year at Jesus College, Cambridge. He married in 1973 and moved to the Isle of Wight three years later, where he settled down as a schoolteacher.

A keen military historian and Sherlock Holmes aficionado, Trow decided to write a novel featuring the Great Detective's Scotland Yard colleague, Inspector Lestrade. Naming him 'Sholto' (the character's first name is never mentioned by Arthur Conan

Doyle), he constructed a tale based loosely on the Jack the Ripper murders, an extremely popular sub-genre in the world of Holmesian pastiche (and one Trow was to delve into fully with his 1988 book, *Lestrade and the Ripper*). He also made the geography of his native island central to the plot, with a walled-up corpse discovered in the picturesque environs of Shanklin Chine.

The Adventures of Inspector Lestrade appeared in 1985. Controversially, it relegated Holmes to a subordinate position as a none-too-bright consulting detective whose talents were apparently exaggerated by the real-life Conan Doyle (who also featured in the book). With its tongue firmly in its cheek, the novel's implausible plot includes a large cast of real and imaginary characters, who variously help and hinder Lestrade as he attempts, somewhat clumsily, to unmask a Victorian serial killer. In a further admixture of fact and fiction, his boss is none other than Sir Melville MacNaghten, Chief Constable of the London Metropolitan Force during the Ripper investigations.

Best described as 'historical romps', Trow's books are characterised by ambitious plotting, eccentric characters and large doses of humour. In *Lestrade and the Hallowed House* (1987), for instance, the detective is called in to investigate the murder of a prominent MP, a bomb in the Houses of Parliament and the kidnapping of the king himself.

During this time, Trow wrote many exhaustively researched biographies on people such as Vlad the Impaler, Kit Marlowe and Derek Bentley, while his second fictional detective series had obvious autobiographical roots. History teacher by day, private detective by night (and at weekends), Peter 'Mad Max' Maxwell first appeared in the punningly titled *Maxwell's House* (1994) in which he sets out to find the killer of a former pupil. *Maxwell's Point* appeared in 2007. *See also* The Detective in British Fiction *and* The Great Detectives.

Selected Works by the Author
The Adventures of Inspector Lestrade (1985, also published in the United States as *The Supreme Adventure of Inspector Lestrade*)
Lestrade and the Leviathan (1987)
Lestrade and the Ripper (1988)
Lestrade and the Sign of Nine (1992)
Maxwell's War (1999)

Mark Campbell

True Crime

A difference between the writers of crime fiction and true crime authors was graphically illustrated at the 2001 awards ceremony for the **Crime Writers' Association** (CWA) Dagger for Non-Fiction, held at the Brewery in the City of London that November. Among the shortlisted, indeed the eventual winner, was *The Infiltrators* by Philip Etienne and Martin Maynard with Tony Thompson, a true account of an undercover exercise mounted by two former members of SO10. Such was the seriousness of the case – and its perpetrators – that the two policemen not only wrote the book pseudonymously but were still in hiding. The press were not told that the authors would be at the ceremony, the authors were not identified among the audience and no photographs were allowed. All this at an event whose whole purpose was publicity. Real criminals, unlike fictional ones, can bite back.

True Crime

The CWA has offered a prize for non-fiction for thirty years. Most prizewinners have been relatively unknown names, although Lady Antonia **Fraser** won in 1996, as four years later did the reformed American convict Edward Bunker, famed as much for his appearance in the film *Reservoir Dogs* (1993) as for his writing. Often the winner has been a journalist. Not infrequently, the true crime writer's investigation has continued despite strenuous opposition from those involved. The first Silver award, to Harry Hawkes in 1978, told of *The Capture of the Black Panther*. The following year's Gold went to Shirley Green's expose of the slum landlord *Rachman*. Two years later, Jacobo Timerman won with *Prisoner without a Name, Cell without a Number*. Both 1998s *Cries Unheard* (Gitta Sereny) and 1999s *The Case of Stephen Lawrence* (Brian Cathcart) probed where the authorities would have preferred no light to shine. John Dickie in 2004 won with *Cosa Nostra*. All these were brave books by determined authors. How much less worrying, one thinks, to win with *The Gunpowder Plot* (Antonia Fraser, 1996), *The Mystery of the Princes* (Audrey Williamson, 1978) or *The Secret Lives of Trebitsch Lincoln* (Bernard Wasserstein, 1988). Winners have ranged from the safely historic, such as *The Passing of Starr Faithfull* (Jonathan Goodman, 1990), to the autobiographical, such as *Mr Blue* (Edward Bunker, 2000).

These winners give an indication of how widely the umbrella of '**true crime**' spreads. But nestling beside these excellent titles on bookshop shelves can be found many cheaply produced, trashily written hack-works in lurid covers. It was ever thus: the equivalents of these sensational tomes screamed out equally blatantly (often as misleadingly) 200 years ago and more. Indeed, a pamphlet was on sale in 1609 telling the true story of Margaret Ferne-seede who ran a brothel near the Tower of London and who slit her husband's throat. The pamphlet's elaborate title began, *The arraignment and burning of Margaret Ferne-seede, for the murder of her late Husband Anthony Ferne-seede, found dead in Packham Field neere Lambeth, having once before attempted to poison him with broth….* In the seventeenth and eighteenth centuries, broadsides, ballads and catchpennies flourished with subjects ranging from poesy and romance through to crime. As the poesy became more syrupy, the crimes became more violent: murder, rape and infanticide. The crudely printed broadsides were often illustrated, frequently with an admonitory drawing of the felon hanging from the gallows but at times with a sketch of the crime itself. Notorious criminals such as Jonathan Wild and Dick Turpin became household names.

The true crime compendium *The Newgate Calendar* began in 1774 but became best known in bound form with an edition published in the 1820s. The *Calendar*, edited by Andrew Knapp and William Baldwin, published 'confessions' and accounts of crimes by those incarcerated in Newgate Prison. The stories were vividly written and illustrated, and the *Calendar* sold well. Other publishers followed suit, combining stories such as 'Maria Marten and the Red Barn Murder' with lesser tales of violence. The tales were simply told, and by the 1870s, their illustrations had become truly shocking. Every issue of the popular *Illustrated Police News* contained frankly hideous pictures of death and torture – excused, of course, by their being printed in a weekly which purported to be a police newspaper. Articles (usually mercifully short) placed side by side with edifying pieces such as 'A Clergyman Flogging a Boy at Grantham', 'Baby Farming at Brixton', 'Five Children Thrown into a Well', 'Horrible Murder by Two Women' and 'A Burglar Bitten by a Skeleton'.

As with the true-crime shelves today, the sale of penny dreadfuls could be justified both by a few sentences of sanctimonious morality printed within and by the concurrent appearance of respectable works such as *The Illustrated London News*,

Charles **Dickens**'s *Household Words* (1850) and the court pages of daily newspapers. Did not Dickens himself write of his experiences in London's opium dens and the rat-infested tenements by the Thames? Did he not accompany the police on midnight prowls? Should the public not be told of crime?

Dickens had his own fictional detective – Inspector Bucket, a minor character in *Bleak House* (1853) – and Wilkie **Collins** had his Sergeant Cuff, but in the early decades of the nineteenth century, the detectives most widely read about were 'true', or at least based on real detectives. In 1827, Thomas Skinner (1770–1847) brought out his *Richmond: Or, Scenes in the Life of a Bow Street Officer*, with a police detective as its hero. Though the book did not sell well, it could rank as Britain's first true crime book – were it not that, in the opinion of most today, Skinner's book is largely fiction masquerading as fact. The following year, in France, saw a far more successful publication, the *Mémoires* of Eugène-François Vidocq. This extraordinary crook-turned investigator had been a thug and a notorious jail-breaker until in a real-life-is-stranger-than-fiction twist, he became the head of the Sûreté in 1812. As poacher-turned gamekeeper, he was supreme. He knew the crooks, he knew where to find them, and find them he did – with his soon to be immortalised cry: 'I am Vidocq, and I arrest you!' That cry and his adventures were immortalised in four volumes of *Mémoires* in 1828 and 1829, and the books were soon translated. Vidocq, like innumerable fictional successors, employed tricks and masterful disguises – or so he claimed in his books, although the truth was probably more brutal. Those books, like many modern celebrity memoirs, were ghost written (probably by Emile Morice and Louis-François L'Héritier). But their impact was colossal. Here was a policeman – a species of being formerly considered by most people as nothing more than a hated agent of the state – presented as hero and adventurer.

In 1829, Peel's Metropolitan Police Act began the replacement of the old Bow Street Runners with a proper Metropolitan Police Force (MPF) of (eventually) some 800 men. It was a typically British, gradual change: the Runners limped on beside the MPF till 1839 and there would not be a Detective Department till 1842. In July 1849, *Chambers Edinburgh Journal* began the serialisation of *Recollections of a Detective Police-Officer* (1856) by the pseudonymous Thomas Waters (serialised at length between 1849 and 1853 and published in yellowback volume form in 1856). 'Waters' was the pseudonym of William Russell, and he borrowed freely from Vidocq in staging dramatic confrontations and writing of detectives who were masters of disguise. By now, Charles Dickens had begun his nocturnal strolls with London's new Detective Department and was enthralling the public with comparatively short but far more believable episodes dramatised in his magazine *Household Words*. He had struck up a friendship with the genuine Inspector Field, through whom he gained access to both the Metropolitan Police and the London's Thames River Police. Rival writers, like William Russell, tended to invent their tales but wrap them in an apparently factual skein and to publish them under factual-seeming titles such as *Recollections of a Private Detective* (1863), *Recollections of a City Detective* (1864) and even, less plausibly, *The Female Detective* (1864). These three were written by the pseudonymous Andrew Forrester Jr. who, like most Victorian writers, found it easier to invent stories than to document actual cases. (Russell, not to be outdone, had continued with *Experiences of a Real Detective* by 'Inspector F' in 1862 and *The Autobiography of an English Detective* in 1863.)

In truth, the work of the real police at that time was a mix of the violent and the humdrum, involving little detection, and it was difficult to pad out such episodes to the length of a book. It was more fitting to report the more lurid crimes succinctly in magazines and newspapers than to expand them to full-length novels. (Even Poe's unbelievable detective, Auguste Dupin, existed only in short-story form.) Britain's Metropolitan Police had a Detective Department but, in the late 1860s, employed less than twenty men. Gradually this changed. In 1878, the Detective Department was reorganised as the Criminal Investigation Department (the name it bears today), and by the mid-1880s, it had expanded to 800 men. But it still had to gain a reputation for efficiency. Criminal gangs, anarchists and Fenians seemed little checked by the forces of law and order. They seemed cleverer than the police, and true crime stories of any length were usually about the outlaw, not the lawman. A spate of murders in 1872 and 1873 caused panic in London, generated pages of reportage, but reflected badly on the police. In 1880, the Fenians bombed Scotland Yard – and got away with it. In the autumn of 1888, a small series of murders was blamed on a man the press dubbed 'Jack the Ripper', and although the police made no progress whatsoever in catching him, the case was sensational enough to launch a deluge of true crime writing. Here was mystery; here was violence; here were thrills.

Even with this story, one of the most famous true crime stories worldwide, writers of the day contented themselves with basic reportage, and it would be left to twentieth-century writers to exploit the case to its full. Similarly, a court case one year later in 1889, that of the alleged murderess Florence Maybrick who was said to have poisoned her husband with arsenic, garnered tremendous press coverage but waited nearly fifty years before it was revisited in a classic crime book – and then a fictional one – when it inspired *Malice Aforethought* (1931) by Francis **Iles**. Much press comment and debate raged in 1889 on the subject of did she/did she not kill him and should she/should she not be hanged. Petitions that her death sentence be commuted poured into the Home Office – with some reason: although Mrs Maybrick undoubtedly had a motive, her husband had been buying and dosing himself with an arsenic-based tonic for over eighteen months. Her defending counsel, Sir Charles Russell (later to become Lord Chief Justice of England) mounted one of the most incompetent defences in legal history. The sentence *was* commuted, but she served fifteen years in jail. The book she wrote on her release, *My Fifteen Lost Years* (1905), added little, and she lived on in near-obscurity till 1941. (Interestingly, a precursor case in 1857 Edinburgh, that of Madeleine Smith who also may or may not have poisoned her lover with arsenic, saw its alleged culprit live to a ripe old age too. Smith died aged ninety-one, and her case may have spawned more books than has Florence Maybrick. Ann Todd portrayed her in a 1949 film.)

Doctor Thomas Neill Cream lived a life stranger and nastier than portrayed in fiction. Twice in America, he was accused but escaped sentence for killing a woman by botched abortion. Then in Chicago in 1881, he administered a fatal dose of strychnine to the husband of his mistress, a crime for which he was sentenced to life imprisonment. But he was released in 1891. He came to London and began killing again, poisoning prostitutes with pills laced with strychnine. He taunted the police with self-advertisement, including an offer to name the 'Lambeth Poisoner' for £30,000, but he pushed his luck too far. He was hanged in November 1892.

That neither Jack the Ripper nor Florence Maybrick launched a flood of true crime books in their own time says much for nineteenth-century attitudes. Their stories would be retold in the twentieth century, along with those of more contemporary crimes and *causes célèbres*. Doctor Crippen was executed in 1910 for poisoning his second wife, Cora Turner, and burying her dissected body in the coal cellar, but what shot his story onto world front pages was the way his escape from England by cruise ship to America was foiled by the new technology of wireless telegraphy. That incident, coupled with his attempt to disguise his wonderfully named mistress Ethel le Neve on board by dressing her as a man, was far more interesting than the actual murder. No crime writer could ask for more. (After her acquittal, Ethel, like Florence Maybrick and Madeleine Smith, went on to live a long life. She died in 1967.)

By contrast, the case of John George Haigh, the acid bath murderer, was sensational because of the way the murders were performed. Haigh killed cold-bloodedly for little gain and attempted to dispose of the bodies by total immersion in a sulphuric acid bath, failing to realise that a victim's plastic dentures would not be dissolved by the acid. Once arraigned for murder, Haigh confessed to eight other killings and was executed in August 1949.

It has long been a British fantasy that the French take a lenient view of the *crime passionnel* (and a French fantasy that the British understand nothing about passion), but when such cases reach British courts, the watching public can be implacable. Certainly, they were about Edith Thompson. Edith, it was alleged, persuaded her young lover Frederick Bywaters to kill her husband by the simple but effective ruse of a pretended street attack. Frederick would knife him and run away, and Edith's evidence would suggest that the murder was an attempted robbery that had gone wrong. Unfortunately, Edith had written some very revealing and compromising letters. But had she incited Frederick to kill her husband? The 1922 jury was in no doubt – reflecting the attitude of a moralistic public – but the jury of history is still out. The case has been filmed, novelised and anthologised.

In fairness to the often censorious British public of yesteryear, we should remember the case of the beautiful Frenchwoman Madame Fahmy who in 1923 shot her playboy husband at the Savoy Hotel. His undoubted and repeated cruelty to her, coupled with a famous defence by Marshall Hall, caused her to be found Not Guilty of either murder or even manslaughter. To deafening cheers, Fahmy walked free. The public was more divided over the case of Ruth Ellis, who in 1955 emptied the chamber of Smith and Wesson 38 into her lover David Blakely, waited beside the body and said, 'Phone the police.' (The man she spoke to replied, 'I *am* a police officer.' It could not happen in fiction.) She had murdered him certainly – but should she hang? Ellis was famously the last woman hanged in Britain, and her case recurs in most true crime anthologies.

True crime books do not confine themselves to murder stories. Just as eighteenth- and nineteenth-century accounts of the thieves Jonathan Wild and Dick Turpin were hugely popular, so have stories of gangland feuds and daring robberies remained a mainstay of the genre. Some are 'written' by the investigating officers (as were, supposedly, those of Richmond, Vidocq and Waters in the nineteenth century), and others by the criminals themselves: the Krays, the Richardsons and the Great Train Robbers have all ghosted their tales, alongside numerous other criminal biographies and confessions. The Train Robbers (who paraded before the cameras for their book launch in 1979) and the Krays and Richardsons and their hangers-on have been written up and filmed often and seem guaranteed to spawn more recreations. There comes a point when fame feeds upon itself, when fact becomes legend and will not die.

Famous trials, especially those which can be presented as miscarriages of justice, are a stock in trade – even if, as in the Hanratty A6 Murder, the miscarriage eventually turns out not to have been a miscarriage at all. (DNA evidence finally proved that, despite the denials which convinced so many for so long, he had been at the scene of the crime after all.) Frequent revisits to the Christie murders – more famous for their address, 10 Rillington Place, than for the name John Christie – have perpetuated the name of Timothy Evans, Christie's neighbour, a man of low IQ who was wrongly hanged for the murder of his wife and daughter, murders later confessed to by Christie. This was a notorious miscarriage of justice, but famous incidents, even if they occur within a minor and uninteresting crime, have a propensity to live on. The botched warehouse robbery by two teenagers in which, when the police had them trapped on the flat roof, one boy pulled out a gun and the other called, 'Let him have it, Chris!', has become immortalised far beyond what they could have imagined at that moment. Christopher Craig was under eighteen, but Bentley had passed that crucial birthday. So Bentley was hanged for murder while his younger companion was only sent to jail.

The appeal of many true crime stories lies in their being true, not in the actual stories. For a fiction writer, they lack strong plot. But they are true, and therein lies their interest. A writer can invent a situation where a woman incites her lover to kill her husband or where a spouse methodically poisons an unwanted partner – but when it happens in real life, it gains extra lustre. In real life, there is always that further question: What actually happened? Did it all come out in court? Did the jury get it right? A crime novelist tells you what happens (even if you have to wait till the last chapter to find out), but a true crime reporter tells you what *seems* to have happened: there remains a nagging doubt. Then you, the reader, become the jury. *See also* Historical Crime *and* Realism and Crime Fiction.

Carol Ann Davis

TV Detectives: Small-Screen Adaptations

With their emphasis on strong characterisation, tight plotting and minute-but-important visual clues, the best detective stories have also made the best television programmes. Figures such as Inspectors Morse and Frost, amateur sleuths Miss Marple and Sherlock **Holmes**, and private eyes James Hazell and Piet van der Valk have all benefited from the attention to detail required for – and necessitated by – the small screen.

It is no surprise that long-running series characters, such as Holmes, Morse and Rebus, have worked so successfully as long-running television series. A readership that is prepared to follow the adventures of their favourite detective year on year as each new book comes out will probably be committed enough to watch television versions of these adventures, and original ones in a similar vein, for as long as the producers see fit to make them.

Very few crime books have a real ensemble cast, in the way that television shows are required to have by definition. Even the most 'authentic' **police procedurals**, such as Graham **Hurley**'s Portsmouth-based series, have a central figurehead (and partner) taking centre stage. This explains why so many of the most enduring British cop shows are original creations designed for the televisual medium. *Z Cars, Dixon of Dock Green* (a spin-off from the 1950 film *The Blue Lamp*) and ***The Bill*** have no obvious literary antecedents, and their large, ever-changing casts guarantee them a degree of longevity. (*The Bill*, first shown in 1984, is still going strong nearly a quarter of a century later.) Straightforward adaptations, even when their source material is prolific, have an inevitable shelf life built into them. They are 'star vehicles', in the way that the ensemble casts of manufactured television shows rarely are.

The first crime novel adapted for television was *The Three Hostages* based on the book by John Buchan, broadcast in six episodes in June–July 1952. However in its early days, BBC favoured original serials and took advantage of Francis Durbridge (1912–1998), already well known for his radio serials. Durbridge had eighteen serials on TV between 1952 and 1980, most run under the banner 'Francis Durbridge Presents'. Durbridge's famous radio detective Paul Temple was eventually transferred to TV in 1969, with Francis Matthews in the title role, but none of the fifty-two hour-long episodes, spread over four series until 1971, were scripted by Durbridge.

With the arrival of commercial TV, British television was swamped with American crime series, but perhaps the most popular home-grown series was *The Saint*, based on the stories by Leslie **Charteris** and featuring Roger Moore, memorably cast in the title role. The series ran for 188 hour-long episodes from 1962 to 1969.

Unsurprisingly, the award for most adapted character goes to Sir Arthur Conan **Doyle**'s world-famous consulting detective. Played on UK television by notable actors such as Peter Cushing, Douglas Wilmer, Guy Henry, Ian Richardson and Jeremy Brett, it is the latter who is often cited as the most accurate impersonator. Others have chosen to play the part in their own, inimitable, style: Rupert Everett, Tom Baker and Richard Roxburgh spring to mind here. Agatha **Christie**'s sleuths have also seen their fair share of screen time, but here the nominees are fewer. David Suchet has no opposition as Poirot, while Joan Hickson eclipses the more recent attempts of Geraldine McEwan and Julia Mackenzie to bring the delightfully eccentric Miss Marple to life.

The unwaning popularity of these genteel detectives is symptomatic of the British viewer's obsession with its own (rose-tinted) history. It seems that people cannot get enough of these old-fashioned whodunits, solved by old-fashioned eccentrics, in old-fashioned settings (country houses, cottages, cobbled streets, church vestries, etc.), preferably shown on Sunday evenings when the evenings are drawing in. How else to explain the popularity of *Midsomer Murders*? Where America has *CSI*, the United Kingdom has the dispiriting *Rosemary and Thyme*.

But it is not all bad news. Despite television's *Inspector Morse* (1987–2000) 'dumbing up' the misogynistic, rough-edged title character of Colin **Dexter**'s books into an intellectual, Mozart-loving aesthete, the series produced a great many finely written episodes that stretched its audience's deductive powers to the full. Romanticised Oxford backdrops and a preponderance of upper-middle-class characters aside, the series broke new ground in its depiction of edgy crime drama masquerading as 'safe' telly for the masses. The brainchild of Kenny McBain, perfect casting in the form of John Thaw (Morse) and Kevin Whately (Lewis), coupled with Barrington Pheloung's sublime incidental music, proved a winning formula from the word go.

By the early 1990s, and with the end in sight, a replacement for Morse was being groomed in the form of *A Touch of Frost* (1992–2008), a leaner variation on the theme, set in a generic Northern town and based on the incident-packed novels of R.D. **Wingfield**. David Jason was cast against type as a spiky copper with a chip on each shoulder, and the stories were grimmer and (often literally) darker than its Tourist Board counterpart. A clever twist had Frost teaming up with a new partner for each case, but otherwise the format was much as before.

The 1990s were a boom for television adaptations. A rare excursion into twelfth-century England (filmed in Hungary) saw Sir Derek Jacobi starring as the monkish sleuth *Cadfael* (1994–1998), based on the books by Ellis **Peters**. Former *Doctor Who* Peter Davison donned a pair of bottle-top spectacles to play Margery **Allingham**'s unruffled *Campion* (1989–1990) – following in the footsteps of Bernard Horsfall in the late 1950s – and Imogen Stubbs was *Anna Lee* (1993–1995), the police officer-turned private eye from the 1980s books by Liza **Cody**.

The twin Queens of the literary crime genre were seemingly never off our screens from the 1980s onwards. Ruth **Rendell**'s soft-spoken Chief Inspector **Wexford** appeared in twenty-three adaptations, from 1987 to 2000, perfectly played by the West Country actor George Baker. P.D. **James**, on the other hand, had to share two actors in the role of her solitary poet detective Adam **Dalgliesh**. Roy Marsden appeared in ten television adaptations from 1983 to 1998, while ex-Professional Martin Shaw took over duties on the more recent versions, *Death in Holy Orders* (2003) and *The Murder Room* (2005).

Recent trends have seen the television crime genre combined with supernatural or fantastical elements, such as the *Jonathan Creek* (1997–2004) and the highly successful *Life on Mars* (2006–2007), and it will be interesting to see whether future adaptations will reflect this. Could the wildly imaginative novels of Jasper **Fforde** ever make it onto British television screens? *See also* Film and Crime: Page to Screen.

Mark Campbell

Twining, James (b.1972)

City businessman–turned thriller writer, James Twining specialises in highly ingenious art world mysteries featuring international art thief Tom Kirk.

103. James Twining.

Twining was born on 13 December 1972 in London. From the age of four, he lived in Paris, and he returned to England in 1974 to study at Merchant Taylors', a public school in Northwood, Middlesex, whose literary alumni include poet Edmund Spenser and Jacobean dramatist John Webster. He then read French Literature at Christ Church College, Oxford, graduating with a first in 1995.

His move into the international business world was entirely expected, and for four years, he worked in the corporate finance department of investment bank SBC Warburg (now USB). His next venture was as co-founder of an e-procurement business, for which he was named as one of eight Best of Young British Entrepreneurs in *The New Statesman* magazine. On selling the business in 2002, Twining found himself temporarily without a job and so started writing a story he had been mulling over for some time. This became *The Double Eagle* (2005).

Twining's fascination with art theft began when he watched the first James Bond film, *Dr No* (1962), in which the title character shows off his 'acquisition' of the recently stolen Goya masterpiece *Portrait of the Duke of Wellington*. Although it was actually taken by a retired bus driver who thought that the vast sums of money paid for it should have been used to subsidise his television licence fee, nonetheless the romantic notion of a criminal mastermind adorning his lair with stolen artwork clearly stuck in the author's mind.

Blending elements from James Bond, *Mission Impossible* and *The Da Vinci Code*, *The Double Eagle* centres on the world's greatest art thief Tom Kirk, now retired but coerced into helping sexy FBI agent Jennifer Browne to track down the thief who stole five gold coins worth $40 million from Fort Knox. The story encompassed many exotic European locales and had more than enough twists, revelations and action set pieces in its 400-odd pages to satisfy the most jaded of airport readers.

Twining's prose style, best described as 'breathless', was ramped up several more degrees for his next novel, *The Black Sun* (2006), again starring Tom Kirk. Instead of gold coins, it is plundered Nazi treasure that is the driving force behind this tale of the Second World War decoding machines, murdered concentration camp survivors and SS secret societies. Considerably longer and more ambitious than its predecessor, the book's complex, globetrotting plot invited further comparison with Dan Brown's 2003 mega-hit *The Da Vince Code*, although the general consensus was that Twining's style was all his own.

His novel *The Gilded Seal* (2007) – which had the working title of *The Napoleon Seal* – bravely tackles Dan Brown head-on with Kirk investigating the theft of a Da Vinci painting from a heavily fortified Scottish castle. The subsequent action takes in London, Paris, New York and Havana in true 007 style.

Selected Works by the Author
The Double Eagle (2005)
The Black Sun (2006)
The Gilded Seal (2007)
The Ivory Key (2009)

Website
www.jamestwining.com

Barry Forshaw

U

Underwood, Michael (1916–1992)

Michael Underwood is the pseudonym of British lawyer and barrister, John Michael Evelyn, who earned a reputation for his methodical investigative novels and created the first female lawyer sleuth, Rosa Epton.

Underwood was educated at Oxford, and his whole working life was in the legal profession. He became a barrister in 1939 and, after his wartime army service, entered the Department of Public Prosecutions in 1946, remaining there until his retirement in 1976. This gave him a detailed and superior knowledge of the legal process which he used with great skill in nearly fifty books. These began with *Murder on Trial* (1954), for which he adopted his mother's maiden name for his writing persona. The book introduced Inspector (later Superintendent) Simon Manton who, in this book and its sequel *Murder Made Absolute* (1955), finds himself investigating death in court, the first of the accused and the second of a barrister. Manton appeared in thirteen novels, all traditional-style investigations. Underwood wrote a similar procedural series, starting with *The Juror* (1975), which introduced Sergeant Nick Atwell who, in some cases, is assisted by his wife, a former police constable. Both series explore the close links between the police investigation and the trial and occasionally show how both can go wrong. For instance, in *The Fatal Trip* (1977), Atwell doubts the guilt of the man he has put on trial and sets out to prove his innocence. Underwood produced five Atwell novels which include some of his best. *Menaces, Menaces* (1976), which also features the lawyer Rosa Epton, is an ingenious puzzle as to how a blackmailer, on trial and under tight security, might somehow continue his crimes.

With *The Unprofessional Spy* (1964), Underwood began a series about barrister Martin Ainsworth who, in this first volume, becomes involved in international **espionage**. Both this book and *The Man Who Died on Friday* (1967), the first of only two novels featuring lawyer Richard Monk, are set against the backcloth of the Cold War and work more as thrillers than crime novels. Underwood returned to more homely territory for the next Ainsworth novel, *A Trout in the Milk* (1971), which involves the murder of a barrister, but returned to Cold War tactics for *Reward for a Defector* (1973).

Rosa Epton had been a legal clerk in these early Ainsworth novels, with only a minor role, but she moved centre stage in *Crime upon Crime* (1980), and thereafter became Underwood's primary series character, with Ainsworth appearing only once more in *A Party to Murder* (1983). Epton gave Underwood the opportunity to explore the problems of a woman in a predominantly man's profession though recognising the increased female freedom of the 1980s and its effect upon life in chambers. Epton is a defence lawyer who frequently represents clients who may be innocent of the crime with which they are charged but who nevertheless lead dubious lives. The series ended with Underwood's last book, *Guilty Conscience* (1992), in which Epton finds herself trying to untangle the complicated relationship between a husband and his wife, who has disappeared.

Underwood usually managed to produce a book a year from 1954 until his death in 1992, and as a consequence, he was able to chronicle changes in society at large and in the legal profession in particular. Although Underwood kept an eye on foreign affairs – even Rosa Epton becomes involved in international intrigue in *A Dangerous Business* (1990) – the majority of his books are traditional crime stories on home ground, well plotted and with dogged and persistent investigative work. He produced several non-series books, most also depicting the due process of law, of which *A Clear Case of Suicide* (1980), in which a successful barrister apparently kills himself, is among his best.

His best books, which have not dated, are those which pit wits between the officers of the law and the perpetrator of the crime. This was especially evident in those non-series books which drew upon domestic situations. Both *Victim of Circumstance* (1979) and *Hand of Fate* (1981) depict husbands devising devious ways to dispose of their wives. Underwood's strength lay not only in his profound knowledge of law and the legal process but also in the psychology of the criminal.

Selected Works by the Author
Cause of Death (1960)
The Crime of Colin Wise (1964)
A Trout in the Milk (1971)
The Juror (1975)
Menaces, Menaces (1976)
The Fatal Trip (1977)
A Clear Case of Suicide (1980)
Death in Camera (1984)

Mike Ashley

Union Jack (and *Detective Weekly*)

One of the most popular and longest lasting of the story papers, this publication is best known for the adventures of the detective Sexton **Blake**. The *Union Jack* ran weekly from 28 April 1894 to 18 February 1933, a total of 2,025 issues. It was then revamped and relaunched as *Detective Weekly* until 25 May 1940, a further 379 issues.

The *Union Jack Library*, as it was initially titled (to avoid confusion with an earlier weekly called *The Union Jack*), was one of many story papers and comic books issued by Alfred Harmsworth during the 1890s, all priced at a halfpenny, in his crusade to publish 'healthy' tales for boys instead of the 'highly immoral' fiction churned out by the publishers of penny dreadfuls. The first editor was Somers Summers, then aged only eighteen, followed by William H. Maas, J.H. Pym, Ernest Goddard, William H. Back, Lewis Carlton and Walter Shute in fairly rapid succession until Harold Twyman took over in 1921 and remained there until 1934.

At the outset, *Union Jack* was much like other story papers. A small chapbook of sixteen pages with very small print in which was a novelette or novella of 16,000–20,000 words, an occasional short story or serial episode plus such reader departments and competitions as could be squeezed in. In later issues, stories often exceeded 20,000 words. The emphasis was on 'stirring' adventures of derring-do starting with 'The Silver Arrow' by Paul Herring. Sexton Blake was introduced from the second number (4 May 1894) with 'Sexton Blake, Detective' by Harry Blyth (1852–1898), who had written the very first Blake story for the *Halfpenny Marvel* a few months

104. Cover of *Union Jack* magazine, advertising a Sexton Blake feature, in January 1931.

earlier. At the start, the Blake stories were few and far between. He appeared in only 79 of the 494 issues of the magazine's first series, which ran to 10 October 1903, after which a new series was created with the price raised to a penny. This early manifestation of Blake was nothing like the detective of later renown. The character was even dropped from the magazine for most of 1903 and 1904, but when he was reintroduced under editor W.H. Back in October 1904, he became a regular and appeared in every issue from 95 (5 August 1905), and it was now that the character was reshaped.

The character was 'owned' by the publisher, and stories were written by a variety of authors, leading to some contradictory facts about the detective's background and whereabouts. There were only a handful of regular writers who developed the core characters. W.J. Lomax was the first to have the detective narrate his own story and to introduce a major villain in 'Nalda the Nihilist' (17 August 1895), and it was Lomax who created Blake's most enduring assistant, Tinker, who first appeared in 'Cunning Against Skill' in the magazine's second series (15 October 1904). Soon after, William Murray Graydon (1864–1946), one of the most productive Blake writers, moved the detective's offices to Baker Street ('The Mystery of the Hilton Royal', 17 December 1904) and introduced Blake's housekeeper Mrs Bardell (19 August 1905) and his dog, Pedro the bloodhound (9 September 1905). Between them, Lomax and Graydon created the Blake his devotees remember.

Andrew Murray (1880–1929) created the villain Count Ivor Carlac in 'The Regent Street Robbery' (28 September 1912). George H. Teed (1886–1938), probably the most popular of the authors, created evil opponents such as Mademoiselle Yvonne Cartier

(25 January 1913), Dr Huxton Rymer (22 March 1913), the Fu Manchu-like Prince Wu Ling (28 June 1913) and, the criminal organisation, the Council of Eleven (30 May 1914). But arguably, the most popular adversary of them all was Zenith the Albino, created by Anthony Skene (1886–1972), who debuted in 'A Duel to the Death' (21 November 1919). This led into the 1920s judged by Blake aficionados as the character's **Golden Age** with many of the authors, especially Teed, Gwyn Evans (1898–1938), Edwy Searles Brooks (1898–1965) and Skene writing at their best. It was also the period when the definitive Blake illustrator, Eric Parker (1898–1934), joined the team, illustrating his first Blake with 995 (7 November 1922). Even though the *Union Jack* had its own rival with the *Sexton Blake Library*, its devotees did not flag and the magazine continued unabated through the decade.

By the early 1930s, however, readership was evidently dwindling and the *Union Jack* was revamped as *Detective Weekly*. Readers were lured to the new magazine by a round-robin serial that began in the last issue of *Union Jack*. *Detective Weekly* was in the larger quarto format, with twenty-four pages and room for a serial episode. The first serial was the reprint of a Leslie **Charteris** novel, *The White Rider* (1928), and later reprinted serials were by Maurice Leblanc, Agatha **Christie**, Valentine Williams (1883–1946) and Earl Derr Biggers, as well as serials by Anthony Skene and John Hunter (1891–1961). Harold Twyman oversaw the change, but editorship was then passed to Len Barry and James Higgins before Jack Hunt ran the magazine from 1935 almost to its demise.

Lewis Jackson (1890–1958) began the magazine with a bang by introducing Blake's ne'er-do-well brother Nigel Blake. Most of the regulars, notably Teed and Skene, continued to contribute. Occasionally, serials were dropped and replaced by a supporting story. These included reprints from American **pulp** magazines with work by Carroll John Daly and Erle Stanley Gardner. For a period (131–250, during 1935–1936), the Blake stories were dropped, and when reintroduced, most of the stories were reprints.

This allowed scope for new characters. The creative G.H. Teed introduced the Shadow Crook in three long adventures later collected in book form. But increasingly after 1936, *Detective Weekly* was filled with reprints either reworked from *Union Jack*, such as Edwy Searles Brooks series featuring Detective Inspector Beeke, known as 'the Grouser', or from its better-selling companion **The Thriller**. Despite its title, Gerald Verner's (1896–1980), serial 'Blake of the Secret Service' (4 July–19 September 1936) had nothing to do with the hero of Baker Street. Occasionally, new material was run, including a serial by Peter **Cheyney**, 'Poison Ivy' (10 April–19 June 1937), a John **Creasey** novella 'Night of Dread' (277, 11 June 1938) and ever-inventive work by G.H. Teed, Rex Hardinge (1902–1990) and Anthony Skene. Even so it was difficult to distinguish *The Thriller* from *Detective Weekly* and, had not the magazine succumbed to the paper rationing of the Second World War, fate would doubtless have intervened.

Long before *Detective Weekly* folded, Sexton Blake was more happily ensconced in the *Sexton Blake Library* and *The Thriller* was providing all and more than *Detective Weekly*. Nevertheless, its passing was a significant moment as the end of the direct successor of the magazine that had fully developed Sexton Blake. *See also* Magazines.

Further Reading
Adrian, Jack. 1986. *Sexton Blake Wins*. Dent.
Harper, Duncan. 1993. *The Sexton Blake Index*, 2nd ed.
Packman, Leonard. 1965. *Sexton Blake Catalogue*. Sexton Blake Circle.

Website
Hodder, Mark. 'Sexton Blake Bibliography', http://www.sextonblake.co.uk/blakebibliography.html.
Nevins, Jess. 'The Sexton Blake Page', http://www.geocities.com/jessnevins/blake.html.

Mike Ashley

Upfield, Arthur (1888–1964)

Arthur Upfield was the English author of several mystery novels set in Australia, to which he had been banished by his father in 1910. Except during the First World War Army Service in Europe and time afterwards in England, Upfield never left his adopted land. Before he began writing his mystery stories in 1924, he avoided cities, preferring to range extensively through vast areas of open country. To support himself, he undertook manual jobs, learning skills from men he worked with. During these years, he amassed a wealth of material about different areas of the continent, its people and wildlife, for his later writing.

His first novel, published in 1928, was one of four without his serial character, Bony. Dissatisfied with an earlier draft of a mystery novel, he rewrote it when he created his detective inspector, Napoleon Bonaparte, based on a half-caste tracker with the Queensland police. The foundations of Bony's character and background are laid in *The Barrakee Mystery* (1928) and developed throughout the twenty-nine novels in which he appears. Conflicts in his personality arise from his parentage. Son of an aborigine mother and a white father, he inherits valuable characteristics from both. His normal behaviour is controlled, with occasional lapses to aboriginal wildness. Despite childhood problems, he is university educated, thoughtful and well read. He is patient and observant, especially of people and the natural world. As a tracker, his skills are rarely surpassed. Kind-hearted and fair, he earns respect and even indulgence for his vanity, when he boasts that he never fails. His stubborn insistence on investigating what, how and when he pleases results in humorous clashes with his superior officers. He is a survivor. Besides coming through floods, sandstorms and other natural disasters, he escapes attempts on his life, including bombing, poisoning, incarceration in a coffin and threats to drown him or throw him from an aeroplane.

The Barrakee Mystery contains many of the elements which make Upfield's writing enjoyable and informative. The background of the New South Wales outback and life on a sheep station is integral to the plot. We learn about aborigines and the snobbery and disdain with which half-castes are treated. Although the mystery solved by Bony has a closed community setting, with clues in the traditional whodunit style, it is intriguing and involves a thrilling race against time. The standard of the Bony novels varies, but all are readable, and many are gripping. Descriptions of landscape, natural phenomena and social settings add much to their attraction, as do Upfield's comments on government failings. Plots range from the whodunit to the thriller, sometimes with elements of horror. Least convincing are those concerning international conspiracies. Characters are generally well drawn, especially those living in remote places and small towns: policemen, government officials, landladies, hotel keepers, stockmen and drunks.

Upfield's work was despised as 'commercial' by the kind of literary critics and authors parodied in *An Author Bites the Dust* (1948). However, he captured the spirit of Australia in his books, succeeding where they failed.

Selected Works by the Author
The Sands of Windee (1931)
The Bone Is Pointed (1938)
Bushranger of the Skies (1940; also published in the United States as *No Footprints in the Bush*)
The Widows of Broome (1950)
The New Shoe (1951)
Venom House (1953)
Man of Two Tribes (1956)
The Will of the Tribe (1962)

Further Reading
Browne, Ray B. 1988. *The Spirit of Australia: The Crime Fiction of Arthur Upfield*. Bowling Green State University Popular Press.
Hawke, Jessica. 1957. *Follow My Dust! A Biography of Arthur Upfield*. Heinemann.

Christine Simpson

V

Vickers, Roy (1889–1965)

Roy Vickers is the adopted form of name of British writer William Edward Vickers, who also wrote as Sefton Kyle, David Durham and John Spencer. Although he wrote over sixty novels and countless short stories, he is almost solely remembered today for his series 'The Department of Dead Ends'.

Vickers was born in Putney, South London, the great-grandson of George Vickers, the noted Victorian publisher of penny dreadfuls and penny newspapers. His younger brother, Lyle, continued the newspaper business, while Vickers trained to be a barrister but he never practiced and instead struggled through several years as a salesman while trying to become a writer. Among his earliest sales was a brief detective series, 'The Exploits of Sefton Kyle' for *The Magpie* in 1913; Vickers later adopting his detective's name as an alias.

During this period, Vickers also worked as a crime reporter, a war correspondent and a ghost writer. It helped him make connections that led to his first book, a rapidly compiled *Lord Roberts: The Story of His Life* (1914), issued within weeks of the Field Marshal's death. The book's publisher, C. Arthur Pearson, gave Vickers an editorial post on *The Novel Magazine*, and at last he began to sell his stories regularly. One early tale, once frequently reprinted, was the railway ghost story 'The Eighth Lamp' (1916).

Vickers's early books are somewhat derivative and formulaic. His first book, *The Mystery of the Scented Death* (1921), owes much to Sax **Rohmer**, while *The Vengeance of Henry Jarroman* (1923) and its sequels show the influence of Alexandre Dumas. *The Whispering Death* (1932), one of his most translated books, is a variant on the master-criminal theme, as is *The Gold Game* (1930). Vickers became extremely prolific, eventually requiring a Dictaphone and two secretaries, and he was not averse to reworking his own plots and characters. Detective Inspector Rason appears in many of his books and stories, but he is seldom the same character, sometimes being brilliant and other times a dupe for the charismatic hero.

To Vickers, the characters are almost always secondary to the plot, and Vickers is acknowledged as one of the most ingenious plotters in the business. On occasions, though, plot and characters come together in a pleasing fusion. *The Exploits of Fidelity Dove* (1924), originally published under the pen-name David Durham (and in that edition an especially rare and collectable volume), tells of a female 'Robin Hood' who, with her coterie of specialists, tackles injustices against those unable to help themselves. A female villain also appears in *I'll Never Tell* (1937), which was adapted for the cinema as *False Evidence* (1937). That and *The Girl in the News* (1937), which was also filmed, both deal with individuals being framed for murder. Among his novels, arguably his best is *Murdering Mr Velfrage* (1950), which uses many cunning ploys to generally obfuscate who has done what to whom.

The stories for which he will long be remembered, though, are those featuring the Department of Dead Ends, a part of Scotland Yard where the detritus of unsolved crimes ends up and where lateral thinking makes connections which may solve two or more crimes at once. The stories started in *Pearson's Magazine* in 1934 with 'The Rubber Trumpet' regarded by many as one of the cleverest contrived crime stories. Vickers continued to add to the series for the next twenty years, so that no single collection includes all the stories, though *The Department of Dead Ends* compiled by E.F. Bleiler in 1978 is the most complete. In addition to the ingenious plots, what makes this series unusual is that it is written more as a matter-of-fact report than as a story, adding verisimilitude to the plot.

Vickers was probably too prolific for his own good and few will spend the time today to find his best books among the chaff. But at his best, he was one of the most inventive writers in the business. *See also* Short Stories.

Selected Works by the Author
The Exploits of Fidelity Dove (stories, 1924, as David Durham)
The Department of Dead Ends (stories, 1947, 1949, 1978)
Six Came to Dinner (1948)
Murdering Mr Velfrage (1950; also published in the United States as *Maid to Murder*)
The Sole Survivor and the Kynsard Affair (1952)
Best Detective Stories (stories, 1965)

Mike Ashley

Villain (film, 1971)

Michael Tuchner, director

'Meet Vic Dakin', claimed the poster, 'then wish you hadn't.' If Richard Burton had made more films like *Villain* and fewer like *Cleopatra* (1963), he might have ended his days as a major movie star rather than a symbol of missed opportunities. Burton's London hard man Vic combines characteristics of both Kray Twins, and the battered-and-boozed, mean-eyed actor makes as distinctive a gangster for Britain as James Cagney was for America or Alain Delon for France. A conniving tough who gets a witness out of the way by telling her to make a cup of tea while he cuts her boyfriend's face off, Vic also shows the traditional sentimental streak by taking his dear old Mum (Cathleen Nesbitt) down to Brighton every weekend and an intolerance for a world grown soft ('we should never have abolished national service'). Vic's fatal mistake comes in moving from his established protection racket into armed robbery, not out of the traditional desire to expand his empire but because he feels middle-aged flabbiness coming on and wants to get back into action to impress his sometime love interest, rent boy-cum-pimp Wolfe Lissoner (Ian McShane). It is a paradox of enlightenment that a gay character in a contemporary film could not be as unpleasant or interesting as Vic Dakin – in a telling moment, he orders his partner to keep the noise down during violent sex so as not to wake up Mum. Made just after *Get Carter* (1971), *Villain* similarly updates the conventions of the British gangland movie into 1970s flares, sideburns and seedy clubs – but without even the icy glamour of the righteous avenger, Carter to rise from the muck as a movie hero. Written by sit-com specialists Dick Clement and Ian La Frenais (both b.1937) (with a subsequent novel and a rewrite by Al Lettieri, 1928–1975, more familiar as a hood actor in *Pulp*, 1972, or *The Getaway*, 1972), its dialogue sounds more authentic than that of television's *The Sweeney* (it may be the first use of the term 'wanker' in a movie) and the plot is a neatly turned anecdote which that pays off with a Burton speech ('who are you looking at?') that prefigures Al Pacino's great restaurant rant in *Scarface* (1983). Director Michael Tuchner, who defected to US television after this striking first film, marshals an awe-inspiring collection of British character actors later lured into sit-coms, cosy television detectives or double-glazing adverts – Joss Ackland as an ulcer-ridden gang boss, Nigel Davenport and Colin Welland as determined plods, Donald Sinden as a sleazy MP caught in an extramarital orgy, Tony Selby and Del Tenney as minders, and Fiona Lewis as a high-class topless tart. The London crime locations are acutely observed and brilliantly used: the bungled smash and grab in an industrial estate is a treat, with Burton blinding a driver by squirting him with a Jif lemon and a booby-trapped suitcase full of cash extruding 5-foot steel arms. Burton is creepy in a fascinating in-depth performance, consumed with hatred for ordinary citizens ('stupid punters – telly all week, screw the wife on Saturday') as he self-destructs by always relying on weaklings who fall apart when the pressure is on.

Kim Newman

Vine, Barbara

See Rendell, Ruth

W

Wade, Henry (1887–1969)

Under the pseudonym Henry Wade, Henry Lancelot Aubrey-Fletcher wrote varied, thoughtful and entertaining crime fiction for thirty years. His career stretched from the heyday of the **Golden Age** to the era when psychological suspense was coming to the fore. He played an important part in the development of the genre, especially (but not only) in the credible depiction of police work and of the ordinary people whose lives are changed by crime. Regrettably, his gifts have long been underestimated by commentators. Aubrey-Fletcher had a distinguished military career during the First World War, and several of his novels reflect his understanding of the impact that conflict had on those who lived through it. *The Dying Alderman* (1930) is a capable early whodunit with neat use of a 'dying message' clue. *Mist on the Saltings* (1933) is even more effective; a study in character which benefited from an evocative setting on the East Anglian coast; it was ahead of its time when compared with most other work being done in the genre at the time. *Released for Death* (1938) presents a sympathetic picture of a criminal exploited, after leaving jail, by an evil former fellow inmate. *Lonely Magdalen* (1940) is even better, offering a realistic yet gripping account of an investigation into the apparently commonplace murder of a prostitute whose body is found on Hampstead Heath. The central part of the book details the dead woman's misadventures in her younger days before the police enquiry resumes following her identification. This masterly novel, like many of Wade's best, features Inspector John Poole, a shrewd and sympathetic Oxford-educated detective whose other cases include a very enjoyable 'inverted mystery'. *See also* Realism and Crime Fiction.

Selected Works by the Author
The Dying Alderman (1930)
Mist on the Saltings (1933)
Constable, Guard Thyself! (1934)
Released for Death (1938)
Lonely Magdalen (1940)
Too Soon to Die (1953)

Further Reading
Shibuk, Charles. 1968. 'Henry Wade' and 'Henry Wade Revisited'. *The Armchair Detective*, vols. 1 and 2.

Martin Edwards

Wainwright, John (1921–1995)

Although now out of print (and, it has to be said, out of fashion), Wainwright's eighty-odd crime books, written over a thirty-year period, made him one of the most prolific crime writers of his generation.

Born in Yorkshire, John William Wainwright served as a rear-gunner in Lancaster bombers during the Second World War, as recounted in his 1978 war memoirs, *Tail-End Charlie*. After the war, he spent twenty years as a policeman in the West Yorkshire constabulary, which gave him the perfect grounding to write crime fiction. (A second book of memoirs, *Wainwright's Beat*, 1978, looked back on his life in the force, while an introductory guide – *Shall I Be a Policeman?* – appeared in 1967.)

Wainwright's first novel was *Death in a Sleeping City* (1965). Drawing on his inside knowledge of police work, and specifically his experiences of organised crime, the book proved popular and was soon followed by a second, *Ten Steps to the Gallows* (1965), which traced similar ground. These early titles, while clearly aimed at a readership hungry for American-style sensationalism, were nonetheless well written and cleverly plotted exercises in police detection. With the memorable titles, such as *The Crystallised Carbon Pig* (1966) and *The Worms Must Wait* (1967), Wainwright kept up a frantic pace, outdoing many of the more established authors of detective novels during this period, such as P.D. **James** or H.R.F. **Keating**.

As Wainwright's popularity grew – he was one of the most borrowed authors from UK public libraries in the 1970s – so his stories became more ambitious. The characterisation grew sharper, the violence more explicit and the general tone more hard-hitting. In reflecting the reality of contemporary policing in all its gory glory, his books became the literary equivalents of popular television series such as *The Sweeney* and *Gangsters*, and in his day, he was as popular as present-day luminaries such as Ian **Rankin** or Reg **Gadney**. His 1981 novel *All on a Summer's Day* equalled the best of R.D. **Wingfield** in its depiction of a crowded and chaotic twenty-four hours inside a Yorkshire police station.

Wainwright adopted one pseudonym, Jack Ripley, which he used for four novels that took a more hard-nosed and satirical view of crime. The first was *Davis Doesn't Live Here Any More* (1971).

His short stories appeared in several anthologies, notably the *Winter's Crimes* series between 1969 and 1986. His non-fiction covers subjects as diverse as protecting your home from burglary, knowing your rights and the study of lapidary (cutting and polishing precious stones), a particular hobby of his. *See also* Police Procedurals.

Selected Works by the Author

As John Wainwright
Death in a Sleeping City (1965)
Talent for Murder (1967)
Freeze Thy Blood Less Coldly (1970)
A Nest of Rats (1977)
All on a Summer's Day (1981)
A Very Parochial Murder (1988)

As Jack Ripley
The Pig Got up and Slowly Walked Away (1971)
My Word You Should Have Seen Us (1972)

Mark Campbell

Waites, Martyn (b.1963)

Martyn Waites was raised in Newcastle and has worked as a stand-up comedian and actor. Although he is often associated with his friend and fellow stand-up comedian (and writer) Mark **Billingham** as key exponents of 'British noir', Waites tends to take a wider and bleaker look at British society, perhaps reflecting his books' setting in Newcastle. Waites's series protagonists are younger and more disillusioned than the sombre, solitary and depressed heroes such as John **Harvey**'s Resnick, Ian **Rankin**'s Rebus or Billingham's Thorne; basically idealistic but with low expectations.

His first series featured the tabloid journalist Stephen Larkin; assigned to cover a gangland funeral in his native Newcastle in Waites's debut novel *Mary's Prayer* (1997), he winds up staying to investigate the suicide of an old flame's friend. In the second Larkin book, *Little Triggers* (1998), he has relocated to Tyneside, working for a news agency, and gets drawn into a ring of powerful people engaged in paedophilia.

The book's title is taken from an Elvis Costello song; all Waites's titles are song titles, *Mary's Prayer* borrowed from the little-known Danny Wilson. The third Larkin novel, *Candleland* (2000, title from Ian McCullough), gives new twists to the classic tale of a teen runaway in a world of drugs and prostitution.

With *Born under Punches* (2003, title from Talking Heads), Waites's work took a leap forwards, expanding to a multi-tiered story featuring a vivid ensemble of lead characters. It showcased his deep feeling for the social roots of crime; Waites has worked as writer in residence in prisons and young offenders' institutions and has run workshops for excluded children. Set during the miner's strike of 1984, *Born under Punches* parallels the destruction of a community with the destruction of individual lives, not all through crime. Most tellingly, Stephen Larkin appears as a young and still idealistic journalist, a sharp contrast for those who had read Waites's earlier books.

He followed up with *The White Room* (2004, title from Cream), set in 1946 Newcastle, which mixed the early years of the child-killer Mary Bell with nineteen-year-old Jack Smeaton, who returns home from the Second World War and falls under the spell of T. Dan Smith, the charismatic and corrupt leader of Newcastle's labour council. The closest comparison to these two novels might be the work of David **Peace**, and although acclaimed critically, with *The White Room* selected by *The Guardian* as a book of the year, they made less commercial impact than they deserved.

Waites switched gears, starting a series featuring another burned-out journalist, Joe Donovan, still haunted by the unexplained disappearance of his young son, which tore his life apart. Set in a Newcastle which boasts a 'Get Carter' city tour, in *The Mercy Seat* (2006, title from Nick Cave), Donovan is drawn into an investigation by a male child prostitute on the run. Waites included graphic scenes of torture, as Donovan assembles a sort of Geordie A-team and uncovers another privileged world of child abuse before discovering a crime whose motivation is surprisingly prosaic. Donovan and his team returned in *Bone Machine* (2007, title from Tom Waits) to deal with white slavers from the former Yugoslavia.

Selected Works by the Author
Mary's Prayer (1997)
Little Triggers (1998)
Candleland (2000)
Born under Punches (2003)
The White Room (2004)
The Mercy Seat (2006)
Bone Machine (2007)

Michael Carlson

Walker, Selina

An editor with a very individual approach to the crime genre, Selina Walker has been a literary handmaiden and facilitator for some of the most impressive novelists in the genre in recent years, with an intuitive grasp of how to obtain the best from a manuscript. She began her publishing career in the production department of William Heinemann. After a ten-year break from the workplace, she read English at University College London as a mature student. Wilkie **Collins**'s *The Moonstone*

(1868) was an early favourite, but she was also an admirer of Dick **Francis**, particularly *Dead Cert* (1962), *Nerve* (1964), *Odds Against* (1965) and especially *For Kicks* (1965). She joined Orion Publishers as an editorial assistant in the 1990s when they were building their crime list, and later joined Transworld as a commissioning editor in 2000. She is now publishing director of Transworld's provocative crime and thriller list with responsibilities across all imprints and publishes the works of Tess Gerritsen and Mo **Hayder** – two of the most uncompromising **women crime writers** in the business. She also acquires widely across the commercial fiction range, historical fiction being her particular passion. When not editing tales of murder and mayhem, she is an enthusiast for trekking and the theatre.

Barry Forshaw

Wallace, Edgar (1875–1932)

Novelist, journalist, playwright and screenplay writer, the legendary Edgar Wallace was an exceptionally prolific author of sensationalist crime fiction, creator of popular characters such as Commissioner Sanders and the Green Archer, and instigator of the original *King Kong* film (1933).

Born in Greenwich, south-east London on 1 April 1875, Richard Horatio Edgar Wallace was cared for by Clara Freeman, wife of a Billingsgate fishmonger; as a child, he was known as 'Richard Freeman'. His real parents, Mary Jane Blair (also called Polly Richards) and Richard Horatio Edgar, were theatre performers. In 1893, he enlisted in the Royal West Kent Regiment, but finding the physical chores too demanding, he transferred to the Royal Army Medical Corps in South Africa. While there he met the Reverend William Caldecott, a Methodist Minister, and celebrated novelist Rudyard Kipling (1865–1936), who both encouraged him to write. Soon Wallace began contributing articles and poems to various journals, which were later collected in *The Mission That Failed* (1898).

In 1899, after a variety of menial jobs, he became the South African Correspondent for Reuters, marrying Ivy Caldecott, the minister's daughter, in Johannesburg in 1901. Tragically, their first child, Eleanor, died of meningitis at the age of two, and the couple returned to England, penniless, whereupon Wallace immediately found work at the *Daily Mail* newspaper as a subeditor.

Their second child, Bryan, was born in 1904, while Wallace was in the Spanish city of Vigo serving as war correspondent in the Russo-Japanese War. While there, he learnt a great deal about the activities of Russian and English spies operating on the Spanish coast, and put his experiences to good use in his first novel, *The Four Just Men* (1905). Detailing the adventures of four rich young men who take the law into their own hands by attempting to assassinate the Foreign Secretary, Wallace published it himself, under the Tallis imprint, and went about organising a newspaper competition to win readers large sums of money. Unfortunately, the expensive cost of advertising the competition, and the inept way in which it was conducted, meant that Wallace was unable to pay out the winnings and was forced to borrow over £5,000 from his begrudging newspaper boss, Alfred Harmsworth.

Wallace was slow to repay this loan, while creditors in South Africa were also clamouring for the repayment of their debts. Wishing to supplement his not ungenerous newspaper income, he began writing short stories featuring Commissioner

Sanders, the governor of a West African colony whose job it was to rule the natives in the style of a minor public school headmaster. The stories, which proved extremely popular, were collected together into *Sanders of the River* (1911). Five more collections followed, and in 1935 a film was made by Alexander Korda, featuring Leslie Banks as Sanders and Paul Robeson as tribal chief Bosambo.

During the first two decades of the 1900s, Wallace wrote quickly and urgently to satisfy his creditors, often selling the rights for his novels for paltry sums to release a constant flow of cash. And while his novels during this time are sometimes rather scantily plotted, they are almost all entertaining. Indeed, it has been said, not without an element of truth, that Wallace wrote best when under pressure.

His third child, Michael, was born in 1916, although two years later he and Ivy were divorced. In 1921, he married his secretary, Violet King, twenty-five years his junior, who bore his fourth child, Penelope Wallace, in 1923. This second marriage seemed to spur the author on to even greater prolificacy. He would often plan and write six novels at a time, usually dictated onto wax cylinders. According to Wallace's biographer, Margaret Lane, one house guest witnessed Wallace dictate an 80,000-word novel, *The Devil Man* (1931), over the course of one weekend. All were stories of crime and detection, occasionally with Gothic horror overtones, and all featured one-off police characters battling a production line of rough henchmen and swarthy villains to solve whatever dastardly crime had been perpetrated that month.

Notable books of this period included *The Green Archer* (1923), in which a sinister masked figure seemingly causes the death of a man staying the night in a haunted castle. *The Mind of Mr J.G. Reeder* (1925) is about an odd-looking man who investigates strange cases for the mysterious Office of the Public Prosecutor. *The Crimson Circle* (1922) depicts a serial killer stalking London. *The Dark Eyes of London* (1924) has a series of apparently accidental deaths that lead the police to a Home for the Blind; it was filmed in 1940 starring Bela Lugosi. The ironic title *The Orator* (1928) features a police inspector who says little but has a very perceptive mind. *Four Square Jane* (1929) features an enterprising female crook.

Ivy died in 1926, a few years before Wallace adapted his 1925 book *The Gaunt Stranger* – about a charismatic-masked assassin who terrorises London – into a stage play, renaming it *The Ringer* (1929). The success of the play led to an honorary appointment as Chairman of the Board at the British Lion film company, and the offer of work in Hollywood. A large proportion of Wallace's books were filmed, including a long series of forty-seven second-feature films, the 'Edgar Wallace Mysteries' produced between 1960 and 1965.

Wallace contributed to the 1932 version of *The Hound of the Baskervilles* starring Robert Rendell as Sherlock **Holmes** and began work on the screenplay of *King Kong* (then just *Kong*), before suddenly falling ill with diabetes. He died in Beverley Hills on 10 February 1932.

In 1969, his youngest daughter Penelope founded the Edgar Wallace Appreciation Society, which still exists today to promote his life and works. *See also* Film and Crime: Page to Screen.

Selected Works by the Author
The Four Just Men (1905)
Sanders of the River (stories, 1911)
Double Dan (1924; also published in the United States as *Diana of Kara-Kara*)
The Mind of Mr J.G. Reeder (stories, 1925)
The Green Archer (1926)
Terror Keep (1927)

The Dark Eyes of London (1929)
The Golden Hades (1929)

Further Reading

Lane, Margaret. 1939. *Edgar Wallace: The Biography of a Phenomenon*. Heinemann.
Lofts, W.O.G. and Adley, Derek. 1969. *The British Bibliography of Edgar Wallace*. Baker.

Website

www.edgarwallace.org

Mark Campbell

Wallis Martin, Julia (b.1956)

Julia Wallis Martin found success with her first novel *A Likeness in Stone* (1997), which was nominated for an Edgar Award and adapted as a peak-viewing two-part drama by the BBC. Apart from her crime fiction, she is the author of a full-length work of non-fiction and a volume of poetry, but it is for her crime novels that she is best known. Her second and third novels, *The Bird Yard* (1998) and *The Long Close Call* (2000), were optioned by Diplomat Films.

In 1977, Wallis Martin was widowed at the age of twenty when her husband was killed in a road accident, an event which not surprisingly shattered her life, causing her for four years to seek solace from mediums – an ordeal which later served to underpin her novel *Dancing with the Uninvited Guest* (2002), but which at the time halted her fledging writing career. It was not until 1986 that she joined Hodder & Stoughton (South Africa) as a commissioning editor, where she ghost-wrote a sports biography *Jumping to Success* (1990) and published a volume of poems *Death Is an Idle Servant* (1992). She returned to England in 1992, and in 1997, Hodder accepted *A Likeness in Stone*.

Tragedy was no stranger to Wallis Martin. Her mother was a suicidal manic-depressive who died when Julia was seventeen. In the days before her death, she told her daughter she was 'glad to be out of it'; life was something, she said, for which she had never quite got 'the knack'.

Undoubtedly, her most personal novel is *Dancing with the Uninvited Guest*, dedicated to her dead husband. Though not a reworking of her own story, the cast comprises psychics and parapsychologists, sceptics and psychiatrists and opens with vulnerable and exploited people believing they have made contact with the afterworld. Attending the séance is a lecturer in parapsychology at the British Institute for Paranormal Research. She is an atheist, but her belief that 'there is nothing on earth for which there is no rational explanation' is challenged by the evidence before her. The eeriest scenes are spookily set in and around a medieval manor house in Northumbria, which seems to ooze menace and malevolent spirits.

The Bird Yard, says Wallis Martin, 'holds a special place in my heart'. It is a complex drama about a search for a missing boy, which leads to a house converted into an aviary – a magical place to the young and vulnerable – but the detective inspector finds it macabre and the criminal psychologist has problems of his own. *The Long Close Call* is more conventional – 'It's about cops and robbers,' declared Wallis Martin insouciantly in a ***Shots*** magazine interview. Telling of a cop hunted after he shoots a bank robber – a cop who has a surprise history of his own – it sold 16,000 copies in its first week. The five-year gap in her published output after 2002 was due to Wallis Martin taking time out to research a PhD at The University of St Andrews.

Selected Works by the Author
A Likeness in Stone (1997)
The Bird Yard (1998)
The Long Close Call (2000)
Dancing with the Uninvited Guest (2002)

Russell James

Walsh, Jill Paton (b.1937)

Few authors have the opportunity to complete work left unfinished by a famous predecessor. When Jill Paton Walsh, herself a distinguished author, was invited to finish a novel begun by Dorothy L. **Sayers**, she felt privileged and daunted. Before the first of her novels for adults was published in 1989, she had long been a writer of children's fiction, for which she won several prizes. In 1993, her first crime novel, *The Wyndham Case*, appeared. Almost entirely set in St Agatha's College, Cambridge, it is a traditional detective story with an amateur detective. Imogen Quy, as college nurse, is well placed to observe staff, students and college politics. Intelligent and caring, she perseveres to find the truth behind a mystery. Although she diligently seeks necessary information, she is sometimes aided by chance. In St Agatha's, two bodies are found at different times. The first death is deemed accidental until the second, definitely murder, occurs. The plot is intricate, involving student rivalries and loyalties and the kidnapping of an elderly Fellow. The terms of the Wyndham bequest are crucial to the denouement.

A Piece of Justice followed after two years. Imogen Quy's hobby of quilting seems irrelevant initially, but is essential to the story which concerns the completion of the biography of a mathematician. Three previous biographers have disappeared, or died, mysteriously. The pursuit of truth takes Miss Quy to Wales, where she happens on part of the solution. It was eleven years before she reappeared in *Debts of Dishonour* (2006). St Agatha's perennial search for funding is swamped by financial scandals caused by an alumnus of the college. Most of the action occurs outside the college, but Imogen Quy manages to discover the truth about two murders in a plot full of twists. *The Bad Quarto* (2007) returns to the Cambridge setting, beloved by the author and her heroine. This book introduces abstruse academic disputes as a possible motive. A performance of an obscure version of Hamlet is significant. What seems like an accident could be a murder, and the solution proves to be a tragedy.

Between the second and third Quy novels, *Thrones, Dominations* (1998) was published – the completion of Sayers's unfinished work. From six chapters, a plot diagram and established characters, Walsh crafted a detective novel which achieved great critical acclaim. P.D. **James** and Ruth **Rendell**, both admirers of Sayers's work, approved of it, admiring the seamless join of the continuation. Following its success, the author wrote *A Presumption of Death* (2002), set in a village during the Second World War. This again uses Sayers's characters, drawing on material from *The Wimsey Papers*, which were published in *The Spectator* in 1939 and 1940 as morale boosters. The plot includes two murders. Harriet Vane struggles to solve them without the support of her absent husband, Lord Peter **Wimsey**. The plot is gripping and the denouement unexpected. Like all the author's work, it is ingenious, well written and has both convincing setting and characters. *See also* Academe, Death in.

Selected Works by the Author
The Wyndham Case (1993)
A Piece of Justice (1995)
Thrones, Dominations (1998) based on material by Dorothy L. Sayers
A Presumption of Death (2002) based on material by Dorothy L. Sayers
Debts of Dishonour (2006)
The Bad Quarto (2007)

Further Reading
Sayers, Dorothy L., and Jill Paton Walsh. 1998. *Thrones, Dominations*. Hodder & Stoughton.
Walsh, Jill Paton, and Dorothy L. Sayers. 2002. *A Presumption of Death*. Hodder & Stoughton.

Christine Simpson

Walters, Minette (b.1949)

Minette Walters began her career auspiciously in 1992 when she won the **Crime Writers' Association** (CWA) John Creasey Award for her first novel *The Ice House*. She went on to produce a string of best-selling psychological thrillers: the second of which, *The Sculptress* (1993), won the Edgar Award, and the third, *The Scold's Bridle* (1994), won the CWA Gold Dagger. Several subsequent novels were shortlisted for prizes, and she achieved a rare double when *Fox Evil* (2002) won her the CWA Gold Dagger for a second time in 2003. Five of her novels have been televised.

Walters did not begin her writing life as a crime fiction practitioner. After graduating from Durham University, she joined IPC Magazines as a subeditor on a romantic fiction magazine, writing articles, short stories and 30,000 word novelettes to help pay the mortgage. She began writing *The Ice House* in 1987, took two years to write it, and another two to sell it. Fortunately, she had used the intervening period to write her second novel and was able to bring that out in 1993. In her non-writing life, Walters devotes a good deal of time to charity work – she has been a school governor, chairman of a PTA and a political candidate and has worked with schools, libraries and prisons – and when she won her second Gold Dagger, she gave the whole of her prize money to Médecins Sans Frontières. She is married with two grown-up children and lives in an eighteenth-century listed manor house in Dorset. As a regular best-selling writer, one might expect Walters to be often in the limelight, but she shuns publicity, hates being photographed and seldom attends celebrity events of any kind. She is sporty (walking, swimming, tennis and sailing), devours crosswords and quizzes and is surprisingly adept at DIY. Rather than mix with the crowd, she prefers to stay at home with her family and other animals (she owns dogs, chickens, sheep and horses). Her idea of perfect bliss, she says, is to decorate a room while listening to Radios 4 and 5.

Her preference for ploughing her own furrow rather than parading at the fair is reflected in her books. Each of her books is a stand-alone thriller; she has no series or recurring characters. Character, though, is a vital element in her work: character and psychology drive the plots. It is the character of the central figure in *The Ice House* – wilful, truculent and unhelpful to the police – which leads them to believe her to be the murderer, despite lack of evidence. One wrong assumption leads to another;

the police even mistake the victim! Similar prejudices in *The Sculptress* mislead practically everyone to believe that the central character, Olive Martin, murdered her own mother and sister. Indeed, it can be said that this theme of too-hasty prejudice runs through Walters's work. *The Scold's Bridle* sees an entire village turn against a woman they see as the 'scold'. Fond of this motif as she is, it would be wrong to think it is the only one Walters has. *The Dark Room* (1995) is a psychological suspense novel which rejuvenates what could have been a hackneyed subject, loss of memory. *The Echo* (1997) tackles homelessness: why was Billy Blake, homeless alcoholic as he may be, found dead of starvation on London's streets? And why was his body found in a garage belonging to a wealthy architect – a woman of unexplained wealth? Are there not worrying similarities with other cases of missing persons? Although this is not her finest book, it once again delivers the Walters trademark mix of a multi-layered plot and an all-too-obvious suspect. Whereas in a Christie novel, one realises that the perpetrator will turn out to be the one person who could not have done it, in a Walters novel, the obvious suspect is the one person who will *not* be guilty.

The Breaker (1998) is as close to a standard police procedural as Walters gets, being about the tracking down of a small town murderer. In *The Shape of Snakes* (2000), she turns a harsh light upon racism – 'breaking all the rules of popular fiction', declared *The Times Literary Supplement*, 'MW asks as much of her readers as many literary novelists, and yet she offers them a book as gripping as any thriller.' In *Acid Row* (2001), she again approaches a fashionable theme – paedophilia – but handles it in her own unique way. *Fox Evil* brings yet another obvious suspect: surely the wealthy landowner killed his wife? Found in her nightclothes with bloodstains on the ground nearby, the inquest says 'death by natural causes', but local gossip in the small and secretive village insists that her husband killed her. Suggestions then emerge that this death could be linked to a mystery from the past – and why, incidentally, is the husband suddenly desperate to locate his only grandchild, illegitimate and adopted? All fingers point in his direction, until a London-based solicitor steps in to defend him against an increasingly relentless campaign. It is a classic Walters concoction.

In 2006, she added to her prize tally with something different: a novella, *Chickenfeed*, which won the Quick Reads Learners' Favourite Award. Relatively modest as this prize is against others she has won, it serves to illustrate the amazing breadth of subject and format Walters produces. Where most best-selling authors – and she certainly is that – tend to find a successful format and stick to it, Walters treats each new book as a fresh exercise. By doing so, she risks disappointing those readers who regard their favourite writers rather as a pair of comfortable slippers to be slipped into without thought. And for any reader, some of Walters's books will seem better than others, but that is a risk that Walters takes. She is not a predictable writer; she is, in effect, a novel writer who happens to write crime. *See also* TV Detectives: Small-Screen Adaptations.

Selected Works by the Author
The Ice House (1992)
The Sculptress (1993)
The Scold's Bridle (1994)
The Shape of Snakes (2000)
Fox Evil (2002)
The Devil's Feather (2005)
The Chameleon's Shadow (2007)

Russell James

Waters, Sarah (b.1966)

Sarah Waters had a meteoric rise to fame on the strength of her first three books, two of which were televised. All three were set in the Victorian era, and while they recreated the swirling atmosphere of the best Victorian gothic fiction, they also startled the reader with their frank and exuberant approach to lesbianism. The novels were masterfully plotted and wonderfully well written, taking the very best of Victorian fiction and re-presenting it fresh for a modern age, and just as it seemed that Waters had this genre for her own, she surprised her readers by leaping forwards in her fourth novel to the twentieth century and the aftermath of the Second World War.

Waters was born and raised in Neyland, Pembrokeshire, and went on to university in Canterbury where she gained a PhD in English Literature. It was while she was working on her PhD thesis on lesbian historical fiction that she was inspired to write her first novel, *Tipping the Velvet* (1998) – the phrase was Victorian slang for cunnilingus. The book won a 1999 Betty Trask Award and was shortlisted for the *Mail on Sunday*/John Llewellyn Rhys Prize, and its lesbian content helped make it a sensational success on television. Set in the 1880s, the story begins as an innocent Victorian romance between a naïve girl who cleans and prepares oysters (the symbolism is obvious) and a Vesta Tilley-like male impersonator in the music hall, but in a typical Waters plot jolt, the girl runs off with her female sweetheart to embark on a raffish journey through the Victorian music hall and high and low London life. Despite its in-your-face lesbianism – sometimes literally – the book swings from Whitstable to Haymarket, from St James's Square to Bethnal Green, and the story ends as it began, a Victorian romance. It is an amazing read.

For her second book, *Affinity* (1999), Waters won the Somerset Maugham Prize and *The Sunday Times* Young Writer of the Year Award, was shortlisted for the *Mail on Sunday*/John Llewellyn Rhys Prize and was runner up for the Welsh Book of the Year Award. The story narrates, first person, the tale of two women: a clairvoyant and medium, Selina Dawes, now in Millbank prison for suspected complicity in a mysterious death and the well-meaning but odd Miss Prior, who comes as a prison visitor and falls beneath her spell. Surely Miss Dawes, a 'Trance Medium', is a fake, no matter how intelligent and appealing she is? Young Miss Prior experiences spirit manifestations and strange happenings. Less of a picaresque romp than *Tipping the Velvet*, it exerts a creepy magnetism and is, as one learns to expect from Waters, expertly researched – almost too researched; it is the only Waters book in which the detailed work (on Victorian prisons) is sometimes visible on the page.

To achieve success with a third novel might seem too much to ask, but it was with *Fingersmith* (2002) that she assured her place as one of Britain's leading fiction writers, appealing to both the literary and the conventional reader. *Fingersmith* was shortlisted for both the Orange Prize and the Man Booker Prize, and it won the **Crime Writers' Association** Ellis Peters Historical Dagger. The book was televised and again was a huge success. This time the research, deep as it was, was submerged and subsumed into the plot. An orphan, Sue, reared among thieves and low life in a hell's kitchen run by Mrs Sucksby, is enticed into a scheme to help one of the young villains seduce and run away with a wealthy heiress. He has already insinuated himself into the wealthy household, and the plan now is for Sue to follow, to become a lady's maid and to help him lure the girl away and incarcerate her in a madhouse. It could be a classic Victorian gothic shocker – but a third of the way through, Waters executes such a staggering plot switch that many who read the book admitted that here they gasped aloud. From this point on – and the book has already been a fine one – the story transforms into brilliant and lurid horror, a melodrama certainly, but a bedazzling noctambulation through Victorian vice. The magazine *Granta* can have had little hesitation when choosing to include Waters as one of their twenty Best Young British Writers of 2003.

In 2006, she brought out her first twentieth-century novel, *The Night Watch*. Set during and after the Second World War, it traces the effect not just of war itself but of romance and relationships in dangerous times. Life may end or change dramatically at any moment. The future may never come. Around the characters rages a war whose outcome will change the world, but these are ordinary people, leading less than ordinary lives. Waters focuses inevitably on the lesbian relationships – there are other relationships in the book – and tells the story backwards, beginning with the surviving characters as they are, with war ended and a numb and sombre peacetime in its place, then moves back to show the events that formed them. It is an unusual approach; it could so easily have failed. It needed boldness, but Waters is a bold novelist.

Waters has occasionally been dismissively assessed as a parodist, a sensationalist or an author who exploits lesbianism for effect. She herself is upfront about her lesbianism and has self-effacingly contributed to the criticism by describing her own work as faux-Victorian melodrama. This is like describing the works of Charles **Dickens** or Wilkie **Collins** as soap operas. Her books are the finest Victorian novels – 'faux' or not – that we have seen for many years. The lesbianism is essential to the plots, and although deliciously enjoyable, it is in no way exploitative or crude. The plots themselves are breathtaking, and her use of language masterly. She is, quite simply, one of the finest writers of recent years. *See also* Feminist Readings in British Crime Fiction *and* Gay and Lesbian Crime Fiction.

Selected Works by the Author
Tipping the Velvet (1998)
Affinity (1999)
Fingersmith (2002)
The Night Watch (2006)

Russell James

Watson, Colin (1920–1982)

The title *Snobbery with Violence* (1971) indicates Colin Watson's attitude to the upper-class settings and characters of much **Golden Age** fiction. He preferred to involve 'ordinary' people in the plots of his crime writing set in a small English town, solidly described.

Watson was born in London. As a teenager, he lived for several years in Lincolnshire, working on local newspapers, before returning to London for a job in advertising. After war-work in Lincoln, in 1947 he returned to journalism, at first as a crime reporter. The settings and characters of his novels owe much to these experiences.

Between 1958 and 1982, Watson produced twelve novels and one short story relating criminal happenings in and around the county town of Flaxborough. The town, which is a port, its surrounding countryside, small towns and villages form a solid, credible background to the stories. This is reinforced by references back to previous events and by the use of characters who appear in several books. Although the plots are best described as 'police procedural', the crimes and investigations are far from conventional. Irreverent, often bawdy humour pervades his writing and sometimes threatens to overwhelm the narrative. Methods of murder are ingenious – bombs, electricity pylons, rejuvenation drugs and acid all play their part. In some books, Watson introduces elements of other styles of popular fiction, among them secret agents, American gangsters, witchcraft and space travel.

These all add problems for the principal investigator, Inspector Walter Purbright. A calm, phlegmatic man, he suffers with great patience the idiocies of his superior, the Chief Constable, and of his assistant, Sergeant Love. Purbright is wary of seemingly respectable people, as professional men in his area are far from model citizens. Much of the humour of the books is based on such characters. One doctor is part of a criminal conspiracy to run a brothel from his surgery, others indulge in medical malpractice. Business men and town officials strive to outdo each other, and their excesses result in some of the more hilarious set pieces. One organises a lavish banquet, which turns into an orgy of almost Rabelaisian proportions. Less obvious in her misdemeanours is Miss Teatime, who settled in Flaxborough when London became too hot for her. She makes money out of ingenious scams. Purbright becomes almost a friend, and she helps in some of his investigations. In one case, she nearly loses her life.

Watson published little apart from his detective fiction. His only other novel, *The Puritan* (1966), is quite different in style, with few touches of humour. Set in the world of journalism, it deals with the disastrous effects that intrusions by the press can have on private lives. There are three published short stories and the critical work, *Snobbery with Violence*. In this latter work, his stated aim was to write about crime and mystery fiction in the previous half century and explore how the genre expressed the attitudes and prejudices of the time. His views on Golden Age writers may displease some readers, but they stimulated Watson to write twelve very original, amusing and entertaining novels. *See also* The Shires: Rural England and Regional Crime Fiction.

Selected Works by the Author
Coffin Scarcely Used (1958)
Bump in the Night (1960)
Hopjoy Was Here (1962)
Charity Ends at Home (1968)
The Flaxborough Crab (1969; also published in the United States as *Just What the Doctor Ordered*)
Snobbery with Violence: Crime Stories and their Audience (non-fiction, 1971)
The Naked Nuns (1975; also published in the United States as *Six Nuns and a Shotgun*)
Plaster Sinners (1980)

Further Reading
Simpson, Christine R. 2002. 'Whatever's Been Going on in Flaxborough?: The Works of Colin Watson'. *CADS* 41: 3–14.

Christine Simpson

Welsh, Louise (b.1965)

Louise Welsh's first novel, *The Cutting Room* (2002), is set in Glasgow, the city where she was a student, later opening a second-hand bookshop. *The Cutting Room* is a classic detective story with a modern twist. The narrator, an auctioneer called

Rilke, turns detective when he finds a disturbing set of pornographic photographs during a routine house clearance. The photographs appear to show a woman before and after she is murdered for the sexual gratification of others. Both she and the deceased former owner of the house become the subjects of Rilke's investigations, which take him from harmless contacts in the antiques trade to dangerous encounters in the criminal underworld.

'I didn't set out to write a crime novel,' Welsh has said, but among the awards she picked up for her debut was the 2002 **Crime Writers' Association** John Creasey Memorial Dagger. The recipient of a Robert Louis Stevenson Memorial Award in 2003 and a *Scotland on Sunday*/Glenfiddich Spirit of Scotland Award in 2004, Welsh was also awarded a Hawthornden Fellowship in 2005.

Her second book was very different. A novella about the last three days of Christopher Marlowe's life, *Tamburlaine Must Die* (2004) was narrated by the playwright himself. It captured the sights, sounds and smells – as well as the language – of sixteenth-century London.

On the surface, *The Bullet Trick* (2006) seemed different yet again a darkly glamorous literary thriller set in the cabaret clubs of present-day Berlin. In fact, its numerous close parallels with *The Cutting Room* establish certain themes and devices as being Welsh favourites. Once again, the detective figure is not a police officer or trained investigator, but, in this case, a conjuror. And the plot turns on visual representations of violence towards women for the entertainment – or benefit – of men. The narrators of both novels are saddled with names that appear deliberately chosen to recall famous figures, in one case real, the German poet Rilke, in the second case fictional, the title character of Poe's great doppelgänger story 'William Wilson'. Wilson, the conjuror-narrator of *The Bullet Trick*, practises prestidigitation in front of his mother's dressing-table mirror:

> Every day when I got home I'd set the panes of the mirror at exactly the right angle, like a precocious teenage masturbator, then set to work. Under my command the army of other Williams stumbled through the same tricks until we had mastered one to perfection. I was the prince of illusion. And even though these doppelgängers might have been tougher or more popular in their worlds than I was in mine, in the world of mirrors it was my decrees that held sway.

The doubles theme surfaces from time to time – there are performing twins and tricks in which two women appear to be the same person – but is not overdone.

Persuaded by a friend of a friend in London to look after an envelope containing damning evidence of wrongdoing, Wilson finds a safe place to keep it in Scotland, then travels to Berlin to take up a conjuring job in a cabaret club. Pursued there by a compromised ex-cop, Wilson finds himself drawn into a world of baffling illusion, sexual confusion and extreme physical danger. The dialogue is sharp enough to cut yourself on, each line neatly setting up the next wisecrack, and the locations, from Berlin's slightly sad clubland to the seedy late-night bars of Glasgow, exude authenticity. *See also* Scottish Crime Fiction.

Selected Works by the Author
The Cutting Room (2002)
Tamburlaine Must Die (2004)
The Bullet Trick (2006)

Nicholas Royle

Wentworth, Patricia (1878–1961)

This astonishingly prolific author is best known for her enduring creation Miss Maud Silver, governess turned private detective, whose investigative career spans thirty-three years and thirty-two books of the romantic cosy type.

Born Dora Amy Elles in Musoorie, Uttarakhand, India, Patricia Wentworth attended the Blackheath High School for Girls in London. Married twice, with one daughter, she settled in Camberley, Surrey, after the death of her first husband. From 1910 to 1915, she wrote novels on non-crime subjects and also produced a volume of poetry (subsequent poetry books followed in 1945 and 1954). In 1923, her first crime novel, *The Astonishing Adventure of Jane Smith*, was published, and the first novel featuring Miss Silver, albeit as a minor character, came out in 1928. After a gap of nine years, the second Miss Silver novel, *The Case Is Closed*, appeared in 1937, and from 1943 onwards Wentworth produced at least one, and sometimes as many as three, every year. Miss Silver's final appearance is in the last novel, *The Girl in the Cellar* (1961). In the late 1930s and early 1940s, Wentworth also produced three novels featuring Inspector Ernest Lamb.

The novels are often set in the conventional and largely middle-class world of the English village or country house, with intelligent, straightforward plotting in the classical manner. The style is also straightforward, and the writing proficient and succinct.

Miss Silver belongs to a group of **Golden Age** spinster sleuths that includes Agatha **Christie**'s Miss Jane **Marple** and Josephine **Tey**'s Miss Lucy Pym. Unlike Miss Marple, with whom she is often compared, Miss Silver is a professional detective who keeps an office in the drawing room of her London home. An essentially Victorian character, with a taste for the paintings of John Everett Millais and James Sant, she undertakes cases for friends as well as strangers (although these usually come through friends' recommendations). Her cases often involve inheritances, family quarrels and long-buried secrets, and her clients are often young people from 'good' families. Miss Silver's intervention ensures that they retain their social status as well as prove their innocence. She relies more on her acute powers of observation and on logic than on intuition. Like Miss Marple, she turns her gentility and unthreatening outward appearance to advantage, listening to gossip and encouraging witnesses to confide in her. She has a predilection for knitting (usually children's clothing) and quoting the Bible and Alfred Lord Tennyson and frequently underscores her investigations with moral lectures.

She has the support of Scotland Yard's Detective Inspector Frank Abbott, and her former pupil, Chief Constable Randal March. Their friendship is socially, rather than professionally based, and her relationship with Frank Abbott is similar to that of Miss Marple and her nephew Raymond West.

Wentworth, who was almost as popular in the 1940s and 1950s as Christie and Sayers, has been largely forgotten. A pity, because her well-made tales, with their engaging protagonist, still hold their own against the works of the two better-known authors. *See also* The Detective in British Fiction; The Shires: Rural England and Regional Crime Fiction; *and* Women Crime Writers.

Selected Works by the Author
Grey Mask (1928)
The Case Is Closed (1937)

The Chinese Shawl (1943)
The Case of William Smith (1948)
Miss Silver Comes to Stay (1949)
The Brading Collection (1950)
The Ivory Dagger (1951)
The Benevent Treasure (1954)
Poison in the Pen (1955)
The Fingerprint (1956)

Laura Wilson

Wexford, Inspector

Unlike the majority of his fictional colleagues, detective Reginald Wexford – the main series character of crime writer Ruth **Rendell** – is a happily married man with a conventional background and a seemingly unprepossessing, almost mundane, personality.

Chief Inspector **Wexford** of the (fictitious) Sussex town of Kingsmarkham first appeared in Rendell's debut, *From Doon with Death* (1964). Accompanied by his partner, the fastidious Detective Inspector (DI) Mike Burden, he investigates the disappearance – and subsequent murder – of one Margaret Parsons, an unglamorous housewife who appeared to hold no secrets and have no enemies. But her lover, the mysterious Doon, throws up a much more remarkable picture of Parsons' past life than any of her neighbours could possibly imagine.

Controversial in its day, the book's main interest is in its clever plotting rather than in the psychology of its characters, and this would become a feature of Rendell's output as the years went on. Her alter ego, 'Barbara Vine', helped restore the balance by concentrating on darker, psychologically nuanced, thrillers. But Wexford's seemingly bland exterior was the perfect camouflage for an occasionally passionate, outspoken, man with surprisingly liberal views – as in his initially sympathetic treatment of the eco-warriors in *Road Rage* (1997).

Wexford, fifty-two and heavy set when we first meet him, is married to Dora, and they have two daughters, Sheila and Sylvia. He also has an aesthetically inclined nephew, Howard Fortune, detective superintendent of Kenbourne Vale CID, who assists him in *Murder Being Once Done* (1972), when Wexford is suffering from a thrombosis. Although in a seriously stable relationship, the detective's interest is nonetheless piqued by the alluring Nancy Lake in *Shake Hands Forever* (1975), but true to the man's innate decorum, he finally chooses fidelity over fun. His youngest daughter, Sheila, is an actress in the RSC and a household name due to the television soap *Runway*, but by the politically motivated of *The Veiled One* (1988), she has become a CND activist and is even arrested for damaging Ministry of Defense property.

As Wexford's crime-solving career continues – twenty-two books and many short stories at the last count – there is some evidence that his character is becoming more cynical of the world around him, especially concerning the motivations of his fellow creatures. By *The Babes in the Wood* (2002), the mysterious drowning of two teenage children and their babysitter in the river Brede near Kingsmarkham has the detective questioning his previously well-entrenched beliefs about human decency. More of a 'whydunit' than a 'whodunit', the novel combines an engaging mystery with the sort of articulate psychological insight more common to the author's non-Wexford stories. *Not in the Flesh* (2007) continues this welcome trend.

On television, George Baker made the part his own in a series of twenty-three adaptations from 1987 to 2000, produced by Graham Benson and Neil Zeiger for independent production company TVS. Based on the novels and short stories, each storyline was told in fifty-minute episodes, ranging from one to four in number, and mostly shown on Sunday evenings. Christopher Ravenscroft played DI Burden, and the series was praised for its acting and production values. Sadly, however, no new episodes have aired since *Harm Done* in 2000. *See also* The Detective in British Fiction *and* TV Detectives: Small-Screen Adaptations.

Mark Campbell

Wheatley, Dennis (1897–1977)

Once dubbed 'The Prince of Thriller Writers' by *The Times Literary Supplement*, Dennis Yates Wheatley wrote some of the best-selling thriller novels of his time, with an inimitable line in the macabre. The only son of a Mayfair wine merchant, Wheatley saw service in the First World War in Flanders, on the Ypres Salient, and in France at Cambrai and St Quentin. He was gassed in a chlorine attack at Passchendaele, which resulted in his invaliding out. He took over sole ownership of the family's wine business in 1926 after his father's death. It was during this time that he began to write short stories, some of which were published or later turned into novels.

The financial slump of the early 1930s took its toll on the business, and by 1932, Wheatley was forced to sell. Influenced by his second wife, Joan Younger, he wrote an intriguing murder mystery *Three Inquisitive People* (1929), introducing his protagonists Duc de Richleau, Rex van Ryn, Richard Eaton and Simon Aron. It would not be published for another ten years, appearing in the omnibus, *Those Modern Musketeers* (1939). The quartet became Wheatley's most popular characters, drawing on the literary influence of Alexandre Dumas. Although the book was initially rejected, Wheatley wrote a second straight thriller, again featuring his modern musketeers, *The Forbidden Territory* (1933), dealing with pre-war Russia under Stalin, which was immediately accepted and published by Hutchinson. The novel allowed Wheatley to trenchantly voice his personal concerns about the threat of communism and his (now highly unfashionable) belief in imperialism. It received critical acclaim from the press and set Wheatley on an unassailable road to success. Without question, Wheatley's most famous book is the celebrated occult thriller *The Devil Rides Out* (1935), in which Simon Aron falls under the power of a high black priest and his three contemporaries attempt to rescue him. It is the first of Wheatley's novels to feature black magic as a theme, an area he would thoroughly strip-mine in his subsequent books. (*The Devil Rides Out* was filmed by Terence Fisher for Hammer Films in 1968 with Christopher Lee as de Richleau.) The setting for *The Golden Spaniard* (1938) is the Spanish civil war and has the quartet involved in a treasure hunt. *Dangerous Inheritance* (1965), set in Ceylon, is the final Duc de Richleau story and is one of the most accomplished.

Such Power Is Dangerous (1933), set in the cut-throat world of Hollywood, was written in seventeen days as part of an experiment. Wheatley had read that Edgar

Wallace had written a novel in one week, and he attempted to emulate him. He was not happy with the final result, but after the success of *The Forbidden Territory*, the pressure from Hutchinson was intense, and so he allowed it to be published without changes.

For most of 1933, Wheatley worked on a novel featuring secret agent, Gregory Sallust, who would appear in a further nine novels. Sallust is a jingoistic Englishman, dashingly handsome, very much a proto-James Bond figure in many ways. He leads a group of men and women away from the anarchy in the city to a supposedly ideal rural retreat. The background to *Black August* (1934) once again channels Wheatley's paranoia regarding communism, as the exuberant narrative deals with a Red Revolution in England set sometime in the future; supposedly 1960. *Contraband* (1936) begins in 1935 with smuggling as the fulcrum of the storyline. Both novels function expertly as launch pads for the Sallust character, but Sallust is at his best in the ensuing seven wartime spy stories. *Scarlet Impostor* (1940) has him dropped into war-torn Germany with the brief to overthrow Hitler – a scenario (in some ways) reminiscent of Household's *Rogue Male* (1939). Controversially, Wheatley portrays Hermann Goring as a largely sympathetic character. *Faked Passports* (1940) picks up minutes after the *Scarlet Impostor* finishes, with Sallust managing to survive and head off to rescue the lovely Erica von Epp, against a colourfully drawn backdrop of Finland and Russia. The series takes in countries such as Norway, France, Budapest and Communist China, culminating with *They Used Dark Forces* (1964) when Sallust becomes imprisoned by a high-ranking magician (Wheatley here utilises Hitler's fascination with the occult).

Wheatley vividly evokes the period of the late eighteenth and early nineteenth centuries in the Roger Brook series. His personal library of over 4,000 books helped finesse his research into appropriate customs, appearances and institutions to achieve verisimilitude. Roger Brook is an historical hero living in the late 1700s, and once again, Wheatley's obvious love of the British empire is reflected in Brook, whom he portrays as a staunch Royalist ready to lay his life on the line for king and country. By now, Wheatley had thoroughly burnished his craft, and *The Launching of Roger Brook* (1947) is written with an energetically detailed style. A young Englishman in France is vying for a young noble lady's affections, managing to become embroiled in French foreign policy. *The Shadow of Tyburn Tree* (1948) is set in Russia, with Brook promoted to Prime Minister Pitt's secret agent; the narrative yokes in Catherine the Great and Queen Matilda of Denmark. The fourth in the series, *The Man Who Killed the King* (1951) conjures the atrocities of the 'reign of terror'.

Wheatley further demonstrated his immense storytelling skills with a trio of Julian Day novels, but among his most fondly remembered endeavours were the four crime dossiers he produced with his friend Joe Links in the 1930s. These were instant bestsellers and were reproduced as 'facsimiles' in the late 1970s. By the time of his death in 1977, it is estimated that Wheatley had sold in excess of fifty million copies of his books worldwide. He unabashedly extolled his forthright opinions on every subject from politics to Satanism (rather in the fashion of a modern writer in line of descent from Wheatley, Frederick **Forsyth**, who share his predecessor's right-wing stance), and today's readers would find many of Wheatley's more extreme views unpalatable. But his novels – unjustly neglected today, despite fitful reissue programmes – shoehorn in elements of luxury, action-fuelled excitement and vivid, larger-than-life characters. The fact that evil is defeated at every turn (unlike much modern fiction) gives his books a particularly comforting quality. *See also* Espionage Fiction *and* Historical Crime.

Selected Works by the Author
The Forbidden Territory (1933)
Black August (1934)
The Devil Rides Out (1935)
Crime Dossiers (1936–1939)
Scarlet Impostor (1940)
They Used Dark Forces (1964)

Mike Stotter

Whitechurch, V[ictor] L[orenzo] (1868–1933)

Whitechurch was an Anglican vicar, the son of a clergyman and a prolific writer of religious books, straight novels and detective and crime fiction. Apart from two early (1901–1903) novels which were crime rather than detection, his six detective novels were published between 1924 and 1932. First was *The Templeton Case* (1924), followed by *The Crime at Diana's Pool* (1927) and *Shot on the Downs* (1927). *Diana's Pool* features (surprise, surprise!) a likeable, observant parson who attaches himself to the police detective and solves the murder. *Shot on the Downs* has pleasant descriptions of the Berkshire Downs (Whitechurch had previously been vicar of Blewbury) and another village parson. After *The Robbery at Rudwick House* (1929), which has no murder, Whitechurch's last two – *Murder at the Pageant* (1930), yet another rural one, and *Murder at the College* (1932), one of the earliest Oxbridge settings in detective novels – are both murder investigations. These novels, while admittedly lacking Freeman Wills **Crofts**'s tight plotting, Agatha **Christie**'s ingenuity, A.E.W. **Mason**'s feeling for romantic adventure and Dorothy L. **Sayers**'s literary distinction, are decently constructed plotwise and pleasant reading even now, and they are still read.

More accomplished, and more significant to a historian of detective fiction, are Whitechurch's short-story collections, three of them, published between 1903 and 1925 (remember that up to perhaps 1914, the short story was the dominant form of detective fiction), and a few uncollected ones. Most have a railway background – there is a tradition of railway enthusiast parsons – and undoubtedly the best collection is *(Thrilling) Stories of the Railway* (1912), fifteen ingenious shorts, mostly crime, nine of them solved by the eccentric Thorpe Hazell, bibliophile, vegetarian, valetudinarian and expert on railway operation. One from this collection, 'Sir Gilbert Murrell's Picture', has often been anthologised (though I am not convinced that the *modus operandi* is practical) and *Thrilling Stories* was reprinted as recently as 1977. Hazell, resourceful and tenacious, may be the earliest 'specialist' detective in fiction, and the stories featuring him would on their own secure Whitechurch's place in the genre. *See also* Literature and Crime Fiction *and* Short Stories.

Selected Works by the Author
The Investigations of Godfrey Page, Railwayac (*Pearson's Weekly*, 1903–4)
(Thrilling) Stories of the Railway (stories, 1912)
The Templeton Case (1924)
The Adventures of Captain Ivan Koravitch (stories, 1925)
The Crime at Diana's Pool (1927)

Whitechurch, V[ictor] L[orenzo]

Shot on the Downs (1927)
The Robbery at Rudwick House (1929)
Murder at the Pageant (1930)
Murder at the College (1932)

Philip Scowcroft

Williams, Alan (b.1935)

The small body of work produced by the writer son of the playwright and actor Emlyn Williams has fallen out of favour. But Alan Williams is among the most impressive in what might be called the Graham **Greene**/Eric **Ambler** school of 'Englishman at bay in sultry climes'. Williams was educated at Stowe, Heidelberg, and King's College, Cambridge. He was in Hungary during the revolt in 1956 and was forced to make his way out of East Germany by clandestine means. Like several of his writing confrères, Williams had some involvement with the **espionage** world, working for a Munich radio station with American intelligence links (and which in turn was targeted by Soviet intelligence). After becoming a journalist, he wrote in Britain for *The Western Mail* and *The Express*, acting as foreign correspondent in the war zones of Vietnam and Algeria. As a badge of honour, on several occasions he was suspected of being a spy.

Long Run South (1962) and *Barbouze* (1963) announced with a flourish that a major new thriller writer had arrived. The former concerns a young Englishman, Rupert Quinn, who is sick of his job and seeking escape in Morocco at the time of the Algerian War. Quinn is offered a job as a courier on a coach tour into the interior, but finds himself unwittingly smuggling arms for the rebels, as well as becoming involved with the seductive Leila, liaison officer for the anti-government forces. This was no 007-style escapist piece: after the brutal torture of Leila, Quinn, despite his crippling fear, manages to survive more through luck than judgement.

Continuing the theme of the Englishman out of his depth à la Greene, *Barbouze* has a newspaperman trying to enjoy a quiet holiday in North Africa and finding himself involved in a brutal and grisly terrorist war. This heady tale of innocence and assassination is couched in a colourful and invigorating literary style that was easily the equal of prestigious forebears such as Greene's *The Confidential Agent* (1939) (even if Williams's writing lacked, as yet, moral force of his mentors). By now, Williams was a master of his craft, ringing changes on themes he had explored repeatedly – notably the moral equivocation of his ambiguous heroes.

With *Snake Water* (1965), Williams tackled a plot that might initially have seemed somewhat shopworn: a fortune in raw diamonds is hidden in the lethal swamps of a South American jungle and a disparate, squabbling group of four people risk everything to acquire them. But such is the freshness and vitality of his treatment that he is able to strip-mine the crucial elements of his narrative, jettisoning the non-essentials. The result is violent and kinetic, yet couched in prose of real elegance (even as the mayhem comes unfeasibly thick and fast: carnivorous crabs, volcanoes and brutal bandits). *The Purity League* (1968), an attack on the self-appointed moral guardians of the era such as Mary Whitehouse and the Christian peer Lord Longford, was a misfire, perhaps because Williams's obvious dislike of his sanctimonious targets overshadowed his attention to the structure of the book. But *The Tale of the Lazy Dog* in 1970 drew praise from no less an authority than Eric Ambler himself (who called it 'superbly exciting'). A team of adventurers and agents in Southeast Asia attempts to pull off an ambitious robbery, and an Irish journalist gets wind of the plan. Apart from the pithy characterisation, the vividly evoked sense of locale marked Williams out as a master of this territory, and *The Beria Papers* (1973) built on the success of the earlier books, with its clever notion of a secret diary written by the former chief of the Soviet secret police before he was executed in the 1950s. The book cleverly synthesised the known facts (Beria was Stalin's right-hand man, with a million armed men at his command and a noted predilection for sadism, rape and mass murder) with the fascinating possibility that he may have kept a diary lasciviously recording his sexual proclivities and murderous atrocities. In Williams's book, the diary sets off a lethal manhunt for those responsible for its release.

Another ingenious melding of truth and fiction can be found in *Gentleman Traitor* (1975), which was based on a conversation that was reported to Williams in which the drunken British spy Kim Philby announced how desperate he was to leave Russia after his defection. Williams's novel has Philby actually doing this, and taking on an assignment in Rhodesia, facilitated by British intelligence (still packed full of old colleagues just as ready as he was to betray his country). His mission ends in confusion and death, but Philby is exuberantly characterised, though the book thankfully lacks Graham Greene's roseate picture of his old colleague. Equally strong work could be found in *The Widow's War* (1978), with a bored ex-soldier and the alcoholic wife of a brutal dictator up against a psychopathic terrorist. The setting, an island wrecked by a volcano, is as memorably realised as anything in Williams's work, though an element of self-parody creeps into this excessive scenario.

Apart from his sheer storytelling ability, Williams continually shored up his novels with a totally persuasive verisimilitude, utilising authentic historical detail to create narratives that generated considerable suspense. While not achieving the immense success of Frederick **Forsyth**, Williams demonstrated, in novel after novel, that he could produce books packed with as much persuasive detail as Forsyth's *The Day of the Jackal* (1971). At the start of the twenty-first century, in a cruelly brief space of time, Williams's achievement has been all but forgotten, and many lesser authors have managed to do what he has not – stay in print. But those willing to seek out his work will find that Williams is a writer whose accomplishments are varied and considerable.

Selected Works by the Author
Long Run South (1962)
Barbouze (1963; also published in the United States as *The False Beards*)
Snake Water (1965)
The Brotherhood (1968; also published in the United States as *The Purity League*)
The Tale of the Lazy Dog (1970)
The Beria Papers (1973)
Gentleman Traitor (1975)
Shah-Mak (1976; also published in the United States as *A Bullet for the Shah*)
The Widow's War (1978)
Dead Secret (1980)
Holy of Holies (1981)

Barry Forshaw

Williams, David (1926–2003)

David Williams's novels are in the tradition of the classic British detective novel (his models were Edmund **Crispin**, Michael **Innes** and Ngaio **Marsh**), and while their plots may not be of the highest quality, his narratives are elegant and readable, matching Williams's own charming personality.

Williams was born in Bridgend (Glamorgan) and educated inter alia at Hereford Cathedral School (Hereford appears, disguised, as Litchester in *Murder in Advent*, 1985). At first pursuing a career in advertising, he (like several others, including W.J. **Burley** and Elizabeth **Lemarchand**) came late to crime writing. He produced, besides a few short stories, some twenty novels from 1976 onwards, several of them written during his slow recovery from a coronary thrombosis, heart bypass surgery and another devastating stroke.

His series detective for nearly twenty years was Mark Treasure – part Welsh, a merchant banker, shrewd, well heeled (he runs a Rolls Royce) and also urbane and civilised, with sundry cultural interests including painting, opera, old buildings and golf. Treasure, who has a delightful actress wife Molly, gets around a bit: *Treasure by Degrees* (1977) visits an agricultural college. *Treasure up in Smoke* (1978) finds him in the Caribbean and *Treasure in Roubles* (1986) finds him in (Soviet) Russia. Investigations nearer home included *Treasure in Oxford* (1988) and *Murder for Treasure* (1980, set in Williams's native South Wales). *Divided Treasure* (1987), with three murders (a fourth is thwarted by Treasure in a helicopter) and an astonishing number of nubile young women, is set in North Wales, and *Advertise for Treasure* (1984) draws on Williams's previous career. With *Last Seen Breathing* (1994) and *Death of a Prodigal* (1995), Williams changed tack, these being police novels featuring Inspector Merlin Parry and Sergeant Gomer Lloyd of the South Wales Police and quite as readable as the Treasure series. The Inspector Parry series ran to six titles before Williams's death in 2003.

Selected Works by the Author
Unholy Writ (1976)
Treasure by Degrees (1977)
Treasure up in Smoke (1978)
Treasure Preserved (1983)
Treasure in Oxford (1988)
Death of a Prodigal (1995)

Philip Scowcroft

Williams, John (b.1961)

John Williams is a highly individual crime novelist, short-story writer, editor, journalist and screenwriter, who sets most of his works in his native city of Cardiff – though his most famous non-fiction work, *Into the Badlands* (1991), journalised his travels into unvisited corners of the United States to visit his favourite crime writers.

It was with non-fiction books that he began. *Into the Badlands* was followed by *Bloody Valentine* (1995, about the murder of a young woman in Cardiff) before his first fiction book, *Faithless* (1997, and atypically set in London), was published. Two short-story collections – *Five Pubs, Two Bars and a Nightclub* (1999) and *Temperance*

105. John Williams.

Town (2004) – followed. Between these two collections, he had produced two Cardiff-based novels: *Cardiff Dead* (2001) and *The Prince of Wales* (2003). Williams deliberately sets his books among the underclass, often in the real-life multi-racial dockland community of Butetown, a hard-pressed area whose fight to survive is harder than that of many deprived urban areas since it exists in a city desperate to shake off its blue-collar history and to be reborn. His books show how these savage changes break the lives of those who live in the affected areas, people almost lost from sight beneath the dirt. Surrounding his drug dealers, pimps and prostitutes is a swarm of ordinary people – not necessarily 'honest, decent, God-fearing people' and certainly not chapel-goers – but real people who are warm and sympathetically explored. Some of his characters recur in different books, because, as for real people in the real city, life does go on. His books also betray another love in his life, the modern music scene, where Williams, inevitably it seems, looks exclusively at the fringes. (Music plays a prominent part in his London and pop culture novel, *Faithless*.)

The fascination of *Into the Badlands* came partly from its being a specific snapshot taken in the summer of 1989, giving detailed portraits of writers such as Eugene Izzi, George V. Higgins, James Crumley and James Lee Burke (and lesser names), and he followed this in 2006 with *Back to the Badlands*, reprising the first work and adding new writers. *Bloody Valentine* was an astonishingly perceptive – and given some of the real-life characters he spoke to, astonishingly brave – reappraisal of an unexplained murder forgotten, it seemed, by everyone until Williams began talking to people who remembered the victim. It remains to be seen whether it will be for his fiction or his non-fiction investigative reportage that Williams will be best remembered.

Selected Works by the Author
Into the Badlands (non-fiction, 1991)
Bloody Valentine (non-fiction, 1995)
Faithless (1997)
Five Pubs, Two Bars and a Nightclub (stories, 1999)
Cardiff Dead (2001)

The Prince of Wales (2003)
Temperance Town (stories, 2004)
Back to the Badlands (non-fiction, 2006)

Russell James

Wilson, Colin (b.1931)

As one of the so-called 'Angry Young Men', Colin Wilson's *The Outsider* (1956) –
an extended essay on the treatment and psyche of the Outsider figure in literature
and art – won him instant critical acclaim. His subsequent writing career has
included a smattering of detective stories.

Born in Leicester on 26 June 1931, as a young man Wilson gravitated towards the
more esoteric areas of psychology and parapsychology; early works included *Religion
and the Rebel* (1957) and *Origins of the Sexual Impulse* (1963). Unfortunately,
a combination of braggadocio and increasingly populist subject areas – serial killers,
ghosts, the paranormal, etc. – meant that Wilson's credibility in intellectual circles
became somewhat damaged. By the time of *Beyond the Outsider* (1965), a sequel to his
barnstorming debut, he was considered by many to be working in areas that (largely
speaking) catered to the crank market.

Encyclopaedia of Murder (1961), *A Casebook of Murder* (1969) and *Order of
Assassins: The Psychology of Murder* (1972) formed a trilogy of true-life criminology.
As regards crime fiction, *The Schoolgirl Murder Case* (1974) and its sequel, *The Janus
Murder Case* (1984), were fairly grubby potboilers featuring one Inspector Saltfleet;
the latter book was an adaptation of Wilson's 1979 stage play *Mysteries*.

His unsettling fictional portrait of a northern psychopath, *The Killer* (1970) was
based on his researches into real-life serial killers, while an earlier trilogy featuring
aspiring writer Gerard Sorme's investigations into the underbelly of 1950s **London**
was a beguiling mixture of eroticism, philosophy and gangland violence (*Ritual
in the Dark*, 1960; *Man without a Shadow*, 1963; and *The God of the Labyrinth*, 1970).

Ultimately, it may be for his fantasy, paranormal and horror books that Wilson will
best be remembered, and for *The Space Vampires* (1976) synthesising all three genres
and forming the basis of Tobe Hooper's misguided 1985 film *Lifeforce*. *See also* Realism
and Crime Fiction.

Selected Works by the Author
The Outsider (1956)
Man without a Shadow (1963; also published in the United States as *The Sex Diary of Gerard Sorme*)
The Killer (1970; also published in the United States as *Lingard*)
The Schoolgirl Murder Case (1974)

Mark Campbell

Wilson, Laura (b.1967)

Laura Wilson's psychological crime books are characterised by strong first-person
narratives that allow the reader to empathise fully with her characters, however
dysfunctional their behaviour.

106. Laura Wilson.

Born in Bethnal Green in the East End of London, Wilson was brought up in Cock-fosters, several miles north, and educated at state and private schools. Her secondary education was spent at an experimental school specialising in an odd concoction of Eastern spirituality and repressive Victorian values – the curriculum including esoteric subjects such as meditation, philosophy and Sanskrit. She then moved into the more conventional environs of Somerville College, Oxford, where she read English literature. Following that, Wilson received a degree in English from University College London, where she wrote a thesis on the influential eighteenth-century author Samuel Richardson (1689–1761), the father of the modern psychological novel.

Although she dallied with a teaching career, Wilson's main job after university was as project editor of a major non-fiction publisher, allowing her to oversee various illustrated reference books on subjects as diverse as gardening, healthcare and art. Fascinated by recent history, she also penned several educational books for children, including *Daily Life in a Tudor House* (1995) and *How I Survived the Irish Famine* (2000), each one a first-person account of life during that period.

Her skill in making history come to life through the eyes of ordinary people allowed her full reign to develop ideas for a grown-up readership. This led to her first adult novel, *A Little Death*, appearing in 1999. Centring on a mysterious triple murder in a musty townhouse in 1955, the narrative backtracks to the late 1890s and the terrible tragedy that strikes a wealthy Victorian family and its repercussions during the Great War and beyond. Deceptively simple in style, the book was shortlisted for the **Crime Writers' Association** Ellis Peters Historical Dagger, in which the judges' panel praised the book's claustrophobic atmosphere and well-delineated characters. The novel was also nominated for an Anthony Award.

Her second offering, *Dying Voices* (2000), confirmed the promise of her debut novel with its engrossing tale of a multi-millionaire's daughter, aged eight when her mother was kidnapped. For twenty years, everyone believes her mother is dead, but when her body is discovered, she has been dead for just forty-eight hours.

Wilson's third book, *My Best Friend* (2001), is arguably her most accomplished. The elegant narrative is recounted by three perfectly realised characters – an obsessive fan, a sparky geriatric and a resilient single mother – to brilliant effect. Combining psychological unease with a fine shading of black humour, Wilson's gripping multi-layered prose is head and shoulders above her contemporaries. Recent works, such as *The Lover* (2004) and *Stratton's War* (2007), have concentrated on the London Blitz as a backdrop (the latter is a striking inaugural volume for a new series).

In January 2007, she became crime fiction critic for *The Guardian*.

Selected Works by the Author
A Little Death (1999)
Dying Voices (2000)
My Best Friend (2001)
Hello Bunny Alice (2003, also known as *Telling Lies to Alice*)
The Lover (2004)
A Thousand Lies (2006)
Stratton's War (2007)
Austerity (2009)

Website
www.laura-wilson.co.uk

Mark Campbell

Wilson, Robert (b.1957)

Robert Wilson is a British writer who has used his experiences living abroad to produce a number of high-quality thrillers, including the Medway series (four novels set in Benin, Africa, and featuring Bruce Medway, a flawed 'fixer' and reluctant detective), perhaps the finest Chandleresque crime series written by an Englishman, and the **Crime Writers' Association** Gold Dagger-winning *A Small Death in Lisbon* (1999).

Wilson's unsettled childhood (an RAF father, moving from base to base) gave him a taste for travel. A desire to write led to an Oxford degree in English. Later, exposure to the crime fiction of both Raymond **Chandler** and Elmore Leonard, together with a year-long trip in Africa and a trading job in Benin, resulted in *Instruments of Darkness* (1995), the first of the Medway novels.

From the first, Wilson's many talents were evident: incisive, often visceral writing, sharp dialogue, characters of flesh and blood, complex plotting and a rare ability to convey the often brutal realities of time and place, in this case of a part of modern Africa riven by political instability and ferocious civil war. Read from the beginning and appreciate Wilson's growing mastery of his craft.

With his next two books, *A Small Death in Lisbon* and his stand-alone spy novel *The Company of Strangers* (2001), Wilson's backdrop of choice moved to Portugal. A novel of hugely impressive depth and scope, *A Small Death* features two interweaving plots that take the reader from the murder of a young girl in 1990s Lisbon to its roots in Portugal's wartime and post-war history.

A similar time span in *Strangers* reveals a fascination with what might be called the 'big' lives of his parents' generation, in this case that of English spy Andrea Aspinall and her passionate and lifelong love affair with German double agent Karl Voss, played out against thrilling background plots first in war-time Lisbon, then in Cold War Germany. The book's conclusion is one of the most moving in crime fiction.

A vibrant Seville is the backdrop to the powerful *The Blind Man of Seville* (2003), the first to feature Inspector Javier Falcón, probably the most complex of current fictional policemen. A crime scene that includes a mutilated corpse almost brings the repressed Falcón to the point of breakdown. Forced to explore the Moroccan connections of the case, he must also confront the 'big' life, this time malign, of his father, through the devastating diaries that interweave with the narrative.

Appearance and reality, the key theme of *Blind Man* returns in new guises in *The Silent and the Damned* (2004), a Falcón investigation into an apparent suicide pact between husband and wife that leads to revelations of both public and private corruption.

Wilson's growing mastery of the literary thriller finds virtuoso expression in *The Hidden Assassins* (2006). A potent mix of murder, a terrorist atrocity, political and media machinations as well as the personal stories of those involved, combine with thematic density and great writing to produce an explosive thriller of the highest order.

Wilson is now writing some of the most fiercely intelligent crime novels of his career. Feted in Europe and the United States, in the United Kingdom he remains under-appreciated and sometimes overlooked, a situation which is gradually changing. *See also* Espionage Fiction *and* Historical Crime Fiction.

Selected Works by the Author
Instruments of Darkness (1995)
The Big Killing (1996)
Blood Is Dirt (1997)
A Darkening Stain (1998)
A Small Death in Lisbon (1999)
The Company of Strangers (2001)
The Blind Man of Seville (2003)
The Silent and the Damned (2004; also published in the United States as *The Vanished Hands*)
The Hidden Assassins (2006)

Website
www.twbooks.co.uk/authors/rwilson.html

Bob Cornwell

Wimsey, Lord Peter

The aristocratic amateur sleuth Lord Peter Death Bredon Wimsey is the most famous (and best-loved) creation of one of the Golden Era's most famous writers, Dorothy L. **Sayers**. He debuted in Sayers's first novel, *Whose Body?* (1923), which introduced many of the main features of Lord Peter: 'His flat, his piano-playing of Bach, his affection for his dotty mother, his profound friendship for his servant Bunter, his nerves shattered by war-service, his man-to-man friendship with Inspector Parker', as Jill Paton **Walsh** noted in her The Dorothy L. Sayers Memorial Lecture in May 2002. As Walsh also observes: 'He is very good at absolutely everything – cricket, incunabula, firsts at Balliol, heroic war service, code-breaking, bell-ringing, disguises, piano-playing, it goes on and on.'

The most significant characters other than Wimsey are his fastidious valet Mervyn Bunter (whom Sayers based partly on P.G. Wodehouse's Jeeves) and Sayers's alter ego, the mystery writer Harriet Deborah Vane who (like Sayers) is Oxford-educated.

Wimsey's relationship with Harriet begins in *Strong Poison* (1930), when she is on trial for the murder of her former lover. Wimsey proves her innocence, naturally, but she refuses his constant offers of marriage, finding him overbearing and arguing that gratitude is not proper grounds for marriage. But in the final Wimsey novel completed in Sayers's lifetime, *Busman's Honeymoon* (1937), they are married.

In the satirical and light-hearted *Murder Must Advertise* (1933), Wimsey goes undercover as a copywriter, Sayers's own profession for seven years. Sayers dashed it off in the middle of writing *The Nine Tailors* (1934), which is considered one of her best works. It involves a remote village, a faceless and handless corpse, a stolen emerald necklace, and bell ringing – the 'nine tailors' being a pattern of bell ringing that is key to the plot.

Although Sayers wrote a number of other novels, her only detective novel without Wimsey was *The Documents in the Case* (1930), co-authored by Dr Eustace Robert Barton (writing under the pseudonym Robert Eustace). Besides the eleven novels and twenty-one short stories featuring Wimsey, she wrote a radio script entitled *A Tribute to Sherlock Holmes on the Occasion of His 100th Birthday* (1954), in which a youthful Wimsey consults Holmes.

After Sayers's death, the unfinished Wimsey novel *Thrones, Dominions* (1998) was completed by Jill Paton Walsh, who also wrote *A Presumption of Death* (2002). The latter was loosely based on 'The Wimsey Papers', a series of letters between members of the Wimsey circle that Sayers wrote for *The Spectator* in 1939 and 1940.

There have been two television adaptations: the first starring Ian Carmichael as Wimsey (1972–1976) and the second featuring Edward Petherbridge, with Harriet Walter as Harriet (1986). *See also* The Detective in British Fiction *and* The Great Detectives: The Mass Appeal of Holmes, Poirot and Wimsey.

Further Reading

Clarke, Stephan P. 1985. *The Lord Peter Wimsey Companion*. Mysterious Press.

Sayers, Dorothy. 1936. 'How I Came to Invent the Character of Lord Peter Wimsey'. *Harcourt Brace News*, 15 July 1936.

Scott-Giles, Charles Wilfrid. 1977. *Wimsey Family: A Fragmentary History Compiled from Correspondence with Dorothy L. Sayers*. Gollancz.

Website

The Dorothy L. Sayers Society, www.sayers.org.uk

Julian Maynard-Smith

Wingfield, R[odney] D[avid] (1928–2007)

Wingfield is solely known for creating the character of the curmudgeonly Detective Inspector William **Frost**, known as 'Jack', whose persona was wonderfully recreated by David Jason for the successful TV series. Wingfield was a very private man and shunned publicity. He wrote only six novels about Frost and life in the fictional Denton police force. The first, *Frost at Christmas* (1984), took twelve years to find a publisher, and first appeared in Canada, whilst the last, *A Killing Frost* (2008), was published posthumously. But Wingfield, who spent many years as a clerk for an oil company, had already spent sixteen years as an author of radio plays for BBC Radio 4. The character of Frost first appeared on radio in 'Three Days of Frost' in February 1977, with Leslie Sands in the title role.

Frost is a surly individual who communicates largely through sarcasm, treating his superiors with large measures of disdain. His dodgy policing methods are firmly 'old school' – although they often get the job done – and he likes working by gut instinct rather than by deduction. He was awarded the George Cross for being shot in the line of duty and is thus tolerated by his immediate boss, the desk-bound Superintendent Mullett. But, as he admits ruefully, it was not through bravery that he stepped in front of the gunman – it was because he was drunk and depressed and could not care what happened to himself.

Wingfield's novels are characterised by their incredibly detailed descriptions of everyday provincial police work. The crimes are a mixture of the trivial and the tawdry, while any helpful leads usually occur through chance encounters (often while working on another case) rather than skilled detection. Glamour is an aspect largely missing from any of the novels, the town of Denton apparently stuck in the icy grip of an endlessly bleak and barren winter.

What impresses the reader most, though, is the sheer humanity of Frost. Here is a man who is sexist, racist and cynical in the extreme, and yet clearly he is on the side of the angels – just. He is prone to lusting after sixteen-year-olds while castigating people who have the same feelings for children a year younger (*Winter Frost*, 1999), but his personal moral code can find him emotionally involved with the cases he is called on to investigate – to the annoyance of Mullett, who considers this deeply unprofessional. Frost is a man with shifting loyalties, though, guided by a sixth sense that invariably lets him down and often stumbling blind in a world that seems to owe him no favours. *See also* Police Procedurals.

Selected Works by the Author

Frost at Christmas (1984)
A Touch of Frost (1987)
Night Frost (1992)
Hard Frost (1995)
Winter Frost (1999)
A Killing Frost (2008)

Further Reading

Ripley, Mike. 'An Appreciation of Rodney Wingfield (and Jack Frost)'. Shots eZine website, http://www.shotsmag.co.uk/features/2008/wingfield/wingfield.html

Mark Campbell

Winspear, Jacqueline (b.1955)

Jacqueline Winspear is the author of a series of delightful books featuring Maisie Dobbs, a psychological investigator. Set in the late 1920s and early 1930s, the books actually have their origin in the First World War.

Winspear grew up in Kent and attended the University of London's Institute of Education. She has worked in academia, publishing and marketing communication. She lives in California after emigrating to the United States in 1990.

Winspear's first book, *Maisie Dobbs* (2003), introduced readers to her resourceful protagonist who (while working as a servant) is caught reading by her employer. Much to her astonishment, her thirst for education is encouraged by Lady Compton and Dr Maurice Blanche, an old friend and mentor. However, the First World War interrupts her studies at Girton College, Cambridge, and Maisie enlists in the nursing services and is sent overseas. After her apprenticeship with Dr Blanche, she becomes a private investigator – and on her first case what appears to be a simple case of infidelity turns out to be much more. Maisie finds herself investigating secrets long buried and being drawn back to the war, her own ghosts, and events that she has tried hard to put behind her. *Maisie Dobbs* was published to considerable acclaim and was nominated for an Edgar Award for Best Novel. It gleaned an Agatha Award and a Macavity Award for Best First Novel.

In the second Dobbs book, *Birds of a Feather* (2004), Maisie is asked to find the daughter of a wealthy grocer who has disappeared. As she begins her enquiries, she discovers that three of the girl's friends have of late died brutally. Once again, Maisie finds that all the answers are to be found in the tragedy of the First World War. While *Maisie Dobbs* showed Winspear's character moving from being a servant to becoming an independent young woman, *Birds of a Feather* is much more of a conventional mystery. Nominated for the Bruce Alexander Award, *Birds of a Feather* won the Dilys Winn Award and the Agatha Award for Best Novel.

Pardonable Lies (2005) sees Maisie trying to determine the truth about a death that took place during the war. Typical of Winspear's work, this is not a clear-cut case, and once again, Maisie finds herself facing the trauma of her First World War recollections. It won the Macavity Award for Best Historical Mystery.

By now, Winspear's expertise with her series character had acquired a comfortable momentum, which was maintained in *Messenger of Truth* (2006) – the death of a controversial artist brings Maisie back once more to the dangerous legacy of the Great War as individuals who do not want the mystery of the death resolved try to silence her.

Customarily told in the third person, the Maisie books showcase a rather unusual character; compassionate and endearing as she utilises Freudian psychology, and as interested in helping her clients as she is in solving her cases. The series incorporates a clever and trenchant series of insights into the period, with a notable sense of the upheaval of wartime and a changing social and economic milieu.

Selected Works by the Author
Maisie Dobbs (2003)
Birds of a Feather (2004)
Pardonable Lies (2005)
Messenger of Truth (2006)

Ayo Onatade

Wire in the Blood (television series, 2002–)

Clinical psychologist Dr Tony Hill and Detective Inspector (DI) Carol Jordan debuted in Val **McDermid**'s novel *The Mermaids Singing*, which won the **Crime Writers' Association** Gold Dagger in 1995. Afterwards they appeared in four further McDermid novels, the latest of which is *Beneath the Bleeding* (2007). All the novels in the series have titles that are quotations from poems by T.S. Eliot.

The characters proved so successful after the first two novels that they generated the ITV show *Wire in the Blood* (named after the second novel in the series, published in 1997), starring Robson Green as Tony Hill and Hermione Norris as Carol Jordan. The fifth series was completed in 2007. The show is produced by Coastal Productions, which is owned by Sandra Jobling and Robson Green. The stories are set in Bradfield, a fictional north-west city reminiscent of Manchester, where Val McDermid has lived for nearly all her adult life. The show is filmed around Green's native Newcastle and other parts of north-east England.

Occasionally compared with *Cracker* (first broadcast 1993) and *Prime Suspect* (1991), the show is dark and gritty, with an emphasis on psychological profiling as the key to unlock the mind of serial killers. Tony Hill often has to overcome resistance from cynical police officers, but while he occasionally makes mistakes, his insights are ultimately crucial to finding the killers. His psychological intuition and unusual working practices are counterbalanced by the pragmatism and police procedural work of Carol Jordan. The sexual chemistry that simmers between the characters never develops into a sexual relationship, because of Tony's psychological hang-ups and the pressures of police work on Carol.

The first series comprised three two-part episodes: 'The Mermaids Singing' (adapted by Patrick Harbinson), 'Shadows Rising' (based on the novel *The Wire in the Blood* and adapted by Alan Whiting) and 'Justice Painted Blind' (an original screenplay by Alan Whiting). Its debut achieved the strongest opening performance figures for any new drama on ITV in 2002, with 8.1 million viewers for the first episode. The show has subsequently won the World Gold Medal for Drama at the New York Television Festival and the RTS Regional Award in 2006, and has been nominated for an Edgar Award from the Mystery Writers of America.

Most of the episodes after the first series were original screenplays; it would not be until 'Torment' (Series 4, episode 2) that there would be another episode based on one of the novels (*The Torment of Others*, 2004, adapted by Guy Burt). Further scriptwriters include Niall Leonard (who wrote the television adaptation of Minette **Walters**'s *The Dark Room*, 1995) and Jeff Povey.

Carol Jordan's character was replaced in Series 4 by DI Alex Fielding, played by Simone Lahbib. An American episode, 'Prayer of the Bone' written by Patrick Harbinson, was filmed in Texas in 2007. *See also* Sexuality in British Crime Fiction *and* TV Detectives: Small-Screen Adaptations.

Episodes
First series (2002): 'The Mermaids Singing'; 'Shadows Rising'; 'Justice Painted Blind'
Second series (2004): 'Still She Cries'; 'The Darkness of Light'; 'Right to Silence'; 'Sharp Compassion'
Third series (2005): 'Redemption'; 'Bad Seed'; 'Nothing but the Night'; 'Synchronicity'
Fourth series (2006): 'Time to Murder and Create'; 'Torment'; 'Hole in the Heart'; 'The Wounded Surgeon'
Fifth series (2007): 'The Colour of Amber'; 'Nocebo'; 'The Names of Angels'; 'Anything You Can Do'
Stand-alone episode (2008): 'Prayer of the Bone'

Julian Maynard-Smith

Wisdom, Julia

Julia Wisdom is an influential editor of modern crime fiction – with a notable line in hard-edged, visceral crime writing – who has guided several authors to some of the most authoritative work of their careers. Wisdom, who came to crime fiction through twin childhood obsessions with Enid Blyton's Famous Five stories and Batman, started her commissioning career at Victor Gollancz Ltd. In 1993, she moved to HarperCollins and is now Publishing Director for HarperFiction. She works with some of the best-loved (and best-selling) authors in the crime and thriller field, from Val **McDermid** and Reginald **Hill** to Michael Crichton, and has brought in award-winning new talent such as Robert **Wilson** and Mark Mills and commercial big-hitters such as Andrew Gross. Recently, she has bought more crime in translation, including Swedish bestseller Camilla Lackberg, and has widened her commissioning base by taking on historical fiction such as John Drake's swashbuckling prequels to *Treasure Island* (*Flint and Silver*, 2008, and *Pieces of Eight*, 2009) and James McGee's *City of Vice*-style *Hawkwood* series (*Ratcatcher*, 2006; *Resurrectionist*, 2007; and *Rapscallion*, 2008). Wisdom has said that crime fiction is a wonderfully broad and flexible area in which to work. 'It can encompass any period and any style, is universally popular and is practised by some of today's most exciting authors. What more could an editor want?'

Barry Forshaw

Wishart, David (b.1952)

David Wishart is a Scottish writer and classicist best known for his series of mysteries set in ancient Rome.

He was born in Arbroath and studied Greek and Latin classics at Edinburgh University. After teaching in a secondary school for four years, he taught English in Greece and the Middle East before returning to Scotland in 1990, where he continued to teach.

Attracted by the growing interest in books with a Roman setting, Wishart put his detailed knowledge to work. He produced two stand-alone novels told in the first person: a fictional autobiography of Virgil in *I, Virgil* (1995) and the story of Nero by his 'advisor on taste', Titus Petronius, in a no-holds-barred account, *Nero* (1996). At the same time, Wishart began his series featuring Marcus Corvinus, a high-ranking Roman who also enjoys the high life, and is drawn to the world of investigation and detection, always a dangerous one in Tiberian Rome in the mid-first century. The series began with *Ovid* (1995), in which Corvinus is asked by Ovid's stepdaughter to arrange for the poet's ashes to be retrieved from Tomis (Constanta, in modern-day Romania), where he had died in exile. When permission is refused, Corvinus, rather unwisely, pursues it further and discovers the history of not only why Ovid was exiled but what really happened at the Teutoburg massacre in AD 9. *Germanicus* (1997) and *Sejanus* (1998) continue the single-name titles that were becoming Wishart's trademark. In the first, Corvinus investigates the death of the military hero Germanicus (father of the later Emperor Caligula), a task which ends in exile, while in the second, he is given posthumous orders by the matriarch Livia to find evidence against the powerful Sejanus. In these novels, Wishart deliberately parallels but reworks the history as presented by Robert Graves in his Claudius books.

Thereafter, Wishart changed direction and converted the series into more conventional historical crime with *The Lydian Baker* (1998), where Corvinus investigates deaths surrounding a newly rediscovered ancient statue. *The Horse Coin* (1999) takes Corvinus to Britain while *Parthian Shot* (2004) finds Corvinus once again caught up in political machinations investigating the death of the Parthian prince Phraates. Otherwise, Corvinus's escapades are set in Italy and frequently involve family and friends. As a consequence, these latter novels have been compared, not always favourably, with the Falco books by Lindsey **Davis**. Both feature an amateur investigator who talks and acts rather like a twentieth-century Philip Marlowe, while trying to survive in an ever more dangerous world. The main difference, though, is that Falco is a plebeian, with no high-and-mighty designs, so that his use of the vernacular is not surprising, whereas Corvinus is of the patrician class, making his street-wise nature out of character. Yet Wishart counterpoints the rather seedy side of Corvinus's life and interests with a vivid recreation of the Roman world and its intrigues, and some creative speculation on the true nature of events. *Illegally Dead* (2008), in which Corvinus investigates the murder of someone who was terminally ill, is the twelfth book in the series. *See also* Scottish Crime Fiction.

Selected Works by the Author
Ovid (1995)
Germanicus (1997)
Sejanus (1998)
Old Bones (2000)
White Murder (2002)
Parthian Shot (2004)
In at the Death (2007)

Website
www.david-wishart.co.uk

Mike Ashley

Women Crime Writers

So many of the great names of mystery fiction are women – historically and in the present – that it might seem unnecessary to distinguish between male and female crime writers. But mystery novels, more than any other genre of fiction, reflect the society their authors know, and since women's experience has been different from men's in most aspects of life, so has their writing. Authors of both sexes have been productive, prosperous and, in the last 100 years at least, famous, but their reception and reputation has been significantly affected by gender.

The appearance of the first English prose novels, such as Daniel Defoe's *Robinson Crusoe* (1719) and Samuel Richardson's *Pamela* (1741), was followed by a flood of fiction. There was an eager audience for this exciting new form of entertainment, and women were eager to supply it, seizing the chance to earn money in one of the few professions open to them, publishing (under pseudonyms) melodramatic, emotional Gothic novels and 'horrid mystery novels' (as a character in Jane Austen's *Northanger Abbey*, 1817, called them). By the mid-nineteenth century, three-volume sagas of sensation, sentiment and suspense, such as *East Lynne* (1861) by Mrs Henry Wood and *Lady Audley's Secret* (1862) by the prolific Mrs M.E. Braddon, appeared under the authors' real name, despite bitter personal criticism of ladies who wrote or read about unfeminine subjects such as murder, robbery, adultery and illegitimacy. The pundits were much less offended by cerebral stories of analytical detection, inspired by the establishment of 'detective police' in 1843 and more often written by men and about men, though Britain's first female detectives both appeared in 1864: Mrs Paschal in *Revelations of a Lady Detective* by the still unidentified 'Anonyma', and the unnamed lady in *The Female Detective* by Andrew Forrester, Jr.

Sherlock **Holmes** made his first bow in 1887. He inspired many other stories of private investigators, including a few by women authors notably C.L. Pirkis (1839–1910) and L.T. Meade (1844–1914). Baroness Emmuska Orczy (1865–1947), the creator of the Scarlet Pimpernel, wrote mysteries including *Lady Molly of Scotland Yard* (1910) and *The Old Man in the Corner* (1909) and Mrs Belloc Lowndes (1868–1947) published fictional reconstructions of several notorious crimes, including *The Lodger* (1913), based around the murders committed by Jack the Ripper. She wrote about a French detective called Hercule Popeau, a name that bears a coincidental similarity to Agatha **Christie**'s Hercule **Poirot**. The publication of *The Mysterious Affair at Styles* (1920) is often said to mark the start of 'the **Golden Age** of crime fiction', which is usually taken as the period between the two world wars.

The typical British women writer of the period used a middle class, usually domestic setting, disrupted by murder, with a hero (always male, often aristocratic) who metaphorically galloped up like a knight in armour to punish the guilty, rescue the virtuous and put everything right again. Explicit details were tactfully omitted, powerful emotions were only hinted at and murder methods tended to be implausibly ingenious. It was very different from the most popular American form of the period, the hard-boiled private eye story, which was copied in Britain almost exclusively by male writers.

Some mystery novels from that time, implausible, artificial and escapist though they often were, remained continuously in print and popular during the next half century; those that survived were by women: Agatha Christie, Dorothy L. **Sayers**, Margery **Allingham** and Ngaio **Marsh**. Yet during the twenty interwar years, their male contemporaries had been equally or more prominent, as review coverage showed. At the time, the detective story was regarded as predominantly a masculine form of entertainment, which was in fact statistically correct, since in the interwar period and still even in the present day, the proportion of published titles written by women has never been more than about one-third. This curiously counterintuitive fact is revealed by Mike **Ripley**, whose calculations are published in his article in ***Shots*** (March 2007). The membership list of The Detection Club, to which the most successful British mystery writers were elected, shows that between 1932, when it was founded, and the end of the Second World War, there were exactly twice as many men as women members.

There was a superficial homogeneity about British women crime writers of the period. To generalise: they were, or took care to seem, respectable, conventional and conformist; crime fiction was by definition non-autobiographical and therefore the genre chosen by women who avoided self-revelation, some because they were retiring by nature (Christie, for example, was notoriously shy). Others had adventurous or even disreputable (by the standards of their day) private lives with things to hide – Dorothy L. Sayers kept the existence of her illegitimate son a lifelong secret. They revealed prejudices that were shared by their readers but shock later generations. There is undisguised anti-Semitism (e.g. in Dorothy L. Sayers and Josephine **Tey**), casual racism and unashamed snobbery. They all wrote books set among the middle or upper classes, which was as implausible then as now since in reality almost all murders are committed on impulse by poor, uneducated men. Above all, there is nostalgia and dislike of change. The women writers of the time were portraying a secure, stable society, which, despite disruption by murder or other unwelcome events, life could eventually return to normal as though nothing had ever gone wrong – a comforting illusion so soon after the horrors of the Great War. Superficial realism and sharp feminine observation make such books a goldmine for historians interested in the minutiae of domestic life. Unpleasant facts such as the looming Second World War were tactfully ignored; so were sex, politics and passion and any uncomfortable or personal truths.

By the late 1930s, the detective story was changing from a puzzle of time and place, motive and opportunity, to a puzzle of character (who and why rather than how and when), but even after the upheavals of the war, most women went on writing about ingenious crimes in middle- or upper-class circles. Many were prodigiously industrious, turning out a book a year or even more. Elizabeth Ferrars wrote more than seventy novels between 1940 and her death in 1995; all were literate, entertaining and posed involving puzzles solved by reasonably lifelike characters. So were books by the even more prolific Lucy Malleson (1899–1973), whose pen-name was Anthony Gilbert. Even those who had other full-time jobs managed to deliver the annual volume, among them Mary Fitt (1897–1959), a lecturer in classical Greek; Josephine **Bell**, a medical doctor; and Gladys **Mitchell**, a teacher. These writers were still following the tradition of their 'Golden Age' elders, not trying to criticise society but to reflect it, or perhaps to create greater understanding of it. For instance, the stereotypical notion of the elderly unmarried woman as a superfluous spinster was subverted when Agatha Christie made a detective of Miss Marple or Patricia **Wentworth** of Miss Silver.

After the end of the Second World War, many women retreated from the world of work and competition to become full-time housewives and mothers. This is not the place to wonder why, but that is what happened, and it is reflected in the crime novels of the period, many of which continued in the classic form of the 1930s. Some of the memorable fiction of the period can now be read in a sociological or historical light, as an implicit argument for the (not yet invented) women's liberation movement. Celia **Fremlin**'s novels vividly portray women in a domestic setting beset by all the mundane problems of husband and children, but not by a career or job. If women were to be involved in detection, it could only be as housewives accidentally caught up in crime or as the detective's amateur helper, for example the wife of Chief Superintendent Henry Tibbett in a series of novels by Patricia Moyes.

Feminism and the women's liberation movement did not take root in Britain until the late 1960s and took a long time to change society. As public perceptions and beliefs changed, the crime novel changed along with them. In the last quarter of the twentieth century, traditional Golden Age-type crime fiction was still being written and eagerly read, but a new generation of women was beginning to escape the traditional bounds of the form, still describing the world they perceived but no longer implicitly confirming its values, in fact often the very reverse. The predominant subtext is no longer conservative but radical, iconoclastic and critical. Subjects that used to be ignored or at most hinted at, such as rape or child abuse, have become part of the mainstream of crime fiction, and women have acquired the characteristics formerly peculiar to male detectives: they can fight, run, climb and sleep around; more importantly, they can be free of domestic obligations. Women private eyes (including P.D. **James**'s Cordelia Gray in *An Unsuitable Job for a Woman* (1972) or Liza **Cody**'s

Anna Lee) are shown as self-reliant women who follow and tackle criminals all alone, although in un-gun-cultured Britain, private detectives do not shoot.

Professional policewomen were slower to appear, the standard male duo of inspired inspector and plodding sergeant remaining far more common in series by men and women alike (e.g. June **Thomson**, Catherine **Aird**, Ruth **Rendell** and many others). Less realistic and less bound by procedure were self-reliant amateur detectives who had other full-time professions, for example journalists (Antonia **Fraser**'s Jemima Shore and Val **McDermid**'s Lindsay Gordon), lawyers (in books by Natasha **Cooper**, Sarah **Caudwell** and Frances Fyfield) and academics (Joan **Smith**'s Loretta Young).

The outlawing of discrimination on grounds of sex in 1975 may not have seemed particularly relevant in a field where women had always been pre-eminent. But in 1987, when American writers complained that *The New York Times* reviewed ninety mysteries by men and seven by women, British women writers realised that they experienced similar discrimination, complaining that nearly all crime fiction reviewers were male and preferred scenes of exploitative sex, gratuitous violence or excessive gore, which at the time no women wrote. They do now; women's experiences and expectations have been transformed, and by the beginning of the twenty-first century, many women writers were producing books full of sex, violence and torture scenes, often painfully – but justifiably – explicit. **Realism** means that crime fiction should be about the poor and deprived; that the detectives will be police officers, bound by routine and overworked, hard to see as knights in shining armour; that evil will flourish. Women writers no longer refrain from writing about paedophilia, the abduction and killing of a child, rape or torture, often using the most explicit descriptions. Few contemporary novelists would say as several women writers of the Golden Age said that they wanted to write books which would comfort their readers. The underlying mood has swung from optimism to an almost apocalyptic vision of society as insecure, continuously under threat, and with most people living in loneliness and fear.

It may be that the early twenty-first-century boom in historical crime novels is driven by the desire to write less unpleasantly, however disagreeable the subject, as in novels about the after-effects of the First World War by Anne **Perry** or Jacqueline **Winspear**. Or perhaps the ever-decreasing distinction between the roles and rights of men and women means that women writers will move on into the last masculine enclave of crime fiction, the military mystery with a cover picture of expensive hardware exploding. At that extreme and its other end, a girl with a ripped bodice, we can still guess the sex of the author. But as the experiences of men and women have become more similar, so has what they write. Until the late twentieth century, it was taken for granted that there was a distinction between the way men and women thought and behaved and many readers could infallibly tell the difference between crime novels by male and female authors. Crime fiction, as we have seen, is a reflection of the society it springs from, and at a 'blind tasting' by experienced crime reviewers in 2006, all guesses as to the gender of an author were wrong. One cannot tell the difference anymore. *See also* Feminist Readings in British Crime Fiction *and* Male Crime Writers.

Further Reading
Caudwell, Sarah. 1981. *Thus Was Adonis Murdered*. Scribner.
Mann, Jessica. 1981. *Deadlier Than the Male*. David & Charles.
Nichols, Victoria, and Susan Thompson. 1988. *Silk Stalkings*. Black Lizard.

Slung, Michelle B. 1975. *Crime on Her Mind*. Pantheon.
Swanson, Jean, and Dean James. 1996. *By a Woman's Hand*. Berkley.
Winn, Dilys. 1979. *Murderess Ink*. Workman Publishing.

Jessica Mann

Y

Yorke, Margaret (b.1924)

One of the most prolific authors of her generation, Margaret Yorke has written
a long-running series of powerful psychological suspense novels that prioritise strong
characterisation over plot exigencies.

The granddaughter of sugar refiner John Lyle, Margaret Beda Larminie was
born in Compton, Surrey, on 30 January 1924. The family lived in Dublin until 1937,
when they moved to Hampshire. Margaret, the eldest of two children and known
affectionately as Peggie, was educated at Priors Field independent girls' school
in Godalming before serving in the Woman's Royal Naval Service until 1945, when
she married Basil Nicholson, and they had two children, Diana and Ian. After
their divorce, she worked as a bookseller and as librarian for two Oxford colleges:
St Hilda's and Christ Church.

Her first novel, *Summer Flight*, appeared in 1957. She wrote under the pseudonym
Margaret Yorke, a name shared by her aunt and her maternal grandmother, and the
book concerned a fugitive from justice and his effect on the inhabitants of a small
village, in particular its vicar. A human interest story, it was followed by several
more volumes in a similar style until, in 1970, Yorke introduced Dr Patrick Grant,
a professor of English literature and part-time sleuth, in the fully fledged crime story
Dead in the Morning.

A consciously old-fashioned whodunit, the book and its protagonist proved popular
enough to spawn four further offerings. The second, *Silent Witness* (1972), was an
Agatha **Christie**-style tale about the mysterious murder of a lowly member of a skiing
party holed up in a snowbound foreign hotel (*cf* Christie's 1939 novel *And Then There
Were None/Ten Little Indians* and her 1952 stage play, *The Mousetrap*). The last in the
series, *Cast for Death* (1975), ended on a dramatic note with the apparent suicide
of Grant's actor friend Sam Irwin, drowned in the Thames.

While writing the Grant series, her 1974 book *No Medals for the Major* signposted
a change of direction. Having exhausted the possibilities of whodunits (which was
by the mid-1970s an overcrowded genre), Yorke revisited her character-based
'problem' novels of the late 1950s and early 1960s with the emphasis firmly on
underlying psychological menace. *The Point of Murder* (1974), for example, sees
Kate Wilson's pent-up frustrations at looking after her elderly mother released
when she spends occasional weekends in a country hotel posing as a widow. A man
she already knows arrives by chance one evening and an affair develops between
them. One weekend, on the way to meet him at the hotel, she stops to help a stranded
motorist who is later murdered and so becomes a witness, hunted down by the

murderer. *The Scent of Fear* (1980), for which she won a Swedish Academy of Detection Award, detailed a secretive young loner's furtive existence in an old woman's isolated house.

Yorke served as Chairman of the **Crime Writers' Association** (CWA), and won the 1993 Golden Handcuffs Award, presented by the UK library service for the most borrowed author, and in 1999, she received the prestigious CWA Cartier Diamond Dagger for lifetime achievement. *See also* The Shires: Rural England and Regional Crime Fiction.

Selected Works by the Author
Dead in the Morning (1970)
Silent Witness (1972)
Grave Matters (1973)
Mortal Remains (1974)
No Medals for the Major (1974)
The Point of Murder (1974; also published in the United States as *The Come-On*)
Death on Account (1979)
The Scent of Fear (1980)
No Fury (1987)
Dangerous to Know (1993)

Mark Campbell

Yuill, P.B.

P.B. Yuill is a pseudonym for journalist Gordon Williams (b.1934) and footballer Terry Venables (b.1943), joint creators of the cockney hard-bitten detective James **Hazell**, protagonist of several hard-boiled 1970s novels as well as a popular Thames television series (1978–1980) starring Nicholas Ball.

Gordon Maclean Williams was born in 1934 in Paisley, Scotland, and moved to London where he worked as a journalist, television scriptwriter and novelist. He is best remembered as the author of *The Siege of Trencher's Farm* (1969), which formed the basis for Sam Peckinpah's controversial film *Straw Dogs* in 1971, but was also nominated for the Booker Prize in 1969 for his gritty depiction of teenage masculinity in *From Scenes Like These* (1968).

Terence Frederick Venables – born on 1943 in Dagenham, Essex – was a professional British footballer who played for various high-profile teams in the 1960s and 1970s, eventually becoming manager of England in the 1996 European Football Championship. His autobiography was ghosted by Gordon Williams, then at Chelsea FC, and the two collaborated – under the rather odd name of 'P.B. Yuill' – to write four popular novels featuring down-to-earth private eye James Hazell, beginning with *The Bornless Keeper* in 1974 (although Hazell's role here is only fleeting).

Hazell was cast from the same mould as *The Sweeney*'s Jack Regan, so it was no surprise when a television series was produced towards the end of the 1970s, featuring Nicholas Ball as the tough central character. The first story was an adaptation of the second Hazell novel, *Hazell Plays Solomon* (1974) and the series ran for twenty-two episodes, achieving cult popularity. *See also* TV Detectives: Small-Screen Adaptations.

Selected Works by the Author
The Bornless Keeper (1974)
Hazell Plays Solomon (1974)
Hazell and the Three-Card Trick (1975)
Hazell and the Menacing Jester (1976)

Mark Campbell

List of Illustrations

1. John Thaw as Inspector Morse in the ITV television series. Carlton TV. Ronald Grant Archive.
2. Margery Allingham at her desk. The Margery Allingham Society.
3. Lisa Appignanesi. Credit Isabelle Boccon-Gibod.
4. Steve Aylett. By permission of the author.
5. Carla Banks. By permission of the author.
6. Simon Beckett. By permission of the author.
7. Mark Billingham. Credit Charlie Hopkinson.
8. Cover of *The Sexton Blake Library*.
9. Victoria Blake. By permission of the author.
10. Nicholas Blincoe. By permission of the author.
11. Stephen Booth. By permission of the author.
12. Chaz Brenchley. By permission of the author.
13. Actors William Hartnell, Richard Attenborough and Harry Ross in *Brighton Rock* (1947). Ronald Grant Archive.
14. Christopher Brookmyre. By permission of the author.
15. Tom Cain. By permission of the author.
16. Ramsey Campbell. Credit Peter Coleborn.
17. A newspaper of 1 January 1926 reports Christie's mysterious disappearance. Hulton Archive. Getty Images.
18. William Wilkie Collins, photographed c.1870. World History Archive. Alamy.
19. Natasha Cooper. By permission of the author.
20. Cover of *Creasey* Mystery Magazine for July 1958.
21. Cover of *Crime Time*, issue 52, 2007.
22. Charles Cumming. Credit Neil Cooper.
23. David Stuart Davies. By permission of the author.
24. Carol Anne Davis. By permission of the author.
25. Lindsey Davis. Credit Michael Trevillion.
26. Autograph fair copy of 'The Adventure of the Missing Three Quarter', first published in *The Strand* magazine in August 1904. The British Library/HIP. Topfoto.
27. Stella Duffy. By permission of the author.
28. Cover of the second issue of the *Edgar Wallace Mystery Magazine,* in September 1964.
29. Martin Edwards. By permission of the author.
30. Ruth Dudley Edwards. By permission of the author.
31. R.J. Ellroy. Copyright 2007 riverstudio.co.uk.
32. Director Alfred Hitchcock contemplates Robert Donat and Lucie Mannheim on the set of *The 39 Steps* (1935). Ronald Grant Archive.
33. Christopher Fowler. By permission of the author.
34. Philip Gooden. By permission of the author.
35. Cover of Mellifont Press's *Sweeney Todd* from the 1930s. Mary Evans Picture Library. Alamy.
36. Lesley Grant-Adamson. By permission of the author.
37. Jon Courtenay Grimwood. By permission of the author.
38. Peter Guttridge. By permission of the author.
39. Maggie Hamand. Credit Philip Wolmuth.
40. John Harvey. By permission of the author.
41. Chris Haslam. By permission of the author.
42. Mo Hayder. By permission of the author.
43. Lauren Henderson. By permission of the author.
44. Reginald Hill. By permission of the author.
45. Cover of the paperback edition of *Saturnalia* (2008) by Lindsey Davis. The Random House Group Ltd.
46. Jeremy Brett and Edward Hardwicke star as Holmes and Watson in *The Return of Sherlock Holmes* (Granada Television, 1987). Granada TV/Album. AKG-Images.
47. Graham Hurley. By permission of the author.
48. Cover of *Hutchinson's Mystery Story Magazine*.
49. Bill James. By permission of the author.
50. Russell James. By permission of the author.
51. Cover of *When Dames Get Tough* (originally published in 1946). Telos Publishing Ltd.
52. Quintin Jardine. By permission of the author.
53. Paul Johnston. By permission of the author.
54. Portrait of Ronald Knox by caricaturist Powys Evans ('Quiz'), 1922. Mary Evans Picture Library. Alamy.

55. Janet Laurence. By permission of the author.

56. Stephen Leather. By permission of the author.

57. Police Constable Neil finds the body of Ripper victim Mary Ann Nicholas in Bucks Row, Whitechapel, in the East End of London. Mary Evans Picture Library. Alamy.

58. Cover of *The London Mystery Magazine*, 1950.

59. Peter Lovesey. Credit Kate Shemilt.

60. Paul McAuley. Credit Georgina Hawtrey-Woore.

61. Val McDermid. Credit Andy Peebles.

62. Cover of *Mackill's* Mystery Magazine in September 1952.

63. John McLaren. By permission of the author.

64. Cover of a war-time issue of *The Strand* magazine.

65. Cover of the first issue of *Mystery Stories* in 1936.

66. Jessica Mann. By permission of the author.

67. Joan Hickson as Miss Marple in *A Pocketful of Rye* (BBC Television, 1985). BBC. Ronald Grant Archive.

68. Ngaio Marsh (right) and Agatha Christie (left) meet at a party at the Savoy Hotel, June 1960. Evening Standard/Hulton Archive. Getty Images.

69. Margaret Murphy. By permission of the author.

70. Barbara Nadel. By permission of the author.

71. Cover of the Modesty Blaise novel, *A Taste for Death* (1969)

72. Gilda O'Neill. By permission of the author.

73. Charles Palliser. By permission of the author.

74. Stuart Pawson. By permission of the author.

75. Portrait of Hercule Poirot by Smithson Broadhead, published in *The Sketch* in 1923. Illustrated London News. Mary Evans Picture Library.

76. James Ellis and Arthur Slater star in *Z Cars* (BBC Television). Ron Spillman. Rex Features.

77. Ian Rankin. By permission of the author.

78. Robert Richardson. By permission of the author.

79. Phil Rickman. By permission of the author.

80. Michael Ridpath. By permission of the author.

81. Mike Ripley. By permission of the author.

82. David Roberts. By permission of the author.

83. Rosemary Rowe.

84. Nicholas Royle. By permission of the author.

85. Cover of the magazine when it was still called *The Saint Detective Magazine*.

86. Zoë Sharp. Credit Andy Butler, ZACE Photographic.

87. Cover of *Wycliffe and the Cycle of Death* (1990), one of W.J. Burley's novels set in Cornwall. Orion Publishing Group.

88. Cover of P.D. James's *A Shroud for a Nightingale* (1971), set on the Sussex-Hampshire border. Faber and Faber.

89. Cover of John Harvey's *Wasted Years* (1993), a Charlie Resnick story set in Nottingham, in the Midlands. The Random House Group Ltd.

90. Cover of Graham Hurley's *Blood and Honey* (2004), set in Dorset. Orion Publishing Group.

91. Cover of *Shots* magazine, Summer 2001.

92. Chris Simms. By permission of the author.

93. Iain Sinclair. By permission of the author.

94. Joan Smith. By permission of the author.

95. Michelle Spring. Credit Mary Bernard.

96. Cath Staincliffe. By permission of the author.

97. Veronica Stallwood. By permission of the author.

98. Cover of *The Strand* magazine for February 1936, advertising a new story by Agatha Christie. Mary Evans Picture Library. Alamy.

99. Cover of *Suspense* magazine, July 1959.

100. Frank Tallis. By permission of the author.

101. Elizabeth Mackintosh, also known as Josephine Tey, photographed in April 1934. Sasha/Hulton Archive. Getty Images.

102. Cover of *The Thriller* magazine, August 1935.

103. James Twining. By permission of the author.

104. Cover of *Union Jack* magazine, advertising a Sexton Blake feature, in January 1931.

105. John Williams. By permission of the author.

106. Laura Wilson. By permission of the author.

Select Bibliography

Books

Benstock, B., and T.F. Staley, eds. 1988. *British Mystery Writers, 1860–1919*. Gale.

_____. 1989a. *British Mystery and Thriller Writers since 1940*. Gale.

_____. 1989b. *British Mystery Writers, 1920–1939*. Gale.

Binyon, T.J. 1989. *'Murder Will Out': The Detective in Fiction*. Oxford University Press.

Breen, J.L., ed. 1981. *What about Murder? A Guide to Books about Mystery and Detective Fiction*. Scarecrow.

_____. 1993. *What about Murder? 1981–1991: A Guide to Books about Mystery and Detective Fiction*. Scarecrow.

Chernaik, W., M. Swales and R. Vilain, eds. 2000. *The Art of Detective Fiction*. Macmillan.

Chibnall, S., and R. Murphy, eds. 1999. *British Crime Cinema*. Routledge.

Church, R., and M. Edwards, eds. 1995. *Anglian Blood: An Anthology of East Anglian Crime Writing*. Rampant Horse.

Earwaker, J., and K. Becker. 2002. *Scene of the Crime: A Guide to the Landscapes of British Detective Fiction*. Aurum.

Forshaw, Barry. 2007. *The Rough Guide to Crime Fiction*. Penguin.

Haycroft, H. 1941. *Murder for Pleasure: The Life and Times of the Detective Story*. D. Appleton-Century.

_____. 1946. *The Art of the Mystery Story: A Collection of Critical Essays*. Biblo and Tannen.

Herbert, R., ed. 2000. *The Oxford Companion to Crime and Mystery Writing*. Oxford University Press.

Johnson, T.W., and J. Johnson, eds. 1981. *Crime Fiction Criticism: An Annotated Bibliography*. Garland.

Kestner, J.A. 2003. *Sherlock's Sisters: The British Female Detective, 1864–1913*. Ashgate.

Klein, K.G., ed. 1994. *Great Women Mystery Writers: Classics to Contemporary*. Greenwood.

Knight, S. 2003. *Crime Fiction, 1800–2000: Detection, Death, Diversity*. Palgrave Macmillan.

Lehman, D. 2000. *The Perfect Murder: A Study in Detection*. University of Michigan Press.

MacDonald, G., ed. 2003. *British Mystery and Thriller Writers since 1960*. Gale.

Maguire, S., and A. Hargreaves, eds. 1999. *Something Wicked, Something New: New Scottish Crime Writing*. Polygon.

Mandel, E. 1984. *Delightful Murder: A Social History of the Crime Story*. Pluto.

Mann, J. 1981. *Deadlier Than the Male: Crime Writing – the Feminine Touch*. David and Charles.

Murch, A.E. 1958. *The Development of the Detective Novel*. Philosophical Library.

Murphy, B.F. 1999. *The Encyclopedia of Murder and Mystery*. St Martin's Press.

Ousby, I. 1976. *Bloodhounds of Heaven: The Detective in English Fiction from Godwin to Doyle*. Harvard University Press.

Panek, L.L. 1979. *Watteau's Shepherds: The Detective Novel in Britain 1914–1940*. Popular Press.

Pederson, J.P., ed. 1996. *St. James Guide to Crime and Mystery Writers*, 4th ed. St. James Press.

Penzler, O., ed. 1978. *The Great Detectives*. Little, Brown.

Priestman, M., ed. 2003. *The Cambridge Companion to Crime Fiction*. Cambridge University Press.

Roth, M. 1995. *Foul and Fair Play: Reading Genre in Classic Detective Fiction*. University of Georgia Press.

Rowland, S. 2000. *From Agatha Christie to Ruth Rendell: British Women Writers in Detective and Crime Fiction*. Palgrave Macmillan.

Salwak, D. 1991. *Mystery Voices: Interviews with British Crime Writers – Catherine Aird, P.D. James, H.R.F. Keating, Ruth Rendell and Julian Symons*. Borgo Press.

Swanson, Jean and Dean James. 1994 (revised, 1996). *By a Woman's Hand*. Berkley.

Symons, J. 1962. *The Detective Story in Britain*. Longmans, Green and Company.

_____. 1992. *Bloody Murder: From the Detective Story to the Crime Novel*, 3rd ed. Mysterious.

Thoms, P. 1998. *Detection and Its Designs: Narrative and Power in Nineteenth-Century Detective Fiction*. Ohio University Press.

Watson, C. 1971. *Snobbery with Violence: Crime Stories and their Audience*. Eyre and Spottiswoode.

Winks, R.W., ed. 1988. *Detective Fiction: A Collection of Critical Essays*. Foul Play Press.

Winn, Dilys. 1979. *Murderess Ink*. Workman Publishing. Revised 1981, Bell.

Journals

Baker Street Journal Steven Rothman, editor
(www.bakerstreetjournal.com)
CADS Geoff Bradley, editor
CrimeSpree Jon & Ruth Jordan, editors
(www.crimespreeemag.com)
Crime Time Barry Forshaw, editor
(www.crimetime.co.uk)
Deadly Pleasures George Easter, editor
(www.deadlypleasures.com)
Mystery File Steve Lewis, editor (currently
in blog format)
Mystery News Lynn Kaczmarek & Chris
Aldrich, editors (www.blackravenpress.com)
Mystery Readers Journal Janet Rudolph, editor
(www.mysteryreaders.org/journal.html)
Mystery Scene Brian Skupin & Kate Stine,
publishers (www.mysteryscenemag.com)
Over My Dead Body (www.overmydeadbody.
com)
Thriller UK (www.thrilleruk.fsnet.co.uk)

Websites

Classic Crime Fiction: www.classiccrimefiction.
com
Crimespot – RSS Feed to all main Crime Blogs:
www.crimespot.net
Crimesquad: http://crimesquad.com/
Crime Time: www.crimetime.co.uk
The Crime Writers' Association:
www.thecwa.co.uk
A Guide to Classic Mystery and Detection:
www.members.aol.com/MG4273/classics.htm
A Guide to Classic Mystery Novels and
Detective Stories: www.mysterylist.com
January Magazine: www.januarymagazine.com
Murder in the Stacks: www.springfieldlibrary.
org/stacks
The Mystery Reader: http://www.
themysteryreader.com/
Mystery Writer: http://writemystery.
blogspot.com/
A Pathfinder on the Evolution of the English
Detective Novel: www.unc.edu/~rdtowery/
detective_novel.htm
Tangled Web UK: www.twbooks.co.uk
Thrilling Detective: http://www.
thrillingdetective.com/
Thrilling Detective Blog: http://
thrillingdetectiveblog.blogspot.com/
Web Mystery Magazine: http://lifeloom.com/
webmysterymagazine.htm

About the Editor and Contributors

Editor

Barry Forshaw is the author of *The Rough Guide to Crime Fiction* (Penguin, 2007) and a contributor to *Film Noir* (Penguin, 2007). He has written for *The Independent*, *The Express* and *The Times*. His book on Italian cinema was published in 2006, and he edits the fiction review *Crime Time*. Besides his specialist area of crime fiction, he writes on film for a variety of magazines and creates booklets for special-edition DVDs. He has contributed to books on literary fiction and film noir. He has acted as a judge for the Crime Writers' Association Dagger Awards.

Contributors

Mike Ashley is a freelance writer and researcher, primarily in the fields of crime fiction, science fiction and fantasy, but exploring all avenues of literary and ancient history. His books include *Starlight Man*, the biography of Algernon Blackwood, *The Age of the Storytellers*, and *The Mammoth Encyclopedia of Modern Crime Fiction* which won the MWA's Edgar Award. He has also written books on the British monarchy and the seven wonders of the world.

Robert Barnard was brought up in Brightlingsea, Essex, and educated in Colchester. After Oxford, he lectured in English at Antwerp during 1961–1962. Moving to Norway, he was professor of English Literature at Tromsø. In 1983, he went full time as a crime writer and moved back to Britain; his celebrated novels include *Sheer Torture* and *Out of the Blackout*. He has published books on Dickens, Christie and Emily Brontë, and in 2007, he and his wife published their *Brontë Encyclopaedia*. He is the recipient of a Cartier Diamond Dagger.

Graham Barnfield is a senior lecturer in journalism at the University of East London. He has a PhD in cultural studies and is a fellow of the Wolfsonian-FIU in Miami Beach, Florida. He is an affiliate editor of *Reconstruction: Studies in Contemporary Culture* and has contributed to numerous publications, webzines, broadcasts and documentaries, including a column on film for *TES New Teacher*.

Leslie Blake is a lecturer in Law at the University of Surrey. A qualified barrister, he specialises in criminal law, public law, housing and environmental health law and notable British trials. He wrote the articles on William Roughhead and Oscar Slater for the *Dictionary of National Biography*.

Geoff Bradley is the editor and publisher of *CADS*, an irregular magazine devoted to the publication of articles about the crime and detective story; the coverage in the magazine is both comprehensive and eclectic. He has been a key administrator for the Crime Writers' Association.

Mark Campbell has written for *Time Out*, *The Independent*, the *Bookseller* and *Sherlock*. He has contributed interviews, articles and reviews for *Crime Time* magazine since 1998 and is the author of *Sherlock Holmes* and *Agatha Christie*. A keen film-maker, he is also artistic director of the Edward Alderton Theatre, Bexleyheath.

Michael Carlson has reviewed for the *The Spectator*, *Daily Telegraph*, *Financial Times* and *Crime Time* (for which he edits the film section) and has written books on Sergio Leone, Clint Eastwood and Oliver Stone. His online column, *American Eye*, appears in *Shots*, and his features on crime writers have appeared in *Bookslut*, *Headpress*, *USA Today* and the *Perth Sunday Times*. As Mike Carlson, he presents sport on television.

Natasha Cooper worked in publishing for ten years, winning the Tony Godwin Memorial Trust Award, before leaving to write her first novel. After six historicals published under another name, she found her natural home in crime. She chaired the Crime Writers' Association from 1999 to 2000. She has judged several literary prizes, broadcasts, speaks at conventions and festivals and reviews for a variety of newspapers and journals, including *The Times Literary Supplement* and the *Toronto Globe and Mail*.

Bob Cornwell is an eclectic and lifelong reader of crime fiction. His reviews, interviews and articles have appeared in *Crime and Detective Stories* (*CADS*), on the Tangled website and in *Shots*, *Crime Time* and *Deadly Pleasures*. He edited *Private Passions, Guilty Pleasures*, a supplement to *CADS* to celebrate its fiftieth issue.

David Stuart Davies is an author, editor and playwright. For ten years, he edited the crime-fiction magazine *Sherlock* and has written two books on the movies of Sherlock Holmes as well as five Holmes novels. He is the supervising editor of Wordsworth's Mystery & Supernatural series. He is on the committee of the Crime Writers' Association and edits their monthly magazine, *Red Herrings*. His wartime detective John Hawke features in three novels, *Forests of the Night*, *Comes the Dark* and *Without Conscience*.

Carol Anne Davis is the author of true crime books such as *Women Who Kill*, *Couples Who Kill*, *Children Who Kill* and *Sadistic Killers*. She is also the author of several realistic crime novels, including *Sob Story*, in which an alienated student teenager is persuaded to write to a long-term prisoner, unaware that he is an about-to-be-paroled killer who plans to kill again.

Martin Edwards has written such Lake District mysteries as *The Coffin Trail* (short-listed for the Theakstons prize for best British crime novel), *The Cipher Garden* and *The Arsenic Labyrinth*. Twice short-listed for CWA Daggers, he has written seven other novels about lawyer Harry Devlin (including *Waterloo Sunset*), plus a stand-alone, *Take My Breath Away*. He completed Bill Knox's last book, *The Lazarus Widow*, and has edited sixteen anthologies. He has published eight non-fiction books, including *Urge to Kill*, a study of homicide investigation.

Terry Fountain founded the crime magazine *ThrillerUK* in 2000 and still edits this, as well as the magazine's website www.thrilleruk. fsnet.co.uk. He has written numerous articles on crime fiction as well as having work published in magazines in Europe and the United States.

Philip Gooden read English at Magdalen College, Oxford, and taught for many years before becoming a full-time writer in 2001. He writes historical mysteries, principally a series featuring Nick Revill, a player with Shakespeare's acting company at the Globe theatre, including *An Honourable Murder*. He also produces reference books on language, most recently *Name Dropping?* and *Faux Pas?*, which won the Duke of Edinburgh's English-Speaking Union Award for the best language book for 2006.

Peter Haining was a Fleet Street journalist and publishing executive before becoming a full-time author in the early 1970s. He wrote biographies of several notorious killers, including *Thomas Corder: The Murder in the Red Barn* and *Sweeney Todd: The Real Story of the Demon Barber of Fleet Street*; a series of books about Sherlock Holmes – *The Sherlock Holmes Scrapbook*, *The Television Sherlock Holmes* and *The Final Adventures of Sherlock Holmes*; as well as a number of best-selling anthologies of crime fiction, notably *The Television Detectives' Omnibus*, *The Crimebusters' Omnibus* and *The Orion Book of Murder*. Peter died in 2007, shortly after delivering his final entries for this book.

Woody Haut was born in Detroit, Michigan, but noir historian Haut has lived in Britain since the 1970s. He is the author of *Pulp Culture: Hardboiled Fiction and the Cold War*, *Neon Noir: Contemporary American Crime Fiction* and *Heartbreak and Vine: The Fate of Hardboiled Writers in Hollywood*. He has also contributed to a variety of periodicals, including *The Observer*, *Financial Times*, *Sight & Sound*, *Crime Time*, *Paradoxa* (US), *Rolling Stock* and *Rolling Stone*. He divides his time between London and the south-west of France.

Lauren Henderson has written seven books in her Sam Jones mystery series (which has been optioned for American television), many short stories and three romantic comedies: *My Lurid Past*, *Don't Even Think About It* and *Exes Anonymous*. Her book *Jane Austen's Guide to Dating* has been optioned as a feature film. She is currently finishing *Kiss Me Kill Me* – the first novel in a YA series. Lauren's books have been translated into over twenty languages. Together with Stella Duffy, she has edited an anthology, *Tart Noir*.

Steve Holland grew up an avid reader of comic strips, children's stories and crime novels and has since spent most of his career writing about them. He is the author of over 1,400 articles and a dozen books relating to crime fiction, comics and pulp culture, including the definitive study of crime paperbacks *The Mushroom Jungle*, nominated for the Anthony Award for non-fiction, and *The Trials of Hank Janson*, nominated for the Silver Dagger Award by the Crime Writers' Association.

Maxim Jakubowski is a former publisher who now writes and edits in both the mystery and the erotica field. He has published over fifty anthologies, and his crime novels include *It's*

You That I Want to Kiss, Because She Thought She Loved Me, On Tenderness Express and *Confessions of a Romantic Pornographer*. He has been the crime reviewer for *Time Out* and *The Guardian*. He runs London's Crime Scene festival and owns the Murder One bookshop.

Russell James is the author of dark multi-layered underworld thrillers largely set in contemporary London. James – 'an acknowledged British master of hard-edged crime' as the *Mail on Sunday* described him – has also compiled and written *The Great Detectives*. He was chairman of the Crime Writers' Association from 2001 to 2002 and is also a crime-fiction critic and journalist.

Michael Jecks is the author of the Templar series of medieval murder stories. He is a judge for the CWA Ian Fleming Steel Dagger and, in the past, organised the CWA Debut Dagger for unpublished authors. He founded the performance group Medieval Murderers and contributes to their annual anthology of linked novellas. He was the chair of the Crime Writers' Association during 2004–2005.

Michael Johnson has run Scorpion Press since 1991, a successful small press publisher of crime fiction in fine bindings. He has friendly contacts with many writers and wrote the overview on crime writers in *Breese's Guide to Modern First Editions* (2000 edition). He devised and contributed to *Masters of Crime: Lionel Davidson and Dick Francis* and has written a study of the espionage novels of Ted Allbeury.

Stephen Jones is the winner of three World Fantasy Awards, four Horror Writers Association Bram Stoker Awards and three International Horror Guild Awards as well as being a seventeen-time recipient of the British Fantasy Award and a Hugo Award nominee. A former television producer/director and genre movie publicist and consultant, he is one of Britain's most acclaimed anthologists with almost 100 books to his credit.

Ali Karim is an assistant editor at *Shots eZine*. He is also a contributing editor to *January Magazine* and *The Rap Sheet* and writes for *Red Herrings*, *Deadly Pleasures* and *Crime Spree* magazines. He is an associate member (and literary judge) for the Crime Writers' Association, International Thriller Writers Inc. and *Deadly Pleasures*' Barry Awards. Karim has contributed to *Dissecting Hannibal Lecter* (edited by Benjamin Szumskyj) and has written *Black Operations*, a violent science-fiction–tinged thriller.

Nick Kimber has written for *CADS*, *A Shot in the Dark*, *Keeler News* and *Notes for the Curious*. He has contributed to *Locked Room Murders* (Crossover Press) and *Wild about Harry* (Ramble House).

Joel Lane is the author of two novels, *From Blue to Black* and *The Blue Mask* (Serpent's Tail), as well as two collections of short stories and two collections of poems. His article on the noir fiction of Cornell Woolrich appeared in the review journal *Wormwood*. He and Steve Bishop have edited an anthology of crime and suspense stories, *Birmingham Noir* (Tindal Street Press).

Jessica Mann has published twenty crime novels, most recently *The Mystery Writer*. She is the author of *Deadlier Than the Male*, a study of feminine crime writing (1981), of *Out of Harm's Way*, the history of the wartime evacuation of children from Britain, and of numerous articles and book reviews. She is the crime fiction reviewer for *The Literary Review*.

Susan Massey is currently at St Andrews University, researching the representation of masculinity in contemporary crime fiction for her PhD, focusing in particular on the work of Ian Rankin, Henning Mankell and George Pelecanos. She is also interested in 'masculinity' in female detectives, such as those created by Sara Paretsky and Stella Duffy.

Val McDermid grew up in a Scottish mining community then read English at Oxford. She was a journalist for 16 years, becoming Northern Bureau Chief of a national Sunday tabloid. As one of Britain's leading crime novelists, she is a winner of The Gold Dagger and many more literary awards throughout the world. In 2007, she won The Stonewall Writer of Year Award, in 2008 saw the 6th series of the ITV series *Wire in the Blood* based on McDermid's books, along with a 3-part ITV drama based on *A Place of Execution*.

Farah Mendlesohn lectures in creative writing at Middlesex University. She was editor of *Foundation* – the international review of science fiction from 2001 to 2005 – and won a Hugo Award for the co-edited *Cambridge Companion to Science Fiction*.

Peter Millar was born in Northern Ireland and read French and Russian at Magdalen College, Oxford. He has been a correspondent for *Reuters*, *The Sunday Telegraph* and *The Sunday Times* in Brussels, East Berlin, Warsaw and Moscow, and was named Foreign

Correspondent of the Year for his reporting on the fall of the Berlin Wall in 1989. He is the author of one non-fiction book and four novels, as well as the translator of several books, fiction and non-fiction, from German. He continues to write for *The Sunday Times* and is a thriller reviewer for *The Times*.

Adrian Muller is a journalist and events organiser specialising in crime fiction. His articles and profiles have been published in books and magazines internationally. Adrian co-founded Britain's Dead on Deansgate convention, and he was one of the originators of *The Times*' crime-fiction supplements. He helped in founding the International Thriller Writers Association, co-hosted Left Coast Crime in Bristol and is the organiser of CrimeFest, an international crime-fiction convention.

Margaret Murphy has written nine psychological crime novels. The grittier themes and faster pace of her more recent books, *The Dispossessed* and *Now You See Me*, are set against the urban landscape of Liverpool. Shortlisted for both the First Blood Award and the CWA Dagger in the Library, she is founder of www.murdersquad.co.uk, CWA Dagger Liaison Officer and former chair of the CWA Debut Dagger. She lectures on writing at LJMU.

Heather O'Donoghue is reader in Old Norse at the University of Oxford and a professorial fellow of Linacre College. Her academic work focuses on Old Norse literature, especially its influence on later poets and novelists, and on the way authors – both medieval and modern – handle complex narratives. She is a regular reviewer of crime fiction in *The Times Literary Supplement* and has acted as a judge for the Crime Writers' Association Duncan Laurie Dagger Awards.

Ayo Onatade has been reading crime and mystery fiction for over thirty years. She helps run the group Mystery Women, and writes for *Reviewing the Evidence*, *Shots eZine* and *CrimeSpree* magazine. She has presented a number of papers on various crime-fiction topics and has a fondness for historical crime fiction as well as books set in Italy and Spain. She has acted as a judge for the Crime Writers' Association Dagger Awards.

Gill Plain teaches English at the University of St Andrews. She is the author of *Twentieth-Century Crime Fiction: Gender, Sexuality and the Body* (Edinburgh University Press) and *Ian Rankin's Black and Blue: A Reader's Guide*

(Continuum). She has also written a critical study of the film career of John Mills and edited a special issue of the journal *Clues* on Scottish crime fiction.

Thalia Proctor gleaned her crime-fiction knowledge from working in every crime bookshop in London during 1989–2004 (Murder One, Crime in Store and Goldsboro Books). She then turned to publishing, first working at Van Lear literary scouts and then moving to Orion. She was then asked to work on the crime list at Little, Brown, where she is currently a desk editor.

Brian Ritterspak is a mainstay of *Crime Time* magazine, where his enthusiasms stretch from the flintiest of hard-boiled fiction to the cosiest of Home Counties mysteries. He writes under a variety of names and bears a strong physical resemblance to another alumnus of this encyclopedia.

Susan Rowland is author of *From Agatha Christie to Ruth Rendell: British Women Writers in Detective and Crime Fiction* and of articles on authors such as Dorothy L. Sayers, Georges Simenon and Sue Grafton for *Crime Time*. She teaches English literature at the University of Greenwich and also publishes on CG Jung and literary theory. She recently made a presentation on myth and detective fiction at St Andrews University.

Nicholas Royle, born in Manchester, is the author of five novels – *Counterparts*, *Saxophone Dreams*, *The Matter of the Heart*, *The Director's Cut* and *Antwerp* – and one short-story collection, *Mortality*, and a novella, *The Enigma of Departure*. Widely published as a journalist, with regular appearances in *Time Out* and *The Independent*, he has also edited twelve anthologies.

Philip L. Scowcroft was for thirty-four years a solicitor in local government service before retirement in 1993. He specialises in crime fiction, military history, sport, transport history and music and has written and lectured extensively on all these subjects. On crime fiction alone, he has written around a thousand articles for ten crime periodicals on both sides of the Atlantic, for societies devoted to crime authors and for partworks on the subject. His *Railways in British Crime Fiction* appeared in 2004.

Chris Simmons is a well-known face on the British crime- and thriller-fiction scene. He has been an über-fan of the genre for many years and is a keen collector of hardbacks and first editions. He co-founded and edits the highly successful UK-based crime and thriller website www.crimesquad.com and is a respected authority on classic crime writers and an active supporter of new writing.

Christine Simpson is an authority on Dorothy L. Sayers and Margery Allingham and has written and lectured on her subjects, as well as acting as editor of The Sayers Society's serial publications for ten years. From 1987, she has contributed to Geoff Bradley's *Crime and Detective Stories* (*CADS*) magazine and has contributed to *The Oxford Companion to Crime and Mystery Writing*.

Mike Stotter is the editor of the website (www.shotsmag.co.uk) for crime and thrillers, *Shots*. Besides working for the Crime Writers' Association, he is member of International Thriller Writers Society and has served as a judge for the Ian Fleming Steel Dagger and the prestigious CWA Gold and Silver Daggers. He is an award-winning children's author for his non-fiction title *The Wild West* and has contributed to various anthologies and encyclopedias covering crime, westerns and science fiction.

Andrew Taylor has won three CWA awards, one of them for the international bestseller *The American Boy* (published in the United States as *An Unpardonable Crime*), a Richard and Judy Book Club selection. His other books include *The Roth Trilogy*, televised as *Fallen Angel* starring Charles Dance and Emilia Fox, the Lydmouth Series set in the 1950s and the Dougal Series. He reviews crime fiction widely, mainly in *The Spectator* and *The Independent*.

Mark Timlin is the creator of the Sharman series of crime novels (which comprises sixteen novels and one collection of short stories) and television series (a pilot and four ninety-minute episodes screened on ITV in 1995/96 and starring Clive Owen as Sharman). He has also written thirteen other novels in various genres and under various noms de plume, plus a number of short stories in magazines and anthologies. He is a feature writer for, among others, *Arena* and *Mojo* magazines, and a crime-fiction reviewer for *The Independent on Sunday*, *Shots* and *Crime Time* magazines and *The Good Book Guide*.

Charles Waring has been the television and music editor of *Crime Time* since 1999. He was born in Evesham, Worcestershire, and educated at Leeds University, where he studied English and music. He began writing professionally in 1996 and now writes regularly for several publications – in addition to being a regular album reviewer for *MOJO* magazine, he is the jazz columnist for *Record Collector* and recently became an editor at *Blues & Soul*. He has also written countless CD liner notes and put together several compilations for record companies.

Laura Wilson has worked as an editor of non-fiction books and written history books for children. Her psychological thrillers have been critically acclaimed, and the first, *A Little Death*, was shortlisted for the Anthony Award for Best Paperback Original in America and the CWA Ellis Peters Award for Historical Crime. Her fifth novel, *The Lover*, was shortlisted for the CWA Gold Dagger for Fiction and the Ellis Peters Award and won the Prix du Polar Européen in France. Her novel, *A Thousand Lies*, was shortlisted for the Duncan Lawrie Dagger. She also reviews crime fiction for *The Guardian*.

Index

Note: Each volume is shown as **1**: or **2**: in boldface, as are the pages for primary entries.

722, 726, 728; as Francis Iles **1**: xx, 261; **2**: **421–422**, 720, 786

Berlins, Marcel **1**: 232; **2**: 776, 777

Bernard, Robert **2**: 713

Biggers, Earl Derr **2**: 795

The Bill TV series **1**: **56–57**, 92; **2**: 548, 608, 788

Billingham, Mark **1**: xxiii, **57–58**, 207, 351; **2**: 497, 608, 695, 730, 801

Bingham, John (Lord Clanmorris) **1**: **59**; **2**: 706, 707

Binyon, T.J. **1**: 2, **60–61**

Birmingham, setting, **1**: 31, 183, 185; **2**: 514, 697

Black Mask magazine **1**: 111, 112; **2**: 771

Black, Benjamin *see* Banville, John

Blackwood, Algernon **1**: 33, 398; **2**: 498, 617

Blackwood's Magazine **2**: 519, 681–682

Blaise, Modesty **1**: 139; **2**: 500, 572–574, 763

Blake, Nicholas [Cecil Day-Lewis] **1**: **61–63**, 203, 405; **2**: 487, 490, 605, 720, 722, 756

Blake, Sexton **1**: 8, **63–67**, 92, 230, 328, 398; **2**: 487, 488, 490, 523–524, 793–795

Blake, Stacey **2**: 771

Blake, Victoria **1**: **68–69**, 307

Blakeborough, John **2**: 710

Bland, Jennifer **2**: 684

Blincoe, Nicholas **1**: **69–70**; **2**: 745, 762, 776

Block, Lawrence **1**: 57, 351; **2**: 626

Bloom, Ursula **1**: 410

Blumenfeld, Simon **2**: 494

Blyth, Harry **1**: 63, 64–66, 398; **2**: 793

Blyth, James **2**: 773

Boast, Philip **1**: 385–386

Bodkin, M. McDonnell **1**: 398

Boland, John **1**: 236, 264; **2**: 469

Bolt, Ben **2**: 723

Bond, James **1**: xxi, 19, 27, 189, 211, 245, 249–250, 252, 266–270, 349, 403; **2**: 479, 546, 657, 687, 774, 816; film adaptations **1**: 251, 300–301; **2**: 474, 650, 791; pastiches

and imitations **1**: 82, 100, 250; **2**: 470, 510, 552, 573

Bonfiglioli, Kyril **1**: **71–72**

Bonner, Hilary **1**: **72–73**

Booth, Stephen **1**: **73–74**, 170; **2**: 608, 705

Boothby, Guy **1**: 398; **2**: 522, 657

Borges, Jorge Luis **2**: 588, 731

Boucher, Anthony **1**: 151, 252, 310

Boulting, John **1**: 41, 81, 262

Bow Street Runners **1**: 107, 357, 384, 385, 386; **2**: 465, 539, 577, 578, 785

Bowers, Dorothy **1**: **74–75**

Bowker, David **1**: 717

Bowker, John **1**: 729

Boyle, Daniel **2**: 428

Boyle, Jimmy **1**: 265

Bradbury, Malcolm **1**: 3

Bradbury, Ray **2**: 757

Braddon, Mary E. **2**: 579, 686, 724, 831

Bradley, Geoff **1**: 97–99; **2**: 525

Bragg, Melvyn **2**: 704

Brahms, Caryl **1**: **75–76**; **2**: 697

Braine, John **1**: 264; **2**: 488

Bramah, Ernest **1**: 203, 398; **2**: 724

Brand, Christianna **1**: 25, **76–78**; **2**: 699, 727, 728

Brandreth, Gyles **1**: 387

Brenchley, Chaz **1**: **78–79**, 172, 307

Brent, Madeleine *see* O'Donnell, Peter

Brett, Simon **1**: **79–80**, 206, 406; **2**: 634, 684, 686, 697, 723, 728

Bridges, Robert **2**: 697

Bridges, Victor **2**: 720

Brighton, setting, **1**: 62, 81–82, 340, 355; **2**: 438, 439, 440, 499, 699, 700, 701, 759, 769, 798

Britton, Paul **2**: 636

Broadbent, Tony **1**: **82–83**

Brock, Lynn **1**: 203

Brontës, The **1**: 48, 321, 326; **2**: 432, 667, 704, 708, 710

Brookmyre, Christopher **1**: xxiii, **83–84**, 266, 351, 406; **2**: 527, 652, 685, 730

Brooks, Edwy Searles **1**: 67; **2**: 771, 795

Broome, Adam **1**: 1, 2; **2**: 713

Brown, Father **1**: 107, 118, 119–121, 135, 137, 176, 203;

2: 450, 486, 517, 522, 526, 682, 701, 706–707, 714, 724–725, 759

Brown, Fredric **2**: 757

Brown, Lizbie **2**: 723

Brown, Molly **1**: 160

Browne, Douglas G. **2**: 700

Bruce, Leo *see* Croft-Cooke, Rupert

Bruen, Ken **2**: 485, 694, 744

Buchan, John **1**: xxi, 83, **86–90**, 126, 189, 191, 245, 247, 261, 267, 312, 314–315, 319, 360, 403; **2**: 470, 487, 488, 524, 682, 683, 685, 699, 715, 717, 718, 772, 773, 789

Buchanan, Eileen-Marie *see* Curzon, Clare

Buckley, Fiona *see* Anand, Valerie

Budd, Jackson **1**: 263

Bude, John **1**: 169; **2**: 605, 701, 704

Bulwer-Lytton, Edward **1**: 217, 327; **2**: 578

Bunker, Edward **2**: 784

Burke, James Lee **2**: 538, 821

Burke, John[athan] **1**: **92**; **2**: 697

Burke, Richard **1**: **92–93**

Burke, Thomas **1**: 384; **2**: 726

Burley, W.J. **1**: **93–94**, 135; **2**: 608, 696, 697, 722, 820

Burn, Gordon **1**: **94–95**

Burnett, Frances Hodgson **2**: 555

Burnett, W.R. **2**: 433, 618, 619

Burns, Alan **1**: **95–96**

Burnside TV series **1**: 56–57

Burrage, A.M. **2**: 618

Burroughs, Edgar Rice **2**: 773

Burroughs, William **2**: 743

Burt, Guy **2**: 829

Burton, Miles *see* Rhodes, John

Burton, William **2**: 578

Busby, Roger **2**: 607

Bush, Christopher **2**: 697

Bush, Geoffrey **2**: 726

Butler, Gerald **1**: 263; **2**: 488

Butler, Gwendoline **1**: **96–97**, 357, 387; **2**: 697, 713, 715

Cadfael, Brother **1**: **84–5**, 137, 206, 222, 357, 383, 385; **2**: 590, 591–594, 680, 790

Cadigan, Pat **2**: 678

Day-Lewis, Cecil *see* Blake, Nicholas
de la Torre, Lillian **2**: 498, 591
De Quincey, Thomas **2**: 493, 681
Dearden, Basil **1**: 264; **2**: 469
Defoe, Daniel **1**: 22, 146; **2**: 577–578, 831
Deighton, Barbara **2**: 711
Deighton, Len **1**: xxi, xxii, 15, 60, 105, 189, 191, **198–201**, 242, 245, 250–251, 267; **2**: 531, 532, 553, 680, 774, 775
Denby, Joolz **1**: 170, **201–202**
Derleth, August **1**: 156
Detection Club **1**: 24, 54, 74, 80, 135, 169; **2**: 422, 452, 453, 456, 462, 463, 502, 529, 676, 728, 734–735, 760, 829
Detective Magazine **1**: 208; **2**: 522, 524
Detective Story Club **2**: 524
Detective Story Magazine **1**: 409; **2**: 522, 523
Detective Weekly magazine **1**: 67; **2**: 523–524, 771, 793, 795
detectives, amateur **1**: 3, 48, 55, 61, 62, 75, 134, 136, 154, 181, **202–206**, 217, 241, 247, 258, 282, 315, 323, 325, 331, 333, 338, 346, 359, 376, 377, 406; **2**: 421–422, 432, 437, 450, 454, 528, 529, 533, 601–602, 604–605, 610, 616, 635, 644, 662, 663, 672, 727, 739, 743, 779, 788, 806, 825, 831, 834; defined 202–203
detectives, armchair **1**: 230–231; **2**: 392, 576, 587, 725
detectives, police **1**: 10, 161, 175, 184–185, 186–188, **202–207**, 216, 313, 363; **2**: 425–426, 434, 457, 503, 504, 540, 547, 556, 563, 579, 604–608, 613, 632, 682, 733, 778, 785, 800; *see also* police procedurals
detectives, private **1**: 3, 34, 40, 105, 112, 118, 121, 123, 125, 144, 155, 161, 176, 185, 192, **202–207**, 216, 231–232, 237, 257, 265, 305, 306, 322, 344, 349, 357, 364, 369, 380, 398–399; **2**: 433, 445, 458, 480–481, 499, 504, 527, 532, 539, 548, 568, 570, 578, 579, 603, 606, 615, 617–622 *passim*, 631, 682, 691, 699,

705, 722, 724, 727, 728, 744, 748, 763, 764, 777–778, 785, 788, 790, 813, 828, 832, 833–834, 836
detectives with disabilities or special talents **1**: 6, 7, 61, 192, 203, 207, 386, 398; **2**: 465, 548, 724, 741, 767, 796
detectives, women **1**: 7, 20, 44–45, 97, 135, 137, 139–140, 141, 148–149, 154–155, 182–183, 185, 188, 204, 215, 233, 239, 241, 257–259, 283–285, 305–306, 316, 331, 374, 388, 397; **2**: 437–438, 466, 479, 500, 510–511, 522, 530, 532–535, 545, 556, 568, 578–579, 613–614, 635, 651, 662, 666, 697, 715, 722, 725, 739, 748, 762–763, 780, 785, 792, 832, 834
Devon setting **1**: 21, 93, 228, 243, 278, 386; **2**: 432, 440, 446, 461, 478, 503, 645, 695–697, 720, 722, 778
Dexter, Colin **1**: 3, 25, 119, 135, 136, 170, 205, **208–212**, 304, 351, 357; **2**: 426–427, 515, 527, 638, 656, 680, 695, 714, 719, 720, 730, 749, 789; *see also* Morse, Inspector
Diamond, Sarah **2**: 722
Dibdin, Michael **1**: 207, **212–215**, 390; **2**: 490, 713, 743–744
Dick, Philip K. **2**: 745; *see also under* Awards
Dickens, Charles **1**: xix, 4, 22, 33, 135, 142, 143, 202–203, **216–220**, 257, 291, 312–313, 327–328, 384, 405; **2**: 486, 494–495, 522, 578–579, 601, 633, 698, 705, 706, 718, 742, 744, 745, 785; attempts to complete *Edwin Drood* **1**: 216, 260, 329; **2**: 699; impact, influence and pastiche **1**: 12, 19, 33, 34, 181, 241, 260, 286; **2**: 581, 627, 765, 775, 810
Dickinson, David **1**: **220**
Dickinson, Peter **1**: **220–221**
Dickson, Carter *see* Carr, John Dickson
Dilnot, George **1**: 208; **2**: 771
Dixon of Dock Green TV series **1**: 105; **2**: 607, 698, 788
Doctorow, E.L. **2**: 481

Doherty, Paul **1**: 207, **222–223**, 385; **2**: 538, 711
Dolphin, Rex **1**: 236
Donachie, David **1**: 387
Donovan, Dick *see* Muddock, James E. Preston
Dorset setting **1**: 249, 403, 725–729
Dostoyevsky, Fyodor **1**: 46, 246; **2**: 557
Doyle, Adrian Conan **1**: 108, 392
Doyle, Arthur Conan **1**: xix, xxii, 22, 23, 66, 119, 121, 191–192, 203, 211, **223–229**, 258, 328, 334, 389–391, 400–401; **2**: 479, 486, 494–495, 522, 525–526, 568, 579, 600, 601, 634, 682, 683, 704, 706, 714, 724, 753–756, 773, 782–783; film/TV adaptations **1**: 261, 262, 391–397; **2**: 597, 789; impact, influence and pastiche **1**: 64, 96, 128, 156, 203, 286, 387, 397–398; **2**: 526, 597, 646, 657, 725, 753–754, 770; *see also* Holmes, Sherlock
Dragnet radio/TV series **2**: 605
Drake, H. Burgess **2**: 498, 499
Drake, John **2**: 830
Dreher, Sarah **1**: 306
Dronfield, Jeremy **2**: 709
drugs and drink **1**: xxiii, 2, 9, 18, 32, 40, 44, 45, 53, 56, 57, 69, 70, 71, 78, 112, 135, 140, 148–149, 159, 165, 185, 197–198, 203, 214, 226, 232, 233, 257, 271, 286, 296, 327, 335, 336, 344, 348, 355, 364, 366, 374, 396, 399; **2**: 440, 450, 457, 472, 492, 493, 511, 519, 521, 543, 548, 550, 565, 567, 571, 588, 606, 613–614, 620, 626, 631, 663, 669–670, 676, 681, 690, 691, 692, 711, 723, 744, 752–753, 761, 774, 802, 808, 811, 819, 820
Drummond, Bulldog **1**: xxii, 90–91, 267; **2**: 488, 568, 756
Du Maurier, Daphne **1**: 153, 202, 261, 265, 328, 381
Dudley, Ernest **1**: 169, **230–231**
Duffy, Margaret **2**: 723
Duffy, Stella **1**: **231–233**, 305, 307, 375; **2**: 652, 686, 727, 745, 763–764
Dumas, Alexandre **2**: 797, 815

Dunant, Sarah **1**: **233–234**;
2: 688

Duncan, Paul **1**: 166

Dupin, C. Auguste **1**: xix,
63–64, 203, 225, 257–258,
389, 393; **2**: 603, 686, 742,
786

Durbridge, Francis **2**: 427,
706, 707, 789

East Anglia, setting **1**: 6, 21,
47, 136, 184, 187, 254, 302,
303, 365, 407; **2**: 436, 454, 551,
608, 696, 722, 747, 765, 780,
802

Eberhart, Mignon G. **1**: 357

Eccles, Marjorie **1**: **234–235**

Eco, Umberto **1**: 328, 385;
2: 597

*Edgar Wallace Mystery
Magazine* **1**: 164, **235–237**;
2: 525, 556

Edinburgh, setting **1**: xxiii, 34,
44, 119, 176, 193, 205, 339,
387, 397, 398–399; **2**: 444–445,
447–448, 516, 528, 530, 608,
625–630, 635, 637, 659, 682,
684, 685, 739, 786

Edric, Robert **1**: **237–238**;
2: 711

Edwards, Martin **1**: 25, 98, 99,
170, 206, **238–240**; **2**: 694, 696,
704, 728, 776–777

Edwards, Ruth Dudley **1**: 3,
136, **240–242**, 346, 406

Efik, Akpan Eyen **1**: 236

Egleton, Clive **1**: **242**

Eglin, Anthony **2**: 723

Egypt, setting, ancient **1**: 223,
384, 385; modern **1**: 131, 255,
318, 344, 388; **2**: 432, 530, 543,
584, 600

Eliot, T.S. **1**: 4, 151; **2**: 828;
quoted **1**: 144; **2**: 486; *see also
under* Awards

*Ellery Queen's Mystery
Magazine* **1**: 105, 158, 370;
2: 480, 481, 513, 517–518, 610,
669, 726

Elliott, William J. **2**: 620

Ellis, Kate **1**: **243**

Ellis, Peter Berresford *see*
Tremayne, Peter

Ellory, R.J. **1**: **243–245**

Ellroy, James **2**: 486, 489, 490;
quoted **1**: 168; **2**: 632, 691

Elton, Ben **1**: 388

Endfield, Cy **1**: 372

erotica **1**: 188, 306–307, 349;
2: 434, 664, 687, 822

espionage and spy fiction **1**:
xxi–xxii, 11, 14, 21, 27, 29,
46, 59, 60, 82, 105, 107, 123,
126, 138–139, 149, 150, 157,
161, 164, 179–180, 189–190,
198–201, 242, **245–253**,
264–265, 266–270, 271–272,
274, 289–290, 296, 298–299,
301, 309, 310, 314, 322, 340,
347, 349, 370, 378, 387, 388,
403–404; **2**: 435, 438–439,
470–471, 473–477, 478–479,
486–487, 500, 505–506, 507,
509–510, 521, 530–531, 532,
541, 546, 547, 552–553, 573,
576, 609, 610–611, 612, 616,
630, 633, 650–651, 671, 680,
687, 690, 697, 699, 701, 707,
708, 713, 716, 721, 723,
772–773, 780, 781–782, 792,
816, 818–819, 826

Essex, setting **2**: 436, 496,
696, 744

Estleman, Loren **1**: 351; **2**: 480

Eustace, Robert **1**: 98; **2**: 522,
677, 726, 755, 826

Evans, Frank Howel **2**:
598–599

Evans, Gwyn **1**: 67, 208

Fabian of Scotland Yard
TV series **2**: 606, 607

Fairlie, Gerard **1**: 91

Fairstein, Linda **1**: 351,

Falkirk, Richard *see* Lambert,
Derek

Falkner, J. Meade **2**: 722

Farnol, Jeffery **1**: 384

Farrer, Katherine **2**: 713

Faulks, Sebastian **1**: 250, 269

Fawcett, E. Douglas **2**: 678

Fawcett, Frank Dubrez **2**:
443, 622

Felix, Charles **2**: 579

Feminism **1**: 2, 3, 168, **254–259**,
284–285, 305, 374–375,
378–379; **2**: 510, 527, 528, 545,
639, 672, 688, 740–741,
746–747, 762–763, 833–834

Ferguson, James *see under*
Rhea, Nicholas

Ferguson, Johnny **1**: 300

Ferrars, Elizabeth **1**: 25, 169;
2: 833

Ferris, Tom *see under* Rhea,
Nicholas

Fforde, Jasper **1**: **260–261**;
2: 678, 790

Fido, Martin **2**: 493–494

Fielding, Henry **2**: 465,
577–578

Fielding, John **1**: 207, 386;
2: 465

films **1**: xx, 8, 15, 16, 19, 21, 27,
32, 38, 41, 44, 49–50, 55, 79,
80, 81–82, 83, 90–91, 101, 105,
113, 115, 116, 122, 123, 128,
130, 132, 139, 146, 157, 161,
162, 164, 165, 173, 181, 189,
190, 197–198, 231, 249–251,
253, **261–266**, 269, 271,
293–295, 300, 301, 308–309,
316, 340, 344–345, 349, 354,
355, 361, 372, 373, 377, 403,
404; **2**: 421, 424, 428, 430,
437, 438, 452, 453, 469–470,
471, 474, 476, 482, 491–492,
500–501, 504, 513, 516, 520,
534, 546, 553–554, 559–560,
566, 569, 570–571, 573, 576,
588, 590, 605, 612, 616, 620,
622, 624, 632, 635, 658,
667–668, 677, 689, 736, 743,
775–776, 778, 781, 787, 788,
791, 798–799, 803–804, 815,
822, 836

film industry **1**: 15, 83, 92, 174,
175, 230, 275, 280, 299, 346,
368, 407–408; **2**: 432, 438, 445,
460, 503, 505, 513, 531–532,
568, 571, 594–595, 597,
663–664, 699, 715, 742,
784, 803

Finney, Jack **2**: 758

Finney, Patricia **1**: 386

Finnis, Jane **1**: 386

Fisher, Michael **1**: 264

Fitt, Mary *see* Freeman,
Kathleen

Fitzgerald, Kevin **2**: 487

Fleming, Ian **1**: xxi, 105,
111, 113, 156, 245, 247, 248,
249–250, **266–270**, 403; **2**: 479,
546, 587, 609, 650, 773, 775;
as fictional character **1**: 83;
impact, influence and
imitators **1**: 157, 189, 211,
245, 251, 252, 301, 348; **2**: 470,
474, 531, 553, 568, 687; *see
also* Bond, James *and under*
Awards

Fleming, Joan **1**: **270–271**

Fletcher, J.S. **2**: 699, 702,
706, 707

Highsmith, Patricia **1**: 25, 189; **2**: 731

Higson, Charlie **1**: 250, 269

Hill, George Roy **1**: 265

Hill, Headon **1**: 66, 398

Hill, Reginald **1**: 186, 205, 206, 351, 357, **378–380**, 405; **2**: 527, 607, 680, 686, 697, 703, 706, 708, 717, 727, 830

Hill, Susan **1**: **381**; **2**: 610

Hillerman, Tony **1**: 26, 357

Hilton, John Buxton **1**: 357; **2**: 704–705; as John Greenwood **2**: 710

Himes, Chester **1**: 345; **2**: 743

Hines, Joanna **1**: **382–383**

Historical mysteries, general **1**: 26, 168, 169, **383–389**; **2**: 434, 481, 498, 611, 680, 704, 710–711, 728, 776, 834; ancient Egypt **1**: 223, 384, 385; ancient Greece **1**: 223; ancient Rome **1**: 194, 207, 259, 385–386; **2**: 499, 662, 830–831; Aztecs, **2**: 480; medieval **1**: 3, 84–85, 206, 207, 222, 324, 341–342, 357, 385–386; **2**: 446, 461, 558, 591–592, 769, 780; Tudor/Elizabethan/Jacobean **1**: 53, 107, 153, 207, 222, 243, 323–324, 329, 386; **2**: 539, 585, 670, 767; 18th Century **1**: 48, 207, 357, 386–387; **2**: 465, 466, 589, 629, 816; Napoleonic/Regency **1**: 107, 183, 384; **2**: 765, 768–769; Victorian/Edwardian **1**: 32, 51, 70, 107, 108, 206, 212, 310, 311, 384, 387, 388; **2**: 431, 432, 484, 504, 540, 557, 581, 584, 589, 705, 760, 762, 783, 809; First World War/1920s **1**: 137, 388; **2**: 504, 539, 828, 834; 1930s **1**: 30, 310, 388; **2**: 458, 653; *see also* Holmes, Sherlock, pastiches *and* Wartime setting

Hitchcock, Alfred **1**: 105, 128, 131, 150, 210, 261–262, 264, 293–294, 349, 354; **2**: 421, 424, 430, 513, 546, 725

Hoare, Tony **1**: 369; **2**: 691, 692,

Hodges, Mike **1**: 265, 308–309; **2**: 482,

Hodgson, William Hope **1**: 398; **2**: 617–618

Hogg, James **1**: 345; **2**: 486, 626

Holdstock, Robert **2**: 618

Holdsworth, Leonard **1**: 236

Holland, Steve **2**: 621, 622

Holliday, Liz **1**: 160

Holmes, Oliver Wendell **2**: 423

Holmes, Sherlock **1**: xix, xx, 22, 119, 120, 121, 156, 176, 203, 211, 223–229, 257, 328, 333–336, **389–391**; **2**: 488, 495, 498, 522, 525–526, 579, 601, 603, 604, 617, 634, 698, 700, 701, 703, 704, 706, 714, 717, 719, 724, 741–742, 753–755, 832

Influence, impact and comparisons **1**: 64, 104, 128, 148, 208, 213, 230, 288, 317, 319, 337–339, 397–398, 400–401; **2**: 429, 439, 534, 594, 598, 728, 759

on film and TV **1**: xx, 166, 191–192, 262, 350, **391–397**; **2**: 597, 620, 630, 658, 682, 687, 788, 804

pastiches, imitations and rivals **1**: 25, 33, 63, 108, 156, 192, 212, 257, 290, 301, 385, 387, **397–398**, 409; **2**: 462, 618, 724, 728, 754, 756, 770, 782–783, 826

studies **1**: 98, 100, 168, 191–192, 349–350; **2**: 453, 694–695

Holms, Joyce **1**: **398–399**

Holt, Hazel **2**: 713, 723

Home-Gall, William **1**: 67

homosexuality *see* gay and lesbian

Horler, Sydney **2**: 772, 773

Hornung, E.W. **1**: 23, 104, 203, 329, 398, **399–401**; **2**: 707, 724, 755, 772, 780

Horowitz, Anthony **1**: 250, 388

horror fiction **1**: 56, 78, 79, 102–103, 136, 147, 155, 172, 181, 221, 271, 275, 299, 349–350, 368, 404, 409–410; **2**: 537–538, 612, 640, 657, 688, 732, 758, 780, 796, 804, 810, 822; *see also* psychic detectives

Horsley, Lee **1**: 316; **2**: 636

Horton, Lesley **1**: **401–402**; **2**: 711, 744

Household, Geoffrey **1**: 25, 245, 248–249, **402–404**; **2**: 487, 721, 722, 774, 816

Howard, Leigh **1**: 264

Hubbard, P.M. **1**: 98, 357, **404–405**

Hubin, Allen J. **1**: 97, 99

Hueffer, Oliver Madox **1**: 208

Hughes, Dusty **2**: 692

Hume, Fergus **1**: 398; **2**: 579

Humour in crime fiction **1**: xxii, 3, 9, 10, 12, 14, 26, 34, 36, 37, 40, 44, 46, 47, 51, 59, 65, 77, 79–80, 84, 87, 88, 93, 110, 136, 158, 174–175, 189–190, 196, 199, 212, 232, 240–241, 260, 295, 345, 346–347, 357, 366, **405–406**; **2**: 426, 434, 460, 481, 483, 504, 514, 549, 584, 610, 615, 652, 683, 685, 728, 745, 774, 783, 811, 824

Hunter, Alan **1**: **406–407**

Hunter, John **1**: 67; **2**: 771, 795

Hurley, Graham **1**: **407–408**; **2**: 721–722, 788

Hush magazine **2**: 524

Hutchinson's Mystery-Story Magazine **1**: **409–410**; **2**: 522, 524

Hyland, Stanley **2**: 706, 707–708

Iles, Francis *see* Berkeley, Anthony

impossible crimes **1**: 2, 8, 26, 33, 106–108, 128, 213, 222, 227, 315, 324, 377; **2**: 433, 513, 524, 683, 700, 728, 762

India, setting **1**: 137, 157, 246, 335, 388; **2**: 452–453, 510, 527

Innes, Brian **2**: **423**

Innes, Hammond **1**: 38, 39, 105; **2**: **424**, 697, 773, 775

Innes, Michael **1**: 1, 2, 174, 205, 406–407; **2**: **425–426**, 487, 517, 526, 603, 712, 719, 726, 743, 820

internet crime *see* computer crimes

Ireland, setting **1**: 26, 46, 47, 63, 149, 164–165, 253, 302, 378; **2**: 595, 609, 665, 682, 690; medieval Ireland **1**: 259, 386; **2**: 780

Ishiguro, Kazuo **2**: **428–429**

Ison, Graham **1**: 351, 388

Israel, setting *see* Middle East

Italy, setting **1**: 6, 39, 110, 212–215, 375–376; **2**: 427, 562–563, 585, 650, 743, 744;

Oakes, Philip, cited **1**: 30, 40
Oates, Joyce Carol **2**: 656,
O'Brien, Martin **2**: **571–572**
Occult Detectives *see* Psychic
　Detectives
O'Connell, Carol **2**: 731
O'Donnell, Elliott **2**: 618
O'Donnell, Michael **2**: 705
O'Donnell, Peter **2**: **572–574**;
　see also Blaise, Modesty
O'Neill, Gilda **2**: **574–575**
Oppenheim, Edward
　Phillips **1**: 247; **2**: **575–577**,
　755, 756, 773
Orczy, Baroness **1**: 384, 398;
　2: 469, 522, 725, 832
Orwell, George **1**: 633, 737;
　quoted **1**: 117, 217, 218, 263,
　401; **2**: 570, 621
Ousby, Ian, cited, **1**: 40, 120
Oxford, setting **1**: 1–4, 6, 19,
　60, 62, 68–69, 110, 119, 133,
　135, 174, 205, 209–210, 256,
　284–285, 321, 339, 352, 370,
　386; **2**: 425, 426–427, 432,
　508, 558, 586, 608, 674–675,
　712–715, 716–717, 719,
　740–741, 749–750, 789, 820

paedophilia **1**: 6, 149, 237; **2**:
　511, 614, 636, 801, 808, 834;
　see also child abuse
Pain, Barry **1**: 23
Palliser, Charles **1**: 328;
　2: **580–581**
Palmer, Frank **2**: 711–712
Palmer, Stuart **1**: 163
Paretsky, Sara **1**: 258, 305;
　2: 511, 746
Pargeter, Edith *see* Peters,
　Ellis
Paris, setting, **1**: 16, 27, 28, 70,
　101, 106, 121, 176, 286; **2**: 479,
　541, 657, 707, 740, 791
Parker, Richard **2**: 487
Parker, Robert B. **1**: 98, 114;
　2: 731
Parks, Tim **2**: 490
Parrish, Frank *see* Longrigg,
　Roger
Parry, Michel **2**: 618
Patrick, Q. **1**: 1
Pawson, Stuart **2**: **582–583**, 711
Peace, David **2**: 490, **583–584**,
　802
Peach, L. Du Garde **2**: 704
Peak District setting **1**: 73–74;
　2: 702, 704–705

Peake, Mervyn **2**: 498, 581
Pearce, Michael **1**: 388;
　2: **584–585**, 756
Pears, Iain **1**: 3, 386; **2**: 491,
　585–586
Pearson, John **2**: **586–587**
Pearson's Magazine **1**: 288;
　2: 522, 523, 617, 726, 756, 798
Pemberton, Max **2**: 678, 773
Penn, John **2**: 697, 715, 721
Penny, Louise **1**: 171
Penny, Rupert **1**: 205
penny dreadfuls **1**: 65,
　327–328; **2**: 486, 523, 578,
　784, 793, 797
Perowne, Barry **1**: 67; **2**: 499,
　669, 721, 772
Perry, Anne **1**: 387, 410; **2**: 497,
　589–590, 704, 834
Perry, Ritchie **2**: 715
Peters, Barbara **2**: 777
Peters, Elizabeth **1**: 385
Peters, Ellis **1**: 25, 84, 137, 170,
　206, 351, 357, 383, 384, 385;
　2: **590–594**, 728, 790; *see also*
　under Awards
Petit, Chris **2**: 487, 494, 497,
　594–595, 736
Petrie, Rhona *see* Curzon,
　Clare
Phillips, Gary **2**: 762
Phillips, Mike **1**: 206;
　2: **595–597**, 636, 743–744
Phillpotts, Eden **1**: 23, 128;
　2: 720
Pike, Barry **1**: 99
Pinkerton, Allan **2**: 579, 755
Pinter, Harold **1**: 248, 284, 340;
　2: 576, 689, 781
Piper, Evelyn **1**: 264
Pirie, David **1**: 397; **2**: **597–598**
Pirkis, C.L. **1**: 257, 397; **2**: 522,
　832
Plater, Alan **1**: 166; **2**: 710
Poe, Edgar Allan **1**: xix, 23,
　61, 64, 203, 225, 227, 288, 350,
　389, 393; **2**: 601, 603, 686, 724,
　760, 786, 812; as character
　1: 765
Poirot, Hercule **1**: xix, 3, 112,
　128, 130, 145, 203, 211, 258,
　316, 319, 334, 336–338, 339,
　397; **2**: 523, 526, 533, 534,
　598–601, 682, 719, 725, 832;
　film/TV adaptations **1**: 132;
　2: 559, 789
police procedurals **1**: 20,
　44–45, 53–54, 56, 57, 73, 97,

148, 158, 161–162, 182, 205,
209, 234, 260, 301, 309, 329,
331, 343, 356, 371, 378,
401–402, 405, 406, 407–408;
2: 427, 439, 449, 503, 506, 514,
515, 527, 545, 556, 561, 565,
572, 595, **603–608**, 613, 640,
644, 684, 709, 711, 716, 733,
743, 745, 748, 770, 776, 788,
808, 811, 829
political thriller **1**: 5, 20, 164,
233, 363; **2**: 508, 584, 595, 630,
772
pornography **1**: 6, 16, 44;
2: 431, 433, 511, 812
Porter, Henry **1**: 253;
2: **609–610**
Porter, Joyce **1**: 206, 405;
2: **610**
Post, Melville Davisson **1**: 384
Postgate, Raymond **2**: 713, 719
Potter, Jeremy **1**: 385
Povey, Jeff **2**: 829
Pratt, Leonard **1**: 67; **2**: 771
Preminger, Otto **1**: 264
Prest, Thomas Peckett **1**: 327;
2: 578
Price, Anthony **1**: 190, 191;
2: 507, **610–611**, 713, 715, 721
Price, Harry **2**: 499
Priestley, J.B. **1**: 153, 354;
2: **612**, 706, 708
Prime Suspect TV series **1**: 37,
258, 259; **2**: 465, 466, 608,
613–615, 829
Prior, Allan **2**: 607
prison setting **1**: 93, 173, 193,
218, 242, 264, 328; **2**: 450, 737,
769, 809
Procter, Maurice **1**: 205, 264,
373; **2**: 606, 608, 709
profiling **1**: 159, 193, 206;
2: 423, 511, 528, 606, 636, 829
Pronzini, Bill **1**: 8, 98
Pryce, Malcolm **2**: **615–616**
Psychic Detectives **1**: 8, 92,
398; **2**: 568, **617–618**, 657, 815
psychological thrillers **1**:
xxiii, 28, 51, 78, 92–93, 154,
263, 290, 291–292, 354; **2**: 439,
511, 560, 656, 772, 807
psychopaths **1**: xx, 157, 185,
193, 202, 356, 372; **2**: 433,
664, 746, 760, 775–776,
819, 822
Puckett, Andrew **2**: 723
pulp fiction **1**: 8, 50, 91, 100,
111, 117, 141, 208, 307, 350,